Rick Steves

EUROPE
THROUGH THE
BACK DOOR

2016

CONTENTS

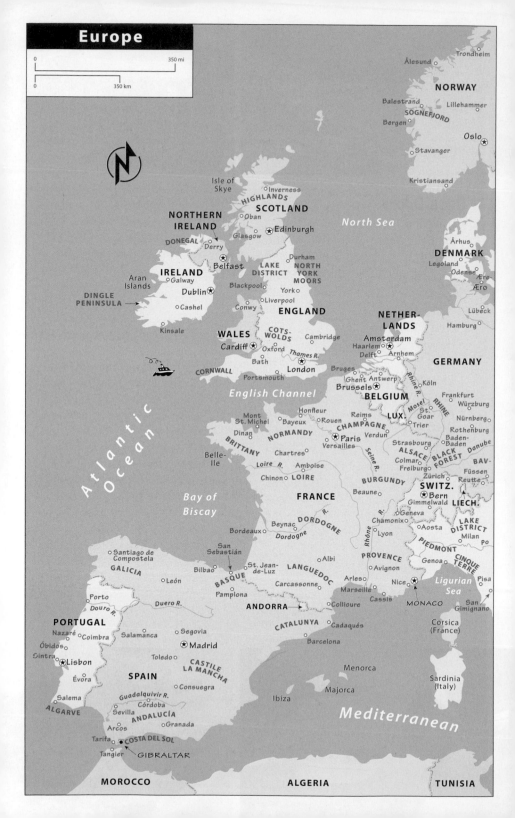

Rick Steves®

EUROPE
THROUGH THE
BACK DOOR

2016

Preface

This guidebook, based on lessons learned from more than 30 years of exploring Europe, is your handbook for traveling smart. With the tips and advice I've assembled here, you can plan, create, and enjoy a trip that will live up to your dreams.

My first five trips to Europe were purely for kicks. I made my share of blunders—I missed train connections, wasted money on dreary hotels and bad restaurants, and showed up at sights after they had closed. But each new trip became smoother than the last. It was clear: I was learning from my mistakes.

While traveling, I saw others making the same costly and time-consuming errors that I'd once made. It occurred to me that by sharing the lessons I'd learned, I could help people enjoy better, easier trips. And I'd have a good excuse to go back to Europe every summer to update my material.

Throughout the late 1970s I taught my "European Travel Cheap" class in Seattle during the school year, and traveled to Europe every summer. I developed a good sense of the fears and apprehensions troubling people before their trips, and I was gathering lots of great "Back Door" discoveries and experiences throughout Europe.

So, in 1980, with all that material, writing the first edition of *Europe Through the Back Door* was easy. I rented an IBM Selectric typewriter, sweet-talked my girlfriend into typing the manuscript, and cajoled my roommate into sketching the illustrations. I gingerly delivered that precious first pile of pages to a printer, and, on my 25th birthday, picked up 2,500 copies.

I sold all those first editions of *Europe Through the Back Door* through my travel classes. With the second edition, in 1981, I got a bit more professional, taking out my personal poems and lists of the most dangerous airlines. I found a distributor who got the book into stores throughout the

Pacific Northwest. The third edition, even though typeset, still looked so simple and amateurish that reviewers repeatedly mistook it for a "pre-publication" edition.

All this time I was supporting myself as a piano teacher. But my recital hall was gradually becoming a travel lecture classroom, and I needed to choose what I would teach: Europe or music. I chose Europe, let my piano students go, and began building my travel business. At the same time, an actual publisher agreed to bring out the fourth edition of *Europe Through the Back Door*. Happily, I could now focus on researching and writing rather than publishing.

Since then I've kept to the same teaching mission—though now this mission is amplified by 90 workmates at my company in Edmonds, Washington, and by technology I never could have dreamed of back when I started. Working together, we've developed a wide-ranging program of travel material—dozens of guidebooks, guided bus tours, a public television series, a weekly public radio program, information-packed apps, personally designed gear, a generous website, and more. Everything we do is designed to inform and inspire American tourists to turn their travel dreams into smooth and affordable reality—and this book is the foundation of our work.

The favorite part of my job remains my on-the-ground research. I spend four months every year in Europe. April and May in the Mediterranean, July and August north of the Alps. I use some of that time to film my TV series, but for the majority of it, I'm alone, eyes and ears open: exploring new places, revisiting old favorites, tracking down leads, collecting experiences, and updating my guidebooks. When I

get home, I can't wait to splice the lessons I've learned from my most recent travels into the book you're about to read.

I still make mistakes with gusto—and take careful notes. Working up a big thirst after a long day of sightseeing in Naples, I come back to the hotel, order a "margarita"...and get a pizza. Sometimes I pretend to screw up, just to see what'll happen. When I get ripped off, I celebrate—the scammer doesn't know who he just ripped off. I'll learn that scam, and pack that lesson—with all the others—into this book.

You can be your own top-notch tour guide—simply equip yourself with the best information. Expect to travel smart... and you will.

Happy travels!

Travel Skills

In Europe, life's very good—even if you're on a budget.

Introduction

Why do I find Europe so endlessly fun and entertaining? Because I know where to look. And I know how to experience more by spending less.

Europe is my beat. For more than three decades, it's been my second home. Sure, I love the biggies...from the Eiffel Tower to "Mad" King Ludwig's castles to Michelangelo's *David*. But even more than the must-see sights, I value the Back Door experiences that Europe has to offer: meeting pilgrims at Santiago, sampling stinky cheese in a Czech town, pondering an ancient stone circle in Dartmoor, and cheering for a high-school soccer team with new friends in Turkey. Looking back on my European travels, having spent much of my adult life living out of a carry-on-sized bag, I'm thankful that, for me, Europe never gets old. When I first started traveling, I wanted to "feel the fjords and caress the castles"...and I still do. My curiosity will always take me back to that wonderful continent.

But many American travelers miss the real Europe because they enter through its grand front door. This Europe greets you with cash registers cocked, $8 cups of coffee, high-rise hotels, and service with a purchased smile. Instead, you can give your trip an extra, more real dimension by coming with me through the back door, where a warm, relaxed, personable Europe welcomes us as friends. Rather than being just part of the economy, we become part of the party.

The first half of this book covers the practical skills of Back Door European travel: how to plan a smart itinerary, pack light, take advantage of public transportation, find good-value accommodations, eat cheaply but well, stay healthy, use technology wisely, avoid theft and scams, save money and time—and best of all, connect with the locals. Even more important than saving you money, my travel tips (which apply whether you're traveling on your own or with a tour group) will steer you toward matchless experiences that become indelible memories. These are the kind of souvenirs you'll enjoy for a lifetime.

The second half of the book gives you a vivid sampling of the experiences awaiting you in each country or region of Europe. With limited vacation time, it's important to understand what each place has to offer. These country introductions will help you sort through the many options so you can come up with a terrific trip, immersing yourself in the Europe of *your* dreams.

GETTING STARTED

Kicking off your European adventure can be a matter of simple logistics (you've got 10 days off in April) or the fulfillment of a lifetime dream (you've always wanted to see where your French grandmother was born). Whether your trip is fueled by practicality or inspiration, the planning part can be instrumental in its success and an enjoyable part of the experience itself. You have a world of choices and plenty to consider.

Stoke Your Travel Dreams

Find out all you can about the destinations you'd like to visit. Many resources are standing by to help inform and inspire your planning. For in-depth itinerary-planning advice, see "Creating an Itinerary" on page 40.

Talk with travelers. Firsthand, fresh information can be good stuff—whether you're at home or in Europe. Travelers love to share the tips and lessons they've learned. Take advantage of every opportunity to confer with fellow travelers who've been to your target destination. Solicit tips and ideas from your Facebook friends.

Keep in mind, however, that all assessments of a place's touristic merit are a product of that person's personality and experiences there. It could have rained on her parade or he may have been sick in "that lousy, overrated city." Every year, I find travelers hell-bent on following bad advice from friends at home. Treat opinions as opinions (except, of course, those found in this book).

Find inspiration online. Trip thrills are on overdrive on the Web, from social networking sites to personal trip blogs to YouTube clips of experiences. Ogle images of places you might want to visit by finding pictures posted by travelers who've been there.

Look through travel books. Spend a couple of hours in the travel section of a bookstore, thumbing through guidebooks. (Make it a date with your travel partner.) Page through coffee-table books with eye-candy pictures of the places you're thinking of visiting. Your hometown library has a lifetime of valuable reading on European culture. Navigate toward nonfiction: Dewey gave Europe the numbers 914 and 940.

Flip through travel magazines. Pick up a few glitzy travel magazines loaded with images of enticing destinations. Try the visually stunning *National Geographic Traveler* (travel advice, trip ideas, and money-saving tips), *Travel & Leisure,* and *Smithsonian* (combines beautiful photography with scholarly articles, often on travel-related topics).

Watch travel shows. Enjoy awe-inspiring art, centuries-old churches, colorful markets, romantically cobbled streets, pristine lakes, and peaceful vineyards. My public television series, *Rick Steves' Europe,* captures the best of Europe in 100 half-hour episodes (ricksteves.com/tv).

Watch movies, TV, and documentaries set in Europe. The Tuscan picnic scene in *Room with a View* will have you packing your bags for Italy. *Downton Abbey* makes English manors and manners enthralling. *The Sound of Music* sends fans singing into the streets of Salzburg, and *Midnight in Paris* will inspire you to stay out after dark in the City of Light. Documentaries can be equally compelling: *The Rape of Europa,* telling the fascinating story of the rescue of Europe's great art from Nazi plunderers, adds an extra dimension to your museum-going. *The Singing Revolution* gives you stirring background on how the people of Estonia literally—and courageously—sang their way to freedom. (For more recommendations, as well as a list of inspiring travel literature, see page 738.)

Take classes. Understanding a subject makes it interesting. To avoid getting "cathedraled" or "museumed" out, take an art history class, especially if you're going to Italy or Greece. A European history class will bring "dull" museums to life, while a conversational language class can be fun and practical. Many of my travel talks are available online (rick steves.com/travel-talks).

Can I Afford It?

Europe is expensive. Prices are high for locals—and even steeper for travelers. But the Back Door style of travel is better because of—not in spite of—your budget. Spending money has little to do with enjoying your trip. In fact, as we can learn from Europeans, even those who don't have much money can manage plenty of *la dolce vita*.

I've been teaching Americans how to travel smart in Europe on a budget for more than three decades, and the tips in this book are tried and tested on the ground every year. The feedback from my readers makes it clear: Enjoying Europe through the back door can be done—by you.

When I reread my trip journals, I'm reminded that the less I spend, the richer the experience I have. So often the best travel memories have cost little or nothing. If you see dancers in Barcelona celebrating their Catalan heritage in the *sardana* circle dance, join in. Talk with a Muslim in Turkey about the separation between mosque and state. In Rome, climb up the Scala Santa Holy Stairs on your knees to learn what it feels like to be a pilgrim. Watch tourists run for their lives from the bulls in Pamplona. At a French produce market, gather a gourmet picnic to enjoy in the garden of a Loire château...or perched in a Provençal hill town amid fields of lavender. Even in London (Europe's most expensive city), you can have a world-class experience by soaking up its many free museums: Visiting the Tate Gallery, British Museum, and National Gallery won't cost you a pence.

Participate in sports and games, and everyone wins. Join the Scotsman who runs your B&B in a game of lawn bowling, the Frenchman who runs your *chambre d'hôte* in a game of *pétanque*, or the Greek who runs your *dhomatia* for a game of backgammon. Even if you don't know the rules, you'll end up with a memory that's easy to pack and costs nothing.

Go with a Group or on Your Own?

Putting together a dream trip requires time and skills. As with any do-it-yourself project, at the outset it's wise to honestly assess whether you want to handle your endeavor (in this case, exploring Europe) on your own. Some people are not inclined to figure things out on a trip, and that's OK. They make their living figuring things out 50 weeks a year,

Free Travel Resources from Rick Steves

This book is just the tip of a flying wedge of information I've produced and designed to make your trip smooth, efficient, and affordable. By tapping into the resources listed below, you'll have access to the collective travel experience of my 90-person staff and legions of smart travelers.

My goal is to inspire, inform, and equip Americans to have European trips that are fun, affordable, and culturally broadening.

RickSteves.com

My mobile-friendly website is *the* place to explore Europe. You'll find thousands of fun articles, videos, photos, and radio interviews organized by country, a wealth of money-saving tips for planning your dream trip, monthly travel news dispatches, my travel talks, my travel blog, and my latest guidebook updates.

Our Travel Forum is an immense, yet well-groomed collection of message boards, where our travel-savvy community answers questions and shares their personal travel experiences. Learn, ask questions, and share your own opinions as you browse topics on each country, other travelers' tips, and reviews of restaurants and hotels. You can even ask one of our well-traveled staff to chime in with an answer.

You'll also find information on our small-group European bus tours, rail passes for independent travelers, and a wide array of guidebooks, luggage, and accessories for sale.

and that's not their idea of a good vacation. These people should travel with a tour...or a spouse.

Tours and cruises are an easy way to see Europe and can make a lot of sense for people with limited time. You don't have to waste any mental energy on where to sleep or how to get to the next town. With a good tour company, you'll enjoy the insights of local guides who'll bring Roman life alive in Pompeii or help you recall recent history in Berlin. And cruises offer the undeniable efficiency of sleeping while you travel to your next destination, allowing you to tour six dynamically different destinations in a single week—provided you're OK with experiencing Europe as day trips in port rather than as a 24/7 immersion course. (For tips on taking tours and cruises smartly, see the Bus Tours & Cruises chapter.)

On a bus tour or cruise, you dip into Europe here and there. But these options tend to show you a veneered version of Europe. If you really want to have an intimate challenge,

Rick Steves' Europe on Public Television

My public television series covers my favorite continent in 100 half-hour episodes, and we're working on new shows every year. To watch episodes online, or for transcripts and other details, see ricksteves.com/tv.

Travel with Rick Steves on Public Radio

My hour-long show, carried by over 200 public radio stations across the US, is a weekly conversation about travel, cultures, people, and the things we find around the globe that give life its extra sparkle (ricksteves.com/radio). I've interviewed European royalty, Irish politicians, and authors such as Salman Rushdie and David Sedaris—and I also take questions from listeners. Years of these interviews are available on our website and through my free Audio Europe app.

Rick Steves Audio Europe

This free app, organized into handy geographic playlists, includes dozens of self-guided audio tours of Europe's top museums, sights, and historic walks, and hundreds of my radio interviews. Download the app to your smartphone or other wireless device, and with one click, you'll have me as your tour guide anytime. Rick Steves Audio Europe is absolutely free, for more details, see ricksteves.com/audioeurope.

Our free audio tours cover the top sights in London, Paris, Rome, Florence, Venice, Vienna, Athens, and other locales.

an educational, experiential time, and a break from being surrounded by a bunch of other Americans, you'll get the most satisfaction from traveling independently. Just as someone trying to learn a language will do better by actually experiencing that culture rather than sitting in a classroom for a few hours, I believe that travelers in search of engaging, enlightening experiences should eat, sleep, and live Europe.

MAKING THE MOST OF YOUR TRIP

On the road, I get out of my comfort zone and meet people I'd never encounter at home. In Europe, I'm immersed in a place where people do things—and see things—differently. That's what distinguishes cultures, and it's what makes travel interesting. By being open to differences and staying flexible, I have a better time in Europe—and so will you. Be mentally braced for some surprises, good and bad. Much of the success of your trip will depend on the attitude you pack.

Don't be a creative worrier. Some travelers actively cultivate pre-trip anxiety, coming up with all kinds of reasons to be stressed. Every year there are air-traffic-controller strikes, train wrecks, terrorist threats, small problems turning into large problems, and old problems becoming new again.

Travel is exciting and rewarding because it requires you to ad-lib, to be imaginative and spontaneous while encountering and conquering surprise challenges. Make an art out of taking the unexpected in stride. Relax—you're on the other side of the world playing games in a continental backyard. Be a good sport, enjoy the uncertainty, and frolic in the pits.

Many of my readers' richest travel experiences have been the result of seemingly terrible mishaps: the lost passport in Slovenia, having to find a doctor in Ireland, the blowout in Portugal, or the moped accident on Corfu.

Expect problems, and tackle them creatively. You'll miss a museum or two and maybe blow your budget for the week. But you may well make some friends and stack up some fond memories. This is the essence of travel that you'll enjoy long after your journal is shelved and your photos are archived in your mind.

KISS: "Keep it simple, stupid!" Don't complicate your trip. Simplify! Travelers can get stressed and clutter their minds over the silliest things, which, in their niggling ways, can suffocate a happy holiday: standing in a long line at the post office on a sunny day in the Alps, worrying about the correct answers to meaningless bureaucratic forms, having a picnic in pants that make you worry about grass stains, sending away for Swedish hotel vouchers. Concerns like these are outlawed in my travels.

People can complicate their trips with clunky camera gear, special tickets for free entry to all the sights they won't see in England, inflatable hangers, immersion heaters, instant

When I see a bunch of cute guys on a bench, I ask 'em to scoot over... and 30 years later, I'm still one of the gang.

coffee, and 65 Handi-Wipes. They ask for a toilet in 17 words and carry a calculator to convert currencies to the third digit. Travel more like Gandhi— with simple clothes, open eyes, and an uncluttered mind.

Head off screwups before they happen. If you make a rental-car reservation six weeks early, have everything in careful order, and show up to pick up your car and it's not there, don't be upset with the car-rental company. You messed up. You didn't confirm the day before. Had you made that smart phone

If people stare... sing cowboy songs.

call—even though you shouldn't have to—the problem would have been ironed out in advance and you would have avoided that annoying hiccup in your travel plans. Don't have a trip marred by other people's mishaps. As your own tour guide, it's your responsibility to double-check things all along the way.

Be militantly humble—Attila had a lousy trip. All summer long I'm pushing for a bargain, often for groups. It's the hottest, toughest time of year. Tourists and locals clash. Many tourists leave soured.

When I catch a Spanish merchant shortchanging me, I correct the bill and smile, *"Adiós."* When a French hotel owner blows up at me for no legitimate reason, I wait, smile, and try again. I usually see the irate ranter come to his senses, forget the problem, and work things out.

"Turn the other cheek" applies perfectly to those riding Europe's magic carousel. If you fight the slaps, the ride is over. The militantly humble and hopelessly optimistic can spin forever.

Ask questions. If you are too proud to ask questions, your trip will be dignified...but dull. Many tourists are too afraid or timid to ask questions. The meek may inherit the earth, but they make lousy travelers. Local sources are a wealth of information. People are happy to help a traveler. Hurdle the language barrier. Use a paper and pencil, charades, or whatever it takes to be understood. Don't be afraid to butcher the language.

Ask questions—or be lost. If you are lost, get help. Perceive friendliness and you'll find it.

Make yourself an extrovert, even if you're not. Be a catalyst for adventure and excitement. Meet people. Make things happen or often they won't. The American casual-and-friendly social style is charming to Europeans who are raised to respect social formalities. While our slap-on-the-back friendliness can be overplayed and obnoxious, it can also be a great asset for the American interested in meeting Europeans. Consider that cultural trait a plus. Enjoy it. Take advantage of it.

Accept that today's Europe is changing. Europe is a complex, mixed bag of the very old, the very new, and every-thing in between. Among the palaces, quaint folk dancers, and dusty museums, you'll find a living civilization grasping for its future while we romantic tourists grope for its past. This presents us with a sometimes painful dose of truth.

Europe is getting crowded, tense, seedy, polluted, indus-trialized, hamburgerized, and far from the everything-in-its-place, fairy-tale land so many travelers are seeking. Hans Christian Andersen's statue has four-letter words scrawled across its base. Amsterdam's sex shops and McDonald's share the same streetlamp. In Paris, armies of Sudanese salesmen bait tourists with ivory bracelets and crocodile purses. Drunk punks do their best to repulse you as you climb to St. Patrick's grave in Ireland, and Greek ferryboats dump mountains of trash into their dying Aegean Sea. A 12-year-old boy in Denmark smokes a cigarette like he was born with it in his mouth. Your must-see cathedral is covered with scaffolding, your must-visit museum is closed for restoration, and your favorite artist's masterpiece is out on loan—probably to the US.

Contemporary Europe is alive and in motion. Keep up! Savor the differences. Europeans' eating habits can be an adjustment. They may have next to nothing for breakfast, mud for coffee, mussels in Brussels, snails in Paris, and din-ner at 10 p.m. in Spain. Beer is room-temperature here and flat there, coffee isn't served with dinner, and ice cubes are only a dream.

Germans wait patiently—in the rain—for the traffic light before they cross an empty street, while Roman cars stay in their lanes like rocks in an avalanche. Trains are speedy but rail strikes are routine.

On town squares, tattooed violinists play Vivaldi while statue-mime Napoleons jerk into action at the drop of a coin. Locals are more attracted to sidewalk cafés and

Extroverts Have More Fun

I'm not naturally a wild-and-crazy kind of guy. But when I'm shy and quiet, things don't happen, and that's a bad rut to travel in. So when I'm on the road I make myself an extrovert...and everything changes. Let me describe the same evening twice—first with the mild-and-lazy me, and then with the wild-and-crazy me.

The traffic held me up, so by the time I got to that great museum I'd always wanted to see, it was 12 minutes before closing. No one was allowed to enter. Disappointed, I walked to a restaurant and couldn't make heads or tails out of the menu. I recognized "steak-frites" and settled for a meat patty and French fries. On the way home I looked into a pub but it seemed dark, so I walked on. A couple waved at me from their balcony, but I didn't know what to say, so I ignored them. I returned to my room and did some laundry.

That's not a night to be proud of. An extrovert's journal would read like this:

I got to the museum only 12 minutes before closing. The guard said no one could enter, but I pleaded with him, saying I'd traveled all the way to see this place. I assured him that I'd be out by closing time, and he gave me a glorious 12 minutes in a hall slathered with Renaissance frescoes. At a restaurant that the guard recommended, I couldn't make heads or tails out of the menu. Inviting myself into the kitchen, I met the cooks and got a firsthand look at what was cookin'. What I chose was delizioso! On the way home, I passed a pub, and, while it seemed uninviting, I stepped in anyway, and was greeted by a guy who spoke broken English. He proudly befriended me, and we shared stories about our kids (he had pictures...and so did I)—while treating me to his favorite brew. As I headed home, a couple waved at me from their balcony, and I waved back, saying "Buon giorno!" I knew it didn't mean "Good evening," but they understood. They invited me up to their apartment. We joked around—not understanding a lot of what we were saying to each other—and had fun. What a lucky break to be welcomed into a local home! And to think that I could've been back in my room doing laundry!

Pledge every morning to do something entirely different that day. Meet people and create adventure—or bring home a boring journal.

mobile-phone shops than medieval cathedrals. The latest government tax or protest march has everyone talking. Today's problems will fill tomorrow's museums. Feel privileged to walk the vibrant streets of Europe as a student—not as a judge. Be open-minded. Absorb, accept, and learn.

If you can think positively, travel smartly, adapt well, and connect with the culture, you'll have a truly rich European trip. So raise your travel dreams to their upright and locked positions, and let this book fly you away.

Rick Steves' Back Door Travel Philosophy

Travel is intensified living—maximum thrills per minute and one of the last great sources of legal adventure. Travel is freedom. It's recess, and we need it.

Experiencing the real Europe requires catching it by surprise, going casual..."through the Back Door."

Affording travel is a matter of priorities. (Make do with the old car.) You can eat and sleep—simply, safely, and enjoyably—anywhere in Europe for $125 a day plus transportation costs. In many ways, spending more money only builds a thicker wall between you and what you traveled so far to see. Europe is a cultural carnival, and time after time, you'll find that its best acts are free and the best seats are the cheap ones.

A tight budget forces you to travel close to the ground, meeting and communicating with the people. Never sacrifice sleep, nutrition, safety, or cleanliness to save money. Simply enjoy the local-style alternatives to expensive hotels and restaurants.

Connecting with people carbonates your experience. Extroverts have more fun. If your trip is low on magic moments, kick yourself and make things happen. If you don't enjoy a place, maybe you don't know enough about it. Seek the truth. Recognize tourist traps. Give a culture the benefit of your open mind. See things as different, but not better or worse. Any culture has plenty to share. When an opportunity presents itself, make it a habit to say "yes."

Of course, travel, like the world, is a series of hills and valleys. Be fanatically positive and militantly optimistic. If something's not to your liking, change your liking.

Travel can make you a happier American, as well as a citizen of the world. Our Earth is home to seven billion equally precious people. It's humbling to travel and find that other people don't have the "American Dream"—they have their own dreams. Europeans like us, but with all due respect, they wouldn't trade passports.

Thoughtful travel engages us with the world. It reminds us what is truly important. By broadening perspectives, travel teaches new ways to measure quality of life.

Globetrotting destroys ethnocentricity, helping us understand and appreciate other cultures. Rather than fear the diversity on this planet, celebrate it. Among your most prized souvenirs will be the strands of different cultures you choose to knit into your own character. The world is a cultural yarn shop, and Back Door travelers are weaving the ultimate tapestry. Join in!

Budgeting & Planning

The best travelers aren't those with the fattest wallets, but those who take the planning process seriously. Jack might jet off to Europe as a free spirit, without much planning and no real itinerary—and return home with a backpack full of complaints about how expensive and stressful it all was. Jill, who enjoys planning and insists on traveling with good information, maps out a detailed day-to-day plan—and returns home with rich stories of spontaneous European adventures. It's the classic paradox of good travel: Structure rewards a traveler with freedom, and "winging it" can become a ball-and-chain of too many decisions, too little information, and precious little time to relax.

In this chapter, I'll help you create a budget for your trip, guide you through the best resources for researching and planning it, give you the scoop on Europe's travel "seasons," and walk you through creating a smart itinerary.

AFFORDING YOUR TRIP

Anticipating costs, knowing your options, and living within your budget are fundamental to a good trip.

I traveled every summer for years on a part-time piano teacher's income (and, boy, was she upset). My idea of "cheap" is simple, not sleazy. I'm not talking about begging and groveling around Europe. I'm talking about enjoying a one-star hotel rather than a three-star hotel ($100 saved), ordering a carafe of house wine at an atmospheric hole-in-the-wall rather than a bottle of fine wine in a classy restaurant ($40 saved), and taking the shuttle bus in from the airport rather than a taxi ($50 saved). There are plenty of ways to keep your expenses in check without compromising your travel experience. In many ways, the less you spend, the more engaged you are with life around you, and the more you actually experience.

Budget Breakdown

Start penciling out your European budget by getting a handle on your biggest expenses.

Airfare: The same round-trip flight between the US and Europe can cost anywhere from $1,000 to $2,000, depending on the time of year and the various fees (such as airport taxes, fuel surcharges, and baggage fees). Traveling outside of peak season alone can save you several hundred dollars per ticket. Understand all of your alternatives (maybe with the help of a good travel agent) in order to make the best choice.

Transportation Within Europe: This can be reasonable if you use Europe's excellent public transportation system (taking advantage of the best deals) or split a car rental among several people.

Trip Costs

In 2016, you can travel comfortably for a month for $5,750 (not including your airfare). If you have extra money, it's more fun to spend it in Europe.

Allow approximately (per person):

$1,000	long-distance transportation (trains, car rental, and short-haul flights)
800	sightseeing and entertainment
200	shopping and miscellany
+3,750	room and board ($125/day)
$5,750	

Students or rock-bottom budget travelers can enjoy a month of Europe for about 40 percent less–$3,200 plus airfare.

Allow approximately (per person):

$800	one-month youth rail pass
500	sightseeing and entertainment
100	shopping and miscellany
+1,800	room and board ($60/day)
$3,200	

And cheap flights—about $100 one-way between most major European cities—can save time and money on long journeys. Within cities, figure about $2-3 for each bus or subway ride. Transportation expenses are generally fixed, but your budget shouldn't dictate how freely you travel in Europe. If you want to go somewhere, do it, making the most of whatever money-saving options you can. You came to travel.

Room and Board: The areas that will make or break your budget—over which you have the most control—are your eating and sleeping expenses. In 2016, smart travelers can thrive on $125 a day for room and board: $75 per person in a $150 hotel double with breakfast, $15 apiece for lunch, and $30 for dinner. That leaves you $5 for cappuccino or gelato. Remember that these prices are averages—Scandinavia, Britain, and Italy are more expensive, while Spain, Portugal, Greece, and Eastern Europe are cheaper. Also, as a general rule, you'll pay less in the countryside and more in big cities.

If $125 per day is too steep for your budget, that's no reason to stay home—you can picnic more and stay at simpler accommodations to get by on less. Make your trip match your budget (rather than vice versa). The key is consuming only what you want to consume. If you want real tablecloths and black-tie waiters, your tomato salad will cost 20 times what it costs in the market. If you want a suite with fancy room service and chocolate on your pillow, you'll pay in a day for accommodations what many travelers pay in a week.

Sightseeing/Entertainment: Admissions to major attractions are roughly $8-20; smaller sights usually charge $2-5. Concerts, plays, and bus tours cost about $30. Don't skimp here. This category powers most of the experiences that all of the other expenses are designed to make possible. And fortunately, some of the best sights are free.

Shopping/Miscellany: Shopping can vary in cost from nearly nothing to a small fortune. Good budget travelers find that this category has little to do with assembling a trip full of lifelong and wonderful memories.

Budget Tips

We Americans are simply not as rich as we have been conditioned to think we are. For a generation, insiders, politicians, and elites have goosed our economy—and now it just no longer responds to further prodding. We're far from poor. We just need to get real with the fact that rather than hopping into a taxi like a German, we'll stand in line for the bus with the Spaniards. Budget travelers need to seek out money-saving options.

Sleep in cheap hotels. I go to safe, central, friendly, local-style hotels, and I shun swimming pools, people in uniforms, and transplanted American niceties in favor of an opportunity to travel as a temporary European. Hotels are pricey just about everywhere in Europe. But, equipped with good information, you can land some fine deals—which often come with the most memories, to boot.

Try inexpensive, unique alternatives to standard accommodations. On recent visits, I slept well in a former medieval watchtower along Germany's Rhine River (Hotel

Kranenturm, $85 double), a room in a private home on the Italian Riviera (Camere Fontana Vecchia in Vernazza, $100 double), and a welcoming guesthouse in Dubrovnik's Old Town (Villa Ragusa, $100 double). If you're willing to rough it, you'll save even more. Consider a renovated jail in Ljubljana (Hostel Celica, $30 for a bunk in a 12-bed dorm) or a summer-only circus tent in Munich ($10 per mattress).

Patronize family-run restaurants with a local following. The best values are not in the places with glossy menus in six languages out front. I look for family-run restaurants away from the high-rent squares, filled with enthusiastic locals and offering a small, handwritten menu in the local language only. You'll get more for your money at mom-and-pop places; they pay less in labor (family members) and care more about their customers.

You can eat well for less nearly anywhere in Europe by taking advantage of daily specials, lunch deals, and early-bird dinners.

Economize where it's expensive and splurge where it's cheap. The priciest parts of Europe (Scandinavia, Britain, and much of Italy) can be twice as expensive as Europe's cheapest corners (Spain, Portugal, Greece, and Eastern Europe). Exercise budget alternatives where they'll save you the most money. A hostel may save you $10 in Crete but $50 in Finland. In Scandinavia I picnic, walk, and sleep on trains, but I live like a king in Portugal or Poland, where my splurge dollars go the furthest. Those on a tight budget manage better by traveling more quickly through the expensive countries and lingering in the cheap ones.

Eastern European hotels are nearly as pricey as in the West, but other items are a relative steal. A mug of Czech beer costs $2 (versus $5 in Britain or Ireland, or $8-10 in Oslo). A ticket for Mozart in a sumptuous Budapest opera house runs $20 (versus $65 in Vienna). And your own private Slovenian guide is $100 for a half-day (versus $200 in London).

Lunch for $10, no problema

Don't take budget tips too far. The true "value" of a trip isn't just a function of how cheaply you travel, but how much you enjoy it. If everyone says, "Portugal is cheap," but your travel dreams feature the Swiss Alps, then *your* best value is in Switzerland.

Learn from the locals. When you're in Europe's priciest corners,

Comparing *Apfels* to *Pommes:*
Relative Prices in Europe's Top Cities

Budget alone should not determine where you go in Europe. People on a shoe-string budget can have a blast in Europe's most expensive countries...if they travel smart. But knowing roughly what you'll pay in various destinations can help you craft a more wallet-friendly itinerary. This chart attempts to compare apples to apples by showing rough costs in US dollars for basic tourist expenses in several of Europe's major cities (and, by way of comparison, my hometown in the USA). Prices are based on midrange hotels and restaurants, second-class trains, and first-class museums. Note that prices in small towns and the countryside are, as a rule, far lower than in the cities listed here.

	Double Room	Main Dish at Dinner	One-Hour Train Ride to a Nearby Town	Museum Entry Fee
Amsterdam	$165	$22	$15	$18
Athens	$115	$15	$5	$17
Budapest, Kraków, Dubrovnik	$120	$15	$5	$8
Copenhagen, Oslo	$160	$25	$21	$15
London	$200	$20	$39	$25
Madrid, Lisbon	$130	$16	$14	$9
Munich	$125	$21	$28	$10
Paris	$190	$25	$19	$15
Prague	$170	$12	$6	$12
Rome	$210	$16	$13	$17
Vienna	$145	$21	$21	$15
Zürich	$195	$28	$25	$10
Seattle	$150	$15	$14	$15

take the high cost of living gracefully in stride by following the lead of people who live there. Instead of paying dearly for dinner at a restaurant, Norwegians "eat out" in the parks, barbecuing their groceries on disposable "one-time grills" ($4 in supermarkets). The last time I was in a restaurant in Oslo, 16 of 20 diners were drinking only tap water. While you'll see crowds of young people drinking beer along Copenhagen's canals, that doesn't mean consumption is higher in Denmark—it's just that many young adults can't afford to drink in the bars, so they pick up their beer at the grocery store and party al fresco. Why not drop by the local equivalent of a 7-Eleven and do the same?

Swallow pride and save money. This is a personal matter, depending largely on how much pride and money you have. Many people cringe every time I use the word "cheap"; others appreciate the directness. Find out the complete price before ordering anything, and say "no thanks" if the price isn't right. Expect equal and fair treatment as a tourist. When appropriate, fight the price, set a limit, and search on. Remember, even if the same thing would cost much more at home, the local rate should prevail. If you act like a rich fool, you're likely to be treated as one.

When young Norwegians "eat out," they drop by the grocery store for a disposable "one-time grill" and head for the park.

Spend money to save time. When you travel, time really is money. (Divide the complete cost of your trip by your waking hours in Europe, and you'll see what I mean. My cost: $20 per hour.) Don't waste your valuable time in lines. In Europe's most crowded cities (especially Paris, Rome, and Florence), easy-to-make reservations and museum passes—which pay for themselves in four visits—let you skirt the long ticket-buying lines. If it costs $1 to use your mobile phone to confirm museum times, but it saves you trekking across town to discover the sight is closed, that's a buck very well spent.

Go communal. If you're traveling with a buddy or small group of friends, pool your money for everyday expenses. Separate checks and long lists of petty IOUs are a pain. Plus, combining costs can save you money; for instance, a group of four often travels more cheaply in a shared taxi or rental car than by subway, bus, or train. Note how much each person contributes, and just assume everything equals out in the long run. Keep track of major individual expenses, but don't worry about who got an extra postcard or cappuccino. Enjoy treating each other to taxis and dinners out of your "kitty," and after the trip, divvy up the remains. If one person consumed $50 or $60 more, that's a small price to pay for the convenience and economy of communal money.

RESEARCHING YOUR TRIP

Europe is always changing, and it's essential to plan and travel with the most up-to-date information. Study before you go. Guidebooks, maps, travel apps, and websites are all key resources in getting started.

While information is what keeps you afloat, too much can sink the ship. So winnow down your resources to what best suits your travel needs and interests. WWII buffs research battle sites, wine lovers brainstorm a wish list of wineries, and MacGregors locate their clan's castles in Scotland.

A word of warning as you hatch your plans: Understand what shapes the information that shapes your travel dreams. Information you seek out yourself is likely to be impartial, whereas information that comes at you is propelled by business (see sidebar on the next page). Many publications and websites are supported by advertisers who have products and services to sell; their information is often useful, but it's not necessarily unbiased. Don't believe everything you read. The power of the printed or pixelated word is scary. Many sources are peppered with information that is flat-out wrong. (Incredibly enough, even this book may have an error.) Some "writers" succumb to the temptation to write travelogues based on hearsay, travel brochures, other books, public-relations junkets, and wishful thinking. A writer met at the airport by an official from the national tourist board learns tips that are handy only for others who are met at the airport by an official from the national tourist board.

Guidebooks and Planning Maps

I am amazed by the many otherwise smart people who base the trip of a lifetime on a borrowed copy of a three-year-old guidebook. The money they save in the bookstore is wasted the first day of their trip, searching for hotels and restaurants long since closed. Guidebooks are $25 tools for $4,000 experiences. As a writer—and user—of guidebooks, I am a big believer in their worth. When I visit somewhere as a rank beginner, I equip myself with a good, up-to-date guidebook. I travel like an old pro, not because I'm a super traveler, but because I have reliable information and I use it.

With a good guidebook, you can come into Paris for your first time, go anywhere in town for less than $2 on the subway, enjoy a memorable bistro lunch for $20, and pay $150 for a double room in a friendly hotel on a pedestrian-only street a few blocks from the Eiffel Tower—so French that when you step outside in the morning, you feel you must have been a poodle in a previous life.

Before buying any guidebook, check the publication date. If it's last year's edition, find out when the new version is due out. Most guidebooks get an update every two or three years. Only a handful of titles (including my most popular books) are actually updated in person each year. The rule of thumb: If the year is not printed on the cover, the guidebook is not updated annually. When I'm choosing between guidebooks for a certain destination, the publication date (often on the copyright page) is usually the deciding factor.

When you pick up your guidebook, choose a map or two for planning purposes. The *Michelin Map Europe 705* provides an excellent overall view of Europe. Many guidebook publishers (including Rough Guides, Lonely Planet, and my series) make maps or combination map-guidebooks. For example, my European planning maps are designed to be used with my guidebooks.

Many guidebook series, including most of my titles, are available as ebooks. While I still consider myself a paper guy, I can see the advantages of going digital. You can effortlessly carry multiple ebooks without adding weight to your bag (great for long, multi-destination trips), and you can buy books on the go (convenient for spur-of-the-moment detours). Someday ebooks may offer more benefits than traditional paper books—including content customized to cover precisely the destinations you want and maps linked to GPS technology so you'll never get lost. But for now, ebooks have limitations. It can be difficult to find the information you're

Understanding the Travel Industry

When sorting through all of the options for your trip, you need to understand that we travelers are consumers—and the travel industry is all about selling us things.

Travel media—TV shows, magazines, newspaper articles, and websites—are careful not to offend advertisers. Just like big business lobbies our government, big travel lobbies the travel media. There's a huge appetite these days in travel journalism for lists. "The Best of This" and "Top Fifty That" are what the typical tourist is gobbling up. Plenty of factors that aren't in your interest shape these reports.

The industry in general is geared toward filling resorts, cruise ships, big tour buses, and fancy hotels. There's very little money to be made from independent travel. Consequently, there's little reason to sing its praises in the glossy media that shape many people's travel dreams.

As it's expensive to promote things, attractions and activities that are free or unprofitable are rarely marketed. It's important to be smart about which information you use to determine your itinerary. Don't be too led on by the attractions promoted by leaflets in your hotel lobby, by advertising disguised as tourist information, or by the recommendations of your commission-hungry concierge.

Enjoy the highly publicized attractions—many of them are popular for a reason. But don't let the promotion lead you away from the wonderful world of travel experiences that lie outside the for-profit travel industry—the ones most likely to put you in touch with the people, nature, and culture of Europe. These dimensions, which no big business is pushing with their slick promotional initiatives, are most likely to be the highlights of your trip.

LEFT Never underestimate the value of an up-to-date guidebook.

RIGHT My planning maps highlight what you want to see...not just the biggest cities.

looking for; flipping from page to page is awkward; and maps—often designed to run across two pages—don't always appear correctly.

While currently just a fraction of guidebook sales are electronic, ebooks are here to stay. But until the perfect digital solution arrives, I believe a printed guidebook remains the most practical format.

Rick Steves Guidebooks

The book you're holding is the foundation of a series of books—written and refined over the last three decades that work together to help smooth your travels and broaden your cultural experience. What makes my guidebooks different from the competition? With the help of my research partners, I update my guidebooks lovingly and in person—many of them annually. In order to experience the same Europe that most of my readers do, I insist on doing my research in the peak tourist season—from April through September. And I'm stubbornly selective, writing about fewer destinations than other guidebooks. For example, Italy has dozens of hill towns, but my Italy book zooms in on the handful that are truly worth the trip. I base my depth of coverage on a place's worthiness, rather than its population or fame.

A trio of my books is best read before your trip. This book, *Europe Through the Back Door,* teaches you the nuts and bolts of how to travel affordably and efficiently, with maximum opportunities to connect to the culture. *Europe 101: History and Art for the Traveler* (co-authored with Gene Openshaw) helps you achieve a deeper understanding of the story of Europe. *Europe 101* was written for smart people who slept through their art history classes before they knew they were going to Europe...and now they're wishing they knew who the Etruscans were.

The next step, ***Travel as a Political Act,*** illustrates how Americans who travel with an open mind and a curious spirit can have the time of their lives and come home smarter—with a keener appreciation for the interconnectedness of the world around them. This trilogy forms a pyramid—similar to Abraham Maslow's "hierarchy of needs"— for the thinking traveler. You start off with the basics: Pack light, stay safe, catch the train, and eat and sleep well. When those needs are met, you can enjoy the art, history, and culture. Finally you reach the pinnacle of travel: gaining a deeper understanding of our place on this delightful planet.

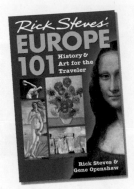

But once you're on the road, you need a blueprint for your actual trip. My take-along **guidebooks** weave my favorite sights, accommodations, and restaurants into trip strategies designed to give you the most value out of every mile, minute, and dollar. As a guidebook writer, I focus on helping you explore and enjoy Europe's big cities, small towns, and regions, mixing must-see sights with intimate Back Door nooks and offbeat crannies. My books cut through the superlatives. Yes, I know you can spend a lifetime in Florence. But you've only got a day and a half, and I've got a great plan. My city, regional, and country guides feature engaging, in-depth, self-guided tours of the top sights, highlighting the great art and history with photos and commentary. My slim **Snapshots** (excerpted from the bigger guidebooks) work well for travelers focused on one destination, and my colorful **Pocket Guides** are designed for travelers visiting Europe's major cities. For the titles in my guidebook series, see the sidebar (opposite).

For some leisure reading laced with inspiration—think of it as a guidebook in disguise—my autobiographical ***Rick Steves Postcards***

from Europe takes you on a private tour of my favorite 2,000-mile loop through Europe: from Amsterdam through Germany, Italy, and Switzerland, with a grand finale in Paris. Woven into this fantasy trip are my favorite stories and experiences from over the years, including my first trip to Europe (my parents forced me to go) and my early "Europe Through the Gutter" adventures.

Rick Steves Guidebook Series

Rick Steves City, Regional, and Country Guides

Amsterdam & the Netherlands	France	Prague & the Czech Republic
Barcelona	Germany	Provence & the French Riviera
Belgium: Bruges, Brussels, Antwerp & Ghent	Great Britain	Rome
Budapest	Greece: Athens & the Peloponnese	Scandinavia
Croatia & Slovenia	Ireland	Spain
Eastern Europe	Istanbul	Switzerland
England	Italy	Venice
Florence & Tuscany	London	Vienna, Salzburg & Tirol
	Paris	
	Portugal	

Rick Steves Snapshot Guides
Excerpted from my bigger country guidebooks, these slim titles zoom in on many of my favorite destinations, including Lisbon, Scotland, the Cinque Terre, and the Hill Towns of Central Italy.

Rick Steves Pocket Guides
These condensed, colorful guides to Europe's top cities, including Amsterdam, Athens, Barcelona, Florence, London, Munich, Paris, Rome, Venice, and Vienna, are formatted to slip easily into your pocket.

Rick Steves Cruise Books
My *Mediterranean Cruise Ports* and *Northern European Cruise Ports* will help you choose and book a cruise, enjoy your time on board, and make the most of your time in port.

Rick Steves Phrase Books
Fun and practical, these guides will help you get along in French, Italian, German, Spanish, and Portuguese (there's a book per language, plus a French/Italian/German combination).

More Rick Steves Books
Europe 101: History and Art for the Traveler
European Christmas
Postcards from Europe
Travel as a Political Act

Need help choosing the right Rick Steves guidebook? Visit ricksteves.com/which-book.

Other Guidebook Series

Every guidebook series has an area of specialization: Some
are great for hotels, but fall down on restaurants. Other series
can't be beat for history and culture. Some guidebooks (like
mine) are more opinionated and selective, choosing only the
most worthwhile destinations in each country and covering
them in depth. Others seek to cover every possible destination you might find yourself in. When I travel in Europe and
beyond—to areas I don't cover in my books—I routinely use
guidebooks from these publishers, and find them helpful.

Lonely Planet: The worldwide standard for a solid
guidebook, Lonely Planet covers most countries in Europe,
Asia, Africa, and the Americas. The Lonely Planet series
offers comprehensive, no-nonsense facts, low- and mid-
budget listings, and helpful on-the-ground travel tips.

Rough Guides: This British series is written by
Europeans who understand the contemporary social scene
better than most American writers. While their hotel listings
can be skimpy and uninspired, the historical and sightseeing
information tends to offer greater depth than others.

Let's Go: Designed for young train travelers on tight
budgets, Let's Go books are written and updated by Harvard
students—making them refreshingly youthful and opinionated. Let's Go has retained its super-low-budget approach, is
the best resource for shoestring travelers, and offers the best
coverage on hosteling and the alternative nightlife scene.

Frommer's Guides: The granddaddy of travel publishing, Arthur Frommer has reinvented his series to be leaner
and more focused on the budget traveler. These books are
especially well attuned to the needs of older travelers, but
some readers may feel like they're being
handled with unnecessary kid gloves.

Eyewitness Travel: These gorgeous
visual guides offer appealing color photos
and illustrations (like cutaway cross-sections
of important castles and churches). They are
great for trip planning and visual learners,
but the written information is scant—I don't
travel with them.

Michelin Green Guides: From a
French publisher, these tall, green books
are packed with color maps and photos, plus
small but encyclopedic chapters on history,
lifestyles, art, culture, and customs. Recent
editions also list hotels and restaurants.

A good guide-
book allows you
to play "tour
guide" and
brings Europe's
museums to life.

Guidebooks: Small, Handy, and Hidden

I often buy several guidebooks for each country I visit, rip them up, and staple the pertinent chapters together into my own personalized hybrid guidebook. On the road, I bring only the applicable pages—there's no point in carrying 100 pages of information on Madrid to dinner in Barcelona.

As I travel in Europe, I've met lots of people with clever book treatments. One couple was proud of the job they did in the name of packing light: cutting out only the pages they'd be using and putting them into a spiral binding. Another couple put their guidebook in a brown-paper-bag book cover so they wouldn't look so touristy (a smart move, I'll admit).

I love the ritual of customizing the guidebooks I'll be using: I fold the pages back until the spine breaks, neatly slice out the sections I want with a box cutter, and then pull them out with the gummy edge intact. I use a monster stapler to "rebind" the sections I'm keeping, then finish it off with some clear, heavy-duty packing tape to smooth and reinforce the spine. Another option is to tear out the chapters you don't need and bring the rest in the original binding. To make things even easier, I've created a line of slide-on laminated covers to corral your pages (pictured; for details see ricksteves.com/shop).

The prominence of a listed place on a Green Guide map is determined by its importance to the traveler, rather than its population. This means that a cute, visit-worthy village (such as Rothenburg, Germany) appears bolder than a big, dull city (like Dortmund). The **Michelin Red Guides** are the hotel and restaurant connoisseur's bibles.

Blue Guides: Known for a dry and scholarly approach, these guides are ideal if you want a deep dive into history, art, architecture, and culture. With the Blue Guide to Greece, I had all the information I needed about every sight and never needed to hire a guide. Scholarly types actually find a faint but endearing personality hiding between the sheets of their Blue Guides.

Cadogan Guides: Readable and thought provoking, Cadogan (rhymes with "toboggan") guides are similar to Blue Guides but more accessible to the typical traveler. They're good pre-trip reading. If you're traveling alone and want to understand tomorrow's sightseeing, Cadogan gives you something productive to do in bed.

Time Out: With titles on many European cities (and several British regions), these guidebooks cover sights, entertainment, eating, and sleeping with an insider's savvy. Written with the British market in mind, they have a hard-hitting, youthful edge and assume readers are looking for the trendy scene.

Online Resources

The Internet has taken much of the mystery and uncertainty out of European travel. Wondering where a certain hotel is in Barcelona? Map it with Google Maps, then check "street view" to get the neighborhood vibe. Thinking about visiting the Eiffel Tower, but worried about getting stuck in a long line? Order advance tickets online. Want to eat at the latest hot spot in Berlin? Get the inside scoop from a local blog.

Start your Web research with the professionals: Every guidebook publisher has a website, as do travel magazines and major newspapers with good travel sections. But don't overlook homegrown talent and opinions from other travelers. Here are some sources to consider:

Tourist Information Websites

Just about every European city has a centrally located tourist information office loaded with maps and advice. This is my essential first stop upon arrival in any town, but you don't need to wait until you get to Europe to access their information. Each European country has its own official tourism website—often a great place to begin researching your trip. Many of these sites are packed with practical information, suggested itineraries, city guides, interactive maps, colorful photos, and free download-able brochures describing walking tours and more. In addition, nearly every European country has a national tourism board, often with an office in the US that you can email or call with specific questions (see the sidebar on the next page for a list).

Resources for Trip Planning

Travel.state.gov: US State Department's official travel site, with foreign entry requirements, travel warnings, and more

RickSteves.com: Destination info, trip-planning advice, travel forum, and a trove of Rick's TV shows, radio interviews, and travel articles

TripAdvisor.com, Yelp.com, and VirtualTourist.com: Traveler reviews of hotels, restaurants, and attractions

Tripshare, Stay.com, and Tripomatic: Itinerary planning, budgeting, and sharing

TripIt app: All-in one travel organizer

Local Websites

I'm a big fan of local websites and blogs loaded with insider tips. Not only do they fill you in on the latest happenings and hot spots, but they help you feel like a native in no time.

Any major city has a host of online resources dedicated to arts, culture, food, and drink. For instance, AOK is a great city guide to Copenhagen, with helpful information on restaurants, nightlife, and neighborhoods (aok.dk). Chew.hu, part of a network of expat sites in Budapest, is a fun read for foodies visiting Hungary. Secrets of Paris, by American-born travel journalist Heather Stimmler-Hall, has a calendar of events, hotel reviews, and a monthly newsletter with dining recommendations and information on exhibits and other Parisian happenings (secretsofparis.com).

One of my favorite resources is Matt Barrett's Athens Survival Guide (athensguide.com). Matt, who splits his time between North Carolina and Greece, splashes through his adopted hometown like a kid in a wading pool, enthusiastically sharing his discoveries and observations on his generous site. Matt covers emerging neighborhoods that few visitors venture into, and offers offbeat angles on the city and recommendations for vibrant, untouristy restaurants.

European National Tourist Offices

Austria: austria.info
Belgium: visitbelgium.com
Croatia: us.croatia.hr
Czech Republic: czechtourism.com
Denmark: visitdenmark.com
Estonia: visitestonia.com
Finland: visitfinland.com
France: franceguide.com
Germany: germany.travel
Great Britain: visitbritain.com
Greece: visitgreece.gr
Hungary: gotohungary.com
Ireland: discoverireland.com
Italy: italia.it
Luxembourg: visitluxembourg.com
Morocco: visitmorocco.com
Netherlands: holland.com
Norway: visitnorway.com
Poland: poland.travel
Portugal: visitportugal.com
Scandinavia: goscandinavia.com
Slovenia: slovenia.info
Spain: spain.info
Sweden: visitsweden.com
Switzerland: myswitzerland.com
Turkey: goturkey.com

Traveler Reviews

To plan a trip, I once relied on travel agents, other travel writers, and the word-of-mouth advice of friends. Those sources are still valid today—but my circle of "friends" has increased exponentially. With the advent of websites and apps such as Yelp.com and TripAdvisor.com, the opinions of everyday travelers are changing the travel industry.

Consumer-generated reviews can be useful throughout

your planning process, allowing you to browse destinations and get a consensus of opinion about everything from hotels and restaurants to sights and nightlife. But the reviews also have some limitations and drawbacks. I've found that the most helpful ideas usually come from the categories for tours, sightseeing experiences, and entertainment. For more on traveler reviews, and how to best use them, see page 209).

CREATING AN ITINERARY

Each spring through my college years, I'd first determine how much time I could get away for, then I'd buy a cheap plane ticket to Europe—and then I'd figure out where I'd actually go. Filling in the blanks between the flight out and the flight home is one of the more pleasurable parts of trip planning. It's armchair travel that turns into real travel.

I never start a trip without having every day planned out. Your reaction to an itinerary may be, "Hey, won't my spontaneity and freedom suffer?" Not necessarily. Although I always begin a trip with a well-thought-out plan, I maintain my flexibility and make changes as needed. An itinerary forces you to see the consequences of any spontaneous change you make while in Europe. For instance, if you spend two extra days in the sunny Alps, you'll see that you won't make it to the Greek Islands. With the help of an itinerary, you can lay out your goals, maximize their potential, and avoid regrettable changes.

Your itinerary depends on several factors, including weather, crowds, geography, timeline, and travel style (are you antsy to see as much as you can, or do you like settling into a place for a few days?) Take the following considerations into account as you build your European itinerary.

Europe by (Tourist) Season

Some people have flexible enough jobs and lifestyles to cherry-pick when to take their vacations, but many others have less choice. Fortunately, Europe welcomes visitors 365 days a year—and each season offers a different ambience and experience.

In travel-industry jargon, the year is divided into three seasons: peak season (roughly mid-June through August), shoulder season (April through mid-June and September through October), and off-season (November through March). Each has its pros and cons. Regardless of when you go, if your objective is to "meet the people," you'll find Europe filled with them any time of year.

Peak Season

Summer is a great time to travel—except for the crowds and high temperatures. Sunny weather, long days, and exuberant nightlife turn Europe into a powerful magnet. I haven't missed a peak season in 30 years. Families with school-age children are usually locked into peak-season travel. Here are a few tips to help you keep your cool:

Arrange your trip with crowd control in mind. Go to the busy places as early or late in peak season as you can. Consider, for instance, a six-week European trip beginning June 1, half with a rail pass to see famous sights in Italy and Austria, and half visiting relatives in Scotland. It would be wise to do the rail pass section first, enjoying fewer crowds, and then spend time with the family during the last half of your vacation, when Florence and Salzburg are teeming with tourists. Salzburg on June 10 and Salzburg on July 10 are two very different experiences.

Seek out places with no promotional budgets. Keep in mind that accessibility and promotional budgets determine a place's fame and popularity just as much as its worthiness as a tourist attraction. The beaches of Greece's Peloponnesian Peninsula enjoy the same weather and water as the highly promoted isles of Santorini and Ios but are out of the way, underpromoted, and wonderfully deserted. If you're traveling by car, take advantage of your mobility by leaving the well-worn tourist routes. The Europe away from the train tracks is less expensive and feels more peaceful and relaxed. Overlooked by the rail pass mobs, it's one step behind the modern parade.

Spend the night. Popular day-trip destinations near big cities and resorts such as Toledo (near Madrid), San Marino

In peak season, sunbathers on Europe's beaches are packed like sardines. In shoulder season, the beaches are wide open.

(near huge Italian beach resorts), and San Gimignano (near Florence) take on a more peaceful and enjoyable atmosphere at night, when the legions of day-trippers retreat to the predictable plumbing of their big-city or beach-resort hotels. Small towns normally lack hotels big enough for tour groups and are often inaccessible to large buses. So they will experience, at worst, midday crowds.

St. Mark's Square in July—no wonder Venice is sinking...but any time of the year, walk a few blocks away and it's just you and Venice.

Prepare for intense heat. Europeans swear that it gets hotter every year. Even restaurants in cooler climates (like Munich or Amsterdam) now tend to have ample al fresco seating to take advantage of the ever longer outdoor-dining season. Throughout Europe in July and August, expect high temperatures—even sweltering heat—particularly in the south.

Don't discount July and August. Although Europe's tourist crowds can generally be plotted on a bell-shaped curve that peaks in July and August, there are exceptions. For instance, Paris is relatively empty in July and August but packed full in June (conventions) and September (trade shows). Business-class hotels in Scandinavia are cheapest in the summer, when travel—up there, mostly business travel—is down.

In much of Europe (especially Italy and France), cities are partially shut down in July and August, when local urbanites take their beach breaks. You'll hear that these are terrible times to travel, but it's really no big deal. You can't get a dentist, and many launderettes may be closed, but tourists are basically unaffected by Europe's mass holidays. Just don't get caught on the wrong road on the first or fifteenth of the month (when vacations often start or finish, causing huge traffic jams), or try to compete with all of Europe for a piece of French Riviera beach in August.

Some places are best experienced in peak season.

Travel in the peak season in Scandinavia, Britain, and Ireland, which rarely have the horrible crowds of other destinations, where sights are too sleepy or even closed in shoulder season, and where you want the best weather and longest days possible. Scandinavia has an extremely brief tourist season—basically from mid-June to late August; I'd avoid it outside this window.

Shoulder Season

"Shoulder season"—generally April through mid-June, September, and October—combines the advantages of both peak-season and off-season travel. In shoulder season, you'll enjoy decent weather, long-enough daylight, fewer crowds, and a local tourist industry still ready to please and entertain.

Shoulder season varies by destination. Because fall and spring bring cooler temperatures in Mediterranean Europe, shoulder season in much of Italy, southern France, Spain, Croatia, and Greece can actually come with near peak-season crowds and prices. For example, except for beach resorts, Italy's peak season is May, June, September, and October, rather than July and August. As mentioned earlier, Paris is surprisingly quiet in July and August.

Spring or fall? If debating the merits of traveling before or after summer, consider your destination. Both weather and crowds are about the same in spring or fall. Mediterranean Europe is generally green in spring, but parched in fall. For hikers, the Alps are better in early fall, because many good hiking trails are still covered with snow through the late spring.

On a budget note, keep in mind that round-trip airfares are determined by your departure date. Therefore, if you fly over during peak season and return late in the fall (shoulder season), you may still pay peak-season round-trip fares.

Off-Season

Every summer, Europe greets a stampede of sightseers. Before jumping into the peak-season pig pile, consider a trip during the off-season—generally November through March.

Expect to pay less—most of the time. Off-season airfares are often hundreds of dollars cheaper. With fewer crowds in Europe, you may find you can sleep for less: Many fine hotels drop their prices, and budget hotels will have plenty of vacancies. And while many B&Bs and other non-hotel budget accommodations may be closed, those still open are usually empty and, therefore, more comfortable.

Numbers and Stumblers

Europeans convey numerical information differently than we do, from measurements to schedules and even dates. Knowing the differences will save needless confusion when planning itineraries or making reservations.

Time and Date

The 24-hour clock (military time) is used in any official timetable. This includes bus, train, and tour schedules. Learn to use it quickly and easily. Everything is the same until noon. Then, instead of starting over again at 1:00 p.m., the Europeans keep on going—13:00, 14:00, and so on. For any time after noon, subtract 12 and add p.m. (18:00 is 6:00 p.m.).

To figure out the time back home, remember that European time is generally six/nine hours ahead of the East/West Coasts of the US. (These are the major exceptions: British, Irish, and Portuguese time is five/eight hours ahead; Greece and Turkey are seven/ten hours ahead.) Europe observes Daylight Saving Time (called "Summer Time" in the UK), but on a slightly different schedule than the US: Europe "springs forward" on the last Sunday in March (three weeks after most of North America) and "falls back" the last Sunday in October (one week before North America). For a handy online time converter, try timeanddate.com /worldclock.

When it comes to dates, remember—especially when making reservations—that European date order is written day/month/year. Christmas 2016, for example, is 25/12/16 instead of 12/25/16, as we would write it.

Written Numbers

A European's handwritten numbers look different from ours. The number 1 has an upswing (1). The number 4 often looks like a short lightning bolt (4). If you don't

---

To save some money, show up late in the day, notice how many open rooms they have (keys on the rack), let them know you're a hosteler (student, senior, artist, or whatever) with a particular price limit, and bargain from there. The opposite is true of big-city business centers (especially in Berlin, Brussels, and the Scandinavian capitals), which are busiest and most expensive off-season.

Enjoy having Europe to yourself. Off-season adventurers loiter all alone through Leonardo da Vinci's home, ponder in Rome's Forum undisturbed, kick up sand on lonely Adriatic beaches, and chat with laid-back guards by log fires in French châteaux. In wintertime Venice, you can be all alone atop St. Mark's bell tower, watching the clouds of your breath roll over the Byzantine domes of the church to a horizon of cut-glass Alps. Below, on St. Mark's Square, pigeons fidget and wonder, "Where are the tourists?"

Off-season adventurers enjoy step-right-up service at shops and tourist offices, and experience a more European

cross your 7 ($\mathcal{7}$), it may be mistaken as a sloppy 1, and you could miss your train. Don't use "#" for "number"—it's not common in Europe.

On the continent, commas are decimal points and decimals commas, so a euro and a half is €1,50 and there are 5.280 feet in a mile. (Britain and Ireland use commas and decimal points like North America.)

Metric Conversion

Expect to confront the metric system in your European travels. Here are some easy ways to guesstimate metric conversions: Since a meter is 39 inches, just consider a meter roughly equivalent to a yard. A kilometer is a bit more than half a mile (1 kilometer = 0.62 mile). A liter is nearly the same as a quart (1.056 quarts, to be exact)—about four to a gallon. A centimeter is about half the distance across a penny (1 inch = 2.54 centimeters), while a millimeter is about the thickness of a penny (1 inch = 25 millimeters). In markets, it's handy to know that 1 ounce = 28 grams, and 2.2 pounds = 1 kilogram.

Converting Temperatures

Europeans measure temperatures in degrees Celsius (zero degrees C = 32 degrees Fahrenheit). You can use a formula to convert temperatures in Celsius to Fahrenheit: Divide C by 5, multiply by 9, and add 32 to get F. If that's too scary, it's easier and nearly as accurate to double the Celsius temperature and add 30. So if it's 27° C, double to 54 and add 30 to get 84° F (it's actually 81° F but that's close enough for me). To convert Fahrenheit to Celsius, subtract 32, divide by 9, then multiply by 5; or take the easy route—just subtract 30 and divide by 2. A memory aid: 28° C = 82° F—balmy summer weather.

Europe. Although many popular tourist-oriented parks, shows, and tours will be closed, off-season is in-season for high culture: In Vienna, for example, the Boys' Choir, opera, and Lipizzaner stallions are in all their crowd-pleasing glory.

Be prepared for any kind of weather. Because much of Europe is at Canadian latitudes, the winter days are short. It's dark by 5 p.m. The weather can be miserable—cold, windy, and drizzly—and then turn worse.

Pack for the cold and wet—layers of clothing, rainproof parka, gloves, wool hat, long johns, waterproof shoes, and an umbrella. Dress warmly. Cold weather is colder when you're outdoors trying to enjoy yourself all day long, and cheap hotels are not always adequately heated in the off-season. But just as summer can be wet and gray, winter can be crisp and blue, and even into mid-November, hillsides blaze with colorful leaves.

Beware of shorter hours. Make the most out of your limited daylight hours. Some sights close down entirely,

European Weather

Make sure to consider weather conditions when you make your travel plans. Europe and North America share the same latitudes and a similar climate. This map shows Europe superimposed over North America (shaded) with latitude lines. Use the map as a general weather guide. For example, London and Canada's Vancouver are located at a similar latitude and are both near the sea, so you can assume their climates are nearly the same. But you can't go by latitude alone. Rome and New York City should have similar weather, but Rome is hotter because it's surrounded by the warm Mediterranean. Inland areas have colder winters, so Prague can get as chilly as Minneapolis. Elevation affects climate as well. For average temperatures, check wunderground.com.

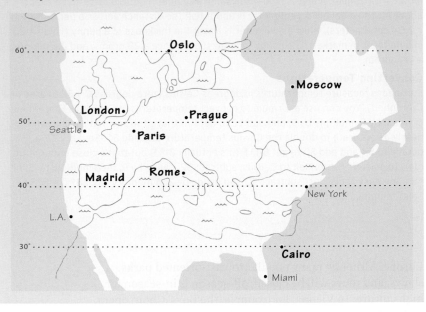

and most operate on shorter hours, with darkness often determining the closing time. Winter sightseeing is fine in big cities, which bustle year-round, but it's more frustrating in small tourist towns, which can be boringly quiet, with many sights and restaurants closed down. In December, many beach resorts shut up as tight as canned hams. While Europe's wonderful outdoor evening ambience survives all year in the south, wintertime streets are empty in the north after dark. English-language tours, common in the summer, are rare off-season, when most visitors are natives. Tourist information offices normally stay open year-round, but have shorter hours in the winter. Opening times are less predictable, so call ahead to double-check hours and confirm your plans.

Itinerary Considerations

When planning your trip itinerary, deal thoughtfully with issues such as weather, culture shock, health maintenance, fatigue, and festivals—and you'll travel happier.

Establish a logical flight plan. It's been years since I flew into and out of the same city. You can avoid needless travel time and expense by flying into one airport and out from another. You usually pay just half the round-trip fare for each airport. Even if this type of flight plan is more expensive than the cheapest round-trip fare, it may save you lots of time and money when surface connections are figured in. For example, you could fly into London, travel east through whatever interests you in Europe, and fly home from Athens. This would eliminate the costly and time-consuming return to London. Plug various cities into flight websites and check the fares. For more on choosing flights, see page 94.

See countries in order of cultural hairiness. If you plan to see Britain, the Alps, Greece, and Turkey, do it in that order so you'll grow steadily into the more intense and crazy travel. If you've never been out of the US, flying directly into Istanbul can be overwhelming. Even if you did survive Turkey, everything after that would be anticlimactic. Start mild—that means England. England, compared to any place but the United States, is pretty dull. Don't get me wrong—it's a wonderful place to travel. But go there first, when cream teas and roundabouts will be exotic. You're more likely to enjoy Turkey, Naples, or Sarajevo if you gradually work your way south and east.

Match your destination to your interests. If you're passionate about Renaissance art, Florence is a must. England's Cotswolds beckon to those who fantasize about thatched cottages, time-passed villages, and sheep lazing on green hillsides. For World War II buffs, there's no more stirring experience than a visit to Normandy. Beer connoisseurs

LEFT In the north, darkness falls early in the winter. This is Oslo at 3:30 p.m.

RIGHT Italy's Cinque Terre villages are empty in the winter...and the good restaurants close for a much-needed extended holiday.

make pilgrimages to Belgium. If you like big cities, you'll enjoy London, Paris, Rome, and Venice. Want to get off the beaten path? Nothing rearranges your mental furniture like a trip to Bosnia's Mostar or Morocco's Tangier.

If you have European roots, a fun part of travel is to discover a kinship with people from the land of your ancestors. I can't tell you how many American Murphys, Kellys, and O'Somethings I meet in Ireland, in search of their roots and a good beer. When in Scandinavia, I feel like I'm among cousins. Then, when I cross the border into Norway, I feel like I'm among brothers and sisters. Because I'm Norwegian, everyone there looks like family.

Don't let well-advertised tourist traps trump more worthwhile sights.

Moderate the weather conditions you'll encounter. For 30 years of travels, my routine has been spring in the Mediterranean area and summer north of the Alps. Match the coolest month of your trip with the warmest area, and vice versa. For a spring and early-summer trip, enjoy comfortable temperatures throughout by starting in the southern countries and working your way north. If possible, avoid the midsummer Mediterranean heat and crowds of Italy and southern France. Spend those weeks in Scandinavia, Britain, Ireland, or the Alps (which may also increase your odds of sun in places prone to miserable weather).

Alternate intense big cities with villages and countryside. For example, break a tour of Venice, Florence, and Rome with an easygoing time in Italy's hill towns or on the Italian Riviera. Judging Italy by Rome alone is like judging America by New York City.

Join the celebration. If you like parties, hit as many festivals, national holidays, and arts seasons as you can (or, if you hate crowds, learn the dates to avoid). This takes some planning. For a calendar of events, try national tourist offices (see list on page 39), and official festival websites (the bigger ones have their own). I've listed some of the major holidays and festivals on my website at ricksteves.com/festivals. An effort to visit the right places at the right times will drape your trip with festive tinsel. Remember to book your room well in advance.

Take advantage of cheap flights within Europe. The recent proliferation of no-frills, low-budget airlines in

Europe is changing the way people design their itineraries. Two decades ago, you'd piece together a trip based on which towns could be connected by handy train trips (or, at most, overnight trains). But these days, it's relatively cheap and easy to combine, say, Portugal, Poland, and Palermo on a single itinerary. For more on cheap flights, see page 105.

Resources for European Events

Timeout.com: Event listings for major European cities

RickSteves.com/festivals: Lists of major festivals and national holidays per country

Sportsevents365.com: Tickets to sporting events and concerts

Minimize one-night stands. Even the speediest itinerary should be a series of two-night stands. I'd stretch every other day with long hours on the road or train and hurried sightseeing along the way in order to enjoy the sanity of two nights in the same bed. Minimizing hotel changes saves time and money, and gives you the sensation of actually being comfortable in a town on the second night.

Leave some slack in your itinerary. Don't schedule yourself too tightly (a common tendency). Everyday chores, small business matters, transportation problems, constipation, and planning mistakes deserve about one day of slack per week in your itinerary. For long trips, schedule a "vacation from your vacation" in the middle of it. Most people need several days in a place where they couldn't see a museum or take a tour even if they wanted to. A stop in the mountains or on an island, in a friendly rural town, or at the home of a relative is a great way to revitalize your tourist spirit.

Assume you will return. This "General MacArthur approach" is a key to touristic happiness. You can't cover all of Europe in one trip—don't even try. Enjoy what you're seeing. Forget what you won't get to on this trip. If you worry about things that are just out of reach, you won't appreciate what's in your hand. I've taken dozens of European trips, and I still need more time. I'm happy about what I can't get to. It's a blessing that we can never see all of Europe.

Your Best Itinerary in Eight Steps

Trying to narrow your choices among European destinations is a bit like being a kid in a candy shop. The options are endless and everything looks delicious (and consuming too much isn't good for you). Start by listing everything you'd like to visit, then turn that list into a smart itinerary by following these steps.

1. Decide on the places you want to see. Start by writing out your wish list ("Places I want to see—London, Alps,

Bavaria, Florence, Amsterdam, Paris, the Rhine, Rome, Venice, Greece"). Then make sure you have a reason for every stop. Don't visit Casablanca because you liked the movie. Just because George Clooney bought a villa on Lake Como doesn't mean you should go there, too.

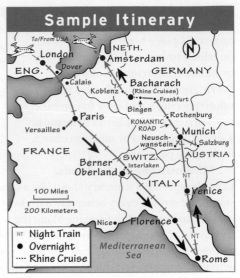

Minimize redundancy. On a quick trip, focus on only one part of the Alps. England's two best-known university towns, Oxford and Cambridge, are redundant. Choose one (I prefer Cambridge).

2. Establish a route and timeline. Circle your destinations on a map, then figure out a logical geographical order and length for your trip. Pin down any places that you have to be on a certain date (and ask yourself if it's really worth stifling your flexibility). Once you've settled on a list, be satisfied with your efficient plan, and focus any more study and preparation only on places that fall along your proposed route.

3. Decide on the cities you'll fly in and out of. Flying into one city and out of another is usually more efficient than booking a round-trip flight. I used to fly into Amsterdam, travel to Istanbul, and then ride two days by train back to Amsterdam to fly home because I thought it was "too expensive" to pay $200 extra to fly out of Istanbul. Now I understand the real economy—in time and money—in breaking out of the round-trip mold. Think carefully about which cities make the most sense as a first stop or a finale. If you'll be renting a car, remember that a one-way drop-off fee can add to your costs.

4. Determine the mode of transportation. Do this not based solely on cost, but by analyzing what's best for the trip you envision. Study the ins and outs of the many ways of getting from point A to point B—whether flying, riding the rails, driving, biking, or hiking.

For example, if you're traveling alone, traversing a huge area, and spending the majority of your time in big cities, it makes more sense to go by train with a rail pass than to mess with a car.

5. Make a rough itinerary. Sketch out an itinerary,

writing in the number of days you'd like to stay in each place (knowing you'll probably have to trim it later). Take advantage of weekends to stretch your time and minimize lost work days.

Carefully consider travel time. Check online to estimate how long various journeys will take by rail (bahn.com) or by car (viamichelin.com). Consider night trains or overnight boats to save time and money.

My rough itinerary, with desired number of days:

3	London
5	Paris
3	Alps
2	Florence
3	Rome (*flight or night boat*)
7	Greece (*flight or night boat*)
1	Bologna
2	Venice (*night train*)
3	Munich/Bavaria
3	Romantic Road/Rhine Cruise
3	Berlin
4	Amsterdam
39	*TOTAL DAYS*

Planning an Itinerary

SEPTEMBER

SUN.	MON.	TUE.	WED.	THUR.	FRI.	SAT.
		1	**2** Mom's Birthday! ☺	**3**	**4** Fly → USA	**5** Arrive London / L
6 London / L	**7** London / L	**8** London; eve train to Paris / P	**9** Paris / P	**10** Paris / P	**11** S.T. Versailles / P	**12** Train to Alps / A
13 Alps / A	**14** Uffizi Closed Train to Florence / F	**15** Florence, see museums / F	**16** Early train to Rome / R	**17** Rome / N.T.	**18** Venice / V	**19** Venice / N.T.
20 Oktoberfest! ☺ Munich / M	**21** Dachau Closed S.T. Neusch. Castle / M	**22** S.T. Salzburg / M	**23** To Romantic Road, Rothenburg / ROT	**24** Train to Rhine, River Cruise / RH	**25** To Amst. / A	**26** Amsterdam / A
27 Fly → Arrive USA	**28** Back to Work ☺	**29**	**30**			

6. Adjust by cutting, streamlining, or adding to fit your timeline or budget. If your rough itinerary exceeds your available time or money, look first to minimize travel time. When you must cut something, cut to save the most mileage. If two destinations are equally important to you and you don't have time for both, cut the place that saves the most miles.

For example, my rough itinerary (on page 51) is too long: I have only 23 days for my trip. Based on miles saved, I cut Greece, and even though I'd like to see both Amsterdam and Berlin, I drop Berlin because it's farther.

Next, I minimize clutter. A so-so destination (Bologna) breaking a convenient night train (Rome-Venice) into two half-day journeys is clutter.

Finally, I trim time from each stop. Five days in Paris would be grand, but I can see the high points in three.

It can also help to consider economizing on car rental or a rail pass. For instance, a 23-day trip can be managed with a 15-day train pass by seeing London, Paris, and Amsterdam before or after using the pass.

My final itinerary, with number of days adjusted to time limitations:

3	*London*
3	*Paris*
3	*Alps*
1	*Florence*
2	*Rome (night train)*
2	*Venice (night train)*
3	*Munich/Bavaria*
2	*Romantic Road/Rhine Cruise*
2	*Amsterdam*
23	*TOTAL DAYS*

7. Fine-tune your itinerary. Study your guidebook. Take advantage of online tools and apps, such as Stay.com, which allow you to browse destinations, map itineraries, and even get advice from friends or fellow travelers. Be sure crucial sights are open the day you'll be in town. Remember that most cities close many of their major tourist attractions for one day during the week (usually Monday). It would be a shame to be in Paris only on a Monday, when

the Orsay is *fermé*. Write out a day-by-day itinerary that takes into account any can't-miss sights, festivals, or markets. Note that when flying from the United States, you'll most likely arrive in Europe on the next day. When returning, you arrive home the same day (or so you hope).

8. Organize and share your itinerary. Whether you want to meet up with friends along the way, let family members know where you'll be, or just corral all your travel details in one place—an itinerary chart saved in a Word document or Excel chart makes it easy to share your plans. Tools such as TripIt can also help; using your confirmation emails, the app creates an itinerary—with maps, directions, and recommendations—that you can access from your smartphone and share.

The Home-Base Strategy

Staying longer in one spot can be a good way to make your trip itinerary smoother, simpler, and more efficient. Set yourself up in a central location and use that place as a base for day trips to nearby attractions.

The home-base approach minimizes set-up time. Changing hotels frequently can be exhausting, frustrating, and time-consuming. Many hotels give a better price, or at least more smiles, for longer stays. Some B&Bs don't accept those staying only one night.

You are freed from your luggage. Being able to leave your luggage in the hotel lets you travel freely and with the peace of mind that you are set for the night. Bags are less likely to be lost or stolen in your hotel than en route.

You feel "at home" in your home-base town. This comfortable feeling takes more than a day to get, and when you're changing locations every day or two, you may never enjoy this important sense of rootedness. Home-basing allows you to become attuned to the rhythm of daily life.

Day-trip to a village, enjoy the nightlife in a city. The home-base approach lets you spend the evening in a city, where there is more exciting nightlife. Most small countryside towns die after 9 p.m. If you're not dead by 9 p.m., you'll enjoy the action in a larger city.

Transportation is a snap. Europe's generally frequent and punctual train and bus systems (many of which operate out of a hub anyway) make this home-base strategy practical. With a train pass, trips are "free"; otherwise, the transportation is reasonable, sometimes with reductions offered for round-trip tickets (especially for "same-day return").

Tracking Your Itinerary

Once I've fine-tuned my itinerary, I put everything into a chart like this one. This system keeps me organized, since I can collect all my reservations, train times, and other trip notes in one place. As I travel, I can see at a glance where I'll be sleeping a week from now, or what time the train leaves on Saturday. Even if you're not a detail person, it pays to be disciplined about this, particularly when you're traveling in peak season or visiting popular spots. And it's handy to give to family, friends, and coworkers who are curious about where you'll be.

Create an itinerary like this, then use it to keep track of your progress as you systematically set up your trip. Work your way through your list and request rooms, slogging away until the entire trip is confirmed. Make any advance train or sightseeing reservations you'll need (for this sample itinerary, I'd reserve the Eurostar and overnight trains ahead of time, as well as tickets for the Eiffel Tower). Then... travel, enjoying a well-planned trip.

Date	Travel	Sleep/Notes
Fri, Sept 4	Fly to London after work (depart 6 p.m.)	Plane
Sat, Sept 5	Arrive London at 11:45 a.m., check in at hotel, take orientation bus tour	Luna Simone Hotel, London (lunasimonehotel.com) Original London Sightseeing Bus Tour is discounted with guidebook
Sun, Sept 6	Sightsee London (Tower of London, Shakespeare's Globe tour, Tate Modern)	Luna Simone Hotel, London Many sights closed today; Speaker's Corner open today only
Mon, Sept 7	See more London (Westminster Abbey, National Gallery, evening play)	Luna Simone Hotel, London Parliament open late; check for discount theater tickets at Leicester Square

Good Home-Base Cities

Here are some of my favorite places to call home, along with the best day trips from each.

Madrid: Toledo, Segovia, El Escorial, and even Sevilla and Córdoba with the AVE bullet trains

Amsterdam: Most of the Netherlands, particularly Alkmaar, Enkhuizen's Zuiderzee Museum, Arnhem's Folk Museum and Kröller-Müller Museum, Delft, The Hague, Scheveningen, and Edam

Copenhagen: Frederiksborg Castle, Roskilde, Helsingør, Odense, and over the bridge to Malmö (Sweden)

Paris: Versailles, Chartres, Vaux-le-Vicomte, Fontainebleau, Chantilly, Giverny, Reims

Date	Travel	Sleep/Notes
Tue, Sept 8	Wrap up London (St. Paul's/ The City, British Museum); take evening train to Paris (6-9:20 p.m.)	Grand Hôtel Lévêque, Paris hotel-leveque.com Confirm Paris hotel before leaving London
Wed, Sept 9	Sightsee Paris (historic core, incl. Notre Dame, Sainte-Chapelle; also Louvre, Eiffel Tower at night)	Grand Hôtel Lévêque, Paris Museums crowded today; Louvre open late
Thu, Sept 10	Sightsee Paris (Champs-Elysées, Rodin Museum, Orsay)	Grand Hôtel Lévêque, Paris Orsay open late
Fri, Sept 11	Side-trip to Versailles	Grand Hôtel Lévêque, Paris Reserve train for tomorrow?
Sat, Sept 12	Take morning train to Swiss Alps (7 a.m.-2 p.m. in Interlaken, transfer in Mannheim and Basel); maybe hike in late afternoon	Olle and Maria's B&B, Gimmelwald (oeggimann@bluewin.ch) Reserve Interlaken-Florence train for Monday?
Sun, Sept 13	Sightsee Alps (breakfast at the Schilthorn Männlichen-Kleine Scheidegg hike)	Olle and Maria's B&B, Gimmelwald If rainy, visit Bern
Mon, Sept 14	Short morning hike and/or visit Trümmelbach Falls, afternoon train to Florence (from Interlaken 1:30-7 p.m.)	Hotel Centrale, Florence (hotelcentralefirenze.it) If rainy, take morning train to Florence (from Interlaken 8:01 a.m.-2 p.m.); on arrival, do walking tour since most museums closed

and so on...

London: Bath, Stonehenge, Cambridge, York, and many others; even Paris is less than three hours away by train

Arles: Pont du Gard, Nîmes, Avignon, and the rest of Provence

Florence: Siena, Pisa, San Gimignano, and many other hill towns

Venice: Padua, Vicenza, Verona, and Ravenna

Munich: Salzburg, "Mad" King Ludwig's castles (Neuschwanstein and Linderhof), the Wieskirche, Oberammergau, and other small Bavarian towns

Sorrento: Naples, Pompeii, Herculaneum, Mount Vesuvius, Amalfi Coast, Paestum, and Capri

High-Speed Town-Hopping

When I tell people that I saw three or four towns in one day, many think, "Insane! Nobody can really see several towns in a day!" Of course, it's folly to go too fast, but many stop-worthy towns take only an hour or two to cover. Don't let feelings of guilt tell you to slow down and stay longer if you really are finished with a town. There's so much more to enjoy in the rest of Europe. Going too slow is as bad as going too fast.

If you're efficient and use the high-speed town-hopping method, you'll amaze yourself with what you can see in a day. Let me explain with an example:

You wake up early in A-ville. Checking out of your hotel, you have one sight to see before your 10 a.m. train. (You checked the train schedule the night before.) After the sight-seeing and before getting to the station, you visit the open-air market and buy the ingredients for your brunch, and pick up a B-burg map and tourist brochure at A-ville's tourist office.

From 10 to 11 a.m. you travel by train to B-burg. During that hour you have a restful brunch, enjoy the passing scenery, and prepare for B-burg by reading your literature and deciding what you want to see. Just before your arrival, put the items you need (camera, jacket, tourist information) into your small daypack. Then, as soon as you get there, check the rest of your luggage in a locker. (Most stations have storage lockers or a baggage-check desk.)

Before leaving B-burg's station, write down the departure times of the next few trains to C-town. Now you can sightsee as much or as little as you want and still know when to comfortably catch your train.

B-burg is great, so you stay a little longer than anticipated. After a snack in the park, you catch the train at 2:30 p.m. By 3 p.m. you're in C-town, where you repeat the same procedure you followed in B-burg. C-town just isn't what it was cracked up to be, so after a walk along the waterfront and a look at the church, you catch the next train out at 5 p.m.

You arrive in D-dorf, the last town on the day's agenda, by 5:30 p.m. A man in the station directs you to a good budget pension two blocks down the street. You're checked in and

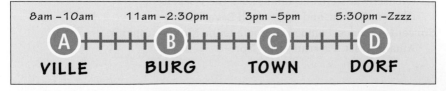

8am –10am   11am –2:30pm   3pm –5pm   5:30pm –Zzzz

A ——— B ——— C ——— D

VILLE   BURG   TOWN   DORF

unpacked in no time, and, after a few horizontal moments, it's time to find a good restaurant and eat dinner. After a meal and an evening stroll, you're ready to call it a day. As you write in your journal, it occurs to you: This was a great sightseeing day. You spent it high-speed town-hopping.

PRIORITIZING YOUR TIME

So much to see, so little time. How to choose? It depends on your interest and your tastes. One person's Barcelona is another person's Bucharest.

The Best and Worst of Europe (with No Apologies)

Good travel writers should make hard choices and give the reader solid opinions. Just so nobody will accuse me of gutlessness, I've assembled a pile of spunky opinions. Chances are that you have too many stops on your trip wish list and not enough time. To make your planning a little easier, heed these warnings. These are just my personal feelings after more than 100 months of European travel. And if you die agree with any of them, you obviously haven't been there.

Let's start with the dullest corner of the British Isles, southern Scotland. It's so boring the Romans decided to block it off with Hadrian's Wall. However, like Venice's St. Mark's Square at midnight and Napoleon's tomb in Paris, Hadrian's Wall itself covers history buffs with goose bumps.

London, York, Bath, and Edinburgh are the most interesting cities in Britain. Belfast, Liverpool, and Glasgow are quirky enough to be called interesting. Oxford pales next to Cambridge, and Stratford-upon-Avon is little more than Shakespeare's house—and that's as dead as he is.

LEFT Geneva's newspaper objects to my "denigrating" its dull city on the Internet.

RIGHT In Switzerland, special scenic trains give you front row seats and the Alps in your lap.

Itinerary Priorities, Country by Country

Use this chart to get ideas on how speedy travelers can prioritize limited sight-seeing time in various countries. Add places from left to right as you build plans for the best of that country in 3, 5, 7, 10, or 14 days. (These suggestions take geographical proximity into account. In some cases, the plan assumes you'll take a night train.) So, according to this chart, the best week in Britain would be spread between London, Bath, Cambridge, and the Cotswolds.

3 Days	5 Days	7 Days	10 Days	14 Days
EUROPE				
Forget it	London, Paris	Amsterdam	Rhineland, Swiss Alps	Rome, Venice
BRITAIN				
London	Bath	Cambridge, Cotswolds	York	Edinburgh, North Wales
IRELAND				
Dublin	Dingle Peninsula	Belfast	Galway/ the Burren	Antrim Coast, Aran Islands
FRANCE				
Paris, Versailles	Normandy	Loire	Dordogne, Carcassonne	Provence, the Riviera
GERMANY				
Munich, Bavarian castles	Rhine Valley, Rothenburg	More Bavaria, Salzburg (Austria)	Berlin	Baden-Baden, Black Forest, Dresden
AUSTRIA				
Vienna	Salzburg	Hallstatt	Danube Valley, Tirol, Bavaria (Germany)	Innsbruck, Hall, Bratislava (Slovakia)

The west coast of Ireland (the Dingle Peninsula), Wales' Snowdonia National Park, and England's Windermere Lake District are the most beautiful natural regions of the British Isles. The North York Moors disappoint most creatures great and small.

Germany's Heidelberg, Ireland's Blarney Stone (slobbered on by countless tourists to get the "gift of gab"), Spain's Costa del Sol, and the French Riviera in July and August are among Europe's most overrated spots. The tackiest souvenirs are found next to Pisa's leaning tower and in Lourdes.

Extra caution is merited in southwest England, a mine-field of tourist traps. The British are masters at milking every tourist attraction for all it's worth. Here are some booby traps: the Devil's Toenail (a rock that looks just like a...toenail), Land's End (pay, pay, pay), and cloying

3 Days	5 Days	7 Days	10 Days	14 Days
SWITZERLAND				
Berner Oberland	Luzern	Bern, Lausanne	Zermatt, Appenzell, scenic rail trip	Lugano and Zürich
ITALY				
Florence, Venice	Rome	Cinque Terre	Civita di Bagnoregio, Siena	Sorrento, Naples, Pompeii, Amalfi Coast
SCANDINAVIA				
Copenhagen, side-trips	Stockholm	Oslo	"Norway in a Nutshell" train trip, Bergen	Helsinki, Tallinn
SPAIN				
Madrid, Toledo	Sevilla, Granada	Barcelona	Andalucía	Costa del Sol, Morocco
PORTUGAL				
Lisbon, Sintra	The Algarve	Évora, Nazaré	Sights near Nazaré, Coimbra	Porto, Douro Valley
EASTERN EUROPE				
Prague	Budapest	Kraków and Auschwitz	Slovenia and Český Krumlov	Dalmatian Coast with Dubrovnik
CROATIA & SLOVENIA				
Dubrovnik	Mostar, Split	Korčula/ Hvar or Montenegro	Lake Bled, Plitvice Lakes	Ljubljana, Rovinj
GREECE				
Athens	Hydra	Delphi	Nafplio, Epidavros, Mycenae	Olympia, Monemvasia, Mani Peninsula

Clovelly (a one-street town lined with knickknack shops selling the same goodies—like "clotted cream that you can mail home"). While Tintagel's castle, famous as the legendary birthplace of King Arthur, offers thrilling windswept and wave-beaten ruins, the town of Tintagel does everything in its little power to exploit the profitable Arthurian legend. There's even a pub in town called the Excali Bar.

Sognefjord is Norway's most spectacular fjord. The Geirangerfjord, while famous as a cruise-ship stop, is a disappointment. The most boring countryside is Sweden's (yes, I'm Norwegian), although Scandinavia's best medieval castle is in the Swedish town of Kalmar.

Norway's Stavanger, famous for nearby fjords and its status as an oil boomtown, is a large port that's about as exciting as...well, put it this way: Emigrants left it in droves to move to the wilds of Minnesota. Time in western Norway is better spent in and around Bergen.

Geneva, one of Switzerland's largest and most sterile cities, gets the "nice place to live but I wouldn't want to visit" award. It's pleasantly situated on a lake—just like Buffalo is. While it's famous, name familiarity is a rotten reason to go somewhere. If you want a Swiss city, see Bern or Luzern. However, it's almost criminal to spend a sunny Swiss day in a city if you haven't yet been high in the Alps.

Bordeaux must mean "boredom" in some ancient language. If I were offered a free trip to that town, I'd stay home and clean the fridge. Connoisseurs visit for the wine, but Bordeaux wine country and Bordeaux city are as different as night and night soil. There's a wine-tourism information bureau in Bordeaux that, for a price, will bus you out of town into the more interesting wine country nearby.

Andorra, a small country in the Pyrenees between France and Spain, is as scenic as any other chunk of those mountains. People from all over Europe flock to Andorra to take advantage of its famous duty-free shopping. As far as Americans are concerned, Andorra is just a big Spanish-speaking outlet mall. There are no bargains here that you can't get at home. Enjoy the Pyrenees elsewhere, with less traffic. Among Europe's other "little countries," San Marino and Liechtenstein are also not worth the trouble.

Germany's famous Black Forest disappoints more people than it excites. If it were all Germany offered, it would be worth seeing. For Europeans, any large forest is understandably a popular attraction. But I'd say the average American visitor who's seen more than three trees in one place would prefer Germany's Romantic Road and Bavaria to the east, the Rhine and Mosel country to the north, the Swiss Alps to the south, and France's Alsace region to the west—all high points that cut the Black Forest down to stumps.

LEFT Kissing the Blarney Stone: Slathered with spit and lipstick, it's a standard stop for typical big-bus tours in Ireland.

RIGHT England's Land's End... pay, pay, pay.

Kraków (Poland) and Budapest (Hungary) are, after
Prague, Eastern Europe's best cities. Bucharest, Romania's
capital, has little to offer. Its top-selling postcard is of the
InterContinental Hotel. If you're heading from Eastern
Europe to Greece, skip Thessaloniki, which deserves its
place in the Bible but doesn't belong in travel guidebooks.

Europe's most scenic train ride is the Glacier Express,
across southern Switzerland from Chur to Zermatt. The
most scenic boat ride is from Stockholm to Helsinki—countless islands and blondes. Europe's most underrated sight is
Rome's ancient seaport, Ostia Antica, and its most misunder-
stood wine is Portugal's *vinho verde* (green wine).

The best French château is Vaux-le-Vicomte, near
Paris. The best Gothic interior is found in Paris' Sainte-
Chapelle church. The top two medieval castle interiors are
Germany's Burg Eltz on the Mosel River, and northern Italy's
Reifenstein, near the Brenner Pass. Lisbon, Oslo, Stockholm,
Brussels, and Budapest are the most underrated big cities.

To honeymoon (or convalesce), try these tiny towns:
Beilstein on Germany's Mosel River; Hallstatt on Austria's
Lake Hallstatt; Varenna on Italy's Lake Como; Ærøskøbing
on an island in south Denmark; and Gimmelwald, high in the
Swiss Alps. Have fun (or get well)!

LEFT Ancient
Ostia Antica,
outside Rome,
is among
Europe's most
underrated
attractions.

CENTER Vaux-
le-Vicomte, near
Paris, gets my
vote for the
most beautiful
château in all
of France.

RIGHT The soar-
ing interior of
Sainte-Chapelle
is the best
lesson in Gothic
you can find.

Paper Chase

Someday, perhaps, travel will be paperless. But we're not there yet, and you'll want to be prepared with the necessary documents and know your insurance options. Here's how you can stay ahead in the inevitable paper chase.

TRAVEL DOCUMENTS

Your trip won't get off the ground if you don't prepare these documents well before your departure date. Give yourself plenty of lead time.

Passports

In much of Europe, the only document a US or Canadian citizen needs is a passport. (The US Passport Card works only for those driving or cruising to Canada, Mexico, Bermuda, and the Caribbean.) And for most American travelers, the only time any customs official looks at you seriously is at the airport as you re-enter the United States.

Getting or Renewing Your Passport: US passports, good for 10 years, cost $135 ($110 to renew). The fee for minors under 16 (including infants) is $105 for a passport good for five years—kids under 16 must apply in person with at least one parent and the other parent's notarized permission. (Parents traveling abroad with children should refer to page 426 for other special document needs.)

You can apply at some courthouses and post offices, as well as municipal buildings, such as your City Hall. For details and the location of the nearest passport-acceptance facility, see travel.state.gov or call 877-487-2778. Processing time varies; the current wait is posted on the State Department website. During busier periods, a six-week wait is common. One or two weeks after you apply, you can check online for the status of your passport application and its estimated arrival date.

If you need your passport in less than six weeks, tack on an additional $60 expediting fee (plus overnight shipping both ways), and you'll get it by mail in two to three weeks. In a last-minute emergency situation, call the above number and speak to a customer-service representative. If you can prove that you have to leave within two weeks (by showing a purchased airline eticket or a letter from work requiring you to travel overseas on short notice), you may be able to receive a passport in a day or so. Make an appointment to go in person to the nearest US Passport Agency and pay the additional $60 fee; they'll issue your new passport in 24 to 72 hours.

Your passport is your most important travel document.

Keep an eye on your passport's expiration date. Most European countries require that your passport be valid for at least three months *after* your ticketed date of return to the United States (Russia requires a six-month window). This means that even if your passport doesn't expire for a few months, you may still be denied entry to a country. Check your destination country's requirements, and if necessary, get your passport renewed before you go. Countries can have surprising entry requirements. For example, the Czech Republic and Poland technically require visitors to carry proof of medical insurance (your health insurance card usually suffices). While it's virtually unheard of that a border guard would actually request this, it's worth knowing about. For requirements per country, see travel.state.gov.

If you're a frequent international traveler, consider the US Customs' Global Entry Program, which lets you bypass passport control at major US airports ($100 fee, globalentry.gov).

Canadian citizens can refer to voyage.gc.ca for Canada-specific passport information.

Traveling with Your Passport: Take good care of your passport, but relax if a night-train conductor asks you to temporarily give it up. When you sleep on an international night train to a non-Schengen country (see sidebar), the conductor may take your passport so you won't be disturbed when the train crosses the border at 3:00 a.m. It's also standard for hoteliers to hold onto your passport for a short time so they can register you with the police (for tips and details, see page 212).

Replacing Your Passport: If you have to replace a lost or stolen passport in Europe, it's much easier to do if you have a photocopy of it and a couple of passport-type photos, either brought from home or taken in Europe. For details on how to get a replacement, see page 338. For tips on preparing and protecting key documents while traveling, see page 66.

Visas

A visa is a stamp placed in your passport by a foreign government, allowing you to enter their country. Visas are not required for Americans or Canadians traveling in Western Europe and most of the East (including the Czech Republic, Slovakia, Poland, Hungary, Slovenia, Croatia, Bosnia-Herzegovina, Montenegro, and the Baltic states).

Both Canadians and Americans need visas to visit Turkey, and must obtain them before entering the country. You can get your "e-visa" online at evisa.gov.tr/en, or visit a Turkish consulate or embassy. US residents pay $20; Canadians pay $60—that's US dollars, not Canadian. However, cruise-line passengers don't need a visa if they are doing day trips in Turkey but spending nights aboard their ship. On the other hand, cruise passengers arriving in Turkey to start their cruise, or staying overnight on Turkish soil after their cruise, must get a visa before their arrival in Turkey. For more information, see turkishembassy.org (Turkey's embassy in the United States) or ottava.be.mfa.gov.tr (Turkey's embassy in Canada).

Travelers to Russia also need visas. The process can be expensive,

European Borders (or Not)

Thanks to a series of treaties known as the Schengen Agreement, today there are no border checks between 26 of Europe's countries: Austria, Belgium, the Czech Republic, Denmark, Estonia, Finland, France, Germany, Greece, Hungary, Iceland, Italy, Latvia, Liechtenstein, Lithuania, Luxembourg, Malta, the Netherlands, Norway, Poland, Portugal, Slovakia, Slovenia, Spain, Sweden, and Switzerland.

Holdouts include the United Kingdom and the Republic of Ireland, as well as some Eastern European countries (such as Croatia, Bosnia-Herzegovina, Montenegro, Russia, and Turkey). Romania and Bulgaria are getting ready to join the Schengen group.

What does Schengen mean for you? When traveling between participating countries, you don't have to stop or show a passport—you'll simply blow past abandoned border posts on the superhighway or high-speed train...souvenirs of an earlier, more complicated era of European travel. Non-Schengen countries still have border checks (for now)—but even in these places, the border crossing is generally just a quick wave-through for US citizens. Schengen or no, you always need to show your passport at your first point of entry into Europe, and to re-enter the US.

and you should begin several weeks in advance. Before applying for a visa, you must first get an official document called a "visa invitation" or a "visa support letter" (generally from a hotel or visa agency). You'll also need to fill out an Electronic Visa Application Form. The embassy does not accept visa applications by mail, so it's smart to use an agency that specializes in steering your

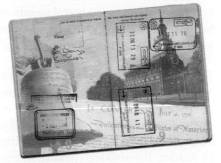

application through the process. Passport Visas Express is one of many such vendors (passportvisasexpress.com). The costs add up; figure about $250 total per person to cover the visa, service fee, and secure shipping. For more details, go to ricksteves.com/russianvisa or see russianembassy.org (which lists Russian consulate locations in Washington, DC; New York; San Francisco; Seattle; and Houston). If you live near one of these consulates, you can save some money (but go through a lot of steps—see embassy website) by applying for your visa in person at the consulate.

For travel beyond Europe, get up-to-date information on visa requirements from your travel agent or the US Department of State (travel.state.gov).

If you do need a visa, it's usually best to get it at home before you leave. If you forget, just about every country has an embassy or consulate (which can issue visas) in the capital of every other European country.

Student Cards and Hostel Memberships

The International Student Identity Card (ISIC), the only internationally recognized student ID card, gets you discounts on transportation, phoning, entertainment, and sightseeing throughout Europe, and includes some basic trip insurance. If you are a full-time student (and can prove it), get one. Your ISIC card can also be used as a prepaid credit card. But, if you're older than 26, you might have trouble using the card in some places. Two other varieties of the card, offering similar discounts, are available, though they're often not honored: for teachers of any age (International Teacher Identity Card, or ITIC) and for non-student travelers under age 26 (International Youth Travel Card, or IYTC). Each card costs $25 and is good for one year from the date of issue. Get yours on the ISIC website (myisic.com), through STA Travel (statravel.com), or from your university foreign-study office.

Travelers who'll be staying at least six nights in official HI hostels should get a hostel membership card from a local hostel or Hostelling International (hiusa.org, tel. 301/495-1240; for more on these cards, see page 226).

Rail Passes and Car Documents

Most rail passes are not sold in Europe and must be purchased before you leave home (for more on rail passes, see the Trains, Buses & Boats chapter). If you're renting a car, be aware that an International Driving Permit is required in Austria, Bosnia-Herzegovina, Greece, Hungary, Italy, Poland, Slovenia, and Spain (get it at AAA before your departure—for $15 plus tax). Even if you aren't renting a car in Europe, bring along your driver's license—it can come in handy if you need to leave a piece of ID to rent a bike or audioguide and you don't want to part with your passport. For specifics, see the Driving & Navigating chapter.

Copying Key Documents

Before your trip, make two sets of photocopies of your valuable documents (front and back). Pack one copy and leave the other copy with someone at home—to email or fax to you in case of an emergency. (Don't photocopy a debit or credit card—instead, keep just the number in a retrievable place.) It's easier to replace a lost or stolen passport, rail pass, or car-rental voucher if you have a photocopy that helps prove you really owned what you lost. Consider bringing a couple of passport-type pictures, which can expedite the replacement process for a lost or stolen passport (to replace a passport, see page 338).

While traveling, guard your photocopies as carefully as you would the originals. I hide mine in a pouch clipped into the bottom of my luggage (don't tell anyone). Some people scan their documents and email them to a Web-based account or store them on a site such as Google Docs for easy access from the road. If you're concerned about having electronic copies floating around in cyberspace, you could put them on a USB flash drive and tuck it into your money belt (a pouch with a strap that you buckle around your waist like a belt and tuck under your clothes—for more info, see page 328). If you're traveling with a companion, carry photocopies of each other's passports and other important documents.

It's also smart to have a backup copy of your itinerary in case you lose the information. You can save hotel and car-rental confirmations online, email a copy of your itinerary to yourself, use an itinerary-storage website (such as TripIt.com), or at the very least, leave the details at home with a friend. You can also write or print, as small as you can read, any phone numbers or email addresses you might need in an emergency, including a list of your reserved hotels, then store this slip of paper in your money belt.

TRAVEL INSURANCE

Travel insurance can minimize the considerable financial risks of traveling: accidents, illness, missed flights, canceled tours, lost baggage, theft, terrorism, travel-company bankruptcies, emergency evacuation, and getting your body home if you die. Each traveler's potential loss varies, depending on how much of your trip is prepaid, the refundability of the air ticket you purchased, your state of health, the value of your luggage, where you're traveling, the financial health of your tour company and airline, and what coverage you already have (through your medical insurance, homeowners or renters insurance, and/or credit card).

For some travelers, insurance is a good deal; for others, it's not. What are the chances you'll need it? How willing are you to take risks? How much is peace of mind worth to you? Take these considerations into account, understand your options, and make an informed decision for your trip.

Insurance Basics

The insurance menu includes five main courses: trip cancellation and interruption, medical, evacuation, baggage, and flight insurance. Supplemental policies can be added to cover specific concerns, such as identity theft or political evacuation. The various types are generally sold in some combination—rather than buying only baggage, medical, or cancellation insurance, you'll usually purchase a package that includes most or all of them. If you want just one type of coverage in particular—such as medical—ask for that (though it might come with a little cancellation or baggage insurance, too). "Comprehensive insurance" covers all of the above (plus expenses incurred if your trip is delayed, if you miss your flight, or if your tour company changes your itinerary).

One of the better changes in recent years is that many companies, such as Travelex and Travel Guard, now offer comprehensive packages that serve as your primary coverage; they'll take care of your expenses regardless of what other insurance you might have (for instance, if you have health insurance through your job). That means they pay first and don't ask questions about your other insurance. This can be a real plus if you want to avoid out-of-pocket expenses.

Insurance prices can vary dramatically, with most packages costing between 5 and 12 percent of the total trip. Age is one of the biggest factors affecting the price: Rates go up dramatically for every decade over 50, while coverage is generally inexpensive or even free for children 17 and under.

Travel agents recommend that you get travel insurance (because they get a commission when you buy it, and because they can be held liable for your losses if they don't explain insurance options to you). While travel agents can give you information and advice, they are not insurance agents—always direct any specific questions to the insurance provider (for a list of providers, see the sidebar).

Travel Insurance Providers

For extensive travel insurance coverage, go with a big-name company. Avoid buying insurance from a no-name company you found online. Consider the package deals sold by:

- **Betins** (betins.com, tel. 866-552-8834 or 253/238-6374)
- **Allianz** (allianztravelinsurance. com, tel. 866-884-3556)
- **Travelex** (travelexinsurance.com, tel. 800-228-9792)
- **Travel Guard** (travelguard.com, tel. 800-826-4919)
- **Travel Insured International** (travelinsured.com, tel. 800-243-3174)

You can compare insurance policies and costs among various providers at **insuremytrip.com** (they also sell insurance; tel. 800-487-4722). The $25 ISIC student identity card (described earlier) includes minimal travel insurance.

Policies available vary by state, and not all insurance companies are licensed in every state. If you have to make a claim and encounter problems with a company that isn't licensed in your state, you don't have a case.

Note that some travel insurance, especially trip-cancellation coverage, is reimbursement-only: You'll pay out-of-pocket for your expenses, then submit the paperwork to your insurer to recoup your money. With medical coverage, you may be able to arrange to have expensive hospital or doctor bills paid directly. Either way, if you have a problem, it's wise to contact your insurance company immediately to ask them how to proceed. Many major insurance companies are accessible by phone 24 hours a day—handy if you have problems in Europe.

Types of Coverage

For each type of insurance that follows, I've outlined some of the key legalese. But be warned—these are only guidelines. Policies can differ, even within the same company. Certain companies and policies have different levels of coverage based on whether you purchase the car rental, hotel, or flight directly on your own or through a travel agent. Ask a lot of questions, and always read the fine print to see what's covered (e.g., how they define "travel partner" or "family member"—your great-aunt might not qualify).

Trip-Cancellation or Interruption Insurance

For me, this is the most usable and worthwhile kind of insurance. It's expensive to cancel or interrupt any prepaid kind of travel, and for a fraction of the trip cost, you can alleviate the risk of losing money if something unforeseen gets in the way. This can be a good value or a bad one, depending on the odds that you'll need to use it. If I think there's a greater than 1-in-20 chance I'll need it (for instance, if I have a loved one in frail health at home), trip-cancellation insurance can be a very good value and provide needed peace of mind. But if I'm healthy and hell-bent on making a trip, I'll risk it and not spend the extra. If it turns out that I need to cancel or interrupt, I'll just have to take my financial lumps—I played the odds and lost.

Before purchasing trip-cancellation or interruption coverage, check with your credit-card issuer; yours may offer limited coverage for flights or tours purchased with the card.

A standard trip-cancellation or interruption insurance policy covers the nonrefundable financial penalties or losses you incur when you cancel a prepaid tour or flight for an acceptable reason, such as:

- You, your travel partner, or a family member cannot travel because of sickness, death, layoff, or a list of other acceptable reasons.
- Your tour company or airline goes out of business or can't perform as promised.
- A family member at home gets sick (check the fine print to see how a family member's pre-existing condition might affect coverage).
- You miss a flight or need an emergency flight for a reason outside your control (such as a car accident, inclement weather, or a strike).

So, if you or your travel partner accidentally breaks a leg a few days before your trip, you can both bail out (if you both have this insurance) without losing all the money you paid for the trip. Or, if you're on a tour and have an accident on your first day, you'll be reimbursed for the portion of the tour you weren't able to use.

This type of insurance can be used whether you're on an organized tour or cruise, or traveling independently (in which case, only the prepaid expenses—such as your flight and any nonrefundable hotel reservations—are covered). Note the difference: Trip *cancellation* is when you don't go on your trip at all. Trip *interruption* is when you begin a journey but have to cut it short; in this case, you'll be reimbursed only for the portion of the trip that you didn't complete. If you're taking a tour, it may already come with some cancellation insurance—ask.

Some insurers won't cover certain airlines or tour operators. Many are obvious—such as companies under bankruptcy protection—but others can be surprising (including major airlines). Make sure your carrier is covered.

It's smart to buy your insurance policy within a week of the date you make the first payment on your trip. Policies purchased later than a designated cutoff date—generally 7 to 21 days, as determined by the insurance company—are less likely to cover tour company or air carrier bankruptcies, pre-existing medical conditions (yours or those of family members at home), or terrorist incidents. Mental-health concerns are generally not covered.

Jittery travelers are fretful about two big unknowns: terrorist attacks and natural disasters. Ask your company for the details. A terrorist attack or natural disaster in your hometown may or may not be covered. You'll likely be covered only if your departure city or a destination on your itinerary actually becomes the target of a terrorist incident within 30 days of your trip. Even then, if your tour operator offers a substitute itinerary, your coverage may become void. As for natural disasters, you're covered only if your destination is uninhabitable (for example, your hotel is flooded or the airport is gone). War or outbreaks of disease generally aren't covered.

You can avoid the question of what is and what isn't covered by buying a costly "any reason" policy. These offer at least partial reimbursement (generally 75 percent) no matter why you cancel the trip. But the premiums are so hefty that these policies appeal mostly to deep-pocketed nervous Nellies.

The rugged, healthy, unattached, and gung-ho traveler will probably forgo trip-cancellation or interruption coverage. I have skipped it many times, and my number has yet to come up. But if you're paying out a lot of up-front money for an organized tour (which is expensive to cancel), if you have questionable health, or if you have a loved one at home in poor health, it's probably a good idea to get this coverage.

Medical Insurance

Before buying a special medical insurance policy for your trip, check with your medical insurer—you might already be covered by your existing health plan. While many US insurers cover you overseas, Medicare does not.

Even if your health plan does cover you internationally, you may want to consider buying a special medical travel policy. Much of the additional coverage available is supplemental (or "secondary"), so it covers whatever expenses your health plan doesn't, such as deductibles. But you can also purchase primary coverage, which will take care of your costs up to a certain amount. In emergency situations involving costly procedures or overnight stays, the hospital will typically work directly with your travel-insurance carrier on billing (but not with your regular health insurance company; you'll likely have to pay up front to the hospital or clinic, then get reimbursed by your stateside insurer later). For non-emergencies, a quick visit to a doctor will likely be an out-of-pocket expense (you'll bring home documentation to be reimbursed). Whatever the circumstances, it's smart to contact your insurer from the road to let them know that you've sought medical help.

Many pre-existing conditions are covered by medical and trip-cancellation coverage, depending on when you buy the coverage and how recently you've been treated for the condition. If you travel frequently to Europe, multitrip annual policies can save you money. Check with your agent or insurer before you commit.

The US State Department periodically issues warnings about traveling to at-risk countries (see travel.state.gov). If you're visiting one of these countries, your cancellation and medical insurance will likely not be honored, unless you buy supplemental coverage.

For travelers over 70 years old, buying travel medical insurance can be expensive. Compare the cost of a travel medical plan with comprehensive insurance (described earlier), which come with good medical and evacuation coverage that can otherwise be very expensive. A travel-insurance company can help you sort out the options. Certain Medigap plans cover some emergency care outside the US; call the issuer of your supplemental policy for the details.

Other Insurance

Evacuation insurance covers the cost of getting you to a place where you can receive appropriate medical treatment

Theft Protection

Theft is definitely a concern when you consider the value of the items we pack along. Laptops, tablets, digital cameras, smartphones, iPods, and ereaders are all expensive to replace.

One way to protect your investment is to purchase travel insurance from a specialized company such as Travel Guard, which offers a variety of comprehensive plans and options that include coverage for theft. Before buying a policy, ask how they determine the value of the stolen objects and about any maximum reimbursement limits for jewelry, electronics, or cameras.

Thieves rifled through this backpack before dumping it—minus any valuables—on the street in Rome.

It's also smart to check with your homeowners or renters insurance company. Under most policies, your personal property is already protected against theft anywhere in the world—but your insurance deductible still applies. If you have a $1,000 deductible and your $500 iPhone is stolen, you'll have to pay to replace it. Rather than buying separate insurance, it may make more sense to add a rider to your existing policy to cover expensive items while you travel.

Before you leave, it's a good idea to take an inventory of all the high-value items you're bringing. Make a list of serial numbers, makes, and models of your electronics, and take photos that can serve as records. If anything is stolen, this information is helpful to both your insurance company and the police. If you plan to file an insurance claim, you'll need to get a police report in Europe. (If dealing with the police is intimidating, ask your hotelier for help.) For tips on avoiding theft while traveling, see the Theft & Scams chapter.

in the event of an emergency. (In a worst-case scenario, this can mean a medically equipped—and incredibly expensive—private jet.) This is usually not covered by your regular medical-insurance plan back home. Sometimes this coverage can get you home after an accident, but more often, it'll just get you as far as the nearest major hospital. "Medical repatriation"—that is, getting you all the way home—is likely to be covered only if it's considered medically necessary. Before purchasing a policy, ask your insurer to explain exactly what's covered before *and after* you get to the hospital.

Keep in mind that medical and evacuation insurance may not cover you if you're participating in an activity your insurer considers to be dangerous (such as skydiving, mountain climbing, bungee jumping, scuba diving, or even skiing).

Some companies sell supplementary adventure-sports coverage.

Baggage insurance—for luggage that is lost, delayed, or damaged—is included in most comprehensive policies, but it's rare to buy it separately. Baggage insurance puts a strict cap on reimbursement for such items as jewelry, eyewear, electronics, and photographic equipment—read the fine print. If you check your baggage for a flight, it's already covered by the airline (ask your airline about its luggage liability limit; if you have particularly valuable luggage, you can buy supplemental "excess valuation" insurance directly from the airline). Check if your homeowners or renters insurance covers baggage. Travelers baggage insurance will cover the deductibles and items excluded from your homeowners policy. Double-check the particulars with your agent. If your policy doesn't cover expensive rail passes, consider Rail Europe's Rail Protection Plan, which must be purchased when you buy your pass (but first check what the plan for your pass actually covers—it may not be a good value).

Flight insurance ("crash coverage") is a statistical rip off that heirs love. It's basically a life insurance policy that covers you when you're on the airplane. Since plane crashes are so rare, there's little sense in spending money on this insurance.

Collision coverage, an important type of insurance for rental cars, is covered on page 159. Collision insurance may be included in some comprehensive travel-insurance plans or available as an upgrade on others.

BEFORE YOU GO

Quite a few things are worth arranging while you're still at home—lining these up before you leave is a big part of having a smooth trip. I've collected my suggestions here, with references for where to find more detailed information elsewhere in the book.

- ❑ Check your **passport expiration;** you may be denied entry into certain European countries if your passport is due to expire within three months of your ticketed date of return. Get it renewed if you'll be cutting it close (see page 62).
- ❑ Make **reservations** well in advance, especially during peak season, for accommodations, popular restaurants, major sights (see page 282), and local guides.

❑ Call your **debit- and credit-card companies** to let them know the countries you'll be visiting, to ask about fees, and more. Get your bank's emergency phone number in the US (but not its 800 number) to call collect if you have a problem. If you don't know your credit card's PIN code, ask your bank to mail it to you (see sidebar on page 182).

❑ Do your homework if you want to buy **travel insurance.** Check whether your existing insurance (health, homeowners, or renters) covers you and your possessions overseas (see page 67).

❑ If you're bringing the **kids,** make sure you have the right paperwork, including a passport for each, a letter of consent if only one parent is traveling, and documentation for adopted children (see page 426).

❑ Make **copies of important travel documents** as a backup in case you lose the originals (see page 66).

❑ **Students** should get an International Student Identity Card (ISIC) for discounts throughout Europe. **Hostelers** who'll be staying at least six nights in official HI hostels should get a membership card (see page 65 for information on both).

❑ If you're planning to buy a **rail pass,** you'll need to get it before you leave the US (see page 119). Rail pass or no, it can also be smart to reserve seats on certain trains before you leave (see page 127).

❑ If you need to bridge several long-distance destinations on your trip, look into cheap **flights within Europe.** For the best fares, book these as far in advance as possible (see page 104).

❑ If you'll be **renting a car,** you'll need a valid driver's license. An International Driving Permit is technically required in Austria, Bosnia-Herzegovina, Croatia, Greece, Hungary, Italy, Poland, Romania, Slovenia, and Spain (see page 157).

❑ If you plan to use your **US mobile phone** in Europe, contact your provider to enable international calling or to "unlock" your phone. Consider signing up for an international calling, text, and/or data plan, and be sure to confirm voice- and data-roaming fees (see page 242).

❑ Get a proper guidebook. If traveling with one of mine, check the **Rick Steves guidebook updates** page for the latest news about your destination (ricksteves.com/update).

❑ Download any **apps** you might want to use on the road, such as translators, maps, and transit schedules. Check out Rick Steves Audio Europe for free, downloadable audio tours of Europe's major sights and hours of travel interviews (via the Rick Steves Audio Europe app or ricksteves.com/audioeurope; for details, see page 19).

❑ Take care of any **medical needs.** Visit your doctor to get a checkup, and see your dentist if you have any work that needs to be done. If you use prescription drugs, stock up before your trip (see page 382). Pack along the prescription, plus one for contact lenses or glasses if you wear them.

❑ Attend to your **household needs.** Cancel your newspapers, hold your mail delivery, and prepay your bills.

❑ Give a **copy of your itinerary** to family or friends.

❑ Make a **list of valuables** that you're bringing (such as electronics). Include serial numbers, makes, and models, and take photos of your items to serve as a record for the police and your insurance company should anything be stolen.

❑ Because **airline carry-on restrictions** are always changing, visit the Transportation Security Administration's website (tsa.gov) for an up-to-date list of what you can bring on the plane with you...and what you must check.

Pack Light

The importance of packing light cannot be overemphasized, but, for your own good, I'll try. You'll never meet a traveler who, after five trips, brags: "Every year I pack heavier." The measure of a good traveler is how light he or she travels. You can't travel heavy, happy, and cheap. Pick two.

ONE BAG—THAT'S IT

My self-imposed limit is 20 pounds in a 9″ × 21″ × 14″ carry-on-size bag (it'll fit in an airplane's overhead bin). At my company, we've taken tens of thousands of people of all ages and styles on tours through Europe. We allow only one carry-on bag. For many, this is a radical concept: 9″ × 21″ × 14″? That's my cosmetics kit! But they manage, and they're glad they did. After you enjoy that sweet mobility and freedom, you'll never go any other way.

No matter your age, you can travel like college kids: light, mobile, and wearing your convertible suitcase/backpack.

You'll walk with your luggage more than you think you will. Before flying to Europe, give yourself a test. Pack up completely, go into your hometown, and practice being a tourist for an hour. Fully loaded, you should enjoy window-shopping. If you can't, stagger home and thin things out.

When you carry your own luggage, it's less likely to get lost, broken, or stolen. Quick, last-minute changes in flight plans become simpler. A small bag sits on your lap on the bus or taxi and stashes easily overhead on an airplane. You don't have to worry about it, and, when you arrive, you can hit the ground running. It's a good feeling. When I land in London, I'm on my way downtown while everyone else stares anxiously at the

luggage carousel. When I fly home,
I'm the first guy the dog sniffs.

These days, you can also save
money by carrying your own bag.
While it's still free to check one bag
on most overseas trips, you'd likely
pay a fee to check two. If you're taking a separate flight within Europe,
expect to be charged to check even
just one bag.

Remember, packing light isn't just about saving time or
money—it's about your traveling lifestyle. Too much luggage
marks you as a typical tourist. It slams the Back Door shut.
Serendipity suffers. Changing locations becomes a major
operation. Con artists figure you're helpless. Porters are a
problem only to those who need them. With only one bag,
you're mobile and in control. Take this advice seriously.

Pack light. You won't have a mule to haul around your bags. (If you do, you're taking advantage of your spouse.)

Baggage Restrictions

Pack light...and pack smart. You can't bring anything potentially dangerous—such as knives, lighters, or large quantities
of liquids or gels—in your carry-on bag. (This list can change
without notice—for details, see "What Can't I Carry On?" on
page 101.) These days I leave my Swiss Army knife at home,
bring smaller bottles of toiletries, and carry on my bag as
usual.

Be aware that many airlines have additional (and
frequently changing) restrictions on the number, size, and
weight of carry-on bags. Some European budget airlines,
such as Ryanair and Air Berlin, use smaller carry-on dimensions than major airlines. (Restrictions can vary from airport
to airport, even on the same airline.) Check your airline's
website for details.

When you carry your bag onto the plane, all liquids, gels,
and aerosols must be in 3.4-ounce or smaller containers, all
of which must fit into one clear, quart-size, plastic zip-top
bag. (If you want to bring a lot of a liquid that can be hard
to find in Europe—like fluoride rinse—pour it into several
smaller containers.) Exceptions are made for certain prescription and over-the-counter medicines, as well as contact-
lens solution (see tsa.gov for details).

If you check your bag, mark it inside and out with your
name, address, and emergency phone number. If you have a
lock on your bag, you may be asked to remove it to accommodate increased security checks, or it may be cut off so the bag

can be inspected (to avoid this, consider a Transportation Security Administration-approved lock, described in the packing list later in this chapter). I've never locked my bag and have never had a problem. Still, just in case, I wouldn't pack anything particularly valuable (such as cash or a camera) in checked luggage.

Backpack or Rolling Bag?

A fundamental packing question is your choice of luggage. Of all the options, I consider only three: 1) a carry-on-size convertible backpack/suitcase with zip-away shoulder straps; 2) a carry-on-size bag with wheels; or 3) an internal-frame backpack.

A convertible backpack/suitcase (see photo on page 80) gives you the best of both worlds—a mobile backpack for traveling and a low-key suitcase when in town. I travel with this bag and keep it exclusively in the backpack mode. While these soft bags basically hang on your shoulders and hips, and are not as comfortable for long hauls as internal-frame backpacks, they work fine for getting from the station to your hotel. And, at 9″ × 21″ × 14″, they fit in the airplane's overhead lockers. I live out of this bag for four months each year—and I absolutely love it.

A 9″ × 21″ × 14″ carry-on bag (with or without wheels) is the ideal size.

Carry-on bags with wheels are well-designed and popular. Many of my staffers prefer this bag; its compact design makes it roomy while keeping it just small enough to fit in the plane's overhead bin (if you don't stuff any expandable compartments). The advantage of a rolling bag over a convertible is that you can effortlessly wheel your gear around without getting sweaty. The drawbacks: Bags with wheels cost $40-50 extra, weigh several pounds more, are awkward to carry up and down stairs, and delude people into thinking they don't need to pack so light. They are cumbersome on rough or uneven surfaces (crowded subways, hiking through a series of train cars, walking to your hotel in villages with stepped lanes, cobbled streets, and dirt paths, and so on)—but they're wonderful in airports, where check-in lines and distances to gates stretch longer than ever. (You can see photos of convertible and rolling bags—and purchase them— at rick steves.com.) A spin-off option is the hybrid bag, which has both wheels and backpack straps—but the wheels add weight when used as a backpack, and having both wheels and straps eats up interior space. Personally, I'd go with either one or the other.

Some younger travelers backpack through Europe with an internal-frame backpack purchased from an outdoor store. These are the most comfortable bags to wear on your back, as the internal frame keeps the weight off your shoulders and balanced over your hips. However, these bags can be expensive and are often built "taller" than carry-on size.

Base your decision on the strength of your back. The day will come when I'll be rolling my bag through Europe with the rest of the gang. But as long as I'm hardy enough to carry my gear on my back, I will.

Pack your bag only two-thirds full to leave room for souvenirs, or bring along an empty, featherweight nylon bag to use as a carry-on for your return flight, and check your main bag through. Sturdy stitching, front and side pouches, padded shoulder straps (for backpacks), and a low-profile color are virtues. I'm not wild about the zip-off day bags that come with some backpacks. I take my convertible backpack and supplement it with a separate day bag that's exactly to my liking.

PACKING 101

How do you fit a whole trip's worth of luggage into a small backpack or suitcase? The answer is simple: Bring very little.

Spread out everything you think you might need on the living-room floor. Pick up each item one at a time and scrutinize it. Ask yourself, "Will I really use my snorkel and fins enough to justify carrying them around all summer?" Not "Will I use them?" but "Will I use them enough to feel good about hauling them over the Swiss Alps?" Frugal as I may be, I'd buy them in Greece and give them away before I'd carry that extra weight over the Alps.

Don't pack for the worst-case scenario. Pack for the best-case scenario and simply buy yourself out of any jams. Bring layers rather than take a heavy coat. Think in terms of what you can do without—not what will be handy on your trip. When in doubt, leave it out. I've seen people pack a whole summer's supply of deodorant or razors, thinking they can't get them there. The world is getting really small: You can buy Dial soap, Colgate toothpaste, Nivea cream, and Gillette razors in Sicily and Slovakia. Tourist shops in

One Carry-on Bag

Here's what I travel with for two months (photos taken naked in a Copenhagen hotel room): convertible 9" × 21" × 14" backpack/suitcase; lightweight nylon day bag; ripped-up sections of several of my guidebooks, notes, maps, journal, tiny pocket notepad; wristwatch; money belt (with debit card, credit card, driver's license, passport, printout of airline eticket, rail pass, cash, sheet of phone numbers and addresses); second money belt clipped inside my bag for "semiprecious" documents; toiletries stuff bag (with squeeze bottle of shampoo, soap in a plastic container, shaver, toothbrush and paste, comb, nail clippers, squeeze bottle of liquid soap for clothes); bag with electronic gear (travel alarm clock, laptop power cord, plug adapter); miscellaneous bag with family photos, tiny odds and ends; light rain jacket; long khaki cotton pants (button pockets), super-light long pants, shorts, five pairs of socks and underwear, two long-sleeved shirts, two short-sleeved shirts, T-shirt; stuff bag with sweater, plastic laundry bag; light pair of shoes; and my smartphone and charger, lightweight laptop, and camera.

major international hotels are a sure bet whenever you have difficulty finding a personal item. If you can't find one of your essentials, ask yourself how half a billion Europeans can live without it. Rather than carry a whole trip's supply of toiletries, take enough to get started and look forward to running out of toothpaste in Bulgaria. Then you have the perfect excuse to go into a Bulgarian department store, shop around, and pick up something you think might be toothpaste.

Whether you're traveling for three weeks or three months, pack exactly the same. To keep your clothes tightly packed and well organized, zip them up in packing cubes, airless baggies, or a clothes compressor. I like specially designed folding boards (such as Eagle Creek's Pack-It Folder) to fold and carry clothes with minimal wrinkling. For smaller items, use packing cubes or mesh bags (one for underwear and socks, another for miscellaneous stuff such as a first-aid kit, earplugs, clothesline, sewing kit, and gadgets).

Go casual, simple, and very light. Remember, in your

travels you'll meet two kinds of tourists—those who pack light and those who wish they had. Say it out loud: "PACK LIGHT PACK LIGHT PACK LIGHT."

What to Pack

I've broken out the contents of your bag into four major categories: clothing, toiletries, travel documents (including money), and electronics. My core packing recommendations are all included on my Packing Checklist (see page 84). At the end of this chapter, I've also included a list of optional bring-alongs. Throughout, an asterisk (*) indicates an item you can purchase online at ricksteves.com.

When getting way off the beaten path—like this traveler, who's staying at a tiny guesthouse in Italy's Civita di Bagnoregio—you'll be glad you're packing light.

Clothing Basics

The bulk of your luggage is filled with clothing. Minimize by bringing less. Experienced travelers try to bring only things that will be worn repeatedly, complement other items, and have multiple uses (for example, since I don't swim much, I let my shorts double as a swimsuit). Pack with color coordination in mind. Neutral colors (black, navy, khaki) dress up easily and can be extremely versatile.

To extend your wardrobe, plan to spend 10 minutes doing a little wash every few nights, or consider a visit to a local launderette, which is in itself a Back Door experience (for details on doing laundry in Europe, see page 395). Choose fabrics that resist wrinkling or look good wrinkled. If you wring with gusto, lightweight clothing should dry overnight in your hotel room.

Many travelers are concerned about appropriate dress. During tourist season, the concert halls go casual. I have never felt out of place at symphonies, operas, or plays wearing a decent pair of slacks and a good-looking sweater or collared shirt. Some cultural events require more formal attire, particularly outside of high season, but the casual tourist rarely encounters these. Women who don't pack a dress or skirt will do just fine with a pair of nice pants.

If you're trying to blend in, realize that shorts are not common streetwear in Europe. They're considered beachwear, to be worn in coastal or lakeside resort towns. No one will be offended if you wear shorts, but you might be on the receiving end of some second glances. Shorts are especially uncommon on older women and in big cities, and the cutoff temperature for "hot enough for shorts" is much higher than in the US. Especially in southern Europe, women can blend in with the locals by wearing Capri pants or a skirt instead; men can pack a pair of as-light-as-possible pants.

Shorts, tank tops, and other skimpy summer attire can also put a crimp in your sightseeing plans. Some churches, mostly in southern Europe, have modest-dress requirements for men, women, and children: no shorts or bare shoulders. Except at the strict St. Peter's Basilica (in Rome) and St. Mark's (in Venice), the dress code is often loosely enforced. If necessary, it's usually easy to improvise some modesty (buy a cheap souvenir T-shirt to cover your shoulders, or carry a wide scarf to wear like a kilt to cover your legs). At some heavily touristed churches in southern Europe, people hand out sheets of tissue paper you can wrap around yourself like a shawl or skirt.

In Britain, they say there's no bad weather... only inappropriate clothing.

It can be worth splurging a little to get just the right clothes for your trip. For durable, lightweight travel clothes, consider ExOfficio, TravelSmith, Tilley, Eddie Bauer, and REI.

But ultimately—as long as you don't wear something that's outrageous or offensive—it's important to dress in a way that makes you comfortable. And no matter how carefully you dress, your clothes will probably mark you as an American. And so what? Europeans will know anyway. To fit in and be culturally sensitive, I watch my manners, not the cut of my clothes.

Here's a rundown of what should go in your suitcase:

Shirts/blouses. Bring up to five short-sleeved or long-sleeved shirts or blouses (how many of each depends on the season) in a cotton/polyester blend. Shirts with long sleeves that roll up easily can double as short-sleeved. Look for a wrinkle-camouflaging pattern or blended fabrics that show a minimum of wrinkles. Synthetic-blend fabrics (such as Coolmax or microfiber) often dry overnight.

Pants/shorts. Bring two pairs: one lightweight cotton and another super-lightweight pair for hot and muggy big cities. Jeans can be too hot for summer travel (and are slow to dry). Many travelers like lightweight convertible pants/shorts with zip-off legs. While not especially stylish, they're functional in Italy, where you can use them to cover up inside

churches while still beating the heat outside. Button-down
wallet pockets are safest (though still not nearly as thief-
proof as a money belt, described later). If you bring shorts,
one pair is probably enough. Shorts can double as a swimsuit
for men when swimming in lakes or the ocean.
Belt. If you need one.
Underwear and socks. Bring five sets (lighter dries
quicker). Bamboo or cotton/nylon-blend socks dry faster
than 100 percent cotton, which lose their softness when
air-dried.
Shoes. Bring one pair of comfortable walking shoes with
good traction. Mephisto, Ecco, and Rieker look dressier and
more European than sneakers, but are still comfortable.
Sturdy, low-profile tennis shoes with a good tread are fine,
too. For a second pair, consider sandals in summer. Flipflops are handy if you'll be using bathrooms down the hall.
Whichever shoes you bring, make sure they are well broken
in before you leave home.
Sweater or lightweight fleece. Warm and dark is best—for
layering and dressing up.
Jacket. Bring a light and water-resistant windbreaker with
a hood. Neutral colors used to look more European than
bright ones, but now everything from azure blue to pumpkin
orange has made its way into European wardrobes. A hooded
jacket of Gore-Tex or other waterproof material is good if
you expect rain. (For summer travel, I wing it without rain
gear—but always pack for rain in Britain and Ireland.)
Tie or scarf. For instant respectability, bring anything
lightweight that can break the monotony and make you look
snazzy.
Swimsuit. To use public pools, you'll need
a swimsuit (men can't just wear shorts; and
in France, men need to wear Speedo-type
swimsuits—not swim trunks).

Sleepwear/loungewear. Comfy streetwear—
such as shorts, leggings, T-shirts, tank tops,
yoga pants, and other lightweight athletic
gear—can be used as pajamas, post-dinner
loungewear, and a modest cover-up to get you
to the bathroom down the hall.
Weather-specific variations. For winter
travel, you can pack just about as light. Wear
heavier, warmer, waterproof shoes. Add a
coat, long johns (quick-drying Capilene polyester or super-light silk), scarf, gloves, hat, and

Packing Checklist

Clothing

❑ 5 shirts: long- & short-sleeve
❑ 2 pairs pants or skirt
❑ 1 pair shorts or capris
❑ 5 pairs underwear & socks
❑ 1 pair walking shoes
❑ Sweater or fleece top
❑ Rainproof jacket with hood
❑ Tie or scarf
❑ Swimsuit
❑ Sleepwear

Money

❑ Debit card
❑ Credit card(s)
❑ Hard cash ($20 bills)
❑ Money belt or neck wallet

Documents & Travel Info

❑ Passport
❑ Airline reservations
❑ Rail pass/train reservations
❑ Car-rental voucher
❑ Driver's license
❑ Student ID, hostel card, etc.
❑ Photocopies of all the above
❑ Hotel confirmations
❑ Insurance details
❑ Guidebooks & maps
❑ Notepad & pen
❑ Journal

Toiletries Kit

❑ Toiletries
❑ Medicines & vitamins
❑ First-aid kit
❑ Glasses/contacts/sunglasses (with prescriptions)

❑ Earplugs
❑ Packet of tissues (for WC)

Miscellaneous

❑ Daypack
❑ Sealable plastic baggies
❑ Laundry soap
❑ Clothesline
❑ Sewing kit
❑ Travel alarm/watch

Electronics

❑ Smartphone or mobile phone
❑ Camera & related gear
❑ Tablet/ereader/media player
❑ Laptop & flash drive
❑ Earbuds or headphones
❑ Chargers
❑ Plug adapters

Optional Extras

❑ Flipflops or slippers
❑ Mini-umbrella or poncho
❑ Travel hairdryer
❑ Belt
❑ Hat (for sun or cold)
❑ Picnic supplies
❑ Water bottle
❑ Fold-up tote bag
❑ Small flashlight
❑ Small binoculars
❑ Small towel or washcloth
❑ Inflatable pillow
❑ Tiny lock
❑ Address list (to mail postcards)
❑ Postcards/photos from home
❑ Extra passport photos
❑ Good book

an extra pair of socks and underwear, since things dry more
slowly. Layer your clothing for warmth, and assume you'll
be outside in the cold for hours at a time. On winter trips, I
bring comfy slippers with leather soles—great for the flight
and for getting cozy in my hotel room.

For warm weather, consider a light, crushable, wide-
brimmed hat for sunny days, especially if you're prone to
sunburn. Lightweight, light-colored clothes are more comfortable in very hot weather.

If you expect rain, you can bring a mini-umbrella or plan
to buy one in Europe. Umbrella vendors, like worms, appear
with the rain. Choose a *collapsible umbrella that's small and
compact, but still sturdy enough to withstand strong winds.
Hard-core vagabonds use a *poncho—more versatile than a
tarp—as protection in a rainstorm, a ground cloth for sleeping, or a beach or picnic blanket.

More Tips for Women

Thanks to our tour guide Joan Robinson for the following tips.
Skirts. Some women bring one or two skirts (knee-length
is appropriate for churches) because they're as cool and
breathable as shorts, but dressier. A lightweight skirt made
with a blended fabric will pack compactly. Make sure it has
a comfy waistband. Skirts go with everything and can easily
be dressed up with a pair of flats and hose (or warm tights if
it's cold).
Underwear and swimwear. Try silk, microfiber, or stretch
lace underwear, which dries faster than cotton, but breathes
more than nylon. Bring at least two bras (what if you leave
one hanging over your shower rail by accident?). A sports bra
can double as a hiking/sunning top. You don't need a bikini
to try sunbathing topless on European beaches—local women
with one-piece bathing suits just roll down the top.
Toiletries. Before cramming in every facial cleanser, lotion,
and cosmetic item you think you might use, ask yourself
what toiletries you can live without for a short time. But do
estimate how many tampons and pads you might need and
bring them with you (unless you're taking a very long trip).
Even though many of the same brands are sold throughout
Europe, you'll have them when you need them, and it's easier
than having to buy a too-small or too-large box in Europe.
Accessorize, accessorize. Scarves give your limited
wardrobe just the color it needs. They dress up your outfit,
are lightweight and easy to pack, and if purchased in Europe,
make a great souvenir. Some women bring a shawl-size scarf

or pashmina to function as a sweater substitute, head wrap, skirt at a church, or even a blanket on a train. Functional, cheap, but beautiful imitation pashminas can be found all over Europe. Vests and cardigans can be worn alone or mixed-and-matched with other clothes to give you several different looks as well as layers for cold weather. Leave valuable or flashy jewelry at home; you can buy cheap costume jewelry in Europe.

Documents, Money, and Travel Info

Organizing your possessions, travel documents, money, guidebooks, and maps is just as important as assembling your wardrobe.

***Money belt (or neck wallet).** This flat, hidden, zippered pouch—worn around your waist (or like a necklace) and tucked under your clothes—is essential for the peace of mind it brings. You could lose everything except your money belt, and the trip could still go on. Get a lightweight one with a low-profile color (I like beige). For more about money belts, see page 328.

Money. Bring your preferred mix of a debit card, a credit card, and an emergency stash of hard US cash (in $20 bills). For detailed recommendations, see page 179.

Documents. Bring your passport; plane, train, and rental car documents or vouchers; driver's license; and any other useful cards (student ID, hostel membership card, and so on). Photocopies and a couple of passport-type photos can help you get replacements more quickly if the originals are lost or stolen (see page 66 for tips on keeping travel documents safe). In your luggage, pack a record of all reservations (print out your hotel confirmation emails). Bring any necessary contact info if you have health or travel insurance. For more information on the travel documents you need, see page 62.

Guidebooks and maps. Pack the travel info you'll need on the ground (or download it into your ereader). I like to rip out appropriate chapters from guidebooks and staple them together (see page 37 for a how-to), or use special slide-on ***laminated book covers.**

***Small notepad and pen.** A tiny notepad in your back pocket or daypack is a great organizer, reminder, and communication aid.

***Journal.** An empty book to be filled with the experiences of your trip will be your most treasured souvenir (for more on journaling, see page 414). Attach a photocopied calendar page of your itinerary. Use a hardbound type designed to last a lifetime, rather than a floppy spiral notebook. My custom-designed Rick Steves Travel Journals are rugged, simple blank books that come in two sizes. Another great brand, with a cult following among travel writers, is Moleskine (moleskine.it).

*Small daypack. A lightweight pack is great for carrying your sweater, camera, guidebook, and picnic goodies while you leave your large bag at the hotel or train station. Don't use a fanny pack—they're magnets for pickpockets.

Toiletries and Personal Items

Even if you check your suitcase on the flight, always carry on essential toiletries, including any prescription medications (don't let the time difference trick you into forgetting a dose).

*Toiletries kit. Because sinks in many hotels come with meager countertop space, I prefer a kit that can hang on a hook or a towel bar. For your overseas flight, put all squeeze bottles in sealable plastic baggies, since pressure changes can cause even good bottles to leak. Pack your own bar of soap or small bottle of shampoo if you want to avoid using hotel bathroom "itsy-bitsies" and minimize waste and garbage.

Medicine and vitamins. Keep medicine in original containers, if possible, with legible prescriptions. See the advice on handling prescriptions in Europe on pages 382 and 392.

*First-aid kit. See sidebar on next page.

Glasses/contacts/sunglasses. Contact-lens solutions are widely available in Europe. Carry your lens prescription, as well as extra glasses, in a solid protective case. If it's a sunny season, pack along sunglasses, especially if they're prescription.

Sealable plastic baggies. Bring a variety of sizes. In addition to holding your carry-on liquids, they're ideal for packing leftover picnic food, containing wetness, and bagging potential leaks before they happen. The two-gallon jumbo size can be used to pack (and compress) clothing or do laundry. Bring extras for the flight home.

*Laundry soap. A tiny box of detergent or a plastic squeeze bottle of concentrated, multipurpose, biodegradable liquid soap is handy for laundry. I find hotel shampoo works fine as laundry soap when I'm

With a hangable toiletries kit, you know the hairs on the toothbrush are yours.

doing my wash in the sink (for tips on doing laundry in Europe, see page 395). For a spot remover, bring a few Shout wipes or a dab of Goop grease remover in a small plastic container.

*Clothesline. Hang it up in your hotel room to dry your clothes. The twisted-rubber type needs no clothespins.

*Small towel/washcloth. You'll find bath towels at all fancy and moderately priced hotels, and most cheap ones. Some people bring a thin hand towel for the occasional need. Washcloths are rare in Europe, so you might want to pack a *quick-drying microfiber one. Disposable wash-cloths that pack dry but lather up when wet (such as Olay's 4-in-1 Daily Facial Cloths) are another option; cut them in half to make them last longer.

*Sewing kit. Clothes age rapidly while traveling. Add a few safety pins and extra buttons.

Small packet of tissues. Stick one of these in your daypack, in case you wind up at a bathroom with no toilet paper.

*Travel alarm/wristwatch. Make sure you have an alarm to wake yourself up (your smartphone, a little clock, etc.). At budget hotels, wake-up calls are particularly unreliable.

Earplugs. If night noises bother you, you'll love a good set of expandable foam plugs. They're handy for snoozing on trains and flights, too.

Hairdryer. These are generally provided in $100-plus hotel rooms. If you can't risk a bad-hair day, buy a cheap, compact hairdryer in Europe or bring a travel-friendly one from home.

Electronics

As you're packing, try to go light with your electronic gear—you want to experience Europe, not interface with it. Of course, some devices are great tools for making your trip easier or better. As the functions of smartphones, tablets, cameras, GPS devices, and ereaders become more similar, think creatively about how you might pare down the number of gadgets you bring on the road.

Traveler's First-Aid Kit

You can buy virtually anything you need in Europe. (You might not find Claritin, though you can get the generic equivalent, loratadine.) But if you'd rather stick with a specific name-brand medication, bring it from home. It's also handy to pack:

- Band-Aids
- hand sanitizer
- antibiotic cream (in Europe, you may need a prescription to buy skin ointments with antibiotics)
- moleskin (to cover blisters)
- tweezers
- over-the-counter pain reliever
- thermometer (if traveling with kids)
- medication for colds and diarrhea (if possible, bring non-liquids)
- prescription medications (preferably in labeled, original containers)

LEFT When traveling with a smartphone, it's cheaper to use Wi-Fi to surf the Web.

RIGHT Wireless hotspots allow you to get online from a park bench.

Note that many of these are high-ticket items; guard them carefully or consider insuring them (see page 72).

Smartphone/mobile phone. Bring your smartphone to keep in touch with folks back home and for accessing resources on the road such as email, travel apps, and GPS. If you just want to make calls or send texts, a simple US mobile phone might work perfectly in Europe—or you can buy a cheap mobile phone to use while you're there. For more on using phones in Europe, see page 242.

Digital camera. Take along an extra memory card and battery, and don't forget the charger and a cable for downloading images.

Tablet, ereader, or portable media player. Download apps, ebooks, and music before you leave home.

Laptop. If you've got a lot of work to do, or want to keep your photoblog updated, a laptop can be worth the weight.

USB flash drive. If you're traveling with a laptop, a flash drive can be handy for backing up files and photos. As an alternative, consider free cloud storage sites—such as Amazon Cloud Drive, Apple iCloud, or Dropbox—that you can access anywhere; see page 407.

GPS device. If you'll be doing a lot of driving and have a portable GPS device at home, you could buy European map data to use on vacation. For details on GPS devices and navigating with a smartphone, see page 175.

Headphones/earbuds. These are a must for listening to music, tuning in to audio tours, or simply drowning out whiny kids on the plane. (I never travel without my noise-canceling Bose headphones.) Bring a Y-jack so you and a partner can plug in headphones at the same time.

Packing Tips from Rick's Readers

Rick's readers—his Road Scholars—have a wealth of travel information to share. To read many more hot-out-of-the-rucksack tips on travel topics (and to contribute your own), visit our Travel Forums at ricksteves.com.

Pencil Pouch: I use a cloth one with a plastic window to corral my passport, itinerary, emergency contact papers, and other important information. I use one of the holes along the edge to clip it inside my bag for extra security.

Backpack Cinch: I "cinch-tied" the opening of my backpack to make it less accessible for would-be thieves (punched holes in the band at the top of the bag and ran an extendable cable lock through the holes, pulled it tight, and locked it).

Dental Floss or **Fishing Line:** Strong, versatile, waterproof, nearly weightless. Tied backpack together when it broke, doubled as a shoelace, etc.

Post-It Notes: To flag guidebooks.

Small Headlamp: Better than a flashlight for reading in bed and frees your hands.

Sleep Machine: In noisy hotel rooms, the sleep machine (which emits various soothing sounds) is a true godsend.

Motion-Detector Alarm: Place near the hotel door or window. If someone moves the door or window, the motion sensor emits a high-pitched sound similar to a fire alarm.

Pillowcase: To put your backpack/travel bag in while you sleep on it on an overnight train. It's another obstacle thieves must overcome.

Washcloths: Dollar-store washcloths are small, thin, and easy to pack in shoes or

Chargers and batteries. Bring each device's charger, or look into getting a charger capable of charging multiple devices at once.

Adapters and Converters

Europe's electrical system is different from ours in two ways: the voltage of the current and the shape of the plug.

American appliances run on 110 volts, while European appliances are **220 volts.** Newer travel accessories and electronic gadgets are "dual voltage," which means they work on both American and European current. If you see a range of voltages printed on the item or its plug (such as "110-220"), you're OK in Europe. Some older appliances have a voltage switch marked 110 (US) and 220 (Europe)—switch it to 220 as you pack.

A few old, cheap American appliances aren't equipped to deal with the voltage difference at all, and they could be damaged or destroyed if plugged directly into a European wall outlet. To make these work, you'd need to buy a separate, bulky converter (about $30), but it's not worth it. With so many dual-voltage gadgets available, I haven't traveled

tiny spaces. They can be disposable or used for future travel. For removing makeup, disposable makeup wipes are another option.

Cotton Bandannas: Use them as hand towels, washcloths, picnic blankets, emergency seat covers, and even towels (use two to dry your entire body). Tie a bandana on your luggage so you can quickly identify it. Although it marks me as American, I'll wear one as a headband or hair scarf, too.

Comfy Slippers: If your feet aren't happy, YOU aren't happy. Pamper them!

Half a Tennis Ball: Works as a stopper in any sink!

Inflatable Hangers: Clothes dry faster.

Wrinkle Wiz: Sprays out the wrinkles after I've unpacked my clothes—no more travel iron!

Binder Clips: I always take a few small, medium, and large binder clips to hang clothes to dry, keep window curtains together, weigh down shower curtains, and keep plastic bags shut.

Disposable Plastic Utensils: Great for taking on an impromptu picnic, or when clean utensils aren't available, a set of plastic silverware is a must to take anywhere.

Travel Blanket: Look for a "parachute blanket" that rolls up into its own nylon bag and has four corner pockets—it can be used for beaches, picnics, and shade in a sunny area. It also serves as an extra blanket at night and even as a pillow when rolled up.

Mailing Tube: To collect prints and posters (cut tube to fit your backpack).

with a separate converter in years. Still not sure? Travel stores offer useful advice on plugs and adapters (such as the "Electrical Connection Wizard" at magellans.com).

Once you've dealt with the voltage, you'll have to consider the ***plug.** A small adapter allows American-style plugs (two flat prongs) to fit into British or Irish outlets (which take three rectangular prongs) or continental European outlets (which take two round prongs). I bring both continental and British adapters (handy for long layovers at Heathrow Airport). Secure your adapter to your device's plug with electrical or duct tape; otherwise it can easily get left behind in the outlet (hotels or B&Bs sometimes have a box of abandoned adapters—ask). Many sockets in Europe are recessed into the wall; your adapter should be small enough so that the prongs seat properly in the socket. (Switzerland uses its own style of electrical plugs: three slim round prongs arranged in a triangular shape. But if you already have an adapter for continental European outlets, it's likely to work in Switzerland, too). If, for some

In Europe, two kinds of adapters fit virtually all outlets: two little round prongs for the continent, three big rectangular ones for Britain and Ireland.

reason, your adapter doesn't work in your hotel, just ask at
the desk for assistance; hotels with unusual sockets will
invariably have the right adapter to loan you.

Some budget hotel rooms have only one electrical outlet,
occupied by the lamp. Hardware stores in Europe sell cheap
three-way plug adapters that let you keep the lamp on while
you charge your camera battery and smartphone.

Optional Bring-Alongs

I don't advocate bringing everything listed here. Choose the
items that fit with your travel style and needs.

Picnic supplies. Bring a plastic plate (handy for dinner in
your hotel room), cup, spoon, fork, and maybe salt and pepper. The Fozzils picnic set folds completely flat (see fozzils.
com). Buy a Swiss Army-type knife with a corkscrew and can
opener in Europe (or bring one from home if you're checking
your luggage on the plane).

*Water bottle. The plastic half-liter mineral water bottles
sold throughout Europe are reusable and work great. If you
bring one from home, make sure it's empty before you go
through airport security (fill it at a drinking fountain once
you're through security).

*Fold-up tote bag. Look for a large-capacity tote bag that
rolls up into a pocket-size pouch. Use it for laundry, picnics,
and those extra souvenirs you want to take back home.

*Small flashlight. Handy for reading under the sheets after
"lights out" in the hostel, late-night trips down the hall,
exploring castle dungeons, and hypnotizing street thieves.
Tiny-but-powerful LED flashlights—about the size of your
little finger—are extremely bright, compact, and lightweight.
Camping-type headlamps also do the trick.

Small binoculars. For scenery or church interiors.

*Inflatable pillow (or neck rest). These are great for snoozing in planes, trains, and automobiles. Some travelers also
swear by an ***eye mask** for blocking out early-rising or late-
setting sun.

Duct tape. A small roll of duct tape can work miracles as a
temporary fix—mending a punctured bag, solving an emergency shoe problem, and so on. Conserve space by spooling
only as much as you might need (less than a foot) around a
short pencil or dowel.

Insect repellent. Bring some along if you're prone to bites
and are going somewhere especially bug-ridden.

*Tiny lock. Use it to lock your backpack zippers shut. Note
that if you check your bag on a flight, the lock may be broken

to allow the bag to be inspected. Improve the odds of your lock's survival by buying one approved by the Transportation Security Administration—security agents can open the lock with a special master key. Or buy plastic zip-ties or *cable locks to secure zippers—be sure to pack fingernail clippers or TSA-approved scissors so you can open them when you arrive.

Office supplies. Bring paper, pens, envelopes (for letter writers), and some sticky notes (such as Post-Its) to keep your place in your guidebook.

> ## Resources for Packing Light
>
> **RickSteves.com/packing:** Rick's packing list and more
> **TSA.gov:** Official list of what you can and cannot carry on
> **Europa.eu/youreurope/citizens/travel:** EU version of TSA website
> **Onebag.com:** More tips on traveling light
>
> ### Apps
> **Packing Pro** and **TripList:** Customizable packing lists with reminders

Address list. If you'll want to mail postcards, you could print your mailing list onto a sheet of adhesive address labels before you leave. You'll know exactly who you've written to, and the labels will be perfectly legible.

Postcards/photos from home. A collection of show-and-tell pictures (either digital or paper) is always a great conversation piece with Europeans you meet.

A good book. There's plenty of empty time on a trip to either be bored or enjoy some good reading. Popular English-language paperbacks are often available in European airports and major train stations (usually costing more than their North American price). An ereader carries lots of books without the additional weight (and you can easily buy more as you go).

Gifts. If you'll be the guest of local hosts, show your appreciation with small, unique souvenirs from your hometown.

*Hostel sheet. These days, sheets are usually included in the price of a hostel, and if they aren't, you can rent one for about $5 per stay. Still, you might want to bring along a sheet (silk is lighter and smaller, cotton is cheaper), which can double as a beach/picnic blanket and cover you up on overnight train rides. See page 227 for hosteling tips.

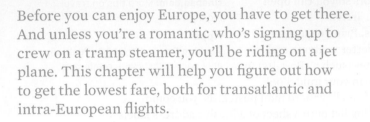

Flying

Before you can enjoy Europe, you have to get there. And unless you're a romantic who's signing up to crew on a tramp steamer, you'll be riding on a jet plane. This chapter will help you figure out how to get the lowest fare, both for transatlantic and intra-European flights.

FLYING TO EUROPE

Your plane ticket to Europe will likely be your biggest trip expense. Because airlines offer fewer flights and sales these days, you'll have to be on your toes to get the best deal.

Researching Flights

If you're not using a travel agent, your first step is to research your options. While each airline has its own website, I prefer to begin my search with a site that compiles a full range of choices.

Flight search engines compare fares available at multiple airlines, online travel agencies, or both, and then sort them by price. I've tested a number of them on a variety of journeys, both transatlantic and within Europe. Surprisingly, I've seen that the industry's big sites—like Priceline and Expedia—can miss good-value results that other sites turned up. Overall, **Kayak** has the best results for both intercontinental and intra-European flights on a combination of mainstream and budget carriers. (However, for cheap flights within Europe, **Skyscanner** has a slight edge—see page 106.)

A couple of sites are better for flights *to* Europe than flights *within* Europe, and some nice features make their results easier to navigate. **Hipmunk** has a lively interface (with a cheery cartoon chipmunk) and a helpful timeline display of available flights, including layovers, to give you an at-a-glance rundown of your options (with an "agony" rating for each). **Vayama** specializes in international flights, and often finds cheaper fares that might not show up elsewhere—but beware that its customer service doesn't have a stellar reputation for handling cancellations and changes.

Booking Your Flight

While it's possible to book your flights on most search sites (they certainly hope you will, to garner their commission), I use them only as a first step. Once I've zeroed in on which airline has the best deal for my trip, I check the airline's own site to compare fares. You can avoid third-party service fees by booking direct, and airlines may offer bonuses (such as extra frequent-flier miles) to those who book direct.

On the other hand, search sites occasionally beat the fares on the airline's official site, sometimes by using "mix and match" journeys to connect the legs of a single trip on multiple airlines. (However, these trips can be difficult to rebook in case of a delay or missed leg—review the schedule carefully, watching out for very tight connections or extremely long layovers.)

For maximum peace of mind, it can be best to book directly with the airline, which can more easily address unexpected problems or deal with rescheduled flights. If you do wind up buying tickets through a third-party site, make sure you carry their phone number with you—you'll need to speak to a person if you have a problem.

Flight-Booking Tips

These days, there's no such thing as a free lunch in the airline industry. (In fact, these days, there's usually no lunch at all.) Before grabbing the cheapest ticket you can find, make sure it meets your travel needs with the best combination of schedule, economy, and convenience.

Buy your tickets at the right time (to the extent possible). Airfares flex like crazy, but in general it's wise to start

---

Flight-Search Guidelines

When searching online for a flight, keep in mind:

- No single flight-search site includes every possible airline—it's always smart to check more than one website.
- If you are flying into a city with several airports, select either "all airports" or simply the city name ("LON" for London) rather than a specific airport name ("LHR" for London Heathrow). If offered, select "include nearby airports"—doing so will return more flight options (for example, Pisa for Florence or Bratislava for Vienna).
- Choosing "flexible dates" lets you see what you might save by flying a few days before or after your ideal time frame.
- When booking, decline extras that you don't want (for example, premium seating—with an extra fee). On each page of the transaction be sure that no boxes are checked unless you want them to be.

looking for international flights four to five months before your trip, especially if you are traveling in spring, summer, or fall. Good deals on travel during winter (November through March) can usually be purchased a month or so in advance, with the exception of winter breaks and holidays, which require even earlier booking. Year-round, it's generally cheaper to book midweek.

All that said, knowing the best time to buy is still a guessing game, though you can improve your chances by taking advantage of some tech tools. Google's **Flight Explorer** (google.com/flights/explore) shows the best prices to your destination in an easy-to-read graph, which you can tailor to your time frame. Several search sites, including Kayak and Expedia, offer similar price-trend graphs.

Be ready to buy. Given how erratic airline pricing can be, you want to be ready to pounce on a good fare when you see it. Waiting to talk with your travel partner could cost you a good fare. As you delay, dates sell out and prices generally go up. Figure out in advance what constitutes a good fare, then grab it when you find it. Long gone are the days when you or your travel agent could put several different reservations on hold while you made a decision.

Consider flying into one city and out of another. Since it rarely makes sense to spend the time and money returning to your starting point, this strategy can be very efficient (see page 50). For most "multicity" flights, the fare is figured simply by taking half of the round-trip cost for each of those ports, though you'll likely save money by using the same airline for each segment.

Be sure of your dates before you book. Changing or canceling your ticket can be very expensive, as airlines can be very aggressive about change fees, with most charging around $250 per ticket per change. Unexpected circumstances can happen to anyone, so understand your ticket's change policies before you buy. (While nonrefundable tickets are cheaper and the most restrictive, even certain types of business and first-class tickets have penalties for changes.)

If you need to alter your return date in Europe, call your airline's European office. If you absolutely must get home

early, go to the airport: If you're
standing at the airport two days
before your ticket says you can go
home, and seats are available, they
may just let you fly.

Pick a seat as early as possible.
Most airlines let you choose your
seat when you book, and most charge
extra for roomier seats. If seat assignments aren't available at booking, ask
about the earliest possible date that
you can call to request your seat (for
example, 90 or 30 days before your
flight)—and put it on your calendar.
Larger or taller travelers may find
it worth the extra cost for the extra
legroom afforded by "Economy Plus"
seats (or whatever your airline calls
their intermediate class between
Economy and Business). For pointers
on which seats are best on specific
airplanes, see SeatGuru.com.

Resources for Air Travel

Kayak.com: Top site (and well-
designed app) for checking flight
options to and within Europe

Skyscanner.com: Best search engine
for cheap flights within Europe

Farecompare.com: Tweets low-fare
alerts tailored to your home airport

Seatguru.com: Airplane-seat maps
and advice

Airlinequality.com: Traveler reviews
of airlines and flights

TSA.gov: Latest US flight rules and
regulations

Apps

TripIt: Itinerary organizer

FlightTrack: Flight-status tracker
with alerts for delays and gate
changes

GateGuru: Detailed airport guides

**Review your ticket information carefully when you
book.** Double-check your dates, times, destinations, baggage
allowance, and exact spelling of your name. Confirm that the
name on your reservation exactly matches the one on your
passport, which can be an expensive hassle to correct later. A
simple second look can give you a chance to fix any mistakes
and save you enormous headaches down the road.

Money-Saving Tips

Here are some additional ideas for finding lower fares online:

Comparison-shop "air plus hotel" promotional deals.
Some airfare aggregators and airlines offer "getaway" deals:
For one low price, you get a round-trip flight to a European
city as well as a few nights' lodging. Given Europe's high
accommodations costs—especially in big cities—this can be a
good value, though you can expect to be put up in a soulless
business hotel.

Sign up for low-fare Twitter and/or email alerts.
Many airfare search sites—as well as the official airline
sites—will email and tweet automated updates about low
fares for specific routes. Airfarewatchdog.com is a free
service that does a particularly good job of finding the
cheapest fares across multiple airlines (including those that

don't show up on most search sites), and limits their alerts
to flights that actually have seats available. The similar
FareCompare.com also tweets alerts specific to your home
airport.

Consider budget European airlines. A few of Europe's
low-cost carriers have flights between the US and Europe;
these don't normally show up in the search results of most
US-based airfare comparison sites. Check the list on page
106 for carriers that serve your European destination, then
find out if they serve any US airports. Be forewarned that
passenger reviews of these carriers' trans-Atlantic flights
are mixed regarding their legroom, onboard services, and
overall comfort—all of which are more important on a long
overseas flight than a quick intra-European hop. Do your
homework before committing to a lengthy flight on one of
these carriers.

Use any scheduling flexibility to your advantage. At
certain times—such as the point at which shoulder season
turns into peak season (and vice versa) for your destination—shifting your flight by one day could save you hundreds
of dollars. And consider that fares are generally a bit cheaper
for travel Monday through Thursday than for weekends.

If your travel dates aren't set, you may be able to score a
great deal. Check out the take-what-you-can-get airfares from
websites such as Lastminute.com and Lastminutetravel.com.
Airfarewatchdog.com and Travelzoo.com keep track of the
latest deals (though Travelzoo lacks a flight-search function).

"Bidding-for-travel" sites like Priceline and Hotwire
are also worth checking. But you're just as likely to stumble
upon deals on the airlines' own websites—particularly if
you sign up for their email alerts. Be aware that deeply
discounted fares generally have serious restrictions; for
example, you can't always choose the time of day to fly. But
the savings could make it worthwhile if your travel dates
are flexible.

Using a Travel Agent

While travel agents may seem like an antiquated notion—or
perhaps only the purview of business travelers and wealthy
jetsetters—even the Web-savviest budget traveler shouldn't
be too quick to rule out using the services of a living, breathing agent. A good travel agent will almost certainly save you
time, may also save you money, and can be a vital ally should
you or your trip run into problems. Like many of my readers,

I value the personal touch and expertise that only an experienced agent can provide.

Now that airline commissions are a thing of the past, many agents charge a $35-150 fee per ticket. In the long run, paying a modest fee could be a worthwhile expense—think of it as a reasonable charge for the hassle of tracking down flight options, and/or a consulting cost for your travel agent's expertise. I enjoy the convenience of calling or emailing my agent, explaining my travel plans, getting a briefing on my options, and choosing the best flight.

Travel agents not only save you the time of looking up your own flights, but sometimes have access to cheaper fares. A good travel agent—especially one who specializes in the region you're traveling to—offers both regular airline fares and discounted consolidator fares. Consolidators are wholesalers who negotiate with airlines to get deeply discounted fares, which they then sell cheaply (but with a markup) to travelers. Be aware that consolidator tickets are "nonendorsable" (meaning that no other airline is required to honor that ticket if your airline is unable to get you home— though this is rarely a problem). And if the airline drops its prices, you are stuck with what was, but no longer is, a cheap fare. If buying a consolidator ticket, check cancellation policies and other restrictions carefully.

You're particularly likely to benefit from using an agent if you're booking a complicated trip (whether coordinating a group and/or a complex, multi-leg itinerary), need to obtain visas for the countries you're visiting, or if you're taking a cruise (most cruise lines prefer that you book through an agent).

An agent can also be helpful in smoothing any bumps in the road. Once, just after boarding my plane in the US and settling in for my flight to London, the flight crew announced that a fire had completely shut down Heathrow. Back in the terminal, you can imagine the chaotic scene as everyone from my flight scrambled to sort out their plans. But I simply called my agent and asked her to get me to my end destination, Berlin, any way but through London. With little fuss, I was rebooked on a flight early the next morning via Amsterdam, and made it to Berlin before noon.

While I use an agent for my plane ticket, car rental, advice on visas, and possibly travel insurance, I turn to a good guidebook for everything else (such as hotel advice). Although an agent may be able to give you tips on Irish

The Fear of Flying

I can understand why many people are afraid to fly. I always think of the little rubber wheels splashing down on a rain-soaked runway and then hydroplaning out of control. Or the spindly landing gear crumbling. Or, if not that, then the plane tilting just a tad, catching a wing tip, and flipping over and bursting into flames.

I overcome these concerns with simple logic. The chances of being in an airplane crash are minuscule. I remind myself that every day, 30,000 commercial planes take off and land safely in the United States alone. While airplanes do crash, entire years go by in which there are no passenger fatalities on any commercial American airline. The pilot and crew fly daily, and they don't seem to be terrified. For more than 30 years, my company has had countless tour-group members fly over to meet us—16,000 tourists a year these days—and, as far as I know, never has one of our travelers even picked up a bruise while flying.

Also consider these statistics: Over the course of a lifetime, a typical American's odds of dying of heart disease are 1 in 6, of being killed in a car accident, 1 in 300...while the odds of dying in an airplane accident are 1 in 7,000. Worldwide, more than a million people die each year in road accidents—about the same as if a fully loaded 747 crashed every four hours. If you worry about safety, the real time to panic is during the drive to the airport.

I comfort my nervousness with the knowledge that flying is a matter of physics and aerodynamics. Air has mass, and the plane maneuvers itself through that mass. I can understand a boat coming into a dock—maneuvering through the water. That doesn't scare me. So I tell myself that a plane's a boat with an extra dimension to navigate, and its "water" (air) is a lot thinner. Also, the pilot, who's still "flying" the plane after it lands, is as much in control on the ground as in the air. Only when he's good and ready does he allow gravity to take over.

Turbulence scares me, too. But a United pilot once told me that he'd have bruises from his seat belt before turbulence really bothered him. Still, every time the plane comes in for a landing, I say a prayer, close my eyes, and take my pen out of my shirt pocket so it won't impale me if something goes wrong. And every time I stick my pen back in my shirt pocket, I feel thankful.

B&Bs or sporadic advice on biking in Holland, it's safe to assume you'll get more helpful information from your guidebook. For intra-Europe flights, do your own search, as a travel agent's reservations networks don't include most of the cheap, no-frills European airlines (see "Flying Within Europe," page 104).

If you're seeking a good travel agent, recommendations from other travelers provide excellent leads. But the right agency doesn't guarantee the right agent. You need a particular person—someone whose definition of "good travel" matches yours. When you contact an agency, ask for their "independent Europe specialist."

Check In and Take Off

To ensure your flight goes as smoothly as possible, heed these tips:

Check in online before heading to the airport. Most carriers allow you to check in and print your boarding pass 24 hours before departure time. This can save you a lot of time at the airport.

It can sometimes be a hassle to check in online for a flight that includes a connection to a different carrier, even if they're partnered (for example, the first leg on Lufthansa and the second leg on United). First try checking in on the website of the company from which you bought the ticket; if that doesn't work, try the other carrier's site. In a pinch, you can check in for the entire journey at the airport, but in rare cases, you may have to wait until your layover to check in for your connecting flight. Don't dawdle—check in as soon as you possibly can.

If checking in online, you may be able to print a scannable boarding pass that you'll pull up on your smartphone when asked to show your pass. This is a fairly hassle-free option—just be sure that your phone is adequately charged before you head to the airport.

Bring your confirmation number and your passport. It's always smart to have your flight-confirmation info on hand (either printed or easily accessed on your smartphone) in case you run into complications at the airport. Take care not to check your passport in your baggage: You're required to show it to the airline before boarding the flight to Europe.

Dress and prep for comfort. Just because you're flying economy class doesn't mean you have to be

What Can't I Carry On?

The list of prohibited carry-on items can change without notice—especially just after a terrorist threat. And while most security rules are similar on either side of the Atlantic, carry-on restrictions can differ between the US and Europe, as well as between any two European countries. Don't assume you know what's allowed. Shortly before your flight, check tsa.gov/travelers, as well as the websites for your airline and any airports you're flying through. (This is an especially good idea if you're flying through London, which often enforces tighter restrictions than other European hubs; see gov.uk/hand-luggage-restrictions.)

Tempted to pick up some duty-free booze or perfume on your way back home? It's no problem if you have a nonstop flight. Passengers with a connection are now permitted to carry liquids (or oil- or liquid-packed foods) in excess of 3.4 ounces if they were purchased in a duty-free shop and are packaged in a "STEB"—a secure, tamper-evident bag. Your STEB sack will be screened when you transfer to your connecting flight. But stay away from liquids in opaque, ceramic, or metallic containers, which usually cannot be successfully screened (STEB or no STEB); you'll have to either place these products in your checked baggage or forfeit them. For more tips, see "Hauling Home Heavenly Wines" on page 324.

miserable. I've never in my life paid for anything more than coach—and many times I've ended up on a full flight, spending nine hours in a middle seat. These aren't ideal conditions for a good night's sleep, but I make it work. Here are my tricks for a comfortable flight in cattle-car "luxury":

• **Dress warm and loose.** I take off my shoes and belt and then cuddle up with a sweater and scarf. A neck rest can do wonders.

• **Wear noise-reduction headphones.** These mute both the rumble of the engines and the mind-numbing chatter of people around me. And with headphones on, I get into conversations only if I want to. This makes the flight much more restful.

• **Board with a fully charged ereader or tablet and lots of reading or writing to do.** This provides me with a mental escape and an opportunity to prepare for my upcoming travels, and it helps the time race by. (It's also important to charge your electronic devices before you board because security checks may require you to turn them on.) Some airlines are beginning to offer charging ports on long-haul flights—even in coach—but I wouldn't count on it.

• **Nap with the help of Ambien (zolpidem).** For me, just a quarter-tablet is good for a couple of blissful hours. When I wake up, I'm thankful for the shut-eye. It enables me to function much better on my first day in Europe.

Use your layovers well. If your flight requires a connection and layover, use the time to charge your mobile devices and handle routine tasks (e.g., if it's your first stop in Europe, get cash at an ATM). With a really long layover, consider a brief excursion downtown—most of Europe's airports are connected to the city center by fast, frequent, and affordable public transit. For key details on Europe's hub airports, see ricksteves.com/hub-airports.

Frequent-Flier Miles

Personally, I don't collect frequent-flier miles. (It's my own quirky hang-up, but I view frequent-flier programs as a cynical way for airlines to produce nothing while prodding their customers to jump through needless hoops and compromise flexibility.) However, for a traveler who's willing to play the game, it can be a useful budget tool.

What began as a way to reward customer loyalty has evolved into a profitable side-business for the airlines, who sell "award miles" to credit-card and other companies (who pass along those miles as incentives to their own customers).

But as more people earn piles of miles, airlines are bumping up the restrictions and additional fees required to claim a seat. Here are some strategies for getting the most travel out of your miles. For more tips, check out flyertalk.com.

Book as far ahead as possible. Airlines reserve only a handful of "award seats" on each flight—and they go fast. The farther ahead you book (ideally months in advance), the more likely you'll get your choice of flights for the fewest miles.

Maximize the miles you earn. For example, booking direct with the airline, rather than on a third-party booking site, might earn you bonus miles. Many credit cards allow you to accrue miles with each purchase you make, flight-related or not. But watch out if you buy your tickets on discount sites—depending on the seat code, some airlines may not credit the full amount of miles to your account.

Know about alliances. Most major airlines belong to one of three gigantic frequent-flier collectives: Star Alliance, SkyTeam, or OneWorld, all of which cover North American airlines as well as European carriers big and small. Before booking, check the latest on which airlines belong to which group (these partnerships are as slippery as political alliances). If you have miles on one airline in the alliance, you can redeem them on any of the others.

The same alliances work for collecting miles. You might not care about earning miles for an SAS or Croatia Airlines flight, but if you give them your United frequent-flier number, the miles go into your United pot.

Redeem miles online if possible. Check if the flight you want is available on the airline's website. If not, try speaking directly with an airline agent. While this can come with a small additional fee, it may be worth it to talk with a live person who has all your options at his or her fingertips—especially if you...

Do some research and know your options. If you try to redeem miles over the phone, the agent might say you're out of luck just because the most straightforward route is sold out. Before you call, make a list (in order of preference) of the connections that would work for your trip, or ask the agent to try a less convenient route. If the direct, nonstop flight you want is full, a flight with connecting stops may still be worth the dollar savings.

If you're a little short on miles, get creative. Look into buying miles from the airline or paying a fee to transfer them from someone else (such as a spouse or relative). While it wouldn't be cost-effective to do this for the entire value of a ticket, it can be worthwhile if you're, say, 2,000 miles short on a 50,000-mile fare. Many airlines also allow you to "pay" for one leg of the ticket with miles and the other in cash.

Watch the expiration date. For many airlines, miles expire at a certain point after you accrue them or if your frequent-flier account remains inactive for too long. It's a good idea to note these expiration dates in your calendar, with a reminder several months ahead. Typically the miles must be redeemed for a ticket before the expiration date, but the flight can occur anytime—even months later. If you've got miles but aren't ready to redeem them, you can usually extend their life by taking advantage of special partner deals listed on your airline's website (send a bouquet of flowers to your mom at a promotional price, pocket the savings, and re-up your miles all at once).

Expect to pay for taxes and booking fees. What were once "free" award seats can now cost as much as $300, depending on the airline and destination. But you're still flying for a small fraction of the full fare.

FLYING WITHIN EUROPE

When I started traveling, no one spending their own money bought one-way airline tickets within Europe. It simply wasn't affordable. But today that kind of thinking is *so* 20th century. Before buying any long-distance train or bus ticket, it's smart to first check the cost of a flight—you might be surprised (for more information, see the sidebar on page 106).

The proliferation of extremely competitive discount carriers has revolutionized European-itinerary planning and turned vagabonds into jetsetters. Because you can make hops just about anywhere on the Continent for roughly $100 a flight, deciding where to go is now mostly just a question of following your travel dreams: You're no longer limited to places within a convenient train ride (or reasonable drive) from each other. It's now entirely feasible to lace together a far-flung trip that ranges from, say, Ireland to Portugal to Sicily, if you please.

Using Budget Airlines

Since Europe deregulated its airways in the 1990s, a flock of budget-conscious, no-frills airlines have taken flight. Some of the most established (such as EasyJet and Ryanair) have route maps that rival their mainstream competitors. Meanwhile, dozens of smaller, niche airlines stick to a more limited flight plan. For a list of many of these carriers—including websites and some of the destinations they serve—see the sidebar on the next page.

Budget airlines typically offer flights between major European cities for $50-250. These days, you can also fly within Europe on major airlines affordably—and without all the aggressive restrictions. You can even find some remarkable, it-must-be-a-typo deals if your timing is right (for example, Ryanair routinely flies from London to any one of dozens of European cities for less than $30). Even after adding taxes and a boatload of fees, these flights can still be a good value. To get the lowest fares, book long in advance. The cheapest seats sell out fast (aside from occasional surprise sales), leaving the pricier fares for latecomers. Of course, it's important to consider the downsides of flying budget airlines (described later).

Europe's no-frills, smaller airlines offer cut-rate fares and scaled-down services.

One-way flights on low-cost airlines are generally just as affordable as round-trips. Consider linking a couple of cheap flights, either with the same or different airlines, to reach your destination. But leave plenty of time for connections—you're on your own if a delay on one airline causes you to miss your next flight on a different airline. Pay attention to which terminal your flights use, as low-cost carriers are often in a different terminal than traditional carriers, and you'll need extra time to get between them. If you're using a budget carrier to connect to your US-bound flight, allow enough of a layover to absorb delays—maybe even an overnight.

Smart vagabonds use low-cost airlines to creatively connect the dots on their itinerary. If there's no direct cheap flight to Florence, maybe there's an alternative that goes to Pisa (1.5 hours away by train); remember that many flight-search websites have a "nearby airports" option that broadens your search. Even adding the cost of the train ticket from Pisa to Florence, the total could be well below the price of a long overland journey, not to mention several hours faster.

Searching for Cheap Flights Within Europe

New no-frills airlines take off every year. Some major European airlines, faced with competition from budget carriers, have even joined the discount-airfare game.

Budget Airlines in Europe

These are just a few of the budget airlines taking to the European skies. To discover more, check out Skyscanner.com, or simply do an online search for "cheap flights" plus the cities you're interested in flying to/from. Note that new airlines appear—and old ones go out of business—all the time.

AIRLINE	DESTINATIONS SERVED	WEBSITE
Aer Lingus	Dublin, Shannon, Cork, Belfast	aerlingus.com
AirBaltic	Riga (Latvia)	airbaltic.com
Air Berlin	Multiple German cities	airberlin.com
Air One	Milan, Venice, Pisa	flyairone.com
Blue Air	Bucharest, Bacău (Romania)	blueairweb.com
Brussels Airlines	Brussels	brusselsairlines.com
CityJet	London City Airport	cityjet.com
Condor	Multiple German cities	condor.com
Darwin Airline	Geneva, Lugano	darwinairline.com
EasyJet	London, Milan, Berlin, Paris, Liverpool, Geneva, Basel, Nice, Toulouse, Edinburgh, Madrid, and more	easyjet.com
Estonian Air	Tallinn	estonian-air.com
Flybe	Manchester, Newquay, Exeter, Southampton, London (southern England); Jersey, Guernsey (Channel Islands)	flybe.com
Germanwings	Multiple German cities	germanwings.com
Helvetic Airways	Zürich, Bern	helvetic.com

Most budget airlines focus on particular hubs (for instance, Norwegian Air has hubs in Oslo, Bergen, Copenhagen, Alicante, London, and Stockholm). When looking for cheap flights, first check airlines that use either your starting point or your ending point as a hub. For example, for a trip from Berlin to Oslo, I'd look at Air Berlin (with a hub in Berlin) and at Norwegian (which has a hub in Oslo). But some airlines forego this "hub-and-spoke" model for a less predictable "point-to-point" schedule.

To find out all your options, use an online search engine that covers everything. My first stop when seeking budget flights is **Skyscanner;** this no-frills website specializes in European budget airlines, and it's a fast way to determine if any of them serve the route you're eyeing. Skyscanner also includes major non-budget carriers.

Several other websites, including the all-purpose **Kayak,** are worth a look. **WhichAirline.com** does a good job of

AIRLINE	DESTINATIONS SERVED	WEBSITE
Icelandair	Reykjavik	icelandair.com
Jet2	Multiple British cities	jet2.com
Jetairfly	Brussels, Liège, Ostend (Belgium)	jetairfly.com
Meridiana	Olbia, Cagliari (Sardinia); Rome and other Italian cities	meridiana.it
Monarch Airlines	Multiple British cities	monarch.co.uk
Niki	Vienna, Salzburg	flyniki.com
Norwegian	Oslo, Bergen, Copenhagen, Stockholm, Alicante, and London	norwegian.no
Pegasus Airlines	Istanbul, Antalya (Turkey)	flypgs.com
Ryanair	London, Dublin, and several other cities	ryanair.com
SmartWings	Prague, Ostrava (Czech Republic)	smartwings.net
Thomsonfly	Connects various British cities to Mediterranean resorts	flights.thomson.co.uk
Transavia	Amsterdam, Rotterdam, Eindhoven	transavia.com
TUIfly	Multiple German cities	tuifly.com
Vueling	Multiple Spanish cities, Amsterdam, Florence, Rome	vueling.com
Widerøe	Oslo	wideroe.no
Wizz Air	Budapest and many other Eastern European cities	wizzair.com
XL Airways	Paris	xlairways.com

searching the budget carriers, and specializes in dredging up creative options for getting the absolutely cheapest fare. The visually engaging **Momondo** automatically searches for flights at nearby airports (read the results carefully to be clear on which airport it's using). **Dohop** has a clean interface and generally good results. You can also check **Flycheapo,** which doesn't include full flight schedules but can tell you which budget airlines fly between any two points.

What's the Catch?

With cheaper airfares come potential pitfalls. These budget tickets are usually nonrefundable and nonchangeable. Many airlines take only online bookings, so you won't have a travel agent to go to bat for you, and it can be hard to track down a staff member to talk to if problems arise. (Read all the fine print carefully, so you know what you're getting into.) Flights are often tightly scheduled to squeeze more flying time out of each plane, which can exaggerate the effects of delays. Deadlines are strictly enforced: If they tell you to arrive at the check-in desk an hour before the flight, and you show up only 50 minutes early, you've just missed your plane. And, as these are relatively young companies, it's not uncommon for budget carriers to go out of business or cancel a slow-selling route unexpectedly—leaving you scrambling to find an alternative.

Since budget airlines are not making much money on your ticket, they look for other ways to pad their profits—bombarding you with ads every step of the way (as you book, via email after you've bought your ticket, on board the plane), selling you overpriced food and drinks on board (nothing's included), and gouging you with fees for everything. For instance, you can get dinged for paying with a credit card (even though there's no option for paying cash), checking in and printing your boarding pass at the airport (instead of online), "priority boarding" ahead of the pack, reserving a specific seat, carrying an infant on board, and—of course—checking bags. The initial fare you see on the website can be misleadingly low, and once you begin the purchasing process, each step seems to come with another unexpected charge.

If you plan to check a bag, pay the fee online when you purchase your ticket—on many budget airlines, the price per bag isn't fixed but gets progressively higher the closer you get to your departure. Be aware that you may have to pay extra to check a bag if it's over a certain (relatively low) weight limit. Don't assume your

EU Passenger Rights

You don't have to be European to benefit from the EU's consumer-protection laws, which are particularly robust when it comes to air travel. The most important one to know: If your European airline is at fault for a sudden cancellation or significant delay—say, if your plane has a mechanical problem—you're entitled to compensation for hotel and food costs you incurred while in air-travel limbo. How much you can be reimbursed depends not only on the length of your delay but on the length of your flight, with an upper limit of €600 (about $830) per traveler.

This law doesn't require airlines to pay up if they've notified you of the change well in advance, but it does apply to any last-minute change of plans, including being moved to an earlier flight. Even US-based carriers are bound by this law for any flights departing *from* the EU.

Not surprisingly, airlines don't automatically fork over these reimbursements—nor are gate agents or customer-service reps likely to inform stranded travelers of their reimbursement rights unless prompted. But all airlines that serve Europe must list the details on their websites (usually under "passenger rights" or "claims," albeit in fine-print legalese). If you need to seek reimbursement, one option is Refund.me, a website that explains what you're entitled to and how to request it. (For a 15 percent commission, this company will also handle the whole process for you.)

bag qualifies as carry-on in Europe; many budget airlines use smaller dimensions than other carriers. To avoid unpleasant surprises, read the baggage policy carefully before you book.

Ryanair, one of the biggest budget carriers, is as famous for its low fares as it is for the creative ways it's devised to nickel-and-dime passengers. For instance, their complicated checked-luggage price schedule varies depending on how many bags you have, how heavy they are, and whether you prebook online—ranging from about $20 for a small bag prebooked off-season to $180 for a bigger bag booked at the airport in peak season, plus about $30 per extra kilogram over 20 kilos (44 pounds).

Another potential headache: Budget airlines sometimes use obscure airports. For example, one of Ryanair's English hubs is Stansted Airport, one of the farthest airports from London's city center. Ryanair's flights to "Frankfurt" actually take you to Hahn, 75 miles away. Sometimes you may even wind up in a different (though nearby) country: For example, a flight advertised as going to Copenhagen, Denmark, might go to Malmö, Sweden, or a flight bound for Vienna, Austria, might land in Bratislava, Slovakia. These are still safe and legal airstrips, but it can take money and time to reach your final destination by public transportation. On the other hand, the money you save on your ticket (compared to using a mainstream carrier into a major airport) often more than pays for the difference.

Even if the name of your budget airline (such as Wizz Air) doesn't exactly inspire confidence, these carriers can get you to many destinations cheaper and a whole lot faster than the train.

Trains, Buses & Boats

In Europe, public transportation works. Over the years, Europeans have invested hugely in their public transit, and it's generally fast and effective. Of course, digging the English Channel Tunnel, building a bridge between Denmark and Sweden, and adding bullet trains all cost money, and train travel is no longer as cheap as it once was. But savvy travelers can still get around on a tight budget.

Europe's commitment to public transportation is not just limited to populated areas; it's widespread. For example, in Scotland's Highlands—way up north—if the population is too sparse to justify a public bus service, citizens needing to get to a remote farmstead are welcome to ride with the postman for the cost of a bus ticket. In Europe, I use this rule of thumb: If there are people here and people there, there's a way to get between them by public transit. I can't think of a favorite European sight that you can't reach by bus, boat, or train.

This chapter pays special attention to the pros and cons of buying rail passes and point-to-point train tickets, figuring out train schedules, and navigating Europe's train stations. Travel by bus and ferry is covered at the end of the chapter; for information on subways, city buses, and taxis, see the City Transportation chapter.

The Benefits of Train Travel

The European train system shrinks what is already a small continent, making the budget whirlwind or far-reaching tour a reasonable and exciting possibility for anyone. The system works great for locals and travelers alike, with well-signed stations, easily accessed schedules, and efficient connections between popular destinations. First-time train travelers get

the hang of it faster than they expect. Generally, European trains go where you need them to go and are fast, frequent, and affordable. Lace this network together to create the trip of your dreams.

Trains connect big cities, but also small towns—such as Manarola—in Italy's Cinque Terre.

For many travelers, the pleasure of journeying along Europe's rails really is as good as the destination. Train travel, though not as flexible as driving, can be less stressful. On a train, you can forget about parking hassles, confusing road signs, speed limits, bathroom stops, and Italian drivers. Watch the scenery instead of fixing your eyes on the road, and maybe even enjoy a glass of the local wine. Compared to flying, rail travel allows more spontaneity. If a town looks too cute to miss, hop out, and catch the next train later.

It's also quite time-efficient, especially with Europe's ever-growing network of super-fast trains. With night trains, you can easily have dinner in Paris, sleep on the train, and have breakfast in Venice. And (with the exception of the Eurostar English Channel train) you don't need to show up early. As long as you're on board when the train leaves, you're on time.

As Americans, we're accustomed to being shoehorned into a cramped car or an economy-class airline seat. On the train, you can walk around, spread out in comparatively wide seats, and easily retrieve an extra sweater from your luggage. The popularity of clean-air laws has made trains even more comfortable, as most trains (and stations) are now smoke-free throughout the European Union.

Trains remain the quintessentially European way to go, and the best option for romantics. Driving to the Austrian lakeside hamlet of Hallstatt is easy, but arriving by train is magical: Hop off at the hut-sized station across the lake, catch the waiting boat, and watch the town's shingled roofs and church spires grow bigger as the mist lifts off the water.

TRAIN TICKETS AND PASSES

A train traveler's biggest pre-trip decision is whether to get a rail pass or stick with point-to-point tickets (or use a mix of both). Many travelers make a costly mistake by skipping over the details of this decision, as rail passes are no longer the sure bet they once were. It pays to know your options and choo-choose what's best for your trip.

Tickets or Passes?

Point-to-point tickets are just that: tickets bought individually to get you from Point A to Point B. It's simplest to buy these in train stations as you travel, but they're becoming easier to purchase online, which can be handy if you need to secure an advance reservation for a certain train.

By contrast, a rail pass covers train travel in one or more countries for a certain number of days (either a continuous span of days or a number of days spread over a wider window of time). Most rail passes available to non-Europeans can only be bought outside Europe, so before your trip, you'll need to sketch out your itinerary, then answer the following questions:

How many days do you expect to ride the train? If you'll be on the train for just one or two days, you almost certainly won't benefit from a pass. The more time you expect to spend on the train, the more likely it is that you'll want a pass.

How many countries will you be visiting by train? The more countries you plan to visit, the more probable it is that you'll save money with a pass. If you're planning a whirlwind trip all around the continent, a pass (or passes) is almost certainly the way to go.

No matter what, it's smart to figure out...

Flight vs. Train?

The availability of inexpensive flights is changing the way travelers plan their itineraries. A decade ago, it would have been folly to squeeze Italy and Norway into a single two-week trip. Today that plan is easy and cheap. So to connect two far-flung cities, what's better? Hopping a flight or riding the rails?

Flying can save both time and money, especially on long journeys. A cheap flight can help a light sleeper avoid spending the night on a rattling train. But if you're focusing on a single country or region and connecting destinations that are closer together, the train is still more practical.

With Europe's high-speed train network getting faster and faster, covering even long distances is a snap. From London to Paris, the Eurostar train can be faster than flying when you consider the train zips you directly from downtown to downtown. Train and car travel, unlike flights, keep you close to the scenery, to Europe, and to Europeans. Ground transportation is also less likely to be disrupted by bad weather, mechanical problems, or scheduling delays.

For more on flying within Europe, see page 104.

Roughly how much would your point-to-point tickets cost? You don't have to laboriously look up exact train fares online—to get a rough idea of what you'd pay for bigger journeys, check the map on page 116. If you're traveling in just one or two countries, you can check the more detailed regional maps at ricksteves.com/cost-maps. Connect the dots and add up the fares to get an approximate cost for your tickets. Don't worry if some of your destinations aren't shown on this map: Ticket prices are mostly based on distance, so you can estimate fares. For example, if you're going to Italy's Orvieto, about halfway between Florence and Rome, it's safe to assume the train fare to Orvieto from either Florence or Rome is roughly half the total shown for the whole Florence-Rome stretch.

Train Travel Tips at RickSteves.com

While this chapter provides a good start in planning your train travel, the Trains & Rail Passes section of my website has even more detailed tips and easy one-stop shopping for rail passes, seat reservations, and point-to-point tickets.

At ricksteves.com/rail you'll find clear, concise advice for figuring out the smartest options for your train trip. Our goal: To create smart con-sumers (and sell a few rail passes) by providing all the information you need to make the best rail-pass deci-sion for your trip. For each European country I cover, you'll get my frank opinion on which passes are usually a good value, handy region-specific ticket-price maps, and useful tips for saving money on point-to-point tickets.

How does your point-to-point ticket cost compare to the price of a pass? Look up the cost of a pass that covers the region you'll be in and the number of days you'll be on the train (see "Choosing Among Passes" on page 120). You may notice that several countries, mostly in southern and eastern Europe, have train fares so low that rail passes rarely beat out point-to-point tickets. If you're sticking to moderate distances in Italy, for example, it's unlikely a pass will save you money. If you're traveling in Germany, however, a pass is quite likely a smart move.

If your price comparison doesn't produce an obvious winner, take a closer look at factors that could tilt your deci-sion one way or another, such as:

• *Sparse rail coverage:* In some areas, such as southern Spain, coastal Croatia, much of Scotland, and all of Greece and Ireland, rail passes make little sense because trains don't reach a lot of places you're planning to go. (To learn whether your destinations are served by train, check online train schedules, described on page 124.)

• *Pricey fast-train supplements:* Passes lose their luster when fees are tacked on. In some countries, passholders are required to pay extra for each trip on a high-speed train. In

First or Second Class?

First class is plusher and roomier, but second class is where you'll make friends.

Nearly every European train has both first- and second-class cars (and some newer fast trains even have one or two extra rungs of "premier" or "executive" fanciness), all going at precisely the same speed. Yet on most trains in most countries, tickets in second class cost about a third less than those in first class.

Many Americans, familiar with the huge difference between first- and coach-class seating on airplanes, are surprised to see just how small the difference is on European trains. Second class is plenty comfortable; it's generally a no-brainer for anyone on a budget. It can also be more fun. Many first-class travelers are businesspeople looking to get work done; you'll have an easier time striking up a conversation in second class. Most Europeans don't travel in first class unless someone else is paying for it.

First class is often less crowded—a significant plus on popular routes at peak times, when it can be hard to find a seat in second class. First class also has wider seats and aisles, and is more likely to have amenities such as air-conditioning and power outlets (though outlets are still rare on Europe's trains, no matter which class). While first class is less conducive to conversation, it's more conducive to napping.

With some rail passes, anyone age 26 or older must buy a first-class pass (youth passes, however, always have a second-class option). Those with first-class passes may travel in second-class compartments, although the conductor may give you a puzzled look. Those with second-class passes can pay the difference in ticket price to upgrade to first (except in Britain).

Italy, for instance, it costs about an additional $15 per ride for mandatory fast-train reservations on most convenient connections between major cities. On the Thalys train that monopolizes direct service from Paris to Brussels or Amsterdam, passholders pay extra fees of up to $55 in second class and $95 in first class. (For more on reservations, see page 127.)

• **First-class-only passes:** A few rail passes don't offer a second-class option for adult travelers. If a first-class pass costs about the same as traveling with second-class tickets, go with the pass for comfort. (For more on the differences between classes, see the sidebar on page 114.)

• **Advance-purchase discounts:** If you don't mind forgoing some spontaneity, you might be able to save money with advance-purchase discounts on point-to-point tickets. But what you save in dollars you will lose in flexibility, as these discounts are usually valid only for nonrefundable, nonchangeable reserved tickets.

• **Convenience:** In countries or regions where reservations usually aren't required, a pass allows you to hop on and off trains without fussing with buying multiple tickets; if all other things are equal, a pass can make sense for ease of travel.

Point-to-Point Tickets

Unlike rail passes, which must be purchased before you get to Europe, it's generally easiest to buy point-to-point train tickets right at the station. But it can be smart to buy in advance for certain trains and destinations, especially if your dates are set and you don't want to risk a specific train journey selling out, or if you're hoping to land an advance-purchase discount.

With a valid rail pass, you just hop on any covered train that doesn't require reservations. But even unreserved point-to-point tickets have some flexibility, since you can still make any number of stops and connections along the most direct route between the starting and ending stations printed on your ticket (within a single country your trip usually just has to be completed within the same calendar day; for many international point-to-point tickets you have two weeks to complete the journey).

Where to Get Train Tickets

You have three main options for buying point-to-point tickets: through a US-based retailer before leaving home (such as ricksteves.com/rail), through the website of one of Europe's national railways, and in person at Europe's train stations (and at some European travel agencies).

US Retailer: You may pay a little more to purchase your ticket through a US retailer than if you were to buy that same ticket in person at a European train station—but for a can't-miss train, the extra cost can be worth it for the peace of mind. (And rail-pass holders who still need tickets and/or seat reservations on certain trains—most notably the Eurostar, Thalys, and any TGV—are smart to get their

Point-to-Point Train Tickets: Cost & Time

This chart shows the cost of second-class train tickets. Connect the dots of your itinerary, add up the cost, compare it with a rail pass, and see what is better for your trip.

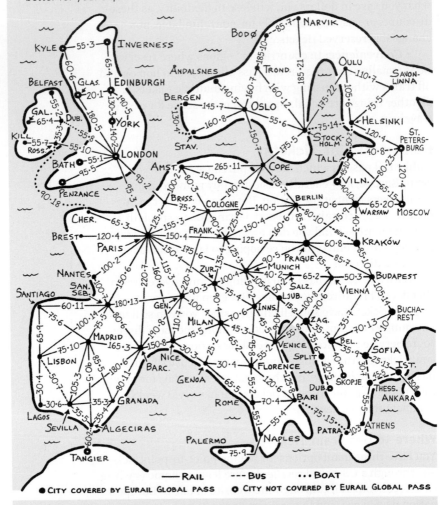

—— RAIL   --- BUS   ••• BOAT

● CITY COVERED BY EURAIL GLOBAL PASS   ○ CITY NOT COVERED BY EURAIL GLOBAL PASS

The **first number** between cities = **approximate cost** in US dollars for a one-way, second-class ticket. For first-class fares, add 50 percent. The **second number** = number of **hours** the trip takes.

Important: Fares given are for the fastest trains on a given route. Actual prices may vary (and may be cheaper). For more detailed regional maps, see ricksteves.com/cost-maps.

passholder-fare tickets through a US-based site, as these fares sell out quite far in advance and aren't available elsewhere online.)

National Railway Websites: Many European national rail companies allow customers to buy tickets online at the going European price (usually for faster classes of trains for which reservations are required, or at least recommended). If you're looking for the cheapest possible ticket between A and B—especially if A and B are in the same country—this is the way to go. Advance tickets can be an especially smart buy for popular high-speed trains (such as France's TGV trains and Italy's Le Frecce trains), which frequently sell out.

Not all national-railway sites are created equal. While some are fairly easy to navigate (such as the German, Austrian, British, French, Irish, Italian, Swedish, and Swiss railway sites), some are difficult or even impossible for foreigners to use (such as the unreliable Spanish railway site).

Your "ticket" may be a barcode on your smartphone, an emailed confirmation code redeemable at the station (in the same country that operates the website you bought it on), or a print-at-home document. Online tickets are valid for a specific date and time and have strict refund restrictions, so read the fine print carefully.

In Europe: Once in Europe, you can simply get tickets at the station, usually without much fuss, either on your day of travel or in advance (for tips, see page 130). This is the best option if you'd prefer to keep your itinerary more spontaneous. You can even get tickets for trains in another country: For example, if your trip starts in Paris, you can buy your Berlin-to-Prague ticket at any Parisian train station (as any Parisian would). Tickets bought at train-station windows tend to be easier to change (or have refunded) than tickets bought online.

In some cities you can avoid trekking to the train station by visiting a neighborhood travel agency or branch office of the national railroad. This convenience may come with an extra fee, but if the agency is easier for you to get to than the train station, buying tickets there can save

Resources for Trains, Buses & Boats

Bahn.com: User-friendly, Europe-wide timetable

Nationalrail.co.uk: Britain-specific train-schedule and ticket-booking site

Railfaneurope.net: Compendium of other national railway websites (click on "Links")

Eurolines.com: Europe's most extensive bus network

Aferry.co.uk: Ferry connections and tickets

Seat61.com: Rail-travel advice; particularly useful night-train info

DB Navigator app: Schedules for trains throughout Europe

lots of time and hassle (and travel agents may have more time and English-language skills than the people behind the train-station counter).

Ticket Prices

European train fares are based primarily on the distance traveled. Each country has its own "euros per kilometer" formula, though the type of train also affects the price (logically, slower trains are usually cheaper than faster ones). For faster classes of trains, however, many European rail companies have moved to a dynamic pricing system—similar to how airfares work—in which a fare can vary depending on demand, restrictions, and how early you purchase.

The quickest way to get a rough idea of what you'd pay for any given train trip in Europe is to check the cost-estimate map on page 116.

Ticket Discounts

If you're buying point-to-point tickets, be aware of the ways you can qualify for a discount (whether buying through a national railway website or in person):

Advance purchase (a week to three months in advance) can save you money in many countries (most notably Austria, Britain, Finland, France, Germany, Italy, Spain, and Sweden), especially for faster or longer rides. In some areas (such as Switzerland and most eastern countries), advance-purchase deals either don't exist or aren't worth the hassle. In most places, for regional or medium-speed trains, tickets cost the same whether they're bought two months or two minutes before the train leaves.

Round-trip tickets can be cheaper than two one-way tickets in some countries (Britain, Ireland, and Spain; sometimes in combination with advance purchase). For many trips within Britain, for example, a "day return" ticket (round-trip in a single day) can be only a little bit more expensive than a single one-way ticket.

Children get ticket discounts in most of Europe (typically about 50 percent off for ages 4-11, sometimes free with an adult). And most rail passes now offer one or two free kids with each adult. Whether you're traveling with tickets or a rail pass, kids under 4 always travel free on your lap (though if there's an empty seat, feel free to use it).

Youths ages 12-25 can buy discount cards in Austria, Belgium, Britain, France, Germany, and Italy.

Seniors can find a few ticket deals, most of which

require a discount card purchased in Europe (discounts start between ages 60 and 67; for details, see page 443).

Off-peak travel (such as midday or midweek) can be cheaper than peak-time journeys (mainly in Britain and France).

Rail Passes

For independent travelers armed with a rail pass, Europe is a playground. You can travel virtually anywhere, anytime, often without any seat reservations. Just step on the right train, sit in an unreserved seat, and when the uniformed conductor comes, flash your pass. High-speed, international, or overnight trains are more likely to require reservations, but despite that chore, a rail pass is still a joy.

All rail passes work in more or less the same way: Every pass covers a specific geographical area (one or more countries), has a fixed number of travel days, and is either good for a continuous block of time (a "continuous pass") or

Do You Speak Rail Pass?

When shopping for a rail pass, you're likely to come across some unfamiliar terms. Here's what they mean in plain English.

Global Pass: The classic "Eurail" pass, letting you travel freely throughout most of continental Europe, from Portugal to Finland to Greece.

Select Pass: Covers four neighboring countries in continental Europe.

Eurail: Brand name under which many European rail passes are sold (though more commonly used as a generic term for any European rail pass).

Continuous pass: Gives you unlimited train travel for the duration of the pass.

Flexipass: Lets you pay for just a certain number of train travel days within a specified window of time (for example, any 10 days within a two-month period).

Saverpass: Discounted pass for groups of two to five people traveling together.

Youth pass: Discounted pass for travelers ages 12-25.

Rail-pass bonuses: Certain boat, bus, and non-train trips that are either covered or discounted with a rail pass.

Benelux: Belgium, the Netherlands, and Luxembourg—collectively treated as one country by rail passes.

Activation: Step required before using your pass for the first time—have it stamped by someone behind a station counter.

Point-to-point ticket: Covers travel from Point A to Point B (may be an open-date ticket, or for a certain train at a certain time).

Couchette (koo-shet): A night-train bunk bed in a compartment (with a blanket, pillow, clean linen, and up to five compartment mates).

Sleeper: Compartment with more privacy than a **couchette,** with one, two, or three beds.

selected days in a window of time (a "flexipass"). Most passes offer "saverpass" deals to people traveling together.

Choosing Among Passes

Carefully compare passes to find the best fit for your itinerary and style of travel. The range of options may seem intimidating, but mostly it's a matter of simply knowing which countries you intend to travel in and for how many days.

Where To? First find the pass that best matches the area you'll be traveling in. If you're planning on covering a lot of ground by train, you probably want a multi-country pass, as it generally makes little sense to cobble together several single-country passes.

A **Global Pass,** covering the widest area, gives you most of Europe by the tail, buying you unlimited travel on all public railways in most of Europe (Britain is the big exception). If you've got a whirlwind trip planned, the Global Pass is probably the best way to go. (You need to essentially travel from Amsterdam to Rome to Madrid and back to Amsterdam to justify the purchase of a one-month Global Pass.)

For a less ambitious multi-country trip, consider a **Select Pass,** which lets you preselect four adjoining countries. If you're traveling just a tad beyond four main countries, consider whether buying one or two extra point-to-point tickets might be cheaper than bumping up to a Global Pass. If a certain **multi-country regional pass,** such as for Scandinavia, happens to fit your plans, it can be even cheaper than a Select Pass.

Virtually every European country has its own **single-country pass.** These are especially worth considering for Britain (which does not participate in the Global Pass or Select Pass) and for Switzerland (where its pass covers more than just trains). The relative value of a single-country pass over individual tickets really varies across Europe, so price it out before buying one.

Flexipass or Continuous? If you plan to linger for a few days at most of your destinations, a **flexipass** makes the most sense, as it lets you pay only for the days on which you actually travel. Most rail

A Global Pass covers most of Europe except Great Britain and some nations in Eastern Europe. A Select Pass lets you narrow the scope to four adjacent countries.

Eurail Countries

FINLAND
NORWAY
SWEDEN
DENMARK
IRELAND
NETH.
BELG. GERMANY
SLOVAKIA
CZECH.
FRANCE
SWITZ. AUST.
HUNG.
SLOV.
ROMANIA
CRO.
PORTUGAL
ITALY
BULGARIA
SPAIN
TURKEY
GREECE

Note: Serbia & Montenegro are not part of Global Pass

passes are of this type. You don't have to decide beforehand which days you'll travel on, but you do have a certain window in which you must use up your train days (usually two months after you start using the pass). You can take as many trips as you like within each travel day, which runs from midnight to midnight (though most direct overnight rides can count as only one travel day on a flexipass—see page 123).

A **continuous pass** can save you money if you plan to travel nearly daily and cover a lot of ground. Global, BritRail, German, and Swiss passes offer this option. If you have a 15-day continuous pass, you can ride the trains as many times as you like for 15 days. The number of days you can travel with a one-month continuous pass depends on the month you start traveling: If you set off on any day in February, the pass is only good for the next 28 days; if you start in July, it's good for 31 days.

For those with open-ended plans, continuous passes can provide an extra sense of flexibility. Let's say you're planning a three-week trip and choosing between two versions of a Global Pass: a 21-day continuous pass and a cheaper 10-days-in-two-months flexipass. For not much more money, the continuous pass gives you the freedom to take any train without wondering if a particular trip justifies the use of a travel day.

Getting the Most Out of a Rail Pass

Many people spend more on their rail pass than they have to. Consider the following tips before you make your purchase:

Stretch a flexipass by paying out of pocket for shorter trips. If you plan to ride the train on, say, eight different days, but two of those days are very short trips, you may save money by getting a six-day pass and buying point-to-point tickets at the station on your short-haul days. Use your flexipass only for those travel days that involve long hauls or several trips. To determine whether a trip is a good use of a travel day, divide the cost of your pass by the number of travel days (or look at what it costs to add a day onto the pass's base price). If the pass you're considering costs about $60 per travel day, it makes no sense to use one of your days for a trip that would otherwise cost $10.

One rail pass is usually better than two. To cover a multi-country trip, it's almost always cheaper to buy one Select Pass or Global Pass with lots of travel days than to buy several country passes with a few high-cost travel days per pass. If you travel over a border (such as Germany to

Switzerland) using separate country rail passes, you'll use up a day of each pass.

Understand your bonuses. Some boat, bus, and other non-train rides—called "bonuses"—are either covered or discounted with any rail pass that covers the appropriate country. A bonus trip is no different from a train trip: To use your flexipass to cover the cost of a bonus boat or bus, you must fill in a travel day on your pass (and you can take as many trips, whether train or non-train, in one travel day as you can squeeze in). These include German Rhine boats, Swiss lake boats and Italy-Greece ferry crossings. Trips offered only at a discount (rather than those that are completely covered by the pass) usually don't cost you a flexipass travel day, but you must use the discount within your pass's validity period.

With careful juggling, a shorter pass can cover a longer trip. For example, if you're on a one-month trip, you don't necessarily need a one-month pass. You may be able to get by with a 21-day continuous pass by starting and/or ending your trip in a city where you'd like to stay for several days or in a country not covered by your pass. On, say, a one-month London-Vienna trip, you could spend a few days in London, take the Eurostar train to Paris (which isn't covered by rail passes), sightsee in Paris for several days, then activate your pass when you leave Paris. Plan for your pass to expire in Vienna, where you can easily spend a few days without the use of a rail pass.

It can make sense to buy a longer pass for a shorter trip. One long, expensive train ride at the end of a 25-day trip can justify jumping from a 21-consecutive-day rail pass to a one-month pass.

Using Your Rail Pass

Rail passes are pretty straightforward but come with a lot of fine print (worth reading). It's important to understand at least the basics before your first day of train travel.

Activate your pass before your first use. You must officially activate your rail pass, in person at a European train station, for it to be valid for train travel. Your pass comes printed with an issue date (usually the day you bought it) and must be activated within six months. For example, if May 24 is stamped on your rail pass as the issue date, you must start the pass by November 23. Never write anything on your rail pass before it's been activated.

Activation is easy: At any European train station, present your rail pass and passport to a railway official at a ticket or

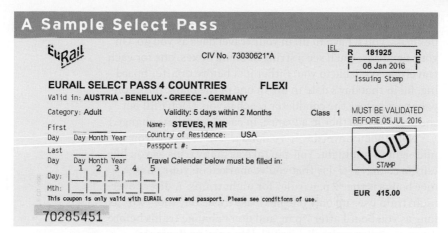

Don't write anything on your rail pass before it's activated. When you're ready to use it, the ticket agent will fill in validity dates and your passport number, and stamp the activation box on the far right. Each day when you take your seat on the train, write down the date in ink (day first, then month) before the conductor comes around.

information window. The ticket agent (not you) writes in your passport number, and the first and last dates of your travel period, and stamps the activation box on the far right. For example, a two-month validity period starting May 15 will end at midnight on July 14. Agents will assume that you intend to use the pass on the same day you are presenting it, so if you're activating it a few days beforehand, write your desired dates (European style, e.g., 15/05/16 - 14/07/16) on a slip of paper to show the agent before handing over the pass. All train trips and non-train "bonuses" (trips on covered or discounted boats and buses) must be started and finished within the valid life of your rail pass. If you have a group pass (i.e., a saverpass), all group members must be present when the rail pass is activated.

You may activate your rail pass before arriving in the (first) country it covers. Let's say you're in Copenhagen with a German rail pass, you're heading to Berlin, and you want the German portion of your route to be covered by your rail pass. At the Copenhagen train station, buy a ticket to the German border and have the agent activate your rail pass at the same time.

Don't get caught with an pass that hasn't been activated: If you forget to do it before boarding, approach the conductor right away to have it done on board (don't be surprised if you're charged a fee of $5-30).

Fill in travel days (for flexipasses) and trip details. With a continuous rail pass, nobody counts how many days you travel during the validated period. But if you're using a flexipass, you'll have to fill in your travel days as you go. On your flexipass, you'll see a string of blank boxes, one for each travel day available to you. Either just before or after boarding, fill in that day's date in ink in one of the blank boxes on your pass before the conductor reaches you. (Don't fill out the dates any farther in advance, in case your plans change.)

Note that a travel day is a calendar day, running from midnight to midnight. You can take as many trips as you like within each travel day that you've marked on your pass. A nice bonus is the "7 p.m. rule" for night trains: A direct overnight train uses up only one flexipass travel day (not two), as long as you board after 7 p.m. and don't change trains before 4 a.m. (you just write the arrival date on your flexipass).

Some passes (continuous or flexi) also require you to fill in your trip destinations on the foldout sheets of your pass cover.

Show your pass if asked. After the train starts, the conductor heads down the aisle, asking for tickets and passes, and checking that they are dated correctly. You may be asked to present your passport, too.

Keep your pass in your money belt. Your rail pass is a valuable slip of paper—if you lose it, it's gone. (Even if you bought the "Rail Protection Plan" when you got your pass, a lost or stolen pass presents a logistical headache.) While some national railways are slowly moving toward paperless ticketing, most rail passes are still only available in old-fashioned hard-copy form. Guard yours carefully.

Looking Up Train Schedules

Riding the rails has become even easier with the advent of user-friendly online timetables. You can instantly find the fastest connections, frequency, and length of a train trip (and learn whether reservations are required). Schedules can also be essential to basic itinerary planning, as they tell you where trains do and don't go.

No matter where you're traveling in Europe, Germany's Deutsche Bahn website at bahn.com should be your first stop for timetable information. (While each country's national rail company has its own website with schedules, the German site has schedules for virtually all of Europe.) I use this site to plan my connections for almost every trip in Europe. Their DB Navigator app is a boon for train travelers with smartphones and tablets.

City Name Variations

English Name	European Name
Athens, Greece	Athina (Greek), Athenes (German)
Bolzano, Italy	Bozen (German)
Bratislava, Slovakia	Pressburg (German), Pozsony (Hungarian)
Basel, Switzerland	Bâle (French)
Bruges, Belgium	Brugge (Dutch)
Brussels, Belgium	Bruxelles (French)
Cologne, Germany	Köln or Koeln
Copenhagen, Denmark	København
Cracow, Poland	Kraków
Dubrovnik, Croatia	Ragusa (Italian and German)
Florence, Italy	Firenze
Gdańsk, Poland	Danzig (German)
Geneva, Switzerland	Genève (French), Genf (German)
Genoa, Italy	Genova
Gothenburg, Sweden	Göteborg
The Hague, Netherlands	Den Haag, 'S Gravenhage
Helsinki, Finland	Helsingfors (Swedish)
Lisbon, Portugal	Lisboa
London, England	Londres (French)
Munich, Germany	München or Muenchen (German), Monaco di Baviera (Italian)
Naples, Italy	Napoli (Italian), Neapel (German)
Nice, France	Nizza (Italian)
Nuremberg, Germany	Nürnberg or Nuornberg
Padua, Italy	Padova
Pamplona, Spain	Iruña (Euskara)
Paris, France	Parigi (Italian)
Prague, Czech Republic	Praha
Rome, Italy	Roma
San Sebastián, Spain	Donostia (Euskara)
Venice, Italy	Venezia (Italian), Venedig (German)
Vienna, Austria	Wien (German), Bécs (Hungarian), Dunaj (Slovene), Vídeň (Czech), Viedeň (Slovak)
Warsaw, Poland	Warszawa (Polish), Warschau (German)

Finding Schedules on the Deutsche Bahn Site

The German railway's online schedule is an invaluable tool
for any European train traveler. Here's how to use it:

1. Start with a station-to-station search. Enter just the
city name, unless you know the name of the specific station
you want. Use complete names: "Rothenburg ob der Tauber"
(not "Rothenburg"); "Jerez de la Frontera" (not "Jerez").
You may encounter unfamiliar versions of city names (for
example, "Praha" instead of "Prague"); the sidebar on the
previous page lists some common variations.

2. If prompted, choose a station. Many cities have
several stations, and you may be asked to specify one from a
drop-down menu. If the city's name spelled in capital letters
is among the options, select it (the site will look up the best
connections for that city, regardless of the station). Main
stations are often called "central," "terminus," or "Hbf" (for
Hauptbahnhof).

3. Enter the date and time. Make your best guess about
when you might travel (using the 24-hour clock). Don't
worry too much about the exact date and time of your train
trips, as schedules for most trains don't vary much (Sundays
are the major exception, when frequency is limited on many
routes). Though most schedules aren't available more than
three months out, you can still get a fairly accurate idea of
trip length and frequency by trying a closer date on the same
day of the week you'll be traveling.

4. Skip the extra search fields. If you're just looking
up schedules, there's no need to fill out any fields beyond the
top ones: Once you've entered the stations, date, and time,
just skip right to "Search." (If you're prompted here to select
from a drop-down list of stations, see #2, above.)

5. Review your options. You'll be given a range of possibilities for your journey. Each one shows the start and end
points (with stations specified), the departure and arrival
times, the duration of the trip, the number of changes, the
types of trains, and whether the train requires a reservation
(indicated by a circled "R").

6. Know where to find more details. Clicking the
arrow symbol next to any of the trip options will give you
more detail, including all transfer points. If you click "Show
intermediate stops," you can see every stop on that route.
Clicking the train number shows all the stops for the entire
route, including those before and/or after your stations.

7. Check for reservation info. "Compulsory reservation" means what it says, while "Please reserve" means

that reservations are recommended but optional (see "Seat Reservations" below). "International supplement" doesn't apply to travelers with rail passes.

The Deutsche Bahn site doesn't show fares for most trains outside Germany and Austria. I wouldn't bother checking exact ticket prices on each country's own national railway site; for estimates, use the map on page 116.

If your destination isn't listed on the Deutsche Bahn site (and if you've spelled it correctly), it likely doesn't have train service. But before giving up—especially for train travel in Spain and Italy—it's a good idea to consult their national railway sites to double-check availability.

For more tips on using the Deutsche Bahn website, head to ricksteves.com/schedules.

Seat Reservations

Some kinds of trains require all passengers to have reservations (which guarantee you a specific seat), and sometimes it's smart to reserve even when it's not compulsory. But many other trains don't require reservations, and the vast majority of trains usually have more than enough seating—so don't make the mistake of over-reserving. Many American travelers waste money and surrender their flexibility after being swayed by US-based agents who profit from exaggerating the need for reservations.

Compulsory Reservations

Your best resource for identifying trains that truly require a reservation is the Deutsche Bahn online schedule—it's objective, complete, and easy to use.

Though relatively few train types require reservations, those that do are among the most popular. They include a few privately run international trains, such as the Eurostar (which connects London with Paris and Brussels), the Brussels-based Thalys, and a handful of special just-for-tourists trains (such as the Norway in a Nutshell route, and several of Switzerland's specially designated scenic trains).

Aside from these one-offs, many countries have at least one category of high-speed train that always requires reservations—most notably France, Italy, Spain, and Sweden. Some countries have a few long-distance must-reserve routes. And you'll need to book ahead (or at least pay a little extra) for a spot on nearly all overnight trains in Europe.

In many cases, these required reservations aren't so much a matter of space constrictions, but a surcharge for the privilege of riding the fastest (or fanciest) train. But on certain routes, seats can sell out quickly (see "How Far Ahead?" below).

Optional Reservations

Reservations can still be a good idea on trains that don't require them. For example, it's wise to reserve at least several days ahead if you are traveling during a peak time (summer, weekends, holidays), on a route with infrequent service, if you need several seats together (a family with children), or for a train you simply cannot afford to miss.

Otherwise, I wouldn't recommend reserving a seat if you don't have to; most slower regional trains don't even give you the option. Most of the time, trains have plenty of seating for everyone, and even if you wind up on a crowded train, the worst-case scenario is that you'll stand a while before a seat frees up.

How to Reserve

For trains that don't need to be booked very far in advance, it's best to simply make all your reservations at one time at any staffed station in Europe.

If you need to lock in your reservations well in advance of your train trip, book them ahead of time from home through a US-based retailer (such as ricksteves.com/rail) or Euraide (euraide.com), a European-based vendor whose prices can be a good value for those who need to book multiple seat reservations in advance.

Seat reservations typically cost anywhere from $5 to $35 (except in Britain, where they're free), with a few more-expensive exceptions, depending on the kind of train they're for, who you buy them from, and whether you're traveling with a rail pass (and sometimes even on which rail pass you have). This cost is included in the price of a point-to-point ticket for any train that requires reservations (dates, times, and seat assignments are built in, just like with an airline ticket), but on trains for which reservations are optional, it's an extra fee.

For more information on passholder reservation fees for popular trains, check the country-specific rail pages at ricksteves.com/rail for any countries you're planning to visit.

How Far Ahead?

Whether you're traveling with a rail pass or just buying tickets as you go, you can purchase seat (or overnight berth) reservations anywhere from an hour to several months in advance.

How far in advance to reserve any given train depends on the inflexibility of your schedule (do you have hotel reservations or a flight to catch?), how many departures in a day could get you there on time (2 or 20?), the likelihood of seats (or at least reservations) selling out, and other factors mentioned above.

Be aware that most trains with compulsory reservations limit the number of seats available to passholders (most notoriously France's TGV trains, which also don't let passholders book seat reservations less than three days before departure). Along some of the most popular routes, such as between Paris and Italy, direct trains run only a few times per day; these can sell out weeks ahead (and the overnight Paris-Italy trains don't accept rail passes at all).

No matter when you're going, I'd recommend booking as far ahead as possible for the following trains:

- Eurostar (London-Paris/Brussels)
- TGV (France's high-speed trains)
- Any direct train between Paris and Italy
- Thalys (high-speed Brussels-based trains)
- City Night Line (fancy night trains based mostly in Germany)

TRAIN STATIONS

Great European train stations still my wanderlust. Stepping off a train in Munich, I stand under the station's towering steel and glass rooftop and study the big, black schedule board crowned by the station clock. It lists two dozen departures. Every few minutes, the letters and numbers on each line spin and tumble as one by one cities and departure times work their way to the top and flutter away.

Whether old or new, bustling European train stations are temples of travel. Just pick a platform...and explore Europe.

A Typical Train Ticket

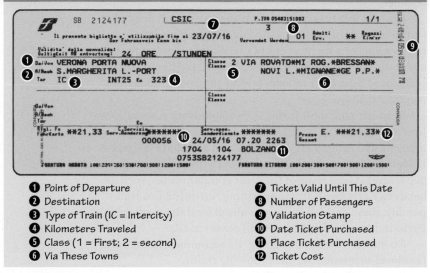

1. Point of Departure
2. Destination
3. Type of Train (IC = Intercity)
4. Kilometers Traveled
5. Class (1 = First; 2 = second)
6. Via These Towns
7. Ticket Valid Until This Date
8. Number of Passengers
9. Validation Stamp
10. Date Ticket Purchased
11. Place Ticket Purchased
12. Ticket Cost

This is a point-to-point ticket for travel in Italy; train tickets across Europe have the same kind of information.

Surrounded by Germany on the move, I notice business-men in tight neckties, giddy teenage girls, and a Karl-Marx-like bum leaning on a *Bierstube* counter. The fast and the slow, the young and the old, we're all in this together—working our way up life's departure board.

There's plenty of romance here, but the hustle and bustle at train stations can also be confusing. Here are some tips on navigating Europe's temples of transportation.

Europe is becoming automated, and savvy travelers save time by using ticket machines: Choose English, then follow the step-by-step instructions.

Buying Tickets at the Station

Nearly every station has at least a few old-fashioned ticket windows staffed by human beings, usually marked by long lines; avoid them by using ticket machines, which almost always offer instructions in English.

The downside to ticket machines: Some won't take American credit cards (even if they claim to), or accept

Key Train Vocabulary

English	French	Italian	German	Spanish
train	train	treno	Zug	tren
ticket	billet	biglietto	Fahrkarte	billete
station	gare	stazione	Bahnhof	estación
main station	gare centrale	stazione centrale	Hauptbahnhof	estación principal
platform/track	quai/voie	binario	Bahnsteig/ Gleis	andén/vía
timetable	horaire	orario	Fahrplan	horario
supplement	supplément	supplemento	Zuschlag	suplemento
delay	retard	ritardare	Verspätung	retraso
strike	grève	sciopero	Streik	huelga
reservation	réservation	prenotazione	Reservierung	reserva
berth/couchette	couchette	cuccetta	Liegeplatz	litera

them only if you key in your card's PIN (for more on credit-card hassles in Europe, see page 190). If the machines won't cooperate with your card, try cash (most machines are labeled according to the kind of payment they accept), or head for the ticket window.

If you opt for a ticket window, try to select the appropriate line—larger stations may have different windows for domestic, international, sleeper cars, or immediate departures. When buying tickets, you can most clearly communicate your intentions by writing what you need and showing it to the ticket agent: destination, date, time, how many people, first or second class.

In person, bridge any communication gap by writing out your plan: departure and destination, date, time (If you want a reservation and/ or a printout of your departure options), how many people, first or second class.

It's often possible to buy tickets aboard the train, but expect to pay an additional fee for the convenience. Be sure to have enough cash in case the conductor can't use your American credit card. If you're buying on board, find the conductor before he finds you; otherwise, your "fee" could turn into a much heftier "fine" for traveling without a valid ticket. Be aware that on most local trains (especially commuter lines), all trains in Switzerland, and many others around Europe, you can be fined for traveling sans ticket, no matter what. Look for warning signs on train doors.

15:37 So*	IC 1958	Weißenfels 16:04 – Naumburg 16:15 – Apolda 16:33 – Weimar 16:45 – Erfurt 17:01 – Gotha 17:26 – Eisenach 17:42 – Fulda 18:36 – Frankfurt (Main) Hbf 19:32 – Darmstadt 20:10 – Bensheim 20:23 – Weinheim 20:34 – Heidelberg 20:50 – Wiesloch-Walldorf 21:02 – Vaihingen 21:26 – Stuttgart Hbf 21:46 ⊘ *auch 13. Jun, nicht 12. Jun, 10., 24. Jul	12
15:37 Mo-Fr*	MRB 54 80275	Leipzig Messe 15:43 ⊘ Delitzsch unt Bf 15:56 – Bitterfeld 16:07 *nicht an allg. Feiertg.	12
15:37 Sa	MRB 54 80277	Leipzig Messe 15:43 – Rackwitz 15:47 ⊘ Delitzsch unt Bf 15:56	12
15:40	ICE 1744	Leipzig/Halle Flughafen ✈ 15:52 – Halle 16:05 – Köthen 16:26 – Magdeburg 16:56 ⊘ Braunschweig 17:49 – Hannover 18:23 – Bremen 19:50 – Oldenburg (Oldb) 20:23	Mo-Sa 18 So 20

Schedule Information

Even if you've looked up your train schedules online in advance, always confirm your plans at the station. Every station has some kind of schedule information available, whether it's in printed or electronic form, or at information counters staffed by people eager (or at least able) to help you. All European timetables use the 24-hour clock (see page 44).

Learning to decipher printed schedules makes life easier on Europe's rails. Posters list all trains that arrive at and depart from a particular station each day. This information is clearly shown in two separate listings: Departures are usually in yellow, and arrivals are normally in white. In some stations, you'll find free schedule booklets listing all their daily departures.

Familiarize yourself with the symbols in schedules that indicate exceptions: Crossed hammers, for instance, mean the train goes only on workdays (daily except Sundays and holidays); a cross signifies that it runs only on Sundays and holidays. Most other symbols are easy enough to guess at: A little bed means the train has sleeping compartments, and crossed silverware indicates a dining car.

Many stations also have either video screens or big flippy boards that list the next several departures. These often befuddle travelers who don't realize that all over the world, the same five easy-to-identify columns are listed: destination, major stops along the way, type of train, track number, and departure time. I don't care what language they're in; without much effort you can accurately guess which column is which.

Stations may also have self-service computer terminals—many of which are ticket machines—where you can

LEFT Posted train schedules clearly indicate departure times, destinations, arrival times, and track numbers.

RIGHT In Munich's train station, departures and arrivals are listed on easy-to-read electronic boards. Railroad staff is standing by to answer your questions.

look up schedule information. These computers are almost always multilingual and can be real time-savers. Use them to understand all your options. Many even print out a schedule tailored to your trip.

Of course, your best authority is the person at the train station information window. Uniformed employees on the platforms and on board the trains can also help.

Other Services

Besides offering travel-related services, most stations are great places to take care of your basic to-do list, with ATMs, grocery stores (usually with longer hours than you'll find in the town center), restaurants, bike-rental kiosks, and shops selling mobile-phone SIM cards.

Baggage Check: Most major stations have storage lockers and/or a luggage-checking service where, for about $3-8 a day, you can leave your bags. People traveling light can fit two bags into one locker, cutting their storage costs in half. In some security-conscious train stations, lockers are no longer in use, and travelers must check their bags at a luggage-deposit desk—often after going through an airport-type security check. You'll pay $5 to $15 per bag. Lock your bag and don't leave valuables inside—both for your own security and because some luggage desks won't accept unlocked bags. In extreme cases, they don't take laptop computers. (I once spent a day in Marseille carrying around my laptop.) Allow plenty of time to retrieve your bag before boarding your train. Bag-check desks come with lines, can close for lunch in smaller stations, and usually aren't open all night—confirm opening and closing times before storing your bag. If the station doesn't offer a place to leave your bag, head to a nearby tourist-information office, hotel, or gift shop. Ask nicely, offer your most charming smile (or a small fee), and you'll likely find someone willing to keep an eye on your things for a few hours.

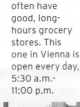

Train stations often have good, long-hours grocery stores. This one in Vienna is open every day, 5:30 a.m.-11:00 p.m.

Internet Access: You will find Wi-Fi hotspots at major train stations throughout most of Europe, sometimes for a fee. Wi-Fi is typically free in the first-class lounge. Finding Wi-Fi on trains is still more serendipitous than reliable, with the exception of high-speed trains on some of the most common business routes.

Tourist Information: Many stations have a tourist information office either in the station or very nearby. Pick up a map, find out about local transit, and double-check the hours of your must-see sights (for more on these offices, see page 274).

Waiting Rooms: Most stations have comfortable waiting rooms, and travelers with fancy tickets often enjoy fancy business or VIP lounges. Before you spend hours idling in one of these rooms, take advantage of the station's services (look up schedules for the next leg of your trip, get groceries) or explore the area around the station. You may well find yourself within a short walk of something really cool. For example, if you're changing trains in Cologne, even on a tight schedule you can easily pop outside for a jaw-dropping look at its cathedral, just across the square. Waiting rooms can be decent last-ditch sleeping options (but guard your valuables).

Transit Connections: Train stations are also major transit hubs, so connections from train to bus, subway, or tram are generally no more difficult than crossing the street. If an airport is nearby, you'll find airport-train or transit services (usually well marked) at the train station.

Buses connect from the station to nearby towns that lack train service. If you have a bus to catch, be quick, since many are intended for commuters and are scheduled to connect with the train and leave promptly.

Getting on the (Right) Train

For many Americans, Europe presents their first experience with a bustling train station, and the task of navigating the system and finding the right train can sound daunting. But anyone who's managed to find their way in a sprawling American airport will find Europe's train stations a snap. As you head for your train, ticket or pass in hand, keep these pointers in mind.

Get yourself to the right station. Many cities have more than one train station: Paris has six, Brussels has three, and even Switzerland's little Interlaken has two. Be sure you know whether your train is leaving from Interlaken East or Interlaken West, even if that means asking what might seem like a stupid question.

Train cars are usually labeled with pertinent information. This is a non-smoking second-class car with video surveillance and room for wheelchairs but not bikes. The eye (top left) means you'll be fined if a ticket patroller catches you without a valid ticket or pass.

Find your track. A few countries publish track numbers in their train schedules, but in most places you'll need to look for your platform information once you get to the station. Upcoming departures are displayed on computer screens or mechanical flippy boards; track information is usually posted about a half-hour before the train departs.

Ask for help. I always ask someone on the platform if the train is going where I think it is. Uniformed train personnel can answer any question you can communicate. Speak slowly, clearly, and with caveman simplicity. Resist the urge to ask, "Pardon me, would you be able to tell me if this train is going to Rome?" Just point to the train or track and say, "Roma?"

Be observant. If the loudspeaker comes on while you're waiting for your train at track 7, gauge by the reaction of those around you whether the announcement affects you. If, after the babble, everyone dashes over to track 15, assume your train is no longer leaving from track 7, and follow the pack.

Allow yourself sufficient time to navigate the station. Stations are generally laid out logically, with numbered tracks lined up in a row. But the biggest stations are so extensive they can take time to cross. Some large stations have entirely separate sections for local and long-distance trains. For example, Madrid's Atocha station is divided into sections for *cercanías* (local trains) and AVE (high-speed, long-distance trains). A Paris train station might have some tracks devoted to Grandes Lignes ("grand lines" to other cities), and others for Transilien (local milk-run trains). At the Frankfurt airport, regional trains depart from

The train on track 5 will stop at Olten, Bern, Thun, and Spiez en route to Interlaken's East Station. But it's two hours late (*später*).

the *Regionalbahnhof,* while long-distance trains use the *Fernbahnhof.* Many large stations also have vast sections devoted to subway trains or regional buses.

Be on guard for pickpockets. With travelers already distracted by announcements and luggage, a busy train station is an ideal work environment for thieves. Wear your money belt, keep your bags in hand, and be very wary of "helpful" locals hanging around ticket machines. For more tips on this, see the Theft and Scams chapter.

Where required, validate your ticket and/or seat reservation before boarding. In France and Italy, most point-to-point tickets and seat reservations aren't valid until you've date-stamped them by inserting them into a machine near the platform (if you've printed tickets at home, they don't need validating). If you have multiple parts to your ticket (for example, a ticket and a reservation), each one must be validated. Watch (or ask) others, and imitate—but don't assume that you can skip this step just because others have, as locals traveling with commuter passes won't be date-stamping them. (No matter where you're traveling, rail passes need to be activated in person at a ticket window before using them for the first time.)

Expect no-hassle boarding. For the vast majority of Europe's trains, you stroll (or dash) right to your boarding platform, ticket or pass in hand, without any check-in formalities. The main exception is the Eurostar English Channel train, which has an advance check-in deadline (30 minutes before departure) and an airline-style security procedure. You may find simple preboarding security or ticket checks in a few other places. In Spain, for instance, your tickets will be checked and luggage scanned before you access the platform to board fast AVE trains. Many stations in Britain now require you to slide your paper ticket or tap your barcode on a turnstile reader both to enter and exit the boarding areas (if you're traveling with a rail pass, just show

A handy diagram showing your train configuration (and at which platform section each car will arrive) can help you decide where to stand while waiting. Understanding this can make the difference between snagging a great seat... or hoofing it to the other end of the train and scrambling for what's left.

it to the attendants at these gates), and train doors close 30 seconds before departure. The Netherlands' *chipkaart* tickets must also be tapped on the card reader both when entering and exiting the station. Across Europe, some night trains have conductors checking tickets at the doors to each car.

Scope out the train ahead of time. The configuration of many major trains is charted in display cases on the platform. As you wait, study the display to note where the first-class, second-class, restaurant, and sleeping cars are, and which cars are going where. First-class cars are always marked with a big "1" on the outside, second-class cars with a "2." Some train schedules will say, in the fine print, "Munich-bound cars in the front, Vienna-bound cars in the rear." Knowing which cars you're eligible for can be especially handy if you'll be competing with a mob for a seat. When expecting a real scramble, I stand on a bench at the far end of the track and study each car as the train rolls by, looking in the windows to note where the empty places are. If there are several departures within an hour and the first train looks hopeless, I'll wait for the next.

Never assume the entire train is going where you are. For long hauls, each car is labeled separately, because cars are usually added and dropped here and there along the journey. I'll never forget one hot afternoon in the center of Spain. My train stopped in the middle of nowhere. There was some mechanical rattling. Then the train pulled away, leaving me alone in my car—in La Mancha. Ten minutes later, another train came along, picked up my car, and I was on my way. To survive all this juggling without any panic, be sure that the city on your car's nameplate is your destination. The nameplate lists the final stop and some (but not all) of the stops in between.

ON THE TRAIN

Once you're on board, it's time to sit back and enjoy the journey.

Find a seat. If you have a seat assignment, locate it and plop yourself down. If you're traveling without a seat reservation, you can claim any unreserved seat. If these are in short supply, take a closer look at the reservation tags posted above the seats or on compartment doors. Each tag shows which stretch of the journey that seat is reserved for. You may well be getting off the train before the seat owner even boards. For example, if you're headed from Luzern to

Strikes

Some travelers worry about getting stranded somewhere because of a strike. But in general, they're nothing to stress about.

Strikes can affect rail service anywhere in Europe (especially in Italy). They're usually announced long in advance in stations and online. Most last just a day, or even just several hours. Anticipate strikes—ask your hotelier, talk to locals, look for signs, check online—but don't feel bullied by them. In theory, train service shuts down, but in reality, sporadic trains lumber down main-line tracks during most strikes (preserving "essential service").

If a strike occurs on your travel day, check the national railway website—special strike schedules are generally posted. Otherwise, head to the station, where the few remaining station personnel can tell you the expected schedule. You'll likely find a workable train to your destination, though it may involve a wait. While it's usually possible to get a refund for reservations affected by a strike, there are no refunds for partially used rail passes.

Know the local word for "strike": *sciopero* (Italian), *grève* (French), *apergia* (Greek), and so on. They're a nuisance but, in many countries, a normal part of life.

Lugano, and you see a seat that's only reserved from Lugano to Milan, it's all yours.

Stow your luggage. In more than 30 years of train travel, I've never checked a bag. Simply carry it on and heave it up onto the rack above the seat or wedge it into the triangular space between back-to-back seats. I've seen Turkish families moving all their worldly goods from Germany back to Turkey without checking a thing. People complain about the porters in the European train stations. I think they're great—I've never used one.

Be savvy with your bags. I assume every train has a thief planning to grab a bag. Store your luggage within sight, rather than at the end of a train car. Before leaving my luggage in a compartment, I establish a relationship with everyone there. I'm safe leaving it among mutual guards. I don't lock my bag, but to be safe, I often clip my rucksack straps to the luggage rack. When a thief makes his move in the darkness of a train tunnel, and the bag doesn't give, he's not going to ask, "*Scusi,* how is your luggage attached?"

Use train time wisely. The time you spend on long train rides can be an opportunity to get organized or make plans for your next destination. Read ahead in your guidebook, write journal entries, delete yesterday's bad photos, double-check your connection information with the conductor, organize your daypack, or write an email home (you don't have to be online to write one). If the train has power outlets (rare but becoming more common), charge your gadgets. Don't, however, get so immersed in chores that you forget to keep an eye out the window for beautiful scenery around the next bend.

Europe's trains are so fast, they pull into stations with squashed birds on their windshields. You'd wait all your life to see a bird squashed onto the windshield of a train back home. I guess with Europe's impressive transportation infrastructure, "DB" stands for "dead bird."

Use WCs—they're free. To save time and money, use the toilets on the train rather than those in the station (which can cost money, and are often less clean). Toilets on first-class cars are a cut above second-class toilets. I "go" first class even with a second-class ticket. Train toilets are located on the ends of cars, where it's most jiggly. A trip to the train's john always reminds me of the rodeo. Some toilets empty directly on the tracks, so never use a train's WC while stopped in a station (unless you didn't like that particular town). A train's WC cleanliness deteriorates as the journey progresses.

Follow local train etiquette. Pay attention to the noise level in your car. If everyone else is speaking in hushed tones, follow suit. Watch for signs indicating that you're sitting in a designated quiet car, where businesspeople come to work and others to nap. No matter where I'm sitting, I make an effort not to be the loudest person in earshot (easily done on the average Italian train, but takes extra awareness in, say, Germany). Resting your feet on the seat across from you without taking your shoes off is perhaps an even graver faux pas.

Talk to locals or other travelers. There is so much to be learned. Europeans are often less open and forward than Americans. You could sit across from a silent but fascinating and friendly European for an entire train ride, or you could break the ice by asking a question, quietly offering some candy, or showing your Hometown, USA, postcards. This can start the conversation flowing and a friendship growing.

Pack a picnic. For the best dining value and variety, stock up at a local deli, bakery, supermarket, or wine cellar before you board; most train stations offer at least one of these. Food sold on the train costs more, with options ranging from a basic coffee and sandwich cart to a more extensive bar car or sit-down dining car (noted on most schedules when available). A few trains offer a "complimentary" meal, in first class only, usually covered by a higher seat-reservation fee.

Strategize your arrival. Use your guidebook to study up on your destination city while you're still on board—it's far more time-efficient and less overwhelming to arrive in a station already knowing how you plan to reach the city center (or your hotel). If you're trying to make a tight connection, it's good to know which platform your next train leaves from. If you don't already have that information, flag down a conductor, who either knows the answer or should be able to look it up for you.

As you approach your destination, have a game plan ready for when you get off the train. Know what you need to accomplish in the station before heading out—e.g., looking up the schedule (and perhaps making seat reservations) for the next leg of your train trip, picking up a map from a trackside information office, hitting an ATM, buying a transit pass, or grabbing provisions from a grocery store (especially if you're arriving late, after most city-center shops and restaurants have closed). If you'll depart from the same station later, pay attention to the layout.

Know where to get off. In Dresden, I twice got off my train too early—at two different suburban stations—before arriving at the central station. Know which station you need before you arrive, and be patient. When arriving in a city (especially on a commuter train), you may stop at several suburban stations with signs indicating your destination's name and the name of the neighborhood (e.g., Madrid Vallecas, Roma Ostiense, or Dresden Neustadt). Don't jump out until you've reached the central station (Madrid Chamartín, Roma Termini, or Dresden Hauptbahnhof)—ask fellow passengers or check your guidebook to find out which name to look for. Learn the local word for "main station."

Be aware that some trains (especially express trains) stop only at a major city's suburban station—if you stay on board, expecting to get off in the center a few minutes later, you'll bypass your destination city altogether. For instance, several trains to "Venice" leave you at Venice's suburban station (Venezia Mestre), where you'll be stranded without a glimpse of a gondola. (You'll have to catch another train to reach the main Venezia Santa Lucia station, on the Grand Canal.) On the other hand, it can be handy to hop out at a suburban station if it's closer to your hotel than the main station. Many trains headed for Barcelona's big Sants station also stop at the Plaça de Catalunya subway station, which is near many recommended accommodations. If you do find yourself at the wrong station, don't despair: It's a safe bet that a city's stations are connected by frequent trains, and probably subway or buses as well.

Sleeping on Trains

The economy of night travel is tremendous. Sleeping while rolling down the tracks saves time and money: For every night you spend on the train, you gain a day for sightseeing and avoid the cost of a hotel.

The first concern about night travel is usually, "Aren't you missing a lot of beautiful scenery? You just slept through half of Sweden!" The real question should be, "Did the missed scenery matter, since you gained an extra day for hiking the Alps, biking through tulips, or island-hopping in the Greek seas?" The answer: No. Maximize night trips.

Your overnight options may look slim, at least at first—as daytime trains speed up and flights within Europe become cheaper, night-train service is being reduced. When you're checking schedules for night trains, pay attention to the details. A connection doesn't have to be direct to be a workable overnight option—it all depends on the timing. If you need to change trains a half hour after boarding, you'll still get some sleep (though rail-pass holders should be aware of the "7 p.m. rule"—see page 124). But if the connection involves getting off at 2:00 a.m....and waiting until 5:30 a.m. for the next leg, that's not a night train, it's a nightmare.

Book your night-train reservation at least a few days in advance. On some popular routes, particularly between Paris and Italy, reservations can sell out weeks in advance, making it worthwhile to commit before you even leave for Europe. For advice on making reservations, see page 127.

Some train travelers are ripped off while they sleep—they're usually the ones who haven't safely stashed their money and valuables in a money belt. You'll hear stories of entire train cars being gassed and robbed in Italy, Spain, and eastern countries. It's extremely rare and I wouldn't lose sleep over it.

Types of Compartments

Most overnight trains offer one or two different ways to sleep; the more comfortably you sleep, the more you pay. For much more on night trains in Europe, go to seat61.com/sleepers.htm.

Couchettes: To ensure a safer and uninterrupted night's sleep, you can reserve a sleeping berth known as a *couchette* (koo-shet). For a surcharge of about $35, you'll get sheets, a pillow, and blankets on a bunk bed in a compartment with three to five other people—and, hopefully, a good night's sleep.

Some trains have more spacious four-berth couchette compartments (two sets of doubles rather than triple bunks for about $50 apiece). This exception aside, most *couchettes* are the same in first and second class.

When booking your *couchette,* you can request the top, middle, or bottom berth. While the top bunk gives you more privacy and luggage space, it can be hotter and stuffier than lower bunks and a couple of inches shorter (a concern if you're six feet or taller). Compartments may be coed or single gender, depending on the route.

As you board, you'll give your *couchette* voucher and rail pass or ticket to the attendant. This is the person who deals with the conductors and keeps out the thieves so you can sleep uninterrupted. In case of a border check (rare in most of Europe these days), you'll either be woken up to show your passport, or your attendant will ask for your passport in advance and handle this task for you.

Private Sleepers: These sleeper compartments are more comfortable but pricier than *couchettes.* Compartments with two or three beds range from about $40 to $150 per person. Single-sleeper surcharges range from $70 to $190.

Sleeping Free

Shoestring travelers just sack out for free, draping their tired bodies over as many unoccupied seats as possible. But trust

LEFT You can rent a *couchette* (bunk bed) on your overnight train. Top bunks give you a bit more room and safety—but B.Y.O.B. & B.

RIGHT They didn't rent a *couchette.*

me: Trying to sleep overnight without a bed can be more lumpy than dreamy. And even free seat "sleeping" isn't always an option, since not all night trains offer standard seats—and many that do require a paid seat reservation. One night of endless head-bobbing, very swollen toes, glaring overhead lighting, a screaming tailbone, sitting up straight in an eternity of steel wheels crashing along rails, trying doggedly—yet hopelessly—to get comfortable, will teach you the importance of finding a spot to stretch out for the night. (If you decide you want a *couchette* after all, seek out a conductor—provided there's a couchette available, you can book one onboard.)

Some older trains have seats that you can pull out to make a bed—assuming your compartment isn't too full. Skilled shoestring travelers know to look for traditional train cars: the kind that have about ten compartments, each with six or eight seats (three or four facing three or four). Some have seats that pull out and armrests that lift, turning your compartment into a bed on wheels. These cars make sleeping free quite manageable, but they're increasingly rare.

If you're determined to avoid paying for a *couchette*, head to the station a day or two ahead of your departure, a few minutes before that night train is scheduled to pull out, and see for yourself if fold-out compartment seats will be an option on your train. If they won't be, book a *couchette*—what you'll spend is less than what you'd waste by arriving at your next destination too fatigued to enjoy it.

BUSES

In most countries, trains are faster, more comfortable, and have more extensive schedules than long-distance buses. But in some countries—especially Greece, Turkey, and parts of Ireland, Croatia, the Czech Republic, Portugal, Spain, and Morocco—buses are often the better (or only) option. Bus trips are usually less expensive than trains—especially in the British Isles—and are occasionally included on your rail pass (where buses are operated by train companies, as many are in Germany, Switzerland, and Belgium). Note that in Great Britain and Ireland, a long-distance bus is called a "coach," while a "bus" provides only in-city transit.

Buses can help you reach places trains don't go.

Use buses mainly to pick up where Europe's great train system leaves off. Buses fan out from the smallest train stations to places trains can't get to. For towns with train stations far from the center (such as hill towns), buses are often scheduled to meet each arrival and shuttle passengers to the main square (often at no extra cost—show your train ticket to the bus driver and see what happens). Many bus connections to nearby towns not served by train are timed to depart just after the train arrives. Miss that connection in a remote place and you'll wait with the ghosts in an empty station until the next train arrives. Bus service can be less frequent on holidays, Saturdays, and especially Sundays.

Schedules

In most countries, bus routes are operated by multiple companies, each with its own timetables and fares. Finding a unified source for schedule and price information can be next to impossible. If you're lucky, the city you're traveling from will have one main bus station that can offer consolidated timetables online. But it's more likely that you'll have to check several websites, run by the various companies that serve the cities you're connecting. If you're going from a small town (with no online timetable) to a big city, try checking the "arrivals" schedules on the big city's website instead. Always confirm the schedule in person.

Learn the code words for deciphering local schedules. For example, in Spain, *pista* or *autopista* means the bus takes the freeway—the fastest option. Buses that are *directa* (direct) are faster than those labeled *semidirecta* or *ruta* (roundabout journeys with several stops en route). Posted schedules list many, but not all, stops on each route. If your intended destination isn't listed, ask at the ticket/information window.

If your trip involves a connection at an intermediate station, don't be surprised if it's difficult to get schedule details for your onward journey. Try calling the tourist information office or bus station in the transfer town (or at your final destination) for details.

Stations and Tickets

It's common for a big city to have a number of smaller bus stations serving different regions, rather than one terminal for all bus traffic. Sometimes a bus "station" can just be an open parking lot with lots of stalls and a tiny ticket kiosk. Your hotel or the local tourist information office can usually point you in the right direction. Larger bus stations have an information desk (and, often, a telephone number) with timetables. In smaller stations, check the destinations and schedules posted on the window of each company's office. Bus-station staffers are less likely to speak English than their train-station counterparts. Bus stations have WCs (often without toilet paper) and cafés that offer quick, forgettable, overpriced food.

For popular routes during peak season, ensure you'll get a seat by dropping by the station to buy your ticket a few hours in advance. If you're downtown, need a ticket, and the bus station isn't central, save time by asking at the tourist information office about travel agencies that sell bus tickets. If you arrive in a city by bus, and plan to leave by bus, it can be convenient to buy your outbound ticket when you arrive.

Riding the Bus

Before you get on a bus, ask the ticket seller and the conductor if you'll need to transfer. If so, pay attention (and maybe even follow the route on a map) to be sure you don't miss your change. When you transfer, look for a bus with the same name/logo as the company you bought the ticket from.

For long trips, your ticket might include an assigned seat. If your bag doesn't fit in the overhead storage space, you may be required to check it under the bus (sometimes for a small fee). Your ride likely will come with a soundtrack: recorded pop music, radio, sports games, movies, or TV shows. Earplugs and/or headphones can go a long way toward preserving your sanity. In most of Europe, smoking is no longer allowed on buses.

Drivers may not speak English. Buses generally lack toilets, but they stop every two hours or so for a short break. Drivers announce how long the stop will be, but if in doubt, ask the driver so you know if you have time to get out. Listen for the bus horn as a final call before departure.

Cheap long-haul buses, such as Eurolines, are a good option for the very budget-conscious. For example, Eurolines' priciest one-way bus fare from Amsterdam to Paris is $70 (compared to $175 second class by train); from Barcelona to Madrid, it's $45 (often as much as $165 by train). Thrifty Megabus operates throughout Great Britain and has some service on the Continent, too. Hippie-type "magic bus" companies such as Busabout offer hop-on, hop-off connections all around Europe—something like a rail pass for buses.

Crossing the English Channel by bus and ferry takes

more than twice as long as the Eurostar train, but costs a small fraction of the price (London to Paris by Eurolines bus: about $25-60 one-way for economy fares booked at least three days in advance).

Package Bus Excursions

These one-day bus tours from big cities into the countryside are designed for sightseeing, but can also serve as useful transportation. For example, rather than buy a train ticket from London to Bath (about $55), consider taking a one-day bus tour from London (about $130) that visits Salisbury, Stonehenge, and Bath. Bring your luggage and leave the tour in Bath before it returns to London, having enjoyed a day of transportation, unforgettable stops, and a live guide bubbling with information. It can be well worth the extra cost, and it's more efficient and faster than lacing together the stops on your own, using a combination of trains and public buses. If you do look into taking a bus tour as transportation, confirm the order of stops with the company (will they be stopping at your end destination last?), and let them know your plans.

FERRIES

Boats can be a romantic mode of European travel. They're particularly useful for Greek or Croatian island-hopping, for Norwegian fjord gawking, or for connecting Scandinavian destinations overnight—saving both time and the expense of a pricey hotel room. But for any ferry ride of more than a couple of hours, it's smart to compare the cost of the ferry trip with the cost of a budget-airline flight.

Most ferries are either big and slow, or small and fast (catamarans). The hulking, slow-moving ferries usually carry cars as well as passengers; run in almost any weather; and tend to be cheaper than catamarans. They have virtually

unlimited deck space for walk-on passengers, though their space for cars is limited.

The sleek, speedy passenger-only catamarans generally cost more but save you time. However, keep in mind that they have to slow down (or sometimes can't run at all) in high winds or other inclement weather. Catamarans have limited seating that can sell out. They're also the less-romantic option, as most require you to stay inside the boat while en route (for safety's sake—they're that fast). Instead of watching the coastline lazily slide by, as you do on slower boats, on fast boats you'll sit inside and peer out through saltwater-spattered windows.

On many islands, big car ferries arrive at a different point (usually farther from the main town) than smaller catamarans (which may drop you right in the town center).

Schedules

Some countries have a national ferry company (such as Croatia's Jadrolinija), but in most places, routes are operated by a variety of smaller companies. You can usually find schedules online; however, particularly in Mediterranean countries, they may not be posted more than a few days before the season starts, making it challenging to plan your midsummer trip in the springtime. It's a good idea to confirm the boat's sailing time at least one day ahead—the boat you found online two months ago might run earlier, later, or less frequently than you'd expected. Service to the smaller Mediterranean islands is particularly seasonal: Routes that run once daily in summer may drop to four days per week in shoulder season and two days per week in winter. At any time of year in the Mediterranean, don't be surprised if actual ferry service bears little resemblance to its published timetable, even if you looked it up yesterday (especially true in Greece).

To search for schedules, check aferry.co.uk for most of Europe; openseas.gr, gtp.gr, or travel.viva.gr for Greek island services; and visitnorway.com/us for Norwegian fjord boats. You can also try searching for the name of the company (if you know it) that operates a particular route.

Getting Tickets

In some cases, you can buy tickets online or at a neighborhood travel agency; for others, you simply show up at the ticket window an hour before departure (tickets generally cost the same whether you buy them in advance or at the last minute). During peak times in popular destinations (July-August, Croatia's Dalmatian Coast, and Greece's more famous islands), get advice from your hotelier, the local tourist information office, or a local travel agency about how far ahead you should book your ticket. If you'll be setting sail very soon after your arrival in Europe, do your research from home, and book a ticket online in advance. Otherwise, the ferry could sell out and you'll be stranded on a castaway isle—or unable to reach it—for longer than you intended. This is particularly important if you're driving a car onto a ferry—in which case you may need to line up hours in advance. (If it's possible to book a space in advance, do so.) Some international ferry routes are covered or discounted with a rail pass (such as Ancona or Bari, Italy, to Patra, Greece; and Sweden to Germany or Denmark).

If you're taking an overnight ferry, consider your sleeping options. A basic passenger ticket is "deck class," meaning you'll simply have to camp out wherever you can find room. You can pay a little more for a seat. A "berth" (bed) costs more, similar to a night train. The more private your lodgings, the more you'll pay, especially if a toilet and shower are included in the compartment. You usually can (and should) reserve overnight accommodations in advance. Some Greek island ferries allow you to reserve beds only upon boarding.

On Board

While many ferry companies tell foot passengers to be at the dock 30 minutes before the boat leaves, there's usually no need to show up that far ahead, especially for short-haul daytime boats. The sole advantage to turning up early is the chance to grab a better seat, which makes a difference only if your ferry happens to have open seating.

On the ferry, you may be able to stow your luggage on a public rack on the boarding level; otherwise you'll haul it up several flights of stairs to the passenger decks. You can buy food and drinks on board most boats. It's not too expensive, but it's usually not top quality, either. Bring your own snacks or a picnic instead. Dining is a featured attraction on just a few ferries, such as the *smörgåsbord* service on Scandinavian overnight cruises. Ferries of all sizes typically have bathrooms on board.

For information about taking a cruise in Europe, see page 456.

Driving & Navigating

While many European travel dreams come with a clickety-clack "rhythm of the rails" soundtrack—and most first trips are best by train—you should consider the convenience of driving. Behind the wheel you're totally free, going where you want, when you want.

Driving is ideal for countryside-focused trips. The super mobility of a car saves you time in locating budget accommodations in small towns and away from the train lines. This savings helps to rationalize the "splurge" of a car rental. You can also play it riskier in peak season, arriving in a town late with no reservation. If the hotels are full, simply drive to the next town. And driving is a godsend for those who don't believe in packing light—you can even rent a trailer.

Every year, as train prices go up, car rental becomes a better option for budget travelers in Europe. While solo car travel is expensive, three or four people sharing a rented car will usually travel cheaper than the same group using rail passes.

This chapter includes my best advice on renting a car without wasting money, tips for what to do if things go wrong, and pointers on driving and navigating Europe's roads and city streets.

RENTING A CAR

Renting a car in Europe tends to be more expensive and more complicated than in the US, due to byzantine insurance options and other additional fees. But making informed choices can help you avoid hassles and save money. Once you're free and easy behind the wheel of a European car, it's all worth it.

Car-Rental Costs

Across Europe, basic rental rates vary from company to company, month to month, and country to country (rentals in Germany tend to be cheaper than average; rentals in Italy tend to be more expensive). The cheapest company for rental in one country might be the most expensive in the next. You'll need to do some comparison-shopping to figure out which one is best for your trip (see "Booking a Car," later).

The basic rates you'll see quoted nearly always include unlimited mileage, value-added tax, and legally required third-party liability insurance. When comparing your options, be sure to factor in the costs of any extras (another driver, a child seat, automatic transmission), especially because they can vary so much across companies and countries.

Here's what to look for:

Tax: The value-added tax (VAT), clear and consistent within each country, generally runs 18-25 percent. Although it's usually included in any rental price you're quoted, it's smart to double-check. Other nonnegotiable fees, such as a "road tax" or "eco tax," also differ per country (road tax is usually less than $5 per day; expect about $5-10 per day for environmental fees, most commonly applied to automatic-transmission cars); if it's not clear whether these taxes are included in a price, ask.

Insurance: Your biggest potential extra cost when renting a car is insurance, even if the rental price supposedly includes insurance. Your credit card may already cover the extra insurance you need, but don't assume it. If you go with the insurance offered by the rental company, figure on paying roughly 30 percent extra, or about $10-30 a day, for a collision damage waiver supplement (described on page 159).

Theft Protection: This charge, about $20/day, is required in Italy; most companies

Car or Train?

Consider these variables when deciding whether your European experience might be better by car or train:

- Geographical range (trains are better if you're covering a wide area)
- Rail coverage (for example, Switzerland is crisscrossed by an extensive train network, whereas Ireland's trains are sparse)
- Urban vs. rural (a car is a pointless hassle in big cities, but helpful in the countryside)
- Number of travelers (a car is usually the cheaper option when shared with more than 2 people)
- Luggage (a car is better if you're bad at packing light)
- Kids in tow (car travel is more flexible, but trains give kids room to move around)

Small car, big scenery

include this in their advertised rates for Italy.

Extra Driver(s): Expect to pay about $5-25/day to add another driver. This is worthwhile if you really plan to share the driving duties; if you let an unlisted driver take the wheel and an accident occurs, your insurance won't cover it.

Child-Safety Seats: Every country has different legal requirements for child-safety seats, and they don't always align with the latest US laws. Ask when booking, and expect to pay about $15-70 per day if you're not bringing a child seat from home.

From sleek German auto-bahns to windy, cliffside Irish lanes, driving is a fun part of European travel.

Other Add-Ons: You'll pay extra for a car with automatic transmission (about 50 percent more than the same car with stick shift), GPS (about $10-30 per day, though often included in more expensive models), winter tires (required in snowy conditions by some countries; often included in basic rental rates), and ski racks. Some companies, such as Avis and Hertz, have started offering Wi-Fi in some cars (roughly $10/day). Emergency roadside assistance is often included in the cost of your rental, but be sure to clarify this, especially if you aren't comfortable changing a tire.

Airport Pickup: In some countries, you'll pay more to pick up a car at the airport or train station than in the town center (10-25 percent extra, or a flat fee of $40-80); for tips on choosing a pickup location, see later.

International Drop-Off Fees: It will generally cost an extra $100-300 to drop the car in a different country. You'll find exceptions, some happy (free) and some outrageous ($1,000+). The farther the distance between your start and end points, the higher the fee (for more on choosing a drop-off point, see later).

Other Fees: Rental companies usually charge extra if you plan to take the car to certain points in eastern Europe (a line that generally follows old Iron Curtain borders). Wintertime driving can carry extra costs beyond the required snow tires. Agencies may tack on vaguely worded extras like "contract fees" or "credit-card fees" that weren't included in your quote. You may not be able to avoid these, but you can at least make sure they don't come as a surprise: Read every bit of fine print, and talk to an agent over the phone before you book if you have questions. Of course, some fees are easily avoided: Return your car on time to avoid late drop-off fees (don't assume you've got a grace period), fill 'er up shortly before returning to avoid refueling fees (see page 171), and return your car in good shape to sidestep a cleaning fee.

Other Driving Costs

When budgeting for your trip, remember that renting a car involves some significant costs beyond what you'll pay the rental agency for the car itself.

Fuel: Paying about $140 a week will get you roughly 700 miles; most rental agencies offer hybrid or diesel cars with better fuel efficiency—ask. Avoid overpaying for gas at the start or finish of your trip (for tips, see page 171).

Tolls: You'll pay tolls figured on the distance you drive (about 12 cents per mile) for expressways in certain countries. Some countries, mostly in central Europe, require drivers to buy a sticker ("vignette") for their window. And in a few countries, freeways really are free (like Germany's autobahn system). For more on tolls and vignettes, see page 169.

Parking: Estimate $35 a day in big cities (more like $40-55/day in London and Paris—don't park there), otherwise it's usually free, or at least fairly cheap.

Ballpark Cost of Renting a Car

This very rough estimate for a one-week car rental includes unlimited mileage. Be aware that base prices for car rentals can flex dramatically with demand, length of trip, location, additional services, and fees.

Fiat Punto (including tax): $230/week

CDW insurance: $140/week ($10-30/day)

Fuel: $140/week ($8/gallon, 40 mpg, 100 miles/day)

Parking: about $35/day for big cities, $5/day for small towns

Freeway tolls: about $0.12/mile (Mediterranean countries) or about $7 for one-time sticker (Austria, Slovenia, Hungary)

Ballpark Total: About $610 a week

Booking a Car

For the best deal on long-term rentals, book in advance from home. If you decide to rent a car while in Europe, try calling around to local car-rental agencies, or book through a local travel agency. When renting a car, you'll need to make a few decisions, including whom to rent from, what kind of car to get, and where to pick it up and drop it off.

Which Rental Company?

These days, most of us start our search on a travel-booking site such as Kayak, Expedia, or AAA. Of course, if you have a favorite car-rental agency at home, consider using the same company in Europe.

When shopping around, don't stop at just comparing

When Booking a Rental Car

Before you commit, make sure you understand these variables:
- What the car company's basic insurance covers
- What they charge for CDW (and the cost of zero-deductible "super CDW" coverage)
- The cost of theft insurance (required in Italy)
- The cost of adding another driver
- One-way rental fees (if you'll be returning the car to a different city)
- Office locations and hours (consider the most efficient pickup and drop-off points)
- Whether it'd be cheaper to pick up the car from an office in the city center
- Whether the agency will deliver the car to your hotel (expect to pay extra)
- The cost of changing your drop-off location or time
- The availability and cost of extras you might want, such as automatic transmission, child-safety seats, GPS, or Wi-Fi
- Age restrictions (if you or any co-drivers are under 25 or over 69)
- Restrictions on driving the car in any countries (particularly in far-eastern Europe)
- Additional charges or local fees, such as mandatory road taxes or winter-tire fees
- Cancellation fees, in case your itinerary changes

initial price quotes. You'll want to determine which company's offer involves the best combination of rates (including all fees and any extras you want), service, and pickup/drop-off locations (with workable office hours) for your trip. Even with the wealth of information that's available online, you may find that it's easier to make a phone call to get all your questions answered.

It's generally an advantage to go with a larger company, with a wider choice of pickup and drop-off locations. Most of the big-time US rental agencies have offices throughout Europe, as do the two major Europe-based agencies, Europcar and Sixt. With these companies, if you get into car trouble, a replacement car is likely to be close at hand. Still, it's smart to make sure you choose a company that thoroughly covers the areas where you'll be driving.

It's also worth considering renting through a consolidator, such as Auto Europe (my favorite) or Europe by Car. These companies compare rates among various companies (including many of the big-name firms), find the best deal, and—because they're wholesalers—pass the savings on to you. You pay the consolidator, and they issue you a voucher to pick up your car in Europe.

With a consolidator as a middleman, it's especially important to ask ahead of time about add-on fees and restrictions, since you might not learn this critical information until you pick up the car. If any dispute arises when you show up at the rental desk, call the consolidator to try to resolve the issue—ask to use the rental office's phone (the consolidator's number is toll-free from any land line). Once you sign off on something with the vendor, it's difficult for the consolidator (or anyone else) to reverse what you've agreed to. If you have a problem with the rental agency, the consolidator may not be able to intervene to your satisfaction, but at least you'll have gotten some help in resolving the problem.

No matter whom you rent through, be sure to hang onto all your paperwork (including the checklist used by the company to check the car's condition when you turn it in) for a few months after the rental period, in case a billing dispute arises.

Choosing a Car

Expect some differences between your typical American rental car and what you'll likely get in Europe, where midrange cars have less passenger room, vast trunk space is unheard of, and manual transmissions are the norm. Automatics are more expensive (usually about 50 percent more) and may only be available if you upgrade to a bigger, pricier car. (Some Americans find automatics worthwhile in Great Britain and Ireland, where it can be enough of a challenge just to learn to drive on the left.) Since supplies are limited, if you must have an automatic, you'll need to arrange it farther in advance than a manual-transmission car. Ideally, skip the automatic and brush up on your shifting skills. It's worth doing some lurching through your hometown parking lot to save the expense (or to be prepared in case your reserved automatic doesn't materialize).

When checking out options for budget rentals, you'll see some familiar makes (Ford, VW)—though not always familiar models of these—as well as some less familiar ones, most commonly Opel, Fiat, Citroën, Peugeot, Renault, Škoda, and Seat ("SAY-aht"). Don't waste time carefully choosing among models, since you're not guaranteed to get the exact car you signed up for, just a "similar" model.

I normally rent the smallest, least-expensive model with a stick shift—not just to save money, but because larger cars are not as maneuverable on Europe's narrow, winding roads.

If you're traveling with more than one other person, it can be worth it to move up to a larger class of car. But if you pack light and have only one other person in tow, the smallest models should have plenty of room, even if it's a little less than what you're used to.

Choosing a Pickup (and Drop-Off) Place and Time

It's best and less stressful to begin your driving experience away from big cities, so try picking up your car away from major destinations. A pleasant scenario for a trip to England would be to start out (sans car) in the smaller city of Bath, rent a car when leaving Bath, explore Britain at your driving leisure, then drop off the car in York and take the train into London, where you can rely on the excellent public transportation system. That way you'd enjoy the three major city stops on your England itinerary—where the last thing you'd want is a car—without paying for one.

That said, beware the possible inconveniences of picking up your car in a truly small town—a tiny regional office almost certainly has a smaller fleet on hand, and the staff may be less equipped to handle the concerns of foreign renters. Don't plan to pick up or drop off your car in a small town on a Saturday afternoon or Sunday—or anywhere on a holiday, when offices are likely to be closed (except for train-station and airport locations).

Picking up a car at an airport usually costs more than picking it up downtown. If you don't need a car immediately after your flight, look into a cheaper rental with a downtown pickup price. But airport pickup may still be worth it; many central car-rental locations have shorter hours (and may close at midday) or are buried in a maze of narrow streets. Also consider traffic—it may be easier to drive away from an airport than a parking garage in the heart of the city. Before choosing a rental location, find it on a map. You may find that a train-station office is handier than a downtown one (though some station pickups come with airport-like fees). Fortunately, airport/train-station fees apply only to your pickup location, not your drop off.

European cars are rented in 24-hour periods, so think carefully about selecting your pickup and drop-off times—if you pick up the car at 10 a.m. on the first day and drop it off at noon on the last day, you'll be charged a whole day's rental for just those two hours. Don't book your pickup time for earlier than you really need the car. If you can, book a drop-off time that falls within that location's office hours (rather than just leaving the keys in an after-hours drop box); it's best to finalize and receive your paperwork in person.

Sometimes it can make a lot of sense to start and end your car rental in different cities. One-way rentals are usually free within the same country (Germany and Portugal are the main exceptions), but dropping off in another country will likely cost you a hefty extra fee. Expect fees of $100-300, but beware that this cost can top $1,000, especially if the start and end points are quite far apart, or if the drop-off point is an out-of-the-way location. Certain places seem to be especially expensive for one-way cross-border trips no matter what (Italy, Spain, Scandinavia, and far eastern Europe). The extra cost of a one-way rental can still be worth it if it saves you a very long drive back to your first country. But if the last leg of your trip isn't too far from the border of the country you started in, a small tweak to your rental plans can save you plenty. Let's say you're renting a car in France for a trip that ends in Barcelona. By simply dropping the car off within France (as close to the border as possible) and hopping a train to Barcelona (roughly $25 per person), you could save hundreds in drop-off fees.

When booking, also ask about your options (and the costs involved) in case you change your plans en route and want to drop off your car at an office in another city or on a different date.

More Tips for Renting a Car

Get quotes for weekly rentals. Typically, the longer you rent, the less it'll cost per day. You may find that renting for a full seven days costs the same as, or even less than, five or six days.

Double-check currency conversions when comparing prices. Some foreign-based rental-company sites use fudged conversion rates that make the price in dollars look cheaper than the price that'll actually show up on your credit-card bill. Convert prices yourself on a conversion site such as oanda.com.

Pay up front. It's almost always smarter to prepay for a rental car when you book, rather than at the agency counter in Europe. Not only are you likely to get a discount, but, assuming that your quote was in dollars, you'll know you're paying the exact amount you were quoted. You'll also avoid getting dinged with an overseas transaction fee on your credit card. If you're purchasing a collision damage waiver from the rental company, that'll likely also be cheaper when paid up front. But beware cancellation fees: Don't pay until your itinerary is firm, and be clear on the company's cancellation policy.

Read the fine print. To minimize the chance of being blindsided when you show up at the rental counter, carefully read your entire reservation voucher before you leave home. Even if you booked the rental over the phone, the agent may well have skipped over certain details (see the sidebar on page 153). Many travelers end up overpaying (or at least worrying they might be overpaying) if they're jetlagged or too eager to hit the road to sort through the details. By asking about fees in advance (and taking along a hard copy of your reservation voucher), you can avoid unpleasant surprises.

Red Tape and Restrictions

Every country has its own take on who can drive—and who can rent—a car. Follow these tips to make sure you'll be able to take the wheel at your destination.

Passports, Driver's Licenses, and International Driving Permits: Whether you're American or Canadian, your passport and driver's license are all you need in most European countries. However, some countries also require an International Driving Permit (IDP). An IDP is an official translation of your US license (making it easier for the cop to write out a ticket). You can get an IDP at your local American Automobile Association or Canadian Automobile Association office ($15 plus the cost of two passport-type photos—OK to bring your own; doesn't require AAA membership). AAA is authorized by the US State Department to issue permits; avoid scam artists peddling overpriced, fake international licenses.

You may hear contradictory information on exactly where you need an IDP. People who sell them say you should have them almost everywhere. People who rent cars say you need them almost nowhere. People who drive rental cars say the IDP is overrated, but can come in handy as a complement to your passport and driver's license. It's a good idea to get one if you'll be driving in Austria, Bosnia-Herzegovina, Croatia, Greece, Hungary, Italy, Poland, Romania, Slovenia, or Spain—countries where you're technically required to carry a permit, since you could be fined if found without one. If all goes well, you'll likely never be asked to show this permit—but it's a must if you end up dealing with the police.

Age Limits: Minimum and maximum age limits for renting a car vary by country, type of car, and rental company. Younger renters can get stuck with extra costs, such as being required to buy extra insurance or pay a surcharge of $15-40 per day (fortunately, there are usually maximum surcharge limits). Most companies will not rent a car to someone under 21 (with some exceptions, depending on the country and type of car), but those who are at least 25 years old should have no problem.

Drivers over 70 may have trouble renting in the Czech Republic, Great Britain, Greece, Northern Ireland, Poland, Slovakia, Slovenia, and Turkey; drivers over 80 may have trouble in Denmark. If you're over 69, you may be required to pay extra to rent a car in the Republic of Ireland, where the official age limit is 75 (although some rental companies will rent to those ages 76-79 if they provide extensive proof of good health and safe driving). If you're considered too young or too old, look into leasing (explained later), which has less stringent age restrictions. (If you're traveling to Ireland, the closest leasing option is in London.)

Crossing Borders: As Europe's internal borders fade, your car comes with the paperwork you need to drive wherever you like throughout most of Europe (always check when booking). But if you're heading to a country in far eastern or southeastern Europe—especially one that still has closed borders (such as Croatia, Bosnia-Herzegovina, or Montenegro), you may need to pay extra—for the rental itself and/or for additional insurance. State your travel plans up front to the rental company when you book. Some companies may have limits on eastward excursions because of the higher incidence of car thefts (for example, you can only take cheaper cars, and you may have to pay extra insurance fees; these limits and fees aren't imposed if you're leasing). When you cross these borders, you may be asked to show proof of insurance (called a "green card"). Ask your car-rental company if you need any other documentation for crossing the borders on your itinerary. It's a bad idea to take your rental car anywhere that's prohibited by your contract, as doing so voids any insurance coverage.

In the mountainous northwest corner of Slovenia, you're just a few miles' drive from both Austria and Italy—and these days, you can cross those borders without stopping.

Some companies allow you to take a rental car from Britain to the Continent or to Ireland, but be prepared to pay high surcharges and extra drop-off fees. If you want to drive on the Continent as well as in Britain and/or Ireland, it'll probably be cheaper to rent separate cars each time, thanks to the high cost of taking cars on ferries (between Ireland and Britain, or between either place and the Continent) or crossing under the English Channel via the pricey Eurotunnel car train.

Insurance and the Collision Damage Waiver (CDW)

When you rent a car, you are liable for a very high deductible, sometimes equal to the entire value of the car. Fortunately, there's usually more than one way to limit your financial risk in case of an accident.

Baseline rates for European rentals nearly always include basic, mandated liability coverage—for accident-related damage to anyone or anything outside the car. (The company may offer additional liability insurance, but I wouldn't buy this without some extenuating reason.)

It's (usually) up to you, however, to decide how to cover the risk of damage to or theft of the car itself. You have three main options, all described below: buying a "collision damage waiver" (CDW) through the car-rental company (easiest but most expensive), using your credit card's coverage (cheapest), or getting collision insurance as part of a larger travel-insurance policy.

If you're renting in either Ireland or Italy, you'll have little choice but to buy the company's CDW. If you need a car for at least three weeks, you're probably better off leasing (described later), which includes zero-deductible collision and theft insurance (and is tax-free to boot).

Note that theft insurance covers just the loss of the car itself, not anything stolen from inside it (for tips on protecting your car from thieves, see page 331).

Car-Rental Company CDW

The simplest solution is to buy a CDW supplement from the car-rental company (it's the main extra included in the "inclusive" rates you'll see in quoted prices). This coverage technically isn't insurance; rather, it's a waiver: The car-rental company waives its right to collect a high deductible from you in the event the car is damaged. Note that this "waiver" doesn't actually eliminate the deductible, but just reduces it. CDW covers most of the car if you're in a collision, but usually excludes the undercarriage, roof, tires, windshield, windows, interior, and side mirrors.

CDW generally costs $10-30 a day (figure roughly 30 percent extra). Sometimes the CDW charge itself is a little less when combined with theft/loss insurance as part of an "inclusive" rental rate—it's often cheaper to pay for this kind of coverage when you book than when you pick up the car.

When purchasing CDW, the reduced deductibles can still be substantial, with most hovering at about $1,000-1,500 (or more, depending on the car type). Most rental companies also offer a second tier of coverage, called "super CDW" or "zero-deductible coverage" to buy down the deductible to zero or near zero (if you didn't opt for this when booking from home, expect to hear a sales pitch from the counter agent). This is pricey—figure about an additional $10-30 per day—but, for some travelers, it's worth the peace of mind.

When comparing rental options online, beware that some European rental agencies quote "basic" rates that include CDW/theft coverage. (In this case, it's not an optional extra, so you can't decline it.) If these CDW-inclusive rates seem too good to be true, they probably are: The unwaived deductible is almost certainly especially high (expect $2,000-3,000)...so you'll have to spend extra to buy the "super CDW" anyway to get the deductible down to a reasonable level. Given these costs, the alternatives to paying for the rental company's CDW are worth considering carefully: credit-card coverage or collision coverage through your travel-insurance provider.

Credit-Card Coverage

Car-company CDW surcharges can seem like a racket when you consider that most credit cards already include collision coverage. By paying with the right credit card, you get zero-deductible collision coverage (comparable to "super" CDW)...likely for free. In other words, if your car is damaged or stolen, your credit card will cover whatever costs you're liable for. The only major downside: If you do end up in an accident, dealing with credit-card coverage can be more of a hassle than what you'd encounter with the car-company CDW. But if a potential headache seems like a worthwhile trade-off for certain—and significant—cost savings, look into this option.

To make this work, first double-check that your credit card does indeed offer this coverage. Remember that restrictions apply and coverage varies between issuers: Get a complete description of the coverage offered by your credit-card company. Ask in which countries it is applicable, which parts of the car (if any) are excluded, the types of vehicles that are eligible, whether it covers theft/loss, the maximum reimbursement allowed (if it's less than the price of the car, the rental company may require you to buy their CDW), and the maximum number of rental days covered (if your rental period exceeds that number, your card won't cover any of the rental). Have them explain the worst-case scenario to you. It can be smart to ask for a "Letter of Coverage"—take a hard copy of it with you to the rental counter in Europe.

Once you've confirmed your credit card's coverage, be sure to decline the CDW offered by your car-rental company. If you accept any coverage offered by the rental agency, you automatically forego your credit-card coverage. (In other words, if you buy CDW that comes with a $1,000 deductible, your credit card will not cover that deductible.) This may also be the case if you book and prepay for a rental that already includes CDW and/or theft coverage—don't sign any rental contract until you're sure that by doing so you're not accidentally accepting the rental company's coverage.

A credit card's collision coverage applies even if the damage happens while the car's being driven by someone else, as long as that other driver, and the cardholder, are both listed as drivers on the rental contract. Remember to use that same card not only to reserve the car, but also to pay for the rental itself, as well as any other related fees you're charged, whether when booking at home, or when picking up or dropping off the car in Europe—switching cards can invalidate the coverage.

If you get in an accident, the rental company will charge your credit card for the value of the damage (up to the deductible amount) or, if the vehicle is stolen, the value of the deductible associated with theft. It's then up to you to seek reimbursement for these charges from your credit-card company when you get home. You'll need to submit the police report and the car-rental company's accident report. (When deciding between rental companies, consider that American-based rental companies can be easier to work with if you have a claim to resolve.)

Be warned that, as far as some rental companies are concerned, by declining their CDW offer, you're technically liable for the full deductible (which can equal the cost of the car). Because of this, the car-rental company may put a hold on your credit card for the full value of the car. This is bad news if your credit limit is low—particularly if you plan on using that card for other purchases during your trip. (Consider bringing two credit cards—one for the rental car, the other for everything else.) If you don't have enough credit on your card to cover the car's value, the rental company may require you to purchase their CDW.

Since most credit cards don't offer collision insurance to their European cardholders, counter agents—especially those unaccustomed to American clients—may be skeptical that declining their CDW is a prudent move (all the more reason to have hard-copy proof of your credit-card coverage on hand). Don't be surprised if you hear a warning about how credit cards provide only "secondary" coverage—that's moot as long as you've declined the rental company's coverage and your own personal car insurance doesn't apply to the country you're in. By clearly understanding the coverage from your credit-card company, you should be set to ward off a hard sell on the rental-company CDW.

Collision Coverage Through Your Travel-Insurance Provider

If you're already purchasing a travel-insurance policy for your trip, adding collision coverage is an option. Travel Guard, for example, sells affordable renter's collision insurance as an add-on to its other policies. It's valid everywhere in Europe except the Republic of Ireland, and some Italian car-rental companies refuse to honor it, as it doesn't cover you in case of theft. If your car-rental company doesn't accept this coverage, and you have to buy other coverage to replace it, Travel Guard will refund your money.

If you do go with an insurer's comprehensive travel coverage, be sure to add the insurance company's name to your rental agreement when you pick up the car. For more on travel insurance, see page 67.

Picking Up Your Car

When you arrive at the rental counter, ask for a copy of the contract in English if it's not provided as a matter of course. If you haven't already paid for the car, know roughly what your quote should be in the local currency. Be sure to decline any offer of "dynamic currency conversion" (explained on page 189).

If you can, avoid prepaying for your first tank of gas (although some offices won't let you out of this). Prepaying for fuel is virtually always a rip-off, since agencies charge far more per gallon than the going rate. The only upside is that you can return the car with a nearly empty tank.

Be sure to check the entire vehicle for scratches or dents.

Photograph all dings and scratches, even the tiniest ones (be sure the date/time stamp is on). Note the fuel level and eyeball the tire pressure. If any damage is not noted on the rental agreement, return to the counter to make adjustments.

Before you drive off, get to know your car. This is tough when you're aching to get out on the road—but take a few minutes, while you're still in the rental agency's parking lot, to try out all the features and gadgets: Run the front and rear windshield wipers and sprayers, figure out whether the headlights come on automatically with the engine, switch the headlights to high-beam, get comfortable with the gearshift, turn on the radio, and so on.

This is also a good time to quiz the rental agent on a few things, including:

- local laws you might not be aware of (for example, whether headlights must be on at all times, where and how kids ride, etc.)
- length of the grace period for drop-off, if any
- how to use anything you can't figure out, such as the wipers, alarm system, lights, radio, GPS, etc.
- what type of fuel the car takes (diesel vs. unleaded), the local term for that fuel, and how to release the gas cap
- location of insurance "green card" and other paperwork
- whether your car has an unexpired toll-highway vignette (if needed)
- info on making repairs and any included emergency roadside services
- location of spare tire and directions for using it (if the car has no spare, ask for a different vehicle)
- whether the car has a breath-testing kit for measuring alcohol levels (required in France, costs around $5)

Before leaving, get instructions for driving to your next stop (or at least to the expressway). Then drive around the parking lot for a few minutes to test rearview mirrors, the gearshift and clutch, and the lights and signals.

Dropping Off Your Car

Be on time to drop off your car—you could be charged an extra day's rent if you show up a little late.

Unless you've already prepaid for a tank of gas, top up your car before returning it—otherwise you may be charged for a full tank, no matter how much gas is actually left. Not only that, but you'll likely be charged more than double what you would have paid at a nearby gas station...and they may pile on an additional "refueling fee" as well. There's no need to wait until you're almost at the rental office to fill up—fuel gauges are very forgiving, so I start watching for a convenient gas station miles before I reach the rental office. Save your final gas receipt as proof that you filled the tank, and don't toss it until you've seen your credit-card bill.

Once you're parked at the rental office, walk around the car with the attendant to be sure there are no new problems. Some drivers take pictures of the returned vehicle as proof of its condition (an especially good idea if you're returning the car at an unstaffed after-hours drop-off point). Ask for a copy of the final condition report and keep it until you've seen your credit-card statement. Unexpected charges that show up on your credit-card statement are easier to dispute if you have good documentation on hand.

If you're relying on your credit card's collision coverage and you have a balance to pay at the returns desk, remember to use that same card (or cash)—using a different card could invalidate your coverage.

ALTERNATIVES TO RENTING

For longer car trips, leasing (or even buying) a car can be more affordable than renting; for short jaunts, you could consider a car-share program. Neither is as widely available as rentals.

Leasing and Buying

Leasing (technically, buying the car and selling it back) gets around many tax and insurance costs and is a great deal for people needing a car for three weeks or more.

Leases are available for periods of up to five and a half months. Prices include all taxes, as well as zero-deductible theft and collision insurance—comparable to a CDW supplement—valid all over Europe, including eastern countries. You won't pay extra for additional drivers or for venturing too far east, and you get to use a shiny new car. Leased cars can most easily be picked up and returned in France, but for an additional fee you can also lease cars in the Netherlands, Belgium, Germany, Switzerland, Spain, Portugal, Italy, and Great Britain.

Europe by Car, which invented leasing more than 50 years ago, still offers good deals. For example, you can lease a Citroën C3 in France for as few as 21 days for about $1,250— about $60 a day. Renault Eurodrive offers similar deals, as does Peugeot Open Europe. In general, the longer you lease the car, the lower the price—a 60-day lease can be as inexpensive as $30 per day.

Although Americans rarely consider this budget option, it's possible to buy a used car for your trip and sell it when you're done. The most common places to buy cars are Amsterdam, Frankfurt, London, and US military bases. In London, check Craigslist (london.craigslist.co.uk), the used-car market on Market Road (Tube: Caledonian Road), and look in London periodicals such as *Loot* (loot.com), which lists used cars (as well as jobs, flats, cheap flights, and travel partners).

Car-Sharing Programs

Car-sharing providers place cars throughout a city, let users rent them for just a few hours or days, and charge no enrollment or annual fees. With these programs, you book your car online (join before leaving home), pick it up at a set location, drive it, then return it to the nearest location. The fee includes insurance, fuel, and GPS, so you can avoid extra insurance charges or having to fill the tank before you return the car. There's no extra fee for drivers ages 21-24, and prices are relatively reasonable—in London a Fiat 500 costs about $9 per hour or $70 per day. Car-sharing makes sense for day trips, but isn't practical for daily use within big cities, where public transportation is a breeze.

Europe's main car-sharing provider is Hertz 24/7 (hertz247.com), currently available in Britain, France, Germany, Spain, Belgium, and the Netherlands. Zipcar operates in a few British cities, as well as Barcelona. Car2go, which rents the smallest Smart model, operates mostly in Germany, but has outposts in a few major cities elsewhere in Europe.

BEHIND THE EUROPEAN WHEEL

Horror stories about European traffic abound. They're fun to tell, but driving is really only a problem for those who make it one. The most dangerous creature on the road is the panicked foreign visitor. Drive defensively, observe, fit in, avoid big-city driving when you can, and wear your seat belt.

Some places are easier to handle than others. The British Isles are good for driving—reasonable rentals, no language barrier, exciting rural areas, and fine roads...and after one near head-on collision scares the bloody heck out of you,

you'll have no trouble remembering which side of the road to drive on.

Other good driving areas are Scandinavia (hug the lip of a majestic fjord as you meander from village to village); Belgium and the Netherlands (yield to bikes— you're outnumbered); Spain and Portugal (explore out-of-the-way villages and hill towns); Germany (enjoy wonderfully engineered freeways much loved by wannabe race-car drivers); Switzerland and Austria (drive down sunny alpine valleys with yodeling on the stereo for auto ecstasy); and Slovenia (a picturesque country with many diverse sights hard to reach by public transit).

Once you're behind the wheel, you may curse the traffic jams, narrow roads, and macho habits, but driving in Europe carbonates your experience. Driving at home is mundane; driving in Europe is memorable.

Driving Tips and Road Rules

The mechanics of driving in Europe aren't all that different from home, but the first day or two can be an adjustment. Below are my top tips for driving safely, and enjoyably, on European roads. (For an A-to-Z index of European-country driving tips, see the website of the British Automobile Association—theaa.com/motoring-advice—and look for "Overseas touring tips.")

Pass as the Europeans do. When you pass other drivers, be bold but careful. On winding, narrow roads, the slower car ahead of you may use turn-signal sign language to indicate when it's OK to pass. This is used inconsistently— and don't rely on it blindly. Be sure you understand the lane markings—in France a single, solid, white line in the middle of the road means no passing in either direction; in Germany it's a double white line.

After a few minutes on the autobahn, you'll learn that you don't linger in the passing lane. For passing, use the left-hand lane on the Continent and the right-hand lane in Britain and Ireland. In some countries (such as France, Germany, and the Netherlands), it's illegal to use the slower lane for passing.

Learn to love roundabouts. In roundabouts, traffic

continually flows in a circle around a
center island. While you'll see them
sporadically throughout continental Europe (where vehicles move
counterclockwise), roundabouts
are everywhere in the British Isles
(where traffic flows clockwise). These
work wonderfully if you follow the
golden rule: Traffic in a roundabout
always has the right-of-way, while
entering vehicles yield. For many, roundabouts are high-
pressure circles that require a snap decision about something
you don't completely understand: your exit. To replace the
stress with giggles, make it standard operating procedure to
take a 360-degree case-out-your-options exploratory circuit.
Discuss the exits with your navigator, go around again if
necessary, and then confidently wing off to the exit of your
choice. (Don't worry. No other cars will know you've been
in there enough times to get dizzy.) When approaching an
especially complex roundabout, you'll first pass a diagram
showing the layout and the various units. And in many cases,
the pavement is painted with the name of the particular road
or town to which the lane leads.

A roundabout:
Take a spin...
or two.

    Drive defensively. Be warned that some Europeans,
particularly Italians and Greeks, make up their own rules
of the road. In Rome, red lights are considered discretion-
ary. On one trip, my cabbie went through three red lights.
White-knuckled, I asked, "*Scusi,* do you see red lights?" He
said, "When I come to light, I look. If no cars come, red light
stupido, I go through. If policeman sees no cars—*no problema*. He agree—red light *stupido.*"

    Know the laws. Many European countries require you
to have your headlights on anytime the car is running, even
in broad daylight. Nearly all countries forbid talking on a
cell phone without a hands-free headset. It's also illegal to
turn right on a red light, unless a sign or signal specifically
authorizes it (most common in Germany). Most countries
require safety seats for children under age three, but a few—
including Ireland and Germany—require booster seats for
older kids. In nearly all countries, children under 12 aren't
allowed to ride in the front seat without a booster seat; a
few ban kids from the front seat no matter what, and some
have these front-seat rules for teens up to age 18. Many
countries require each car to carry a reflective safety vest or
kit with a reflecting triangle (typically supplied by the rental

company). In France, all cars need to have an unused Breathalyzer on board (supplied if your rental starts in France, but ask about this if you're picking up the car elsewhere). In many cities, cars must meet a certain emission standard in order to enter. Your car-rental company should be aware of these rules—just ask. Or you can research them on the US State Department's travel website (travel. state.gov, search for your country in the "Learn about your destination" box, then click "Travel and Transportation").

Don't drink and drive. The legal blood-alcohol limit is lower across the Continent and in Ireland than in the US, and punishment ranges from steep fines to imprisonment. Europe takes its DUI laws seriously, and so should you.

Learn the signs. All of Europe uses the same simple set of road symbols (see graphic). It takes just a few minutes to learn them. Many major rest stops have free local driving almanacs (or cheap maps) that explain such signs, roadside facilities, and exits.

Steer clear of big-city centers. Don't use a car for city sightseeing. Park your car and use public transportation or taxis (see "Parking," later).

Cities across Europe have taken measures to discourage urban driving. For example, to drive anywhere in downtown London or Stockholm, you'll pay a "congestion charge." You'll pay a toll to drive into Oslo and Bergen—but because of their automated systems, you may not know it until you get a bill two months later.

Car traffic is banned altogether in many Italian city centers, including Rome, Naples, Florence, Pisa, Lucca, Siena, San Gimignano, Orvieto, and Verona. Don't drive or park anywhere you see signs reading *Zona Traffico Limitato* (ZTL, often shown above a red circle). If you do, even briefly by accident, your license plate will be photographed, usually without your knowledge, and a hefty ticket—or

tickets, if you did it multiple times—will be waiting for you at home (for advice on handling tickets, see "If Something Goes Wrong," later). If your hotel is within a restricted area, ask your hotelier to register your car or direct you to legal parking.

Avoid heavy traffic times. Europeans have the same rush hours we do, especially in the north. Mediterranean resort areas are extremely congested on summer weekends.

To save time, use expressways. The shortest distance between any two European points is the *Autobahn/strada/ route/cesta*. Some prefer the more scenic national highway systems (*route nationale* in France). These small roads can be a breeze, or they can be dreadfully jammed up.

In many countries, expect to pay to use expressways (via tolls or vignettes). It's free to drive on expressways in some countries, such as nearly all highways in Great Britain and Germany's famous autobahn. But on major expressways in much of Mediterranean Europe—including Italy, France, Spain, Portugal, Greece, and Croatia—you'll periodically encounter toll booths; fees are based on the distance you drive (about 12 cents/mile, or roughly $7 per hour). Other countries don't use toll booths, but instead require drivers to buy a permit sticker (called a "vignette") to display in their windshields. You'll pay about $45 for the highway permit decal for Switzerland (good for a year). Other countries requiring highway vignettes have short-term permits (7-10 days) for $10-20 (Austria, Bulgaria, Czech Republic, Hungary, Romania, Slovakia, and Slovenia), as well as monthly and annual permits. You can usually buy the toll sticker at border crossings, gas stations, and post offices (check to see if your rental car already has one that hasn't yet expired). If you don't have one, you'll soon meet your first local...in uniform. Fines for not displaying the correct sticker start at around $150.

Although tolls can add up (for example, it's about $90 to get from Paris to the French Riviera, and about $55 from Rome to Naples),

Resources for Driving & Navigating

Viamichelin.com: Reliable route planner with good estimates of driving times and distances

Maps.google.com: Online maps with excellent Street View feature

theaa.com/motoring-advice: Country-by-country driving tips and local road laws

Apps

City Maps 2Go: Detailed, searchable offline city maps that read your current location

Waze: Crowd-sourced navigation and traffic info, including cheapest nearby gas

Navfree: Free offline maps with turn-by-turn directions

OffMaps: Offline maps showing points of interest

the fuel and time saved on European expressways justifies the expense. Note that in any country, if you're skipping the expressways and sticking to secondary roads, you don't need to buy a toll sticker or otherwise pay for road use.

Assume that Big Brother is watching. In many countries, traffic is monitored by automatic cameras that check car speed, click photos, and send speeders tickets by mail. It's smart to know—and follow—the area speed limit.

Parking

The best advice for avoiding parking hassles in Europe: Use common sense, and if you're unclear on the rules, ask locals. Park carefully—Europe's narrow streets are responsible for more than their fair share of insurance claims.

Street Parking: Learn what the pavement markings mean (different curb colors can mean free parking—or no parking), look for signs indicating where and when you can't park, and double-check with a local that your car's parked legally. Don't assume that an absence of meters means you can leave your car there: You may need to get a timed ticket from a nearby pay-and-display machine, or display a parking-clock disc that allows you to use free, time-limited spots (see photo).

Lots and Garages: "Parking" is the European word for a parking lot or garage, universally marked with a blue *P* sign. In midsize towns, I generally just pull into the most central and handy lot I can find. In bigger cities, I avoid the center (often an unpleasant grid of one-way streets) and head straight to a parking lot outside the core. In an effort to make well-touristed places more pedestrian-friendly, many cities have stopped providing any parking at all in the city center. Look for huge government-sponsored park-and-rides on the outskirts of town, where local transit will zip you easily into the center—commonly, the affordable parking fee includes a transit ticket (or the transit is cheap and the parking itself is free).

Parking Prices: Just like

Some areas use cardboard or plastic "parking clocks" instead of parking meters. They often come with rental cars or can be bought cheaply at gas stations, newsstands, or tobacco shops. Park, set the clock for the current time, and leave it on your dash. A street sign indicates how much time you have (parking here is limited to 2 hours, Mon-Fri, 8:00 a.m.-6:00 p.m and Sat, 8:00 a.m.-1 p.m.). The clock establishes when you arrived. In Germanic countries, where they're widely used, ask for a *Parkscheibe*.

at home, the bigger the city, the more you'll pay for parking. Small towns don't usually charge more than $10 per day (and are likely to have free limited-time spots), whereas in bigger cites you'll pay upwards of $35-$55 per day. Street parking can be cheaper than parking in a lot or garage, but often comes with a time limit too short for sightseeing. In smaller towns, you may find a cheaper hourly rate by parking farther away from the big-name sight. Parking machines on the street or at unstaffed garages often don't accept American magnetic-stripe credit cards, and many don't give change, so keep plenty of coins and bills on hand.

Overnight Stops: If parking overnight, it's crucial to choose a safe, well-traveled, and well-lit spot for your car. Ask your hotelier about parking options (and rules governing overnight parking); the hotel may offer a permit or free spot, whether in their own lot or through an agreement with a neighbor.

Filling the Tank

The cost of fuel in Europe (about $8 a gallon) sounds worse than it is. Distances are short, petite cars get great mileage, and, when compared to costly train tickets (for the price of a two-hour train ride, you can fill your tank), expensive gas is less of a factor. You'll be impressed by how few miles you need to travel to enjoy Europe's diversity.

Pumping gas in Europe is as easy as finding a gas station (the English word "self-service" is universal), sticking the nozzle in, and pulling the big trigger. Paying, however, can be more complicated, because some pay-at-the-pump machines won't accept most American magnetic-stripe credit cards (most common in the UK, France, and Scandinavia; see page 190). Be prepared to pay cash. If you're traveling on rural highways, automated gas stations may be the only ones open on Sundays, holidays, and late at night—fill up ahead of time.

Fuel prices are listed by the liter (about a quart, four to a gallon). As in the US, most cars take unleaded, but diesel is widely in use. In many countries, the pumps are color-coded to help you find the right kind of gas. In Europe, regular gas is marked "95" while super or premium gasoline is usually designated "97" or "98." Unleaded gas is called *essence*, *petrol*, or *benzine*, while diesel is known as *gasoil, gasol, gaz-oil, gasolio, gasóleo, dieselolie, mazot, motorina, nafta,* or just plain *diesel* (ask about the proper local term when you rent your car). Pay extra attention in Spain, where gasoline is *gasolina* and diesel is sometimes called *gasóleo*.

Freeway gas stations are more expensive than those in towns, but sometimes (e.g., during lunchtime siesta) only freeway stations are open. Giant suburban supermarkets often offer the cheapest gas.

If Something Goes Wrong

Some travelers obsess about the possibility of a car accident while driving in Europe. Most come back bragging about their road skills and missing the freedom of the autobahn. Those who do have a mishap usually tell me it was the result of a tight squeeze in a parking garage. Still, it's good to know what to do if you hit a bump in the road. Figure out where to find your rental company's emergency service number *before* you need it (it's likely on a windshield sticker, your keychain, and the rental paperwork).

Traffic Accidents

If there's major damage to your vehicle, call your rental company's 24-hour roadside assistance line. If the accident involves another car, you'll need to show your driver's license and insurance "green card" to the other driver and/or the police. Fill out the European Accident Report form that the agency includes with your rental documents. If you're going to submit an insurance claim, notify your insurer as soon as possible, and file a police report—and get copies of that report—even if no other cars are involved. Both steps must happen within your policy's time limit. If the police refuse to write up a report ("it's only a scrape"), ask your hotelier to help you type up a report, take it to the police station, and ask them to stamp it. It's a good idea to take photos of the damage to your car and the license plate of any other vehicles involved.

Flat Tires and Mechanical Problems

Rental companies typically include roadside assistance or a towing service in the event your car becomes undrivable (sometimes for a fee). Ask about this possibility when you pick up the car.

If your car has a serious issue, in theory, you should be able to swap it out for a replacement car at the rental company's nearest office. In reality, it may not be so convenient, especially if you break down in the middle of nowhere. If that happens, call your 24/7 roadside assistance number right away...then expect a wait for the tow truck. (If you rented through a consolidator, they may be of some help in speeding things up—but call roadside assistance first.) The repair will be covered by the rental company as long as it's clear it was the car's fault, not yours. It's worth noting that burnt clutches account for the vast majority of breakdowns experienced (and paid for) by American drivers in Europe— go easy on the transmission.

Traffic Tickets

Just because there was no police car in sight when you ran a red light (or ignored the speed limit, drove into a restricted zone, or even tailgated too closely) doesn't mean you weren't caught—Europe's traffic cameras are every- where. Quite likely, you won't know about the infraction until months later, when a letter arrives in your mail and/or a charge shows up on your credit card.

You likely won't get a chance to dispute a fine. Europe doesn't have "traffic courts"—you're simply expected to pay up. In some cases, the fine may be automatically billed to your credit card. In other cases, the rental agency may charge you $50 just for providing your address to local authorities.

Of course, many renters just ignore any notices that show up months after their trip. It's understandable—paying the fine may not be all that straightforward, and it's not as if Interpol's on your tail. But be aware that an unpaid ticket can follow you for years, and you'll likely be forced to pay it the next time you rent a car in Europe (especially if it's in the same country).

NAVIGATING

After more than 30 years of driving in Europe—pre- and post-GPS—I've collected a carload of knowledge and tricks for navigating the roads. Most of these tips apply to navigat- ing cities and towns on foot, too.

Paper Maps

Drivers need detail, especially when focusing on a specific region. The free maps you get from your car-rental com- pany usually don't cut it. Better maps and atlases are sold at European gas stations, bookshops, newsstands, and tourist shops.

I like Michelin maps, but the cost for individual maps can add up. Consider the popular and relatively inexpensive Michelin road atlases for each country (with good city maps and detailed indexes). Though they can be heavy, atlases are compact, a good value, and easier for drivers to use than big foldout maps.

Sometimes the best regional maps are available locally. For example, if you're exploring your roots in the Norwegian fjord country, Cappelens 1:200,000 maps are detailed enough to help you find Grandpa Ole's farm. Other quality European brands include Hallwag, Freytag Berndt, Marco Polo, Berndtson & Berndtson, AA (Britain's AAA-type automobile club), Road Editions (for Greece), and Kod & Kam (for Croatia and Slovenia).

Like most goats, I appreciate a good, old-fashioned map.

Each map has a legend that indicates navigational as well as sightseeing information, such as types of roads, scenic routes and towns, ruined castles, hostels, mountain huts, viewpoints, and so on. Good maps even include such specific details as tolls and opening schedules of remote mountain roads.

21st-Century Maps

Digital maps offer several benefits over paper maps. They show your current location at all times, suggest the fastest way between Point A and Point B, give turn-by-turn directions, consider traffic conditions when creating routes, and offer fairly accurate estimates of how long the drive (or ride, or walk) will take.

When renting a car in Europe, you have several options for your digital navigator: Use the mapping app that's already on your cellular-connected device or download a mapping app that's designed to be used offline. You can also rent a GPS device with your rental car (or bring your own GPS device from home).

Using Mapping Apps on Your Mobile Device

If you want to use your mobile device for pulling up maps or routes on the fly, for turn-by-turn directions, or for traffic updates, you'll need an international data plan (see page 243). But just using GPS to locate your position on a map does not require an Internet connection (and therefore does not require Wi-Fi or cellular data). This means that once you have the map in your phone, you can navigate with it all day long without incurring data-roaming charges.

Using Your Default Mapping App: Since the mapping app you use at home (such as Google Maps or Apple Maps) works just as well for navigating Europe, it can make a lot of sense to use it on your trip. It's already installed on your device, you're familiar with it, you don't have to do any prep work, and it can alert you to current road conditions and transit disruptions.

The most economical approach when using these apps is to download as much information as possible while you're on Wi-Fi. Google Maps' "save map to use offline" feature is useful for this, allowing you to view and even zoom in on a map when you're offline (though you can't search for an address or get directions). Apple Maps doesn't offer a save-for-offline feature, though it does automatically cache (save) certain data. So if you bring up the maps you need or plan your route while on Wi-Fi in the morning, the app may end up caching those maps and not using data roaming to call them up during the day (no guarantees, though).

No matter which app you're using, view the maps in standard view (not satellite view) to limit the data demands for each map, and resist the temptation to talk to your phone, as its voice recognition is data-heavy. And consider bringing a car charger for your device, since the mapping service—even just its offline positioning system—gobbles up battery life.

Using a Third-Party Offline Mapping App: A number of well-designed apps allow you much of the convenience of online maps without any costly demands on your data plan. City Maps 2Go is one of the most popular of these; OffMaps and Navfree also offer good, zoomable offline maps—similar to Google Maps—for much of Europe (some apps are better for driving, while others are better for navigating cities on foot). You need to be online to download the app, but once that's done, the maps are accessible anywhere (note that you won't get turn-by-turn directions, which require a data connection).

For much more fully featured GPS apps for your mobile phone, check out those from TomTom, Garmin, CoPilot, and other GPS device makers, though European maps for these tend to be very expensive.

GPS Devices

If you'll be traveling without a smartphone or data-roaming plan, you may want to rent a GPS device with your car. Some drivers even prefer using a dedicated GPS unit over a phone-based mapping app—not only to avoid the data-roaming fees, but because a stand-alone GPS can be easier to operate (important if you're driving solo). The downside: It's expensive—around $10-30 per day. Also, your car's GPS unit may only come loaded with maps for its home country; if you need additional maps, ask. Make sure your device's language is set to English before you drive off.

If you have a portable GPS device at home, you can take that instead. Many American GPS devices come loaded with US maps only—you'll need to buy and download European maps before your trip. This option is far less expensive than paying for the rental company's unit, and you'll have the ease of traveling with a familiar device. (Before purchasing, check that the maps available through the manufacturer are detailed enough for the areas you're visiting.)

Tips for Using Digital Maps

Once on the road, stay on your toes, and remember that digital maps are fallible. Check the settings to see whether it's defaulting to the "most direct" or the "most scenic" route—a distinction that can translate into hours of extra driving. Some GPS units receive wireless traffic reports, then modify your route to help you avoid upcoming traffic jams; however detours onto back roads can wind up costing you even more time.

Even if I'm using a GPS, I always make it a point to also have a road map handy and at least a vague sense of my route. One time, driving from St. Moritz to Lugano via Italy's Lake Como, I realized my GPS had just directed me right past the Lugano turnoff. Hitting the brakes and checking my paper map, I figured out that the GPS was aiming to send me on the freeway, then on a ferry across the lake. I stuck with the "slower" roads on the correct side of the lake—and arrived an hour earlier. The lesson: Digital maps are most useful in conjunction with a good map and some common sense.

Tips for Navigators

Here are some general tips for finding your way:

Navigate intelligently. Study the roads and major interchanges you'll be using before you set out. If you're headed for a small or midsize town, know which big city is nearby (and most likely to be signposted) to keep you headed in the right direction. In some countries, road numbers can help you find your way: For example, take road A-1 to London, then B-23 to Bristol, then C-456 to Bath. In other countries, locals (and local signs) ignore the road numbers, so you'll navigate by town name. Signs are often color-coded: yellow for most roads, green or blue for expressways, and brown for sightseeing attractions. When leaving a city, look for "all directions" signs (*toutes directions, alle Richtungen,* etc.) pointing you out of town.

Know the local road-naming conventions. Normally, the more digits the road number has, the smaller it is. In Britain, M-1 is a freeway, A-34 is a major road, and B-4081 is a secondary road. Most international European expressways are designated with an "E" (similar to the "I" designation on American freeways), but they may also be labeled on maps and signs with their national letters (for example, the main route between Paris and Lyon is known as both A-6 and E-15). Since road numbers can change, you should also navigate by town names.

Get directions. When you call ahead to confirm your room, ask your hotelier for detailed directions on how to reach the place. Many hotels give precise driving directions and/or GPS coordinates on their websites. If possible, figure out your arrival route on a map before you enter the city limits. While some small towns helpfully post signs directing you to individual hotels, in many cases you're on your own.

Look for clues to the town center. You can drive in and out of strange towns fairly smoothly by following a few basic signs. Most European towns have signs directing you to the "old town" or the center (such as *centrum, centro, centar, centre-ville, Zentrum, Stadtmitte*). The tourist office, normally right downtown, will usually be clearly signposted (*i, turismo, VVV,* or various abbreviations that you'll learn in each country). The tallest spire often marks the center of the old town. Park in its shadow and look for the tourist information office.

Consider hiring cabbies. Even if you have a rental car, cabbies can be handy when you're driving lost in a big city. Many times I've hired a cab, showed him an elusive address, and followed him in my car to my hotel.

Think metric. European countries (except the UK) use kilometers instead of miles. One kilometer is six-tenths of a mile. To convert kilometers to miles, cut the kilometers in half and add 10 percent of the original number (90 km/hour = 45 + 9 miles = 54 miles—not very fast in Europe).

Do the math yourself: 140 km/hour = 84 mph. Or 360 km = 216 miles. Some people prefer to drop the last digit and multiply by 6 (if 80 km, multiply 8 × 6 = 48 miles), though this can be challenging with large numbers (340 km × 6 = ?). Choose whichever formula works for you.

Figure out the length of your trip. When estimating how long a drive will take, figure you'll average 100 kilometers per hour on expressways (about the same as going 60 mph back home). Determining how much ground you can cover off the freeway is a crapshoot. I use a trick an Irish bus driver taught me: Figure a minute for every kilometer (covering 90 km will take you about an hour and a half). Double that for slow, curvy roads, such as in Italy's Dolomites or Amalfi Coast.

Money

Life in 21st-century America has become a plastic experience. For many of us, days can go by when we don't use any cash. We swipe our credit card at the drug store or tap our debit card's PIN code at the gas pump, and we're on our way.

In Europe, however, day-to-day spending can be more cash-based. There I rely mostly on cash, though I appreciate the convenience that credit cards offer.

Pay with Plastic or Cash?

For me, it all comes down to maximizing ease and minimizing fees. I pay for as much as possible with cash, using a bank that charges no or low fees for international ATM transactions, and withdrawing large amounts at each transaction. I never exchange dollars for foreign cash at a currency exchange booth, and I don't bother getting euros, pounds, or whatever prior to my trip. When I arrive in Europe, I head for an ATM at the airport, load up on cash, and keep it safe in my money belt.

I use my credit card sparingly: to book hotel reservations, to buy advance tickets for events or sights, to cover major expenses (such as car rentals or plane tickets), and to pay for things online or near the end of my trip (to avoid another visit to the ATM). Cash is the best— and sometimes only—way to pay for bus fare, taxis, and local guides. If you'll be shopping a lot or settling

Use euros in Euroland: Austria, Belgium, Cyprus, Estonia, Finland, France, Germany, Greece, Ireland, Italy, Latvia, Lithuania, Luxembourg, Malta, the Netherlands, Portugal, Slovakia, Slovenia, and Spain.

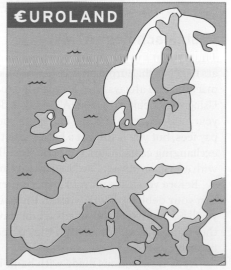

€UROLAND

bills at pricey business-class hotels, you might use your credit card more than I do—but you'll still be better off using cash for smaller purchases.

Because merchants pay commissions to credit-card companies, small European businesses (B&Bs, mom-and-pop cafés, gift shops, and more) often prefer that you pay in cash. Vendors might offer you a discount for paying with cash, or they might not accept credit cards at all. Having cash on hand can help you avoid a stressful predicament if you find yourself in a place that won't accept your credit card.

A dependence on plastic reshapes the Europe you experience. Pedro's Pension, the friendly guide at the cathedral, and most merchants in the market don't take credit cards. Going through the Back Door often means using hard local cash. Minimizing debit- and credit-card use also guards against card fraud or theft: The less you use your cards, the less likely your information will be stolen.

Remember, you're on vacation. Don't get stressed about money in Europe; just spend it wisely.

CASH

When I first started traveling in Europe, I'd convert my traveler's checks into cash at American Express—the convivial, welcoming home to American travelers abroad. When changing dollars into francs in Paris, it felt so good to lose money to that smiling, English-speaking person at the desk. Now with ATMs, the euro, and the general shrinking of the economic world, AmExCo is a dinosaur.

Cash Machines (ATMs)

Throughout Europe, ATMs are the standard way for travelers to get cash. European ATMs work like your hometown machine and always have English-language instructions. Using your debit card at an ATM takes dollars directly from your bank account at home and gives you foreign cash. You'll pay fees, but you'll still get a better rate than you would exchanging cash dollars at a bank. Ideally, use your debit card with a Visa or MasterCard logo to take money out of ATMs.

Before you leave on your trip, confirm with your bank that your debit card will work in Europe and alert them that you'll be making withdrawals while traveling—otherwise, they might freeze your card if they detect unusual spending patterns.

ATM transactions made with bank-issued debit cards

come with various fees. Your bank may levy a flat $2-5 transaction fee each time you use an out-of-network ATM, and/or may charge a percentage for the currency conversion (1-3 percent), on top of Visa and MasterCard's 1 percent fee for international transactions.

When possible, withdraw your cash from bank ATMs located outside banks—a thief is less likely to target a cash machine near surveillance cameras, and if your card is munched by a machine, you can go inside for help.

Most bank ATMs in Europe don't charge a usage fee, but stay away from "independent" ATMs, which have high fees and may try to trick users with "dynamic currency conversion" (see page 189). These ATMs (labeled with names such as Travelex, Euronet, Moneybox, Cardpoint, and Cashzone) are often found next to bank ATMs in the hope that travelers will be too confused to notice the difference.

If your US bank charges a flat fee per transaction, make fewer visits to the ATM and withdraw larger amounts. (Some major US banks partner with European bank chains, meaning that you can use those ATMs with no fees at all—ask your bank.) Quiz your bank to figure out exactly what you'll pay for each withdrawal (for a list of questions, see page 189).

Welcome to Euroland

Nineteen EU member countries—and more than 330 million people—use the same currency, the euro. With euros, tourists and locals can easily compare prices of goods between countries. And we no longer lose money or time changing money at borders.

Not all European countries have switched to euros. As of now, major EU holdouts are the United Kingdom, Denmark, and Sweden (Norway and Switzerland also have their own currency, but aren't EU members). Despite the currency's recent trouble, several Eastern European countries that have joined the EU—including the Czech Republic, Poland, Hungary, Croatia, Romania, and Bulgaria—are committed to adopting the euro sometime in the future. For now, these countries still use their traditional currencies.

Even in some non-Euroland countries, the euro is commonly used. Montenegro and Kosovo are not in the EU, but the euro is their official currency. In Switzerland, some ATMs give euros, most prices are listed in both Swiss francs and euros, and travelers can get by with euro cash. But if you pay in euros, you'll get a rotten exchange rate. Ideally, if you're in a non-euro country for more than a few hours, get some local currency instead.

Since European keypads have only numbers, you'll need to know your personal identification number (PIN) by number rather than by letter. Plan on being able to withdraw money only from your checking account. You are unlikely to be able to dip into your savings account or transfer funds between accounts from a European ATM.

Bringing an extra ATM card provides a backup if one is

ATM Basics

Before you go:
- Inform your bank of your travel dates in Europe (see sidebar on page 189 for questions you should ask).
- European ATMs will take funds only from checking accounts—not savings—so make sure your checking account balance is high enough before you go.
- Bring at least one credit card and one debit card, ideally with a Visa or Master-Card logo. Some travelers carry an extra card, in case one gets demagnetized or eaten by a temperamental machine.
- Make sure you have a four-digit PIN number (no letters) for all of your cards, even your credit card. Request a PIN if you don't know it (allow time for your bank to mail it).

When making a withdrawal:
- Try to use ATMs at banks during banking hours. If there's a problem, someone in the bank can probably help.
- Avoid non-bank ATMs. "Independent" ATMs—brands such as Travelex, Cashzone, Cardpoint, YourCash, or Euronet—charge outrageous fees.
- Grab your cash and card quickly; some ATMs suck back the cash after 30 seconds.
- Take out large amounts of money at one time to avoid frequent ATM trips and repeated withdrawal fees.

How to use a European cash machine: Insert card, pull out cash.

- Don't use your credit card to withdraw cash unless it's an emergency; you'll be charged a high cash-advance interest rate from the minute you pull out the money.

If your card doesn't work:
- Try a different ATM. (Do not re-enter your PIN if the ATM eats your card.)
- Try a lower amount; the ATM may have a withdrawal limit.
- Try later. Your card's 24-hour withdrawal maximum is based on US time, or your bank's network may be temporarily down.

If all else fails:
- Use your emergency dollars stashed in your money belt.
- Use your credit card to get a cash advance (you'll need your credit-card PIN for the ATM).
- Have a friend or relative wire you money via Western Union (see page 187).
- Contact the nearest American embassy/consulate; they can help arrange a wire transfer.

demagnetized or eaten by a machine. Make sure your card won't expire before your trip ends. You do not need a chip-and-PIN card (described later) to use a European ATM—your standard magnetic stripe card will work fine.

Before you go, ask your bank how much you can withdraw per 24 hours, and consider adjusting the amount. Some travelers prefer a high limit that allows them to take out more cash at each ATM stop, while others prefer to set a lower limit as a security measure, in case their card is stolen. To avoid excess per-transaction fees, I usually go with a higher maximum.

Remember that you're withdrawing a different currency than dollars; for example, if your daily limit is $300, withdraw just 200 euros. Many frustrated travelers have walked away from ATMs thinking their cards were rejected, when actually they were asking for more cash in euros than their daily limit allowed.

Be aware that many foreign ATMs have their own limits. If the ATM won't let you withdraw your daily maximum, you'll have to make several smaller withdrawals to get the amount you want. Note that few ATM receipts list the exchange rate, and some machines don't dispense receipts at all.

In some countries (especially in Eastern Europe), an ATM may give you high-denomination bills, which can be difficult to break. My strategy: Request an odd amount of money from the ATM (such as 2,800 Czech *koruna* instead of 3,000). If the machine insists on giving you big bills, go to a bank or a major store to break them.

If you're looking for an ATM, ask for a *distributeur* in France, a "cashpoint" in the UK, and a *Bankomat* just about everywhere else. Many European banks have their ATMs in a small entry lobby, which protects users from snoopers and bad weather. When the bank is closed, the door to this lobby may be locked. In this case, look for a credit-card-size slot next to the door. Simply insert or swipe your debit or credit card in this slot, and the door should automatically open. For a list of common ATM scams, see the sidebar on page 186.

Cash and Currency Tips

Avoid (or at least minimize) cash exchange. The financial industry does a masterful job of hiding the fact that you lose money each time you change it. On average, at a bank you lose 8 percent when you change dollars to euros or another foreign currency. When you use currency exchange booths such as Forex or Travelex at the airport, you lose around 15 percent. If you must change cash in Europe, the postal banks inside post offices usually have the best rate.

Don't buy foreign currency in advance. Some tourists just have to have euros or pounds in their pockets when they step off the airplane, but smart travelers don't bother and know better than to get lousy stateside exchange rates. Wait until you arrive at your destination; I've never been to an airport in Europe that didn't have plenty of ATMs.

Leave the traveler's checks at home. I cashed my last traveler's check long ago. They're a waste of time (long lines at slow banks) and money (fees to get them, fees to cash them). ATMs are the way to go.

Use local cash. Many Americans exclaim gleefully, "Gee, they accept dollars! There's no need to change money." But the happy sales clerk doesn't tell you that your purchase is costing about 20 percent more because of the store's terrible exchange rate. Without knowing it, you're changing money—at a lousy rate—every time you buy something with dollars.

Figure out currency conversions. Local currencies are all logical. Each system is decimalized just like ours. There are a hundred "little ones" (cents, pence, groszy, stotinki) in every "big one" (euro, pound, złoty, lev). Only the names have been changed—to confuse the tourist. Examine the coins in your pocket soon after you arrive, and in two minutes you'll be comfortable with the nickels, dimes, and quarters of each new currency.

You don't need to constantly consult a currency converter. While you can do real-time conversion with an app, I've never bothered. You just need to know the rough

For information about using traveler's checks…see the 1995 edition of this book.

exchange rates. I see no need to have it figured to the third decimal.

Very roughly determine what the unit of currency (euros, kroner, Swiss francs, or whatever) is worth in American dollars. For example, let's say the exchange rate is €1 = $1.20. If a strudel costs €5, then it costs five times $1.20, or about $6. Ten euros is about $12, and €250 = $300 (figure 250 plus about one-fifth more). Quiz yourself. Soon it'll be second nature. Survival on a budget is easier when you're comfortable with the local currency.

Assume you'll be shortchanged. In banks, restaurants, at ticket booths, everywhere—expect to be shortchanged if you don't do your own figuring. Some people who spend their lives sitting in booths for eight hours a day taking money from strangers have no problem stealing from clueless tourists who don't know the local currency. For 10 minutes I observed a man in the Rome subway shortchanging half of the tourists who went through his turnstile. Half of his victims caught him and got their correct change with apologies. Overall, about 25 percent didn't notice and probably went home saying, "*Mamma mia,* Italy is really expensive."

Coins can become worthless when you leave a country. Since big-value coins are common in Europe, exporting a pocketful of change can be an expensive mistake. Spend them (on postcards, a newspaper, or food or drink for the train ride), change them into bills, or give them away. Otherwise, you've just bought a bunch of souvenirs. Note, however, that while euro coins each have a national side (indicating where they were minted), they are perfectly good in any country that uses the euro currency.

Bring along some US dollars. While you won't use it for day-to-day purchases, American cash in your money belt comes in handy for emergencies, such as when banks go on

Avid coin collectors have the joy of filling in coin books with the eight denominations of euro coins from 22 different countries (including the tiny nations of Vatican City, Monaco, and San Marino). Europhiles can buy these books in Europe and chart their travels by gradually completing the collection.

ATM Scams

While ATM fraud happens more often in the US than in Europe, it pays to be alert. Remember, try to use ATMs at banks—thieves shy away from surveillance cameras. And watch out for these common ATM scams:

Card Skimmers: Criminals attach a skimming device to the card reader and place a camera nearby to capture your keystrokes as you enter your PIN. Usually, the crooks sell the information to others, who make a new card and use it to withdraw money at a later date. Beat this scam by inspecting the front of the ATM: If anything looks crooked, loose, or damaged—or if the entry to the card slot bulges out dramatically—it could be a sign of a skimming device. And always cover your hand as you enter your PIN.

Card Traps: Thieves insert a thin ribbon of tape into the card slot. The loop traps the card so you think it's been "eaten" by the ATM. Then a Good Samaritan arrives, telling you that you can retrieve your card by retyping your PIN. (While you do it, he memorizes your code.) Or there is a sign asking you to enter your PIN twice if there is trouble. Since your card still won't eject, you eventually leave to call your bank. As soon as you're gone, the criminal removes your card and uses it with your PIN to withdraw money. If your card gets stuck, look for a trapping device—and never re-enter your PIN.

Money Grabbers: These scammers work in pairs—the first one distracts you after you've entered your card and PIN; the second one grabs your cash. There are many clever ruses used to distract you. The scammer may pretend to sell you a newspaper; she may place a €5 bill at your feet and tell you that you dropped some money; or she may ask you for a charitable donation. Sometimes the scammers are children. Pay attention to strangers loitering near the machine, and remember that you're most vulnerable just after you have entered your PIN and the withdrawal amount.

strike or your ATM card stops working. I carry several hundred US dollars as a backup (in denominations of easy-to-exchange 20s). I've been in Greece and Ireland when every bank went on strike, shutting down without warning. But hard cash is hard cash. People always know roughly what a dollar is worth. If local banks don't have exchange services, you can always find exchange desks at major train stations or airports.

Get back to dollars at the end of your trip. If you have foreign cash left at the end of your trip, change it into dollars at the European airport or simply spend it at the airport before you fly home. You might get a few more dollars from your hometown bank for that last smattering of foreign bills, but it's clean and convenient to simply fly home with nothing but dollars in your pocket.

Wiring Money

What if your credit and debit cards don't work, you're out of emergency cash, and you don't have a travel partner who can loan you money? Don't panic. It's easy for someone in the US to wire you some cash. Western Union has thousands of agents at banks, travel agencies, post offices, train stations, airports, currency exchange offices, and supermarkets in Europe. As long as you still have your passport, a friend or relative can go online at westernunion.com, transfer money with a credit card, and call you back with your Money Transfer Control Number (MTCN). Then you present your passport and the control number to a Western Union agent, who gives you the cash. If your friend or relative prefers, he or she can make the transfer in person at a Western Union office in the US or by calling toll-free 800-225-5227. There's a hefty fee and a poor exchange rate, but the cash can be ready for pickup in a matter of hours.

> ## Money Resources
>
> **Ftc.gov/idtheft:** Advice on bank card theft and more
> **Oanda.com:** Currency conversion tool
> **Bankrate.com:** Compares bank card fees
>
> ### Apps
> **Your bank's mobile app**
> **ATM Hunter:** Finds the nearest ATMs
> **Currency Converter** or **XE Currency:** Real-time currency conversion

It's trickier if you've lost your passport. Western Union lets your financial angel set up a "secret question" that only you can answer to confirm your identity. Or you can use a slower US State Department service that wires money to an embassy or consulate for pickup during business hours (see travel.state.gov). For more on what to do if you've lost your passport, see page 338.

If your situation is dire and you can't get anyone to wire you money, ask the consulate about a "repatriation loan." Usually this is enough money to cover a night's lodging and a plane ticket home. Your passport will be stamped "Valid for Return to US Only" until your loan is repaid. Don't even think about stiffing Uncle Sam—after six months the State Department forwards the paperwork to the Treasury Department and the IRS.

CREDIT CARDS

American credit cards work throughout Europe (at hotels, larger shops and restaurants, travel agencies, car-rental agencies, and so on); Visa and MasterCard are the most widely accepted. American Express is less common, and the Discover card is unknown in Europe. It's a good idea to bring an extra card as a backup (especially if you're renting a car and using your card to cover CDW insurance—see page 159 for more). Although most of Europe is switching to new technology that may cause your US card to be rejected in some self-service machines, it shouldn't cause you too much hassle (see "Chip-and-PIN Cards," later).

Plastic fans should realize that when you use your credit card, you're buying from businesses that have enough slack in their prices to cover credit-card processing fees (2-5 percent). In other words, those who travel mostly with plastic may enjoy the convenience, but they pay for it with higher prices.

Fees (and How to Avoid Them)

Travelers returning from Europe often open their mail to discover they paid more for their trip than they thought they had. Over the last decade, banks have dramatically increased their fees for overseas transactions. While these fees are legal, they're basically a slimy way for credit-card companies to wring a few more dollars out of their customers.

Visa and MasterCard levy a 1 percent fee on international transactions, and some banks that issue those cards also tack on a currency conversion fee (additional 1-3 percent). These are similar to the fees associated with using your debit card for ATM withdrawals (described earlier).

So, how can a smart traveler avoid—or at least reduce—these fees? Here are a few suggestions.

Ask about fees. Banks are required to break out international transaction fees as line-items on your statement, helping you to see exactly what you're paying. But by the time you get your statement, it's too late—so it's smart to make a call before your trip to get the whole story. Quiz your bank or credit-card company about the specific fees that come with using their card overseas (see sidebar).

Transaction Fees Add Up

It pays to shop around for the best rates, both for debit-card ATM withdrawals and credit-card transactions. Consider these examples and you'll see how fees can really add up over the length of your trip.

$300 ATM withdrawal (with debit card)

	Bank A	Bank B
Flat fee	$3	$5
Currency conversion fee	$6 (2%)	$0 (0%)
ATM out-of-network fee	$2	$2
Total fees	$11	$7

$600 credit-card purchase

	Bank A	Bank B
International transaction fee	$6 (1%)	$6 (1%)
Bank currency conversion fee	$12 (2%)	$0 (0%)
Total fees	$18	$6

If you're getting a bad deal, get a new card. Some companies offer lower international fees than others—and some don't charge any at all. If you're going on a long trip, do some research and consider taking out a card just for international purchases. Capital One has a particularly good reputation for no-fee international transactions on both its credit cards and its debit cards linked to a checking account. Most credit unions have low-to-no international transaction fees. Bankrate has a good comparison chart of major credit cards and their currency-conversion fees (search "conversion fees" at bankrate.com).

Avoid dynamic currency conversion (DCC). Some European merchants and hoteliers—capitalizing on the fact that many Americans are intimidated by unusual currencies—cheerfully charge you for converting their prices to dollars before running your credit card. Dynamic currency conversion may seem like a nice perk, but you'll actually end up paying more. The dollar price is usually based on a lousy exchange rate set by the merchant—and to make matters worse, even though you're paying in "dollars," your credit-card issuer may still levy its standard foreign-transaction fee. The result: The "convenience" of seeing your charge in dollars comes at a premium.

These DCC charges are becoming more common, especially in Ireland, Spain, and Portugal—and they're also popping up in large department stores that cater to tourists in cities such as London and Paris. Some merchants may disagree, but according to Visa and MasterCard policies, you have the right to decline this service at the store and have your credit-card transaction go through in the local currency. If you're handed a receipt with two totals—one in the local currency and the other in US dollars—circle or

Card Questions

Before your trip, notify your credit-card company and your bank (for debit cards) that you'll be traveling in Europe. This will ensure that they don't decline your foreign transactions. While you have them on the phone, ask these questions.

The Basics:
- Will my card work in the countries I'm traveling to?
- What fees do you charge for withdrawals or purchases made in Europe? Is it a percentage, a flat fee, or both?
- Are other currency conversion or foreign transaction fees tacked on?
- If my credit/debit card is lost or stolen, what is my liability?
- What phone number should I call if there's an emergency?

For Debit Cards:
- What is my daily limit for ATM withdrawals in Europe? (Change your limit, if necessary.)
- Do you have partner banks in Europe whose ATMs I can use without a fee?

For Credit Cards:
- Request a PIN if you don't have one (sometimes required for purchases in Europe).

checkmark the amount in the local currency before you sign. If your receipt shows the total in dollars only, ask that it be rung up again in the local currency. If the merchant refuses to run the charge again, pay in cash, or mark the receipt "local currency not offered" and warn the clerk that you will be disputing the charges with your bank.

Lately, some ATMs are also trying to confuse customers by presenting DCC in misleading terms. If an ATM offers to "lock in" or "guarantee" your conversion rate, choose "proceed without conversion." Other prompts might say "You can be charged in dollars: Press YES for dollars, NO for euros." Always choose the local currency in these situations.

Don't bother with prepaid cards. It's possible to buy prepaid "cash cards"—which you load with funds before you leave, then use like any other credit or debit card—but they come with high fees and aren't worth considering for most trips.

The Bottom Line: Here's the best formula for saving money as you travel. Pay for most items with cash (use a bank that charges low rates for international ATM transactions, and withdraw large amounts at each transaction—keeping the cash safe in your money belt). When using a credit card, use a card with low international fees, and make sure your transactions are charged in the local currency—not dollars. Then smile and enjoy your trip, feeling very clever for avoiding so much unnecessary expense.

Chip-and-PIN Cards

Europe—and the rest of the world—is adopting a new system for credit and debit cards. While handy for locals, these chip-and-PIN cards are causing a few headaches for American visitors: Some machines that are designed to accept chip-and-PIN cards simply don't accept US credit cards. This news is causing some anxiety among American travelers, but really: Don't worry. While I've been inconvenienced a few times with self-service machines that wouldn't accept my card, it's never caused me any serious trouble. Here's the scoop:

Today, outside the US, the majority of all cards are chip cards. These "smartcards" come with an embedded security chip (in addition to the magnetic stripe found on American-style cards). To make a purchase

When Europeans buy something with their chip-and-PIN card, they insert the card in a machine like this one, then type in their PIN.

with a chip-and-PIN card, the cardholder inserts the card into a slot in the payment machine, then enters a PIN (like using a debit card in the US) while the card stays in the slot. The chip inside the card authorizes the transaction; the cardholder doesn't sign a receipt.

Some of my readers tell me their American-style cards have been rejected by some self-service payment machines in Great Britain, Ireland, Scandinavia, France, Switzerland, Belgium, Austria, Germany, and the Netherlands. This is especially common with machines at train and subway stations, toll roads, parking garages, luggage lockers, bike-rental kiosks, and self-serve gas pumps. For example, after a long flight into Charles de Gaulle Airport, you'll find you can't use your credit card at the ticket machine for the train into Paris. Or, while driving in rural Switzerland on a Sunday afternoon, you discover that the unattended gas station only accepts chip-and-PIN cards.

In most of these situations, a cashier is nearby who can process your magnetic-stripe card manually by swiping it and having you sign the receipt the old-fashioned way. Many payment machines take cash; remember you can always use an ATM to withdraw cash with your magnetic-stripe debit card. Other machines might take your US credit card if you also know the card's PIN—almost every card has one (request the number from your bank before you leave, and allow time to receive it by mail). In a pinch, you could ask a local if you can pay them cash to run the transaction on their card.

Most hotels, restaurants, and shops that serve Americans will gladly accept your US credit card. During the transaction, they may ask you to type in your PIN rather than sign a receipt. Some clerks in destinations off the beaten track may not be familiar with swiping a credit card; either be ready to give them a quick lesson, or better yet, pay with cash.

In a few cases, you might need to get creative; drivers in particular need to be aware of potential problems when filling up at an unattended gas station, entering a parking garage, or exiting a toll road...you might just have to move on to the next gas station or use the "cash only" lane at the toll plaza.

Those who are really concerned can apply for a chip card in the US. Major US banks, such as Chase, Citi, Bank of America, US Bank, and Wells Fargo, are beginning to offer credit cards with chips—but most of these come with a hefty annual fee. Technically, most of these are "chip-and-signature" cards, for which your signature verifies your identity, not the true "chip-and-PIN" cards being used in Europe. So while Europeans punch in their codes when making a purchase, you will sign a paper receipt when you present your American chip card.

The problem with these American chip-and-signature cards is that they are not configured for all offline transactions (in which the card is securely validated for use even without a real-time connection to the bank). Your American chip-and-signature card will work at some self-service machines, such as those in the Paris Métro or London Tube stations. But it won't work for offline transactions at Dutch train ticket machines, French toll roads, or out-of-the-way Swiss gas stations. Often there's no way of knowing if your chip-and-signature card will work for self-service payment until you try it—so look for a cashier or have cash for a backup.

If you really want a chip card, ask your financial institution if it plans to offer one soon, and find out if the card is "chip-and-signature" or "chip-and-PIN." With either type, be sure you memorize the PIN for your card in case a card reader requires it. Even if your bank says the PIN is only for cash withdrawals, ask for it anyway—it might work for some offline transactions.

Some credit unions are beginning to roll out true chip-and-PIN cards that work for nearly all transactions, online or offline. One no-fee card is the GlobeTrek Visa, offered by Andrews Federal Credit Union in Maryland (open to all US residents, see andrewsfcu.org). Another is the EMV Visa Platinum Card offered by the State Department Federal Credit Union in Washington, DC (sdfcu.org).

Slowly the US is making the transition to chip-and-signature cards. Visa and MasterCard have asked US banks and merchants to use chip-based cards by late 2015; those who don't make the switch may have to assume the liability for fraud. Experts estimate up to 50 percent of US cards will have a chip by the beginning of 2016. When your bank next renews your credit card, it's likely there will be a chip in it.

Bank Card Security
As with preventing other kinds of theft, the key to averting fraud is to protect your personal information.

Protect your credit and debit cards. Take to Europe only the credit and debit cards that you expect to use, plus a backup, and keep them safely in your money belt. Upon returning home, verify the balance and charges on your debit and credit cards. Some travelers monitor balances as they travel, though accessing a financial account online can be risky (see page 259). For tips on money belts and foiling pickpockets, see page 328.

Safeguard your PIN code. Memorize your personal identification number; you'd be surprised how many people foolishly write it on their card. "Shoulder surfing"—a thief watching you as you type your PIN into a keypad—is a common problem. When entering your PIN, carefully block other people's view of the keypad, covering it with your free hand.

Use your debit card only at ATMs. Because a debit card pulls funds directly out of your bank account, potential charges incurred by a thief are scary—it's *your* money that's gone, and it will stay gone until the fraudulent use is investigated by your bank. For that reason, I use my debit card only for cash-machine withdrawals. To make purchases, I pay with cash or a credit card.

What to do if your card is lost or stolen. Report it immediately by making a collect call to your credit-card company (see the sidebar on page 339 for details), as your liability is linked to timely reporting. You'll likely be on the hook for only $50, but it's still worrisome. If you're concerned about this, talk to your bank about setting a daily withdrawal limit for your ATM or debit card; you'll have to weigh the convenience of withdrawing large amounts of euros from your accounts...against the risk of a crook doing the same. Note that this limit applies to cash-machine withdrawals, not purchases.

TIPPING

Tipping in Europe isn't as automatic and generous as it is in the United States, but in many countries, tips are appreciated, though not expected. As in the US, the proper amount depends on your resources, tipping philosophy, and the circumstances. That said, there are big tippers and there are misers the world over. Tipping varies by country, but some general guidelines apply.

At restaurants, check the menu to see if service is included; if it isn't, a tip of 5-10 percent is normal (for more on tipping at restaurants, see page 368). For taxis, round up the fare (see page 270). At hotels with porters, pay the porter a euro for each bag he carries; it's nice (but not required) to leave a small tip in your room for the housekeeping staff when you depart.

Tipping for special service is optional. Guides who give talks at public sights or on bus or boat tours often hold out their hands for tips after they give their spiel. If I've already paid for the tour or admission to the sight, I don't tip extra (but if you want to tip, a euro or two is enough for a job well done). In general, if someone in the service industry does a super job for you, a tip of a couple of euros is appropriate...but not required.

When in doubt, ask. The French and British generally tip hairdressers, the Dutch and Swedish usually don't. If you're not sure whether (or how much) to tip for a service, ask your hotelier or the tourist information office; they'll fill you in on how it's done on their turf.

Sleeping

Europe offers a wide range of accommodations: hotels (from small to large, and simple to swanky), cozy B&Bs, characteristic guesthouses, cheap hostels, and rental apartments, plus creative accommodations such as monasteries, campgrounds, free couches, and house-swaps. There's certain to be a perfect home-away-from-home for you. First we'll cover the basics of choosing and reserving a room. Then we'll take a spin through the various types of lodging.

FINDING THE RIGHT ROOM

Whether you're booking accommodations for your entire trip months in advance, or rolling into town after dark and finding a room on the fly, these tips will help you choose what's best for you and your budget.

Independent Traveler Seeks Good-Value Accommodations

People often ask me how I choose which hotels to list in my guidebooks. There's no secret trick to it: I walk through the most inviting neighborhood in town, snoop around each hotel and grab their price lists, and jot down some notes. By the end of the day, the best-value hotels stand out. What's striking to me is how little correlation there is between what you pay and what you get. I recently spent a day in Amsterdam, scaling the stairs and checking out the rooms of 20 different hotels, all offering double rooms for $100-230 a night. What I found is that you are just as likely to spend $150 for a big, impersonal place on a noisy highway as you are to spend $100 for a charming, family-run guesthouse on a bikes-only stretch of canal.

I look for places that are clean, central, relatively quiet at night, reasonably priced, friendly, small enough to have a hands-on owner and stable staff, run with a respect for local traditions, and not listed in other guidebooks. Obviously, meeting every criterion is rare, and many hotels fall short of perfection—sometimes miserably. But if I can find a place with, say, six of these eight criteria, it's a keeper. I'm more impressed by a convenient location and a fun-loving philosophy than flat-screen TVs and a pricey laundry service.

My favorite type of European hotel: well-located, small, friendly, charming, and moderately priced.

It pays to choose your accommodations thoughtfully. Expensive hotels can rip through a tight budget like a grenade through a dollhouse. I hear people complaining about that "$300 double in Frankfurt" or the "$400-a-night room in London." They come back from their vacations with bruised and battered pocketbooks, telling stories that scare their friends out of international travel and back to Florida or Hawaii one more time. True, you can spend $400 for a double, but I never have. That's three days' accommodations for me.

As far as I'm concerned, spending more for your hotel just builds a bigger wall between you and what you traveled so far to see. If you spend enough, you won't know where you are. Think about it. "In-ter-con-ti-nen-tal." That means the same everywhere—designed for people who deep-down inside wish they weren't traveling, people spending someone else's money, people who need a strip of paper over the toilet promising them no one's sat there yet. It's uniform sterility, a lobby full of stay-press Americans, English menus, and lamps bolted to tables.

Europe's small, midrange hotels may not have room service, but their staffs are more interested in seeing pictures of your children and helping you have a great time than in thinning out your wallet.

Budget Tips

The majority of Americans traveling in Europe want to sleep in moderately priced hotels. Most of the accommodations I recommend in my guidebooks fall into this category. Keep these things in mind when searching for a good-value hotel that suits your budget:

Comparison-shop. It's smart to email several hotels

to ask for their best price. This is especially helpful when dealing with the larger hotels that use "dynamic pricing," a computer-generated system that predicts demand for particular days and sets prices accordingly: High-demand days will often be more than double the price of low-demand days. Compare their offers and make your choice.

Book directly with the hotel. Skip the middleman, such as a hotel-booking website or the tourist information office's room-finding service. Booking services extract a commission from the hotel, which logically closes the door on special deals. If you book directly with the hotel, it doesn't have to pay a cut to that intermediary. This might make the hotelier more open to giving you a deal. For tips on getting the best deals online, see page 208.

Try to wrangle a discount for a longer stay or payment in cash. If you plan to stay three or more nights at a place, or if you pay in cash rather than by credit card (saving the hotelier the credit-card company's fee), it's worth asking if a discount is available.

If it's off-season, bargain. Prices usually rise with demand during festivals and in July and August. Off-season, try haggling. If the place is too expensive, tell them your limit; they might meet it. Or consider arriving without a reservation and dropping in at the last minute to try to score a deal.

Think small. Larger hotels are usually pricier than small hotels or B&Bs, partly because of taxes (for example, in Britain, once a B&B exceeds a certain revenue level, it's required to pay an extra 20 percent tax to the government). Hoteliers who pay high taxes pass their costs on to you.

Know the exceptions. Hotels in northern Europe are pricier than those in the south, but you can find exceptions. In Scandinavia, Brussels, and Berlin, fancy "business hotels" are desperate for customers in the summer and year-round on weekends, when their business customers stay away. Some offer amazing deals through the local tourist information offices. The later your arrival, the better the discount.

Don't consume above your needs. Know the government ratings. A three-star hotel is not necessarily a bad value, but if I stay in a three-star hotel, I've spent $60 extra for things I don't need. Amenities such as

Europe's cheap, no-character hotels cater to local business travelers interested in going home with some of their per diem still in their pockets.

air-conditioning, elevators, private showers, room service, a 24-hour reception desk, and people in uniforms each add $10 apiece to your room cost. Before you know it, the simple $90 room is up to $150. Then, additional charges can pile on top of this already inflated room rate. For example, most moderately priced hotels offer Wi-Fi free to their guests, while the expensive places are more likely to charge for it.

Check the prices on the room list, and figure out how to get the best-value rooms. Room prices can vary tremendously within a hotel according to facilities provided. On their websites (and near their reception desks), most places post a room summary that lists each room, its bed configuration, facilities, and maximum price (for one and for two people), sometimes broken down by season (low, middle, high). Also read the breakfast, tax, and extra-bed policies. By studying this information, you'll see that, in many places, a shower costs less than a bath, and a double bed is cheaper than twins. In other words, an inattentive couple who would have been just as happy with a shower and a double bed can end up paying more for an unneeded tub and twins. If you want a cheap room, say so. Many hoteliers have a few unrenovated rooms without a private bathroom; they usually don't even mention these, figuring they'd be unacceptable to Americans.

Put more people in a room. Family rooms are common, and putting four in a quad is much cheaper than two doubles. Many doubles come with a small double bed and a sliver of a single, so a third person pays very little.

Avoid doing outside business through your hotel. Go to the flamenco show and get the ticket yourself. You'll learn more, save money, and be more likely to sit with locals than with a bunch of tourists. So often, tourists are herded together—by a conspiracy of hotel managers and tour organizers—at gimmicky folk evenings featuring a medley of cheesy cultural clichés kept alive only for the tourists. You can't relive your precious nights in Sevilla. Do them right—on your own.

Avoid hotels that require you to buy meals. Many national governments regulate hotel prices according to class or rating. In order to overcome this price ceiling (especially at resorts in peak season, when demand exceeds supply), hotels might require you to buy dinner—or your choice of lunch or dinner—in their dining room. It's generally called "half-board," "half-pension," or *demi-pension*. While this might not be expensive, I prefer the freedom to explore and sample the atmosphere of restaurants in other neighborhoods. Breakfast is often included in the room rate, but in some countries it's an expensive, semi-optional tack-on. If you want to opt out of a pricey hotel breakfast, ask if it's possible when you book the room.

RESERVING A ROOM

I used to travel with absolutely no reservations. A daily chore was checking out several hotels or pensions and choosing one. Europe was ramshackle, things were cheap, and hotel listings were unreliable and unnecessary. Now, like hobos in a *Jetsons* world, budget travelers need to think one step ahead.

To Reserve or Not to Reserve?

Every Europe-bound traveler has to make a decision: Am I willing to sacrifice spontaneity for the comfort of knowing exactly where I'll sleep each night? Decide which of the following scenarios best suits your style.

Want maximum choice and peace of mind? Book far in advance. Most travelers find that it's worth booking ahead to get into the most popular, best-value hotels. In fact, lately I've been getting aced out by my own readers at my favorite accommodations. So when I want to be certain to get my first choice, I reserve several weeks (or even months) in advance. For peak-season travel, on national holidays, during big festivals, and when visiting big, popular cities (such as London, Paris, Madrid, Venice, and so on), I make my reservations as soon as I can pin down a date. (To check holiday and festival dates, go to ricksteves.com/festivals.)

Happy with a mix of predictability and flexibility? Call ahead as you travel. If you don't want to book everything far in advance, but also don't want to simply show up without a room, calling a day or two ahead while on the road can be a good compromise. This works best when there's relatively little demand for rooms (in shoulder or off-season, or in less-crowded places). In these situations, my standard room-finding tactic is to telephone in the morning to reserve my room for that night. I travel relaxed, knowing a good place is holding a room for me.

Family-run hotels offer the warmest welcome and the best value.

Prefer maximum spontaneity? Find rooms as you travel. There's nothing more liberating than choosing which town to visit only when you step onto the rail platform, or veering off course from your itinerary just to get away from the clouds or crowds. But doing this makes it less likely you'll find a room that matches your budget and priorities. Even those who generally skip reservations should at least reserve their arrival night in Europe (as jet-lagged room-finding can be stressful). Several tips for this strategy are explained later, under "Reserving Rooms as You Travel."

Making Reservations

If you decide to reserve rooms in advance, here are the basics.

Requesting a Reservation

It's usually easiest to book your room through the hotel's website. Many have a reservation-request form built right in. (For the best rates, always use the hotel's official site and not a booking agency's site.) If there's no reservation form, or for complicated requests, send an email (see next page for a sample request). Most hotels are accustomed to guests who speak only English. The hotelier wants to know:
- the number and type of rooms you need
- the number of nights you'll stay
- your date of arrival (use the European style for writing dates: day/month/year)
- your date of departure
- any special needs (twin beds vs. double bed, crib, bathroom in the room vs. down the hall, air-conditioning, quiet, view, ground floor or no stairs, and so on)

Make sure you mention any discounts—for Rick Steves readers or otherwise—when you make the reservation.

Confirming a Reservation

Most places will request a credit-card number to hold your room. While you can email it (I do), it's safer to share that confidential info via a phone call, two emails (splitting your number between them), or the hotel's secure online reservation form. On the small chance that a hotel loses track of your reservation, bring along a printed copy of their confirmation.

When making reservations, communicate your needs clearly to your hotelier.

Sample Room Request

From: rick@ricksteves.com
Sent: Today
To: info@hotelcentral.com
Subject: Reservation request for 19-22 July

Dear Hotel Central,

I would like to reserve a room for 2 people for 3 nights, arriving 19 July and departing 22 July. If possible, I would like a quiet room with a double bed and private bathroom.

Please let me know if you have a room available and the price.

Thank you!
Rick Steves

Small B&Bs, which often don't accept credit cards, may not require a deposit; however, in places where no-shows are epidemic, some B&B owners request that you put money down to hold a room (it's becoming easier to do this, thanks to PayPal). Especially during slow times, some establishments will hold a room without a deposit if you promise to arrive early in the day. The earlier you arrive, the better your chances of a room being held for you. If you end up running a little late, call again to assure the owners that you're coming.

Canceling a Reservation

If you must cancel your reservation, it's courteous—and smart—to do so with as much notice as possible, especially for smaller family-run places. Request confirmation of your cancellation in case you are accidentally billed.

Be warned that cancellation policies can be strict; read the fine print or ask about these before you book. For example, if you cancel on short notice, you could lose your deposit, or be billed for one night or even your entire stay. Internet deals may require prepayment, with no refunds for cancellations.

Reconfirming a Reservation

Always call to reconfirm your room reservation a few days in advance. This gives you time to improvise in the unlikely event that something has gone wrong with your reservation. For smaller hotels and B&Bs (which may not have a 24-hour reception desk), I call again on my day of arrival to tell my host what time I expect to get there; this is especially important to do when arriving late (after 5 p.m.).

Reserving Rooms as You Travel

While most travelers prefer to nail down room reservations long in advance, you can blow like the wind freely through Europe if you want, finding beds on the fly.

Your approach to room-finding will be determined by whether it's a "buyer's market" or a "seller's market"—based on the current demand. These trends can be obvious (a beach resort will be crowded in summer, empty in winter); in other cases, a guidebook or local tourist information office can tip you off. Sometimes you can arrive late, be selective, and even talk down the price. Other times you'll happily accept anything with a pillow and a blanket.

These tricks work for me:

Travel with a good list of hotels. Even the most footloose and fancy-free traveler shouldn't totally wing it. Bring along a good guidebook so you at least have a sense of your options (and the general price range in town) when you begin your search.

The early bird gets the room. When you anticipate crowds (weekends are worst) on the day you want to check in, call or arrive at the hotel at about 9 or 10 a.m., when the receptionist knows who'll be checking out and which rooms will be available. For instance, I would leave Florence at 7 a.m. to arrive in popular, crowded Venice early enough to get a decent choice of rooms. If the rooms aren't ready until noon, take one anyway. Leave your luggage behind the desk; you can relax and enjoy the city, then move in later. Consider the advantage of overnight train rides—you'll arrive, if not bright, at least early.

Shop around. When going door-to-door, the first place you check is rarely the best. It's worth 20 minutes of shopping around to find the going rate before you accept a room. You'll be surprised how prices vary as you walk farther from the station or down a street strewn with B&Bs. Never judge a hotel by its exterior or lobby. Lavish interiors with shabby exteriors are a cultural trait of Europe (blame the landlord who's stuck with rent control and therefore doesn't invest in fixing it up, not the hotel). If you're traveling with a companion, one of you can watch the bags over a cup of coffee while the other runs around.

Ask to see the room before accepting. Then the receptionist knows the room must pass your inspection. He'll have

LEFT Private rooms are often the best deal going.

RIGHT Ask your friend who runs today's hotel to call tomorrow's hotel to make you a reservation in the native language.

to earn your business. Notice the bellhop is given two keys. You asked for only one room. He's instructed to show the room that's harder to rent first. It's only natural for the hotel receptionist to try to unload the most difficult-to-sell room on the easiest-to-please traveler. Somebody has to sleep in it. If you ask to see both rooms, you'll get the better one. When you check out a room, point out anything that deserves displeasure. The price may come down, or they may show you a better room. Think about heat and noise. Some towns never quiet down. I'll climb a few stairs to reach cheaper rooms higher off the noisy road. A room in back may lack a view, but at least you'll sleep in peace.

Consider hotel runners. As you step off the bus or train, you'll sometimes be met by hotel and B&B runners wielding pictures of their rooms for rent. My gut reaction is to steer clear, but these people are usually just hardworking entrepreneurs who lack the location or write-up in a popular guidebook that can make life easy for a small hotel or B&B owner. If you like the guy and what he promises, and his rooms aren't too far away, follow him to take a look. You are obliged only to inspect the room. If it's good, take it. If it's not, leave. You're probably near other budget accommodations anyway. Before setting out, establish the location very clearly, as some of these people have good places located miserably far out of town. Especially in Eastern Europe, room hawkers might not be affiliated with a hotel at all; they're simply renting out vacant rooms in their own homes. If nothing else, taking the room for a night is an easy way to buy more time to seek out an even better option for the remainder of your stay.

Use room-finding services only if necessary. Popular tourist cities usually have a room-finding service at the train station or tourist information office. They have a listing of that town's "acceptable" available accommodations. For a fee of a few dollars, they'll get you a room in the price range and neighborhood of your choice. Especially in a big city, the service can be worth the price to avoid the search on foot.

But I generally avoid room-finding services unless I have no listings or information of my own. Their hotel lists normally make no judgments about quality, so what you get is potluck. The stakes are too high for this to be acceptable. (Remember the exception: In certain northern European cities—such as Brussels and some Scandinavian capitals—room-booking services can sometimes land you a deeply discounted room in an upscale business-class hotel.)

Since most room-finding services profit from taking a "deposit" that they pocket, hotel managers may tell the room-finding service they're full when they aren't. These places know they'll fill up with travelers who book direct, allowing the hotelier to keep 100 percent of the room cost.

In recent years, many tourist information offices have lost their government funding and are now privately owned. This creates the absurdity of a profit-seeking tourist information "service." Their previously reliable advice is now colored with a need to make a kickback. Some room-finding services work for a group of supporting hotels. Only if you insist will you get information on cheap sleeping options such as dormitories or hostels. And beware: Many offices labeled "tourist information" are just travel agencies and room-booking services in disguise.

Follow taxi tips. A great way to find a place in a tough situation is to let a cabbie take you to his favorite hotel. They are experts.

Let hotel managers help. Have your current hotelier call ahead to make a reservation at your next destination. If you're in a town and having trouble finding a room, remember that nobody knows the hotel scene better than hotel managers do. If one place doesn't have a vacant room, the manager often has a list of neighborhood accommodations or will even telephone a friend's place around the corner. If the hotel is too expensive, there's nothing wrong with asking where you can find a budget place. The priciest hotels have the best city maps (free, often with other hotels listed) and an English-speaking staff who can give advice to the polite traveler in search of a cheap room. I find hotel receptionists to be understanding and helpful.

Leave the trouble zone. If the room situation is impossible, don't struggle—just leave. An hour by car, train, or bus from the most miserable hotel situation anywhere in Europe is a town—Dullsdorf or Nothingston—with the Dullsdorf Gasthaus or the Nothingston Inn just across the street from the station or right on the main square. It's not full—never has been, never will be. There's a guy sleeping behind the reception desk. Drop in at 11 p.m., ask for 14 beds, and he'll say, "Take the second and third floors—the keys are in the doors." It always works. Oktoberfest, Cannes Film Festival, St-Tropez Running of the Girls, Easter at Lourdes—your bed awaits in nearby Dullsdorf. If you anticipate trouble finding a room, consider staying at the last train stop before the crowded city.

HOTELS

I normally stay in a hotel. But rather than the predictable cookie-cutter comfort of a modern chain hotel, I prefer a small, independently owned hotel in the center of town. Perhaps the single most important factor for me in selecting a hotel   assuming it's in my price range—is location. I also count on character. Part of the fun of travel is enjoying a friendly and characteristic hotel in an exciting destination.

Room Types and Costs

Most European hotels have lots of doubles and a few singles, triples, and quads. Traveling alone can be expensive, especially when staying in older hotels, where singles (except for the rare closet-type room that fits only one twin bed) are simply doubles used by one person—so they cost about the same as a double. Most hotels offer family deals, which means that parents with young children can easily get a room with an extra child's bed or a discount for larger rooms. Teenagers are generally charged as adults, while kids under age five sleep almost free. Hotels cannot legally allow more people in the room than are shown on their price list. Hotels often charge a daily room tax of about €1-4 per person per night. Some hotels include it in the price list, but most add it to your bill.

Room prices vary within each hotel depending on size and whether the room has a tub or a shower, and twin beds or a double bed. A room with a bathtub costs €10-15 more than a room with a shower and is generally larger. Hotels are inclined to give you a room with a tub because they often have more rooms with tubs than with showers; be sure to specify if you have a preference.

A room with a European double bed (which is smaller than an American queen) is usually cheaper than one with twins, though twin rooms tend to be larger. If you want any room for two but you say "double," they'll think you'll only take a double bed. To keep all my options open (twin and double), I ask for "a room for two people." On the other hand, it can also help to specify "one big bed for two people" if you want the cost benefit of a double bed. (Most hoteliers understand "double bed" in English, but here's some local lingo: *französische Liege* in German, *un lit de cent-soixante* in French, *matrimoniale* in Italian, and *matrimonial* in Spanish). At many hotels—especially in the north and in Eastern Europe—a "double bed" is two twin beds pushed together, sometimes sheeted as one big bed.

A triple comes with a double or queen-size bed plus a sliver-sized single (or sometimes with three singles). Quad rooms usually have two double beds.

Breakfast: Hotels generally offer some kind of breakfast, usually served from about 7:30 to 10 a.m. in the breakfast room near the front desk. Continental breakfast is usually coffee, tea, or hot chocolate and a roll that's firmer than your mattress. Breakfasts in Eastern Europe and northern countries can be a bit heartier, with fruit, yogurt, cereal, and more. (For details, see page 371.) Breakfast may or may not be included in room rates: Pay attention when comparing prices between hotels. This per-person charge can add up, particularly for families. While hotels hope you'll buy their breakfast, it's optional unless otherwise noted; to save money, head to a nearby bakery or café instead.

Budget Hotels: What's a Cheap Room?

Europe has many inexpensive accommodations, ranging from traditional old hotels to unremarkable chains. Older places can be dingy and a bit run-down, but they're usually central, friendly, safe, and government-regulated, offering good-enough-for-the-European, good-enough-for-me beds. Chain hotels can make up for a lack of character with good prices and convenient locations. In a typical budget European hotel, a double room costs an average of $110 a night. You'll pay about $80 at a pension in Madrid, $100 at a simple guesthouse in rural Germany or a B&B on the Croatian coast, and $150 for a two-star hotel in Paris or a private room in a Bergen pension. This is hard-core Europe:

fun, cheap, and easy to find, particularly in Italy, France, Spain, Portugal, and Greece.

A typical room in an old-fashioned, low-end hotel has a simple bed; a rickety, old, wooden (or new, plastic) chair and table; a freestanding closet; a small window; old wallpaper; a good sink under a fluorescent light; a mysterious bidet; a view of another similar room across a tall, thin interior courtyard; peeling plaster; and a tiled or wood floor. The light fixtures are very simple, often with a weak ceiling light. Naked fluorescent is common in the south. You might have a TV, but likely not a telephone. While more and more European hotels are squeezing boat-type prefab showers and toilets into their rooms, the cheapest places still offer only a toilet and shower or tub down the hall, which you share with a handful of other rooms.

You'll climb lots of stairs, as a hotel's lack of an elevator is often the only reason it can't raise its prices. You'll be given a front-door key because the desk is not staffed all night. If the hotel is located on the higher floors of a multipurpose building, press the button with your hotel's name by the main entrance to ring the bell, and you'll be buzzed in.

This type of cheap hotel usually has clean-enough but depressing shower rooms, with hot water normally free and constant (but, in very rare cases, available only through a coin-op meter or at certain hours). The WC has toilet paper, but might have a missing, cracked, or broken lid. At a few hotels, you might be charged $3-5 for a towel and a key to the shower room. The cheapest hotels are run by and filled with people from the Two-Thirds World.

I want to stress that there are places I find unacceptable. I don't mind dingy wallpaper, stairs, and a bathroom down the hall, but I won't compromise when it comes to safety and being able to get a decent night's sleep.

A typical budget hotel room: tidy, small, affordable

The hotel I'm describing may be appalling to many Americans; to others, it's charming, colorful, or funky. To me, "funky" means spirited and full of character(s): a caged bird in the TV room, grandchildren in the backyard, a dog sleeping in the hall, no uniforms, singing maids, a night-shift man tearing breakfast napkins in two so they'll go further, a hand-written neighborhood history lesson on the wall, different furniture in each room, and a willingness to buck the system when the tourist board starts requiring shoeshine machines in the hallways. An extra $40-50 per night will buy you into cheerier wallpaper and less funkiness.

Unfortunately, older, traditional hotels are becoming an endangered species. As Europe becomes more affluent, land in big cities is becoming so expensive that cheap hotels can't survive and are being bought out, gutted, and turned into modern hotels. More and more Europeans are expecting what were once considered "American" standards of plumbing and comfort. A great value is often a hardworking family-run place that structurally can't fit showers in every room or an elevator up its spiral staircase. Prices are regulated, and regardless of how comfy and charming it is, with no elevator and a lousy shower-to-room ratio, it is—and will remain—a cheap hotel.

1977: It slowly dawns on Rick that cheap beds aren't always good beds.

Finding a Hotel

Your hotel, and the neighborhood it inhabits, can color your travel experience. Landing in the right place merits a little research.

Guidebooks

A trusted guidebook remains the best place to start your search for a great hotel. Professional guidebook writers take their jobs seriously, offering detailed hotel reviews and their best advice on the sleeping scene. Find and use a guidebook whose travel philosophy matches yours. (For a rundown of various guidebooks, see page 31.) Get the most current edition possible—but even with the newest editions, don't be surprised if rates have increased slightly since the book was published.

Hotel Websites

If a guidebook's write-up of a particular hotel appeals to you, visit the hotel website to glean additional information, check prices, and view photos of the rooms. Some hotels (especially chain or business hotels) offer discounts only if you book on their website. Here are some tips for getting the best deal online: Midweek prices are generally higher than weekend rates, and Sunday nights can be surprisingly cheap. The rates for a particular room for a specific date can change from day to day or week to week (like airline tickets), making it difficult to know when to book. On the hotel's online reservation form, punch in the dates you're considering to see what the going rate is. Look for special offers. For the best deals, book at least three weeks in advance, prepay in full, and hope you don't have to change your plans (since promotional rates are often nonrefundable).

Hotel-Booking Websites

Big hotel-booking websites (see sidebar) can provide a wealth of information about the types of hotels available and the range of prices. But what you won't easily find on these sites are links to individual hotels—that's because the big guys want you to book through them (or their partners) for a fee. Using a booking service costs the hotel about 20 percent and logically closes the door on special deals. Instead, once you've identified a promising option, do a Google search to find the hotel's own website. You'll get more complete information, and you may save money by booking direct.

Other Online Sources

Sites such as Mobissimo.com and Hotelscombined.com compile prices from travel agencies, consolidators, and hotel websites. (If you find a deal you like, still go to the hotel's website to book a room.) If your travel dates are flexible, consider the deep discounts available on sites such as Priceline, EuroCheapo, and RatesToGo. Also consider the "air plus hotel" packages described on page 97.

Traveler Reviews

User-generated travel review websites—such as TripAdvisor, Booking.com, and Yelp—have quickly become huge players in the travel industry. These days, few travelers plan a trip without consulting online reviews. And I use them, too. But—as with any source of information—it's important to be an informed consumer.

The primary advantage of review sites is that you can

Resources for Booking Hotels

Yelp.com and **TripAdvisor.com:** Travelers' hotel reviews

Expedia.com, Booking.com, and **Venere.com:** Hotel-booking websites good for initial research (it's best to book directly with hotel)

Mobissimo.com, Hotelscombined.com, and **Kayak.com:** Search engines that check multiple hotel sites so you can compare rates

Bidroom.com: Hotels bid on your specs to give you the best price

Priceline.com, Eurocheapo.com, and **Ratestogo.com:** Deep discounts for flexible travelers

Apps

Hotel Tonight and **Blink:** Last-minute hotel deals in major cities

Modern Chains: Good Value, Less Character

Hotel chains may lack personality, but provide predictable comfort and can be a good choice for families who need triple or quad rooms. Here are some options.

Hotel Chain	Description	Website
Hotel F1	Cheap, mostly in France	hotel1.com
Ibis Hotels	Sterile rooms throughout Europe	ibishotel.com
easyHotel	Economical, basic lodging in major cities	easyhotel.com
Holiday Inn	Family hotels throughout Europe	ihg.com
Mercure Hotels	Cushier but pricier, all over Europe	mercure.com
Novotel Hotels	250 business-class hotels across Europe	novotel.com
Travelodge	Accommodations in Ireland and the UK	travelodge.co.uk
Premier Inn	650 hotels in UK and Ireland	premierinn.com
Jurys Inn	Locations in Britain and Ireland	jurysinns.com

get actual reports—good and bad—from travelers who have experienced the hotel, restaurant, tour, or attraction. Instead of trusting the business' own information, or the advice of one travel writer, you get a broader base of opinion. If you scan reviews of a hotel and see several complaints about noise or a rotten location, it tells you something important that you'd never learn from the hotel's own website.

My hotelier friends in Europe are in awe of how influential these sites have become. If you run a small hotel and want to stay in business, you have no choice but to work with review sites. While these sites offer a convenient way to reach potential customers, some charge dearly for that service (for example, by charging for good placement and photos). And users who check reviews, then click through to book a room, are redirected to a booking agency that charges a hefty commission, which is passed along to the guest.

While these sites work hard to weed out bogus users, my hunch is that a significant percentage of user reviews are posted by friends or enemies of the business being reviewed. (To increase your odds of getting accurate reports, consider the site's screening process. For example, to review a hotel on TripAdvisor, you just need an email address; on Booking.com, you must have actually stayed there. Perhaps not coincidentally, I've found Booking.com's rankings more reliable than TripAdvisor's.)

Reviews can be skewed in other ways, too. A charming host can garner good reviews from appreciative guests who overlook other, substantial flaws. I find more and more small hotels offering a free breakfast to people who promise to write kindly about them on TripAdvisor. Conversely, several hoteliers have told me that occasionally guests threaten them with a bad review unless the hotel gives them a big discount.

Review sites can become an echo chamber, where one or two well-located, flashy businesses camp out atop the ratings. Travelers use it, like it, and rave about it, creating a self-perpetuating cycle of positive reviews. Meanwhile, a better, more affordable, and more authentic alternative may sit ignored, tucked down a side street. Perhaps for this reason, I find review sites' restaurant recommendations skew to very touristy, obvious options. Try this experiment: Check the TripAdvisor rankings for your hometown restaurants. In my town, the top-ranked places are pretty evenly split between tourist traps and legitimately great eateries.

Review sites are only as good as the judgment of their reviewers. And someone reviewing a hotel can't judge it on a curve because, in most cases, they've only experienced that one hotel in that town. When updating my guidebooks, I spend hours each day personally visiting dozens of hotels. Only through that legwork can I be confident that I've narrowed down all of the well-run places in town to the handful that are the best values for my readers. Curious, I recently checked out some top-rated TripAdvisor listings in various towns, when stacked up against their competitors, some are gems, while just as many are duds. I've also seen fine-value small hotels that score low on TripAdvisor, presumably because they haven't been reviewed as often.

Don't get me wrong: Review sites can be an invaluable tool for planning a trip. I see them as a perfect complement to a thoughtfully updated guidebook. If a hotel or restaurant is well reviewed in a guidebook or two, and also gets good ratings on one of these sites, it's likely a winner.

Hotel Tips

This section covers what you can expect—and what may be unexpected—when it comes to European hotels. Many of these tips also apply to the other types of accommodations described later in this chapter.

Check-In

When you check in at a hotel, with or without an advance reservation, establish the complete and final price of your room. Know what's included and what taxes and other charges (breakfast, extra fee for air-conditioning) will be added. More than once, when checking out, I've been given a bill that was double what I expected. Dinners were required, and I was billed whether I ate them or not, or so I was told—in very clear Italian.

At check-in, hotels may take your passport for the night so they can register you with the police. This is normal. Hotels throughout Europe must do this paperwork for foreign guests, and busy receptionists like to gather passports and register them all at the same time when things are quiet. Although it's unreasonable to expect a receptionist to drop whatever he or she is doing to register me immediately, I politely ask if I can pick up my passport in two hours. I just don't like having my passport in the hotel lobby's top drawer all night long.

Reconfirm how long you intend to stay when you check in. If you think you may want to stay a night or two longer than your initial reservation, discuss it with the receptionist up front. Don't assume your room is yours indefinitely once you're in.

Your Room

In a typical room, you'll find a TV and phone, and—increasingly—Wi-Fi (ask for the Wi-Fi password and network name at the desk when you check in). To turn on your TV, press the channel-up or channel-down button on the remote. If it still doesn't work, see if there's a power button on the TV itself, then press the up or down button again.

As Europe gets hotter, more hotels are offering rooms with air-conditioning. (But be aware that regulations may prohibit turning on the air-conditioning between October and May.) Most A/C units come with a remote control, similar to one for a TV. The various remotes have basically the

LEFT An A/C remote lets you cool off the room without even getting out of bed.

RIGHT French hotels sometimes come with Lincoln Log pillows.

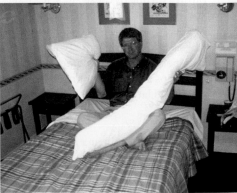

same features, including. a fan icon (click to toggle through wind power), louver icon (click for steady air flow or waves), sunshine and snowflake icons (generally just cold or hot is possible: cool in summer, heat in winter), two clock settings (to determine how many hours the air-conditioning will stay on before turning off, or stay off before turning on), and temperature control (20 degrees Celsius is comfortable).

Be prepared for regional differences in bedding. In France, some hotel beds have irregular pillows (shaped like a wedge or a log). To get an American-style pillow or extra blankets, look in the closet or ask at the desk. In alpine countries and in northern Europe, many hotels use covered duvets instead of a top sheet; don't be confused if your top sheet is "missing."

For details on hotel-room bathrooms, see page 397.

Hotel Help

In the lobby, there's nearly always a lounge with a TV, a phone, a guest computer, and a clerk at the desk who can be a great help and source of advice. Hotels are in the business of accommodating people. If you need another blanket or an electrical adapter, just ask.

Hoteliers know their city well, and can point you to the nearest tourist office, launderette, grocery store, restaurant, or show. They'll call a taxi for you, make restaurant reservations, telephone your next hotel, or give you driving instructions for your departure.

Pick up the hotel's business card. In the most confusing cities, the cards come with a little map. Even the best pathfinders can get lost in a big city, and not knowing where your hotel is can be scary. With the card, you can hop into a cab and be home in minutes. Most hotels give out free city maps.

Many hoteliers can book bus tours for you (though they usually get a commission, so they might be biased in their recommendation). In Florence, hoteliers can make museum reservations for the Uffizi Gallery and for Michelangelo's *David*; ask when you book your room. If you arrive in town early or need to leave late, any good hotel will store your bag for you (without charge) while you sightsee.

Hotel Hassles

Even at the best hotel, things can go awry. You may be on your dream trip, but you're still in the real world. Take a deep breath, and remember that things go wrong at home, too. If you state your concern to your hotelier politely, you'll more likely be dealt with kindly.

When you enter a hotel room for the first time, survey it for problems. Is the bathroom dirty and moldy? Is the window latch broken and unsafe? Are you next to a noisy elevator? Is the room too small? If the room you're shown doesn't meet your standards, ask to see a different one. It's easier to change rooms before you've settled in.

It can be disappointing to arrive at a hotel and find that your room is in a less desirable annex or in a partner hotel. If you feel the hotel has misrepresented its offer, it can help (though it's not essential) to show them a copy of their confirmation email. You don't need to stay.

Just as it happens at your house, hotels experience mechanical breakdowns. Sinks get clogged, hot water turns cold, toilets gurgle and smell. The air-conditioning dies when you need it most. The Wi-Fi doesn't work. The elevator refuses to budge. Report your concerns calmly at the front desk. For more complicated problems, don't expect instant results. In the rare case that something is stolen from your room, report your loss to the hotelier (see page 329 for tips on safeguarding your hotel-room belongings).

Occasionally travelers encounter bedbugs—tiny blood-sucking insects that live in bedding and come out at night. To avoid infestation, check mattress seams for specks of blood before you unpack—or your first sign of trouble will be mysterious, itchy welts (similar to mosquito bites) on your legs and arms. These critters are

The 🔑 to Keys

Tourists spend hours fumbling with old skeleton keys in rickety hotel doors. The haphazard, nothing-square construction of old hotels means the keys need babying: Don't push them in all the way. Lift the door in or up. Try a little in, quarter turn, and farther in for full turn. Always turn the top of the key away from the door frame to open it. Some locks take two key revolutions to open.

Leave the key at the desk before heading out for the day, but confirm when reception closes. Some hotels lock up after their restaurant closes, after midnight, or during their weekly "quiet day" and expect you to keep the key to the outside door with you to get in after hours.

Plastic key cards (the size of a credit card) are becoming standard at many European hotels. If there's no slot to insert the card into, try simply touching the card to your door's keypad. Once inside the room, you may have to insert your card into a slot near the door to turn on the lights. This green measure is intended to prevent potentially energy-wasting guests from leaving the lights on when they're not in the room.

a nuisance, but they don't spread disease. Bedbugs can show up even at fine hotels, brought in by the last guest. Don't automatically assume that the hotel is overrun with them. Report the problem, and see how it's dealt with. Changing rooms should be enough.

Mosquitoes can also be pests. In warm climates, make sure there's a window screen; if there isn't, think twice about leaving your window open all day for ventilation. Insect repellent can help. Warning: If you leave your window open and forget to close it when darkness falls, the light of your room can attract a vast swarm of bugs.

Europe seems to excel in thin-walled rooms, narrow streets that amplify traffic noise, and people who party until the wee hours in formerly romantic piazzas. I always consider these problems before settling into a room. If you suspect night noise will be a problem, ask for a room in the back or on an upper floor. Some travelers customarily ask for a quiet room when they book or reconfirm their reservation; if you wait to ask until you arrive, the quietest rooms might already be occupied. On the other hand, if you'd happily put up with some street noise to look out onto a square, be sure to ask for a view (which might cost extra). If you're a light sleeper, skip the view (and bring earplugs, too).

"Too many stairs!" is a common complaint. In general, European hotels have more stairs and fewer elevators than we're used to. Think of it as exercise, and pack light. Keep in mind that floors of buildings are numbered differently in Europe. The bottom floor is called the ground floor, and what we call the second floor is a European's first floor. So if your room is on the second floor (European), bad news—you're on the third floor (American). On the bright side, higher floors generally have better views and less street noise than lower ones. If you must have an elevator or ground-floor room, confirm that one is available when you book.

Hotel elevators in Europe tend to be minuscule. Sometimes only one person with a backpack can fit at one time (couples can split up, sending bags up separately for the other person to retrieve). In the elevator, push whatever's below "1" to return to the ground floor.

If you're trying to dial out from your room but the phone won't work, try calling (or visiting) the reception desk. They might have to open up an outside line for you on the switchboard, or they can tell you if you have to dial an access number first. If the hotel has Wi-Fi, ask whether you need to pay to use it, and request the network name and password.

(For a rundown on telephones and Internet access, see the Staying Connected chapter.)

If you're in southern Europe and having trouble getting a problem solved at your hotel, ask to see the complaint book, which the hotelier is legally required to show you on request. Sometimes even just asking to see the complaint book will inspire the hotelier to see that your problem is fixed. If you've had a good experience, jot a friendly note in the hotel's guest book; conscientious hoteliers love to show these off to arriving guests.

Unfriendly staff can taint your stay, but don't let them ruin your trip. If you have difficulties to bring up, keep checking to see if a sympathetic or more capable staff member comes on shift, or just be persistent (kind but firm) with whomever you have to deal with. Generally the hotel staff doesn't like to have complainers overheard by other customers, so it can be effective to state your problems clearly and reasonably with witnesses around. The staff may accommodate you just to shut you up.

Above all, keep a positive attitude. Remember, you're on vacation. If your hotel is a disappointment, spend more time out enjoying the city you came to see.

Checkout

When you pay for your room is up to the hotel and you (normally I pay upon departure). If surprise charges pop up on your bill, ask the hotelier to explain each item you're not sure about. Some charges are legitimate; for example, in touristy areas, hotels charge a per-day tax that everyone has to pay. To avoid preventable charges, don't use the hotel-room phone to make international calls unless you have an international phone card (described on page 256), and even then, ask first to be sure the hotel won't charge you to dial that "toll-free" access number.

Some hoteliers have credit-card readers that mysteriously break when you want to check out, requiring you to pay in cash. Or you might be charged extra if you want to pay with your credit card. If you settle up your bill the night before you leave—or even better, the day before, when there's a manager present—you'll have time to discuss and address any points of contention.

BED-AND-BREAKFASTS

Between hotels and hostels in price and style is a special class of accommodations: bed-and-breakfasts (B&Bs). These are small, warm, and family-run, and offer a personal touch at a reasonable price. They are the next best thing to staying with a family, and even if hotels weren't more expensive, this budget alternative can be your best bet.

Don't confuse European bed-and-breakfasts with their rich cousins in America. B&Bs in the US are usually frilly, fancy places, very cozy and colorful but as expensive as hotels. In a European B&B, rather than seven pillows and a basket of jams, you get a warm welcome and a good price.

Each country in Europe has these friendly accommodations in varying degrees of abundance, facilities, and service. While we commonly refer to them as bed-and-breakfasts, some include breakfast and some don't. They have different names from country to country, but all have one thing in common: They satisfy the need for a place to stay that gives you the privacy of a hotel and the comforts of home at a price you can afford.

Despite the benefits, B&Bs aren't for everyone. Some either don't allow kids or require them to be over a certain age (often around ages 8-12). Rooms may be tucked away in attics or perched at the top of several flights of stairs—a negative for those with mobility issues. It's not uncommon for B&Bs to require two-night stays, especially in popular weekend getaway spots. Some B&Bs only accept cash as payment, while others add a service fee to your bill if you pay with plastic. But if these restrictions don't bother you, a B&B can be an ideal place to spend the night.

While information on more established places is available in many budget-travel guidebooks, the best leads are often found locally, through tourist information offices, or even

LEFT A special bonus when enjoying Britain's great B&Bs: You get your own temporary mother.

RIGHT In most British towns, B&Bs line up along the same street—find one, and you've found a dozen.

from the man waiting for his bus or selling apples. Especially in the British Isles, each B&B host has a network of favorites and can happily set you up in a good B&B at your next stop.

Many times, the information is brought to you. I'll never forget struggling off the plane on my arrival in Santorini. Fifteen women were begging me to spend the night. Thrilled, I made a snap decision and followed the most attractive offer to a very nice budget accommodation.

The "part of the family" element of a B&B stay is determined entirely by you. Chatty friendliness is not forced on guests. Depending on my mood and workload, I am often very businesslike and private during my stay. On other occasions, I join the children in the barn for the sheep-shearing festivities.

B&Bs by Region

The British Isles

Britain's B&Bs are the best of all. As the name indicates, a breakfast comes with the bed, and (except in London) this is no ordinary breakfast (for details, see page 580). While you are finishing your coffee, the landlady (who by this time is probably on very friendly terms with you) may present you with her guest book, inviting you to make an entry and pointing out others from your state who have stayed in her house. Your hostess will sometimes cook you a simple dinner for a good price, and if you have time to chat, you may get in on an evening social hour. When you bid her farewell and thank her for the good sleep and full stomach, it's often difficult to get away. Determined to fill you with as much information as food, she wants you to have the best day of sightseeing possible.

Never judge a B&B by its name. Like most in Britain, this one is non-smoking and comes with numerous pleasant extras.

If you're going to the normal tourist stops, your guidebook will list some good B&Bs. If you're venturing off the beaten British path, you don't need (or want) a listing. The small towns and countryside are littered with places whose quality varies only in degrees of wonderful. I try not to choose a B&B until I have checked out three. Styles and atmosphere vary from house to house, and besides, I enjoy looking through European homes.

Britain rates its B&Bs using a diamond system (1-5) that considers

Private Rooms to Rent

Private rooms throughout Europe can cost as little as $40-60 per person, which sometimes includes breakfast and sometimes does not—confirm when you reserve.

For more on staying in European homes, see page 232.

In...	Look for...
Great Britain & Ireland	bed-and-breakfast
Norway/Sweden	rom or rum
Denmark	værelser
Germany/Austria	Zimmer
France	chambre (d'hôte)
Italy	(affitta) camere
Spain	casa particular
Portugal	quarto
Greece	dhomatia
Croatia/Slovenia	sobe
Poland	pokoje
Eastern Europe	Zimmer or "rooms"

cleanliness, furnishings, and decor. But diamond definitions are pretty squishy. Few B&Bs make a big deal of the ratings, and fewer tourists even know the system exists.

Ireland has essentially the same system of B&Bs. They are less expensive than England's and if anything, even more "homely" (cozy). You can expect a big breakfast and comfortable room, often within an easy walk of the town center.

Germany and Austria

Look for *Zimmer Frei, Privatzimmer,* or *Gästezimmer.* These are very common in areas popular with travelers (such as Austria's Salzkammergut Lake District and Germany's Rhine, the Romantic Road region, and southern Bavaria). Especially in Austria, one-night stays are discouraged. Most *Privatzimmer* cost about $40 per person and include a hearty breakfast. *Pensionen, Gasthäuser,* and *Gasthöfe* are similarly priced small, family-run hotels. Don't confuse any of these with a *Ferienwohnung,* which is a self-catering apartment rented out by the week or fortnight.

France

The French have a growing network of *chambres d'hôte* (CH) where residents, mainly in the countryside and in small towns, rent double rooms for about the price of a cheap hotel ($80-120), but with breakfast included. Some CHs post *chambre* signs in their windows, but most are listed only through tourist information offices. While your hosts likely won't speak English, they will almost always be enthusiastic and happy to share their home. If you want to stay in a countryside house *(gîte)*, visit gite.com or gites-de-france.com for options.

Italy

Check out Italy's good alternatives to its expensive hotels—look for *albergo, locanda,* and *pensione.* (While these are technically all bunched together now in a hotel system with star ratings, you'll still find these traditional names to be synonymous with simple, budget beds.) Private rooms, signposted as *camere libere* or *affitta camere,* are fairly common in Italy's small towns. Small-town bars are plugged into the B&B grapevine. Breakfasts are usually included, and you'll sometimes get a kitchenette in the room. Drivers can try *agriturismi,* rooms in farmhouses in the countryside. Weeklong stays are preferred in July and August, but shorter stays are possible off-season. For a sampling, visit agriturismoitaly.it or do an Internet search for *agriturismo.*

Bed-and-breakfast travelers scramble at the breakfast table.

Scandinavia

These usually luxurious B&Bs—advertised as a *rom, hus rum,* or, in Denmark, *værelser*—cost about $45 per person. By Scandinavian standards, these are incredibly cheap. If your Scandinavian B&B is serving breakfast, eat it. Even at $15, it's a deal by local standards and can serve as your best big meal of the day. Some hosts provide a roll of foil so you can pack up a lunch from the breakfast spread. If that sounds like a good idea, just ask.

Spain and Portugal

Travelers get an intimate peek into their small-town, whitewashed worlds by renting *camas* and *casas particulares* in Spain and *quartos* in Portugal. In rural Iberia, wherever there's tourism, you'll find these budget accommodations.

Breakfast is rarely included. *Hostales* and *pensiones* are easy to find, inexpensive, and, when chosen properly, a fun part of the Spanish cultural experience. These places are often family-owned, and may or may not have amenities like private bathrooms and air-conditioning. Don't confuse a *hostal* with a hostel. A *hostal* is an inexpensive hotel, not a hostel with bunks in dorms.

Guidebook listings will lead you to friendly Croatian *sobe* hosts eager to invite you into their homes.

Greece

You'll find many $60-per-room *dhomatia*. Especially in touristy coastal and island towns, hardworking entrepreneurs will meet planes, ferries, and buses as they come into town at any hour. In Greek villages with no hotels, ask for *dhomatia* at the town taverna. Forget breakfast.

Croatia and Slovenia

In these countries—where mass tourism and overpriced resort hotels reign—private rooms are often the best deal in town (no breakfast). You'll notice signs advertising *sobe* (rooms) everywhere you look, or you can book one through a travel agency (10-30 percent extra). You'll generally pay extra if you stay less than three nights. Along the Dalmatian Coast, *sobe* skimmers meet every arriving ferry, targeting backpackers and eager to whisk you away to see their room. In the Slovenian countryside, look for tourist farms *(turistične kmetije)*, where you can sleep in a family's farmhouse for remarkably low prices. Croatia's Istria region has similar *agroturizams*.

APARTMENT RENTALS

Whether you're in a city or the countryside, renting an apartment, house, or villa can be a fun and cost-effective way to delve into Europe. A short-term rental is a great alternative to a hotel, especially if you plan to settle in one location for several nights. Options run the gamut, from French *gîtes* to Tuscan villas to big-city apartments in the heart of town. Prices vary depending on the season, size, location, and quality of the accommodation. For stays longer than a few days, you can usually find a rental that's comparable to—or even cheaper—than a hotel room with similar amenities.

Apartments and houses for rent are generally roomier than hotel rooms and come with kitchens and common areas to gather in; some have laundry facilities. Rentals can be especially cost-effective for groups. Two couples traveling together can share a two-bedroom apartment, which often ends up being less expensive than a pair of hotel rooms. Groups of backpackers find that splitting the price of a cheap apartment can cost less than paying for several bunks at a youth hostel. You can further your savings by cooking your own meals instead of going out. If you enjoy eating in restaurants, consider stocking your kitchen with breakfast food or picnic-lunch supplies and saving your money for nice dinners out.

For families, an apartment is a huge benefit. Kitchens make it easier and cheaper to dine in and feed picky eaters. Laundry machines let you do the family wash. With more than one room, parents of younger children can hang out and chat while their kids slumber (as opposed to being trapped in a hotel room with the lights out at 8 p.m.). If you have teenagers, you can leave them to eat dinner in the apartment while you go out to a restaurant—they'll feel independent (perhaps enjoying a little screen time without parents), and you'll get a night on the town with your partner.

In general, I find that if you're staying somewhere for four nights or longer, it's worth considering an apartment or rental house. Three nights is borderline. To me, anything less than that isn't worth the extra effort involved in settling into an apartment (arranging key pickup, buying groceries, figuring out the neighborhood without the help of a hotelier, etc.). Plus, many apartments require minimum stays—typically three to seven nights (note that you'll likely pay more per night if staying less than a week, and you can sometimes negotiate better deals if renting for longer). If you can work it into your itinerary, consider settling in a rental for a full week. This gives you an opportunity to really get to know the town and take advantage of day-trip possibilities. (Good home-base cities are also ideal apartment-rental cities—see the list on page 54.)

The rental route isn't for everyone. First off, you're generally on your own. While the apartment owner or manager might offer some basic assistance, don't expect them to provide all the services of a hotel reception desk. If you like fresh towels and daily sheet changes, stay in a hotel. Your apartment likely won't be serviced or cleaned during a one-week stay unless you pay extra (though places generally have cleaning supplies—ask about this when you check in). Remember that the lack of these services is what keeps rentals affordable.

Finding an Apartment

Sometimes you'll deal directly with the apartment owner; in other cases, you might work with an agency that maintains a network of rentals. (Agencies may actually own the apartments, or they can act as a go-between.)

Aggregator Websites

Websites such as Booking.com, Airbnb, VRBO, and FlipKey let you browse properties and correspond directly with European property owners or managers. (There's even an aggregator of some of these aggregators—AlltheRooms.com —but their results appear in a long list that can be overwhelming to sort through.) Owners pay a fee to list their places and include photos and loads of other information (number of bedrooms and bathrooms, amenities, etc.) to help you make your decision.

Airbnb and sites such as Roomorama also list rooms in private homes (for more on using Airbnb to stay in someone's home, see page 233). These websites charge a booking fee (6-12 percent) but alleviate worries about fraud by collecting payment when you book, then waiting until you check in to release the funds to owners. Airbnb also allows hosts and guests to rate each other. To help renters feel safer, hosts who opt to share a government-issued ID and online profile with Airbnb can display a "Verified ID" icon with their listing.

Once you've found a property that looks appealing, contact the owner for more information. Most sites provide a form for entering your contact info, travel dates, and number of people in your traveling party. Within a few days, you'll hear back from the owner about availability and pricing.

These sites have their pros and cons. Booking with property owners takes a little more effort, but cutting out the middleman decreases cost and bureaucracy. Because you're working directly with the owner, you'll probably get a slightly better deal than if you go through an agency, which takes a commission. On the flip side, these sites require a little more legwork. You have to filter through a lot of properties, and you might have a lot of back-and-forth with several owners about amenities, policies, and other info.

Rental Agencies

If combing through listings and contacting homeowners sounds like too much effort, consider going through a rental agency. Using an agency is convenient, the places they list have been prescreened, and their staff will work with you to find an appropriate accommodation. For instance, if you have a larger family or you're not sure what neighborhood you want to be in, it might be easier to talk to a rental agency, convey your needs, and see what they come up with. The downside is that you'll pay more for the rental to cover the agency's costs.

Rental agencies such as Interhome.us and the more upscale Rentavilla.com list places all over Europe. Other agencies concentrate on a certain region or city. For example, Prague-stay.com focuses on apartments in Prague while France: Homestyle (francehomestyle.com) lists Parisian apartments and country houses in the Loire. To find a rental in a specific region, simply search for "vacation rental" or "holiday rental" and the town you're interested in, then browse your options.

Renting an Apartment

Before you commit to a rental, be clear on the details. Check out the location on a map so you know how convenient—or inconvenient—it is. Ask about the neighborhood and what's nearby. If you plan on driving, find out about parking. If you have kids, ask if there are playgrounds or parks nearby. Many European apartments involve some climbing; confirm what floor the apartment is on and whether the building has an elevator. If the owner or agency is anything but helpful, skip to the next place on your list.

When you make a reservation, you'll probably have to pay a deposit, which can range from 10 to 50 percent of the rental cost. Many places require you to pay the entire balance before your trip (such as 30 days prior to your stay), or upon arrival. Ideally the owner will accept credit cards (which offer some fraud protection), but some places will add a credit-card fee. And some rentals don't accept credit cards and will instead ask you to make your deposit securely online via PayPal, or to send a personal check.

Be warned: You're renting a place sight unseen, so check for scams before sending money. You can do this by searching online for the lister's name, address, or email to see if anything suspicious pops up. For a fee, VRBO offers a rental guarantee that protects you for up to $10,000 if you're the victim of fraud, or if the owner misrepresented the property (for example, if your 200-square-foot studio facing a dumpster looks nothing like the photos of the spacious two-bedroom apartment with "lovely garden views" you thought you were renting). The fee for the guarantee starts at $39 and depends on the price of the rental.

Before you send a deposit, request a rental agreement, which usually includes the house rules and the cancellation policy. Read the document carefully and clear up any questions you have with the owner or agency. Rentals tend to have much more rigid cancellation policies than hotels (30 days is common, but it can be longer), even in circumstances beyond your control. For example, when the volcano erupted in Iceland in 2010, one of my staffers had to delay her trip to Spain by a few weeks. While the apartment she had booked in Madrid was able to accommodate her new itinerary, she was still charged for the original dates (even though she ended up staying two fewer nights). Some homeowners might be more lenient and let you out of your contract in an emergency. It's always worth asking.

If you think your plans might change, consider staying in a hotel, where you can usually cancel just a few days beforehand without paying a penalty. You can also protect your investment by purchasing trip-cancellation insurance (see page 69).

Upon Arrival

Apartments, especially those in big cities, can be tricky to find. Unlike hotels, you can't expect taxi drivers and people on the street to be able to point you in the right direction. Make sure you nail down directions to the rental prior to your arrival. (House numbers often have no obvious correlation to one another; for example, in Italy, #28 may be directly across the street from #2.)

You'll also need to arrange a time and place to meet the property owner or manager and pick up the keys. That person will show you around the rental and may be able to give you tips about the neighborhood (grocery stores, pharmacies, and good places to eat). But once they leave, you probably won't see them again.

On departure, it's generally expected that you leave the place clean and in good condition. If you don't, you may lose some or all of your security deposit. Some places may ask you to do minimal cleaning before you leave (for instance, stripping off bed linens or emptying the fridge).

HOSTELS

Europe's cheapest beds are in hostels. Several thousand hostels provide beds throughout Europe for $20-40 per night. Most hostels are set in good, easily accessible locations.

As Europe has grown more affluent, hostels have been remodeled to provide more plumbing and smaller rooms. Still, hostels are not hotels—not by a long shot. Many people hate hostels. Others love them and will be hostelers all their lives, regardless of their budgets. Hosteling is a philosophy. A hosteler trades service and privacy for a chance to live simply and communally with people from around the world.

For students, travelers on a budget, solo travelers, groups or families who can take a whole room, and those hoping to meet other travelers, hostels can be a great option.

Official Hostels vs. Independent Hostels

There are two different types of hostels: official and independent.

Official hostels belong to the same parent organization, Hostelling International, and share an online booking site (hihostels.com). They used to adhere to various rules (such as a 5 p.m. check-in, lockout during the day, and a curfew at night), but nowadays are more flexible. If you plan to spend at least six nights at official HI hostels, you'll save money if you buy a membership card before you go ($28/year for full benefits, free if you're under 18 and $18 if you're 55 or over, stripped-down $18 emembership does not include frills such as insurance and currency exchange; available at your local student-travel office, any HI hostel office, or Hostelling International; hiusa.org, tel. 240/650-2100). If you think you may not spend six nights at HI hostels, don't buy the card in advance. Nonmembers who want to stay at III hostels can sometimes get an "international guest card" at their first hostel and pay about $5 extra per night for a "welcome stamp." Once you have six welcome stamps on your card, you become a member. As independent hostels become a more popular option, this "pay-as-you-go" system for official hostels makes sense for many travelers (rather than buying your membership up front).

Independent hostels tend to be more easygoing and colorful, but not as predictably clean or organized as official hostels. Independent hostels don't require a membership card or charge extra for nonmembers, and generally have fewer rules. Many popular European destinations have wild and cheap student-run hostels that are popular with wild and cheap student travelers, but some independent hostels are tame and mature. Hostelworld.com is the standard way backpackers search and book hostels these days, but also try hostelz.com and hostels.com.

If you're staying at a mix of both official and independent hostels—as most hostelers do—*Let's Go* guidebooks offer the best all-around listings (letsgo.com).

> ## Hosteling Terms
>
> **Dormitory:** Group room with multiple beds, usually bunk beds, and lockers for storage. You'll pay to rent one bed and will sleep in a room shared with strangers.
>
> **Private/Family Room:** Private rooms with one, two, three, or more beds. You'll pay to rent every bed in the room, which will be used only by you and your traveler partners.
>
> **Mixed Dorm:** Dormitory open to both genders.
>
> **Shared Bathroom:** You'll share a bathroom down the hall (like the locker room at the gym).
>
> **En Suite:** The room has a private bathroom, not one down the hall. This can apply to either a dorm room or a private/family room.

Hosteling Tips

Unless noted, these tips apply to both official and independent hostels.

A youth hostel is not limited to young people. You may assume hostels aren't for you because, by every standard, you're older than young. Well, many countries have dropped the word "youth" from their hostels, and for years Hostelling International has given "youths" age 55 and over a membership discount. Even the last holdout, the German state of Bavaria, has finally dropped its youths-only restriction. If you're alive, you're young enough to hostel anywhere in Europe (with the rare exception of some independent hostels that have age cutoffs of around 40). The average hosteler is 18-26 years old, but every year there are more seniors and families hosteling. As a reader wrote on my website: "My partner and I stayed in a 'youth' hostel for the first time by Lake Como and thought we'd be the oldest people there. Not so! At our table was a 60-ish couple from Sydney and a 79-year-old British woman who was backpacking alone through Europe. All three were a delight, but especially the backpacker, who said she stays in hostels for the evening company."

Hostels provide "no frills" accommodations in clean dormitories. Hostels were originally for hikers and bikers, but that isn't the case these days—some newer hostels are downright plush. Still, expect humble conditions. At official hostels, the sexes are segregated, with 4 to 20 people packed in a room full of bunk beds. Many independent hostels have both segregated and mixed dorms. Hostels often have a few doubles for group leaders and couples, and rooms for families are increasingly common (and affordable). Strong, hot showers are the norm, but some very rustic, off-the-beaten-path hostels (or mountain huts) might have no showers at all.

Bedding is usually included. Pillows and blankets are provided. Sheets are typically included in the cost, but occasionally you'll be asked to pay about $5 extra to rent them. Hostelers who are used to bringing their own sleep sack should check ahead before packing it. Concerned about bedbugs, many hostels now require you to use their linens even if you have your own.

Many hostels offer meals, meeting places, and information. A simple breakfast is often included in the price of your bed. Hearty, super-cheap meals are served at an extra cost, often in family-style settings. A typical dinner is fish sticks and mashed potatoes seasoned by conversation with new friends from Norway to New Zealand. The self-service kitchen, complete with utensils, pots, and pans, is a great budget aid that comes with most hostels. Larger hostels even have small grocery stores. International friendships rise with the bread in hostel kitchens.

The hostel's recreation and living rooms are my favorite. People gather, play games, tell stories, share information, read, write, and team up for future travels.

Hostels: Meet, drink, and be merry.

Solo travelers find a family in every hostel and can always find a new travel partner; those with partners do well to occasionally stay in a hostel to meet some new companions.

Most hostel lobbies are littered with brochures and posters about local tours, events, and public transportation. There's generally Wi-Fi or a guest computer.

One of Europe's hostels: $30 a night, your own kitchen, a million-dollar view of the Swiss Alps, and lots of friends.

Get to know your host. The people who live in and run hostels (sometimes called "wardens" in Britain) do their best to strictly enforce rules, quiet hours, and other regulations. Some are loose and laid-back, others are like Marine drill sergeants, but they all work toward the noble goal of enabling travelers to better appreciate and enjoy that town or region. While they are often overworked and harried, most hostel employees are fine people who enjoy a quiet cup of coffee with an American and are happy to give you some travel tips or recommend a special nearby hostel. Be sensitive to the many demands on their time, and never treat them like hotel servants.

Hostels have drawbacks. Some hostels—especially official ones—have strict rules. Some lock up during the day (usually from 10 a.m. to 5 p.m.), and a few may have a curfew at night, when the doors are locked. Keep in mind that a curfew can be a big advantage—hostels that don't have curfews, especially in big cities, are more likely to have hostelers (often drunk and rowdy) returning at ungodly hours. The sounds you'll hear just after everyone's turned in remind me of summer camp—giggles, burps, jokes, and strange noises in many languages. Snoring is permitted and practiced openly.

Hostel rooms can be large and packed. School groups (especially German) can turn hostels upside down (typically weekends during the school year and weekdays in the summer). Try to be understanding (many groups are disadvantaged kids); we were all noisy kids at one time. Get to know the teacher and make it a "cultural experience."

Theft can be a problem in hostels, but try this simple safeguard: Wear your money belt (even while sleeping), and don't leave valuables lying around (but no one's going to steal your tennis shoes or journal). Use the storage lockers that are available in most hostels.

Be skeptical about hostel ratings. The ratings on hostel-booking websites can help you get a feel for a hostel, but shouldn't be the end-all in your decision making. What matters most to me are a hostel's ratings in the areas of safety, location, and character. Seek a hostel where you and your belongings will be secure, in a central location (or easily linked to the center by public transit), and with a good vibe (if other people enjoy their time there, you likely will too). I don't pay much attention to ratings for cleanliness or helpfulness of the staff (which can be negatively influenced by former five-star hotel guests who weren't ready for a hostel experience).

Hostel selectively. I've hosteled mostly in northern Europe, where hostels are more comfortable and the savings over hotels more exciting. (This is particularly true in Scandinavia, where you find lots of Volvos in hostel parking lots; locals know that hostels provide the best—and usually only—$30 beds in town.) I rarely hostel in the south, where hostels are less common and two or three people can sleep just as cheaply in a budget hotel.

Big-city hostels are the most overrun by young backpackers. Rural hostels, far from train lines and famous sights, are usually quiet and frequented by a more mature crowd. If you have a car, use that mobility to visit places without train service and enjoy some of Europe's overlooked hostels.

Getting a hostel bed in peak tourist season can be tricky. The most popular hostels fill up every day. Most hostels will take telephone or email reservations. I always call or email ahead to try to reserve and at least check on the availability of beds. But don't rely solely on advance reservations, because many hostels hold some beds for drop-ins. Try to arrive early. If the hostel has a lockout period during the day, show up before the office closes in the morning; otherwise, line up with the scruffy gang for the 5 p.m. reopening, when any remaining beds are doled out.

In most hostels, there are dorm rooms for boys...and dorm rooms for girls.

Some hostels have a reservation system where, for a small fee, you can reserve and pay for your next hostel bed before you leave the last one. You can also book Hostelling International locations online (hihostels.com,

$3 nonrefundable booking fee plus 6 percent nonrefundable deposit per location booked, balance due at hostel on arrival, 10 percent discount for members at check-in); they accept Visa and MasterCard and also sell hostel membership cards. Book at least a day ahead.

Hostel bed availability is unpredictable. Some obscure hostels are booked out on certain days six months in advance. But I stumbled into Oberammergau one night during the jam-packed Passion Play festival and found beds for a group of eight.

Look for unique hostel experiences. Hostels come in all shapes and sizes, and some are sightseeing destinations in themselves. There are castles (Bacharach, Germany), moored ships and a converted jumbo jet (Stockholm), alpine chalets (Gimmelwald, Switzerland), lakefront villas (Lugano, Italy), former prisons (Stockholm and Ljubljana, Slovenia), medieval manor houses (Wilderhope Manor, England), and former choirboys' dorms (St. Paul's, London). Survey other hostelers and hostel employees for suggestions.

Stockholm's floating youth hostel, the *af Chapman*

Hostel-Style Alternatives

Hostels aren't the only places to find low-cost rooms in Europe. Depending on where you're traveling, you might land a bed in a convent, school, or youth camp.

In Italy, some cities have religious institutions that rent out rooms. The beds are twins and English is often in short supply, but the price is right. The Church of Santa Susanna's website maintains a list of such places in Rome and beyond (santasusanna.org, select "Coming to Rome"). Since sisters and monks are less likely than hotel staff to speak English, email or fax your reservation—or consider using monasterystays.com to book your stay for you, although they do exact a fee from the monastery for this service.

If you can't bunk with pilgrims, try snoozing with students. In London, which seems to have the highest hotel prices in Europe, the University of Westminster opens its dorm rooms to travelers from June through mid-September. Located in several high-rise buildings scattered around central London, the rooms—some with private baths—come with access to well-equipped kitchens and big lounges (westminster.ac.uk/business). University College London (ucl.ac.uk/residences) and the London School of

Economics (lsevacations.co.uk) also rent out dorm space in the summer.

In the cheap-sleeps circus, nothing beats Munich's venerable International Youth Camp Kapuzinerhölzl (a.k.a. "The Tent"). From June to early October, they offer 400 spots on the wooden floor of a huge circus tent—and they never fill up. You can rent a mattress or bed, or you can pitch your own tent. Blankets, hot showers, lockers, a kitchen, and Wi-Fi are all included; breakfast is a few euros extra. It can be a fun but noisy experience—kind of a cross between a slumber party and Woodstock (the-tent.com).

STAYING IN EUROPEAN HOMES

There is no better way to get to know a new country than to stay in a home. Whether paying a host for a spare room or crashing on your neighbor's cousin's couch, bunking with locals can provide some of the richest, most memorable travel experiences (and it's cheap, to boot). For those aware of the trade-offs, it can be a great option.

Being a guest in a European home isn't all that different from being a guest in an American one. That said, clear communication and a focus on being considerate are even more critical when trying to bridge a linguistic or cultural divide. People who are OK with welcoming strangers in their home are usually friendly, interested in others, and eager to show off their town. You'll likely be greeted with genuine enthusiasm, whether you're paying a fee or staying for free. Many hosts happily provide maps, sightseeing and transit information, and advice on how to make the most of your time.

But some awkwardness is inevitable—expect to make a faux pas or two. Limit your embarrassing blunders by doing your cultural homework—ask around and look online for pointers on guest etiquette in the country you're visiting. Follow your host's lead—if they're not wearing shoes in their house, leave yours at the door. Be aware of what makes for touchy conversation, and do your best to get squared away on geopolitical basics—e.g., Scotland isn't in England, and Bratislava is no longer in "Czechoslovakia." To bridge a wide language gap, try to learn the elements of that country's nonverbal communication: What means "OK" in the US can mean something quite the opposite in some parts of Europe. Communicate your plans clearly: how long you expect to stay, whether you'll be there for dinner in the evening, and where to leave the key in the morning.

Before you arrange to stay with someone in their house, be aware of the potential downsides. Consider what you may have to give up for your free or cheap bed. At a hotel, B&B, or hostel, you have no social obligations to your host. But if someone's putting you up, it could be perceived as rude to return late at night and leave first thing in the morning. If your host invites you to dinner, do your best to accept—but remember to budget your sightseeing time accordingly. If you accept a bed from someone (especially if it's free), it's polite to give your hosts plenty of advance warning of your arrival and not flippantly change plans at the last minute.

> ## Resources for Apartments and House Stays
>
> **Home-exchange-usa.com**, **Home Exchange.com**, and **Intervacus. com:** Swap a stay in your home for one in your European destination
> **Airbnb.com:** Broad range of room rentals
> **Couchsurfing.org:** Local offerings of free places to sleep
> **Agriturismoltaly.It:** Rural rentals in Italy
> **Gite.com** and **gites-de-france.com:** Countryside rental homes in France

If you're sleeping where others live, there's a decent chance you'll find yourself in a workaday suburb, or at least far from old-town charm or sights you came to see. Thanks to Europe's excellent public-transit network, you'll probably be able to reach the city center on your own, but that commute will cost you time and money.

Room-Finding Services

If you're looking for a cheap or free home to call home, consider one of the services that mediate between travelers and hosts.

Cheap Beds in Private Homes

Airbnb makes it reasonably easy to find a place to sleep in someone's home. Beds range from air-mattress-in-living-room basic to plush-B&B-suite posh. Most listings offer at least a spare room to yourself, and many are for entire apartments. The listings have plenty of pictures, easy ways to sort your options according to your preferences, and feedback from previous travelers. All arrangements, including payment, are handled via their website, and safety is taken seriously. The site provides a round-the-clock emergency hotline and waits until after you've checked in to pay the host, giving you a chance to back out. Hosts tend to be convivial and accommodating, but are usually more interested in earning some money with their spare square footage than making new friends. A similar site worth checking out is 9flats.com.

Couchsurfing

If you want a place to sleep that's free, Couchsurfing.org, a free-to-join network of travelers, is a vagabond's alternative to Airbnb. It lists millions of outgoing members—more than 72,000 in Paris alone—who host fellow "surfers" in their homes for free. Most do this out of a sincere interest in meeting interesting people, and many of them are in it for the good karma, having couch-surfed themselves. This service is a boon for laid-back, budget-minded extroverts who aren't too picky about where they rest their head. Most surfers are in their 20s and traveling solo, but plenty are a decade or two older, or traveling in small groups.

Travelers and hosts alike post profiles on the website, listing basic information (usually a photo, age, languages spoken, and interests). When seeking a "couch" (often precisely that, but can be anything from floor space to a spare room), travelers browse listings for the city they're headed to and, based on a sense of compatibility, contact a potential host several days to several weeks in advance to confirm specifics. Once you're in town, the host usually makes time to introduce you to the city, whether taking you on a walk past the big sights or out on the town to introduce you to friends (everyone pays their own way, though many surfers buy their host a thank-you drink or gelato). Most surfers will tell you that they enjoy the conviviality even more than the free accommodation.

Safety is, of course, a concern of any smart couch surfer. While the Couchsurfing site makes an effort toward this end (offering plenty of safety tips, listing references from travelers and hosts on member profiles, and allowing hosts to pay for name and address verification), travelers must still be on alert for creeps and scammers—they're certainly out there. My best tip for crashing with strangers: Always arrive with a backup hostel, hotel, or Couchsurfing host in mind; if you don't feel comfortable with your host, just leave (after all, it's free). Don't worry about hurting their feelings. Never let budget concerns take you outside your comfort zone.

Other Accommodation Options

If you've got more time and stamina than money, consider Workaway.info, which connects you with families or small organizations offering room and board in exchange for volunteer work, usually manual labor (gardening, carpentry, painting) for about five hours a day, five days a week. For more on volunteer opportunities, see page 480.

If you believe that travel is about bringing people together, consider joining a cultural-exchange organization, which lets you stay with hosts in their home (described on page 480). Note that while travelers do get a free bed with their hosts, the focus is much less about providing accommodation than an opportunity to connect. Guests are there to spend the bulk of their visit with their hosts, not off sightseeing.

Crashing with Friends and Family

Staying with a friend, relative, or friendly stranger not only stretches your budget (usually along with your belly), but your cultural horizons. And now that it's so easy to connect and stay in touch online, travelers are finding more and more chances to crash with old or new friends.

Try and dig up some European relatives, friends, friends of relatives, or relatives of friends. No matter how far out on the family tree they are, unless you're a real jerk, they're tickled to have an American visitor in their nest. I email my potential host, telling them when I'll arrive and asking if they'd be free to meet for dinner while I'm there. They answer with "Please come visit us" or "Have a good trip." It's obvious from their response (or lack of one) if I'm invited to stop by and stay awhile.

Especially if you're traveling solo and reasonably extroverted, you're likely to make new friends on the road. When people meet, they invite each other to visit. Exchanging email addresses or Facebook names is almost as common as a handshake in Europe. If you have a business or personal card, bring a pile. Some travelers even print up a batch of personal cards for their trip. Once invited to visit, I warn my new friends that I may very well show up some day at their house, whether it's in Osaka, Auckland, Santa Fe, or Dublin. When I have, it's been a good experience.

Don't be afraid to follow up with indirect contacts. I have dear "parents away from home" in Austria and London. My Austrian "parents" are really the parents of my sister's ski instructor. In London, they are friends of my uncle. Neither relationship was terribly close—until I visited. Now we are friends for life.

If you're afraid of being perceived as a freeloader, remember that both parties benefit from such a visit. A Greek family is just as curious and

The Europeans you visit don't need to be next-of-kin. This Tirolean is the father of my sister's ski teacher. That's close enough.

interested in me as I am in them. Equipped with hometown postcards, pictures of my family, and a bag of goodies for the children, I make a point of giving as much from my culture as I am taking from the culture of my host. I insist on no special treatment rather than to be treated simply as part of the family. If I ask for a favor, I make it as easy as possible for my host to say no. I try to help with the chores, I don't wear out my welcome, and I follow up each visit with postcards or emails to share the rest of my trip. I reimburse my hosts for their hospitality with a bottle of wine, a bunch of flowers, or a thank-you letter from home, possibly with photos of all of us together.

House Swapping

Many families enjoy this great budget option year after year. They trade houses (sometimes cars, too—but most draw the line at pets) with someone at the destination of their choice. People who've tried house swapping rave about the range of places they've enjoyed for free, and about the graciousness and generosity of their swap-mates.

Swapping works best for people with an appealing place to offer, and who can live with the idea of having strangers in their home, touching their stuff. Unsurprisingly, those living in swanky Manhattan apartments and beachside villas have the best pick of options in Europe, but you don't need to live in an obvious vacation spot or a mansion to find a workable exchange. Your guests may appreciate the pace of a smaller town (especially if you offer your car) and may be less interested in luxury or location than in finding a suitable place that's available when they are.

Good places to start are HomeExchange.com, HomeLink (home-exchange-usa.com), or Intervac Home Exchange (intervacus.com). Once you've found a potential host, expect to be in fairly close contact with them as you finalize the swap. Be very clear about your expectations, agree on how you'll handle worst-case scenarios, and get the details pinned down before you leave. Be triple-sure about where to find the key and how to open the door, find out beforehand how to get to the nearest grocery store, make sure your host family leaves instructions for operating the appliances, make arrangements in advance for phone and Internet charges, and ask about any peculiarities with the car you'll be driving. Veteran house swappers report that by the time these logistics are all worked out, it usually feels less like you'll be swapping with strangers, and more like you've made a new, conveniently located friend.

CAMPING EUROPEAN STYLE

Camping, like hosteling, is a great way to meet Europeans. But although camping is the middle-class European family way to travel—and can be the cheapest way to see Europe—relatively few Americans take advantage of Europe's 10,000-plus campgrounds. Those who do camp in Europe give it rave reviews.

"Camping" is the international word for campground. In Europe, local tourist information offices have guides and maps listing nearby campgrounds. In the US, we think of campgrounds as being picturesque outposts near a lake or forest. By contrast, European campings are often located within or on the outskirts of an urban center and can range from functional (like park-and-rides) to vacation extravaganzas, with restaurants and mini water-parks. In general, European campgrounds are less private than the American version and forbid open fires. But they rarely fill up, and if they do, the "Full" sign usually refers to motorhomes and trailers. A small tent can almost always be squeezed in somewhere.

Campgrounds generally mirror their surroundings. If the region is overcrowded, dusty, dirty, unkempt, and chaotic, you're unlikely to find an oasis behind the campground's gates. A sleepy Austrian valley will probably offer a sleepy Austrian campground. "Weekend campings" are rented out on a yearly basis to local urbanites. Too often, weekend sites are full or don't allow what they call "stop-and-go" campers (you). Camping guidebooks indicate which places are the "weekend" types.

Prices: Prices vary according to facilities and style—sometimes it's by the tent, the person, or the vehicle. Expect to spend $13-16 per night per person. In big cities, the money you save on parking alone will pay for your campsite (leave your car at the campground and take the bus downtown).

Registration and Regulations: Camp registration is easy. As with most

Many campgrounds offer bungalows with kitchenettes and four to six beds. Comfortable and cheaper than hotels, these are particularly popular in Scandinavia.

Out of Options (or Money)?

This book is not a vagabonding guide, but things happen: You run out of money, you get into town too late to find a room, or volcanic ash strands you somewhere without a place to stay. I once went 29 out of 30 nights without paying for a bed. It's not difficult...but it's not always comfortable, convenient, clean, safe—or legal.

A bench with a view

I no longer lug a sleeping bag around, but if you'll be vagabonding a lot, bring a light bag—you'll find plenty of places to roll it out. Just keep your passport with you, attach your belongings to you so they don't get stolen, and use good judgment in your choice of a free bed. Faking it until the sun returns can become, at least in the long run, a good memory.

The Great Outdoors: Some large cities, such as Amsterdam and Athens, are flooded with tourists during peak season—and some of those tourists spend their nights dangerously in city parks. Most cities enforce their "no sleeping in parks" laws only selectively. Away from the cities, in forests or on beaches, you can pretty much sleep where you like. In my vagabonding days, I found summer nights in the Mediterranean part of Europe mild enough that I was comfortable with just my jeans, sweater, and hostel sheet.

Train Stations: Assuming the station stays open all night, it can be a free, warm, safe, and uncomfortable place to hang your hat. Most popular tourist cities in

hotels, you show your passport, fill out a short form, and learn the rules. Quiet is enforced beginning at 10 or 11 p.m., and checkout time is usually noon. English is the second language of campings throughout Europe, and most managers will understand the monoglot American.

Services: There's usually space to pitch a tent or park a camper van, motorhome, or trailer (caravan). Most campgrounds have laundry facilities and great showers with metered hot water—carry coins and scrub quickly. Larger campgrounds may have a grocery store and café (a likely camp hangout with an easygoing European social scene).

Equipment: You can bring your gear with you—or buy it when you get there. Tents, sleeping bags, and cooking supplies are cheaper at large European superstores than at specialty backpacking stores. European campers prefer a very lightweight "three-season" sleeping bag and a closed-cell sleeping pad. I'd start without a stove, keeping meals simple

Europe have stations whose concrete floors are painted nightly with a long rainbow of sleepy vagabonds. Some stations close for a few hours in the middle of the night, and everyone is always cleared out at dawn before the normal rush of travelers converges on the station. Any ticket or train pass entitles you to a free night in a station's waiting room: You're simply waiting for your early train. For safety, lock your pack in a station locker or check it at the baggage counter.

Trains: Success hinges on getting enough room to stretch out, and that can be quite a trick (see page 142). It's tempting but risky to sleep in a train car that seems to be parked for the night in a station. No awakening is ruder than having your bedroom jolt into motion and roll toward God-knows-where. If you do find a parked train car to sleep in, check to see when it's scheduled to leave. Some rail-pass holders get a free if disjointed night's sleep by riding a train out for four hours and catching a different train back for another four hours.

Airports: After a late landing, crash on an airport sofa rather than waste sleeping time looking for a place that will sell you a bed for the remainder of the night (for a guide to airport slumber, try sleepinginairports.com). Frankfurt's airport is served conveniently by the train and is great for sleeping free—even if you aren't flying anywhere. A few large airports have sterile, womblike "rest cabins" that can be rented for as few as four hours or overnight at the price of a cheap hotel room (for example, see yotel.com for London's Heathrow and Gatwick airports and Amsterdam's Schiphol airport).

Tents and Dorms: Big, crowded cities such as London, Paris, Munich, Venice, and Copenhagen run safe, legal, and nearly free sleep-ins (in tents or huge dorms) during peak season.

by picnicking and enjoying food and fun in the campground café. You can always buy a stove later.

Safety: Campgrounds, unlike hostels, are remarkably theft-free. Campings are full of basically honest, middle-class European families, and someone's at the gate all day. Most people just leave their gear in their vans or zipped inside their tents.

Kids: A family can sleep in a tent, van, or motorhome a lot cheaper than in a hotel. Camping offers plenty to occupy children's attention, namely playgrounds that come fully equipped with European kids. As your kids make friends, your campground social circle widens. Campgrounds are filled with

For a "room" with a view on a tight budget, pitch your tent in a secluded mountain valley.

Europeans in the mood to toss a Frisbee with a new American friend (bring a nylon Woosh Frisbee).

RV Camping: David Shore, co-author of *Europe by Van and Motorhome* (see sidebar), gives consults on finding and renting the right camper vehicle (shorecam@aol.com). Each country has companies specializing in camper van and motorhome rentals. Look for one with a pickup and drop-off location that makes sense for your itinerary. For example, Origin Campervans is centrally located in Lille, France (origin-campervans.com). McRent (mcrent.eu) has 50 rental depots across Europe. London-based Wild Horizon (wildhorizon.co.uk) can meet you or provide transfers from UK airports. Keep in mind that picking up your RV or campervan in Germany could save you 19 percent, since German rental companies don't charge VAT tax if you rent for 31 days or longer.

With an RV, you can often find free places to park and sleep—such as rest stops on national motorways (look for a big blue and white "P" sign).

Turn-Key Camping: Some services offer virtually turn-key camping, renting sites already set up for you with a tent, trailer, or mobile home outfitted with linens and kitchen gear. Two British companies are a good place to start: Eurocamp (eurocamp.co.uk) and Canvas Holidays (canvasholidays.co.uk) contract with campgrounds across continental Europe.

"Free" Camping: Low-profile, pitch-the-tent-after-dark-and-move-on-first-thing-in-the-morning free camping is usually allowed even in countries where it is technically illegal. Use common sense, and don't pitch your tent in carefully controlled areas such as cities and resorts. It's a good idea to ask permission when possible. Never leave your gear and tent unattended without the gates of a formal campground to discourage thieves. With a camper van or motorhome, no stealthiness is required—you can sleep overnight in any legal parking space.

Resources for Camping

Let's Go **guides:** Good instructions on getting to and from European campgrounds

Eurocampings.co.uk: Details and user reviews on more than 9,000 campgrounds.

TheAA.com: Britain's AAA-type auto club lists camp sites throughout Europe.

Roadtripeurope.com: Travelers David Shore and Patty Campbell wrote the book on European camping (free, personal consultation, free shipping for Rick Steves readers).

Staying Connected

One of the most common questions I hear from travelers is, "How can I stay connected in Europe?" The short answer is: more easily and cheaply than you might think.

These days, traveling abroad with a mobile phone, tablet, or laptop (or some combination of the three), makes it easier than ever for you to inexpensively communicate on the run and keep in touch with friends and family back home. Plus, having a mobile device on hand can help you make the most of your travel time. You can pull up maps when you're lost, enhance sightseeing with audio tours and podcasts, call a restaurant for reservations while riding the bus, or buy advance tickets for a blockbuster museum and have them sent right to your phone.

In this chapter, I cover the ins-and-outs of making phone calls, getting online, and sending text messages while traveling in Europe. I explain how to set up and bring your own mobile device with you, and share some cheap (and even free) ways to use it. And if you want to untether completely, I'll show you how public phones and computers can keep you connected. Finally, I discuss ways to keep your personal data safe while traveling.

One way or another, going to Europe is no longer a trip to the dark side of the moon.

USING YOUR MOBILE DEVICE IN EUROPE

Many travelers enjoy the convenience of bringing their own mobile phone to Europe. Some people also prefer to bring a tablet or laptop for emailing or blogging, uploading or editing photos, reading, and watching videos in their down time. Using your mobile device abroad isn't hard, and with a little preparation, you can text, make calls, and access the Internet without breaking the bank.

Unfortunately, all of this information can be cloaked in technical jargon. I'll try to keep it simple—when possible. One distinction you need to know up front are the two ways to connect: through a cellular network or via Wi-Fi. A **cellular network** is a paid service provided by your telecom company, available almost everywhere. **Wi-Fi** is generally a free (or low cost) service that's only available at hotspots.

Your Basic Options

I recommend bringing at least a phone. Even with near-universal Internet access, smart travelers still use the telephone. I call museums to see if an English tour is scheduled, restaurants to check if they're open or to book a table, hotels and car-rental agencies to confirm reservations, and so on. (For tips on communicating over the phone with someone who speaks another language, see page 352.) Having a phone on hand is also useful when you're traveling with a group. It's comforting to know you can make a quick phone call or send a text if you get separated, need to make plans, or if there's an emergency.

When it comes to staying connected, here are your basic options, all of which are explained in this chapter. Choose the best option for you, after considering how you plan to use your device.

1. Bring your own phone and sign up for an international/global plan. For most travelers, who don't visit Europe as frequently or for as long as I do, it's easiest to set up your own mobile phone with a basic international calling and/or data plan that's customized to your needs—and it doesn't have to cost an arm and a leg. You get to travel with all of your contact information and your US phone number, making it easy to connect with folks back home. With the cost of international plans dropping, more and more travelers are willing to pay for the freedom to call, text, and go online anytime, anywhere. (To set up an international plan, see below.)

2. Bring your own phone and do everything over Wi-Fi. More budget-conscious travelers can forego their carrier's international plans altogether and do everything over Wi-Fi. Not only can you use Wi-Fi to get online, but you can also make phone calls and send text messages at no charge. Sounds great—but you've got to find a hotspot first (see page 245).

3. Buy a European SIM card. This option works best for people who plan to make a lot of calls while traveling. You buy a European SIM card (a microchip that stores your phone number and other data) to insert in your current phone—or into a cheap mobile phone that you buy for your trip. This gives you a European number—and the same local rates Europeans enjoy (see page 254).

4. Leave the devices at home. Of course, you can still travel abroad without any of your mobile devices. You can check email or browse websites using public computers and Internet cafés, and make calls from your hotel room and/or public phones (see page 256).

Bad-Value Options: Many car-rental companies, mobile phone companies, and even some hotels offer the option to rent a mobile phone with a European number. This is a terrible value, as hidden fees (such as high per-minute charges) can add up.

Resources for Staying Connected

Countrycallingcodes.com and **how tocallabroad.com:** Dialing how-tos

Ricksteves.com/travel-forum: Tips from my readers, including a section on technology

Apps

Skype, FaceTime, Google+ Hangouts, and **Viber:** Video, voice, and text services for mobile devices

iMessage and **WhatsApp:** Instant messaging for text, images, and video

Setting Up International Service on Your US Phone

Roaming with your own phone outside the US generally comes with extra charges, whether you are making voice calls, sending texts, or accessing data (going online over a cellular network rather than Wi-Fi, a.k.a., "data roaming"). If you plan to bring your own phone to Europe, start by assessing how you will to use it—whether you will be making a few or a lot of phone calls, sending and receiving text messages, and how freely and frequently you'll want to get online to check email, look up websites, access maps, get driving directions, or use other mobile apps.

Researching and Choosing an International Plan

If you're taking your own phone to Europe, look into your carrier's offerings for global calling, texting, and data.

What to Ask Your Carrier About

Pay-As-You-Go Rates: Ask about the pay-as-you-go voice calling, text messaging, and data rates for the countries you're visiting. If you don't plan to access the cellular network for calls, texts, or data, it may be cheaper to forego an international plan, and simply pay the standard rates if you need to use your phone in an emergency.

Voice Calling Plans and Rates: Find out how much it would cost to set up an international calling plan for the length of your trip. Ask about the cost for voice calls from Europe to the US, as well as voice calls within Europe. Rates may vary depending upon the country you're visiting.

Text Messaging Plans and Rates: Find out how much it costs to both send and receive text messages and what kinds of messaging plans your carrier offers.

Data Plans and Rates: Research your carrier's international data plans. Most offer a certain number of megabytes for a flat fee. When assessing how much data you'll need, consider that 100 megabytes lets you view about 500 websites, send/receive about 1,200 emails, stream about 30 minutes of standard-definition video, download about 150 maps (turn-by-turn directions eat up way more data), or upload about 150 posts to social media (these are ballpark numbers; actual numbers vary greatly depending on which apps/websites you're using, your device, etc.). Keep in mind that you'll likely use far less data on the road than you do at home.

You can pay as you go on your normal plan for all three services. But the costs can add up (on average, about $1.50/ minute for voice calls, 50 cents to send text messages, 5 cents to receive them, and $20 to download one megabyte of data).

Travelers who want to stay connected at a lower cost can sign up for an international service plan through their carrier. Most offer some sort of global calling plan that cuts the per-minute cost of phone calls and a flat-fee data plan that includes a certain amount of megabytes. Your normal plan may already include international coverage, as T-Mobile's does. It's a fairly painless process:

1. Confirm that your phone will work in Europe. Nearly all newer phones work fine abroad (as do older phones purchased through AT&T and T-Mobile), but it's smart to check with your carrier if you're unsure.

2. Research your provider's international rates. Plan pricing varies wildly by carrier. Call your provider or check their website for the latest pricing (see the sidebar above for tips and sample rates).

3. Activate international service. A day or two before

Sample International Plans

These are the international plans being offered by each major carrier as of early 2015. Plans and rates change constantly; for the latest, check with your provider.

Plan Overview	Voice	Text	Data
AT&T			
3 pricing tiers: $30/$60/$120	$30 plan: $1/min. $60 plan: $0.50/min. $120 plan: $0.35/min.	Unlimited	$30 plan: 120MB $60 plan: 300MB $120 plan: 800MB
SPRINT			
Separate plans for voice and data; no texting plan	$5/mo. plan includes calls for $0.99/min.	Pay as you go: $0.50 to send, $0.05 to receive	$40/40MB $80/85MB
T-MOBILE			
International coverage included in Simple Choice Plan	$0.20/min.	Unlimited	Unlimited
VERIZON WIRELESS			
Separate plans for voice and data; no texting plan	$5/mo. Includes calls for $0.99-$1.50/min.	Pay as you go: $0.50 to send, $0.05 to receive	$25/100MB

you leave, log on to your mobile phone account or call your provider to activate international roaming for voice, text, and/or data (whichever features you plan to use), and sign up for any international plans.

4. Cancel international service when you get home. When you return from your vacation, cancel any add-on plans that you activated for your trip.

Getting Online with Your Mobile Device

With any laptop, tablet, or smartphone, you can get online via a Wi-Fi signal, which is usually free. If you have a mobile phone (smartphone or basic) or a cellular-enabled computer, you can get online over a cellular network, but you'll usually have to pay for it.

The most cost-efficient way to get online is to log on to Wi-Fi hotspots during your trip. Even if you have an international data plan, you're better off saving most of your online tasks for Wi-Fi. In this section I give you tips on finding hotspots in Europe, as well as advice for conserving your cellular data allotment.

Free Public Wi-Fi in Europe

Some destinations offer free public Wi-Fi at well-trafficked locations. Here's a sampling.

Barcelona: The city has more than 700 free "Barcelona WiFi" hotspots—just look for a blue-and-white diamond logo with a "W" (bcn.cat/barcelonawifi/en).

Dublin: "Dublin Free WiFi" provides more than a dozen hotspots around town (dublincity.ie/main-menu-services-business/dublin-free-wifi).

Germany's Cities: In **Berlin,** more than 100 "Public Wi-Fi Berlin" hotspots at locations such as Gendarmenmarkt, Hackescher Markt, and Potsdamer Platz, let you log on for 30 minutes per day—look for "KD WLAN Hotspot +" or "30 Min Free WIFI" (kabeldeutschland.de/wlan-hotspots). In **Munich,** you'll find more than a dozen free "M-WLAN" hotspots, including at Marienplatz, Karlsplatz, and Odeon Square (search for "M-WLAN" at muenchen.de). The national tourist board's "Youth HotSpot" app pinpoints free Wi-Fi around the country.

Helsinki: Visitors will find free outdoor hotspots throughout the city center. Just look for the "Helsinki City Open" network (no passwords or registration required).

Italy's Cities: Register once for "Free ItaliaWi-Fi," and you can access hotspots at participating municipalities throughout Italy, including Rome, Florence, Venice, Pisa, and Livorno (at freeitaliawifi.it, you'll find a list of network names to look for in each location). You'll need to enter a credit card number, but you won't be charged, and your card number will not be saved. After creating a user name and password, you'll get two hours of free access per day. Visitors to **Florence** will find free Wi-Fi at most major squares, such as Piazza della Signoria, and those who purchase the Firenze Card museum pass get 72 hours of free Wi-Fi at city-run hotspots (firenzecard.it). In

If you plan to use any new apps on your device—such as language translators, ebook readers, or transportation or mapping apps—it's smart to download or update them before your trip, when bandwidth isn't an issue.

Finding Wi-Fi in Europe

Most accommodations in Europe offer free Wi-Fi, but some—especially expensive hotels—charge a fee. In some hotels, Wi-Fi works great; in others, the signal is less reliable or doesn't work well (or at all) beyond the lobby (many European hotels are in old buildings with thick stone walls). Often it's good enough to shoot off an email, but too slow to stream movies or make a video call.

If Wi-Fi is important to you, ask about it when you book—and check that it'll be available in your room. As soon as I arrive at a hotel, I ask at the desk for the password and network name (in case several are in range), so I can log on right away.

When you're out and about, your best bet for finding free Wi-Fi is often at a café. They'll usually tell you their Wi-Fi

Rome, you can browse free for an hour a day on any trams (and at tram stops) with an "ATAC WiFi" logo.
Lisbon: You'll find free Wi-Fi throughout the Metro system (look for the "ON-FI" network) and in the food court at the Armazéns do Chiado shopping center.
London: It's smart to get an account with "The Cloud," a free (but sometimes slow) Wi-Fi service found in many convenient spots, including most London train stations and many museums, coffee shops, cafés, and shopping centers. Use their FastConnect app to locate hotspots (register and download app via thecloud.co.uk). "O2 Wifi" hotspots let you connect for free for two hours in busy locales such as Trafalgar Square, Leicester Square, and Piccadilly (o2wifi.co.uk). In Tube stations, you can hop online and use the free Virgin Media portal, which provides transit updates (but to surf beyond that, you'll need to buy a Wi-Fi pass; my.virginmedia.com/wifi).
Madrid: Plaza Mayor has free Wi-Fi, and more public spaces may offer it soon. You can get online on all Madrid buses and trains—look for signs that say "Wi-Fi gratis."
Paris: "Paris Wi-Fi" offers more than 250 free hotspots around the city. Convenient hotspots include the park alongside Notre-Dame, Place des Vosges in the Marais, Champ de Mars park near the Eiffel Tower, and Esplanade des Invalides. Your connection expires after two hours, but you can immediately reconnect (paris.fr/wifi).
Vienna: "Wien.at Public WLAN" hotspots are located throughout the city, including at Stephansplatz, on Danube Island, and along Mariahilfer Strasse. You'll need to enter a mobile number; after that, you'll receive a text message with a password for registration (go to wien.gv.at, and search for "WLAN").

password if you buy something. As in North America, most McDonald's and Starbucks in Europe offer free Wi-Fi.

You may also find Wi-Fi here and there throughout the day—for example at tourist offices, in city squares (e.g., Marienplatz in Munich), within major museums (e.g., the Tate Modern in London), at public-transit hubs (such as many of London's train stations), and aboard some trains and buses (for instance, Austria's RailJet or on Portugal's long-distance buses). You may need to register or accept terms of service to get online, and some networks limit browsing time (see the sidebar for a rundown of public Wi-Fi in some European cities).

Using Data Roaming Smartly

Using data roaming on your cellular network is handy for times when you can't find Wi-Fi. But while convenient, data roaming is also potentially expensive, depending on your international plan rates. You'll want to be conscious of how much data you're using, since you're probably paying for a limited amount of bandwidth. Still, data roaming can be worth it when you're out and about, need to get online, and don't want to waste your valuable vacation time hunting for a Wi-Fi hotspot.

Budgeting your data is easy if you follow these tips:

Avoid using your cellular network for bandwidth-gobbling tasks. Skyping, downloading apps, and watching YouTube all eat up megabytes and can wait until you're on Wi-Fi. (You're on a Wi-Fi network when you see the symbol for Wi-Fi in the corner of your screen—it looks like a half-rainbow.) If you use a navigation app like Google Maps, there are ways to do so without using any cellular data (see page 174). If you're lost and need to access a map and turn-by-turn directions, do so sparingly.

Keep track of data usage. Upon arrival in Europe, it's smart to start tracking how much data you're using. On your device's menu, look for an item like "cellular data usage" or "mobile data" and reset the counter at the start of your trip so you can see how many megabytes you've consumed. Some carriers automatically send a text message warning if you approach or exceed your limit and will let you upgrade your package without penalty.

Limit automatic updates in your email and other apps. By default, many mobile apps are set to constantly check for a data connection and update information. You can cut your data use by switching off this feature in your various apps. Start with your email: Go to your device's email settings and change them from "auto-retrieve" to "manual," or from "push" to "fetch." This means that you will have to manually download (or "fetch") your messages when you're on Wi-Fi rather than having them automatically downloaded (or "pushed") to your device. If you receive an email with a large photo, video, or other file, wait until you're on Wi-Fi to view it.

Other apps—such as news, weather, social media, and sports tickers—also automatically update. On some devices, you can select which apps are allowed to update via the cellular network. It's smart to disable these features in most of your apps so that they'll only update when you're on Wi-Fi.

Disconnect from your cellular network altogether. Because there are still ways that you can accidentally burn through data, I like the additional safeguard of manually turning off data roaming or cellular data (either works) whenever I'm not using it—check under "cellular" or "network," or ask your service provider how to do it. Then, when

Alternatives for Getting Online

If traveling with a laptop or tablet, you'll typically use Wi-Fi to get online throughout Europe. But if you need something more than Wi-Fi, here are some alternatives.

Ethernet: The fastest and most secure way to get online is through a wired Ethernet connection. High-speed Ethernet jacks are available at some hotels. To connect, simply string an Ethernet cable, which looks like an oversized phone cord, from the jack to your laptop (but not smartphone or tablet, since these lack Ethernet ports). If you don't have a cable, ask to borrow one at reception.

Mobile Hotspots: A mobile hotspot is a device that connects to a cellular data network, enabling you to have near-constant Internet access on your laptop or tablet. It comes in two forms: either as a USB dongle (works on computers with a USB port) or a standalone Wi-Fi hotspot that's about the size of a deck of cards (works with any Wi-Fi-enabled device; your device connects to the hotspot via Wi-Fi and the hotspot connects to the Internet via a cellular network). Hotspots can be pricey, as they require a data plan and likely a contract.

Mobile hotspots are available through your carrier. You can also buy an unlocked mobile hotspot, then purchase a SIM card with data at your destination (explained later, under "Using a European SIM Card.") Or consider renting a hotspot, such as the XCom Global MiFi, which wirelessly connects up to 10 devices for a high fee ($15/day plus $30 shipping; includes the hotspot and all data roaming charges).

Connecting Through Your Smartphone: Many smartphones can be used as a hotspot, which lets laptops, tablets, and other devices piggyback on your phone's cellular data connection (ask your service provider whether and how it works on your phone). This works well if you don't want to buy or rent a dedicated mobile hotspot, but remember that you'll be using cellular data, which can get expensive depending on your international data plan.

you need to get online but can't find Wi-Fi, simply turn it on long enough for the task at hand, then turn it off again. Another way to ensure you're not accidentally using data roaming is to put your device in "airplane" or "flight" mode, and then turn your Wi-Fi back on when needed (this disables phone calls and texts, as well as data).

If you're traveling with an unlocked smartphone (explained later), you can buy a SIM card that also includes data; this can be cheaper than data roaming through your home provider.

Internet Calling and Messaging

A cheap way to stay in touch while traveling is to use Internet calling/messaging apps, such as Skype, Apple's FaceTime and iMessage, or Google+ Hangouts. Many

How to Dial

Many Americans are intimidated by dialing European phone numbers. You needn't be. It's simple, once you break the code.

Calling Internationally

Whether you're phoning from a US landline, your own mobile phone, a Skype account, or a number in another European country (e.g., Spain to Italy), you're making an international call. Here's how to do it:

1. Dial the **international access code.**
   - 011 if calling from a US or Canadian landline or mobile phone; if dialing from a mobile phone, you can enter a + instead of the 011 (press and hold the 0 key).
   - 00 if calling from a number in any European country; if dialing from a mobile phone, you can enter a + instead of the 00.
2. Dial the **country code.**
   - For example, dial 39 if you're calling Italy or 33 for France (see the chart on page 253 for a list of country codes).
3. Dial the **phone number.**
   - If the number begins with a 0, drop it (except for Italy).
   - In some countries, it's normal for phone numbers to have varying lengths (for instance, a seven-digit phone number and an eight-digit mobile number).

Calling Domestically

If you're calling from one number to another within the same European country (either from a landline or with a local mobile phone or SIM card), simply dial the phone number, including the initial 0 if there is one.

In the US, we're accustomed to seven-digit phone numbers and three-digit area codes, but European phone numbers and calling standards are a bit harder to predict. Phone numbers and area codes can vary in length, even within the same country, and mobile phones utilize their own sets of prefixes.

In some countries, much like at home, you can choose to drop the area code if dialing landline to landline within the same area code, while in other countries, you

travelers use a mix of these apps, based on what their friends and family are already using at home.

To use these apps for free, all you have to do is log on to a Wi-Fi network, then connect with any of your friends or family members who are also online and signed into the same service. Although it's possible to use these apps over a cellular network, doing so when traveling can burn through your data allowance, especially if you're making a video call.

Internet calling makes it easy to keep in touch for free.

must dial the full number, even if calling across the street. But I keep things simple by always just dialing the full phone number, including the area code or prefix.

Examples

The chart on page 253 lists country codes for most of Europe. If you get stuck, see countrycallingcodes.com or howtocallabroad.com for more help. Remember that if you're dialing from a mobile phone, you can enter a + instead of the international access code (011 or 00) by pressing and holding the 0 key.

- To call a Munich hotel (tel. 089/264-349) from your Berlin hotel phone, dial 089/264-349. To dial it from your hotel in Italy, enter 00, then 49 (Germany's country code), then 89/264-349 (area code—without its initial 0—and number).
- To call a Paris hotel (01 47 05 49 15) from your US home phone, dial 011, then 33 (France's country code), then 1 47 05 49 15 (the hotel's phone number minus its initial 0).
- To call a Madrid hotel (915-212-900) from a friend's house in Germany, dial 00, then 34 (Spain's country code), then 915-212-900.
- To call a Florence museum (055-238-8651) from your US mobile phone (whether you're in Florence or the US), dial +, then 39 (Italy's country code), then 055-238-8651 (phone number with its 0).

Calling Home

Whether dialing from a mobile phone or landline, this is how to call the US or Canada from Europe:

1. Dial **00,** Europe's international access code, or enter + from any mobile phone.
2. Dial **1,** the country code for the US and Canada.
3. Dial the **phone number,** including area code.

So to call my office in Edmonds, Washington, from anywhere in Europe, I dial 00-1-425-771-8303; or, from a mobile phone, +-1-425-771-8303.

Voice and Video Calls

Skype, Viber, FaceTime, and Google+ Hangouts let you make both voice and video calls. Skype and Viber are available for most devices, including PCs, Macs, Apple's iOS devices, and Android and Windows phones. The Hangouts app is preloaded on Android devices, and anyone with a Google account can install it for free (as a plug-in on their computer's browser, or as an app). FaceTime, built into iOS devices, works especially well for contacting other Apple users.

The biggest hurdle travelers face with Internet calling is finding a Wi-Fi signal that's strong enough for a smooth call. With a solid signal, the sound quality is much better than a standard phone connection; but with a weak signal, the video and audio can be choppy and freeze up. If you're struggling with your connection, try turning off the video and sticking with an audio-only call.

Skype, Viber, and Hangouts also work for making calls from your computer to telephones worldwide. Most services charge just a few cents per minute (you'll have to pre-buy some credit). For example, I use Skype to call ahead from home and reserve hotels, or while I'm traveling to confirm tomorrow's reservation without paying high fees. This is also a good, affordable way for folks back home to call you at a European number (if you don't have your US phone with you or don't want to be charged for receiving a call). Just give them your hotel-room phone number (or your European mobile number), and they can call you using Skype/Viber/Hangouts for much cheaper than dialing direct from their US landline or mobile phone.

Messaging

When you're in Europe, text messaging over the cellular network generally costs money, with some carriers charging per message. So if you want to send a couple of messages to check in with family and friends back home, it's smart to use an app that allows you to send text messages over Wi-Fi.

Apple's iMessage lets you send text, images, and video clips to other Apple users for free over Wi-Fi, just like at home. But if you want to use the iPhone's messaging app to send a text message via a cellular network or to contact a non-Apple user, you'll use data roaming. To avoid accidentally sending a text message when iMessage isn't available, go to Settings, then Messages, and turn off the "Send as SMS" option.

Several similar apps are available, all of which allow you to send a text message, image, or video clip to any other person using that app:

- **Google+ Hangouts** (free, requires Google account; available for Android, iOS, and most Web browsers)
- **What's App** (no account needed per se and free to download but 99 cents/year after that to keep it active; available for virtually all kinds of phones but doesn't work between computers)
- **Viber** (free, no account needed; available for nearly all kinds of phones as well as Windows and Mac computers)
- **Facebook Messenger** (free, requires Facebook account; available on most platforms)

Phoning Cheat Sheet

Just smile and dial, using these rules.

Calling a European number
- **From a mobile phone** (whether you're in the US or in Europe): Dial + (press and hold 0), then country code and number*
- **From a US/Canadian number:** Dial 011, then country code and number*
- **From a different European country** (e.g., German number to French number): Dial 00, then country code and number*
- **Within the same European country** (e.g., German number to another German number): Dial the number as printed, including initial 0 if there is one

* Drop initial 0 (if present) from phone number in all countries except Italy

Calling the US or Canada from Europe
Dial 00, then 1 (country code for US/Canada), then area code and number; on mobile phones, enter + in place of 00

Country	Country Code	Country	Country Code
Austria	43	Italy	39 [2]
Belgium	32	Latvia	371
Bosnia-Herzegovina	387	Montenegro	382
Croatia	385	Morocco	212
Czech Republic	420	Netherlands	31
Denmark	45	Norway	47
Estonia	372	Poland	48
Finland	358	Portugal	351
France	33	Russia	7 [3]
Germany	49	Slovakia	421
Gibraltar	350	Slovenia	386
Great Britain & N. Ireland	44	Spain	34
Greece	30	Sweden	46
Hungary	36 [1]	Switzerland	41
Ireland	353	Turkey	90

[1] For long-distance calls within Hungary, dial 06, then the area code and number.

[2] When making international calls to Italy, do not drop the initial 0 from the phone number.

[3] For long-distance calls within Russia, dial 8, then the area code and number. To call the US or Canada from Russia, dial 8, then 10, then 1, then the area code and number.

Using a European SIM Card

While using your American phone in Europe is easy, it can get expensive. And unreliable Wi-Fi can make the reality of keeping in touch via a service like Skype more frustrating than it should be.

If you anticipate heavy phone or data use, consider traveling with a mobile phone fitted with a European SIM card. This gives you a European mobile number and access to cheaper rates than you'd get through your US carrier, even with an international plan. Generally with a European SIM card, it's free to receive domestic texts and calls, about 2-20 cents/minute to make domestic calls and calls within the EU, and 5-15 cents to send a text within the EU. For the best rates, buy a new SIM card every time you arrive in a new country.

To get a European SIM, you'll need to do the following:

1. Make sure you're equipped with a proper phone. You'll need either a European phone or an unlocked phone in order for a European SIM card to work (some phones are electronically "locked" so you can't switch SIM cards). Check with your carrier—it's possible the phone you have is already unlocked, as this feature is becoming more common in newer models. Otherwise, you can try asking your provider if they'll unlock it for you. Remember that as long as you have a European SIM in your own phone, you won't be reachable at your regular US number.

If it's not possible to unlock your phone, you can buy an unlocked phone either before your trip or at your destination (it's around $40 for a basic unlocked phone). It's also possible to buy an inexpensive mobile phone in Europe that already comes with a SIM card. While these phones are generally locked to work with just one provider (meaning you couldn't switch to another European SIM if traveling to other countries), they may be even cheaper ($20 or less, and often with enough prepaid calling credit to make the phone itself virtually free). If shopping for a phone in Europe, use the European term "mobile" (pronounce it the way Brits do—rhymes with "smile") or "handy" (common in German-speaking areas).

Finally, you may already have an old, unused mobile phone in a drawer somewhere. It's probably locked, but your provider may be willing to send you a code to unlock it.

2. Shop around for a SIM card. SIM cards are sold in Europe at mobile-phone shops, department-store electronics

counters, some newsstands, and even
at vending machines. Costing about
$5-10, they usually include about that
much prepaid calling credit, with no
contract and no commitment. Certain
brands –including Lebara and
Lycamobile, both of which operate
in multiple European countries—are
reliable and provide cheap international calls, including to the US.

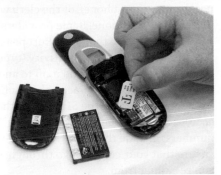

Your phone's
SIM card is
sometimes
hiding behind
the battery.

If you have a smartphone, look
for a SIM card that also includes data. Expect to pay about
$15-30 for a SIM that includes one month of data within the
country you bought it. Be aware that many smartphones
(especially iPhones) use smaller micro-SIM or nano-SIM
cards. Make sure you get the right size card for your phone.

Before buying a SIM card, ask the clerk about rates for
calls within the country; to and from other countries you'll
be visiting; and, if you plan on calling home, to the US and
Canada. Also check the rates for data use and for sending/
receiving a text message (called an "SMS" in Europe). Make
sure you get rates for data and texting both within and
outside the card's home country. Rates can vary wildly from
brand to brand and store to store.

3. Set up your SIM card. Once you buy your SIM card,
ask the clerk to insert it, set it up, and make a test call to be
sure it's working properly. Turning on the phone, you'll be
prompted to enter the SIM PIN, which you may be asked
to enter every time you start up the phone. If text or voice
prompts are in another language, ask the clerk whether
they can be switched to English. Also find out how to check
your credit balance (usually you'll key in a few digits and hit
"Send"). Remember to record your new phone number so you
can pass it on to friends and family.

Note that many countries require you to register the
SIM card with your passport as an antiterrorism measure. If
that's the case, it may take an hour or two after submitting
the information before you can use the phone.

4. Top up your SIM card. When you run out of credit,
you can top it up at newsstands, tobacco shops, mobile-
phone stores, or many other businesses (look for the SIM
card's logo in the window). Tell the clerk how much credit
you want. You'll either get a voucher with instructions (in
most cases, to top up credit, you'll punch in a long string of

numbers on your phone), or the clerk will send the credit directly to your phone. Some providers let you top up online.

Tips: Be aware that most European SIM cards expire after a certain period of inactivity (typically 3-12 months), so use up the credit or hand it off to another traveler. Also, be sure to save your contacts' phone numbers in the phone itself, rather than on the SIM card; otherwise, you'll lose access to them when you switch SIMs. When storing phone numbers, include the plus (+) sign and the country code to ensure that your calls will go through, regardless of where you're calling from.

CUTTING THE CORD: TRAVELING WITHOUT A MOBILE DEVICE

If you prefer to travel without a mobile device, you can stay in touch using public telephones and computers.

Landline Telephones

You can make phone calls from your hotel, public phones, and call shops.

Phones in your hotel room can be great for local calls and for calls using cheap international phone cards (described in the sidebar on the opposite page). Otherwise, they can be an almost criminal rip-off. Most hotels charge a fee for placing local and "toll-free" calls as well as long-distance and international calls—always ask for the rates before you dial. Since you'll never be charged for receiving calls, it's better to have someone from the US call you in your room, rather than the other way around. Note that smaller, B&B-type accommodations often don't have a landline in each room.

Relatively few phone booths remain in Europe... and those that do generally take phone cards rather than coins.

While public pay phones are on the endangered species list, you'll still see phone booths and banks of phones in post offices and train stations. Pay phones generally come with multilingual instructions. Most public phones in Europe work with insertable phone cards (described in the sidebar). While some card phones also accept coins, most don't. Press the "follow-on call" button (rather than hanging up) to make another call without losing your credit.

You'll see many cheap call shops that advertise low rates to faraway lands, often in train-station neighborhoods. While these target immigrants who want to call home cheaply, tourists can use them, too. You'll be assigned to your own private sweatbox, make the call, and pay the bill when you're done. Before making your call, be clear on the rates. For example, the listed price may be per *unit,* rather than per minute—if there are 10 "units" in a minute, your call costs 10 times what you expected.

Internet Cafés and Public Computers

In Europe, finding a place to get online without a mobile device isn't difficult. A number of hotels have a computer in the lobby for guests to use. Otherwise, head for an Internet café, where you can pay to use a public computer. Even towns without an Internet café usually offer some way to get online—at libraries, bookstores, post offices, tourist offices, and so on. Ask your hotelier for the nearest place.

European computers typically use non-American keyboards. Most letters are the same as back home, but a few are switched around, and many of the command keys are labeled in a foreign language. Many European keyboards have an "Alt Gr" key (for "Alternate Graphics") to the right of the space bar; press this to insert the extra symbol that appears on some keys. Europeans have different names for, and different ways to type, the @ symbol; check the sidebar on the next page to see a few. If you can't locate a special character (such as the @ symbol), simply copy it from a Web page and paste it into your email message.

Often a simple keystroke or click of the mouse can make the foreign

Types of Phone Cards

Europe uses two types of telephone cards. You can find them at many post offices, newsstands, street kiosks, tobacco shops, and train stations.

Insertable Phone Cards: These cards, which can only be used at pay phones, are available in most countries (but not Britain). To use them, simply take the phone off the hook, insert the card, wait for a dial tone, and dial away. The phone displays your credit ticking down as you talk. Each European country has its own phone card—so your German card won't work in an Austrian phone.

International Phone "Cards": These cards let you make inexpensive calls—within Europe, or to the US, for pennies a minute—from nearly any phone, including the one in your hotel room. You'll either get a prepaid card with a toll-free number and a scratch-to-reveal PIN code, or just a code printed on a receipt. If the voice prompts aren't in English, experiment: Dial your code, followed by the pound sign (#), then the phone number, then pound again, and so on, until it works. National telecom companies in some countries (including Germany and Great Britain) levy a hefty surcharge for using one of these cards from a pay phone—which effectively eliminates any savings. But you can still use them cheaply from your hotel.

Typing @ on European Keyboards

Language	Name of @ Sign	Pronounced	How It's Typed
French	*signe arobase*	seen-yuh ah-roh-bahz	Alt Gr + 0
German	*At-zeichen;* also *Klammeraffe* ("monkey hug") or *A-Affenschwanz* ("A with a monkey tail")	eht-TSĪKH-ehn	Alt Gr + Q
Italian	*chiocciola* ("snail")	kee-OH-choh-lah	Alt Gr + @
Spanish and Portuguese	*arroba*	ah-ROH-bah	Alt Gr + 2

keyboard work like an American one. Many computers have a box in the lower right-hand corner of the screen where you can click and select which type of keyboard you prefer. If not, ask the clerk for help.

You can even make Internet calls on some public computers. Most European Internet cafés have microphones and webcams built into their machines. With a Google or Skype account (most public computers have Skype installed), you can just log on and chat away.

INTERNET SECURITY ON THE ROAD

Whether you're accessing the Internet with your own device or at a public terminal, using a shared network or computer comes with the potential for increased security risks and can open you up to cyber attacks.

While you shouldn't be freaked out about your computer use on the road, travelers who are too careless with their digital information can open themselves up to significant hassle and expense. Aim for a middle ground of cautiousness, and protect your computer and your personal information by heeding the following tips.

Safety Tips for Traveling with Your Own Device

If you're taking your devices on the road, be aware that gadget theft is an issue in Europe. Not only should you take precautions to protect your devices from thieves (see page 328 for tips), but you should also configure them for maximum security so that if they are stolen, your personal data will stay private.

First, check that you're running the latest version of your device's operating system and security software. Next, consider tightening your security settings. At the very least, make sure your device is password- or passcode-protected so thieves can't access your information if it's stolen. If it's already protected, consider decreasing the time it takes for the screen to lock when not in use—while it's annoying to have to keep entering your code, that's not nearly as annoying as identity theft (you can relax your security settings once you're home). For an extra layer of security, consider setting passwords on apps that access key info (such as email or Facebook).

Many laptops have a file-sharing option. Though this setting is likely turned off by default, it's a good idea to check that this option is not activated on your computer, so that people sharing a Wi-Fi network with you can't access your files (if you're not sure how, search online for your operating system's name and "turn off file sharing"). Newer versions of Windows have a "Public network" setting (choose this when you first join the network) that automatically configures your computer so that it's less susceptible to invasion.

Once on the road, use only legitimate Wi-Fi hotspots. Ask the hotel or café for the specific name of their network, and make sure you log on to that exact one. Hackers sometimes create bogus hotspots with a similar or vague name (such as "Hotel Europa Free Wi-Fi") that shows up alongside a bunch of authentic networks. It's better if a network uses a password (especially a hard-to-guess one) rather than being open to the world. If you're not actively using a hotspot, turn off Wi-Fi so that your device is not visible to others.

Safety Tips for Using Public Computers

It's perfectly safe to use a public computer for tasks that don't require you to log in to an account. For instance, checking train schedules, maps, or museum hours doesn't pose a security risk. The danger lies in accessing personal accounts that require you to enter a login and password (such as email, Facebook, or any ecommerce site).

If you're traveling with your own device, try to make that device your sole means of accessing personal accounts. But if you'll be relying on hotel-lobby computers or Internet cafés, keep in mind that you have no idea who used that computer last—or who will hop on next. Public computers may be loaded with damaging malware, such as key logger programs that keep track of what you're typing—including passwords.

If you do need to access personal accounts on a public computer, make sure that the Web browser you use doesn't store your login information. If you have the option of opening an "incognito" or "private" browser window, use it. When you sign in to any site, look for ways to ensure that the browser forgets your user name and password after you log out: For instance, you should click the box for "public or shared computer" or unclick any box that says "stay signed in" or "remember me." It's also a good idea to clear the Internet browser's cache, history, and cookies after you're done, so fewer artifacts of your surfing session remain—especially if you've accessed sensitive information (under the browser's "Options" or "Preferences" settings, look for a "Privacy" or "Security" category).

Europe's Internet cafés, often open long hours, allow travelers to get online.

Finally, consider setting up two-step verification for your most important accounts. This requires you to enter not just a password but a second code whenever you log in using an unfamiliar computer (available with many Web-based email and social-networking sites).

Accessing Personal Information Online

While you're away, you may be tempted to check your online banking or credit-card statements, or to take care of other personal-finance chores. Internet security experts advise against accessing these sites entirely while traveling.

Definitely refrain from logging in to personal financial sites on a public computer. But even if you're using your own mobile device at a password-protected hotspot, any hacker who's logged on to the same network may be able to see what you're up to (chances are remote—but it's possible). If you need to access banking information, it's best to do so on a hard-wired connection (i.e., using an Ethernet cable in your hotel room). Otherwise, try to log in via a cellular network, which is safer than a Wi-Fi connection.

Even if you avoid accessing bank accounts during your trip, you may still need to enter your credit card information online, such as for booking museum or theater tickets. If so, make sure that the site is secure. Most browsers display a little padlock icon to indicate this; also check that the page's URL begins with "https" instead of "http." Never send a credit-card number (or any other sensitive information) over a website that doesn't begin with "https."

It's also important to be careful if emailing personal information. Don't send your credit-card number in one email message. It's better to call or fax. Some people send their credit-card number in two halves, via two separate email messages. For extra security, a few banks, such as Citi and Bank of America, allow their customers to create virtual account numbers, which are one-time or short-term numbers linked to their regular credit card.

City Transportation

Shrink and tame big cities by mastering their subway and bus systems—you'll save time, money, and energy. Europe's public-transit systems are so good that many urban Europeans go through life never learning to drive. Their wheels are trains, subways, trams, buses, and the occasional taxi. If you embrace these forms of transportation when visiting cities, you'll travel smarter.

Buses can give you a tour of the town on the way to your destination. Subways are speedy and never get stuck in traffic jams. With the proper attitude, taking public transit can be a cultural experience, plunging you into the people- and advertisement-filled river of workaday life.

This chapter offers tips on using subways, buses, and taxis. For information on taking trains, long-distance buses, and ferries, read the Trains, Buses & Boats chapter.

PUBLIC TRANSIT TIPS

Even if you've never used public transit in your hometown, these tricks can help you quickly master your transportation options in Europe's cities. You'll have the city by the tail, without having to shell out for taxis.

Get a transit map. With a map, anyone can decipher the code to easy, affordable urban transportation. Paris and London have the most extensive—and the most needed—subway systems. Pick up a schematic map at the tourist office or subway ticket window, ask for one at your hotel, or print one off a website. Many city maps, even free ones, include a basic transit map. To help you plot your travel, major transit systems offer online journey planners, and many sights list the nearest bus or subway stop on their websites and brochures. Apps for the London Tube, Paris Métro, and other subway systems offer digital plans of public-transit networks that work offline and save you from having to unfold an unwieldy map on a busy platform.

Learn what's covered by a ticket. In many cities, the same tickets are good on the subway, trams, and buses, and include transfers between the systems; in other places, you'll need to buy a new ticket each time you transfer. If a ticket seems expensive, ask what it covers—$4 may seem like a lot until you learn it's good for a round-trip, two hours, or several transfers.

Consider your ticket options. Your choices, which vary per city, are individual tickets, multi-ticket deals, passes, and reloadable cards. You'll pay the most per ride by buying individual tickets, but this can be the way to go if you'll be taking only a few rides or prefer to get around mainly on foot.

If you're committed to using public transit, the following options will cut your per-ride costs and save you time (because you won't have to stand in a ticket line every time you travel):

- Multi-ticket deals offer you a set number of tickets—most notably Paris' 10-ticket *carnet*—that you can use anytime and share with companions, even on the same ride (unlike passes and cards, which can be used by only one person at a time).
- Passes allow unlimited travel on all public transport for a set number of hours or days; a 24-hour pass usually costs less than four single fares. Some passes cover sights as well or offer admission discounts. Before you buy, plan how you'll get the most use out of your pass during its period of validity.

Reloadable cards, such as Stockholm's prepaid SL-Access card, require a deposit to buy, subtract the cost of your rides when you use it, and can be topped off when the balance runs low.

LEFT Public transit—the European treat

RIGHT If you take advantage of public transportation, you can zip quickly, effortlessly, and inexpensively around Europe's most congested cities.

You can buy tickets, passes, and cards at subway ticket-machines or windows, and, depending on the city, on the bus (usually for exact change and at a slightly higher cost than the ticket-machine price), at newsstands, or in tourist offices. Ask about discounts if you're young, old, or traveling with children.

> ## Transportation Apps
>
> **MetrO:** Route planner for subways, buses, trams, and trains
> **Uber:** Find and order a taxi in major cities

Don't try to travel for free. Many European subways, buses, and trams use the honor system, patrolled sporadically by ticket checkers—some are in uniform, others rove incognito, but all mean business. If you're caught without a valid ticket, you'll most likely have to pay a hefty fine.

If confused, ask for help. Europe's buses and subways are filled with people who are more than happy to help lost tourists locate themselves. Confirm with a local that you're at the right platform or bus stop before you board. If you tell them where you're going, the driver or passengers sitting around you will gladly tell you where to get off.

Expect pickpockets. While public transportation feels safe, savvy riders are constantly on guard. Per capita, there are more pickpockets on Europe's subway trains and buses than just about anywhere else. They congregate wherever there are crowds or bottlenecks: on escalators, at turnstiles, or at the doors of packed buses or subway cars as people get on and off. If there's a hubbub, assume it's a distraction for pickpockets—put a hand on your valuables. Be on the lookout, wear your money belt, and you'll do fine. (For tips on avoiding theft, see the Theft and Scams chapter.)

SUBWAYS

Most of Europe's big cities are blessed with an excellent subway system, and wise travelers know that learning this network is key to efficient sightseeing. European subways go by many names: "Metro" is the most common term on the Continent, but Germany and Austria use "U-Bahn." For Scandinavia, it's the "T-bane" in Oslo, "T-bana" in Stockholm, and "S-tog" in Copenhagen. In London, it's the "Tube" (to the British, a "subway" is a pedestrian underpass). In big subway

systems, shops are clustered at larger stops.

Subways generally operate from about 6 a.m. until midnight. They rarely follow a specific schedule, but just pass by at frequent but irregular intervals. Most systems have electronic signs noting when the next train will arrive.

Here are tips for smooth sailing on Europe's subways:

Study your map. Subway maps are usually included within city maps and are posted prominently at the station and usually on board. A typical subway map is a spaghetti-like tangle of intersecting, colorful lines. The individual lines are color-coded, numbered, and/or lettered (and even named, in the case of London); their stations, including those at either end of the line, are also indicated. These end stations—while probably places you'll never go—are important, since they tell you which direction the train is headed and appear (usually) as the name listed on the front of the train.

A few cities (like Rome) have just two or three subway lines, while London has over a dozen. Some cities' subways share the tracks with express commuter trains (such as Paris' RER and Germany's S-Bahn), which make fewer stops and can usually get you across town faster.

Plan your route. Determine which line you need, the name of the end station in the direction you want to go, and (if necessary) where to transfer to another line. In the station, you'll use this information to follow signs to reach your platform. (See the sidebar on the next page for a step-by-step sample trip.) When in doubt, just ask someone.

Validate your ticket. Once you buy a ticket, you may need to validate it in a turnstile slot (don't forget to retrieve it)—watch to see what others do. If you have an all-day or multi-day ticket, you may need to validate it only the first time you use it, or not at all (ask when you buy it). If there's no turnstile at the station, it doesn't mean the subway is free; if you're caught

As you'll constantly be reminded on London's Tube... mind the gap.

As you enter the subway station, insert your ticket into the slot to open the turnstile. After validating your ticket, remember to reclaim it.

A Sample Subway Trip

Let's say you want to go from your hotel to the art museum on the other side of town. Your hotel is a five-minute walk from the Napoleon station on the A line. Note that the A line has two end stations: Outer Limits to the north and Suburb del Sud to the south. The art museum is on the B line, so you'll need to transfer at the

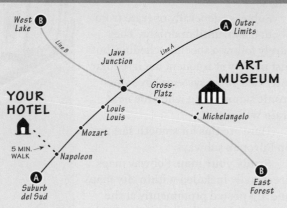

station where these two lines intersect: Java Junction.

Here's how you'll do it:

1. Entering the subway at the Napoleon station, follow signs to trains going in the direction of Outer Limits (the northern end station).
2. Ride three stops to Java Junction, where you get off to transfer to line B.
3. Follow signs to line B, in the direction of East Forest (the end station).
4. Ride the train two stops to the Michelangelo station.
5. Use the neighborhood map in the station to choose the exit closest to the museum.

Congratulations—you've survived your first European subway trip!

traveling without a valid ticket, you'll be fined, usually on the spot. Don't throw away your ticket too soon—you might need to insert it in a turnstile to exit the system (the machine might keep your ticket if it's used up). Once you're out, toss or tear used tickets to avoid confusing them with unused ones.

Keep alert. Follow signage carefully as you navigate through the station. Confirm that you're at the right platform—heading in the right direction—before boarding. Subways can get packed during rush hour. Try to steer clear of crowds and commotion; there are usually fewer people in the first and last cars.

Stick together. If you're with a companion or group, make sure everyone knows the name of your final stop before boarding, stays close together, and agrees on a game plan in case you get separated. If a subway is about to depart as you arrive on the platform, don't rush to catch it and risk leaving behind your companions; subways run frequently, and it's far easier to wait for the next departure than to reconnect with your split-up group.

Get off at the right place. Once on the train, follow along with each stop on your map. Newer cars may have an electronic screen showing the next stop. Sometimes the driver or an automated voice announces the upcoming stop—but don't count on this cue, as a foreign name spoken by a native speaker over a crackly loudspeaker can be difficult to understand. Keep an eye out the window as you pull into each station; the station's name will be posted prominently on the platform or along the wall. If the train is crowded, move close to the doors one stop before you want to exit. When the train stops, the doors may open automatically, or you may need to open them yourself by pushing a button or pulling a lever. Don't panic—watch others and imitate.

Subway Etiquette

- On escalators to and from platforms, stand on the right, pass on the left.
- When waiting at the platform, stand to either side of the opening doors, out of the way of people exiting the train. Board only after everyone who wants to leave is off.
- Talk softly on board. Listen to how quietly Europeans communicate and follow their lead.
- On a crowded train, try not to block the exit (unless your stop is next). If you're at the door of a packed train when it reaches a stop, step out of the car and off to the side, let others off, then get back on.

If you need to transfer, follow the signs. Changing from one subway line to another can be as easy as walking a few steps to an adjacent platform—or a bewildering wander via a labyrinth of stairs and long passageways. Subway systems are clearly signed—just follow along (or ask a local for help).

Exit the station. When you arrive at your destination station, follow exit signs up toward street level, keeping an eye out for posted maps of the surrounding neighborhood to help you get your bearings. Bigger stations have multiple exits, signposted by street name or nearby landmarks. Choosing the right exit will help you avoid extra walking and unnecessary forays through busy intersections. Some travelers carry a pocket compass to help them get oriented when they surface from the subway.

When using public transit (buses or the underground), take full advantage of posted signs and maps to save needless searching and walking (for instance, know exactly where your bus stops or which underground exit of many leaves you closest to your destination). And thoughtful neighborhood maps help you get oriented upon arrival.

BUSES

Getting around town on city buses is a little more compli-cated than using the subway, but has its advantages. Since you're not underground, it's easier to stay oriented, see the landmarks, and enjoy the vibrant street life out the window. In fact, some public bus routes are downright scenic—Paris' bus #69 gives you a great sightseeing introduction for just the cost of a transit ticket. Bus stops are more closely spaced than subway stops—meaning the bus is useful even for short hops and usually gets you closer to where you need to go. Some buses go where the subway can't, such as the top of Castle Hill in Budapest.

Like subways, city buses run frequently, especially during peak hours (if a bus is packed, wait for the next one). Although night buses run less frequently and follow limited routes, they're useful for night owls who don't want to spring for a taxi. The main disadvantage of buses is that they're slowed down by traffic, so try to avoid taking them during rush hour.

In many cities, hop-on, hop-off tourist buses connect the major sights; these are generally privately operated (for details, see page 276). The focus of this section is on public city buses.

To travel smartly by bus, follow these tips:

Plan your route. You can usually get a bus map and schedule from local tourist or transit offices, print them off the bus system's website, or use a public-transit app. Many bus stops have their routes and timetables posted, and some have electronic signs noting how many minutes until the next bus arrives.

Confirm the essentials before you board. Find out if you need to have a ticket in advance or if you can buy it on the bus. Make sure you're getting on the right bus going in the right direction. Before you get on, mention your destina-tion to a local or the driver. Smile and ask, for example, "Vaticano?"

Validate your ticket. Usually you enter at the front of the bus and show your ticket to the driver, or validate it by inserting it into an automated time-stamp box. Observe and imitate what the locals do.

Get off at the right stop. Bus stops, like subway stops, are named

(usually for a cross street or nearby landmark), but their names are often difficult to see from a moving bus. It can be tricky to get off where you intend, so it pays to stay alert: Have a sense of how long a ride is going to take, and know the names of the stops coming up right before yours (and the one right after yours, so you'll know if you've gone too far). If possible, sit near the door, so you can hop out easily. On a cross-town trip, you'll have time to enjoy the sights. As you ride, follow along the route on your map, looking for landmarks along the way: monuments, bridges, major cross streets, and so on. If you're uncertain about your stop, get the attention of the driver or another passenger and ask, "Prado?" (For extra credit, preface your request with the local word for please.) Then wait for them to signal to you when the bus reaches the Prado.

In bike-friendly cities such as Amsterdam and Copenhagen, buses often let you off directly into busy bicycle lanes. Look carefully in both directions, as you exit.

Signal for your stop. Some buses pull over at every stop, while others only stop by request; this means you can't necessarily navigate by counting stops. If in doubt, look for a pull cord or a button with the local word for "stop," and use it to signal that you want to get off at the next stop.

TAXIS

Taxis are underrated, scenic time savers that zip you effortlessly from one sight to the next (except during rush-hour traffic, when they're stuck like everyone else). I enjoy cab rides. Many of my favorite insider tips and most interesting conversations have come from chatting up taxi drivers. But don't trust their advice blindly; cabbies can get kickbacks for recommending (and delivering you to) a particular restaurant or attraction.

While cabs are expensive for the lone budget traveler, a group of three or four people can often travel cheaper by taxi than by buying bus or subway tickets. Taxis are especially cheap in Mediterranean countries and Eastern Europe. You can go anywhere by cab in downtown Lisbon or Athens for about $15.

The ride-booking service Uber is also available in a number of European cities, including London, Paris, Prague, Barcelona, and Vienna, and rides can be cheaper than taxis. Like at home, you request a car via the Uber app on your mobile device, and the fare automatically gets charged to your credit card. But you'll need an Internet connection to request a car, so it's best to do it when you're on Wi-Fi (unless you have a data roaming plan).

Tipping: For a typical ride, round up to the next euro on the fare (to pay a €13 fare, give €14); for a long ride, to the nearest 10 (for a €76 fare, give €80). If the cabbie hauls your bags and zips you to the airport to help you catch your flight, you might want to toss in a little more. But if you feel like you're being driven in circles or otherwise ripped off, skip the tip.

Avoiding Taxi Scams

Though many Americans are wired to assume that taxi drivers in other countries are up to no good, I've also found that most drivers are honest. Sure, scams happen. But with the right tips and a watchful eye, you'll get where you want to go without being taken for a ride.

Be extra careful at airports and train stations. Dishonest cabbies often lurk at major transit points, ready to take advantage of travelers who are jet-lagged and travel-weary—just when they're most susceptible to getting ripped off. If you don't want to worry about getting conned the minute you arrive at a new destination, plan ahead. In many cities, you can arrange for an airport shuttle bus to pick you up at the airport and zip you straight to your hotel (you can ask your hotelier for a recommended service). Another option, much cheaper than a taxi ride, is taking public transportation into town. Recently, I took a speedy train from Rome's airport to the train station downtown, then caught a bus from there to my hotel. It took me less than an hour, and while a taxi would have cost me about $65, I paid about $50—for the train fare and a handy transit pass that lasted me all week. If you want to take a taxi from the airport, it's better to head for the official taxi stand and join the queue rather than flag one down.

Always choose a well-marked cab. It should have a big, prominent taxi-company logo and telephone number. Avoid using unmarked beaters with makeshift taxi lights on top.

These Sorrento cabbies hire by the hour and would love to show you around.

In some cities, it's easy to flag down a cab; in any city, you can find cabs at a taxi stand. These stands are often listed as prominently as subway stations on city maps; look for the little *T*s (or ask a local to direct you to the nearest one).

When you need a ride from a hotel or restaurant, you can have the staff call a taxi for you (or use a taxi-finding app to order one yourself). This can dramatically decrease your odds of getting ripped off, but be aware that in many places, the meter starts ticking from the time the call is received. Note that if you have an early morning flight to catch, it'll save you some stress (and cost nothing beyond the usual supplements) to have your hotelier book a cab for you the day before.

Establish a price or rough estimate up-front. It's usually best to make sure the cabbie uses the taxi meter. But for certain standard trips (such as to or from the airport), it can be common for the cabbie to use a set price. Know the going rate—ask your hotelier or the tourist office in advance how much a taxi ride should cost to your destination. You can check your guidebook or worldtaximeter.com for estimated taxi fares in larger cities.

Sometimes tourists wrongly accuse their cabbies of taking the long way around or adding unfair extras. But what can seem like a circuitous route may still be the shortest, given pedestrianized zones and one-way streets. And many supplements are legit, based on the time of day (nights, early mornings, and weekends), amount of baggage, extra people, airport taxes, port fees, and so on.

In cities such as London, Paris, and Barcelona, meters are tamper-proof. That said, even cabbies with honest meters have ways of overcharging tourists. One common trick is for cabbies to select the pricier "night and weekend" rate on their meter during a weekday. An explanation of the different meter rates should be posted somewhere in the cab, often in English; if you're confused about the tariff, ask your cabbie to explain. If you suspect foul play, following the route on your map or conspicuously writing down the cabbie's license information can shame a cad into being honest.

Pay with small bills. Using small bills minimizes your chance of getting ripped off. If you only have a large bill, state the denomination out loud as you hand it to the cabbie. They can be experts at dropping your €50 note and then showing you a €20. Count your change. If, for whatever reason, I'm charged a ridiculous price for a ride, I put a reasonable sum on the seat and say good-bye. Don't be intimidated by a furious cabbie.

Taking a Taxi Between Cities

While a budget traveler would generally never dream of hiring a taxi for a trip between cities, it can actually be a fairly good value. For example, if you're headed somewhere that's a long train trip but a short drive away, a taxi can be an affordable splurge, especially if the cost is split between two or more people.

Consider the time you'll save over public transportation— for example, one hour of sweat-free, hotel-door-to-hotel-door service versus two sticky hours on stop-and-go public transit, including transfers to and from the train or bus station. Simply ask any cabbie what they'd charge (it could be an hourly rate or even an off-meter flat rate—they know you have a cheap public-transit alternative and might be willing to strike a deal if they want the work). Or ask at your hotel if they have a line on any car or taxi services that do the trip economically. See if you can find a driver who's accustomed to taking tourists on these trips. While not technically guides, these drivers are often willing to provide some basic commentary on what you're seeing and might even suggest some interesting stops along the way.

Sightseeing

After months of planning, you're finally on the ground in Europe, and the real work—and joy— begins: sightseeing. This is when it pays to have a thoughtful plan. The pointers in this chapter will help you get oriented to your surroundings; make the most out of your sightseeing time; navigate museums, churches, castles, and other sights smartly; and find your way off the beaten path.

GETTING ORIENTED

Whether tackling big cities or quaint villages, you don't want to feel like a stranger in a strange land (even though that's exactly what you are). Getting oriented is especially important in big cities—which, for many travelers, are the most intimidating part of a European trip. Visitors who decide to wing it in Europe's large cities invariably waste time—and miss out. Here are your best resources for getting acclimated to a new place.

Guidebooks and Maps

Have a good guidebook for wherever you're traveling. If you haven't shown up with one, get one; they're sold at news-stands, major sights, English bookstores, and the English sections in large bookstores (see page 31 for a rundown of guidebooks).

While guidebooks come with basic maps of big cities, these are generally small and intended only to give you an overview. A detailed, foldout map can save you endless time and frustration; I make a point of picking one up immediately upon arrival. (You can almost always get a decent map free or cheaply at the local tourist office—described later.) If choosing a city sightseeing map, make sure the city center is detailed enough, because that's where you'll be spending most of your time. If you'll be relying heavily on public transit, get a map that shows not just subway stations, but bus and tram lines and stops. For an extended stay in a sprawling city, it can be worth paying extra for a sturdier, more detailed map. Or consider using a mapping app on your smartphone (for details, see page 174).

Your first stop in a new town: the tourist information office

Study your map to understand the city's layout. Relate the location of landmarks—your hotel, major sights, the river, main streets, the train station—to each other. Use any viewpoint, such as a church spire, tower, or hilltop, to understand the lay of the land and see where you're going next.

Tourist Information Offices

No matter how well I know a town, my first stop is always the tourist information office. Nearly any place with a tourist industry has an information service for visitors on the main square, in the City Hall or public library, at the train station, or sometimes at airports or freeway entrances. You don't need the address—just follow the signs. A normally busy but friendly and multilingual staff gives out sightseeing information, reserves hotel rooms, sells concert or theater tickets, and answers questions.

Prepare a list of questions ahead of time. Write up a proposed sightseeing schedule. Find out if it's workable or if you've left out any important sights. Confirm closed days and free-admission days. If necessary, get ideas on where to eat and sleep, though keep in mind that their advice can be biased. Many tourist offices aren't nonprofit services— they're businesses that sell things and work on fees and commissions.

Entertainment Guides

Big European cities bubble with entertainment, festivities, and nightlife. But these events won't come to you. New in town and unable to speak the native language, travelers can be oblivious to a once-in-a-lifetime event erupting just across the bridge. A periodical entertainment guide is the key. Every big city has one, either in English (such as *What's On in*

Oslo or *Time Out,* which has editions in many cities) or in the local language, but easy to decipher (such as the *Pariscope* weekly in Paris).

Printed guides may be available at the tourist office (where they're often free), at newsstands, English-language bookstores, or at the front desk of big, fancy hotels (look like a guest and help yourself). Many guides can also be found online.

Events are posted on city walls everywhere. They may be in a foreign language, but that really doesn't matter when it reads: *Weinfest, Música Folklórica, 9 Juni, 21:00, Piazza Maggiore, Entre Libre,* and so on. Figure out the signs—or miss the party.

Other Resources

If you find yourself in a town with no guidebook coverage or tourist office, glance through a postcard rack to get a quick overview of the town's most famous sights. Even the most mundane town will feature whatever's worth seeing on its postcards.

Firsthand advice is available from hotel staff, B&B hosts, hostel employees, and other travelers. Glean advice from the couple seated next to you at breakfast, chat with the waiter who serves you lunch, or ask a shop owner for tips.

You can also find help online: Search Twitter for the scuttlebutt on local events, poll your social-network friends for advice, or choose restaurants with the help of user-review sites like Yelp and TripAdvisor (see page 38).

TOURS

Organized tours are a great way to acclimate to a new city and learn about its history and highlights. Not only do tours provide a city overview, but they also give you an idea of what to revisit later in your stay. Especially in big cities, you'll find tours of all kinds, from guided walks to bus rides that let you hop on and off at will. And in a number of places, audio tours are available for those who prefer a DIY approach.

Guided Walking Tours

These are my favorite introduction to a city. Since they focus on just a small part of a larger whole (generally the old town center), they are thorough. The tours are usually conducted in English by well-trained guides who are sharing their town for the noble purpose of giving you an appreciation of its history, people, and culture—not to make a lot of money. Walking tours are personal, inexpensive, and a valuable education. They're nearly always time and money well spent.

In major European cities, you'll see advertisements from start-up companies offering "free" walking tours. While the tours are indeed free, tipping is expected; in fact, the guides don't earn money unless you tip. On these free tours, guides—generally expat students who have memorized a script—tend to emphasize stories over a strictly academic approach, and are known to take liberties with historical events and characters. And they may spend your valuable time heavily promoting their company's other tours (which are not free). Personally, I'd rather support tours offered by established companies, and pay up front for hard-working guides whose goal is to make the city's history come alive. But these free tours can be enjoyable, and for travelers on a budget, they provide an affordable way to get to know a place.

Try a guided walk to learn about a town that's probably a thousand years older than your hometown.

Bus Orientation Tours

Many cities have fast-orientation bus tours that take you around the city on a double-decker bus. Riding in the open air atop a two-story bus, you get a feel for the city's layout as the major sights roll on by; most buses include live or recorded narration. Many are structured as hop-on/hop-off tours with a circular route that connects the top sights; with an all-day pass, you can hop off to visit a sight, then catch a later bus to continue the route.

You might even go topless on some hop-on, hop-off buses.

Bus tours usually cost about $30-40. Some can be a disappointing rip-off; others are a great sightseeing tool. If you're short on time, have limited mobility, or would appreciate an overview before diving into a city, they can be worth the money. If I had only one day in a big city, I might spend half of it on one of these tours.

But before you shell out for

a ticket, consider a few key factors: route, quality of narration, and for hop-on/hop-off buses, frequency. The best-value hop-on/hop-off tours leave several times an hour, visit sights I actually want to see, and feature an engaging live guide (if the guide is good, I'll stay on for the entire route). Be wary of overcrowded buses—if space is full on top, you may have no choice but to be crammed into the (potentially hot and stuffy) lower level. It's worth waiting for the next bus if that will get you space on an upper level, where views come from a higher vantage point and aren't marred by smeared windows. The best scenario is enjoying the view from a top-less bus on a sunny day.

Many cities also offer a public bus (e.g., Paris' bus #69 or Berlin's bus #100) or boat route (Amsterdam has several, Venice has the Grand Canal) that connects the city's major sightseeing attractions; you can ride these as if they were low-cost (unguided) tour buses/boats. Tourists buy the one-day pass and make the circuit at their leisure (for more on city buses, see page 268.)

Local Guides

For the price of four seats on a forgettable city bus tour with recorded narration, you can often hire your own private guide for a personalized city tour (most cost-effective if you're traveling with a group). Every city has a long list of English-speaking professional guides who earn their living giving tours. They hire out by the day or half-day and generally follow a national guide service fee schedule (about $200 per half-day, which can mean two to four hours—ask when you book). In my research, I've grown accustomed to relying heavily upon these experts and generally find them well worth the investment. You can find recommendations for good local guides in guidebooks, on travel websites, and from the local tourist information office. Although it's possible to drop by the tourist office when you're in town and arrange

Guides bring museums and castles to life.

a guide, it's better to email or call the office in advance; typically, the office will give you a guide's contact information and you'll book the guide yourself by email or phone. When I meet particularly good independent guides, I include their contact information in my guidebooks.

Hiring a private guide is an especially good value in Eastern Europe,

where guides tend to be young, intelligent, and enthusiastic—and charge half as much. The best guides are often those whose tours you can pick up at a specific sight. They usually really know their museums, castles, cathedrals, or town.

Self-Guided Walks and Audio Tours

If you don't want to join an organized tour or spring for a local guide, a printed self-guided walk or audio tour can provide direction and meaning to your wanderings through a new city or museum.

Many tourist offices offer do-it-yourself walking-tour leaflets that provide turn-by-turn directions for an orientation walk around town. Or consider purchasing one of the many "turn right at the fountain"-type guidebooks that include carefully written collections of self-guided walks through major cities. Many of my guidebooks include these types of walking tours.

Some tourist offices offer audio tours to accompany their self-guided walks, and most major museums offer room-by-room audioguides. In many cases you'll borrow or rent a device preloaded with the audio content, but at some museums you can download the tours on the spot to your mobile device. To access the tour, simply log onto the museum's Wi-Fi network with your device. While this sounds complicated, it generally works great.

With an audio tour, you can immerse yourself in a wonderful sight, enjoying its visual wonder while listening to information that gives it all meaning. Before you leave for Europe, it's worth checking online to see what kinds of digital content you can download in advance to enhance your trip. Using Google or the iTunes store, search for sights and cities you'll be visiting. For instance, Versailles offers helpful podcasts for touring the extensive palace grounds (chateauversailles.fr). Remember to bring earbuds.

I've produced free, self-guided audio versions of my walking tours of the major sights in Athens, Florence, London, Munich, Paris, Rome, Venice, Vienna, and other places (download the Rick Steves Audio Europe free mobile app). These user-friendly, easy-to-follow, fun, and informative audio tours are available for museums (for instance, Paris' Louvre and Orsay, Florence's Uffizi), churches (St. Paul's in London, St. Peter's in Rome, the Basilica of St. Francis in Assisi), ancient sites (Athens' Acropolis, Rome's Colosseum), my favorite neighborhoods (historic Paris, London's Westminster, Venice's Grand Canal), and much more. Compared to live tours, audio tours are hard to beat: No guide will stand you up, the quality is reliable, you can take the tour exactly when you like, and they're free.

Minivan Excursions

Some of Europe's top sights are awkward to reach by public transportation, such as the *châteaux* in the Loire, the *Sound of Music* sights outside Salzburg, the D-Day beaches of Normandy, the rural meadows of Cornwall, or the Lascaux cave paintings in France's Dordogne. For roughly $50-60 per half-day, an organized tour not only whisks you effortlessly from one hard-to-reach-without-a-car sight to the next, but gives you lots of information as you go. (Or, if you have a car, consider picking up the brochure for a well-thought-out tour itinerary and doing it on your own.)

Minivan tours—such as this one, to the Rock of Gibraltar—can be an ideal way for non-drivers to reach certain sights.

If you have a choice between a big, 50-seat bus (a "coach") and a minivan, I'd generally recommend the minivan. While typically a bit more professional and comfortable, big-bus tours are often also boring and impersonal. With a smaller group, you're likely to have a more engaging, entertaining guide and more camaraderie as you roll.

SIGHTSEEING STRATEGIES

Westminster Abbey, the Eiffel Tower, the Sistine Chapel—these are the reasons you came to Europe. They're also the reason millions of other tourists are here as well. Nothing kills a sightseeing buzz like waiting in line for hours to get into a popular sight or being crammed into a room, squinting up at Michelangelo's masterpiece. If you plan ahead, the sights you dreamed of seeing won't disappoint.

Be Strategic and Selective

Set up an itinerary that allows you to fit in your must-see sights, but be realistic about what you can accomplish in a day. As you make your plan, note the specifics of the sights on your list, especially their closed days and any evening hours (which can help extend your sightseeing day). Check the weather report a few days out and plan your indoor/outdoor time accordingly. Arrange your sightseeing to cover a larger city systematically and efficiently, one neighborhood at a time.

Save yourself for the biggies. Don't overestimate your powers of absorption. Rare is the tourist who doesn't become somewhat jaded after several weeks of travel. At the start of my trip, I'll seek out every great painting and cathedral I can. After two months, I find myself "seeing" cathedrals with a sweep of my head from the doorway, and I probably wouldn't cross the street for another Rembrandt. Don't burn out on mediocre castles, palaces, and museums. Sightsee selectively.

When possible, visit major sights in the morning (when your energy is best), and save other activities for the afternoon. Don't put off visiting a must-see sight; even if you've double-checked hours, places can close unexpectedly for a strike or restoration. On holidays, expect reduced hours or closures. In summer, some sights may stay open late. Off-season, many attractions have shorter hours.

For more spontaneous day-planning, you could turn to your smartphone for help. Location-based apps such as Foursquare, Tripomatic, and Triposo all point you toward sights and venues within walking distance (to limit your data usage, just enable data roaming as needed, then disable it between stops—see page 247). Each has its own advantages—for example, Foursquare also includes restaurants, and takes other users' recommendations into account; Tripomatic shows opening hours and user ratings, and meshes with an itinerary-planning tool; and Triposo sorts your options by time of day, and works well offline.

Avoiding Lines and Crowds

Plenty of people queue up in long lines at Europe's most popular sights. As far as I'm concerned, there are two IQs for travelers: those who queue...and those who don't. If you plan ahead, you can avoid virtually every line that tourists suffer through. The following tricks aren't secrets. They're in any good, up-to-date guidebook. Just read ahead.

Timing Is Everything

In many cities, a number of sights tend to be closed on the same day of the week (usually Sunday, Monday, or Tuesday).

It's Tuesday at Versailles, and these people now have time to read their guidebooks, which warn: "On Tuesday, many Paris museums are closed, so Versailles has very long lines."

In high season, any major sight that's open when everything else is closed is guaranteed to be crowded. For example, Versailles is very crowded on Tuesdays, when many of the biggest museums in Paris are closed.

Many museums are free one day a month—a great deal for locals who can nip in and see small parts of a museum without paying the full fare. But for visitors, it's generally worth paying the entrance fee to avoid the hordes on a museum's free day. The Sistine Chapel feels more like the Sardine Chapel when it's open and free on the last Sunday of the month.

At popular sights, it can help to arrive early or go late. This is especially true at places popular with cruise excursions and big-bus tour groups. At 8 in the morning, Germany's fairy-tale Neuschwanstein Castle is cool and easy, with relaxed guides and no crowds; come an hour later and you'll either wait a long time, find that tickets are sold out, or both. (You can book online for the castle as well.)

Many sights are open late one or two nights a week—another pleasant time to visit. For instance, London's Tate Modern stays open Friday and Saturday evenings, when you'll enjoy Matisse and Dalí in near solitude. Very late in the day—when most tourists are long gone, searching for dinner or lying exhausted in their rooms—I linger alone, taking artistic liberties with some of Europe's greatest works in empty galleries.

Shortcuts

Even at the most packed sights, there's often a strategy or shortcut that can break you out of the herd, whether it's a side entrance with a shorter wait, a guided tour that includes last-minute reservations, a better place in town to pick up your ticket, or a pass with line-skipping privileges (explained later).

Grand as the Louvre's main entrance is, that glass pyramid stops looking impressive as you wait—and wait—to get through security. You can't bypass security checks, but you'll encounter shorter lines if you go in through the less crowded underground entrance.

In Milan, you can take a

The Eiffel Tower comes with long lines for those who didn't book online in advance. With my reservation and appointment in hand, I was escorted directly to the elevator, while this long queue of tourists waited. (None of them had my guidebook.)

bus tour that includes an easy stop at Leonardo's *Last Supper*, normally booked up more than a month in advance.

At St. Mark's Basilica in Venice, you can either snake slowly through an endless line, or go instead to a nearby church to check a large bag or backpack—then walk right to the front of the basilica's line, show your bag-claim tag, and head on in (go figure). Check your guidebook for sight-specific insider tips.

Making Advance Reservations

Certain sights are almost always jammed, all day long, throughout most of the year (many in older edifices that weren't built to accommodate the demands of mass tourism). Fortunately, many popular sights sell advance tickets that guarantee admission at a certain time (often with a small booking fee that's well worth it). While hundreds of tourists are sweating in long lines, those who've booked ahead can just show up at their reserved entry time and breeze right in. It's worth giving up some spontaneity in order to save time. In some cases, getting a ticket in advance can simply mean buying your ticket earlier on the same day. For example, if you buy your ticket for the Tower of London at a souvenir stand, you can skip the long line at the sight. For other sights, you may need to book weeks or even months in advance.

Some sights are notorious for grueling waits. These include the Eiffel Tower, Rome's Vatican Museum, Barcelona's Picasso Museum, and Florence's famous galleries—the Accademia (Michelangelo's *David*) and the Uffizi (the showcase for Italian Renaissance art). At these places, lines are completely avoidable by making advance reservations. After learning how simple this is and seeing hundreds of annoyed tourists waiting in lines without a reservation, it's hard not to be amazed at their cluelessness. As soon as you're ready to commit to a certain date, book it.

At many great galleries, such as the Uffizi in Florence, you can wait in line for two hours...or book ahead for an appointment and walk right in. Remember: Lines like this are not for the entry turnstile, but for the ticket booth.

Note that some sights require reservations, such as the Reichstag in Berlin, Leonardo's *Last Supper* in Milan, Giotto's Scrovegni Chapel in Padua, and the Borghese Gallery in Rome. For some of these, the reservations system is aimed not so much at coping with vast crowds, but toward moving people in and out efficiently.

Reserving Sights in Advance

At some of Europe's most popular sights, reservations are required; at others, reservations are very smart. This list of major sights you can book ahead isn't comprehensive; check your guidebook for details on the sights you plan to visit.

Austria
Schönbrunn Palace, Vienna

France
Eiffel Tower, Paris
Orsay Museum, Paris
Picasso Museum, Paris
Versailles, near Paris
Château at Chenonceau, Chenonceaux
Cro-Magnon Caves, Dordogne

Germany
Reichstag, Berlin*
Neuschwanstein Castle, Bavaria
Historic Green Vault, Dresden

Great Britain
Tower of London
London Eye
Madame Tussauds Waxworks, London
Stonehenge, near Salisbury*
Jorvik Viking Centre, York
Lennon and McCartney Homes, Liverpool

Hungary
Hungarian Parliament, Budapest

Italy
Vatican Museum (including Sistine Chapel), Rome

Borghese Gallery, Rome*
Uffizi Gallery, Florence
Accademia Gallery, Florence
Brancacci Chapel, Florence*
Last Supper, Milan*
South Tirol Museum of Archaeology (Ötzi the Iceman), Bolzano
Scrovegni Chapel, Padua*

The Netherlands
Anne Frank House, Amsterdam
Rijksmuseum, Amsterdam
Van Gogh Museum, Amsterdam

Poland
Auschwitz-Birkenau Memorial*

Spain
Sagrada Família, Barcelona
La Pedrera, Barcelona
Park Güell (Monumental Zone), Barcelona
Casa Lleó Morera, Barcelona
Picasso Museum, Barcelona
Alhambra, Granada
Salvador Dalí House, Cadaqués*
Altamira Caves, near Santillana del Mar

Indicates sights requiring reservations

Sightseeing Passes and Combo-Tickets

Many tourist destinations offer a citywide sightseeing pass (or "tourist card"), which includes free or discounted entrance to many or most sights for a certain amount of time (usually intervals of 24 hours). Many of these deals also include free use of public transit, a brief explanatory booklet, and a map.

In some places, passes can save you serious time and money; in others, you'd have to sightsee nonstop to barely break even. Do the math: Compare the price of the pass to the total of what you'd pay for individual admissions. But remember: Time is money. These passes are almost always worthwhile if they allow you to bypass long admission lines.

For instance, Paris' Museum Pass covers many top sights (the Louvre, Orsay, Notre-Dame Tower, and Versailles) and allows you to skip ticket-buying lines. The Madrid Card may not save you a lot of money, but it can help you avoid high-season lines at the Royal Palace and the Prado.

Combo-tickets combine admission to a larger sight with entry to a lesser sight or two that few people would pay to see. The bad news: You have to pay for multiple sights to visit one. The good news: You can bypass the line at the congested sight by buying your ticket at a less-popular sister sight. You can wait up to an hour to get into Rome's Colosseum or Venice's Doge's Palace—or buy a combo-ticket (at another participating yet less-crowded sight) and scoot inside.

Whether you have a combo-ticket or pass, never wait at the back of the line if there's any chance you can skip it. Don't be shy: March straight to the front and wave your pass or ticket. If you really do have to wait with everyone else, they'll let you know.

Visiting Sights Smartly

Some people walk into Europe's major museums, churches, and ancient sights, gawk for a few minutes, then walk out. But with a little preparation and know-how, your sightseeing will go much smoother—and take on more significance. Here's what you can expect at Europe's major sights.

Security Check: Some important sights have metal detectors or conduct bag searches that will slow your entry, and a few will confiscate the same sharp items and full water bottles that you're not allowed to carry on board a plane.

Tickets: As you approach the ticket window, study the list of prices. You could have a choice of individual tickets, combo-tickets, or passes. You may be eligible for discounts if you're young, old, or with children (have proof of ID, student card, etc.). Be prepared to pay cash, particularly for inexpensive sights.

For Rome's Colosseum, buy a combo-ticket 150 yards away at the Palatine Hill—which never has a line—and skip directly past the not-so-smart travelers pictured here.

Museums may have special exhibits in addition to their permanent collections. Some exhibits are included in the entry price, while others come at an extra cost (which you may have to pay even if you don't want to see the exhibit).

Your ticket may allow in-and-out privileges (e.g., for a

lunch break outside the museum); if this is important to you, ask.

Entry Procedure: Entering a major sight is similar to arriving at a new town—you need to get oriented. Hit the information desk for a brochure or map, find out about any special events and tours, and ask about any temporary room or wing closures.

Checkroom: Most sights offer a checkroom or lockers (usually free or with a small deposit), and many require you to check daypacks and coats. They'll be kept safely. If you have something you can't bear to part with, stash it in a pocket or purse. To avoid checking a small backpack, carry it under your arm like a purse as you enter. (From a guard's point of view, a backpack—which could bump against artwork—is generally a problem while a purse is not.)

Touring the Sight: Many sights offer audioguide tours with recorded descriptions in English. If the audioguide isn't included with admission, you can ask to listen to it for a couple of minutes to gauge the quality before paying for it. If you bring along a Y-jack and an extra pair of earbuds, you may be able to share the same audioguide with a companion. Other sights offer downloadable audio tours which you'll listen to on your own mobile device. (For more on audio tours, including my free ones, see "Self-Guided Walks and Audio Tours," earlier.)

Guided tours in English are most likely to be available during peak season (they may be included with your admission). If you're interested, check online or call ahead to be sure your visit will coincide with a tour.

Some sights run short films that are generally well worth your time. I make it standard operating procedure to ask when I arrive at a sight if there is a film in English (some come with audioguides that always offer English).

Stroll with a chatty curator through Europe's greatest art galleries, thanks to digital audioguides.

Once inside, hit the highlights first, then go back to other things if you have the time and stamina. Expect changes—items can be on tour, on loan, out sick, or shifted at the whim of a curator. If the painting you crossed the Atlantic to see isn't on the wall, ask a museum staffer if it's been shifted to another location.

Most sights stop selling tickets and start shutting down rooms or sections 30 to 60 minutes before closing. Guards usher people out, so don't save the best for last. Get to the far end early, see the rooms that are first to shut down, and work your way back toward the entry.

My favorite time at a major sight is the lazy last hour, when the tourists clear out. On a recent visit to the Acropolis, I showed up late and had the place to myself in the cool of early evening. Other blockbuster sights like St. Peter's Basilica and the Palace of Versailles can be magical just before closing.

Photography: Flashes are often banned in museums, but taking photos without a flash is usually allowed. Look for signs or ask. Flashes damage oil paintings and delicate artifacts, and distract others in the room. Even without a flash, a handheld camera or mobile device will take a decent picture (or buy postcards or posters at the museum bookstore).

Services: Bigger sights usually have a café or cafeteria (a good place to rejuvenate during a long visit). The WCs at sights are free and usually clean; make a point of using them whether you think you need to or not.

TYPES OF SIGHTS

From modern museums to centuries-old churches, Europe is rich with attractions both new and old. Here are some tips for navigating Europe's various sights.

Museums

Europe is a treasure chest of great art and history. For some, visiting the world's greatest museums is the highlight of a European trip. For others, "museum" spells "dull." But you don't need to know how a Ferrari works to enjoy the ride. Paintings are like that. You can just stroll through a gallery and bask in the color scheme. That said, it doesn't hurt to keep in mind the following.

Learn about art and history. In my student days, I had to go to the great art galleries of Europe because my mom said it would be a crime not to. Touring places like the National Archaeological Museum in Athens, I was surrounded by people looking like they were having a good time—and I was convinced they were faking it. I thought, "How could anybody enjoy

At the Louvre, it's worth fighting through crowds of amateur paparazzi to see the *Venus de Milo...* who's ready for her close-up.

that stuff?" Two years later, after a class in classical art history, that same museum was a fascinating trip into the world of Pericles and Socrates, all because of some background knowledge. Pre-trip studying makes art and artifacts more fun. When you understand the context in which things were made, who paid for it and why, what the challenges of the day were, and so on, paintings and statues become the closest thing to a time machine Europe has to offer.

With a good guidebook, you stand a chance of finding Michelangelo's *Slaves* in the Louvre.

Don't miss the masterpieces. A common misconception is that a great museum has only great art. But only a fraction of a museum's pieces are masterpieces worthy of your time. You can't possibly cover everything—so don't try. With the help of a tour guide or guidebook, focus on just the museum's top attractions. Most of Europe's major museums provide brief pamphlets that recommend a greatest-hits plan. With this selective strategy, you'll appreciate the highlights while you're fresh. If you have any energy left afterward, you can explore other areas of specific interest to you. For me, museum going is the hardest work I do in Europe, and I'm rarely good for more than two or three hours at a time. If you're determined to cover a large museum thoroughly, try tackling it in separate visits over several days.

Find your favorites. On arrival, look through the museum's collection handbook or the gift shop's postcards to make sure you won't miss anything of importance to you. For instance, I love Salvador Dalí's work. One time I thought I was finished with a museum, but as I browsed through the postcards...Hello, Dalí. A museum staffer was happy to show me where this Dalí painting was hiding. I saved myself the disappointment of discovering too late that I'd missed it.

A victim of the Louvre

Some sights make it easy for you to find your favorites; e.g., London's National Gallery has a computer-study room where you can input your interests and print out a tailored museum tour.

Eavesdrop. If you're especially interested in a particular piece of art, spend a half hour studying it and listening to each passing tour guide tell his or her story about *David* or the *Mona Lisa*. They each do their own research and come up with a different angle to share. Much of it is true. There's nothing wrong with this sort of tour freeloading. Just don't stand in the front and ask a lot of questions.

Take advantage of my free audio tours. Rick Steves Audio Europe includes self-guided tours of the finest museums in many of Europe's greatest cities. These can make your museum going easier and more meaningful (see page 19).

Churches, Synagogues, and Mosques

European houses of worship offer some amazing art and architecture—not to mention a welcome seat and a cool respite from the heat. You may be there just to see the Caravaggio over the side altar, but others are there as worshippers. Be a respectful visitor.

A modest dress code (no bare shoulders or shorts) is encouraged at most churches, but is enforced at some larger churches and most mosques. If you are caught by surprise, you can improvise, such as using maps to cover your shoulders and tying a jacket around your hips to cover your knees. (Throughout the Mediterranean world, I wear a super-lightweight pair of long pants rather than shorts for my hot and muggy big-city sightseeing.) At Turkish mosques, women must cover their heads and wear clothing that shields their legs and arms; everyone needs to remove their shoes.

At active places of worship, visitors may not be allowed inside for one or more time periods throughout the day. If you are already inside, you may be asked to leave so as not to disturb the congregation. Check your guidebook's listing to avoid showing up at a church or mosque when it's closed for worship. Some services are open to the public. One of my favorite experiences in Great Britain is to attend evensong—a daily choral service—at a grand cathedral (see page 581).

Some churches have coin-operated audio boxes that describe the art and history; just set the dial to English, insert your coins, and listen. Coin boxes near a piece of art illuminate the work (and present a better photo opportunity). I pop in a coin whenever I can. It improves my experience, is a favor to other visitors trying to appreciate a great piece of art in the dark, and is a little contribution to that church. Whenever possible, let there be light.

Boning Up on Europe's Relics

Centuries ago, relics were an important focus of worship. These holy relics, often bones, were the "ruby slippers" of the medieval age. They gave you power—got your prayers answered and helped you win wars—and ultimately helped you get back to your eternal Kansas.

The bones of monks were venerated, and sometimes even artistically arranged in crypts and chapels. In **Rome's** Capuchin Crypt, hundreds of skeletons decorate the walls to the delight—or disgust—of the always wide-eyed visitor. The crypt offers unusual ideas in home decorating, as well as a chance to pick up a few of Rome's most interesting postcards. A similar Capuchin Crypt is a highlight of many visits to **Palermo** in Sicily. In **Évora**, Portugal, osteophiles make a pilgrimage to the macabre "House of Bones" chapel at the Church of St. Francis, lined with the bones of thousands of monks.

TOP Even in death, Italians know how to look cool.

BOTTOM Head to Hallstatt's Bone Chapel.

Overcrowding in cemeteries has prompted unusual solutions. Austria's tiny town of **Hallstatt** is crammed between a mountain and a lake. Space is so limited that bones get only 12 peaceful buried years in the church cemetery before making way for the newly dead. The result is a fascinating chapel of bones in the cemetery. Hallstatt stopped this practice in the 1960s, about the same time the Catholic Church began permitting cremation.

Kutná Hora's ossuary, an hour by train from Prague, is decorated with the bones of 40,000 people, many of them plague victims. The monks who stacked these bones 100 years ago wanted viewers to remember that the earthly church is a community of both the living and the dead.

Some cities, such as Paris and Rome, have catacombs. Many cities opened up a little extra space by de-boning graveyards, which used to surround medieval churches. During the French Revolution, **Paris** experienced a great church cemetery land grab. Skeletons of countless Parisians were dug up and carefully stacked along miles of tunnels beneath the city.

Seekers of the macabre can bone up on Europe's more obscure ossuaries, but any tourist will stumble onto bones and relics. Whether in a church, chapel, or underground tunnel in Europe, you might be surprised by who's looking at you, kid.

Ancient Sites and Ruins

Climbing the Acropolis, communing with the druids at Stonehenge, strolling the Croatian shore in the shadow of Emperor Diocletian's palace in Split, tracing the intricate carvings on a Viking ship—the remnants of Europe's distant past bring a special thrill to those of us from the New World.

But the oldest sites are also the most likely to be initially underwhelming, especially if it's been a while since your last history class. On its own, the Roman Forum is just a cluster of crumbling columns and half-buried foundations. You've heard about it all your life, you've spent good money to get here, and your first thought upon entering is..."This is it?"

Ancient sites come to life with your imagination, aided by information. Bring a guidebook that's heavy on historical background, and consider hiring a local guide. For some well-known places you can get books that cleverly use overlays to visually mesh the present with the past. To fire up your imagination before your trip, watch a movie or read a book set in the time and place of any site you're excited to see. Once you're there, mentally reconstruct arches and repaint facades. Clad your fellow tourists in togas. Fill a ruined cathedral with the chants of cowled monks while inhaling imaginary incense.

Many major ancient sites (especially in Greece) have both an archaeological site and a nearby museum full of artifacts unearthed there. You can choose between visiting the museum first (to mentally reconstruct the ruins before seeing them) or the site first (to get the lay of the ancient land before seeing the items found there). In most cases, I prefer to see the site first, then the museum. However, crowds and weather can also help determine your plan. If it's a blistering hot afternoon, tour the air-conditioned museum first, then hit the ruins in the cool of the early evening. Or, if rain clouds are on the horizon, do the archaeological site first, then duck into the museum when the rain hits.

Castles

Castles excite Americans. Fortresses perch on hilltops from Ireland to Israel, and from Sweden to Spain, lining the Loire and guarding harbors throughout the Mediterranean.

While some of Europe's castles are fairy-tale wonderful (such as Neuschwanstein in Bavaria), others are massive, crumbling hulks (Rheinfels on the Rhine). Relatively few castles are furnished; most of their original furnishings disappeared long ago. Some castles have little more than a ticket booth, while others (like England's Warwick) have jousting competitions, catapult demonstrations, museums of medieval armor and artifacts, and well-stocked gift shops. There are even entire towns built in and around medieval castles, like Carcassonne in France.

Before visiting a castle, do your research; check to see if tours are offered. If you're visiting a ruined castle, wear good walking shoes. Bring a small flashlight if there are tunnels; claustrophobics beware. Learn the various parts of the castle; you'll appreciate your visit more if you can tell the difference between a dungeon and a donjon (a.k.a. the keep; the main tower that's the refuge of last resort if the castle is attacked).

Europe's castles generally fall into one of two categories: medieval fortresses (built to withstand sieges) and castle-palaces (residences and luxury châteaux for royalty and nobility).

With the advent of cannons, even the sturdiest medieval castles became obsolete. Many fell into ruin, used as quarries to build more practical things. You'll enjoy the best concentration of medieval ramparts and dark dungeons by touring the Rhine in Germany. To see a castle being built today with methods used in the 13th century, visit Guédelon in France (about two hours south of Paris).

From the 16th century through the 19th-century Romantic era, the rich and famous built castle-palaces as residences, culminating in Europe's most opulent palace—Versailles, just outside of Paris, and its most fanciful—King Ludwig II's Neuschwanstein. Walt Disney made Ludwig's fairy-tale castle his trademark, and the rest is history.

Travelers tramping through Europe's castles will encounter a muddle of medieval bunker mentality and Romantic renovation. While confusing, this weird mix makes for great sightseeing.

Open-Air Folk Museums

Many people travel in search of the old life and traditional culture in action. While we book a round-trip ticket into the romantic past, those we photograph with the Old World balanced on their heads are struggling to dump that load and climb into the modern world. In Europe, most are succeeding.

The easiest way to see the "real local culture" is by exploring open-air folk museums. True, it's culture on a lazy Susan, with an often sanitized, romanticized version of

Europe's Coolest Castles

Visiting Europe can overwhelm you with too many castles to tour in too little time. To help you prioritize, here are my favorite castles.

Carcassonne (France): Europe's greatest Romanesque fortress-city, medieval Carcassonne is a 13th-century world of towers, turrets, and cobblestones—a walled city and Camelot's castle rolled into one.

Storm Carcassonne early or late.

Warwick Castle (England): The best castle in Britain, this 14th- and 15th-century fortified shell holds an 18th and 19th-century royal residence surrounded by dandy gardens—a fairy-tale fortress that's entertaining from dungeon to lookout.

Burg Eltz (Germany): Lurking in a mysterious forest, this is my favorite European castle. Once the fortified home to three big landlord families, it retains its medieval furnishings and ambience.

Rheinfels Castle (Germany): This mightiest of Rhine castles, built in 1245, rumbles with ghosts from its hard-fought past—it withstood a siege by 28,000 French troops in 1692, but was destroyed by the French Revolutionary army a century later.

Warwick Castle—for kings and queens of any age

Towering Eltz Castle, on Germany's Mosel River

Even in ruins, Rheinfels is mighty.

Shimmering Château de Chillon

Reifenstein Castle, rugged inside and out

Sintra's hilltop ruins, where the winds of the past really howl

At the Ehrenberg ruins, grab a sword fern and unfetter your imagination.

Château de Chillon (Switzerland): This wonderfully preserved 13th-century castle is set romantically at the edge of Lake Geneva.

Reifenstein Castle (Italy): Situated below the Brenner Pass, Reifenstein once bottled up a strategic valley leading to the easiest way across the Alps—and features the best-preserved medieval castle interior I've ever seen.

Moorish Ruins of Sintra (Portugal): The desolate ruins of a 1,000-year-old Moorish castle is a medieval funtasia of scramble-up-and-down-the-ramparts delights and atmospheric picnic perches with vast Atlantic Ocean views.

King's Castles (Germany's Bavaria): The fairy-tale extravagance of Neuschwanstein Castle is proof that Bavaria's King Ludwig II was just "mad" about 19th-century Romanticism. Downhill, nestled near Alpsee lake, is the more stately Hohenschwangau Castle, Ludwig's boyhood home.

Ehrenberg Ruins (Austria): An ensemble of brooding ruins near the sleepy town of Reutte, Ehrenberg comprises four castles that once made up the largest fort in Tirol.

Neuschwanstein, the greatest of "Mad" King Ludwig's fairy-tale castles

Europe's Best Open-Air Folk Museums

Popularized in Scandinavia, these folk museums are now found all over the world, though the best ones are still in the Nordic capitals.

Scandinavia

Skansen (Stockholm, Sweden): One of the best in Europe, with more than 100 buildings from all over Sweden, craftspeople at work, feisty folk entertainment, and an Arctic camp complete with reindeer and Lapp dancing.

Funen Village (Den Fynske Landsby, near Odense, Denmark): Life in the 18th century.

The Old Town (Den Gamle By, Århus, Denmark): Danish town life in the 1700-1800s, 1920s, and 1970s.

Norwegian Folk Museum (Bygdøy, near Oslo, Norway): Norway's first, with 150 old buildings from all over Norway and a 12th-century stave church.

Maihaugen Folk Museum (Lillehammer, Norway): Norway's best, with folk culture of the Gudbrandsdal Valley.

Seurasaari Island (near Helsinki, Finland): Reconstructed buildings from all over Finland.

The Netherlands, Germany, and Switzerland

Dutch Open-Air Folk Museum (Arnhem, Netherlands): Holland's first and biggest.

Zuiderzee Open-Air Museum (Enkhuizen, Netherlands): Lively reconstruction of Dutch traditions lost forever to land reclamation.

Vogtsbauernhof Black Forest Open-Air Museum (Gutach, Germany): Farms filled with exhibits on traditional dress and lifestyles.

Ballenberg Swiss Open-Air Museum (near Interlaken, Switzerland): Fine collection of old Swiss buildings, arranged roughly as if in a huge map of Switzerland.

Hungary

Skanzen (Szentendre, near Budapest, Hungary): Traditional architecture from around Hungary.

Hollókő (near Budapest, Hungary): Old-fashioned village where people still live.

Great Britain and Ireland

Blists Hill Victorian Town (Ironbridge Gorge, England): Unrivaled look at life in the early days of the Industrial Revolution, with the world's first iron bridge and a glimpse at the factories that lit the fuse of our modern age.

Beamish Open-Air Museum (northwest of Durham, England): Life in northeast England in 1900.

St. Fagans National History Museum (near Cardiff, Wales): Traditional Welsh ways of life.

Ulster Folk and Transport Museum (near Belfast, Northern Ireland): Traditional Irish lifestyles and buildings from all over Ireland.

Bunratty Folk Park (near Limerick, Ireland): Buildings from the Shannon area and artisans at work.

Muckross Traditional Farms (near Killarney, Ireland): Three working farms, a schoolhouse, and other buildings from the 1930s and 1940s.

LEFT Traditional culture is kept alive in Europe's open-air folk museums.

RIGHT At Stockholm's open-air folk museum, you may be entertained by this rare band of left-handed fiddlers.

an area's preindustrial lifestyle. But these museums can be simultaneously fun and enlightening—a magic carpet ride through a culture's past. In more and more places they provide your only chance for a close-up look at the "Old World."

An open-air folk museum collects traditional buildings from every corner of a country or region, then carefully reassembles them in a park, usually near the capital or a major city. Log cabins, thatched cottages, mills, old schoolhouses, shops, and farms come complete with original furnishings and usually a local person dressed in the traditional costume who's happy to answer any of your questions about life then and there. In the summer, these museums buzz with colorful folk dances, live music performances, and craft demonstrations by artisans doing what they can to keep the cuckoo clock from going the way of the dodo bird. Some of my favorite souvenirs are those I watched being dyed, woven, or carved by folk-museum artists. To get the most out of your visit, start by picking up a list of that day's special exhibits, events, and activities at the information center, and take advantage of any walking tours.

Folk museums teach traditional lifestyles better than any other kind of museum. As our world hurtles past 250 billion McDonald's hamburgers served, these museums will become even more important. Of course, they're as realistic as Santa's Village, but how else will you see the elves?

BECOMING A TEMPORARY EUROPEAN

Many travelers tramp through Europe like they're visiting the cultural zoo. "Ooh, that guy in lederhosen yodeled! Excuse me, could you do that again in the sunshine so I can get a good picture?" It's important to stow your camera, roll up your sleeves, and enjoy the real thing.

By developing a knack for connecting with locals and

their culture, we become temporary Europeans, members of the family—approaching Europe on its level, accepting and enjoying its unique ways of life. When I'm in Europe, I become the best German or Spaniard or Italian I can be. I consume wine in France, beer in Germany, and small breakfasts in Italy. While I never drink tea at home, after a long day of sightseeing in England, "a spot of tea" really does feel right. Find ways to really be there. Here are some ideas to consider:

Hit the back streets. Many people energetically jockey themselves into the most crowded square of the most crowded city in the most crowded month (St. Mark's Square, Venice, July)—and then complain about the crowds. If you're in Venice in July, walk six blocks behind St. Mark's Basilica, step into a café, and be greeted by Venetians who act as though they've never seen a tourist.

Play where the locals play. A city's popular fairgrounds and parks are filled with families, lovers, and old-timers enjoying a cheap afternoon or evening out. European communities provide their heavily taxed citizens with wonderful athletic facilities. In Britain, check out a public swimming pool, called a "leisure center." While tourists outnumber locals five to one at the world-famous Tivoli Gardens, Copenhagen's other amusement park, Bakken, is enjoyed purely by Danes. Disneyland Paris is great, but Paris' Parc Astérix is more French.

Take a stroll. Across southern Europe, communities relax with a *paseo,* or stroll, in the early evening. Stroll along. Join a *Volksmarch* in Bavaria to spend a day on the trails with people singing "I love to go a-wandering" in its original language. Mountain huts across Europe are filled mostly with local hikers. Most hiking centers have alpine clubs that welcome foreigners and offer organized hikes.

Go to church. Many regular churchgoers never even consider a European worship service. But any church would welcome a traveling American. And an hour in a small-town church provides an unbeatable peek into the community, especially if you join them for coffee and cookies afterwards. I'll never forget going to a small church on the south coast of

Mass with the sun's rays, daily in St. Peter's

Connecting with the Culture

Generally speaking, Europeans enjoy getting to know Americans—all it takes to connect is a friendly smile and genuine curiosity. Take advantage of one of the many programs and organizations set up to help bridge the cultural divide.

Meet-the-Locals Programs: Several European cities have English-speaking volunteer greeters who belong to the Global Greeter Network (globalgreeter network.com). Greeters are screened extensively, but aren't trained as historical experts. Instead, they introduce visitors to their city by spending a few hours sharing their insider knowledge—their favorite hidden spots, how to navigate public transit, where to find the best bargains, etc.

A few bigger cities have more formal programs that put travelers in direct touch with locals. Dublin, the City of a Thousand Welcomes, brings volunteers and first-time visitors together for a cup of tea or a pint (free, cityofathousand welcomes.com). In Paris, the group Meeting the French organizes dinners in private homes and workplace tours to match your interests or career (fee, meetingthefrench.com). Visitors to Copenhagen can enjoy a home-cooked meal with a family through Dine with the Danes (fee, dinewiththedanes.dk).

Conversation Clubs: Across Europe, most large cities, and even many small towns, have informal English-language conversation clubs, usually meeting weekly or monthly in a public space (search online or ask at the tourist information office). You may well be the only native speaker there—if so, expect an especially warm welcome. For instance, in Rothenburg, Germany, the English Conversation Club meets on Wednesdays at Mario's Altfränkische Weinstube am Klosterhof. After 9 p.m., when the beer starts to sink in, the crowd grows, and everyone seems to speak that second language a bit more easily.

Casual Meetups: While primarily designed to connect travelers with overnight hosts, Couchsurfing.org also lists "day hosts" who are happy to just meet up with like-minded visitors and swap travel stories (see page 234). Meetup.com is another free means of finding people with shared interests in a given city. Such cored events are hikes, picnics, museum tours, cocktail evenings, and more.

Cooking Schools: These give you not just a taste of the culinary traditions of the area you're visiting, but also a hands-on feel for what happens in European kitchens—along with a skill you can take home. Many include a trip to local markets. You can find one-day European cooking classes at the International Kitchen (theinternationalkitchen.com).

Portugal one Easter. A tourist stood at the door videotaping the "colorful natives" (including me) shaking hands with the priest after the service.

Be an early bird. Throughout Europe—on medieval ramparts, in churches, produce markets, alpine farmsteads, and Riviera villages—the local culture thrives while the tourists sleep. In Germany, walk around Rothenburg's fortified wall at breakfast time, before the tour buses pull in and turn the town into a medieval theme park. Crack-of-dawn joggers and walkers enjoy a special look at wonderfully medieval cities as they yawn and stretch and prepare for the daily onslaught of the 21st century. By waking up with the locals on the Italian Riviera in the off-season, you can catch the morning sun as it greets a sleepy village, breathe in the damp, cool air...and experience a rare Italian silence. Among travelers, the early bird gets the memories.

Root for your team. For many Europeans, the top religion is soccer. Getting caught up in a sporting event is going local. Whether enjoying soccer in small-town Italy or hurling in Ireland, you'll be surrounded by a stadium crammed with devout fans. Buy something to wear or wave with the hometown colors to help you remember whose side you're on.

Challenge a local to the national pastime. In Greece or Turkey, drop into a teahouse or taverna and challenge anyone to a game of backgammon. You're instantly a part (even a star) of the café or bar scene. Normally the gang will gather around, and what starts out as a simple game becomes a fun duel of international significance.

Contact an equivalent version of your club. If you're a member of a service club, bridge club, professional association, or international organization, make a point to connect with your foreign mates.

See how the locals live. Residential neighborhoods rarely see a tourist; ride a city bus or subway into the suburbs. Browse through a department store. Buy a copy of the local *Better Homes and Thatches* and use it to explore that particular culture. Get off the map. In Florence, most tourists stick to the small section of the city covered by the ubiquitous tourist maps. Wander beyond that, and you'll dance with the locals or play street soccer with the neighborhood gang. In Helsinki, rather than sweat with a bunch of tourists in your hotel's sterile steam room, ride the public bus into a working-class neighborhood to a rustic-and-woody $14 sauna. Surrounded by milky steam, knotty wood, stringy blond hair, and naked locals, you'll have no idea which century you're in. But one thing is clear: You're in Finland.

Drop by a university. Mill around a university and check out the announcement boards. Eat at the college cafeteria. Ask at the English-language department if there's a student learning English whom you could hire to be your

Make your trip worth more by cranking up the experiences. Attending a sporting event anywhere in Europe—like this soccer match in Germany—puts you in touch with the local spirit for little money. If you're wearing a lei with colors, be sure you root for the right team. *Auf geht's Deutschland!*

private guide. Be alert and even a little bit snoopy. If you stumble onto a grade-school talent show—sit down and watch it.

Join in. When you visit the town market in the morning, you're just another hungry shopper, picking up your daily produce. Traveling through the wine country of France during harvest time, you can be a tourist taking photos—or you can pitch in and become a grape-picker. Get more than a photo op. Get dirty. That night at the festival, it's just grape pickers dancing—and their circle could include you.

If you're hunting cultural peacocks, remember they fan out their tails best for people...not cameras. When you take Europe out of your viewfinder, you're more likely to find it in your lap.

LEFT Connect with people. Greeks and Turks love a game of backgammon.

RIGHT Blend into Europe: Shop at the town market.

Outdoor Adventure

Europe is a treasure chest of great art and history. But it's also a continent filled with natural beauty—often overlooked by tourists busy sprinting from sight to sight, or searching for the perfect souvenir. A day in the great outdoors can be just as culturally fulfilling as time spent in a church or museum—and much more invigorating.

If you're an energetic person, make a point to be active in Europe. Whether walking through the city core or speeding down an alpine luge, there are plenty of ways to get your heart pumping while savoring some of Europe's outdoor attractions.

HIKING AND WALKING

From casual city strolls to pleasant day hikes to multiday alpine treks, Europe is a walker's paradise.

City Walking (and Dodging)

It's easy to get in a lot of walking time in Europe's cities and towns. Skip public transport (or save it for the end of the day, when your feet are crying for mercy), and get a literal feel for a place.

When putting together a walking itinerary, look for ways to splice in some top sights. In Rome, for example, winding up to the top of Gianicolo Hill rewards you with a lovely park and superb city views—and along the way you can knock off Bramante's Tempietto church, one of the jewels of the Italian Renaissance. In any city, a walking tour can help you get oriented (described on page 275).

Be prepared—bring good, well-broken-in walking shoes, and realize that pounding the pavement all day can result in blisters (see page 390 for remedies). Pace yourself—concrete and cobblestones take their toll on feet much sooner than dirt trails do.

Be on your toes: Walking in cities can be dangerous, and jaywalking can have serious consequences (scores of pedestrians are run down on the streets of Paris each year). Drivers are aggressive, and politeness has no place on the roads of Europe. Cross streets carefully, but if you wait for a break in the traffic, you may never make it to the other side. Look for a pedestrian overpass or underpass, or when all else fails, just shadow a local—one busy lane at a time—across that seemingly impassable street. In some cities, such as Amsterdam, watch out for bikes as well as cars.

Day Hiking

You don't need to go far into the wild to find a slice of natural Europe to explore on foot. England's Cotswolds are walkers' country. The English love to walk the peaceful footpaths that shepherds walked back when "polyester" meant two girls. A two-hour trek connecting two thatched-roof towns in the Cotswolds affords intimate backyard views of farms in action: rabbits popping up in fields, ducks bull up in millponds, and black-and-white cows jostling for space at troughs. Southern France's Cap Ferrat has well-maintained foot trails, perfect for short, view-struck walks above the Mediterranean.

The Dolomites, Italy's dramatic mountainous rooftop, serve up alpine thrills with Italian sunshine. Europe's largest high alpine meadow, Alpe di Siusi, spreads high above Bolzano. A gondola whisks visitors up to the park from the valley below. Within the park, buses take hikers to and from key points along the tiny road, all the way to the foot of the postcard-dramatic Sasso peaks. Meadow walks are ideal for flower lovers and strollers, while chairlifts provide springboards for more demanding hikes.

Perhaps my favorite place to hike is in Italy's Cinque Terre. The five towns that make up the Cinque Terre are strung together by a series of trails that form a national park. Hiking these trails—a seven-mile, five-hour journey—is one of the most exhilarating experiences in Italy. Take it slow...smell the cactus flowers and herbs, listen to birds, and enjoy spectacular vistas on all sides.

Even those who know a Rocky Mountain

Thanks to well-maintained trails, walking in Italy's Dolomites can be a walk in the park—with more spectacular scenery.

High find something special about the Swiss Alps. On one side of you, lakes stretch all the way to Germany. On the other stands the greatest mountain panorama in Europe—the peaks of the Eiger, Mönch, and Jungfrau. And up ahead you hear the long, legato tones of an alphorn, announcing that a helicopter-stocked mountain hut is open, it's just around the corner...and the coffee schnapps is on. That's the kind of magic that awaits anyone who makes the effort to get high in the Alps.

Outstanding national parklands are scattered throughout Europe, offering wonderful ways for visitors to commune with nature. Hikers enjoy nature's very own striptease as the landscape reveals itself in an endless string of powerful poses. Most alpine trails are free of snow by July, and lifts take less rugged visitors to the top in a sweat-free flash. Trails are generally well kept and carefully marked, and precise maps are readily available. Throughout the Alps, trail markers are both handy and humiliating. Handy, because they show hours to hike rather than kilometers to walk to various destinations. Humiliating, because these times are clocked by local senior citizens. You'll know what I mean after your first hike.

If you plan on taking day hikes, look for walking and hiking books on that region. Ask for advice from the national tourist offices of the countries you will visit (find a

Resources for Hiking, Biking & Climbing

Era-ewv-ferp.com: European Ramblers' Association's country-specific advice and maps of Europe's walking paths

Ramblers.org.uk: Group walks all over Britain, from casual strolls to bracing treks

LDWA.org.uk: Long Distance Walkers Association in United Kingdom

Countrywalkers.com: Guided or self-directed hiking itineraries

TrailDino.com: Links to hiking trails around the world

Europebicycletouring.com: Tips and tours from a 20-year vet of cycling in Europe

Reading
Sunflowerbooks.co.uk: Guides for walking and touring

Cicerone.co.uk: Reliable guidebooks for walkers, bikers, trekkers, and climbers

Alpine trail signs show where you are, the altitude in meters, and how long in hours and minutes it takes to hike to nearby points.

Lift Lingo

Europeans, and especially the Swiss, have come up with a variety of ways to conquer alpine peaks and reach the best viewpoints and trailheads with minimum sweat. Known generically as "lifts," each of these contraptions has its own name and definition.

Cogwheel Train: A train that climbs a steep incline using a gear system, which engages "teeth" in the middle of the tracks to provide traction. Also known as "rack-and-pinion train" or "rack railway." In German, it's a *Zahnradbahn* (*train à cremaillère* in French and *ferrovia a cremagliera* in Italian).

Funicular: A car that is pulled by a cable along tracks up a particularly steep incline, usually counterbalanced by a similar car going in the opposite direction (meaning you'll pass the other car exactly halfway through the ride). Funiculars, like cogwheel trains, are in contact with the ground at all times. In German, it's a *Standseilbahn* (*funiculaire* in French and *funicolare* in Italian).

Cable Car: A large passenger car, suspended in the air by a cable, which travels between stations without touching the ground. A cable car is generally designed for skiers and holds a large number of people (sometimes dozens at a time), who generally ride standing up. When a cable car reaches a station, it comes to a full stop to allow passengers to get on and off. In German, it's a *Seilbahn* (*téléphérique* in French and *funivia* in Italian).

Gondola: Also suspended in the air by a cable, but smaller than a cable car—generally holding fewer than 10 people, who are usually unable to sit. Gondolas move continuously, meaning that passengers have to hop into and out of the moving cars at stations. Also, while cable-car lines usually have two big cars—one going in each direction—gondolas generally have many smaller cars strung along the same cable. In German, it's a *Gondel* (*télécabine* in French and *telecabine* in Italian).

list on page 39). Tourist offices often have booklets of local self-guided hikes. You can also look into local groups that offer walks to see if one of their scheduled hikes fits with your itinerary. For example, German groups routinely plan *Volksmärsche* and welcome participation. In Great Britain, the Ramblers extend guest privileges to nonmembers who want to try one of the group walks they lead every week; see the sidebar below for other resources.

Hard-core hikers invest in detailed maps (1:100,000 or 1:50,000)—look for OS Ordnance Survey (Britain), Michelin (throughout Europe), IGN's Blue series (good for France), Touring Club Italiano (Italy), and Die Generalkarte (Germany). Make sure the map shows general elevation gain with contour lines and/or indicates the steepness of roads.

Hut Hopping

The hikers' shelters spaced along the European trail system make walking trips a simpler proposition: There's no need to carry a tent, stove, or cooking utensils. Hundreds of huts exist to provide food and shelter for hikers. Using a smart network of trails and mountain huts spaced one convenient day's hike apart, you could walk from France to Slovenia without ever coming out of the Alps. At mountain villages, you can replenish your food supply or enjoy a hotel bed and a restaurant meal.

Resources for Hut Hopping

Sac-cas.ch: List of more than 150 hiker huts run by the Swiss Alpine Club

Aacuk.org.uk: Austrian Alpine Club English website, with links to other clubs and hut directories by country

Reading
100 Hut Walks in the Alps (Kev Reynolds, 2010)

Most alpine huts serve hot meals and provide bunk-style lodging. Many huts require no linen and wash their blankets annually. I'll never forget getting cozy in my top bunk while a German in the bottom bunk said, "You're climbing into zee germs of centuries." Serious hut-hoppers hike with their own sheets or hostel-style sheet sack.

In the Alps, look for the word *Lager,* which means they have a coed loft full of $30-a-night mattresses.

BIKING

Some travelers are surprised when I tell them to consider biking in Europe. I explain that it gets you close to the ground and close to the people. Europeans love bicycles, and they are often genuinely impressed when they encounter Americans who reject the view from the tour-bus window in favor of huffing and puffing on two wheels. Your bike provides an instant conversation piece, the perfect bridge over a maze of cultural and language barriers.

City Biking

While my schedule usually won't allow a week-long pedal in the Loire Valley, I'll often do day trips in or around cities.

LEFT Bike tours are a fun, informative, and healthy way to see great cities with an entertaining guide.

RIGHT Use your bike lock correctly. I learned this lesson the hard way, and suffered the embarrassment of returning just one wheel to my bike-rental place.

I feel local, efficient, and even smug with my trusty and well-fitted bike. Especially during rush hour, I can get across town faster on my bike than by taxi or tram.

Europe's cities are striving to become more bike-friendly. Dozens of them have joined a European Union initiative to make bicycles on par with cars as a form of urban transport. The progress is gradual. Some cities (such as Rome and Athens) are not yet set up well for bikers, but quite a few (particularly Stockholm, Amsterdam, Copenhagen, Lucca, Florence, Salzburg, Munich, and Bruges) are a delight on two wheels, offering an extensive network of well-marked bike lanes. In these cities, rather than relying on walking or public transportation, consider making a bike your mode of transport. Bikes cut transit times in half compared to walking, giving you more time to spend at the sights.

Rental bikes are bargains at $15-25 per day (the best deals are for multiple days); helmets aren't always available. Bike-rental shops generally provide strong locks. Always lock the frame (not the wheel) to the permanent rack. Bike thieves can be bold and brazen.

Many places (including Barcelona, Copenhagen, Dublin, London, Paris, Stockholm, and Vienna) have citywide programs in which hundreds of free or very cheap loaner bikes are locked to racks around town. While tourists can easily take advantage of these programs in cities like London and Vienna, in other places (Dublin), the systems are designed mostly for residents (some require a membership or only take European-style chip-and-PIN credit cards). Also, the bikes are very basic, sometimes in disrepair, and often plastered with ads. If you're serious about biking, pay to rent a good one from a shop instead.

For a quick but meaningful spin around town, consider a bicycle tour. Guided bike tours are popular in cities throughout Europe (especially Amsterdam, Barcelona, Bruges, Paris,

Munich, Berlin, and Budapest), as well as many bike-friendly countryside areas. You'll get a young, entertaining, often foul-mouthed, sometimes informative guide who will give you a breezy introduction to the city and a close-up look at back streets few tourists ever see. The various companies—generally started by disgruntled employees of other bike-tour companies—are highly competitive, and come and go all the time. Tours are typically fun, reasonable (about $25-30), good exercise, and an easy way to meet other travelers as well as get a new angle on an old city.

Countryside Biking

Biking in the boonies (using a small town as a springboard) is extremely popular in Europe. Thanks to the law of supply and demand, you can generally count on finding bike-rental shops wherever there are good bike-tripping options: along the Danube, the Rhine, and other idyllic river valleys; around Ireland's Dingle Peninsula; on Greek islands; and in the Alps for mountain biking on service roads.

In many countries (especially France, Germany, Austria, Belgium, and the Netherlands), train stations rent bikes and sometimes have easy "pick up here and drop off there" plans. For instance, if you ride the train into Amsterdam, rent a bike at the station for a few days to get around the city...and out into the tulip fields and windmills.

Longer Bike Trips

If you're interested in long-distance biking, figure out how much of Europe you want to see. With an entire summer free, you can cover a lot of ground on a bike. But with a month or less, it's better to focus on a single country or region.

Consider bringing your bike from home, but be sure to check your airline's baggage policies for fees and restrictions.

LEFT Wherever biking is fun, you'll find shops renting bikes and helmets.

RIGHT Anyone can enjoy a gentle pedal through some of Europe's flat and inviting countryside.

It could cost you $100-400 to bring your bike, and you may need to reserve a spot for it when you book your plane ticket. But if you're planning to ride a bike for more than a week, the cost of bringing your own may beat the cost of renting one in Europe, where bikes are more expensive than in the US. And having your own bike means you'll know that it works well for you. Carry along the tools you'll need to get your bike back into riding form, so you can ride straight out of your European airport.

Unless you love bike camping, it makes sense to stay in hostels, hotels, or B&Bs, since it frees you from lugging around a tent and sleeping bag. If you'd rather let someone else carry your gear, try a bike tour (offered by REI and many other companies).

Don't be a purist. Taking your bike on a train can greatly extend the reach of your trip, and there's nothing so sweet as taking a train away from the rain and into a sunny place.

You can find many good books on cycling in Europe, along with online info (such as europebicycletouring.com).

MORE ACTIVITIES

Adventure travel continues to be a major trend in the tourism industry. While I'm not going to suggest you drop everything to climb the Matterhorn, Europe has plenty of thrills and chills to carbonate a stodgy vacation. From marveling at Cappadocia's otherworldly landscape from the basket of a hot-air balloon, to paddling a boat in Norway's breathtaking Sognefjord, outdoor escapes abound.

Riding a Luge

The *Sommerrodelbahn* ("summer toboggan run") is one of the most exhilarating alpine experiences. You take a lift up to the top of a mountain, grab a wheeled sled-like go-cart, and scream back down the mountainside on a banked course made of concrete or metal. Then you take the lift back up and start all over again.

Operating the sled is simple: Push the stick forward to go faster, pull back to apply the brake. Novices quickly find their personal speed limits. Most are cautious on their first run, speed demons on their second...and bruised and bloody on their third. A woman once showed me her travel journal illustrated with her husband's dried, five-inch-long luge scab. He had disobeyed the only essential rule of luging: Keep both hands on your stick. To avoid getting into a bumper-to-bumper traffic jam, let the person in front of you get way ahead before you start. You'll emerge from the course with a windblown hairdo and a smile-creased face.

You've got several luge options. In the French mountain resort of Chamonix, at the base of Mount Blanc, two concrete courses run side by side (the slow one marked by a tortoise and the fast one marked by a hare). In Austria, south of Salzburg on the road to Hallstatt, you'll pass two metal courses: one near Wolfgangsee (scenic with grand lake views) and one at Fuschlsee (half as long and cheaper).

In Germany and Austria, near "Mad" King Ludwig's Neuschwanstein Castle, you'll find two courses. One is in Austria, just beyond Biberwier (under Zugspitze, Germany's tallest mountain); the Biberwier Sommerrodelbahn is the longest in Austria at 4,000 feet. And just a mile from Neuschwanstein is Germany's Tegelberg course—because it's metal rather than concrete, it's often open when the other course has closed at the least sprinkle of rain.

Hot-Air Ballooning

A few years ago, I learned that even if I wasn't blessed with wings, I've got an abundance of hot air—and I can fly quite well with little more than that. I've always loved Cappadocia in central Turkey, so I took a majestic hot-air balloon ride over the fairy-chimney formations of that exotic landscape. From the moment our basket slipped from the land into the sky, I gazed in wonder, mesmerized at the erosion-shaped countryside and spectacle of colorful balloons gliding around me. As I stood in the basket of my balloon, the rhythmic bursts of flame punctuated the captain's jokes while warming my wide eyes. Illogically, the stripes on his epaulets made me feel safe as we lifted off.

You'll also find hot-air balloon companies in France's most popular regions (Burgundy, the Loire, Dordogne, and Provence are best suited for ballooning). These offer a bird's-eye view of France's sublime landscapes as you sail serenely over châteaux, canals, vineyards, Romanesque churches, and villages.

These trips aren't cheap

City Thrills

Surfing in Downtown Munich: Far from the nearest stretch of coast, surfers "hang ten" in Munich's English Garden, in the rapids of the city's little man-made river. While seeking their thrills, the surfers provide great entertainment for the ever-present crowd that gathers to watch from a bridge.

Skiing in Edinburgh: If you'd rather be skiing, the Midlothian Ski Centre, just outside Edinburgh, has a brush-skiing hill with a chairlift, two slopes, a jump slope, and rentable skis, boots, and poles. While you're actually skiing over what seems like a million toothbrushes, it feels like snow skiing on a slushy day. It's open nearly year-round (except, ironically, when it snows). Beware: Local doctors are used to treating an ailment called "Hillend Thumb"—digits dislocated when people fall and get tangled in the brush.

Boating in Madrid: When it's sizzling, Madrileños head to majestic Retiro Park, where active types can rent a rowboat and traverse a big lake in its center (El Estanque). At midday on Saturday and Sunday, the area around the lake becomes a street carnival, with jugglers, puppeteers, and lots of local color. Other city parks offer rental rowboats at lakes (e.g., London's Hyde Park and Paris' Bois de Vincennes). Paddle boats are popular in many cities, too.

(about $200 in Turkey and $275-390 in France), but they give lots of travelers a fine memory and stunning pictures.

Canoeing and Kayaking

If you're near a lake or river, consider exploring the area by boat. Some of Europe's natural wonders are best seen from the water. For example, in France's unpretentious port town of Cassis, you can kayak to its exotic fjords of translucent blue water in the calanques—the narrow inlets created by the prickly extensions of cliffs that border the shore. These spiky pinnacles are located along the 13 miles of coast between Cassis and Marseille (you can get there by hiking or boat cruise, too).

When I'm in the Dordogne region of France, one of my rituals is exploring the riverside castles and villages by canoe. I can't think of a more relaxing way to enjoy great scenery while getting some exercise. Delights are revealed around each bend, and you can pop ashore whenever you like. There's always a place to stow the canoe, and plenty of welcoming villages. Two of the most picturesque are La Roque-Gageac, a strong contender for "cutest town in

France," and Beynac, a perfectly preserved medieval village that winds, like a sepia-tone film set, from the shore to the castle above.

You can rent plastic boats—which are hard, light, and indestructible—from many outfits in this area for a reasonable price ($16-24 for two-person canoes, $22-30 for one-person kayaks). It's OK if you're a complete novice—the only whitewater you'll encounter will be the rare wake of passing tour boats...and your travel partner frothing at the views.

Shopping

Shopping in Europe can be fun, but don't let it overwhelm your trip. All too often, slick marketing and clever displays can succeed in shifting the entire focus of your vacation toward things rather than experiences. I've seen half the members of a guided tour of the British Houses of Parliament skip out to survey an enticing array of plastic "bobby" hats, Big Ben briefs, and Union Jack panties. Stay in control, and don't let your trip become just one more glorified shopping spree.

The thrill of where you bought something can fade long before the item's usefulness does. Even thoughtful shoppers go overboard. I have several large boxes in my attic labeled "great souvenirs." On the other hand, a few well-chosen items—a hand-painted tile from Siena, Provençal fabric from Nice, a fine old print from Athens—can help you capture the essence of a place for years to come.

WHERE TO SHOP

Avoid the souvenir carts outside of big monuments, where the goods tend to be overpriced and cheesy. Do your shopping in places that offer a fun cultural experience as well.

Outdoor Markets

The most colorful shopping in Europe—and a fun way to feel the local vibe—is at its lively open-air markets. A stroll along Portobello Road, arguably London's best street market, has you rubbing elbows with antique buffs and people who brake for garage sales. In Florence, the sprawling San Lorenzo Market has stalls of garments, accessories, and leather jackets ranging from real to vinyl. Even a place as overrun with international visitors as Istanbul's Grand Bazaar still has tourist-free nooks and crannies that offer a glimpse into the real Turkey. Jump into the human rivers that flow in these venues.

Other good markets are Amsterdam's Waterlooplein, Madrid's El Rastro, and Paris' Puces St. Ouen. Remember that flea markets anywhere have soft prices. Bargain like mad (see "Successful Haggling," later). Pickpockets love flea markets—wear your money belt and watch your day bag.

Department Stores

While Europe's large department stores may seem daunting at first, they're generally laid out much like ours. Most are accustomed to wide-eyed foreign shoppers and have some English-speaking staff. The store directory (usually near the elevators or escalators) often includes English. Many department stores have a souvenir section, with standard local knickknacks and postcards at far lower prices than you'll find in cute little tourist shops.

In Paris, visit Galeries Lafayette or Printemps. Harrods is London's most famous and touristy department store, but locals prefer Liberty on Regent Street. In Italy, an upscale department chain is La Rinascente, and in Spain, El Corte Inglés is everywhere. Berlin's mammoth Kaufhaus des Westens (KaDeWe) has a staff of 2,100 to help you sort through its vast selection of 380,000 items.

Neighborhood Shops and Boutiques

The best shopping districts not only offer interesting stores, but also let you feel the pulse of the city. In Rome, an early evening stroll down Via del Corso takes you past affordable shops—and the city's beautiful people. For top fashion—and top people-watching—stroll the streets around the Spanish Steps.

The narrow streets near Vienna's cathedral are sprinkled with old-fashioned shops that seem to belong to another era—just the place to pick out an old print or an elegant dirndl. London's best and most convenient shopping streets are in the West End and West London (roughly between Soho and Hyde Park).

In Paris, a stroll from the Bon Marché department store to St. Sulpice allows you to sample smart clothing boutiques and clever window displays while enjoying one of the city's more attractive neighborhoods. For more eclectic, avant-garde boutiques, peruse the artsy shops of the Marais. Or head to the Champs-Elysées and peek into Louis Vuitton,

Guerlain, and Mercedes-Benz; you don't have to buy the glitz to feel *très* French.

Museum Gift Shops

Gift shops at major museums (such as the Picasso Museum in Barcelona) are a bonanza for shoppers. Consider picking up books, prints, unusual posters, decorative items, or clever knickknacks featuring works by your favorite artist or commemorating a historic event or sight. Museum gift shops are also a good source for books you may not see elsewhere. Before accumulating too much to easily carry, keep in mind that many things (like prints and posters of universally loved art) can be ordered fairly cheaply online from home.

SHOPPING TIPS

Here are some tips for shopping in Europe—from buying souvenirs and clothes to bargaining your way to the best price.

Souvenir Strategies

Shop smart, and remember that your most prized souvenirs are your memories

Comparison shop at home. Do some research if you're looking for a particular high-end item overseas (and be aware that you can often find a similar item of better quality for a cheaper price at home). Before heading off to buy a Turkish carpet in Istanbul, learn the going rate, types of materials, and signs of quality, if only to avoid advertising your inexperience

Concentrate your shopping in countries where your dollar will stretch. You'll find the best bargains in Turkey, Morocco, Portugal, Spain, Greece, and Eastern Europe. For the price of a skimpy doily in Di Italia, you can get a lace tablecloth in Spain.

Restrict your shopping to a stipulated time. Form an idea of what you want to buy in each country. Set aside one day to shop in each country, and stick to it. This way you can avoid drifting through your trip thinking only of souvenirs.

Choose good souvenirs. I look for local crafts, such as hand-knit sweaters in Portugal or Ireland, glass in Sweden, painted beehive panels in Slovenia, or lace in Belgium. I also

Boxloads of *Davids* await busloads of tourists.

like books published in Europe; these are a great value all over the Continent, with many editions that are impossible to find in the US. Other good souvenirs are strange stuffed animals (at flea markets), CDs of music I heard live, posters (one sturdy tube stores 8-10 posters safely), and clothing.

Lighten your load. Larger stores can arrange shipping for you, or you can ship packages home yourself (see "Shipping Things Home," later). Or simply wait for the last country you visit to go hog-wild and fly home heavy. One summer I had a 16-pound backpack and nothing more until the last week of my trip, when I hit Spain and Morocco and managed to accumulate two sets of bongos, swords, a mace, and a camelhair coat...most of which are now in boxes in my attic.

Remember the paperwork. If you intend to claim a Value-Added Tax (VAT) refund, you'll need to get the right documents from the merchant. For details on VAT as well as US customs regulations, see "VAT Refunds, Customs, and Shipping" on page 318.

Clothes Shopping

Many travelers enjoy shopping for wearable souvenirs in Europe, where the fashions can be quite different from back home. Options range from hole-in-the-wall boutiques to grand department stores to colorful street markets.

Europe-wide chains such as Mango and C&A have stylish, affordable selections. They can offer good value, especially for designer-inspired clothing. In addition, each country has its own popular chains (such as Topshop in Britain). Fashions vary by store and by country, so if you see an item you like, grab it rather than wait to pick it up at a later stop—you might never see that same style or color again. Some women like buying high-quality underwear and camisoles in Italy or France; browse for them at any large department store.

European department stores (such as Paris' regal Galeries Lafayette) can be as interesting as what's on sale.

Street markets also offer clothing. Remember that prices are often soft—especially if it's near the end of the day, you're paying cash, and you're buying multiple items (such as several scarves). Don't be afraid to bargain.

No matter where you buy,

be aware that the US, the UK, and continental Europe all use slightly different sizing conventions. For specifics, see the clothes-sizing conversion chart. Also note that European clothes are generally cut to fit more snugly than American clothes. Be prepared to swallow your pride and go up a size or two. If you wear a size medium leather jacket back home, you might need a large or extra-large in Italy.

Successful Haggling

In much of the Mediterranean world, the price tag is only an excuse to argue. Bargaining is the accepted and expected method of finding a compromise between the wishful thinking of the merchant and the tourist. In Europe, bargaining in shops is common only in the south, but you can fight prices at flea markets and with street vendors anywhere. (Note that bargaining applies to goods, not to food sold at stands or outdoor produce markets.)

Here are a few guidelines to help you get the best bargain.

Determine if bargaining is appropriate. It's bad shopping etiquette to "make an offer" for a tweed hat in a London department store. It's foolish not to at a Greek outdoor market. To learn if a price is fixed, show some interest in an item but say, "It's just too much money." You've put the merchant in a position to make the first offer. If he comes down even 2 percent, there's nothing sacred about the price tag. Haggle away.

Shop around to find out what locals pay. Prices can vary drastically among vendors at the same flea market, and even at the same stall. If prices aren't posted, assume there's a double price standard: one for locals and one for you. If only tourists buy the item you're pricing, see what an Arab, Spanish, or Italian tourist would be charged. I remember thinking I did well in Istanbul's Grand Bazaar, until I learned my Spanish friend bought the same shirt for 30 percent less. Merchants assume American tourists are rich, and they know what we pay for things at home.

Determine what the item is worth to you. Price tags can be meaningless and serve to distort your idea of an item's true worth. The merchant is playing a psychological game. Many tourists think that if

You can troll for quirky souvenirs at flea markets.

Clothes Sizing Conversion

These conversion tables are very general guidelines; sizes vary considerably by country and brand. I've also included shortcuts for figuring out sizes. When a range is given (e.g., shoe size 36-37), it means that the European size straddles the American one (half-sizes are rare on the Continent)—look for a 36 that runs large, or a 37 that runs small.

WOMEN

Pants, Dresses & Suits

US	2	4	6	8	10	12	14	16	18	20
Europe	32	34	36	38	40	42	44	46	48	50
UK	6	8	10	12	14	16	18	20	22	24

Shortcut: From US to Europe—add 30; from US to UK—add 4.

Blouses & Sweaters

US	32(S)	34(S)	36(M)	38(M)	40(L)	42(L)
Europe	40	42	44	46	48	50
UK	34	36	38	40	42	44

Shortcut: From US to Europe—add 8; from US to UK—add 2.

Shoes

US	5½	6	6½	7	7½	8	8½	9	9½	10
Europe	35-36	36	37	37-38	38	38-39	39	40	41	42
UK	3	3½	4	4½	5	5½	6	6½	7	7½

Shortcut: From US to Europe—add about 31; from US to UK—subtract 2½.

MEN

Suits & Jackets

US/UK	34	36	38	40	42	44	46	48	50	52
Europe	44	46	48	50	52	54	56	58	60	62

Shortcut: From US to Europe—add 10; US and UK use the same sizing.

they can cut the price by 50 percent they are doing great. So the merchant quadruples his prices and the tourist happily pays double the fair value. The best way to deal with crazy price tags is to ignore them. Before you even see the price tag, determine the item's value to you, considering the hassles involved in packing it or shipping it home.

Determine the merchant's lowest price. Merchants hate to lose a sale. Work the cost down, but if it doesn't match with the price you have in mind, walk away. That last amount the merchant hollers out as you turn the corner is often the best price you'll get. If *that* price is right, go back and buy.

Shirts

US/UK	14(S)	14½(S)	15(M)	15½(M)	16(L)	16½(L)	17(XL)
Europe	36	37	38	39	40	41	42

Shortcut. From US to Europe—multiply by 2 and add about 8; US and UK use the same sizing.

Shoes

US	7½	8	8½	9	9½	10	10½	11	11½	12
Europe	39	39-40	40	41	42	43	44	45	45-46	46
UK	7	7½	8	8½	9	9½	10	10½	11	11½

Shortcut: From US to Europe—add about 32-34; from US to UK—subtract about ½.

CHILDREN

Clothing

US/UK	2	4	6	8	10	14/13	16/15
Europe	1	2	5	7	9	10	12

Shortcut: From US to Europe—subtract 1-2 for smaller children and subtract 4 for juniors; US and UK use the same sizing.

Girls' Shoes

US	9½	10	11	12	13	1	2	3	4
Europe	26	26-27	27-28	28-29	30	31	32-33	33-34	35
UK	8	8½	9½	10½	11½	12½	13½	1½	2½

Shortcut: From US to Europe—for sizes up to 13 add 16-17, and for sizes 1 and up add about 30; from US to UK—subtract about 1½, except sizes 1 and 2, to which you'll add 11½.

Boys' Shoes

US	11½	12	12½	13	1	2	3	4	5
Europe	29	29-30	30-31	31	33	34	35	36	37-38
UK	11	11½	12	12½	13½	1½	2½	3½	4½

Shortcut: From US to Europe—for sizes up to 13 add 17½-18, and for sizes 1 and up add about 32; from US to UK—subtract about ½, except size 1, to which you'll add about 12½.

Prices often drop at the end of the day, when merchants are considering packing up.

Curb your enthusiasm. As soon as the merchant perceives the "I gotta have that!" in you, you'll never get the best price. He assumes Americans have the money to buy what they really want.

Employ a third person. Use your friend who is worried about the ever-dwindling budget or who doesn't like the price or who is bored and wants to return to the hotel. This trick can work to bring the price down faster.

Impress the merchant with your knowledge. He'll respect you, and you'll be more likely to get good quality.

Istanbul has very good leather coats for a fraction of the US cost. Before my trip I talked to some leather-coat sellers and was much better prepared to confidently pick out a good coat in Istanbul.

Ask for a deal on multiple items. See if the merchant will give you a better price if you buy in bulk (three necklaces instead of one). The more they think they can sell, the more flexible they may become.

Offer to pay cash at stalls that take credit cards. You can expect to pay cash for most things at street markets, but some merchants who sell pricier goods (nice jewelry, artwork, etc.) take credit cards, too. They're often more willing to strike a deal if you pay cash, since they don't lose any profit to credit-card fees.

Show the merchant your money. Physically hold out your money and offer him "all you have" to pay for whatever you are bickering over. He'll be tempted to just grab your money and say, "Oh, OK."

Obey the rules. Don't hurry. Bargaining is rarely rushed. Make sure you are dealing with someone who has the authority to bend a price downward. Bid carefully. If a merchant accepts your price (or vice versa), you must buy the item.

If the price is too much, leave. Never worry about having taken too much of the merchant's time. Merchants are experienced businesspeople who know they won't close every deal.

VAT REFUNDS, CUSTOMS, AND SHIPPING

For serious shoppers, it's worth knowing the ins and outs of tax refunds on your major purchases, and how to bring these items home (either in your luggage or by shipping them).

Claiming Back Value-Added Tax (VAT)

Every year, tourists visiting Europe leave behind millions of dollars of refundable sales taxes. For some, the headache of collecting the refund is not worth the few dollars at stake. But if you do any extensive shopping, consider that the refund is hard cash—free and fairly easy to claim. You just

VAT Rates and Minimum Purchases Required to Qualify for Refunds

Country of Purchase	VAT Standard Rate*	Minimum in Local Currency	Approx. Min. in US Dollars
Austria	20%	€75.01	$98
Belgium	21%	€125.01	$163
Croatia	25%	740 HRK	$148
Czech Republic	21%	2,001 CZK	$112
Denmark	25%	300 DKK	$51
France	20%	€175.01	$228
Germany	19%	€25	$33
Great Britain	20%	£30	$48
Greece	23%	€120	$156
Hungary	27%	52,001 HUF	$260
Ireland	23%	No minimum	No minimum
Italy	22%	€155	$202
Netherlands	21%	€50	$65
Norway	25%	315 NOK	$53
Poland	23%	200 PLN	$67
Portugal	23%	€61.35	$80
Slovenia	22%	€50.01	$65
Spain	21%	€90.15	$117
Sweden	25%	200 SEK	$33
Switzerland	8%	300 CHF	$273

* EU VAT standard rates are set by member countries and can fluctuate. Your refund will likely be less than the rate listed above, especially if it's subject to processing fees.

have to bring your passport along on your shopping trip, get the necessary documents from the retailer, and track down the right folks at the airport, port, or border when you leave. (This gives you something to do while you're hanging around waiting for your flight.)

The standard European Union Value-Added Tax ranges from 15 to 25 percent per country. Exact rates change; you can double-check with merchants when you're there.

Unlike business travelers, tourists aren't entitled to refunds on the tax they spend on hotels and meals. Still, you can get back most of the tax you paid on merchandise such as clothes, cuckoos, and crystal. You're not supposed to use your purchased goods before you leave Europe—if you show up at customs wearing your new Italian shoes, officials might look the other way, or they might deny you a refund.

To get any refund, your purchase has to be above a certain amount—ranging from about $30 to several hundred dollars, depending on the country (except in Ireland, which has no minimum). Typically, you must ring up the minimum at a single retailer—you can't add up your purchases from various shops to reach the required amount—so if you're doing a lot of shopping, you'll benefit from finding one spot where you can buy big. If you'll be in Europe for a long time, shop near the end of your trip. You need to collect your refund within three months of your purchase.

The details on how to get a refund vary per country, but generally you'll need to follow the same basic steps:

Bring your passport along. You'll likely be asked to present your passport when you make the purchase, in order to start the refund process.

Shop at stores that know the ropes. Retailers choose whether to participate in the VAT-refund scheme. Most tourist-oriented stores do; often you'll see a sign in the window or by the cash register (if not, ask). It'd be a shame to spend big bucks at a place and not have a chance of getting a refund.

Get the documents. When you make your purchase, have the merchant fill out the necessary refund document, often called a "tax-free form." Make sure the paperwork is done before you leave the store so there's nothing important missing. If they leave any blanks for you to fill out, be sure you understand what goes where. Attach your receipt to the form and stash it in a safe place.

Some stores may offer to handle the rest of the hassle for you (if they provide this service, they likely have some sort of "Tax Free" sticker in the window). If you're charming and at the right store, try talking the merchant into mailing your documents for you and reimbursing your credit card on the spot. You may also be able to take your paperwork to a nearby third-party agency to get an immediate cash refund (minus a commission for the quick service; these tend to be located at money-exchange counters near touristy land-marks). In either case, you'll still need to get the documents stamped at the border, then mail them back; if they never receive the documents, they'll charge the refund to your credit card.

If the store ships your purchase to your home, you can still collect a refund (or you may even be able to avoid paying the VAT in the first place). However, shipping fees can be pricey enough to wipe out most of what you'd save in VAT. I wouldn't mail a purchase home just to avoid paying the VAT, but if you're having things shipped anyway, ask for the refund at the shop. (Depending on the country, you may still have to handle some VAT-related red tape—ask the merchant.)

Bring your paperwork and purchases to the airport or border crossing, and arrive early. Assuming you left the store with your purchase, receipt, and VAT paperwork (but no refund), you'll need to get the refund processed before going home. If you've bought merchandise in a European Union country, process your documents at your last stop in the EU, regardless of where you made your purchases. So if you buy sweaters in Denmark, pants in France, and shoes in Italy, and you're flying home from Greece, get your documents stamped at the airport in Athens. (If the currencies are different in the country where you made your purchase and where you process your refund—say, pounds and euros—you may have to pay an extra conversion fee.) And don't forget—Switzerland, Norway, and Turkey are not in the EU, so if you buy in one of those countries, get your documents stamped before you cross the border.

Get your documents stamped at customs. At your point of departure, find the local customs office, and be prepared to stand in line. In smaller airports, ports, and less-trafficked border crossings, finding the right customs agent can be tough. If you run out of time and have to leave without the stamp, you're out of luck. At customs, an export officer will stamp your documents and may ask you to present your unused goods to verify that you are, indeed, exporting your purchase—if your purchases are inside your checked luggage, stop by customs before you check it. (Some retailers, particularly those in Scandinavia, will staple and seal the shopping bag to keep you from cheating.)

Collect the cash—sooner or later. Once you get your form stamped by customs, it takes one more step to get your money back. If your purchases were bought from a merchant who works with a refund service such as Global Blue or Premier Tax Free, find their offices inside the airport. These services take a cut of your refund (about 4 percent), but save you further fuss and delay. Present your stamped document, and they'll likely give you your refund in cash, right then and there. Otherwise, they'll credit the refund to your credit card (within two billing cycles; see globalblue.com or premiertaxfree.com). Other services may require you to mail the documents—either from home, or more quickly, just before leaving the country (using a postage-free, pre-addressed envelope—just drop it in a mailbox after getting your customs stamp). Then you wait. It could take months. Look for a refund on your credit-card statement, or for a check in the mail. If the refund check comes in a foreign currency, you may have to pay $30 or so to get your bank to cash it.

Don't count on it. My readers have reported that, even when following all of the instructions carefully, sometimes the VAT refund just doesn't pan out. (For example, they have all the paperwork ready when they get to the airport—but can't find the customs official to process it.) These problems seem most prevalent in Italy. Your best odds are to buy from a merchant who knows how to deal with the red tape for you—but even that is not infallible.

Only you can decide whether VAT refunds are worth the trouble. As for me, my favorite trip souvenirs are my photos, journal, and memories. These are priceless—and exempt from taxes and red tape.

Customs for American Shoppers

Customs regulations vary depending on whether you are bringing items home on the plane with you, or mailing them to a US address. To check US customs rules and duty rates, visit cbp.gov, click on "Travel," and then "Know Before You Go."

Bringing Things Home in Your Luggage

You are allowed to take home $800 worth of items per person duty-free in your luggage, once every 31 days (family members can combine their individual $800 exemptions on a joint declaration). The next $1,000 is taxed at a flat 3 percent. After that, you pay the individual item's duty rate. You can also bring in duty-free a liter of alcohol (slightly more than a standard-size bottle of wine; you must be at least 21), 200 cigarettes, and up to 100 non-Cuban cigars. Household effects intended for personal use, such as tableware and linens, are also duty-free.

Because food items can carry devastating diseases or pests, they are strictly regulated. You may take home vacuum-packed cheeses; dried herbs, spices, or mushrooms; and canned fruits or vegetables, including jams and vegetable spreads. Baked goods, candy, chocolate, oil, vinegar,

mustard, and honey are OK. Fresh fruits and vegetables
(even that banana from your airplane breakfast) are not
permitted. Meats are generally not allowed; however, canned
meat is allowed if it doesn't contain any beef, veal, lamb, or
mutton. Just because a duty-free shop in an airport sells a
food product, it doesn't mean it will automatically pass US
customs. Be prepared to lose your investment.

Of course, you'll need to carefully pack any bottles of
wine, jam, honey, oil, and other liquid-containing items in
your checked luggage, thanks to limits on liquids in carry-
ons (though there's an exception for some foods and wine
purchased at a duty-free shop; see sidebar). For tips on bringing duty-free liquids onto the plane, see "What Can't I Carry
On?" on page 101.

Shipping Things Home

While it's fun to shop in Europe, it's not fun to have more
things to carry. Consider shipping your shopping bounty
back home so you don't have to lug your purchases around
while you're traveling.

Customs regulations for items you ship amount to 10 or
15 frustrating minutes of filling out forms with the normally
unhelpful postal clerk's semi-assistance. Be realistic in your
service expectations. European postal clerks are every bit as
friendly, speedy, and multilingual as American postal clerks.

From Europe, you can mail one package per day to yourself in the US, worth up to $200 duty-free (mark it "personal
purchases"). If you mail an item home valued at $250, you
pay duty on the full $250, not $50. When you fill out the
customs form, keep it simple and include the item's value
(contents: clothing, books, souvenirs, poster, value $100). For
alcohol, perfume containing alcohol, and tobacco valued at
more than $5, you will pay a duty. You can also mail home all
the "American Goods Returned" you like (e.g., clothes you
packed but no longer need)
with no customs concerns—
but note that these goods
really must be American (not
Bohemian crystal or a German
cuckoo clock), or you'll be
charged a duty. If it's a gift
for someone else, they are
liable for customs fees if it's
worth more than $100 (mark
it "unsolicited gift").

If you accu-
mulate a box's
worth of dead
weight, mail it
home and keep
on packing light.

Hauling Home Heavenly Wines

Wine lovers wandering through Europe face a continual dilemma: Savor the memories or haul a few favorite bottles home?

Despite the global-goods-on-demand world we live in today, your neighborhood wine shop can't always track down the wine you enjoyed at that Parisian café or Spanish tapas bar. Some wineries only sell their wine within their country, which makes it tempting to bring a few bottles home.

The downside, of course, is the schlepping—the scary prospect of a bottle breaking in your suitcase or the weight of the box dragging you down as you trudge through the airport. And there's the chance that the wine won't taste quite as exquisite when you're sipping it in your kitchen as it did on that piazza in Siena. You might be better off seeing wine like art—something to be enjoyed, marveled at, and remembered.

Before you purchase a bottle to carry home, ask the server whether the wine is exported to your home state. Or take a picture of the label with your phone—you can even email it to your hometown wine shop to find out if they can have the wine waiting for you when you return.

But if you can't resist bringing wine home, keep these tips in mind.

Pack softly and carry a hard suitcase. Per TSA regulations, if you purchase liquor from a duty-free shop and it's able to be screened (i.e., not in an opaque, metallic, or ceramic bottle) and is in a secure, tamper-evident bag (called a STEB), you can transport it in your carry-on (a STEB can also be used for transporting foods packed in liquid or oil—if purchased at the airport duty-free shop). If not, you'll have to pack it carefully in checked luggage. This works most of the time if the bottles are thickly padded with clothing in a hard-sided suitcase (though bottles can still break); they'll also have to endure the extreme cold (or heat) of the cargo hold.

Divide and conquer. If you're traveling with a partner, divide the bottles among your bags (each bottle of wine weighs about three pounds, so five bottles means 15 extra pounds). Bring a spare fold-up tote bag or duffle for your clothes that are displaced by the wine.

Know your limits. If you bring back more than one liter, customs regulations require you to pay duty tax based on the percent of alcohol (generally $1-2 per liter for wine). Couples get away with three standard 750 ml bottles, adding up to 2¼ liters. There's also a small federal excise tax.

Tell the truth. Be up front if you're over the limit. You may even benefit—sometimes the special customs lines move faster than the nothing-to-declare ones. If your wine is for personal use, the agents might not even tax you. It won't happen all the time, but many wine-obsessed travelers report that this can be the case.

It's fairly painless to use regular postal services; it can be expensive but convenient. You can usually buy boxes and tape at the post office. A box the size of a small fruit crate costs about $40 by slow boat. Post offices in some countries have limits on how big or heavy your packages can be. In Germany and Great Britain, any surface-mail package for overseas delivery is limited to 2 kilograms, or about 4.5 pounds (but for books only, Great Britain allows up to 5 kilograms, or 11 pounds). For heavier packages, you must use their postal services' affiliated package services. From France, you can ship surface packages up to 30 kilograms (about 66 pounds). The fastest way to get a package home from Italy is to use the Vatican post office—or take it home in your suitcase. Every box I've ever mailed from Europe has arrived—bruised and battered but all there—within six weeks. To send precious things home fast, I use DHL; they have offices in any big city.

Theft & Scams

The odds are in your favor for enjoying a perfectly safe and incident-free trip to Europe. But anybody, whether at home or abroad, can experience unexpected problems, from inadvertently leaving your backpack on the train to getting pickpocketed in a crowd. By taking a few common-sense precautions, you'll greatly improve your chances of having a smooth trip.

PICKPOCKETING AND THEFT

Europe is safe when it comes to violent crime. But it's very "dangerous" in terms of petty theft: Purse-snatching, phone-grabbing, and pickpocketing are rampant in places where tourists gather. Thieves target Americans—not because they're mean, but because they're smart. Americans have all the good stuff in their bags and wallets. Loaded down with valuables, jetlagged, and bumbling around in a strange new environment, we stick out like jeweled thumbs. If I were a European street thief, I'd specialize in Americans—my card would say "Yanks R Us."

If you're not constantly on guard, you'll have something stolen. One summer, four out of five of my traveling companions lost cameras in one way or another. (Don't look at me.) In more than 30 summers of travel, I've been mugged once (in a part of London where only fools and thieves tread); my various rental cars have been broken into a total of six times (broken locks, shattered windows, lots of nonessential stuff taken); and one car was hot-wired (and abandoned a few blocks away after the thief found nothing to take). But not one of my hotel rooms has ever been rifled through, nor any of my money-belt-worthy valuables ever stolen.

Many tourists get indignant when ripped off. If it happens to you, it's best to get over it. You're rich and thieves

LEFT In Spain, just say "No, gracias" to women trying to thrust sprigs of rosemary on you for a tip.

RIGHT Outer backpack compartments are easy pickings for thieves.

aren't. You let your guard down and they grab your camera. It ruins your day and you have to buy a new one, while they sell it for a week's wages on their scale. And the score's one to nothing. It's wise to keep a material loss in perspective.

Remember, nearly all crimes suffered by tourists are nonviolent and avoidable. Be aware of the pitfalls of traveling, but relax and have fun. Limit your vulnerability rather than your travels.

Be Prepared

Before you go, you can take some steps to minimize your loss in case of theft.

Make photocopies and/or take photos of key documents—your passport, rail pass, car-rental voucher, itinerary, prescriptions (for eyewear and/or medicine), and more—to bring along. For a backup, email these photos to yourself and/or leave a copy with loved ones in case you lose your copy and need to have one sent to you. You could also bring extra passport pictures if you have some laying around.

If you have expensive electronics (camera, tablet, smartphone, etc.), consider getting theft insurance (see page 72). As I mentioned earlier in the book, make a list of serial numbers, makes, and models of your pricey gear and take photos of it, in case it'll help you settle an insurance claim. As you travel, back up your digital photos and other files frequently.

Leave your fancy bling at home. Luxurious luggage lures thieves. The thief chooses the most impressive suitcase in the pile—never mine.

Avoiding Theft

If you exercise adequate discretion, stay aware of your belongings, and avoid putting yourself into risky situations (such as unlit, deserted areas at night), your travels should be about as dangerous as hometown grocery shopping. Don't travel fearfully—travel carefully.

Here's some advice given to me by a thief who won the lotto.

Wear a money belt. A money belt is a small, zippered fabric pouch on an elastic strap that fastens around your waist, under your pants or skirt. I never travel without one—it's where I put anything I really, really don't want to lose. Wear it completely hidden from sight, tucked in like a shirttail—over your undies and shirt, under your pants. Most people wear the pouch over their stomach, but if you find it more comfortable, slide it around to the small of your back. (And some people prefer to use a neck pouch instead, worn like a necklace but under their shirt.) Each traveler should carry his or her own credit and debit cards and a stash of emergency cash in their own money belt.

If you need to access your money belt, just reach casually into your pants (ignoring the curious glances of onlookers) and pull it out.

With a money belt, all your essential documents are on you as securely and thoughtlessly as your underwear. Have you ever thought about that? Every morning you put on your underpants. You don't even think about them all day long. And every night, when you undress, sure enough, there they are, exactly where you put them. When I travel, my valuables are just as securely out of sight and out of mind, around my waist in a money belt. It's luxurious peace of mind. I'm uncomfortable only when I'm not wearing it.

Those who travel with nothing worth stealing except for what's in their money belt are virtually invulnerable. But money belts don't work if they're anywhere but under your clothes. I once met an American woman whose purse was stolen, and in her purse was her money belt (that juicy little anecdote was featured in every street-thief newsletter). If you pull out your money belt to retrieve something, always remember to tuck it back in. And don't use a fanny pack as a money belt—thieves assume this is where you keep your goodies.

Never leave a money belt "hidden" on the beach while you swim (ideally, leave it locked up in your room). In hostels or on overnight trains, wear your money belt when you sleep. You can even shower with it (hang it—maybe in a plastic bag—from the nozzle or curtain rod). Keep your money-belt contents dry and sweat-free by slipping them into a plastic sheath or baggie before zipping them into the belt.

You don't need to get at your money belt for every euro. Your money belt is your deep storage—for select deposits and withdrawals. For convenience, carry a day's spending money in your pocket (a button-down flap or Velcro strip sewn into your front or back pocket slows down fast fingers). Make sure it's an amount you're prepared to lose. Lately, I haven't even carried a wallet. A few bills in my shirt pocket—no keys, no wallet—I'm on vacation!

Leave your valuables in your hotel room. Expensive gear, such as your laptop, is much safer in your room than with you in a day bag on the streets. While hotels often have safes in the room (or at the front desk), I've never bothered to use one, though many find them a source of great comfort. Theft happens, of course, but it's relatively rare—hoteliers are quick to squelch a pattern of theft. That said, don't tempt sticky-fingered staff by leaving a camera or tablet in plain view; tuck your enticing things well out of sight.

Establish a "don't lose it" discipline. Travelers are more likely to inadvertently lose their bags than to have them stolen. I've heard of people leaving passports under pillows, bags on the overhead rack on the bus, and cameras in the taxi. Always take a look behind you before leaving any place or form of transport. At hotels, stick to an unpacking routine, and don't put things in odd places in the room. Run through a mental checklist every time you pack up again: money belt, passport, mobile phone, electronic gear, charging cords, toiletries, laundry, and so on. Before leaving a hotel room for good, conduct a quick overall search—under the bed, under the pillows and bedspread, behind the bathroom door, in a wall socket...

Tour of a Money Belt

Packing light applies to your money belt as well as your luggage. Here's what to keep in it:

Passport: The item you least want to lose en route.

Rail Pass: It's as valuable as cash.

Driver's License: Necessary if you want to rent a car, and useful as non-passport collateral for rentals (bikes, audioguides, and so on).

Cards: Debit and credit cards.

Cash: Store big bills in your money belt.

Plastic Sheath: Keep money-belt contents dry by placing them in something protective—even a plain old plastic baggie.

Just-In-Case Information: List of important phone numbers, email addresses, hotels, and any other itinerary details.

Secure your bag, gadgets, and other valuables when you're out and about. Thieves want to quickly separate you from your valuables, so even a minor obstacle can be an effective deterrent. If you're sitting down to eat or rest, loop your daypack strap around your arm, leg, or chair leg. If you plan to sleep on a train (or anywhere in public), clip or fasten your pack or suitcase to the seat, luggage rack, or yourself. Even the slight inconvenience of undoing a clip deters most thieves. While I don't lock the zippers on my bag, most zippers are lockable, and even a twist-tie, paper clip, or key ring is helpful to keep your bag zipped up tight—the point isn't to make your bag impenetrable, but harder to get into than the next guy's.

Never set down valuable items—such as a camera, mobile device, wallet, or rail pass—on a train seat or restaurant table, where they are easy to swipe. Keep these tucked away. When using your phone at a café, don't place it on the bar after your call: Put it in your front pocket (then return it to a safer place before you leave). Make it a habit to be careful with your things; it'll become second nature.

Some thieves can even be so bold as to snatch something right out of your hands. For instance, if you're holding up a smartphone to take a picture of the Eiffel Tower, a thief can grab it and run—and he can navigate his escape route far better than you can.

One way to minimize this risk is to keep valuable devices attached to you or your bag (this also reduces the chance of accidentally leaving something behind). For instance, make sure your camera strap is looped around your chest or wrist, even when snapping a photo, or use a lanyard to attach gadgets to your daypack. Many bags, including mine, have an interior tag that makes for a handy attachment point. Otherwise, feed straps through zipper pulls or a sturdy safety pin hooked to the inside of your bag. To attach a lanyard to a smartphone case, try looping a thin ribbon between any two holes in the case, then attaching a lanyard to the ribbon loop.

If your mobile device disappears, you're not just out the cost of the device—but also the photos and personal data stored on it. Given the much higher risk of theft and loss while on the road, it's smart to take extra precautions to protect your data before your trip: Make sure you've installed a "find my phone"-type app, and consider setting up stronger data precautions (see page 258 for details).

Stay vigilant in crowds and steer clear of

commotions. Go on instant alert anytime there's a commotion; it's likely a smokescreen for theft. Imaginative artful-dodger thief teams create a disturbance—a fight, a messy spill, or a jostle or stumble—to distract their victims. For more on this, see "Scams and Rip-Offs," later.

Crowds anywhere, but especially on public transit and at flea markets, provide bad guys with plenty of targets, opportunities, and easy escape routes.

Be on guard in train stations, especially upon arrival, when you may be overburdened by luggage and overwhelmed by a new location. Take turns watching the bags with your travel partner. Don't absentmindedly set down a bag while you wait in line; always be in physical contact with your stuff. If you check your luggage, keep the claim ticket or locker key in your money belt; thieves know just where to go if they snare one of these. On the train, be hyper-alert at stops, when thieves can dash on and off—with your bag. City buses that cover tourist sights (such as Rome's notorious #64) are happy hunting grounds. Be careful on packed buses or subways; to keep from being easy pickings, some travelers wear their day bag against their chest (looping a strap around one shoulder). Some thieves lurk near subway turnstiles; as you go through, a thief might come right behind you, pick your pocket and then run off, leaving you stuck behind the turnstile and unable to follow. By mentioning these scenarios, I don't want you to be paranoid...just prepared. If you keep alert, you'll keep your valuables, too.

Leave a note for honest finders. Accidents happen, and even the most cautious traveler can leave something behind. Maximize your chances of getting it back by taping a tiny note with your email address to any item you really don't want to lose, making it easy for a kind soul to return it.

Theft-Proofing Your Rental Car

Thieves target tourists' cars—especially at night. Don't leave anything even hinting of value in view in your parked car. Put anything worth stealing in the trunk (or, better yet, in your hotel room). Leave your glove compartment open so the thief can look in without breaking in. Choose your parking place carefully. Your hotel receptionist knows what's safe and what precautions are necessary.

Make your car look as local as

You can judge the safety of a European parking lot by how it glitters.

possible. Leave no tourist information lying around. Put a local newspaper under the rear window. More than half of the work that European automobile glass shops do is repairing windows broken by thieves. Before I choose where to park my car, I check to see if the parking lot's asphalt glitters. In Rome, my favorite hotel is next to a large police station—a safe place to park.

If you have a hatchback, leave the trunk covered during the day. At night, roll back the cover so thieves can see there's nothing stored in the car. Many police advise leaving your car unlocked at night. "Worthless" but irreplaceable things (journal, memory cards full of photos, etc.) are stolen only if left in a bag. It's better to keep these things with you, or if need be, lay them loose in the trunk.

Be alert to "moving violations." In some urban areas, crude thieves reach into windows or even smash the windows of occupied cars at stoplights to grab a purse or camera.

SCAMS AND RIP-OFFS

Europe is a surprisingly creative place when it comes to travel scams. Many of the most successful gambits require a naive and trusting tourist. But don't think it can't happen to more sophisticated travelers, too. There are many subtle ways to be scammed—a cabbie pads your fare, a shop clerk suddenly inflates prices, or a waiter offers a special with a "special" increased price. Be smart: Know what you are paying for before handing over money, and always count your change. (For tips on avoiding taxi scams, see page 270.)

Scam artists come in all shapes and sizes. But if you're cautious and not overly trusting, you should have no problem. Here are some clever ways European crooks bolster their cash flow.

Such a Deal!

If a bargain seems too good to be true...it's too good to be true.

The "Found" Ring: An innocent-looking person picks up a ring on the ground in front of you and asks if you dropped it. When you say no, the person examines the ring more closely, then shows you a mark "proving" that it's pure gold. He offers to sell it to you for a good price—which is several times more than he paid for it before dropping it on the sidewalk.

The "Friendship" Bracelet: A vendor approaches you

and aggressively asks if you'll help him with a "demonstration." He proceeds to make a friendship bracelet right on your arm. When finished, he asks you to pay a premium for the bracelet he created just for you. And, since you can't easily take it off on the spot, you feel obliged to pay up. (These sorts of distractions by "salesmen" can also function as a smokescreen for theft– an accomplice is picking your pocket as you try to wriggle away from the pushy vendor.)

Salesman in Distress: A well-spoken, well dressed gentleman approaches you and explains that he's a leather jacket salesman, and he needs directions to drive to a nearby landmark. He chats you up ("Oh, really? My wife is from Chicago!") and soon you've made a new friend. That's when he reaches in his car and pulls out a "designer leather jacket" which he'd like to give to you as a thank you for your helpfulness. Oh, and by the way, his credit card isn't working, and could you please give him some cash to buy gas? He takes off with the cash, and you later realize that you've paid way too much for your new vinyl jacket.

Money Matters

Any time money changes hands, be alert, even when using ATMs (see "ATM Scams," page 186.) For general tips on keeping your cards safe, see "Bank Card Security" on page 192. When dealing with the public, keep your cards in your sight, or much easier and safer, pay cash. But even paying with cash can have its challenges.

Slow Count: Cashiers who deal with lots of tourists thrive on the slow count. Even in banks, they'll count your change back with odd pauses in hopes the rushed tourist will gather up the money early and say *"Grazie."*

Switcheroo—You Lose: Be careful when you pay with too large a bill for a small payment. Clearly state the value of the bill as you hand it over. Some cabbies or waiters will pretend to drop a large bill and pick up a hidden small one in order to shortchange a tourist. Get familiar with the currency and check the change you're given.

Talkative Cashiers: The shop's cashier seems to be speaking on her phone when you hand her your credit card. But listen closely and you may hear the sound of the phone's camera shutter, as she takes a picture of your

In Berlin, the police teach the public the latest shell-game scam. On the streets of Europe, anything that seems too good to be true…is.

card. It can make you want to pay cash for most purchases, like I do.

Meeting the Locals

I want my readers to meet and get to know Europeans—but watch out for chance encounters on the street.

The Attractive Flirt: A single male traveler is approached by a gorgeous woman on the street. After chatting for a while, she seductively invites him for a drink at a nearby nightclub. But when the bill arrives, it's several hundred dollars more than he expected. Only then does he notice the burly bouncers guarding the exits. There are several variations on this scam. Sometimes, the scam artist is disguised as a lost tourist; in other cases, it's simply a gregarious local person who (seemingly) just wants to show you his city. Either way, be suspicious when invited for a drink by someone you just met; if you want to go out together, suggest a bar (or café) of your choosing instead.

Oops! You're jostled in a crowd as someone spills ketchup or fake pigeon poop on your shirt. The thief offers profuse apologies while dabbing it up—and pawing your pockets. There are variations: Someone drops something, you kindly pick it up, and you lose your wallet. Or, even worse, someone throws a baby into your arms as your pockets are picked. Assume beggars are pickpockets. Treat any commotion (a scuffle breaking out, a beggar in your face) as fake—designed to distract unknowing victims. If an elderly woman falls down an escalator, stand back and guard your valuables, then...carefully...move in to help.

The "Helpful" Local: Thieves posing as concerned locals will warn you to store your wallet safely—and then steal it after they see where you stash it. If someone wants to help you use an ATM, politely refuse (they're just after your PIN code). Some thieves put out tacks and ambush drivers with their "assistance" in changing the tire. Others hang out at subway ticket machines eager to "help" you, the bewildered tourist, buy tickets with a pile of your quickly disappearing foreign cash. If using a station locker, beware of the "Hood Samaritan" who may have his own key to a locker he'd like you to use. And skip the helping hand from official-looking railroad attendants at the Rome train station. They'll help you find your seat...then demand a "tip."

Young Thief Gangs: These are common all over urban southern Europe, especially in the touristy areas of Milan, Florence, and Rome. Groups of boys or girls with big eyes, troubled expressions, and colorful raggedy clothes politely mob the unsuspecting tourist, beggar-style. As their pleading eyes grab yours and they hold up their pathetic message scrawled on cardboard, you're fooled into thinking that they're beggars. All the while, your purse or backpack is being expertly rifled. If you're wearing a money belt and you understand what's going on here, there's nothing to fear. In fact, having a street thief's hand slip slowly into your pocket becomes just one more interesting cultural experience.

Appearances Can Be Deceiving

The sneakiest pickpockets look like well-dressed business-people, generally with something official-looking in their hand. Some pose as tourists, with daypacks, cameras, and even guidebooks. Don't be fooled by looks, impressive uniforms, femme fatales, or hard-luck stories.

Fake Charity Petition: You're at a popular sight when someone thrusts a petition at you. It's likely a woman or a teen who, often pretending to be deaf, will try to get you to sign an official-looking petition, supposedly in support of a charity (the petition is often in English, which should be a clue). The petitioner then demands a cash donation. At best, anyone who falls for this scam is out some euros; at worst, they're pickpocketed while distracted by the petitioner.

Phony Police: Two thieves in uniform—posing as "Tourist Police"—stop you on the street, flash their bogus badges, and ask to check your wallet for counterfeit bills or "drug money." You won't even notice some bills are missing until after they leave. Never give your wallet to anyone.

Room "Inspectors": There's a knock at your door and two men claim to be the hotel's room inspectors. One waits outside while the other comes in to take a look around.

In your wallet, you've got a little cash...and this funny note to the thief (with a fake 50-euro bill on back—see next page). Cut it out and take it along.

DEAR THIEF...

ENGLISH: Sorry this contains so little money. Consider changing your profession.

ITALIANO: Mi spiace per te che ci siano così pochi soldi. Sara' meglio che cambi lavoro.

FRANCAIS: Je suis désolé d'avoir si peu d'argent. Considérez un changement de carrière.

DEUTSCHE: Tut mir leid dass meine Geldbörse so wenig Geld enthält. Vielleicht sollten Sie sich einen neuen Beruf auswählen.

ESPAGÑOL: Lamento que encuentre tan poco dinero. Vaya pensando en cambiar de trabajo.

While you're distracted, the first thief slips in and takes valuables left on a dresser. Don't let people into your room if you weren't expecting them. Call down to the hotel desk if "inspectors" suddenly turn up.

The Broken Camera: Everyone is taking pictures of a famous sight, and someone comes up with a camera or cell phone and asks that you take his picture. But the camera or cell phone doesn't seem to work. When you hand it back, the "tourist" fumbles and drops it on the ground, where it breaks into pieces. He will either ask you to pay for repairs (don't do it) or lift your wallet while you are bending over to pick up the broken object.

The Stripper: You see a good-looking woman arguing with a street vendor. The vendor accuses her of shoplifting, which she vehemently denies. To prove her innocence, she starts taking off her clothes—very slowly. Once she's down to her underwear, the vendor apologizes and she leaves. Suddenly all the men in the crowd find out that their wallets have "left," too, thanks to a team of pickpockets working during the show.

LOSING IT ALL... AND BOUNCING BACK

You're winging your way across Europe, having the time of your life, when you make a simple mistake. You set your bag down next to your café chair, and before you know it...your bag is gone. Unfortunately, today's the day you tucked your passport, credit cards, and extra cash in your bag instead of in your money belt. That sinking feeling is the realization that you've lost everything but the euro or two in your pocket.

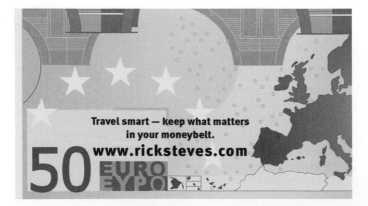

Travel smart — keep what matters in your moneybelt.
www.ricksteves.com

Odds are, this won't ever happen to you. But a little bit of advance preparation can make even this worst-case scenario a minor bump in your European adventure.

Don't panic. First of all, take a breath. Panic clouds your judgment. And don't beat yourself up: No matter how careful, any traveler can get ripped off or lose a bag. I once met a family in Amsterdam who managed to lose all their bags between the airport and their first hotel, and they went on to have a very successful trip. A positive attitude can be a great asset.

Ask for help. If you're in a country where little English is spoken, enlist the help of a local English speaker to assist you in making phone calls or explaining the situation to officials. Try your hotelier or someone at the tourist office. Even in the smallest towns, someone is likely to know at least a little English. Fellow travelers you've met and even family or friends back home can also be sources of help.

For emergency help (for any reason—police, medical, and fire), dial 112 from any phone. This toll-free number is the European Union's version of 911. In many cases, operators are able to answer in English.

File a police report. Find a police officer and report the theft or loss. Having a police report may help with replacing your passport and credit cards, and is a must if you file an insurance claim for a lost rail pass or expensive travel gear. The police may be able to direct you to a local travelers' aid office or Red Cross-like organization. And if you're lucky, someone may actually turn in your bag. That happened to me one time. My stolen bag showed up at the police station—turned in by a Good Samaritan who found it discarded after the thief rifled through its contents. Thieves don't want your clothes or your bag. They want only what they can resell, and they discard the rest.

Lost It All? Follow These Steps

1. File a police report, either on the spot or later. You'll need it to file an insurance claim for a lost or stolen rail pass or travel gear, and it can help with replacing your passport or credit and debit cards.

2. Replace your passport at the nearest embassy or consulate; they're located in the country's capital and sometimes also in major cities (find locations online: travel.state.gov for Americans, passportcanada.gc.ca for Canadians; if you need help getting online for free, try your hotelier or the tourist-info office).

3. Cancel and replace your credit and debit cards. Toll-free numbers (listed by European country) are available at the websites for Visa and MasterCard. You can also call these 24-hour US numbers collect:

   Visa: 303/967-1096
   MasterCard: 636/722-7111
   American Express: 336/393-1111

Gather critical information. In the best situation, you've got photocopies of your important documents on you. If you don't have your bank or embassy's contact information, look it up online (if Internet access is a problem, explain the situation to your hotelier or a staffer at the tourist office, and ask if you can use their office computer). Your hotelier or a tourist-office staffer should also be able to help you place necessary collect or toll-free calls. Retrieve information you've stored online, or solicit help from folks back home. Be careful about emailing passport and credit-card numbers. If you need important documents, have them sent by fax to a trusted location.

Replace your passport. This is top priority. Without a passport, you can't leave the country, and you'll find it difficult to check into a new hotel or receive wired funds. You'll need to go in person to the closest embassy or consulate (in the capital and sometimes major cities, too).

You may be able to make an appointment at the embassy or consulate, or you may need to show up during open hours and wait your turn. If you can, save time by printing the required forms off their website and filling them out before you go. Having a photocopy of your passport can help; if you don't, embassy staff can look up your previous passport records, interview you and your travel partners, and even call contacts at home to verify your identity.

Americans can find embassy and consulate information at travel.state.gov. Every US consulate operates an American Citizen Services (ACS) office, which aids Americans traveling abroad in coping with natural disasters, receiving money, and replacing passports (if calling from Europe, dial 00-1-202/501-4444; in the US, call 888/407-4747). A replacement passport costs $140 and can generally be issued within a few days, or faster if you make a good case that you need it right away. If you don't have the funds, the embassy will help you contact someone at home who can wire money directly to the embassy. If no one can wire the money, the embassy staff may waive the fee or give you a "repatriation loan"—just enough funds to cover the new passport and get you back home.

If you're Canadian, you'll need to report the loss or theft to the local police, as well as your nearest embassy or consulate. Canadian authorities will conduct an investigation into the circumstances, which may delay the processing of your request. You must complete an application form and a statutory declaration concerning the lost/stolen passport, supply two passport photos and documentary proof of Canadian citizenship, and pay a $190 CAD fee (for more information, see passportcanada.gc.ca).

Cancel debit and credit cards. Within two days, cancel your lost or stolen debit and credit cards (meeting this deadline limits your liability to $50) and order replacements. Visa, MasterCard, and American Express all have global customer-assistance centers, reachable by collect call from anywhere (see sidebar on page 337). You'll need to know the name of the bank that issued the card; the card type (classic, platinum, or whatever); the card number; the primary and secondary cardholders' names; the cardholder's name exactly as printed on the card; billing address; home phone number; circumstances of the loss or theft; and identification verification (your birth date, your mother's maiden name, or your Social Security number—memorize this, don't carry a copy). If you are the secondary cardholder, you'll also need to provide the primary cardholder's identification-verification details.

Your bank can generally deliver a new card to you in Europe within two to three business days. Some may even be able to wire cash to keep you going or pay for your hotel room directly. Ask about these extra services. It's also possible to transfer money from a bank in the US to a bank in Europe, but this may take several days to accomplish—you'll probably have the new cards faster. (For information on wiring money, see page 187.)

Replace travel documents. Point-to-point rail etickets can often be reprinted from any computer or at the station, but tickets purchased at the station and printed on special ticket paper probably can't be replaced. Unfortunately, you can't replace a rail pass—you'll need to either purchase a new pass (most likely sent from home) or new tickets to complete your trip. (If you bought Rail Europe's Rail Protection Plan, you may be able to get a partial refund when you get home.) There's no need to replace printed copies of airline reservations—once you have your new passport, the airline can easily look up your reservation when you arrive at the airport.

Try to regenerate any other documents you might have been carrying in your pack, such as hotel and car-rental confirmations. If you don't have these stored somewhere, such as in your email or with a friend at home, call the hotel or car-rental agency and explain your predicament.

Rearrange travel plans. Depending on how long it takes to get your passport replaced—and how far you have to travel to reach an embassy or consulate—you'll probably need to rearrange your travel plans. Call or email to cancel and reschedule hotels and flights as soon as possible to avoid losing deposits or paying change fees (explaining the situation may help). If you're stuck without cash or credit cards for a few days, see if your bank or a family member back home can pay for your hotel stay.

Replace travel gear. Once you've started the process of replacing your passport and credit and debit cards, you can think about replacing travel gear such as your camera, phone, or tablet. Depending on your insurance policy, you may be able to get reimbursed for part of the replacement cost when you get home (see page 72). Decide which items are critical enough to your trip to replace immediately (flea markets, thrift shops, and cheap department stores are great for bargains). If you need to have something sent from home, try second-day US-Europe services (though figure on four days for delivery to a small town).

Refill prescriptions. Bring in a copy of your prescription to a pharmacy—if you don't have it, try contacting your doctor's office by phone or email. They can usually fax or email a copy to you in Europe (see page 392 for more on filling prescriptions). Your optometrist can do the same for your prescription eyewear.

Replace a rental-car key. If you lose the key to your rental car, call the car-hire company with your rental agreement number and your exact location. Be prepared for considerable expense and a delay: You will be charged $200 or more for a replacement key, and you may need to wait 24 to 48 hours for delivery of new keys or even a different vehicle.

Make the best of the situation. Getting everything straightened out can take a while. Be flexible and patient. It may not help at the time, but try to remember that your loss will make for a good story when you get home. Like a friend of mine says, "When it comes to travel, Tragedy + Time = Comedy."

Hurdling the Language Barrier

You're probably wondering: How can you connect with the locals if you can't communicate in their language? You'll be surprised at how easy it is. Over the years, I've collected tips and tricks on how travelers who speak only English can step right over that pesky language barrier. Still, it always helps to be able to communicate—even just a few phrases—in the local tongue. In this chapter, you'll learn how to simplify your English and communicate creatively to get your points across and your needs met.

Communication also goes beyond words: It helps to know the meaning of various common gestures (and what to avoid doing).

A fear of the language barrier keeps many people (read: English speakers) out of Europe, but the "barrier" is getting smaller every day. Over the last 30 years, an entire generation of Europeans has grown up speaking more English than ever. English really has arrived as Europe's second language. According to studies, half of all Europeans now speak English. Historically, many European signs and menus were printed in four languages: German, French, English, and—depending on where you were—Italian, Spanish, or Russian. But there's been a shift. In the interest of free trade and efficiency, the European Union has established English as Europe's standard language of commerce. Now most signs are printed in just two languages:

These signs in Amsterdam's airport don't even bother with Dutch.

the native language for locals and English for everyone else. In some airports, signs are now in English only.

CONFESSIONS OF A MONOGLOT

While it's nothing to brag about, I basically speak only English. Of course, if I spoke more languages, I could enjoy a much deeper understanding of the people and cultures I visit. Still, speaking only English, I've enjoyed researching my guidebooks, leading tours, and making my TV shows, as well as navigating through wonderful vacations—getting transportation, finding rooms, eating well, and seeing the sights. However, while you can manage decently with the blunt weapon of English, you'll get along in Europe better if you learn and use a few basic phrases and polite words.

Having an interest in the native language wins the respect of those you'll meet. Pocket-size two-language dictionaries are cheap and sold throughout Europe. Get a good phrase book, and start your practical vocabulary growing right off the bat. My phrase books (for French, Italian, German, Spanish, Portuguese, and French/Italian/German) are the only ones on the market designed by a guy who speaks just English (that's why they're so helpful). They are both fun and practical, with a meet-the-people and stretch-the-budget focus. Mr. Berlitz knew the languages, but he never stayed in a hotel where he had to ask, "Where can I hang my laundry?" These phrase books—written by travelers for travelers—have what you need to communicate during your vacation.

Spend bus and train rides learning. Start studying the language when you arrive—or sooner. I try to learn five new words a day. You'd be surprised how handy it is to have a working vocabulary of even 50 words. Take advantage of everyday conversations to learn the language. You're surrounded by expert, native-speaking tutors in every country. Let them teach you.

While Americans are notorious monoglots, many

LEFT You don't have to speak Danish to understand this sign.

RIGHT If your taxi driver is going too fast, my phrase books will help you say, "If you don't slow down, I'll throw up."

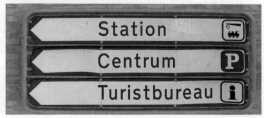

Europeans are very good with languages. Make communication easier by choosing a multilingual person to speak with. Businesspeople, urbanites, well-dressed young people, students, and anyone in the tourist trade are most likely to speak English. Many Swiss grow up trilingual, and many young Scandinavians and Eastern Europeans speak several languages. People speaking minor languages (Dutch, Norwegians, Czechs, Hungarians, Slovenes) have more reason to learn English, German, or French since their linguistic world is so small. All Croatians begin learning English in elementary school, and—since their TV programming is subtitled—they listen to Americans talk for hours each day. Scandinavian students of our language actually decide between English and "American." My Norwegian cousin speaks with a touch of Texas and knows more slang than I do.

Dutch is close enough to English that most any tourist can decipher this sign: It tells the opening hours (10:00 a.m. to 12:00 p.m., then 2:00 p.m. to 5:00 p.m.) on *Maandag* (Monday), *Woensdag* (Wednesday), *Vrydag* (Friday), and *Zaterdag* (Saturday).

We English speakers are the one group that can afford to be lazy, because English is the world's linguistic common denominator. When a Greek meets a Norwegian, they speak English. (What Greek speaks Norwegian?)

Imagine if each of our states spoke its own language. That's close to the European situation, but they've done a great job of minimizing the communication problems you'd expect to find on a small continent with such a Babel of Tongues. Most information a traveler must understand (such as road signs, menus, telephone instructions, and safety warnings) is printed either in English or in universal symbols. Europe's uniform road-sign system (see page 168) enables drivers to roll right over the language barrier. And rest assured that any place trying to separate tourists from their money will explain how to spend it in whatever languages are necessary. English always makes it.

Dominant as English may be, it's just good manners to start every conversation by politely asking, "Do you speak English?," "*Parlez-vous anglais?*," "*Sprechen Sie Englisch?*," or whatever. If they say "No," then I do the best I can in their language. Usually, after a few sentences they'll say, "Actually, I do speak some English." (One thing Americans do well is put others at ease with their linguistic shortcomings.) Your European friend is doing you a favor by speaking your language. The least we can do is make our English simple and clear.

USING SIMPLE ENGLISH

English may be Europe's lingua franca, but communicating does require some skill. If you have a trip coming up and don't speak French yet, be realistic, and don't expect to become fluent by the time you leave. Rather than frantically learning a few more French words, the best thing you can do at this point is to learn how to communicate in what the Voice of America calls "Special English."

Speak slowly, clearly, and with carefully chosen words. Assume you're dealing with someone who learned English out of a book—reading British words, not hearing American ones. They are reading your lips, wishing it were written down, hoping to see every letter as it tumbles out of your mouth. If you want to be understood, talk like a Dick-and-Jane primer. Choose easy words and clearly pronounce each syllable (po-ta-to chips.) Try not to use contractions. Be patient—when many Americans aren't easily understood, they speak louder and toss in a few extra words. (Listen to other tourists talk, and you'll hear your own shortcomings.) For several months out of every year, I speak with simple words, pronouncing... very...clearly. When I return home, my friends say (very deliberately), "Rick, you can relax now, we speak English fluently."

Can the slang. Our American dialect has become a super-deluxe slang pizza not found on any European menu. The sentence "Can the slang," for example, would baffle the average European. If you learned English in a classroom for two years, how would you respond to

Translating Foreign Websites

Monolinguists will appreciate the fact that many European websites offer the option to view their pages in English (often by clicking on a tiny British or American flag). For Web pages that are available only in the native language, a website translator can help.

Google's Chrome browser detects when a Web page is in a foreign language and asks if you want it to be translated to English. While automated translation can be less than perfect, this feature can open up a whole new world of local information for travelers. For example, before my last trip to Copenhagen, I used Chrome's translator to read piles of restaurant reviews written by Danish users.

Google lends a hand even if you use a different Web browser (such as Internet Explorer). Whenever you Google a page that's in a foreign language, you'll see a "Translate this Page" link next to the URL in your search results. Click on this link for a rough version in English. You can also cut and paste any text into Google Translate (translate.google.com) for an instant translation; click the speaker icon to hear the foreign words spoken aloud.

The Google Translate app also translates text it reads with your device's camera, as well as speech and handwriting; you can save favorite words to access when you don't have an Internet connection.

the American who uses expressions such as "sort of like," "pretty bad," or "Howzit goin'?"

Keep your messages grunt-simple. Make single nouns work as entire sentences. When asking for something, a one-word question ("Photo?") is more effective than an attempt at something more grammatically correct ("May I take your picture, sir?"). Be a Neanderthal. Strip your message naked and drag it by the hair into the other person's mind. But even Neandertourists will find things go easier if they begin each request with the local "please" (e.g., *Bitte,* toilet?").

Translation Resources

Translate.google.com: Translates from foreign language to English and vice versa

Apps

Google Translate: Translates speech, handwriting, and even text (such as on a sign) photographed with your device's camera

Lonely Planet Fast Talk: Pronounces a selection of foreign phrases

Use internationally understood words. Some Americans spend an entire trip telling people they're on *vacation,* draw only blank stares, and slowly find themselves in a soundproof, culture-resistant cell. The sensitive communicator notices that Europeans are more likely to understand the word *holiday*—probably because that's what the English say. Then she plugs that word into her simple English vocabulary, makes herself understood, and enjoys a much closer contact with Europe. If you say *restroom* or *bathroom,* you'll get no relief. *Toilet* is direct, simple, and understood. If my car is broken in Portugal, I don't say, "Excuse me, my car is broken." I point to the vehicle and say, "Auto kaput."

TIPS ON CREATIVE COMMUNICATION

Even if you have no real language in common, you can have some fun communicating. Consider this profound conversation I had with a cobbler in Sicily:

"Spaghetti," I said, with a very saucy Italian accent.

"Marilyn Monroe," was the old man's reply.

"*Mamma mia!*" I said, tossing my hands and head into the air.

"Yes, no, one, two, tree," he returned, slowly and proudly.

By now we'd grown fond of each other, and I whispered, secretively, "*Molto buono,* ravioli."

He spat, "Be sexy, drink Pepsi!"

Waving good-bye, I hollered, "*No problema.*"

"*Ciao,*" he said, smiling.

Risk looking goofy. Even with no common language,

rudimentary communication is easy. Butcher the language if you must, but communicate. I'll never forget the clerk in the French post office who flapped her arms and asked, "Tweet, tweet, tweet?" I understood immediately, answered with a nod, and she gave me the airmail stamps I needed. At the risk of getting bird-seed, I communicated successfully. If you're hungry, clutch your stomach and growl. If you want milk, "moo" and pull two imaginary udders. If the liquor was too strong, simulate an atomic explosion starting from your stomach and mush-rooming to your head. If you're attracted to someone, pant.

Make an educated guess and go for it. Can you read the Norwegian: "Central Sick House"? Too many Americans would bleed to death on the street corner looking for the word "hospital."

Be melodramatic. Exaggerate the native accent. In France, you'll communicate more effectively (and have more fun) by sounding like Maurice Chevalier or Inspector Clouseau. The locals won't be insulted; they'll be impressed. Use whatever French you know. But even English spoken with a sexy French accent makes more sense to the French ear. In Italy, be melodic and exuberant, and wave

Öffnungszeiten

VOM 4. JULI AN

Montag:	*08:30 - 13:00 u. 14:00 - 18:30*
Dienstag:	*08:30 - 13:00 u. 14:00 - 18:30*
Mittwoch:	*08:30 - 13:00* GESCHLOSSEN
Donnerstag:	*08:30 - 13:00 u. 14:00 - 18:30*
Freitag:	*08:30 - 13:00 u. 14:00 - 18:30*
Samstag:	*08:30 - 13:00 u. 14:00 - 18:30*

Hurdle the language barrier by thinking of things as multiple-choice questions and making educated guesses. This sign on a shop in Germany lists times. The top word can only mean "open times" or "closed times." I'd guess it lists hours open from (vom = from, if it rhymes, I go for it) the Fourth of July. Those six words on the left, most of which end in *tag*, must be days of the week (think *guten tag* or soup of the tag). Things are open from 8:30-13:00 *und* from 14:00-18:30 (24-hour clock). On *Mittwoch* (midweek), in the afternoon...something different happens. Since it can only be open or closed, and everything else is open, you can guess that on Wednesdays, *nach Mittag*, this shop is *geschlossen!*

those hands. Go ahead, try it: *Mamma mia!* No. Do it again. *MAMMA MIA!* You've got to be uninhibited. Self-consciousness kills communication.

Make logical leaps. Most major European languages are related, coming from (or at least being influenced by) Latin. Knowing that, words become meaningful. The French word

International Words

As our world shrinks, more and more words leap their linguistic boundaries and become international. Sensitive travelers develop a knack for choosing words most likely to be universally understood ("auto" instead of "car"; "kaput" rather than "broken"; "photo," not "picture"). They also internationalize their pronunciation. "University," if you play around with its sound (oo-nee-vehr-see-tay), can be understood anywhere. The average American really flunks out in this area. Be creative.

Communication by analogy is effective. Anywhere in Europe (except in Hungary), "Attila" means "crude bully." When a bulky Italian crowds in front of you, say, "*Scusi,* Ah-tee-la" and retake your place. If you like your haircut and want to compliment your Venetian barber, put your hand sensually on your hair and say "Casanova." Nickname the hairstylist "Michelangelo."

Here are a few internationally understood words. Remember, cut out the Yankee accent and give each word a pan-European sound ("autoboooos," "Engleesh").

Hello	Auto	Disneyland (wonderland)
No	Autobus	Nuclear
Stop	Taxi	Toilet
Kaput	Tourist	Police
Ciao	Beer	English
Bye-bye	Coke, Coca-Cola	Telephone
OK	Tea	Photo
Mañana	Coffee	Photocopy
Pardon	Vino	Disco
Rock 'n' roll	Chocolate	Computer
Mamma mia	Picnic	Sport
No problem	Self-service	Internet
Super	Yankee, Americano	Central
Sex/Sexy	Hercules (strong)	Information
Oo la la	Casanova (romantic)	University
Moment	Attila (mean, crude)	Passport
Bon voyage	Fascist	Bill Gates
Restaurant	Elephant (a big clod)	Obama
McDonald's	Michelangelo (artistic)	Holiday (vacation)
Bank	Rambo	Gratis (free)
Hotel	Communist	America's favorite four-
Post (office)	Amigo	letter words
Camping	Europa	

The European Babel of Tongues

Most of Europe's many languages can be arranged into one family tree. Many of them have the same grandparents and resemble each other more or less like you resemble your siblings and cousins. But occasionally, an oddball uncle sneaks in whom no one can explain.

Romance Countries: Italy, France, Spain, and Portugal

The Romance family evolved from Latin, the language of the Roman Empire ("Romance" comes from "Roman"). Few of us know Latin, but being familiar with any of the modern Romance languages helps with the others. For example, your high school Spanish will help you learn some Italian.

Germanic Countries: British Isles, Germany, Netherlands, and Scandinavia

The Germanic languages, though influenced by Latin, are a product of the tribes of northern Europe (including the Angles and Saxons)—

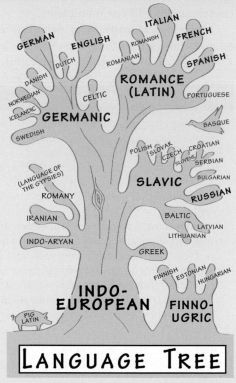

people the ancient Romans called "barbarians" because they didn't speak Latin. German is spoken by all Germans and Austrians, and by most Swiss. The people of Holland and northern Belgium speak Dutch, a close relative to German. While Dutch is not *Deutsch*, a Hamburger or Frankfurter can almost understand an Amsterdam newspaper. The Norwegians, Danes, and Swedes can read each other's magazines and enjoy their neighbors' TV shows.

for Monday (our "day of the moon") is *lundi* (lunar day). The Germans say the same thing—*Montag*. *Sonne* is sun, so *Sonntag* is Sunday. If *buon giorno* means good day, *zuppa del giorno* is soup of the day. If *Tiergarten* is zoo (literally "animal garden") in German, then *Stinktier* is a stinky animal—a skunk—and *Kindergarten* is children's garden. Think of *Vater*, *Mutter*, *trink*, *gross*, *gut*, *rapide*, *grand*, *económico*, *delicioso*, and you can *comprender mucho*.

Many letters travel predictable courses (determined by the physical way a sound is made) as related languages drift apart over the centuries. For instance, *p* often becomes *v* or *b*

Slavic Countries: Czech Republic, Poland, Slovakia, Slovenia, Croatia, and More

Most Eastern European countries (except Hungary, Romania, and the Baltics) speak Slavic languages. While these languages are more or less mutually intelligible, spellings change as you cross borders; for example, Czech *hrad*, or castle, becomes Croatian *grad*. Farther east—in Serbia, Russia, Ukraine, Bulgaria, and elsewhere—the language sounds similar, but is written with the Cyrillic alphabet. The Baltic languages, Latvian and Lithuanian, are distantly related to Slavic tongues.

Finno-Ugric Countries: Hungary, Finland, and Estonia

Hungarian, Finnish, and Estonian are more closely related to Asian languages than to European ones—likely hinting that the Hungarians, Finns, and Estonians share ancestors from Central Asia.

Multilingual Countries and Regions

Switzerland has four official languages: German, French, Italian, and Romansh (an obscure Romance tongue); most Swiss are at least bilingual. Because the region of Alsace, on the French-German border, has been dragged through the mud during several tugs-of-war, most residents speak both languages. Belgium waffles (linguistically), with the southern half (the Walloons) speaking French and the rest speaking Dutch.

Europe's Underdog Languages

Every year on this planet, a dozen or so languages go extinct. But thanks to Europe's recent determination to celebrate diversity, its underdog languages—once endangered—are thriving once more.

The Basques, who live where Spain, France, and the Atlantic all touch, speak Euskara—mysteriously unrelated to any other European language.

England is surrounded by a "Celtic Crescent." In Scotland, Ireland, Wales, and Brittany (northwestern France), the old Celtic language survives. Seek out these old Celtic remnants in proud gift shops and bookstores, Gaelic pubs, and the Gael tachts (districts, mostly in Western Ireland, where the old culture is preserved by the government).

in the neighboring country's language. Italian menus always have a charge for *coperto*—a "cover" charge.

Read and listen. Read time schedules, posters, multilingual signs (and graffiti) in bathrooms and newspaper headlines. Develop your ear for foreign languages by tuning in to the other languages on a multilingual tour. It's a puzzle. The more you play, the better you get.

A notepad can work wonders. Words and numbers are much easier to understand when they're written rather than spoken (especially if you mispronounce them). My back-pocket notepad is my constant travel buddy. To repeatedly communicate something difficult and important (such as medical instructions, "I'm a strict vegetarian," "boiled water," "well-done meat," "your finest ice cream," or "I am rich and single"), have it written in the local language on your notepad.

Assume you understand and go with your educated guess. My master key to communication is to treat most problems as multiple-choice questions, make an educated guess

A Yankee-English Phrase Book

Oscar Wilde said, "The English have really everything in common with the Americans—except, of course, language." On your first trip to Britain, you'll find plenty of linguistic surprises. I'll never forget checking into a small-town bed-and-breakfast as a teenager on my first solo European adventure. The landlady cheerily asked me, "And what time would you like to be knocked up in the morning?" I looked over at her husband, who winked, "Would a fry at half-eight be suitable?" The next morning I got a rap on the door at 8:00 and a huge British breakfast a half hour later.

Hmm... Where's the "exit"?

Traveling through Britain is an adventure in accents and idioms. Every day you'll see babies in prams and pushchairs, sucking dummies as mothers change wet nappies. Soon the kids can trade in their nappies for smalls and spend a penny on their own. "Spend a penny" is British for a visit to the loo (bathroom). Older British kids enjoy candy floss (cotton candy), naughts and crosses (tic-tac-toe), big dippers (roller coasters), and iced lollies (popsicles), and are constantly in need of an Elastoplast or sticking plaster (Band-Aid).

It's fun to browse through an ironmonger's (hardware store) or chemist's shop (pharmacy), noticing the many familiar items with unfamiliar names. The school-supplies section includes sticky tape or Sellotape (adhesive tape), rubbers (erasers), and scribbling blocks (scratch pads). Those with green fingers (a green thumb) might pick up some courgette (zucchini), swede (rutabaga), or aubergine (eggplant) seeds.

In Britain, fries are chips and potato chips are crisps. A beefburger, made with mince (hamburger meat), comes on a toasted bap (bun). For pudding (dessert), have some gateau or sponge (cake).

The British have a great way with names. You'll find towns with names like Upper and Lower Piddle, Once Brewed, and Itching Field. This cute coziness comes through in their language as well. Your car is built with a bonnet and a boot rather than a hood and trunk. You drive on motorways, and when the freeway divides, it becomes a dual carriageway. And never go anticlockwise (counterclockwise) in a roundabout.

at the meaning of a message (verbal or written), and proceed confidently as if I understood it correctly. At the breakfast table the waitress asks me a question. I don't understand a word she says, but I tell her my room number. Faking it like this applies to rudimentary things like instructions on customs forms, museum hours, and menus. With this approach I find that 80 percent of the time I'm correct. Half the time I'm wrong, but I never know it, so it doesn't really matter. So 10

Gas is petrol, a truck is a lorry, and when you hit a tailback (traffic jam), don't get your knickers in a twist (make a fuss), just queue up (line up).

A two-week vacation in Britain is unheard of, but many locals holiday for a fortnight in a homely (homey) rural cottage, possibly on the Continent (continental Europe). They might pack a face flannel (washcloth), torch (flashlight), and hair grips (bobby pins) in their bum bag (never a fanny pack!) before leaving their flat (apartment).

Don't take British road signs personally.

On a cold evening it's best to wear the warmest mackintosh (raincoat) you can find or an anorak (parka) with press studs (snaps). You can post letters in the pillar box and give your girlfriend a trunk (long distance) call. If you reverse the charges (call collect), she'll say you're tight as a fish's bum. If she witters on (gabs and gabs), tell her you're knackered (exhausted) and it's been donkey's years (ages) since you've slept. After washing up (doing the dishes) and hoovering (vacuuming), you can go up to the first floor (second floor) with a neat (straight) whisky and a plate of biscuits (cookies) and get goose pimples (goose bumps) just enjoying the view. Too much of that whisky will get you sloshed, paralytic, bevvied, wellied, popped up, ratted, or even pissed as a newt.

All across the British Isles, you'll find new words, crazy humor, and colorful accents. Pubs are colloquial treasure chests. Church services, sporting events, the Houses of Parliament, live plays featuring local comedy, the streets of Liverpool, the docks of London, and children in parks are playgrounds for the American ear. One of the beauties of touring Great Britain is the illusion of hearing a foreign language and actually understanding it—most of the time.

Somehow, "Broken TV" just doesn't have the same ring to it.

percent of the time I really blow it. My trip becomes easier—
and occasionally much more interesting.

Desperate Telephone Communication

Getting a message across in a language you don't speak
requires some artistry. It takes something closer to wiz-
ardry on a telephone, where you won't have any visual aids
(your dynamic hand and facial expressions, for example). In
attempting a phone conversation, speak slowly and clearly,
pronouncing every syllable. Keep it very simple—don't clutter your message with anything more than what's essential.
Don't overcommunicate—many things are already understood and don't need to be said. (See? Those last six words
didn't need to be written.) Use international or carefully
chosen English words. When all else fails, let a local person
on your end (such as a hotel receptionist) do the talking after
you explain to him (with visual help, if needed) the message.

Let me illustrate with a hypothetical telephone conversation. I'm calling a hotel in Barcelona from a phone booth
in the train station. I just arrived, read my guidebook's list
of budget accommodations, and I like Pedro's Hotel. Here's
what happens:

Pedro answers, "Hotel Pedro, grabdaboodogalaysk."

I ask, "Hotel Pedro?" (Question marks are created
melodically.)

He affirms, already a bit impatient, "*Sí*, Hotel Pedro."

I ask, "*Habla* Eng-leesh?"

He says, "No, dees ees Ehspain." (Actually, he probably
would speak a little English or would say "*momento*" and get
someone who did. But we'll make this particularly challenging. Not only does he not speak English, he doesn't want to...
for patriotic reasons.)

Remember not to overcommunicate. You don't need to tell
him you're a tourist looking for a bed. Who else calls a hotel
speaking in a foreign language? Also, you can assume he's got
a room available. If he's full, he's very busy and he'd say "complete" or "no hotel" and hang up. If he's still talking to you, he
wants your business. Now you must communicate just a few
things, like how many beds you need and who you are.

I say, "OK." (OK is international for, "Roger, prepare
for the next transmission.") "Two people"—he doesn't
understand. I get fancy, "*Dos* people"—he still doesn't get
it. Internationalize, "*Dos* pehr-son"—*no comprende*. "*Dos*
hombre*"—nope. Digging deep into my bag of international
linguistic tricks, I say, "*Dos* Yankees."

Tongue-Twisters (or "Tongue-Breakers")

These are a great way to practice a language -and break the ice with the Europeans you meet. Here are some that are sure to challenge you and amuse your new friends.

GERMAN

Fischer's Fritze fischt frische Fische, frische Fische fischt Fischer's Fritze.

Fritz Fischer catches fresh fish, fresh fish Fritz Fischer catches.

Ich komme über Oberammergau, oder komme ich über Unterammergau?

I am coming via Oberammergau, or am I coming via Unterammergau?

ITALIAN

Sopra la panca la capra canta, sotto la panca la capra crepa.

On the bench the goat sings, under the bench the goat dies.

Chi fù quel barbaro barbiere che barberò così barbaramente a Piazza Barberini quel povero barbaro di Barbarossa?

Who was that barbarian barber in Barberini Square who shaved that poor barbarian Barbarossa?

FRENCH

Si ces saucissons-ci sont six sous, ces six saucissons-ci sont trop chers.

If these sausages are six cents, these six sausages are too expensive.

Ce sont seize cents jacinthes sèches dans seize cent sachets secs.

There are 1,600 dry hyacinths in 1,600 dry sachets

SPANISH

*Un tigre, dos tigres, tres tigres comían trigo en un trigal. Un tigre, dos tigres, tres tim \ *

One tiger, two tigers, three tiu \ \ ate wh \ \ \ \ \ wheatfield. One tiger, two tigers, three tigers.

Pablito clavó un clavito. ¿Qué clavito clavó Pablito?

Paul stuck in a stick. What stick did Paul stick in?

PORTUGUESE

O rato roeu a roupa do rei de Roma.

The mouse nibbled the clothes of the king of Rome.

Se cá nevasse fazia-se cá ski, mas como cá não neva não se faz cá ski.

If the snow would fall, we'd ski, but since it doesn't, we don't.

Excerpted from Rick Steves Phrase Books—full of practical phrases, spiked with humor, and designed for budget travelers who like to connect with locals.

Happy Talk

English	French	Italian	German	Spanish
Good day.	Bonjour.	Buon giorno.	Guten tag.	Buenos dias.
How are you?	Comment allez-vous?	Come sta?	Wie geht's?	¿Cómo está?
Very good.	Très bien.	Molto bene.	Sehr gut.	Muy bien.
Thank you.	Merci.	Grazie.	Danke.	Gracias.
Please.	S'il vous plaît.	Per favore.	Bitte.	Por favor.
Do you speak English?	Parlez-vous anglais?	Parla inglese?	Sprechen Sie Englisch?	¿Habla usted inglés?
Yes./No.	Oui./Non.	Si./No.	Ja./Nein.	Sí./No.
My name is ____.	Je m'appelle ____.	Mi chiamo ____.	Ich heisse ____.	Me llamo ____.
What's your name?	Quel est votre nom?	Come si chiama?	Wie heissen Sie?	¿Cómo se llama?
See you later.	Á bientôt.	A più tardi.	Bis später.	Hasta luego.
Good-bye.	Au revoir.	Arrivederci.	Auf Wiedersehen.	Adiós.
Good luck!	Bonne chance!	Buona fortuna!	Viel Glück!	¡Buena suerte!
Have a good trip!	Bon voyage!	Buon viaggio!	Gute Reise!	¡Buen viaje!
OK.	D'accord.	Va bene.	OK.	De acuerdo.
No problem.	Pas de problème.	Non c'è problema	Kein Problem.	No hay problema.
Everything was great.	C'était super.	Tutto magnifico.	Alles war gut.	Todo estuvo muy bien.
Enjoy your meal!	Bon appétit!	Buon appetito!	Guten Appetit!	¡Qué aproveche!
Delicious!	Délicieux!	Delizioso!	Lecker!	¡Delicioso!
Magnificent!	Magnifique!	Magnifico!	Wunderbar!	¡Magnifico!
Bless you! (after sneeze)	À vos souhaits!	Salute!	Gesundheit!	¡Salud!
You are very kind.	Vous êtes très gentil.	Lei è molto gentile.	Sie sind sehr freundlich.	Usted es muy amable.
Cheers!	Santé!	Salute!	Prost!	¡Salud!
I love you.	Je t'aime.	Ti amo.	Ich liebe dich.	Te quiero.

"OK!" He understands that you want beds for two Americans. He says, *"Sí,"* and I say, "Very good" or *"Muy bien."*

Now I need to tell him who I am. If I say, "My name is Mr. Steves, and I'll be over promptly," I'll lose him. I say, "My name Ricardo (ree-KAR-do)." In Italy I say, "My name Luigi." Your name really doesn't matter; you're communicating just a password so you can identify yourself when you walk through the door. Say anything to be understood.

He says, "OK."

You repeat slowly, "Hotel, *dos* Yankees, Ricardo, coming *pronto,* OK?"

He says, "OK."

You say, *"Gracias, adiós!"*

Twenty minutes later you walk up to the reception desk, and Pedro greets you with a robust, "Eh, Ricardo!"

EUROPEAN GESTURES

In Europe, while some gestures can help you communicate, others can contribute to the language barrier. For example, if you count with your fingers, in Europe remember to start with your thumb, not your index finger (if you hold up your index finger, you'll probably get two of something).

The "thumbs up" sign popular in the United States is used widely in most of Europe to say "OK" (it also represents the number one when counting). The "V for victory" sign is used in most of Europe as in the United States, but may get you a punch in the nose in parts of Britain, where it's an obscene gesture (if you make the "V" with your palm toward you.)

Some cultures also indicate "yes" and "no" differently: In Turkey, they shake their heads as Americans do, but someone may also signal "no" by tilting their head back. In Bulgaria and Albania, "OK" is indicated by happily shaking your head left and right—as if you were signaling "no" in the US.

Here are a few more common European gestures, their meanings, and where you're likely to see them.

Fingertips Kiss: Gently bring the fingers and thumb of your right hand together, raise to your lips, kiss lightly, and joyfully toss your fingers and thumb into the air. This gesture is used commonly in France, Spain, Greece, and Germany as a form of

praise. It can mean sexy, delicious, divine, or wonderful. Be careful—tourists look silly when they overemphasize this subtle action.

Hand Purse: Straighten the fingers and thumb of one hand, bringing them all together and making an upward point about a foot in front of your face. Your hand can be held still or moved a little up and down at the wrist. This is a common and very Italian gesture for a query. It is used to say "What do you want?" or "What are you doing?" or "What is it?" or "What's new?" It can also be used as an insult to say "You fool." The hand purse can also mean "fear" (France), "a lot" (Spain), and "good" (Greece and Turkey).

Very delicious!

Hand Shake: "Expensive" is often indicated by shaking your hand and sucking in like you just burned yourself.

Cheek Screw: Make a fist, stick out your index finger, and (without piercing the skin) screw it into your cheek. The cheek screw is used widely and almost exclusively in Italy to mean good, lovely, beautiful, or delicious. Many Italians also use it to mean clever. But be careful: In southern Spain, the cheek screw is used to call a man effeminate.

Eyelid Pull: Place your extended forefinger below the center of your eye and pull the skin downward. In France and Greece this means "I am alert. I'm looking. You can't fool me." In Italy and Spain, it's a friendlier warning, meaning "Be alert, that guy is clever."

Forearm Jerk: Clench your right fist and jerk your forearm up as you slap your right bicep with your left palm. This is a rude phallic gesture that men throughout southern Europe use the way many Americans "give someone the finger." This jumbo version of "flipping the bird" says "I'm superior" (it's an action some monkeys actually do with their penises to insult their peers). This gesture is occasionally used by rude men in Britain and Germany as more of an "I want you" gesture about (but never to) a sexy woman.

Chin Flick: Tilt your head back slightly and flick the back of your fingers forward in an arc from under your chin. In Italy and France, this means "I'm not interested, you bore me," or "You bother me." In southern Italy it can mean "No."

Eating

Eating in Europe is sightseeing for your taste buds. Every country has local specialties that are good, memorable, or both. Whether it's Wiener schnitzel in Vienna, *salade niçoise* in Nice, or wurst in Würzburg, a country's cuisine is as culturally important as its museums. But just as there are tricks for sightseeing, there are also ways to maximize your culinary journey.

Much of my experience lies in eating well cheaply. Galloping gluttons thrive on $25 a day—by picnicking. Those with a more refined palate and a little more money can mix picnics with atmospheric and enjoyable restaurant meals and eat well for $50 a day.

This $50-a-day budget includes a $15 lunch (cheaper if you picnic or eat fast food), a $30 good and filling restaurant dinner (more with wine or dessert), and $5 for your chocolate, cappuccino, and gelato needs. (This assumes that breakfast is included with your hotel room; if you have to buy breakfast, have a picnic lunch...or eat less gelato.) If your budget requires, you can find a satisfying dinner for $20 or less anywhere in Europe. If you have more money, of course, it's delightful to spend it dining well.

A fun neighborhood restaurant: no English menus, no credit cards, but good food, good prices, and a friendly staff

RESTAURANTS

Restaurants are the most expensive way to eat. They can pillage and plunder a tight budget, but it would be criminal to pass through Europe without sampling the specialties served in good restaurants.

The truth is that European restaurants are no more expensive than American ones. The cost of eating is determined not by the local

standard, but by your personal standard. Many Americans can't find an edible meal for less than $30 in their hometown, but their next-door neighbors enjoy eating out for half that. If you can enjoy a $15 meal in Boston, Chicago, or Seattle, you'll eat well in London, Rome, or Helsinki for the same price. Every year I eat about 100 dinners in Europe. My budget target is $15 for a simple, fill-the-tank meal; $30 for a good restaurant dinner; and $50 for a splurge feast. Forget the scare stories. People who spend $60 per person on dinner in Dublin and then complain either enjoy complaining or are fools. Let me fill you in on filling up in Europe.

Finding a Restaurant

Average tourists are attracted—like moths to a light bulb—to the biggest neon sign that boasts, *We speak English and accept credit cards*. Wrong! I look for a handwritten menu in the native language only, with a small selection. This means the kitchen is cooking what was fresh in the market that morning for loyal return customers (and not targeting tourists).

A reliable guidebook can be a good starting point for finding a great place to eat. Most guidebooks list restaurants by neighborhood and locate them on a map, allowing you to peruse a selection of places near your hotel or a major sight. Guidebook listings can help you select a restaurant based on its specialty, ambience, or cost. There are even guidebooks targeted specifically at foodies, such as *The Food Lover's Guide to Paris*.

Techie travelers report they're generally pleased with the restaurant advice they've found on user-generated review websites and apps such as Yelp and TripAdvisor. And their online maps are handy when you're tired and hungry: Just whip out your smartphone and find an eatery nearby. In addition, many cities have websites and blogs where

A small, handwritten menu in the local language is a good sign.

residents post their own restaurant reviews, though these sites aren't always in English. Also, bear in mind that while restaurants can be highly rated on a site or app, they can—as a result—get overwhelmed with customers and the quality can slide. For advice on getting the most out of traveler-review sites, see page 209.

For advice on getting the most out of traveler-review sites, see page 209.

> **Eating Apps**
>
> **Yelp:** Reviews and online maps for restaurants with local touch
> **TripAdvisor:** Huge collection of restaurant reviews but has tourist bias
> **Happy Cow:** Restaurant reviews and online maps for vegetarians and vegans

Another way to find a good restaurant is to ask your hotel receptionist or even someone on the street for a good place—not a good place for tourists, but a place they'd take a friend. Or leave the tourist center and stroll around until you find a restaurant with a happy crowd of locals. Be snoopy; look at what people are eating. After a few days in Europe, you'll have no trouble telling a genuine hangout from a tourist trap.

Many European cities have a bustling, colorful "restaurant row," a street or square lined with characteristic eateries--such as Rue des Bouchers in Brussels, Rue Mouffetard in Paris, Rua das Portas de Santo Antão in Lisbon, Leidsedwarsstraat in Amsterdam, Campo de' Fiori in Rome, Adrianou street in Athens, and Prijeko street in Dubrovnik. The restaurants on these streets usually have straightforward menus of tourist-pleasing dishes, superficial elegance, and gregarious hawkers out front trying desperate sales pitches to lure in diners. Most of these places are tourist traps with overpriced food and rotten service; but others are frequented by natives and can offer great ambience and decent value. A good guidebook tip from a trusted native, or simply an eye for choosing the local favorite can help you figure out which is which.

Keep in mind that restaurants and pubs don't usually serve meals continuously throughout the day. Restaurants often close in the late afternoon (about 2 p.m.) and then reopen at dinner; pubs stay open all day, but serve only drinks and snacks between lunch and dinner. For those in-between times, you'll find plenty of snack bars and cafés happy to feed you.

Restaurant Etiquette

For expensive places, it's smart to reserve a table in advance. You drop by to reserve, call ahead, or—for many high-end places—you can reserve online. When entering a restaurant without reservations, I head toward any table that isn't

marked "reserved." I try to catch a
server's eye and signal to be sure it's
OK for me to sit there. It also lets him
know I'm ready to look at a menu.
If the place is full, you're likely to
simply be turned away: There's no
"hostess" standing by to add your
name to a carefully managed waiting
list. Since European diners take their
time with a meal, it's impossible to
predict how quickly the tables will turn over. You might see
people milling around outside a popular place hoping for a
table to free up, but it's basically a chaotic, self-managing
system—not monitored by any restaurant staff.

These days, the
Germans are
splitting their
bratwurst and
kraut, too.

While portions may be expensive, they're often huge and
splittable. A key challenge of budget eating is ordering just
enough to fill you, while leaving nothing on your plate. If a
single main dish is enough for 1.5 people (as many are), split
it between yourself and your travel partner, and supplement
it with a bowl of soup or something small. Waiters are generally understanding and accommodating; the prices are high
for Europeans, too. But be careful in France, where splitting
meals at restaurants can be frowned upon; instead, head for
a café, where it's perfectly acceptable to share meals or order
just a salad or sandwich, even for dinner. At any place, it's
fine to split a dessert, saving money and calories.

In Europe, the meal is routinely the event of the evening.
At good restaurants, service will seem slow. Meals won't
always come simultaneously—it's fine to start eating when
served. Many Europeans will spend at least two hours enjoying a good dinner, and, for the full experience, so should you.
Fast service is considered rude service. If you need to eat and
run, make your time limits very clear as you
order.

Share fine
things.
Restaurateurs
are happy
to bring one
dessert and as
many spoons
as needed.

Of course, each country has its own quirks
when it comes to dining. Spaniards eat dinner
very late (after 9 p.m.). In Italy, it's common to
be charged a *pane e coperto* ("bread and cover"
charge) just to sit down. In Portugal, appetizers (olives, bread, etc.) that are automatically
brought to your table are not free—if you
touch them, you pay for them. If you see a
Stammtisch sign hanging over a table at a
German restaurant, it means that it's reserved
for regulars.

Vegetarians

Vegetarians find life a little frustrating in Europe. Very often, Europeans think "vegetarian" means "no red meat" or "not much meat." If you are a strict vegetarian, you'll have to make things very clear. Write out the appropriate phrase (see below), keep it handy, and show it to each waiter before ordering your meal.

Salad bars are abundant and great for vegetarians.

Vegetarians have no problem with continental breakfasts, which are normally meatless anyway. Meat-free picnic lunches are delicious, since bread, cheese, and yogurt are wonderful throughout Europe. Have some healthy snacks (such as nuts or fresh produce) on hand, in case you can't find a suitable meal.

It's in restaurants that your patience may be minced. Big-city tourist office brochures list restaurants by category. In any language, look under "V." For a good meal, seek out a vegetarian restaurant (most big cities have them; check a website such as happycow.net for ideas), or browse the menus at some fine-dining restaurants, many of which pride themselves on offering at least one good vegetarian option. In my guidebooks, whenever possible, I make it a point to list a good vegetarian restaurant in each city.

Cafeterias (such as the bright, cheery, fresh, affordable ones you'll find on the top floor of major department stores) are a good option for vegetarians, since you can see exactly what you're getting and select an assortment of foods that suit your diet.

Each country has its own quirks. Italy seems to sprinkle a little meat in just about everything. German cooking normally keeps the meat separate from the vegetables. Hearty German salads, with bacon, cheese, and eggs, are a vegetarian's delight. Vegetarians will love antipasti buffets, salad bars, and ethnic restaurants throughout Europe.

Refer to the list below to communicate these **key vegetarian phrases:** "We are (I am) vegetarian. We (I) do not eat meat, fish, or chicken. Eggs and cheese OK."

German: *Wir sind (Ich bin) Vegetarier. Wir essen (Ich esse) kein Fleisch, Fisch, oder Geflügel. Eier und Käse OK.*

French: *Nous sommes (Je suis) végétarien. Nous ne mangeons (Je ne mange) pas de viande, poisson, ou poulet. Oeufs et fromage OK.*

Italian: *Siamo vegetariani (Sono vegetariano/a). Non mangiamo (mangio) nè carne, nè pesce, nè polli. Uova e formaggio OK.*

Spanish: *Somos vegetarianos (Soy vegetariano/a). No comemos (No como) ni carne, ni pescado, ni pollo. Los huevos y el queso OK.*

The no-smoking rules seem to be working in restaurants all over Europe these days, but watch out if you're seated outdoors, where smokers congregate to light up.

Ordering Your Meal

Finding the right restaurant is only half the battle. You also need to order a good meal. Most European restaurants post their menus outside. Check the price and selection before entering. If the menu's not posted, ask to see one. Be aware that in France, the word *menu* means a fixed-price meal (as does *menù* in Italian, *Menü* in German, and *menú* in Spanish); instead you want *la carte* (to order à la carte). Several other languages also use variations on the word "card" to mean "menu": *Speisekarte* in German, *la carta* in Spanish, and so on.

Ordering in a foreign language can be fun, or it can be an ordeal. Ask for an English menu—if nothing else, you might get the waiter who speaks the most English. Many waiters can give at least a very basic translation—"cheekin, bunny, zuppa, green salat," and so on. A menu reader or phrase book (like my five-language series) is helpful for those who want to avoid ordering sheep stomach instead of lamb chops. If you have allergies, carry a handwritten card in the local language that states "I am allergic to" followed by the problem foods; a native speaker (such as your hotelier) can help you with this.

If you don't know what to order, go with the waiter's recommendation or look for your dream meal on another table and order by pointing. People are usually helpful and understanding of the poor and hungry monoglot tourist. If they aren't, you probably picked a place that sees too many of them. Europeans with the most patience with tourists are the ones who rarely deal with them.

People who agonize over each word on the menu season the whole experience with stress. If you're in a good place, the food's good. Get a basic idea of what's cooking, have some fun with your server, be loose and adventurous, and just order something.

To max out culturally, my partner and I order two different meals: one high risk and one low risk. We share, sampling twice as many

If you have dietary restrictions, write them out on a card. Flash it while ordering and you'll get what you want.

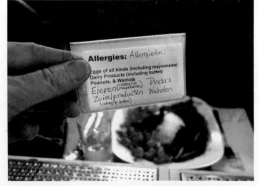

dishes. At worst, we learn what we don't like and split the chicken and fries. My tour groups cut every meal into bits, and our table becomes a lazy Susan. If anything, the waiters are impressed by our interest in their food and very often they'll run over with a special treat for all of us to sample—like squid eggs. With a gang of 10 travelers, I once ordered all 10 pizzas on the menu to come one after the other, each cut into 10 slices. We took our time, the waiters had fun, we savored a great variety, and everything was hot...it was the cheapest 10-course meal in Rome.

The "tourist *menu*" (*menu* in France, *menù turistico* in Italy) is popular in restaurants throughout Europe's tourist zones, offering confused visitors a no-stress, three-course meal for a painless price that usually includes service, bread, and a drink. You normally get a choice of several options for each course. Locals rarely order this, but if the options intrigue you, the tourist *menu* can be a convenient way to sample some regional flavors for a reasonable, predictable price.

In restaurants throughout Europe, lunch generally costs less than dinner. (If you want to stretch your budget by mixing picnics and restaurant meals, your euros will go farther if you have lunch at restaurants and picnics for dinner.) Seek out the various deals, such as the daily special—a great value. Small eateries in most countries offer this fresh, economical "*menu* of the day." Recognize the native term (*menu del día* in Spain, *plat du jour* in France, *menù del giorno* in Italy, *dagens rett* in Sweden). These are often limited to early seatings (with the time—usually before 7:30 p.m.—posted on the door and in the menu). Some classy restaurants in bigger cities in Britain and Ireland offer early-bird specials (order before 6:30 or 7:00 p.m.); having an early, nice dinner before attending a play or concert feels just right.

If you're a foodie, do some research and learn what's in season (or ask your server). In the summer, French onion soup and cheese fondue are only for tourists. White asparagus and porcini mushrooms are a treat for your palate in season...but come out of the freezer the rest of the year.

The best values in entrées are usually chicken, fish, and

MENU TURISTICO € 19,00

ANTIPASTO di MARE

PRIMI PIATTI
RISOTTO alla PESCATORA
SPAGHETTI alla MARINARA
SPAGHETTI allo SCOGLIO
TRENETTE al PESTO

SECONDI PIATTI
PESCE ai FERRI
FRITTO MISTO
GRIGLIATA di CARNE

CONTORNI
PATATE FRITTE o INSALATA

This Italian *menù turistico* includes a seafood starter plate (*antipasto di mare*), then you get to choose a first course (*primi piatti*), a second course (*secondi piatti*), and a side dish (*contorni*, either French fries or salad)... all for €19.

veal. Sometimes, rather than getting entrées, my travel partner and I share a memorable little buffet of appetizers—they're plenty filling, less expensive, and more typically local than entrées. Drinks (except for wine in southern Europe) and desserts can be the worst value. Skipping those, you can enjoy some surprisingly good $15 meals.

Drinks

If your budget is tight and you want to save $5-10 a day, never buy a restaurant drink. Beverages can sink a tight budget.

Europeans generally drink bottled water—for taste, not health. But as their cost of living increases, so do their requests for tap water. Once in an Oslo restaurant, I counted 16 of 20 diners drinking tap water. They were charged $1 a glass, but it was still a substantial savings over a $6 Coke.

For a good dining value, I look for a chalkboard daily special *(menu del día)*.

To get tap water at a restaurant, you may need to be polite, patient, inventive, and know the correct phrase. Availability of (and willingness to serve) tap water varies from country to country; you'll pay for it in Belgium (and in Denmark, too, unless you order an additional beverage). It's sometimes considered a special favor, and while your glass or carafe of tap water is normally served politely, occasionally it just isn't worth the trouble, and it's best to put up with the bottle of Perrier or order a drink from the menu.

Bottled water is served crisp and cold, either with or without carbonation, usually by happier waiters. Some Americans don't like the bubbly stuff, but I do. Learn the local phrase for *con/avec/mit/con*/with gas or *senza/sans/ohne/sin*/without gas (in Italian, French, German, and Spanish, respectively), and you'll get the message across. Acquire a taste for *acqua con gas*. It's a lot more fun (and read on the label what it'll do for your rheumatism).

German pubs don't serve minors beer—but many locals do.

Drink like a European. Cold milk, ice cubes, and coffee with (rather than after)

your meal are American habits. Insisting on any of these in Europe will get you strange looks and a reputation as a crazy American. Order local drinks, not just to save money but to experience the culture and to get the best quality and service. The timid can always order the "American waters" (Coke, Fanta, and 7-Up), sold everywhere.

Trying regionally produced alcohol can be a great cultural experience—and brings out fun and fascinating facets of my favorite continent. In Scotland, locals are passionate about finding and describing the whisky that fits their personality. Each guy in the pub has "his" whisky. And the flavors (fruity, peppery, peaty, smoky) are much easier to actually taste than their wine-snob equivalents.

In France, geography plays a big part in their liquid pride. *Terroir* (pronounced "tehr-wah") is a uniquely French concept. *Terroir* is "somewhere-ness," a combination of the macro- and microclimate, soil, geology, and culture (the accumulated experience of the people and their craft). The French don't call a wine by the grape's name. Two wines can be made of the same grape, but be of very different character because of their *terroir*. A real Chablis made from the Chardonnay grape is better than Chardonnays made elsewhere because of its *terroir*.

Drinking locally produced alcohol has another advantage: It's cheaper than your favorite import. A shot of the local hard drink in Portugal will cost a dollar, while an American drink would cost more than the American price. Drink the local stuff with local people in local bars; it's a better experience than having a Manhattan in your hotel with a guy from Los Angeles. Drink wine in wine countries and beer in beer countries. Sample the regional specialties. Let a local person order you her favorite. You may hate it, but you'll never forget it.

Tap Water in Five Languages

Italian: *acqua del rubinetto*
French: *une carafe d'eau*
German: *Leitungswasser*
Spanish: *agua del grifo*
Portuguese: *água da torneira*

In other languages, just do the international charade: Hold an imaginary glass in one hand, turn on the tap with the other, and make the sound of a faucet. Stop it with a click of your tongue and drink it with a smile.

Paying the Bill

To get the bill, you'll have to ask for it (catch the waiter's eye and, with raised hands, scribble with an imaginary pencil on your palm). Before it comes, make a mental tally of roughly how much your meal should cost. The bill should vaguely resemble the figure you expected. (It should at least have the same number of digits.) If the total is a surprise, ask to have it itemized and explained. Some waiters make the same

Interpreting the Bill

Examine this sample Italian restaurant bill to get used to the charges you'll see in Europe.

Check each line item. Be sure you understand what each charge was for. You don't have to speak fluent Italian to recognize *minestrone* or *spaghetti carbonara*. Even *insalata mista* isn't a stretch if you remember that you ate a mixed salad. But if it says *"4 birre"* and you don't remember drinking four beers, ask for an explanation (or an apology).

Pane e coperto ("bread and cover" charge) is a mandatory amount charged per customer just to sit down. Common in Italy, this is relatively rare in other countries—though (sadly) it's beginning to catch on at touristy restaurants in other popular destinations, such as Prague.

A legitimate **servizio** (service) charge of 10 percent has been added. You don't need to leave a big tip (but if you were pleased with the service,

VIA GARIBALDI 37, ROMA

Ristorante Colosseo

DI RICARDO STEFANO

	IMPORTO
pan e coperto (×2)...	4,00
insalata caprese.....	6,00
ins. mista..........	4,00
spaghetti carbonara...	6,00
minestrone........	8,00
frutta...........	4,00
tiramisú..........	5,00
vino rosso (bottiglia)...	12,00
acqua min. (litro).....	4,00
totale............	53,00
servizio 10%.......	5,30
totale........	**€58,30**
documento	

RICEVUTA FISCALE
COPIA PER IL CLIENTE

you'd add a euro or two for each person in your party). In many cases, rather than adding the 10 percent at the end of the bill, the menu prices already include the service charge (in which case, the menu might say *"servizio incluso."*)

Also notice that Europeans use a comma as a decimal point—so €58,30 is the same as €58.30.

Now hand over your cash and wait for the change...and don't leave until you get the correct amount back. When you collect your change, you can leave the tip on the table, or better, give the tip directly to your server.

Or you can pay with exact change, including the tip, and indicate you don't need any back. For this meal, I'd hand the server €60, smile, say *grazie*, and wave my hand to suggest she should keep the change.

"innocent" mistakes repeatedly, knowing most tourists are so befuddled by the money and menu that they'll pay whatever number is scrawled across the bottom of the bill.

I pay cash for my meals. But if you use a credit card, don't be surprised if your waiter brings a mobile card reader to the table. These machines cut down on fraud since your card never leaves your sight. Be aware that you may have to enter the card's PIN rather than sign a receipt (see page 190). Many restaurants in Germany won't take a credit card, and in Denmark they may tack on an extra fee if you use one—ask.

Tipping

Restaurant tips are more modest in Europe than in America. In most places, 10 percent is a big tip. If your bucks talk at home, muzzle them on your travels. As a matter of principle, if not economy, the local price should prevail. Please believe me—tipping 15 or 20 percent in Europe is unnecessary, if not culturally ignorant.

Tipping is an issue only at restaurants that have waiters and waitresses. If you order your food at a counter (in a pub, for example), don't tip.

At table-service restaurants, the tipping etiquette and procedure vary slightly from country to country. But in general, European servers are well paid, and tips are considered a small "bonus"—to reward great service or for simplicity in rounding the total bill to a convenient number. In many countries, 5-10 percent is adequate.

In Mediterranean countries, the "service charge" (*servizio* in Italian, *service* in French, *servicio* in Spanish) can be handled in different ways. Sometimes the menu will note that the service is included ("*servizio incluso*"), meaning that the prices listed on the menu already have this charge built in. When the service is not included ("*servizio non incluso*"), the service charge might show up as a separate line item at the end of your bill. Fixed-price tourist deals (a.k.a. *menu*) include service.

In northern and eastern Europe, the menu or bill is less likely to address the "service charge," but you can usually assume that it's included in the prices (see the "Tipping Standards by Country" sidebar on the next page for details).

Virtually anywhere in Europe, you can do as the Europeans do and (if you're pleased with the service) add a euro or two for each person in your party. In very touristy areas, some servers have noticed the American obsession with overtipping—and might hope for a Yankee-size tip. But

Tipping Standards by Country

COUNTRY	AMOUNT	GENERAL RULE
Austria	10%	Service is included, but it's common to tip 10 percent after a good meal.
Belgium	Round up	Service is included, although it's common to round up the bill.
Croatia	5-10%	Tip about 5-10 percent after a good meal.
Czech Republic	5-10%	Your bill will state—in English—whether or not service is included. In most cases it's not, so round up the bill by adding 5-10 percent and paying in cash. Speaking just a few Czech words will get you better service (if you greet your waiter in English, he'll want a 15 percent tip).
Denmark	10%	Tip about 10 percent.
Estonia	5-10%	Round up for good service (though never more than 10 percent).
Finland	0-10%	A service charge is included in your bill. If the service is exceptional, you can tip 5-10 percent.
France	0-5%	Prices include a service charge, so most French never tip. For exceptional service, you could tip up to 5 percent—but don't feel guilty if you skip it.
Germany	10%	It's common to tip after a good meal, usually 10 percent.
Great Britain	10-15%	Check the menu or bill to see if service is included; if not, tip about 10 percent (up to 15 percent in London). Many London restaurants list a 12.5 percent "optional" tip on the bill, but you should tip only what you feel the service warrants.
Greece	Round up	Round up—about €1 for a drink, and €2-6 for a meal.
Hungary	0-10%	Most Budapest restaurants automatically tack on a 10-20 percent service charge. No additional tip is necessary. If service isn't included, tip about 10 percent.
Ireland	0-10%	Check the menu or your bill to see if the service is included; if not, tip about 10 percent.
Italy	5-10%	A 10 percent service charge (*servizio*) is usually built into your bill. If you wish, you can add an extra €1-2 for each person in your party. If *servizio* is not included, tip up to 10 percent.

COUNTRY	AMOUNT	GENERAL RULE
Netherlands	5-10%	Service is included, although it's common to round up the bill by about 5-10 percent after a good meal. In bars, rounding up to the next euro ("keep the change") is appropriate.
Norway	10%	Tip about 10 percent. If there is a "service charge" on your bill, it goes to the owner, so you should still leave a tip.
Poland	5-10%	At some tourist-oriented restaurants, a 10-15 percent "service charge" may be added to your bill, in which case an additional tip is not necessary; otherwise tip 5-10 percent.
Portugal	5-10%	Service is included, but if you are pleased with the waitstaff, it's customary to leave 5 percent in family-run places and around 10 percent in upscale restaurants.
Slovenia	0-10%	At some touristy restaurants, a 10-15 percent "service charge" may be added to your bill—in which case an additional tip is not necessary. Otherwise tip 5-10 percent.
Spain	0-10%	If you order at a counter—such as sampling tapas at a bar—there's no need to tip (you can round up a few small coins if you wish). At restaurants with table service, most Spaniards tip nothing or next to nothing; a service charge is generally included. For good service, you can tip up to 5 percent. If service is not included (servicio no incluido), you could tip up to 10 percent.
Sweden	10%	Tip about 10 percent.
Switzerland	Round up	Service is included, although it's common to round up the bill after a good meal.
Turkey	10%	Tip about 10 percent. Some upscale restaurants may include a "service charge" on the bill; this goes to the owner, not the server—so still tip about 10 percent.

the good news is that European servers and diners are far more laid-back about all this than we are. Any tip is appreciated, the stakes are low, and it's no big deal if you choose the "wrong" amount.

Typically, it's better to hand the tip to the waiter when you're paying your bill than to leave it on the table, particularly in busy places where the wrong party might pocket the change. Servers prefer to be tipped in cash even if you pay with your credit card (otherwise the tip may never reach your server); in many cases, there isn't even a line on the credit-card receipt for a tip.

In Germanic countries, it's considered discreet and classy to say the total number of euros you'd like the waiter to keep (including his tip) when paying. So, if the bill is €41, hand him €50 while saying, "45." You'll get €5 back and feel pretty European.

CAFÉS AND BARS

On my last trip to Italy, I savored a peaceful moment in Siena's great square, Il Campo, sipping a glass of *vin santo* as the early evening light bathed the red-brick stone. My five-euro drink gave me a front-row seat at the best table on the square, and for a leisurely hour I soaked up the promenading action that nightly turns Il Campo into "Il Italian Fashion Show."

Public squares like Il Campo are the physical and cultural heart of Europe's cities and towns. For Europeans, these bustling squares proclaim "community." Defined by stately architecture and ringed by shops and cafés, squares are the perfect venue for café-sitting, coffee-sipping, and people-watching. Promenaders take center stage, strolling and being seen, while onlookers perch on the periphery. To play your part, tether yourself to one of the café tables parked around any square, order a drink, and feel the pulse of the passing scene. Don't be in a

In European cafés, menus are two-tiered: cheaper at the bar, more expensive at a table.

Listino Prezzi

BEVANDE CALDE	€ (al banco)	€ (al tavolo)
Caffè espresso	0.80	1.60
Caffè d'orzo	0.80	1.60
Caffè decaffeinato	0.80	1.60
Caffè corretto		
Macchiatone	1.00	1.80
Cappuccino	1.30	2.60
Cappuccino decaffeinato	1.30	2.60
Caffèlatte	1.30	2.60
Tè e infusi (tazza)	1.30	2.60
Camomilla (tazza)	1.80	2.60
Cioccolata (tazza)		
Latte (bicchiere)	0.80	1.60
Caffè freddo	1.30	2.60
Tè freddo	1.80	2.60
Ponce		

PASTICCERIA dolce e salata		
Pasticceria (al pezzo)	0.80	2.00
Panini imbottiti	2.60	4.20
Panini farciti	2.60	4.20
Piadine		
Tramezzini	1.70	2.10
Toast	2.10	3.10
Toast farciti	2.60	3.80
Pizzette		
Schiacciate	3.00	4.20

hurry—spending endless hours sitting in an outdoor café is the norm.

In many countries, you'll pay less to stand and more to sit. In general, if you simply want to slam down a cup of coffee, it's cheapest to order and drink it at the bar. If you want to sit a while and absorb that last museum while checking out the two-legged art, grab a table with a view, and a waiter will take your order. This will cost you about double what it would at the bar. (Sometimes an outdoor table is more

Breakfast Basics

The farther north you go in Europe, the heartier the breakfasts. Heaviest are the traditional British fry and Scandinavian buffet breakfasts. Throughout the Netherlands, Belgium, Germany, Austria, Switzerland, and Eastern Europe, expect a more modest buffet—but still plenty of options (rolls, bread, jam, cold cuts, cheeses, fruit, yogurt, and cereal). In these countries, there's a good chance of finding hard-boiled eggs, but scrambled or fried eggs are relatively rare. As you move

The continental breakfast: bread, jam, and coffee

south and west (France, Italy, Spain, and Portugal), skimpier "continental" breakfasts are the norm. You'll get a roll with marmalade or jam, occasionally a slice of ham or cheese, and coffee or tea.

If your breakfast is sparse, supplement it with a piece of fruit and a wrapped chunk of cheese from your rucksack stash. Orange juice fans pick up liter boxes in the grocery store and start the day with a glass in their hotel room. If you're a coffee drinker, remember that breakfast is the only cheap time to caffeinate yourself. Some hotels will serve you a bottomless cup of a rich brew only with breakfast. After that, the cups acquire bottoms. Juice is generally available at breakfast, but in Mediterranean countries, you have to ask for it, and you'll probably be charged.

In many countries, breakfast is included in your hotel bill, though if you make prior arrangements with the hotelier, you may be able to skip breakfast and pay a lower price for the room. If breakfast costs extra, it's often optional, and you can usually save money and gain atmosphere by buying coffee and a roll or croissant at the café down the street or by brunching picnic-style in the park.

I'm a big-breakfast person at home. But when I feel the urge for a typical American breakfast in Europe, I beat it to death with a hard roll. You can find bacon, fried eggs, and orange juice, but it's nearly always overpriced and disappointing.

Few hotel breakfasts are worth waiting around for. If you need to get an early start, skip the breakfast.

expensive than an indoor one.) If you're on a budget, always confirm the price for a sit-down drink. While it's never high profile, there's always a price list posted somewhere inside with the two- or three-tiered price system clearly labeled (cheap at the bar, more at a table, still more at an outside table). If you pay for a seat in a café with an expensive drink, that seat's yours for the afternoon if you like. Lingering with your bar-priced drink on a nearby public bench or across the street on the beach is usually OK—just ask first.

If you're a coffee lover, it pays to know the ground rules. In some coffee bars (especially in Italy), you pay for your drink at the cash register, then take your receipt to the bar, where you'll be served. In Italy, if you ask for *un caffè*, you'll get espresso. Cappuccino is served to locals before noon and to tourists any time of day. (To an Italian, cappuccino is a breakfast drink, and drinking anything with milk or cream after eating anything with tomatoes is a travesty.) A *caffè latte* is an espresso mixed with hot milk with no foam and served in a tall glass (ordering just a *latte* gets you only hot milk). While the French call espresso with lots of steamed milk *un café au lait*, you can get specific by asking for *un grand crème* if you want a big cup or *un petit crème* for a smaller one.

If you're hankering for the closest thing to brewed coffee in Italy, try a *caffè americano*, which is espresso diluted with hot water. A similar drink in France is called *un café allongé*. Cafés in Britain, Germany, and Scandinavia are more likely to serve brewed coffee, though there are plenty of espresso places these days. Turkish coffee is unfiltered coffee, with the grounds mixed right in. It's popular in the eastern Mediterranean—typically drunk as a digestive after dinner and sometimes after lunch.

As a traveler, you naturally want to take in as many sights as you can every day. But make time in your itinerary to simply drop yourself into a café chair for a few hours. Enjoying life like the Europeans do—watching the world go by—is one of the best and most relaxing ways to go local.

BUDGET FOOD OPTIONS

There are plenty of strategies for stretching your food budget on the road. While cafeterias, street stands, and "to go" meals are not high cuisine, they're undeniably cheap. And in my book, there's no better travel experience than a picnic sourced from local markets and grocers.

Cheap Eats

Europe offers a bounty of options for eating inexpensively:

Cafeterias: "Self-service" is an international word. You'll find self-service restaurants in big cities everywhere, offering low-price, low-risk, low-stress, what-you-see-is-what-you-get meals. A sure value for your euro is a department-store cafeteria. These places are designed for the shopper who has a sharp eye for a good value. At a salad bar, grab the small (cheap) plate and stack it like the locals do—high. Hungry sightseers also appreciate the handy, moderately priced cafeterias they'll find in larger museums.

Institution-Affiliated Eateries: If your wallet is as empty as your stomach, find a cheap, humble cafeteria that's associated with (and subsidized by) a local institution—such as a university, City Hall, church, hospital, charity, senior center, fire station, union of gondoliers, retired fishermen's club, and so on. (These are sometimes called "mensas.") Profits take a back seat to providing good food at a good price—and many of these eateries welcome the public to pull up a chair. Options range from a semi-swanky City Hall cafeteria in Oslo, to student canteens in university towns (such as Salzburg, Austria), to Poland's dreary-looking but cheap-and-tasty "milk bars." Don't be afraid to take advantage of these opportunities to fill yourself with a plate of dull but nourishing food for an unbeatable price in the company of locals. University cafeterias (generally closed during summer holidays) also offer a surefire way to meet educated, English-speaking young people with open and stimulating minds. They're often eager to share their views on politics and economics, as well as their English, with a foreign friend.

Bakeries and Sandwich Shops: Bakeries are a good place to pick up basic sandwiches, tiny pizzas, or something equally cheap and fast but with more of a regional flavor (such as savory pasties in England or a *croque-monsieur* sandwich in France). Britain's Pret à Manger, Norway's Deli de Luca, and Spain's Pans & Company are chains that sell good, healthful sandwiches, salads, and pastries. Local deli-like shops are popular in many parts of Europe; try a *traiteur* in France or a *rosticceria* in Italy. The business lunch crowd invariably knows the best place for an affordable fill-the-tank bite.

Street Food: Every country has its own equivalent of the hot-dog

Cafeteria leftovers: even cheaper than picnics...

LEFT Eat where the immigrants do, and you'll save plenty of money.

RIGHT All around Europe, Industrial Age iron-and-glass market halls—such as Florence's venerable Mercato Centrale—are finding new life hosting trendy restaurants.

stand, where you can grab a filling bite on the go—French *crêperies,* Greek souvlaki stands, Danish *pølse* (sausage) vendors, Italian *pizza rustica* takeout shops, Dutch herring carts, and Turkish-style kebab and falafel kiosks in Germany (and just about everywhere else). A falafel (fried chickpea croquettes wrapped in pita bread) is a good vegetarian option that's also popular with meat eaters. Of all of these options, the ubiquitous kebab stand is my favorite. The best ones have a busy energy, and a single large kebab wrapped in wonderful pita bread can feed two hungry travelers for €4. Don't miss the *ayran*—a healthy yogurt drink popular with Turks—which goes well with your kebab. In general, if there's a long line at a particular stand, you can bet that customers appreciate the value that vendor provides.

Ethnic Eateries: Throughout wealthy northern Europe, immigrant communities labor at subsistence wages. Rather than eat bland and pricey local food, they (along with savvy residents and travelers) go cheap and spicy at simple diners, delis, and take-away stands serving Middle Eastern, Pakistani, and Asian food. These places usually offer the cheapest hot meals in town.

McEurope: Fast-food restaurants are everywhere. Yes, the hamburgerization of the world is a shame, but face it—the busiest and biggest McDonald's in the world are in Tokyo, Rome, and Moscow. The burger has become a global thing. You'll find Big Macs in every language—it isn't exciting (and costs more than at home), but at least at McDonald's you know exactly what you're getting, and it's fast. A hamburger, fries, and shake can be fun halfway through your trip. For a change of pace, you'll also find KFC, Subway, and Starbucks almost everywhere.

American fast-food joints are kid-friendly and satisfy the need for a cheap salad bar and a tall orange juice. They've grabbed prime bits of real estate in every big European city. Since there's no cover charge, this is an opportunity to savor a low-class paper cup of coffee while enjoying some high-class people-watching (unless you're at Starbucks, where your paper cup will be high class, too). Many offer free Wi-Fi as well.

Each country also has its equivalent of the hamburger stand (I saw a "McCheaper" in Switzerland). Whatever their origin, they're a hit with youths and a handy place for a quick, cheap bite to eat.

Picnics, Markets, and Supermarkets

There is only one way left to feast for $10-15 anywhere in Europe: picnic. You'll eat better, while spending half as much as those who eat exclusively in restaurants.

I am a picnic connoisseur. While I'm the first to admit that restaurant meals are an important aspect of any culture, I picnic almost daily. This is not solely for budgetary reasons. It's fun to dive into a marketplace and deal with locals in the corner grocery or market. Europe's colorful markets overflow with varied cheeses, meats, fresh fruits, vegetables, and still-warm-out-of-the-bakery-oven bread. Many of my favorite foods made their debut in a European picnic.

To busy sightseers, restaurants can be time-consuming and frustrating. After waiting to be served, tangling with a menu, and consuming a budget-threatening meal, you walk away feeling unsatisfied, knowing your money could have done much more for your stomach if you had invested it in a picnic. Nutritionally, a picnic is unbeatable. Consider this example: cheese, thinly sliced ham, fresh bread, peaches, carrots, a cucumber, a half-liter of milk, and fruit yogurt or a freshly baked pastry for dessert.

To bolster your budget, I recommend picnic dinners every few nights. At home, we save time and money by raiding the refrigerator to assemble a pickup dinner. In Europe, the equivalent is the corner deli, bakery, or grocery store. When staying several nights, I cozy up a hotel room by borrowing plates, glasses, and silverware from the breakfast

You can save on your food budget by visiting the corner bakery and picnicking on the grass or a bench.

Pique-nique

room and stocking the closet with my favorite groceries (juice, fruits and vegetables, cheese, and other munchies). If your hotelier posts signs prohibiting picnicking in rooms (most likely in France), you'll easily be able to find plenty of other atmospheric places to eat. But if you picnic in your room anyway, be discreet and toss your garbage in a public waste receptacle.

There is nothing second-class about a picnic. A few special touches will even make your budget meal a first-class affair. Proper site selection can make the difference between just another meal and *le pique-nique extraordinaire*. Since you've decided to skip the restaurant, it's up to you to create the atmosphere.

Try to incorporate a picnic brunch, lunch, or dinner into the day's sightseeing plans. For example, I start the day by scouring the thriving market with my senses and my camera. Then I fill up my shopping bag and have breakfast on a riverbank. After sightseeing, I combine lunch and a siesta in a cool park to fill my stomach, rest my body, and escape the early afternoon heat. It's fun to eat dinner on a castle wall enjoying a commanding view and the setting sun. Some of my all-time best picnics have been lazy dinners accompanied by medieval fantasies in the quiet of after-hours Europe.

Mountain hikes are punctuated nicely by picnics. Food tastes even better on top of a mountain. Europeans are great picnickers. Many picnics become potlucks, resulting in new friends as well as full stomachs.

Only a glutton can spend more than $15 for a picnic feast. In a park in Paris, on a Norwegian ferry, high in the Alps, at an autobahn rest stop, on your convent rooftop, or in your hotel room, picnicking is the budget traveler's key to cheap and good eating.

Picnic Tips

Here are some tricks for picnicking like a pro:

Picnic Supplies: Pack resealable plastic baggies (large and small). Buy a good knife with a can opener and cork screw in Europe (or bring it from home, if you plan to check your luggage on the plane). In addition to being a handy plate, fan, and lousy Frisbee, a plastic lid makes an easy-to-clean cutting board. A dishtowel doubles as a small tablecloth, and a washcloth or wet wipe helps with cleanup. A disposable shower cap contains messy food nicely on your picnic cloth. Bring a plastic, airline-type drink cup and spoon for cereal and a fork for takeout salad. Some travelers get immersion heaters (buy in Europe for a compatible plug) to make hot drinks to go with munchies in their hotel room.

Drinks: There are plenty of cheap ways to wash down a picnic. If you're tired of filling your water bottle, you can buy drinks in supermarkets and corner grocery stores. Liter bottles of Coke are inexpensive, as is wine in most countries—and local wine gives your picnic a nice touch. Neighborhood wine shops have a great selection— and most will open your bottle if you forgot your corkscrew.

Stretching Your Money: Bread has always been cheap in Europe. (Leaders have learned from history that when stomachs rumble, so do the mobs in the streets.) Cheese is a specialty nearly everywhere and is, along with milk and yogurt, one of the Continent's most affordable sources of protein. The standard low-risk option anywhere in Europe is Emmental cheese (the kind with holes, what we call "Swiss"). Buy fruit and veggies that are in season; see what's inexpensive and plentiful in the produce section or market. Anything American is usually pricey and rarely satisfying. Cultural chameleons eat and drink better and cheaper.

LEFT This happy gang is living simply and well on the cheap: enjoying a picnic in Assisi, the hometown of St. Francis.

RIGHT Kick back and munch a picnic dinner in your hotel room.

Markets

Nearly every town, large or small, has at least one colorful outdoor or indoor marketplace. Assemble your picnic here; you'll probably need to hit several stalls to put together a complete meal. Make an effort to communicate with the merchants. Know what you are buying and what you are spending. Whether you understand the prices or not, act like you do (observe the weighing process closely), and you're more likely to be treated fairly. Gather your ingredients in the morning, as markets typically close in the early afternoon.

Farmers markets are a fun source for healthy picnic snacks.

Learn the measurements. The unit of measure throughout the Continent is a kilo, or 2.2 pounds. A kilo (kg) has 1,000 grams (g or gr). One hundred grams (a common unit of sale) of cheese or meat tucked into a chunk of French bread gives you about a quarter-pounder.

Food can be priced in different ways. Watch the scale when your food is being weighed. It'll likely show grams and kilos. If dried apples are priced at €2 per kilo, that's $2.80 for 2.2 pounds, or about $1.25 per pound. If the scale says 400 grams, that means 40 percent of €2 (or 80 euro cents), which is a little over $1.

Not everything is strictly priced by the kilogram. Read the little chalkboard price carefully: Particularly in the case of specialty items, you might see things priced by the ¼ kg, ½ kg, 100 g, 500 g, and so on. Or an item could be priced by the piece (*Stück* in German, *la piéce* in French, *pezzo* in Italian), the bunch, the container, and so on. If the pâté seems too cheap to be true, look at the sign closely. The posted price is probably followed by "100 gr."

If no prices are posted, be wary. Travelers are routinely ripped off by market merchants in tourist centers. Find places that print the prices. Assume any market with no printed prices has a double price standard: one for locals and a more expensive one for tourists.

I'll never forget a friend of mine who bought two bananas for our London picnic. He grabbed the fruit, held out a handful of change, and said, "How much?" The merchant took the equivalent of $4. My friend turned to me and said, "Wow, London really is expensive." Anytime you hold out a handful of money to a banana salesman, you're just asking for trouble.

Point, but don't touch. Most produce stands and outdoor markets are not self-service: Tell the vendor (or point to) what you want, and let the merchant bag it and weigh it for you. It's considered rude for a customer to touch the goods.

Want only a small amount? You'll likely need only one or two pieces of fruit, and many merchants refuse to deal in such small quantities. The way to get what you want and no more is to estimate what it would cost if the merchant were to weigh it and then just hold out a coin worth about that much in one hand and point to the apple, or whatever, with the other. Have a Forrest Gump look on your face that says, "If you take this coin, I'll go away." Rarely will he refuse the deal.

Appreciate the cultural experience. Shopping for groceries is an integral part of everyday European life for good reasons: People have small refrigerators (kitchens are tiny), value fresh produce, and enjoy the social interaction.

Supermarkets and Grocery Stores

I prefer local markets, but American-style supermarkets, many of which hide out in the basements of big-city department stores, are a good alternative. Some of them are very upscale. Common European chains include Aldi, Carrefour, Co-op, Despar, Dia, Konzum, Lidl, Mercadona, Migros, Monoprix, Morrisons, Sainsbury's, Spar, and Tesco. Corner grocery stores give you more color and a better price—but are less efficient and have a smaller selection.

If it's late in the day, you may be able to score some deals. One night in Oslo I walked into an ICA supermarket just before closing to discover that they'd marked down all the deli food by 50 percent. Back in my hotel room, I ate my cheapest meal in Norway—roast chicken and fries at almost US prices.

At the supermarket, put your banana on the scale, push the banana button, rip off the price sticker, and stick it on your banana.

Ready-made food: Many supermarkets offer cheap packaged sandwiches, while others have deli counters where you can get a sandwich made-to-order. Just point to what you want. Most supermarkets offer a good selection of freshly prepared quiche, fried chicken, and fish, all for takeout.

Produce: Don't be intimidated by the produce section. It's a cinch to buy a tiny amount of fruit or vegetables. Many have an easy push-button pricing system: Put the banana on the scale, push the picture of a banana (or enter the banana bin number), and a sticky price tag prints out. You could weigh and sticker a single grape. In Spain and Italy, if there is no one to serve you, the store provides plastic gloves for you to wear while picking out your produce (a bare hand is a no-no).

Drinks: Milk in the dairy section is always cheap and available in quarter, half, or whole liters. Be sure it's normal drinking milk. Strange white liquid dairy products in look-alike milk cartons abound, ruining the milk-and-cookie dreams of careless tourists. Look for local words for "whole," "half," or "light," such as *voll, halb,* or *lett.* Nutritionally, a half-liter provides about 25 percent of your daily protein needs. Get refrigerated, fresh milk. Or look on the (unrefrigerated) shelves for the common-in-Europe but rarer-in-America "long life" milk. This milk—which requires no refrigeration until it's opened—will never go bad...or taste good.

European yogurt is delicious and can often be drunk right out of its container. Fruit juice comes in handy liter boxes (look for "100% juice" or "no sugar" to avoid Kool-Aid clones). Buy cheap by the liter, and use a reusable half-liter plastic mineral-water bottle (usually found next to the soft drinks) to store what you can't comfortably drink in one sitting.

If it's hot outside, don't expect the soft drinks, beer, or wine to be chilled—most supermarkets sell these at room temperature.

Sweets: To satisfy your sweet tooth (or stock up on gifts for the folks back home), check out the dessert and candy section. European-style "biscuits" (cookies)—made by companies such as Lu, Bahlsen, or McVities—are usually a good value, as are candy bars that might cost twice as much at airport gift shops.

Supermarket Etiquette: Bring your own shopping bag or use your empty daybag, or expect to pay extra for the store's plastic bags. You may even have to pay €1 to use a shopping cart—although you'll get your deposit back when you return the cart to its rack. Sometimes the store's plastic shopping baskets will have wheels and pull-out handles as a handy alternative.

It's easiest to pay cash at checkout, but if you want to use your credit card, be sure you know the PIN—the clerk may ask you to enter it (clerks may also ask for photo ID). No one will bag your groceries for you; expect to be bagging and paying at the same time. It's smart to start bagging immediately to avoid frustrating the shoppers behind you.

Health & Hygiene

Understandably, two big concerns of American travelers are staying healthy and adjusting to European plumbing. Take comfort: Doctors, hospitals, launderettes, and bathrooms aren't *that* different in Europe. And dealing with them is actually part of the fun of travel. This chapter provides information on staying healthy while traveling, dealing with jet lag, and finding medical treatment, along with tips on hygiene—from doing your laundry to mastering European bathrooms.

STAYING HEALTHY

Before You Go

When you're scrambling around getting organized before a trip, remember to also get your medical business in order. Your health is critical to your enjoyment of your trip.

Get a checkup. Just as you'd give your car a good checkup before a long journey, it's smart to meet with your doctor before your trip, particularly if you have any medical concerns. Ask for advice on maintaining your health on the road. Obtain recommended immunizations and discuss proper care while traveling for any pre-existing medical conditions. Get any prescriptions you might need (described on the next page). If you have health concerns, pack a copy of your records, including your latest EKG or X-rays; a flash drive that can be attached to a necklace or keychain is a handy way to carry this data. If you have a medical device or condition that will affect airport screening, print and pack a notification card from tsa.gov, which allows you to discreetly describe your situation to the agent.

It's also a good idea to figure out if your health insurance covers you internationally or whether you might need to buy special medical insurance (for details, see page 71).

Pack your prescriptions. If you take regular prescriptions—or have health problems that could flare up on your trip—bring a letter from your doctor describing the condition and any prescription medications you may need, including the generic names of the drugs. It's best to bring a big enough supply to cover your entire trip, along with a copy of your prescription just in case you need more while you're abroad. Bring pharmaceuticals in their original containers (clearly labeled), and pack them in your carry-on bag (don't stow them in checked luggage in case it gets lost).

Visit the dentist. Get a dental checkup well before your trip. Emergency dental care during your trip can be expensive, time consuming...and painful. I once had a tooth crowned by a German dentist who knew only one word in English, which he used in question form—"Pain?"

Take extra precautions for exotic locations. No vaccinations are required for travel in Europe. But if you're heading to more exotic destinations, such as Morocco, Russia, or Turkey, ask your doctor about any shots or medicine you might need, or consult a travel-medicine physician. Only these specialists keep entirely up-to-date on health conditions for travelers around the world. Tell the doctor about every possible destination on your vacation itinerary, confirmed or not. Then you can have the flexibility to take that impulsive swing through Turkey or Morocco knowing that you're prepared medically and have the required shots. Ask the doctor about vaccines against hepatitis A (food- or water-borne virus) and hepatitis B (virus transmitted by bodily fluids), antidiarrheal medicines, and any additional precautions. Countries "require" shots in order to protect their citizens from you and "recommend" shots to protect you from them. If any travel vaccines or medications are recommended, take that advice seriously. The Centers for Disease Control offers updated information on every country (cdc.gov/travel).

Resources for Staying Healthy

CDC.gov/travel: Trip preparation and health advice

IAMAT.org: International directory of English-speaking doctors

Tripprep.com: Health advice and planning guide

mPassport app: Directory of English-speaking doctors and hospitals, and translations for medical terms and medications

Conquering Jet Lag

Anyone who flies through multiple time zones has to grapple with the biorhythmic confusion known as jet lag. Flying from the US to Europe, you switch your wristwatch six to nine hours forward. Your body says, "Hey, what's going on?" Body clocks don't reset so easily. All your life you've done things on a 24-hour cycle. Now, after crossing the Atlantic, your body wants to eat when you tell it to sleep and sleep when you tell it to enjoy a museum.

Too many people assume their first day will be made worthless by jet lag. Don't prematurely condemn yourself to zombiedom. Most people I've traveled with, of all ages, have enjoyed productive—even hyper—first days. You can't avoid jet lag, but by following these tips you can minimize the symptoms.

Leave home well rested. Flying halfway around the world is stressful. If you leave frazzled after a hectic last night and a wild bon-voyage party, there's a good chance you won't be healthy for the first part of your trip. An early-trip cold used to be a regular part of my vacation until I learned this very important trick: Plan from the start as if you're leaving two days before you really are. Keep that last 48-hour period sacred (apart from your normal work schedule), even if it means being hectic before your false departure date. Then you have two orderly, peaceful days after you've packed so that you are physically ready to fly. Mentally, you'll be comfortable about leaving home and starting this adventure. You'll fly away well rested and 100 percent capable of enjoying the bombardment of your senses that will follow.

Use the flight to rest and reset. In-flight movies are good for one thing—nap time. With a few hours of sleep during the transatlantic flight, you'll be functional the day you land. When the pilot announces the European time, reset your mind along with your wristwatch. Don't prolong jet lag by reminding yourself what time it is back home. Be in Europe.

On arrival, stay awake until an early local bedtime. If you doze off at 4 p.m. and wake up at midnight, you've accomplished nothing. Plan a good walk until early evening. Jet lag hates fresh air, daylight, and exercise. Your body

Jet lag hits even the very young.

may beg for sleep, but stand firm: Refuse. Force your body's transition to the local time.

You'll probably awaken very early on your first morning. Trying to sleep later is normally futile. Get out and enjoy a "pinch me, I'm in Europe" walk, as merchants set up in the marketplace and the town slowly comes to life. This may be the only sunrise you'll see in Europe.

Consider jet-lag cures. The last thing I want to do is promote a pharmaceutical, but I must admit that the sleep aid Ambien (generic name zolpidem) has become my friend in fighting jet lag. Managing a good seven hours of sleep a night in Europe (or after flying home) hastens my transition to local time. That way, I'm not disabled by sleepiness that first afternoon and can stay awake until a decent bedtime. Ambien can have side effects, and if misused, can be habit-forming; consult with your doctor, and read and follow the directions carefully.

Other travelers rave about melatonin, a hormone that helps recalibrate your internal clock (available over the counter in the US, but illegal in some European countries).

Bottom Line: The best prescription is to leave home unfrazzled, minimize jet lag's symptoms, force yourself into European time, and give yourself a chance to enjoy your trip from the moment you step off the plane.

Staying Healthy While Traveling

Using discretion and common sense, I eat and drink whatever I like when I'm on the road. I've stayed healthy throughout a six-week trip traveling from Europe to India. By following these basic guidelines, I never once suffered from Tehran Tummy or Delhi Belly.

Take precautions on the flight. Long flights are dehydrating. I ask for "two orange juices with no ice" every chance I get. Eat lightly, stay hydrated, and have no coffee or alcohol and only minimal sugar until the flight's almost over. Avoid the slight chance of getting a blood clot in your leg during long flights by taking short walks hourly. While seated, flex your ankles and don't cross your legs. Some people are more prone to clots (factors include obesity, age, genetics, smoking, and use of oral contraceptives or hormone replacement therapy).

Eat nutritiously. The longer your trip, the more you'll be affected by an inadequate diet. Budget travelers often eat more carbohydrates and less protein to stretch their travel dollars. This is the root of many health problems. Protein

European Water

I drink European tap water and any water served in restaurants. Read signs carefully, however: Some taps, including those on trains and airplanes, are not for drinking. If there's any hint of nonpotability—a decal showing a glass with a red "X" over it, or a skull and crossbones—don't drink it. Many fountains in German-speaking countries are for drinking, but others are just for show. Look for *Trinkwasser* ("drinking water") or *Kein Trinkwasser* ("not drinking water").

The water at many European public fountains is safe to drink...unless your travel partner has dirty hands.

The water (or, just as likely, the general stress of travel on your immune system) may, sooner or later, make you sick. It's not necessarily dirty. The bacteria in European water are different from those in American water. Our bodily systems—raised proudly on bread that rips in a straight line—are the most pampered on earth. We are capable of handling American bacteria with no problem at all, but some people can go to London and get sick. Some French people visit Boston and get sick. Some Americans travel around the world eating and drinking everything in sight and don't get sick, while others spend weeks on the toilet. It all depends on the person.

East of Bulgaria and south of the Mediterranean, do not drink untreated water. Water can be sanitized by boiling it for 10 minutes or by using purifying tablets or a filter. Bottled water, beer, wine, boiled coffee and tea, and bottled soft drinks are safe as long as you skip the ice cubes. Coca-Cola products are as safe in Egypt as they are at home.

helps you resist infection and rebuilds muscles. Get the most nutritional mileage from your protein by eating it with the day's largest meal (in the presence of all those essential amino acids). Supplemental super-vitamins, taken regularly, help me to at least feel healthy.

Use good judgment when eating out (and outside Europe). Avoid unhealthy-looking restaurants. Meat should be well cooked (unless, of course, you're eating sushi, carpaccio, etc.) and, in some places, avoided altogether. Have "well done" written on a piece of paper in the pertinent language and use it when ordering. Pre-prepared foods gather germs (a common cause of diarrhea). Outside of Europe, be especially cautious. When in serious doubt, eat only thick-skinned fruit...peeled.

Keep clean. Wash your hands often, keep your nails

clean, and avoid touching your eyes, nose, and mouth. Hand sanitizers, such as Purell, can be helpful. However, since they target bacteria, not viruses, they should be used as an adjunct to, rather than a replacement for, hand washing with soap and warm water.

Practice safe sex. Sexually transmitted diseases are widespread. Obviously, the best way to prevent acquiring an STD is to avoid exposure. Condoms (readily available at pharmacies and from restroom vending machines) are fairly effective in preventing transmission. HIV is also a risk, especially among prostitutes.

Exercise. Physically, travel is great living—healthy food, lots of activity, fresh air, and all those stairs! If you're a couch potato, try to get in shape before your trip by taking long walks. People who regularly work out have plenty of options for keeping in shape while traveling. Biking is a great way to burn some calories—and get intimate with a destination. Though running is not as widespread in Europe as it is in the US, it's not considered weird either. Traveling runners can enjoy Europe from a special perspective—at dawn. Swimmers will find that Europe has plenty of good, inexpensive public swimming pools. Whatever your racket, if you want to badly enough, you'll find ways to keep in practice as you travel. Most big-city private tennis and swim clubs welcome foreign guests for a small fee, which is a good way to make friends as well as stay fit.

Get enough sleep. Know how much sleep you need to stay healthy (generally 7-8 hours per night). If I go more than two nights with fewer than six hours' sleep, I make it a priority to catch up—no matter how busy I am. Otherwise, I'm virtually guaranteed to get the sniffles.

Give yourself psychological pep talks. Europe can do to certain travelers what southern France did to Vincent van Gogh. Romantics can get the sensory bends, patriots can get their flags burned, and anyone can suffer from culture shock.

Europe is not particularly impressed by America or Americans. It will challenge givens that you always assumed were above the test of reason, and most of Europe on the street doesn't really care that much about what you, the historical and cultural pilgrim, have waited so long to see.

Take a break from Europe, whether it's a long, dark, air-conditioned trip back to California in a movie theater; a pleasant sit in an American embassy reading room surrounded by eagles, photos of presidents, *Time* magazines, and other Yankees; or a visit to the lobby of a world-class hotel, where any hint of the traditional culture has been lost under a big-business bucket of intercontinental whitewash. It can do wonders to refresh the struggling traveler's spirit.

Women's Health Issues

For specific advice on women's health, I turned to Rick Steves' Europe *researcher Risa Laib, who wrote the following section based on her experiences traveling solo (and pregnant) through Europe.*

You can find whatever medications you need in Europe, but you already know what works for you in the US. It's easiest to B.Y.O. pills, whether for cramps, yeast infections, or birth control. Some health-insurance companies issue only a month's supply of birth control pills at a time; ask for a larger supply for a longer trip. Tampons and pads, widely available in Europe, are sold—for more than the US price—at supermarkets, pharmacies, and convenience stores. You may not see the range of brands and sizes typical in American supermarkets, so if you're used to a particular type, it's simpler and cheaper to bring what you'll need from home.

Yeast and Urinary Tract Infections (UTIs): Women prone to yeast infections should bring their own over-the-counter medicine (or know the name and its key ingredient to show a pharmacist in Europe). Some women get a prescription for fluconazole (Diflucan), a powerful pill that cures yeast infections more quickly and tidily than creams and suppositories. If you get a yeast infection in Europe and need medication, go to a pharmacy. If you encounter the rare pharmacist who doesn't speak English, find an English-speaking local woman to write out "yeast infection" for you in the country's language to avoid an embarrassing charade.

Your bladder can react to a sudden change in diet, especially increases in alcohol, coffee, or juice. If you experience UTI symptoms, drink plenty of water and use a general pain reliever. If symptoms persist, a pharmacist in Europe should be able to help.

Traveling When Pregnant: Some couples want to time conception to occur in Europe so they can name their child Paris, Siena, or wherever. (Be thoughtful about this, or little Zagreb may harbor a lifelong grudge against you.) Consider bringing a pregnancy test from home to help you find out when you can celebrate.

If you'll be traveling during your first pregnancy, rip out a few chapters from a book on pregnancy to bring along; it can be hard in Europe to find books in English on pregnancy. If you want certain tests done (such as an amniocentesis), ask your doctor when you need to be home.

Traveling in the first trimester can be rough for some women: Morning sickness can make bus or boat rides especially unpleasant, and climbing all those stone stairs can be exhausting. Packing light is more essential than ever. You might find it easier to travel in the second trimester, when your body's used to being pregnant and you're not yet too big to be uncomfortable.

Wear comfortable shoes that have arch supports. If you'll be traveling a long time, bring loose clothing (with elastic waistbands) and shoes a half size larger to accommodate your changing body. Keep your valuables (cash, passport, etc.) in a neck pouch rather than a constricting money belt.

Pace yourself and allow plenty of time for rest. If problems pop up, go to a clinic or hospital (for more, see "Medical Care in Europe," later).

Seek out nutritious food (though some of it may make you nauseated, just as in America). Picnics, with drinkable yogurt, are often healthier than restaurant meals. Pack baggies for carrying snacks. Bring prenatal vitamins from home, plus a calcium supplement if you're not a milk drinker.

It's actually pleasant to be pregnant in Europe. People are particularly kind. And when your child is old enough to understand, she'll enjoy knowing she's already been to Europe—especially if you promise to take her again.

Basic First Aid

Be proactive to stay well. If you do get sick, take action to regain your health. For a list of first-aid items to pack from home, see page 88.

Headaches and Other Aches: Tylenol (or any other over-the-counter pain reliever) soothes headaches, sore feet, sprains, bruises, Italian traffic, hangovers, and many other minor problems. If you're buying it overseas, Europeans may be more familiar with the term "paracetamol" (pare-ah-SEET-ah-mall).

Swelling: Often accompanying a physical injury, swelling is painful and delays healing. Ice and elevate any sprain periodically for 48 hours. A package of frozen veggies works as a cheap ice pack. If your foot or leg is swollen, buy or borrow a bucket and soak the affected area in cold water, or sit on the edge of a cool swimming pool. Take an anti-inflammatory drug like ibuprofen (Advil, Motrin). Use an Ace bandage to

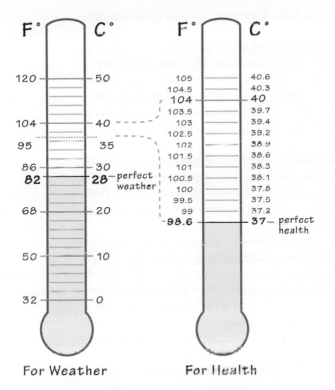

F° C°   F° C°

120 — 50   105 — 40.6
              104.5 — 40.3
              104 — 40
104 — 40   103.5 — 39.7
              103 — 39.4
95 — 35   102.5 — 39.2
              102 — 38.9
              101.5 — 38.6
86 — 30   101 — 38.3
82 — 28 — perfect weather   100.5 — 38.1
              100 — 37.8
              99.5 — 37.5
68 — 20   99 — 37.2
              98.6 — 37 — perfect health
50 — 10
32 — 0

For Weather   **For Health**

Europe takes its temperature using the Celsius scale, while we opt for Fahrenheit. For weather, remember that 28°C is 82°F—perfect. For health, 37°C is just right.

immobilize, reduce swelling, and provide support. It is not helpful to "work out" a sprain—instead, cut back on activities that could aggravate the injury.

Fever: A high fever merits medical attention, particularly for children. A normal temperature of 98.6° Fahrenheit equals 37° Celsius. If your thermometer reads 40°C, you're boiling at 104°F. You can use Tylenol to bring down a fever, along with putting cold washcloths on your forehead for relief.

Colds: It's tempting to go, go, go while you're in Europe—but if you push yourself to the point of getting sick, you've accomplished nothing. Keep yourself healthy and hygienic. If you're feeling run-down, check into a good hotel, sleep well, and force fluids. (My trick during the hectic scramble of TV production is to suck on vitamin C with zinc tablets.) Stock each place you stay with boxes of juice upon arrival. Sudafed (pseudoephedrine) and other cold capsules are usually available, but may not come in as many varieties.

Abrasions: Clean abrasions thoroughly with soap to prevent or control infection. Bandages help keep wounds clean but are not a substitute for cleaning. A piece of clean cloth can be sterilized by boiling for 10 minutes or by scorching with a match.

Blisters: Moleskin, bandages, tape, or two pairs of socks can prevent or retard problems with your feet. Cover any irritated area before it blisters. Many walkers swear by Body Glide, a solid anti-chafing stick sold in running shops and sporting-goods stores. For many, Band-Aid's Friction Block stick is a lifesaver for preventing blisters in spots where your shoe rubs against your foot.

Motion Sickness: To be effective, medication for motion sickness (Dramamine or Marezine) should be taken one hour before you think you'll need it. These medications can also serve as a mild sleep aid. Bonine also treats motion sickness but causes less drowsiness.

Diarrhea: Get used to the fact that you might have diarrhea for a day. (Practice that thought in front of the mirror tonight.) If you get the runs, take it in stride. It's simply not worth taking eight Pepto-Bismol tablets a day or brushing your teeth in Coca-Cola all summer long to avoid a day of the trots. I take my health seriously, and, for me, traveling in India or Mexico is a major health concern. But I find Europe no more threatening to my stomach than the US.

I've routinely taken groups of 24 Americans through Turkey for two weeks. With adequate discretion, we eat everything in sight. At the end of the trip, my loose-stool survey typically shows that five or six travelers coped with a day of the Big D and one person was stuck with an extended weeklong bout.

To help avoid getting diarrhea, eat yogurt, which has enzymes that can ease your system into the country's cuisine.

If you get diarrhea, it will run its course. Revise your diet, don't panic, and take it easy for 24 hours. Make your diet as bland and boring as possible for a day or so (bread, rice, boiled potatoes, clear soup, toast without butter, weak tea). Keep telling yourself that tomorrow you'll feel much better. You will.

If loose stools persist, drink lots of water to replenish lost liquids and minerals. Bananas are effective in replacing potassium, which is lost during a bout with diarrhea.

Don't take antidiarrheal medications if you have blood in your stools or a fever greater than 101°F (38°C)—you need a doctor's exam and antibiotics. A child (especially an infant) who suffers a prolonged case of diarrhea also needs prompt medical attention.

Good news for your health: Europe has become enthusiastic about not smoking. These days most countries prohibit smoking in enclosed public spaces. Cigarette packages make it really clear: "Smoking kills"; and Berlin's subway—like much of Europe—is now smoke-free.

I visited the Red Cross in Athens after a miserable three-week tour of the toilets of Syria, Jordan, and Israel. My intestinal commotion was finally stilled by a recommended strict diet of boiled rice and plain tea. As a matter of fact, after five days on that dull diet, I was constipated.

Constipation: With all the bread you'll be eating, constipation, the other side of the intestinal pendulum, is (according to my surveys) as prevalent as diarrhea. Get exercise, eat lots of roughage (raw fruits, leafy vegetables, prunes, or bran tablets from home), and everything will come out all right in the end.

Medical Care in Europe

If you're worried about getting sick while traveling, rest assured: Most of Europe offers high-quality medical care that's as competent as what you'll find at home. The majority of Europe's doctors and pharmacists speak at least some English, so communication generally isn't an issue.

Emergencies

If an accident or life-threatening medical problem occurs on the road, get to a hospital. For serious conditions (stroke, heart attack, bad car accident), summon an ambulance. In most countries, you can call 112, the European Union's universal emergency number for ambulance, fire department, or police. Most countries also have a 911 equivalent that works as well. Or you can ask your hotelier, restaurant host, or whoever's around to call an ambulance (or a taxi for less dire situations).

Be aware that you will likely have to pay out of pocket for any medical treatment, even if your insurance company provides international health care coverage. A visit to the emergency room can be free or cost only a nominal fee, or it can be expensive, depending on where you are and what treatment you need. Make sure you get a copy of your bill so that when you return home, you can file a claim to be reimbursed. If you purchased travel insurance to serve as your primary medical coverage, call the company as soon as possible to report the injury. They can usually work directly with the hospital to get your bills paid (for information on travel insurance, see page 71).

Minor Ailments

If you get sick on your trip, don't wait it out. Find help to get on the road to recovery as soon as possible. Here are your options if you have a non-emergency situation:

Pharmacies: Throughout Europe, people with a health problem go first to the pharmacy, not to their doctor. European pharmacists can diagnose and prescribe remedies for many simple problems, such as sore throats, fevers, stomach issues, sinus problems, insomnia, blisters, rashes, urinary tract infections, or muscle, joint, and back pain. Most cities have at least a few 24-hour pharmacies from which you can pick up what you need and be on the mend pronto.

When it comes to medication, expect some differences between the way things are done in Europe and at home. Certain drugs that you need a prescription for in the US are available over the counter in Europe. Some drugs go by different names. And some European medications can be stronger than their counterparts in the US, so follow directions and dosages carefully. Also, topical remedies are common in Europe; if you're suffering from body aches and pains, or any swelling, don't be surprised if a pharmacist prescribes a cream to apply to the problem area. If you need to fill a prescription—even one from home—a pharmacy can generally take care of it promptly. If a pharmacist can't help you, he or she will send you to a doctor or a health clinic.

Clinics: A trip to a clinic is actually an interesting travel experience. Every year I end up in a European clinic for one reason or another, and every time I'm impressed by its efficiency and effectiveness.

A clinic is useful if you

Regardless of the local word for "pharmacy" (*farmacia* in Spanish, *Apotheke* in German, *pharmacie* in French), you can always look for the green cross.

need to be checked for a non-emergency medical issue, get some tests done, or if your problem is beyond a pharmacist's scope. Clinics in Europe operate just like those in the US: You'll sign in with the receptionist, answer a few questions, then take a seat and wait for a nurse or doctor.

A trip to a clinic may be free or cost a small fee. Expect to pay this fee up front, whether you're covered through your health insurance company or a special travel policy. Make sure you get a copy of the bill so you can file a claim when you return home.

House Calls: If you're holed up sick in your hotel room and would rather not go out, the hotel receptionist can generally call a doctor who will come to your room and check you out. This option is generally more expensive than dragging yourself to a pharmacy or clinic.

Finding Medical Help

To locate a doctor, clinic, or hospital, ask around at places that are accustomed to dealing with Americans on the road—such as tourist offices and large hotels. Most embassies and consulates maintain lists of physicians and hospitals in major cities (go to usembassy.gov, select your location, and look under the US Citizens Services section of that embassy's website for medical services information).

If you're concerned about getting an English-speaking and Western-trained doctor, consider joining IAMAT, the International Association for Medical Assistance to Travelers. You'll get a list of English-speaking doctors in more than 90 member countries who charge affordable, standardized fees for medical visits (membership is free but donation is requested, fee pricing on website, pay provider directly at time of visit, iamat.org, tel. 716/754-4883).

LAUNDRY

I met a woman in Italy who wore her T-shirt frontward, backward, inside-out frontward, and inside-out backward, all to delay the laundry day. A guy in Germany showed me his take-it-into-the-tub-with-you-and-make-waves method of washing his troublesome jeans. But you don't need to go to these extremes to have something presentable to wear. Do laundry in your hotel room, find a launderette, or splurge on full-service laundry.

Washing Clothes in Your Room

One of my domestic chores while on the road is washing my laundry in the hotel-room sink. I keep it very simple, using hotel laundry bags to store my dirty stuff, washing my clothes with hotel shampoo, and improvising places to hang things. But you can pack a self-service laundry kit: a plastic or mesh bag with a drawstring for dirty clothes; concentrated liquid detergent in a small, sturdy, plastic squeeze bottle wrapped in a sealable baggie to contain leakage; and a stretchable "travel clothesline" (a double-stranded cord that's twisted, so clothespins are unnecessary). To make things easier, I bring a quick-dry travel wardrobe that either looks OK wrinkled or doesn't wrinkle. (I test-wash my shirts in the sink at home before I let them come to Europe with me. Some shirts dry fine; others prune up.)

Most European hotels prefer that you not do laundry in your room. Some bathrooms are even equipped with a multilingual "no washing clothes in the room" sign (which, after "eat your peas," may be the most ignored rule on earth). Interpret hoteliers' reticence as "I have lots of good furniture and fine floors in this room, and I don't want your drippy laundry ruining things." But as long as you wash carefully and are respectful of the room, go right ahead.

Sometimes a hotel will remove the sink and tub stoppers in an attempt to discourage washing. Bring a universal drain-stopper from home, try using a wadded-up sock or a pill-bottle lid, or line the sink with a plastic bag and wash in it. Some travelers create their own washing machine with a large, two-gallon sealable baggie: soak in suds for an hour, agitate, drain, rinse.

Wring wet laundry as dry as possible to minimize dripping. Other than a clogged toilet, there's little a hotelier likes seeing less than a pool of water on their hardwood floors. Rolling laundry in a towel and twisting or stomping on it can be helpful (but many accommodations don't provide new towels every day).

Whistler's laundry

Hang clothes in a low-profile, nondestructive way. Suspend them over the bathtub or in a closet. The maid hardly notices my laundry. It's hanging quietly in the bathroom or shuffled among my dry clothes in the closet. Separate the back and front of hanging clothes to speed drying. Some travelers pack inflatable

hangers. Don't hang your clothes out the window—hoteliers find it unsightly, and you might find it has blown away when you return from dinner. Laid-back hotels will let your laundry join theirs on the lines out back or on the rooftop.

Smooth out your wet clothes, button shirts, set collars, and "hand iron" to encourage wrinkle-free drying. If your shirt or dress dries wrinkled, hang it in a steamy bathroom or borrow an iron and ironing board from the hotel (nearly all have loaners). A piece of tape is a good ad hoc lint-brush. In very hot climates, I wash my shirt several times a day, wring it, and put it on damp. It's clean and refreshing, and (sadly) in 15 minutes it's dry.

Go ahead and ask! There's a good chance you can share the clothesline in the B&B's backyard or on the hotel's roof.

Using a Launderette

For a thorough washing, ask your hotel to direct you to the nearest launderette. In Western Europe, nearly every neighborhood has one; in Eastern Europe, launderettes are much less common. It takes about an hour and $10-15 to wash and dry an average size load. (Many hostels have coin-op washers and dryers or heated drying rooms.)

Better launderettes have coin-op soap dispensers, change machines, English instructions, and helpful attendants. Others are completely automated—but many of these have pictogram instructions that usually aren't too hard to parse. Look around for a sign listing the "last wash" time, and stick to it. When it's closing time, an attendant might come by to evict you, or the machines may simply stop operating.

Many of Europe's launderettes are completely unstaffed—it's just you, sparse English instructions, and dirty clothes.

While the exact procedure varies, it usually includes the same steps as you'd encounter at a launderette at home. If you're planning on visiting a launderette, you could pack one or two small detergent boxes, although you can typically buy some at the launderette from an automated dispenser. The soap compartments on most washers have three reservoirs: for pre-wash, the main wash cycle (normally at the top of the washer), and fabric softener. (Don't put your main soap into the pre-wash compartment, or it'll be washed away before its time.)

While you might be able to pay

at the washer itself, it's more likely that you'll have to insert your money at a central unit. Note the number of your machine, then type that number into the central unit and put in your coins (use exact change if possible—some machines don't give change). Sometimes a central unit dispenses tokens, which you then insert in the machine.

Select your cycle, either at the machine itself or at the central unit. Below I've listed some of the cycles you're likely to see. The first number is the temperature in Celsius for the first cycle (pre-wash), the second is the temperature for the second cycle (main wash), and the third is how long the whole thing lasts.

45° / 90° / 55 m	whites (very hot)
45° / 60° / 50 m	colors (hot)
45° / 45° / 40 m	permanent press (warm)
— / 30° / 30 m	nylon (lukewarm)
— / 20° / 25 m	delicates (cold)

Some washing machines have a built-in spin cycle; however, others leave clothes totally soaked. In this case, you'll need to put your wet clothes in a special spin-dry machine (usually called a "centrifuge" or something similar) to wring out excess water before moving them to the dryer.

Drying time is generally available in smaller units (5- or 10-minute increments) rather than as a full cycle. Most machines let you choose the drying temperature: low (cool and slow); medium (warmer but still slow); and high (speedy but shrinky). Because both washers and dryers at

Sample Laundry Instructions

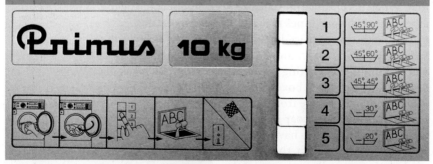

This laundry machine hurdles the language barrier with completely pictographic instructions: Insert your laundry, close the door, select the program, add the soap, and insert coins to start. The five buttons on the right let you select the washing program: The first water temperature (in Celsius) is for the pre-wash cycle, and the second is for the wash cycle. The pictures tell you where to put the soap and softener for each program (notice that the last two skip the pre-wash—no soap needed in compartment A).

launderettes can be unpredictable, hand wash anything that you value dearly.

While waiting for your clothes, use the time to picnic, catch up on postcards and your journal, or chat with other customers. Launderettes throughout the world seem to give people the gift of gab. Many launderettes have Internet access or Wi-Fi (or ask about an Internet café nearby). If you ask attendants sweetly, they might be willing to transfer your clothes to the dryer, allowing you to slip out for some bonus sightseeing. (In these cases, it's appropriate to thank them by offering a small tip.)

Hiring It Out: Truly full-service places, which fold and sometimes even iron your laundry, are easier—just drop it off and come back in the afternoon—but more expensive. Also pricey, but handiest of all: You can hire your hotel to do your laundry.

Regardless of the cost, every time I slip into a fresh pair of pants, I figure it was worth the hassle and expense.

EUROPEAN BATHROOMS

Bathrooms in Europe are nothing to be fearful of. In most cases, they will feel familiar and comfortable. But European bathrooms and plumbing can have their share of quirks. Just keep an open mind, and remember that nothing beats a good bathroom story when you get home.

Your Hotel Bathroom

In Europe, don't expect big bathrooms. Many hotels have tiny facilities that have been retrofitted into the corner of an already modest-size room. Counter space is often limited, and showers can be surprisingly tight, especially if you're a larger person. Be careful bending over to pick up a dropped bar of soap—you might just hit your head on the toilet or sink. In some bathrooms, you may see a mysterious porcelain thing that looks like an oversized bedpan. That's a bidet. Tourists who aren't in the know use them as anything from a launderette to a vomitorium to a watermelon-rind receptacle to a urinal. Locals use them in lieu of a shower to clean the parts of the body that rub together when they walk. Go ahead and give it a try. Just remember the four S's—straddle, squat, soap up, and swish off.

When traveling in Europe, you may need to lower your towel expectations. Like breakfast and people, towels get smaller as you go south. In simple places, bath towels are not replaced every day, so hang them up to dry and reuse. This is also catching on with bigger hotels—even fancy ones—which, in an effort to be eco-friendly, post a sign explaining that they'll replace towels left on the floor, but not those that are hanging to dry. In my experience, pricey hotels rarely stay true to this promise; your towels will probably be replaced no matter where you leave them. On the other end of the spectrum, dorm-style accommodations don't provide towels or soap at all, so you'll have to B.Y.O. Also, most European hotels don't supply washcloths. If a washcloth is part of your bath ritual, pack a quick-drying one along in your suitcase.

Shower Strategies

Americans are notorious (and embarrassing) energy gluttons—wasting hot water and leaving lights on as if electricity were cheap. Who besides us sings in the shower? European energy costs are shocking, so many accommodations try to conserve where they can.

Hot-Water Hiccups: Most of the cold showers Americans take in Europe are cold only because they don't know how to turn the hot water on. You'll find showers and baths of all kinds. The red knob is hot and the blue one is cold—or vice versa. Unusual showers often have clear instructions posted. Study the particular system, and before you shiver, ask the receptionist for help.

There are some very peculiar tricks. For instance, in Italy and Spain, "C" is for *caldo/caliente*—hot. In Croatia, look for the switch with an icon of a hot-water tank (usually next to the room's light switch). The British "dial-a-shower" features an electronic box under the showerhead—turn the dial to select how hot you want the water and to turn on or shut off the flow of water (this is sometimes done with a separate dial or button). If you can't find the switch to turn on the shower, it may be just outside the bathroom.

No matter where you are in Europe, get used to taking shorter showers. Some places, especially modest accommodations, furnish their bathrooms with little-bitty water heaters that are much smaller than the one in your basement. After five minutes, you may find your hot shower turning very cold.

Handheld Showers: In Europe, handheld showers are common. Sometimes the showerhead is sitting

European showers: Each one has its own personality.

loose in a caddy; other times it's mounted low on the tub. Not only do you have to master the art of lathering up with one hand while holding the showerhead in the other, but you also have to keep it aimed at your body or the wall to avoid spraying water all over the bathroom. To avoid flooding the room, you may find it easier to just sit in the tub and shower that way.

Budget-Hotel Showers: Hostels and budget hotels can offer interesting shower experiences. In some places, the line between shower and bathroom is nonexistent, and there's no shower curtain. The water simply slides into a drain in the middle of the bathroom.

A few hostels and budget hotels actually have coin-operated showers. If you run into one of these, it's a good idea to have an extra token handy to avoid that lathered look. A "navy shower," using the water only to soap up and rinse off, is a wonderfully conservative method, and those who follow you will more likely enjoy some warm *Wasser* (although starting and stopping the water doesn't start and stop the meter).

Shower Cords: The cord that dangles over the tub or shower in many hotels is not a clothesline; only pull it if you've fallen and can't get up. (But if the cord hangs outside the tub or shower, it probably controls the light—good luck with this.)

Shared Showers: The cheapest hotels often feature a shared toilet and shower "down the hall." To batlioholics, this sounds terrible. Imagine the congestion in the morning when the entire floor tries to pile into that bathtub! Remember, only Americans "need" a shower every morning. Few Americans stay in these basic hotels; therefore, you've got what amounts to a private bath—down the hall.

Over the years, I've observed that even the simplest places have added lots of private showers. For example, a hotel originally designed with 20 simple rooms sharing two showers may now have been remodeled with private showers in 14 of its rooms. That leaves a more reasonable six rooms rather than 20 to share the two public showers. Those willing to go down the hall for a shower enjoy the same substantial savings with much less inconvenience.

Finding Places to Shower: If you are vagabonding or spending several nights in transit, you can buy a shower in "day hotels" at major train stations and airports, at many

Throughout southern Europe, even the cheapest hotel rooms come with a bidet. Europeans use them to stay clean without a daily shower.

freeway rest stops, and in public baths or swimming pools. Most Mediterranean beaches have free, freshwater showers all the time. I have a theory that after four days without a shower, you don't get any worse, but that's another book.

Toilet Trauma

Every traveler has one or two great toilet stories. Foreign toilets can be traumatic, but they are one of those little things that can make travel so much more interesting than staying at home. If you plan to venture away from the international-style hotels in your Mediterranean travels and become a temporary resident, "going local" may take on a very real meaning.

Squat Toilets: The vast majority of European toilets are similar to our own. But in a few out-of-the-way places, you might find one that consists simply of porcelain footprints and a squat-and-aim hole. If faced with one, remember: Those of us who need a throne to sit on are in the minority. Throughout the world, most humans sit on their haunches and nothing more. Sometimes called "Turkish toilets," these are more commonly found in, well, Turkey.

Flummoxing Flushers: In Europe, you may or may not encounter a familiar flushing mechanism. In older bathrooms, toilets may come with a pull string instead of a handle (generally with the tank affixed to the wall rather than the toilet itself). In modern bathrooms, you may see two buttons on top of the tank—one performs a regular flush, the other (for lighter jobs) conserves water. In Great Britain, you'll likely come across the "pump toilet," with a flushing handle that doesn't kick in unless you push it just right: too hard or too soft, and it won't go. (Be decisive but not ruthless.)

Toilet Paper: Like a spoon or a fork, this is another Western "essential" that many people on our planet do not use. What they use varies. I won't get too graphic, but remember that a billion civilized people on this planet never eat with their left hand. While Europeans do use toilet paper, WCs may not always be well stocked. If you're averse to the occasional drip-dry, carry pocket-size tissue packs (easy to buy in Europe) for WCs sans TP. Some countries, such as Greece and Turkey, have very frail plumbing. If you see a wastebasket adjacent to the toilet

One of Europe's many unforgettable experiences is the rare squat-and-aim toilet.

with used toilet paper in it, that's a sign that the local sewer has a hard time handling TP. (The rule of thumb in those places: Don't put anything in the toilet unless you've eaten it first.)

Paid Toilets: Paying to use a public WC is a European custom that irks many Americans. But isn't it really worth a few coins, considering the cost of water, maintenance, and cleanliness? And you're probably in no state to argue, anyway. Sometimes the toilet is free, but the person in the corner sells sheets of toilet paper. Most common is the tip dish by the entry—the local equivalent of about 50 cents is plenty. Caution: Many attendants leave only bills and too-big coins in the tray to bewilder the full-bladdered tourist. The keepers of Europe's public toilets have earned a reputation for crabbiness. You'd be crabby, too, if you lived under the street in a room full of public toilets. Humor them, understand them, and carry some change so you can leave them a coin or two.

Women in the Men's Room: The female attendants who seem to inhabit Europe's WCs are a popular topic of conversation among Yankee males. Sooner or later you'll be minding your own business at the urinal, and the lady will bring you your change or sweep under your feet. Yes, it is distracting, but you'll just have to get used to it—she has.

Getting comfortable in foreign restrooms takes a little adjusting, but that's travel. When in Rome, do as the Romans do—and before you know it, you'll be Euro-peein'.

Finding a Public Restroom

I once dropped a tour group off in a town for a potty stop, and when I picked them up 20 minutes later, none had found relief. Locating a decent public toilet can be frustrating. But with a few tips, you can sniff out a biffy in a jiffy.

Coin-op Toilets on the Street: Some large cities, such as Paris, London, and Amsterdam, are dotted with coin-operated, telephone-booth-type WCs on street corners. Insert a coin, the door opens, and you have 15 minutes of toilet use accompanied by Sinatra Muzak. When you leave, the entire chamber disinfects itself.

Some cities have free, low-tech public urinals (called *pissoirs*) that offer just enough privacy for men to find relief... sometimes with a view. Munich had outdoor urinals until the 1972 Olympics and then decided to beautify the city by doing away with them. What about the people's needs? There's a law in Munich: Any place serving beer must admit the public (whether or not they're customers) to use the toilets.

LEFT This high-tech public toilet offers a free, private place to do your business.

RIGHT Going local

Restaurants: Any place that serves food or drinks has a restroom. No restaurateur would label his WC so those on the street can see, but you can walk into nearly any restaurant or café, politely and confidently, and find a bathroom. Assume it's somewhere in the back, either upstairs or downstairs. It's easiest in large places that have outdoor seating—waiters will think you're a customer just making a quick trip inside. Some call it rude; I call it survival. If you feel like it, ask permission. Just smile, "Toilet?" I'm rarely turned down. American-type fast-food places are very common and usually have a decent and fairly accessible "public" restroom. Timid people buy a drink they don't want in order to use the bathroom, but that's generally unnecessary (although sometimes the secret bathroom door code is printed only on your receipt).

Even at American chains, be prepared for bathroom culture shock. At a big Starbucks in Bern, Switzerland, I opened the door to find an extremely blue space. It took me a minute to realize that the blue lights made it impossible for junkies to find their veins.

Public Buildings: When nature beckons and there's no restaurant or bar handy, look in train stations, government buildings, libraries, large bookstores, and upper floors of department stores. Parks often have restrooms, sometimes of the gag-a-maggot variety. Never leave a museum without taking advantage of its restrooms—they're free, clean, and decorated with artistic graffiti. Large, classy, old hotel lobbies are as impressive as many palaces you'll pay to see. You can always find a royal retreat here, and plenty of soft TP.

Photography & Sharing Your Trip

If my hotel was on fire and I could grab just one thing as I escaped, it would be my digital camera with its memory card filled with photos. Every year I ask myself whether it's worth the worry and expense of mixing photography with my travels. After I return home and relive my trip through those pictures, the answer is always "Yes!"

Photographs aren't just treasured mementos that spark memories of your journey. They're also the best way to tell others about the places you've been and what you've experienced, whether you share your pictures and thoughts on the fly via social media, or collect them in scrapbooks.

TRAVEL PHOTOGRAPHY

Since I spend four months a year in Europe, I usually prefer to bring a compact point-and-shoot camera to keep things as lightweight as possible. There are trade-offs—smaller cameras have smaller lenses, and the image quality can suffer slightly. But many people find that since they can slip the camera into a pocket, they're more likely to take it everywhere...and use it more. Serious photographers can consider more elaborate digital SLR cameras (with interchangeable lenses and a satisfying, old-fashioned shutter click). These cameras are bulky, but produce beautiful, professional-looking images. If you prefer the portability of a point-and-shoot but like the advanced features of a DSLR, consider a mirrorless interchangeable-lens digital camera. These cameras offer better image quality than point-and-shoots, but aren't as large as DSLRs and allow you to swap out lenses.

You can use a smartphone or tablet to take decent-enough pictures, but to commemorate your dream trip, you'll likely want to take better-quality, higher-megapixel photos with a dedicated camera.

Some people prefer to capture Europe in motion. Pocket-sized video cameras (such as ones from Sony, Panasonic, and Kodak), along with the proliferation of video cameras built into digital cameras and smartphones, make shooting and sharing vacation videos easier than ever.

Accessories and Gadgets

Like many hobbies, photography allows you to spend endless amounts of money on accessories. The following are particularly useful to the traveling photographer. But be careful not to take so much gear on your trip that you become a slave to your gadgets.

Memory: Travel with enough digital memory to cover your entire trip. Memory cards come in different types (Secure Digital is most common, but there's also CompactFlash and Sony's Memory Stick) and different sizes (up to 64 gigabytes). Memory is so cheap now, I'd spring for one of the bigger cards, but buy them at home; they're readily available in Europe but more expensive. You'll need higher-capacity cards if you plan to record lots of video.

For more tips on saving and backing up images—especially on a long trip—see "Managing Images on the Road," later.

Batteries: Some digital cameras come with a battery that can be recharged; others take AA batteries (which the camera will burn through amazingly quickly). Rechargeable or lithium AA batteries last much longer than disposable alkalines and are significantly cheaper in the long run—you can buy a good set of rechargeable nickel-metal hydride (NiMH) batteries and a charger for about $20. Before you buy, make sure the charger will work in Europe (look for the voltage numbers "110V" and "220V"), and take an adapter to plug it in (for details, see "Electronics," page 88). Be aware that you cannot pack loose lithium batteries in your checked luggage—but you can carry spare rechargeable batteries in your carry-on as long as they're sealed inside a plastic zip-lock bag or in their original packaging.

Mini-tripod: Because the flash on my camera gives a harsh image, I prefer to use existing light—which often requires a tripod. A conventional tripod is too large to lug around Europe. A mini-tripod screws into most cameras, sprouts three legs, and holds everything perfectly still for slow shutter speeds, timed exposures, and automatic shutter-release shots. (About five inches high, it looks like a small lunar-landing module; some are flexible enough to wrap around posts.) Those without a mini-tripod can use a tiny beanbag or a sock filled with rice, or get good at balancing their camera on anything solid and adjusting the tilt with the lens cap or strap. If you're planning to use a mini-tripod, master your delayed shutter release button or consider bringing a shutter release cable (if your camera accepts one).

SLR Lenses and Filters: No-frills photographers will stick with the midrange lens that comes with the camera; serious shutterbugs can look into zoom, wide-angle, or image stabilization lenses. If you invest in a zoom lens, get one that covers both ends of the visual range—close ups to long shots. A 24-105 mm lens gives you a great medium-wide angle that zooms to a medium-telephoto. Make sure all your lenses have a haze or UV filter. It's better to bang and smudge up your filter than your actual lens. The only other filter you might use is a polarizer, which eliminates reflections and enhances color separation, but you can lose up to two stops of light with it. Don't use more than one filter at a time, and don't go cheap. You're placing another layer of glass in front of your shooting lens. If the filter is poor, your images will not be as sharp as they should be. Some photographers suggest using a lens shade in daylight; it keeps stray light off the front of the camera to prevent "lens flare" and enhances the color saturation of your images.

Tissue, Cleaner, and Lens Cap: A lens-cleaning tissue and a small bottle of cleaning solution are wise additions (use cleaning solution sparingly and only for greasy spots—too much cleaner can damage your lens). If you have an SLR, protect your lens with a cap that dangles on its string when you're shooting.

TV Adapter Cable: Many cameras come with a cable that allows you to plug directly into a TV set. If you're staying at a hotel in Europe with a modern TV, you can enjoy a big-screen digital slideshow while you're still on the road.

You can take remarkably clear low-light shots—like this, serene twilight image of Moscow's Red Square—with the help of a mini-tripod.

Camera Case: When you're not using your camera or camcorder, keep it in a small, padded case inside your day bag. If you have a DSLR or extra accessories, you may need a dedicated bag. A functional and economical way to tote your gear is in a small nylon stuff bag (the type made for hikers). I steer clear of formal camera bags, which are bulky and attract thieves.

Managing Images on the Road

Even if you have plenty of space on your camera's memory card, it's always wise to back up your images. One year, I took some of the best photos I can remember at Chartres Cathedral in France, when the setting sun brought life to the expressions on the delicately carved faces of the Gothic statues. Afterward, I celebrated with a *salade de gésiers* of bouncy lettuce and chicken innards, washed down with a life-is-good carafe of red house wine. Back at my hotel, as I sorted through my intimate moments with those statues through the viewing screen of my camera, I accidentally erased everything on my memory card. That night, I learned several important lessons: 1) Never cull photos with a wine buzz, and 2) Be vigilant about backing up. You never know what might happen, from leaving your camera on a train to dropping your memory card in a puddle. Here are some tips for dealing with images while you travel.

Be selective. Travelers on an extended trip, who record a lot of video, or are just plain shutter happy, may run out of card space. The easiest solution is to edit your images ruthlessly and often, keeping only the very best shots. (The people who watch your slideshow later will thank you for it.) Get in the habit of doing this periodically, even if space isn't an issue, to avoid bringing home an overwhelming number of photos. If you cull photos and are still short on space, you may need to transfer your photos onto another medium (see tips below), then empty your memory card so you can reuse it.

Dump images onto a laptop or tablet. Since I usually travel with a laptop, I can simply upload my photos to my computer every so often (if your computer lacks a card reader, remember to bring a cable so you can connect your camera to your laptop). For added safety, you can back up photos from your laptop to a high-capacity USB flash drive or upload them to a photo-sharing service such as Flickr or Snapfish.

Use other media. If you want to save or back up photos,

but you're traveling *sans* laptop, you have several options. The Apple camera connection kit makes it easy to download media from your digital camera to an iPad. You can also consider a photo backup device like the HyperDrive Colorspace UDMA, a palm-sized (but pricey) gadget that has a memory-card reader, hard drive, and color screen. If you use a smartphone or tablet to take pictures or videos, a device like MediaShair Hub USB On-the-Go allows you to wirelessly transfer content to an external hard drive.

Consider lower resolution. If you plan to use your photos only for emailing or posting to a website, and if you're certain you won't want to print any of your photos, you can squeeze more images on your memory card by taking photos at a lower resolution. In order to get double the shots on my memory card, I sometimes shoot at the grainier "basic" level rather than the memory-gobbling fine-resolution level. But I've sometimes regretted taking lower-resolution images—such as when I've captured a really great shot, but the resolution is too low to make a large framed print.

Remember the cloud. Apple, Amazon, and Dropbox allow you to store digital content (photos, videos, documents, music, books) in their "clouds" (their networks). With Apple's iCloud, owners of newer iPhones have an automatic image backup system built in. All you have to do is activate the iCloud settings on your phone. Then, whenever you're at a Wi-Fi hotspot, your phone will automatically send your latest pictures to the cloud, which in turn pushes those images to other iCloud-enabled devices (iPad, home computer, etc.) the next time they're connected to the Internet. The iCloud will hold your last 1,000 images and saves new photos for 30 days (so eventually you must edit and permanently save the images you want). With both Apple and Amazon, the first 5 GB of storage is free (about 2,000 photos); with Dropbox the first 2 GB of data is free. Additional storage is available at a price for all three services.

Resources for Travel Photography

Cnet.com, Steves-digicams.com, and **Dpreview.com:** Digital camera reviews

Photosecrets.com and **BBC.com/travel/photography:** Tips on taking good photos

Snapfish, Shutterfly, Picasa, Flickr, and **LiveShare:** Store and share photos

YouTube and **Vimeo:** Store and share video

SlideShare, Powerpoint, and **Prezi:** Online presentation tools for slideshows

iCloud, Amazon Cloud Drive, and **Dropbox:** Cloud storage for digital photos

Tricks for a Good Shot

Most people are limited by their photographic skills, not by their camera. Understand your camera. Devour the manual. Take experimental shots, make notes, and see what happens. If you don't understand f-stops or depth of field, find a photography class or book and learn (for tips on taking better pictures, visit photosecrets.com and bbc.com/travel/photography). Camera stores sell good books on photography in general and travel photography in particular. I shutter to think how many people are underexposed and lacking depth in this field.

Find a creative new angle.

A sharp eye connected to a wild imagination will be your most valuable piece of equipment. Develop a knack for what will look good and be interesting after the trip. The skilled photographer's eye sees striking light, shade, form, lines, patterns, texture, and colors.

Look for a new slant to an old sight. Postcard-type shots are boring. Everyone knows what the Eiffel Tower looks like. Find a unique or different approach to sights that everyone has seen. Shoot the bell tower through the horse's legs, or lay your camera on the floor to shoot the Gothic ceiling.

Capture the personal and intimate details of your trip. Show how you lived, whom you met, and what made each day an adventure (a close-up of a picnic, your favorite taxi driver, or the character you befriended at the launderette).

Vary your perspective. You can shoot close, far, low, high, during the day, and at night. Don't fall into the rut of always centering a shot. Use foregrounds to add color, depth, and interest to landscapes.

The Vatican Museum staircase: Have fun with composition.

Maximize good lighting. Real photographers get single-minded at the "magic hours"—early morning and late afternoon—when the sun is very low, light is rich and diffused, and colors glow. Plan for these times. Grab bright colors. Develop an eye for great lighting; any time of day, you may luck into a perfectly lit scene. Some of my best photos are the result of great lighting, not great subjects.

Get close. Notice details.

Eliminate distractions by zeroing in on your subject. Get so close that you show only one thing. Don't try to show it all in one shot. For any potentially great shot, I try several variations—then delete the ones that don't pan out.

People are the most interesting subjects. It takes nerve to walk up to people and take their picture. It can be difficult, but be nervy. Ask for permission. (If you don't speak the language, point at your camera and ask, "Photo?") Your subject will probably be delighted. Try to show action. A candid is better than a posed shot. Even a "posed candid" shot is better than a posed one. Give your subject something to do. Challenge the kid in the market to juggle oranges. Many photographers take a second shot immediately after the first portrait to capture a looser, warmer subject. The famous war photographer Robert Capa once said, "If your pictures aren't good enough, you're not close enough." My best portraits are so close that the entire head can't fit into the frame.

Buildings, in general, are not interesting. It does not matter if Karl Marx or Beethoven was born there—a house is as dead as its former resident. As travel photographers gain experience, they take more people shots and fewer buildings or general landscapes.

Expose for your subject. Even if your camera is automatic, your subject can turn out to be a silhouette. Get those faces in the sun or (even better) lit from the side.

When shooting a portrait, the sun should be behind you. Have the sunlight hit the subject's face at an angle by making sure it's coming over your right or left shoulder. This creates dramatic highlights and shadows on the subject's face. Avoid shooting outdoor portraits during the lighting "dead

LEFT Vary your perspective—add extra depth with a foreground.

RIGHT Fill the lens with your subject.

The best people shots are up close and well lit, with a soft background.

LEFT Capture the magic with just the right light.

RIGHT Back lighting "puts an edge" on your subject.

zone," between 11 a.m. and 2 p.m. If you have to shoot then, use your camera's flash to fill the shadows that form in the eye sockets, under the nose, and under the chin. High-end cameras have an adjustable power setting on the flash. Use it to get the right ratio of sunlight to fill light.

Don't be afraid to handhold a slow shot. Tripods enable you to take professional shots that could compete with those at the museum gift shop. But most major museums prohibit you from using a tripod or a flash (which ages paintings). Despite these restrictions, you can take good shots by holding your camera as still as possible. If you can lean against a wall, for instance, you become a tripod instead of a bipod. Placing your elbows on a flat surface also helps. Wait until you breathe out to take the picture (when you hold your breath, your body shakes more). Use a self-timer or a shutter release cable, which clicks the shutter more smoothly than your finger can. With these tricks, I get good pictures inside a museum at 1/30 of a second. Many digital cameras use "image stabilization" to help in these situations. (And if you still can't get that perfect shot, go to the gift store. Nearly every important museum has a good selection of top-quality cards and prints at reasonable prices.)

Bracket shots when the lighting is tricky. The best way to get good shots in difficult lighting situations is to "bracket" your shots (take several different pictures of the same scene, slightly varying the exposure settings for each one). You can simply delete the unsuccessful attempts. Automatic cameras usually meter properly up to 8 or 10 seconds, which makes night shots easy, though bracketing may still be necessary.

Once Back Home...

Relive your trip by organizing, editing, improving, and sharing your digital images.

First, come up with a system to keep your photos organized on your computer. You can simply create folders and subfolders, or you can use a more advanced photo-organizing program, such as Google's free Picasa, which also includes editing and sharing features.

It's always smart to look at your pictures and see if you can improve them. While a basic photo-editing program probably came with your camera, serious shutterbugs use Adobe Photoshop Elements (an easy-to-use program for novices) or Adobe Photoshop (for more advanced work). You can't imagine how much better your photos will look until you use this software.

When it comes time to share your images, you have many options, from making prints of your favorite shots to putting them online (see the next section).

SHARING YOUR TRIP

Back in the '70s and '80s, I eagerly shared my travel experiences through slideshows. Even that method was high-tech compared to my earliest travels—on my first trip at age 14, I collected and logged my journey in a file of several hundred numbered postcards, each packed with notes. Those days of slow, static 20th-century methods are now long gone, replaced by a slew of fast, interactive advancements in social media, online programs, and websites.

Social Media

While on the road and back at home, I interact with thousands of readers via my Facebook page. Each night, my favorite bedtime reading is the comments from my followers. It's become a fun way for us to experience Europe together.

With social-networking tools, you can share real-time travel stories by posting quick updates—a simple task

Resources for Trip Sharing

Twitter, Instagram, Facebook, and **Pinterest:** Share image and word snippets of your experiences

WordPress and **Blogger:** Easy-to-use blogging sites

TravelPod and **MapQuest Travel Blogs:** Blogging sites geared toward trip sharing

Picasa, Flickr, SmugMug, and **Instagram:** Share photos

YouTube, Vimeo, and **Vine:** Share videos

MyPublisher: Create high-quality, custom-bound scrapbooks

Postagram and **SnapShot Postcard:** Send postcards via snail mail with pics from your smartphone

PhotoGram: Create and send digital postcards

thanks to Wi-Fi and mobile apps. You can post photos and videos, add descriptions, and receive instant feedback in the form of comments, reposts, and likes. Easy photo uploading makes Facebook ideal for the non-tech-savvy. And many social media applications are compatible; for example, most allow simultaneous posting to Facebook and Instagram.

Twitter lets you share (or tweet) pictures and text tidbits from your mobile device as you travel. The website and mobile app Pinterest, a virtual bulletin board, lets you collect, share, and store pictures and videos by pinning them to various "boards."

With any social media tool, be selective as you update. You want to fascinate, not bore or annoy your friends and family. It's also important not to unwittingly share your whereabouts with strangers or advertise that your home is unguarded, especially when you're traveling. Be sure to check the privacy settings for every application and device you use. Most applications are not automatically set to "private"; you'll have to activate the privacy settings yourself.

Blogs

While social media is optimal for quick updates, blogging is the best option for lengthy storytelling. Maintaining a blog of your travels is the perfect way to document your journey, as well as entertain family and friends with your adventures.

First, decide on a blog host. Popular choices are WordPress and Blogger. Both are free and relatively easy to use, with templates and customization options. You can post text, photos, audio, video, slideshows, links, and more; sync with Facebook and Twitter; set your blog to automatically publish at staggered times; and have multiple people contribute to one blog. For on-the-go access, both blogging platforms have apps that let you post right from your mobile device.

Several travel-oriented websites are geared specifically for trip sharing, offering features such as maps, statistics, and itineraries to document your travels. TravelPod and MapQuest Travel Blogs offer free hosting for blogs and journals, with quick and easy sharing to Facebook and Twitter. You can build your itinerary, chart your route on an interactive map, and add photos, videos, and stories to create a shareable overview of your journey. Mobile apps allow you to update either site on the go, and each also offers the option to print your trip as a book. Other hosts include TripNTale, Mobilytrip, and MyTripJournal.

Sharing via Snail Mail

If you prefer to share your trip the low-tech way—by sending picture postcards and brief "Wish you were here!"-type messages, you'll find that European post offices can be handy and efficient or jam-packed and discouraging, depending on the country. In general, small-town post offices can be less crowded and more user-friendly. If possible, avoid the Italian male...I mean, mail. Service is best north of the Alps.

Don't assume you have to wait in a long line for a few postcard stamps—they're often sold in machines at post offices. Sometimes you can buy them at neighborhood newsstands, gift shops that sell cards, or your hotel's front desk. (Write your postcards before getting stamps—you may be in the next country by the time you're ready to mail them.)

If you need to have something sent from home, have it addressed to you at a hotel you'll arrive at when it does; your hotelier will be happy to hold it for you. Allow 10 days for a letter; to speed things up, try second-day US-Europe services (such as DHL), though figure on four days for delivery to a small town. If you're not staying at a hotel (for instance, if you're camping or caravanning), you can have mail sent to any city's post office, addressed to you in care of "Poste Restante"; for convenience, pick a small town with only one post office and no crowds.

Whichever host you choose, here are some guidelines for creating a memorable blog:

- When posting stories online, think about interactive elements that combine entertaining, insightful text with engaging videos and photos.
- Consider embedding slideshows (a presentation sharing site like SlideShare.net can help) or links to related websites and resources.
- Include amusing tidbits or interesting quotes to spice up your stories.
- If struggling for inspiration, consider implementing a certain theme or ongoing elements like a "picture of the day."

Online Photo and Video Sharing

Photos and videos take you there in a way that words cannot. Multimedia-sharing sites let you unleash your images to friends and family—without holding them captive in a dark room. With any of these trip-sharing possibilities, editing your photos before posting online will improve their impact.

Picasa, Flickr, and **SmugMug:** These tools help you organize and edit your photos online. You can then share your trip pics through Web albums or import them into your

Journaling

The best way to document your trip as you travel is to pick up a pen and put your experiences to paper. Even in my days as a vagabond backpacker, I was a keen and disciplined journal writer. Journaling the old-fashioned way has no limits, word counts, or caps on creativity.

Great travel journals describe both the inner and outer journey—your physical surroundings and sensory experiences as well as your emotions and thoughts at the time. Transcribing intimate details into your journal will allow you to revisit a place time and time again, whether shared with others or kept to yourself.

Be selective in choosing a journal. I prefer a minimalist booklet with empty pages, lightweight yet stiff enough to both protect the pages and give me something solid to write on in the absence of a table. Consider a bound book; spiral notebooks tend to fall apart. I write in black ink or mechanical pencil, allowing my simple words to be the focus. Carry your journal with you so you can write throughout the day—while at a bus stop or waiting for a restaurant meal, for instance. If pressed for time while on the go, keep a pocket notebook handy to jot down brief moments or fleeting thoughts. You can expand on these and add them to your actual journal when you have time.

As you write, avoid guidebook-type data and instead focus on the sentimental effects and imagery of your experiences. You don't have to give a chronological account of your journey. In fact, you probably shouldn't. Consider just sitting somewhere interesting and writing about your surroundings or focusing an entry on a specific topic: strange cultural customs or a touching moment, for instance. Throwing in creative essays will sharpen your ability to observe and understand the culture you visited.

Most importantly, don't write just to write. Ten years from now, you won't feel the need to recall the mediocre meal you grabbed at that café or the quality of the hotel's complimentary breakfast. Leave out the boring stuff. You want to include specific details that define the character of a place as well as your personal response. Throw in sketches, mementos, little paper souvenirs like maps and old tickets—anything that takes you back to that moment. Combining these personal touches with candid accounts and reflective musings will create a travel souvenir you'll forever cherish.

social-networking sites. Some even let you create videos from your photos and upload them straight to YouTube.

Instagram: This app lets you put fun filters on images and share them with friends, creating a river of pictures that documents your travels.

YouTube, Vimeo, and **Vine:** The de facto video-sharing site, YouTube offers high-quality, free video hosting with detailed privacy controls. Vimeo has no bandwidth or time limits, so you can customize your videos and embed them into any website or blog. Vine allows you to upload video or record and edit six-second looping clips to share instantly with your followers.

Your friends will enjoy seeing photos of the different characters you meet.

Scrapbooks and Photo Books

Creating a tangible scrapbook of travel photos and anecdotes allows you to personally share your journey with loved ones at home.

After selecting the best photos from your trip, you can either visit an online publishing service to create a custom book, or you can make a scrapbook the old-fashioned way (print your favorites and put them into an album or book).

Creating a digital scrapbook is simple—a few clicks and personal touches, and you've got your own coffee-table masterpiece. Each year at Rick Steves' Europe, we hold a contest for our tour members to see who's created the best digital scrapbook of their recent trip with us (the top prize is a free tour). For lots of great inspiration for making digital trip scrapbooks, peruse the award-winning entries at ricksteves.com/tours.

Snapfish and Shutterfly are just two of the easy-to-use sites where you can upload, view, organize, and edit photos, then order prints, photo books, cards, posters, and more.

One of my favorite tools is MyPublisher, which lets you create high-quality, custom-bound, professional-looking scrapbooks. Download the site's free photo book application and customize to your heart's desire.

Travel Styles

Embracing new experiences is a lot easier to do if you're well prepared. This chapter addresses the special concerns and interests of solo travelers (including issues specific to women), families, seniors, and travelers with disabilities.

TRAVELING SOLO

I've talked to too many people who put off their travel dreams because they don't want to do it by themselves. If you want to go to Europe but don't have a partner, consider gathering the courage to go it alone. There are plenty of people to meet as you travel, and single travelers often enjoy a montage of fun temporary partners throughout their trip.

Traveling solo has its pros and cons—and for me, the pros far outweigh the cons. When you're on your own, you're independent and in control. You can travel at your own pace, do the things that interest you, eat where and when you like, and splurge where you want to splurge. You don't have to wait for your partner to pack up, and you never need to negotiate where to eat or when to call it a day. You go where you want, when you want, and you can get the heck out of that stuffy museum when all the Monets start to blur together. If ad-libbing, it's easier for one to slip between the cracks than two.

Traveling without a tour, you'll have the locals dancing with you—not for you.

Of course, there are downsides to traveling alone: When you're on your own, you don't have a built-in dining companion. You've got no one to send ahead while you wait in line, help you figure out the bus schedule, or commiserate with when things go awry.

Traveling alone immerses you in Europe.

And traveling by yourself is usually more expensive. With a partner, accommodations cost less because they're shared. Rarely does a double room add up to as much as two singles. If a single room costs $80, a double room will generally be about $100—a savings of $30 per night per person. Other things become cheaper too when you're splitting costs, such as groceries, guidebooks, taxis, storage lockers, and more.

But when you travel with someone else, it's natural to focus on your partner—how you're getting along, whether she meant it when she said she wasn't hungry—and tune out the symphony of sights, sounds, and smells all around you. Traveling on your own allows you to be more present, more open to your surroundings. You'll meet more people—you're seen as more approachable. You're more likely to experience the kindness of strangers.

Solo travel is intensely personal. You can discover more about yourself at the same time you're discovering more about Europe. Traveling on your own is fun, challenging, vivid, and exhilarating. Realizing that you have what it takes to be your own guide is a thrill known only to solo travelers. Your trip is a gift from you to you.

Traveling Alone Without Feeling Lonely

For many people contemplating their first solo trip, their biggest fear is that they'll be lonely. Big cities can be cold and ugly when the only person to talk to is yourself. And being sick and alone in a country where no one knows you is a sad and miserable experience.

Fortunately, combating loneliness in Europe is easy. The continent is full of travelers and natural meeting places, especially in peak season (the built-in camaraderie of other travelers is harder to come by in winter).

Meeting People: You'll run across vaga-buddies every day. If you stay in hostels, you'll have a built-in family (hostels are open to all ages). Or choose small pensions and B&Bs,

Traveling with a Partner

Though I love trekking through Europe by myself, there's nothing like that special lifelong bond that forms between you and the person you've dined with, slept with, and trudged around in the rain with for two weeks straight in a foreign land.

A group of travel buddies defending Caesar's empire atop Hadrian's Wall in Britain

But your choice of travel partner is critical—it can make or break a trip. Traveling with the wrong partner can be like a bad blind date that lasts for weeks. I'd rather do it alone. One summer I went to Europe to dive into as many cultures and adventures as possible. I planned to rest when I got home. My partner wanted to slow life down, get away from it all, relax, and escape the pressures of the business world. Our ideas of acceptable hotels and how much time we wanted to spend eating were quite different. The trip was a near disaster.

Traveling together greatly accelerates a relationship—especially a romantic one. You see each other constantly and make endless decisions. The niceties go out the window. Everything becomes very real; you're in an adventure, a struggle, a hot-air balloon for two. The experiences of years are jammed into weeks. If you haven't traveled with your companion before, consider a trial weekend together before merging dream trips. Any shared trip is a good test of a relationship—often revealing its ultimate course. I'd highly recommend a little premarital travel.

Many people already have their partner—for better or for worse. Couples should take particular care to minimize the stress of traveling together by recognizing each other's need for independence. Too many couples do Europe as a three-legged race, tied together from start to finish. Have an explicit understanding that there's absolutely nothing selfish, dangerous, insulting, or wrong about splitting up occasionally. This is a freedom too few travel partners allow themselves. Doing your own thing for a few hours or days breathes fresh air into your togetherness, making those shared experiences all the more memorable.

where the owners have time to talk with you. At most tourist sights, you'll meet more people in an hour than you would at home in a day. If you're feeling shy, cameras are good icebreakers; offer to take someone's picture with his or her camera.

Take a walking tour of a city (ask at the tourist office). You'll learn about the town and meet other travelers, too. If you're staying in a hostel, check its message board—some hostels arrange group tours.

It's easy to meet people on buses and trains. When you meet locals who speak English, find out what they think—about anything. Take your laundry and a deck of cards to a

launderette and turn solitaire into gin rummy. You'll end up
with a stack of clean clothes and interesting conversations.

Play with kids. Thumb wrestle. Learn how to say "pretty
baby" in the local language. If you play peek-a-boo with a
baby or fold an origami bird for a kid, you'll make friends
with the parents as well as the child.

Try meeting up with other solo travelers through social
media. Like-minded individuals can find one another on
meetup.com, whose worldwide members welcome visitors
to wide-ranging events such as photography walks, happy
hours, and weekend skiing. Interface with your social media
connections to find out if anyone has friends or family in
the destinations that you'll be traveling to, then drop them
a note about your upcoming visit. Also consider joining a
hospitality-exchange network, such as Servas (see page 480),
or Couchsurfing, its more low-key alternative (page 234).

Eating Out: I like the old-fashioned, face-to-face social
media option of just saying to someone you meet, "Would
you like to meet up for dinner?" Some countries have special
meals that are more fun to experience with others. You could
invite someone to join you for, say, a rijsttafel dinner in the
Netherlands, a smorgasbord in Scandinavia, a fondue in
Switzerland, a paella feast in Spain, or a spaghetti feed in an
Italian trattoria. Wondering whom to ask? People with Rick
Steves guidebooks are like an extended family in Europe. My
readers are on the trail of the same travel thrills, and happy
to share in the adventure.

If you're dining alone, consider alternatives to formal
sit-down meals. Try a self-service café, a local-style fast-food
restaurant, or a small ethnic eatery. Visit a supermarket
deli and get a picnic to eat in the square or a park. Get a
slice of pizza from a takeout shop and munch it as you walk,
people-watching and window-shopping. Eat in the members'
kitchen of a hostel; you'll always have companions. Make it a
potluck.

A restaurant feels cheerier
at noon than at night, and
a maître d' is more likely to
seat a solo diner (especially a
woman) at a favorable table
for lunch than for dinner.
If you like company, eat
in places so crowded and
popular that you have to share
a table, or ask other single

Please book
+ big smile =
plenty of friends

travelers if they'd like to join you. Assume that many couples would enjoy a third party at their dinner table to stoke the conversation.

If you eat alone, be busy. Use the time to learn more of the language. Practice your verbal skills with the waiter or waitress (when I asked a French waiter if he had kids, he proudly showed me a picture of his twin girls). Read a guidebook, a novel, or the *International New York Times*. Do trip planning, draw in your journal, or scrawl a few postcards to the folks back home.

An afternoon at a café is a great way to get some writing done; for the cost of a beverage and a snack, you'll be granted more peace and privacy than at a public fountain or other open space.

Evenings: Experience the magic of European cities at night. Go for a walk along well-lit streets. With gelato in hand, enjoy the parade of people, busy shops, and illuminated monuments. You'll invariably feel a sense of companionship when lots of people are around. Take advantage of the wealth of evening entertainment: concerts, movies, puppet shows, and folk dancing. Some cities offer tours after dark. You can see Paris by night on a river cruise.

During the evening, visit a café with Wi-Fi and send travel news to your friends and family. You'll find friendly answers in your inbox the next time you have the opportunity to get online.

If you like to stay in at night, get a room with a balcony overlooking a square. You'll have a front-row seat to the best show in town. Read novels set in the country you're visiting. Learn to treasure solitude. Go early to bed, be early to rise. Shop at a lively morning market for fresh rolls and join the locals for coffee.

Tips for Solo Women Travelers

Thanks to my female staffers and their friends for assembling their top tips for women.

Every year, thousands of women, young and old, travel to Europe on their own. You can, too, by using the same good judgment you use at home. Begin with caution and figure out as you travel what feels right to you. Create conditions that are likely to turn out in your favor, and you'll have a safer, smoother, more enjoyable trip.

Theft and harassment are two big concerns for women. If you've traveled alone in America, you're more than prepared for Europe. In America, theft and harassment are especially scary because of their connection with assault. In Europe, you'll rarely, if ever, hear of violence. Theft is past tense (as in, "Where did my wallet go?"). As for experiencing harassment, you're far more likely to think, "I'm going to ditch this guy ASAP" than, "This guy is going to hurt me."

Stay in hostels to swap tales and advice with other adventurous women.

Here are some tips for safe and pleasant travels:

Use street smarts. Be self-reliant and well prepared, so that you don't need to depend on someone unless you want to—carry cash, a map, a guidebook, and a phrase book. Walk purposefully with your head up; look like you know where you're going. If you get lost in an unfriendly neighborhood, be savvy about whom you ask for help; seek out another woman or a family, or go into a store or restaurant to ask for directions or to study your map.

When you use cash machines, withdraw cash during the day on a busy street, not at night when it's dark with too few people around.

Be proactive about public transportation. Before you leave a city, consider visiting the train or bus station you're going to leave from, so you'll know where it is, how long it takes to reach it, if it feels safe, and what services it has. Reconfirm your departure time. If you're leaving late at night and the train station is sketchy, hang out in your hotel's lounge until you need to head for the station. Cafés are also a safe and productive place to wait.

When taking the train, avoid sleeping in empty compartments. You're safer sharing a compartment with a family. If available, rent a *couchette* for overnight trains. For a small surcharge, you'll stay with like-minded roommates in a compartment you can lock, in a car monitored by an attendant. You'll wake reasonably rested with your belongings intact.

It's possible to ask for a female roommate on overnight trains. (You'll have better luck if the train isn't crowded.) On some trains, couchettes are divided by gender (unless your party takes the whole compartment). Certain countries, such as Spain, are better about accommodating requests than others. On France's night trains, a one-bed compartment closest to the conductor is set aside for women, but it's the most expensive type of accommodation. In general, ask what your options are, make the request to bunk with other women, and hope for the best—but don't count on it.

Unless you're fluent in the language, accept the fact that you won't always know what's going on. Though it might seem worrisome, there's a reason why the Greek bus driver drops you off in the middle of nowhere. It's a transfer point, and another bus will come along in a few

minutes. You'll often discover that the locals are looking out for you.

Learn how to deal with European men. In small towns, men are often more likely to speak English than women. If you never talk to men, you could miss out on a chance to learn about the country. So, by all means, talk to men. Just choose the man and choose the setting.

In northern Europe, you won't draw any more attention from men than you do in America. In southern Europe, particularly in Italy, you'll get more attention than you're used to, but it's usually in the form of the "long look"—nothing you can't handle. But be aware that in the Mediterranean world, when you smile and look a man in the eyes, it's often considered an invitation. Wear dark sunglasses and you can stare all you want.

Dress modestly to minimize attention from men. Take your cue from what local women wear. For young women, even wearing a shapeless sack and sensible shoes may not ward off unwelcome advances. Try to stay with a group when exploring, and avoid walking alone at night, particularly in unlit areas with few people around. Don't be overly polite if you're bothered by someone; it's important to create boundaries to protect yourself. Use facial expressions, body language, and a loud firm voice to fend off any unwanted attention. If a man comes too close, say "no" firmly and loudly in the local language. That's usually all it takes.

If you feel like you're being followed or hassled, trust your instincts. Don't worry about overreacting or seeming foolish. Start screaming and acting crazy if the situation warrants it. Or head to the nearest hotel and chat up the person behind the desk until your would-be admirer moves on. Ask the hotelier to call you a cab to take you to your own hotel, hostel, or B&B.

Wear a real or fake wedding ring, and carry a picture of a real or fake husband. There's no need to tell men that you're

Books for the Woman Traveling Alone

Practical Advice

Gutsy Women: Travel Tips and Wisdom for the Road (Marybeth Bond, 2007): Funny, instructive, and inspiring ideas for solo travelers

A Journey of One's Own: Uncommon Advice for the Independent Woman Traveler (Thalia Zepatos, 2003): Recommendations on everything from trekking in Nepal to handling sexual harassment

Safety and Security for Women Who Travel (Sheila Swan and Peter Laufer, 2004): Tips on self-protection

Traveling Solo: Advice and Ideas for More than 250 Great Vacations (Eleanor Berman, 2008): Advice on specific destinations for women

Wanderlust and Lipstick: The Essential Guide for Women Traveling Solo (Beth Whitman, 2009): Empowering tales for nervous newbies from experienced women travelers

Tales from the Road

The Best Women's Travel Writing: True Stories from Around the World (Levinia Spalding, ed., published annually): An anthology of funny and inspirational tales

Expat: Women's True Tales of Life Abroad (Christina Henry de Tessan, ed., 2002): A collection of stories about how the reality of life abroad matches up to the fantasy

Go Your Own Way: Women Travel the World Solo (Faith Conlon and others, eds., 2007): Cultural revelations mixed with advice for the female traveler

A Woman's Europe: True Stories (Mary-lu Ili Dand, ed., 2004): Europe from a totally female point of view

Humor

Sand in My Bra and Other Misadventures: Funny Women Write from the Road (Jennifer L. Leo, ed., 2003): Travel shenanigans

The Unsavvy Traveler: Women's Comic Tales of Catastrophe (Rosemary Caperton, Anne Mathews, and Lucie Ocenas, eds., 2001): A collection of humorous and cathartic misadventures

traveling alone, or whether you're actually married or single. Lie unhesitatingly. You're traveling with your husband. He's waiting for you at the hotel. He's a professional wrestler who retired from the sport for psychological reasons.

If you're arranging to meet a guy, choose a public place. Tell him you're staying at a hostel: You have a 10 p.m. curfew and 29 roommates. Better yet, bring a couple of your roommates along to meet him. After the introductions, let everyone know where you're going and when you'll return.

By using common sense, making good decisions, and above all else, having confidence in yourself and your ability to travel on your own, you'll be rewarded with rich experiences—and great stories to tell your friends.

FAMILY TRAVEL

When parents tell me they're going to Europe and ask me where to take their kids, I'm tempted to answer, "to Grandma and Grandpa's on your way to the airport."

It's easy to make the case against taking the kids along. A European vacation with kids in tow is much more about playgrounds and petting zoos than about museums and churches. And traveling with kids is expensive. Out of exhaustion and frustration, you may opt for pricey conveniences like taxis and the first restaurant you find with a kid-friendly menu. Two adults with kids spend twice as much to experience about half the magic of Europe per day than they might without.

But if you can afford it and don't mind accomplishing less as adult sightseers, traveling with your children can be great family fun, creating piles of lifelong memories. Moreover, it's great parenting, as it helps get kids comfortable with the wider world.

With kids, you'll live more like a European and less like a tourist. Your children become your ambassadors, opening doors to new experiences and relationships. Your child will be your ticket to countless conversations. Some of your best travel memories may be of your son floating a wooden boat alongside Parisian *garçons* in the great pond at Luxembourg Garden, or of your daughter kicking a soccer ball with kids at a park in Madrid. Let them race their new Italian friends around Siena's main square, the Campo, while you sip your Campari.

European families, like their American counterparts, enjoy traveling. You'll find kids' menus, hotel playrooms, and kids-go-crazy zones at freeway rest stops all over Europe. Traveling with an infant or toddler

Leave the Kids at Home?

If you and your partner have 20 days for a family vacation, are on a budget, and are dreaming of adult time in Europe, consider this plan: Go for 10 days without the kids and really enjoy Europe as adults rather than parents—the savings from leaving them at home will easily cover top-notch child care. Then fly home and spend the other 10 days with your kids—camping, at a water park, or just playing at home. (If your kids have an adult relative somewhere else in the US whom they'd enjoy getting to know better, offer to fly him or her to your house to kid-sit while you're gone.)

can be challenging, but parents with a babe-in-arms will generally be offered a seat on crowded buses and sometimes allowed to go to the front of the line at museums.

The key to a successful European family vacation is to slow down and to temper expectations. Don't overdo it. Tackle one or two key sights each day, mix in a healthy dose of pure fun, and take extended breaks when needed. If done right, you'll take home happy memories to share for a lifetime.

Conquering peaks on your rental mountain bike (as my proud son Andy did here in Switzerland) and connecting with local families can leave your own family with the most important souvenirs—lifelong memories of times shared together.

At What Age Can I Take the Kids?

My children are young adults now, but after taking them to Europe every year for their first 20 years, it's fun to think back about our European trips during different stages of their childhood. When they were grade-schoolers, our trips were consumed with basic survival issues, such as eating, sleeping, and occupying their attention. By the time they entered their teens, the big challenge became making our trips educational and fun.

Some parents won't take their kids abroad until they are old enough to truly enjoy the trip. My rule of thumb is that children should be able to stand a day of walking, be ready to eat what's in front of them, and be comfortable sleeping in strange beds. They should be able to carry their own day-packs with some clothes, a journal, and a couple of toys. I've found that a child is ready for an international trip at about the same age they're ready for a long day at Disneyland.

Grade-school kids are often the easiest travelers, provided you schedule some kid-friendly activities every day. They're happiest staying in rural places with swimming pools and grassy fields to run around in.

High-schoolers feel that summer break is a vacation they've earned. If this European trip is not *their* trip, you become the enemy. Make it their trip, too, by asking for their help—give each child who's old enough a location to research. Kids can quickly get excited about a vacation if they're involved in the planning stages. Consider your teen's suggestions and make real concessions. A day of shopping or at the beach might be more fun than another ruined abbey.

Prepping Your Kids

Before you leave home, get your kids enthusiastic about what they'll be seeing in Europe. Encourage them to learn about the countries, cities, sights, and people they'll be visiting. Look online for articles, photos, and video clips to pique their curiosity.

Read books, both fiction and nonfiction, set in the place you're going, such as *The Diary of Anne Frank* for Amsterdam or *The Thief Lord* for Venice. For younger kids, check out M. Sasek's delightfully illustrated *This Is* series on various European destinations (*This is Venice*, *This is Edinburgh*, and so on). Watch movies, such as *The Sound of Music* for Salzburg, *The Red Balloon* for Paris, or *The Secret of Roan Inish* for Ireland. Your hometown library can be a great resource for age-appropriate books and movies.

Get a jump on foreign phrases. Type out the top 20 or so and put them on the fridge for everyone to learn. Get the *10 Minutes a Day* language book for your destination, which comes with preprinted sticky word labels that your kids will enjoy plastering around the house.

Try to relate your children's hobbies or favorite games to the place you're visiting (draw pictures of the Eiffel Tower, play dominoes saying the numbers in Italian). Give your kids the chance to try out foreign specialties in advance by eating at ethnic restaurants, or get a cookbook and make meals together at home. Many US cities host celebrations of different cultures—look for festivals held by local communities of Greeks, Italians, Hungarians, or whatever group might be vibrant in your town or relevant to your travels.

Travel Documents for Kids

You'll need the proper documents—even babies need passports. For a child of any age, take an official copy of his or her birth certificate, along with a photocopy of his or her passport. These documents are especially important if you have a different last name than your child. For parents of adopted children, it's a good idea to bring their adoption decree as well. Keep these documents separate from your passports, as they'll be a huge help if you end up needing to get a replacement passport for your child.

If you're traveling with a child who isn't yours (say, a niece or grandson), bring along a signed, notarized document from the parent(s) to prove to authorities that you have permission to take the child on a trip. Even a single parent traveling with children has to demonstrate that the other parent has given approval. Specifically, the letter should grant permission for the accompanying adult to travel internationally with the child. Include your name, the name of the child, the dates of your trip, destination countries, and the name, address, and phone number of the parent(s) at home.

You may want to bring extra passport photos with you. Since infants and toddlers change so quickly, carry pictures that were taken for the passport, as well as ones taken close to your departure date.

Most parents hold onto their kids' passports, but if you have older children who'll be out on their own, you could get them a money belt or neck pouch for carrying their cash and ID.

For younger kids, drape a lanyard around their necks with emergency contact information, or consider ordering custom dog tags (see dogtagsonline.com). Another option is an ID Inside wristband, with a hidden pocket that holds a disposable ID card (id-inside.com). You can easily switch out the ID card, updating your hotel name and contact info as you go. When you're out sightseeing, if you suddenly realize you left your child's ID at the hotel and you need to improvise, you can write your phone number on a piece of paper to tuck into your child's pocket or inside the bottom of her shoe. In a pinch, you could write your contact number—gently—on your child's arm with a pen or magic marker.

Resources for Family Travel

Ciaobambino.com: Mom-written, destination-focused advice

Travelforkids.com: Fun things to do with kids worldwide

Travelswithbaby.com: Baby and toddler travel tips

Minitime.com: Trip-planning resources for travel with babies and kids

Deliciousbaby.com: Tips on how to make travel with kids fun

Reading

Cadogan Guides' *Take the Kids* and Fodor's *Around* series

Family on the Loose: The Art of Traveling with Kids (Bill Richards and E. Ashley Steel, 2012)

Take Your Kids to Europe (Cynthia Harriman, 2007)

Travels with Baby: The Ultimate Guide for Planning Travel with Your Baby, Toddler, and Preschooler (Shelly Rivoli, 2014)

What to Bring

The amount and type of gear you need depends on the age of your child. Since a baby on the road requires a lot of equipment, the key to happiness is a rental car or a long stay in one place. If you're visiting friends or family, they may be able to borrow a car seat, stroller, and travel crib so you won't have to pack it. If you have older kids, let them know they'll be hauling their own luggage through airports and down cobblestone streets. Pack as light as you can, and think hard about what you'll really need (based on your experience taking trips near home).

With little kids, I found having the best gear was more important than packing light. We would rent a car because taking everyone and everything on trains would have been miserable. Once the kids were older, however, I insisted on being mobile, and we had a family ethic whereby everyone carried their own stuff...so they'd better pack light. (This book's packing tips apply to teens just as much as to adults.)

Infants and Toddlers: It's helpful to have a stroller and a baby carrier. Umbrella strollers can easily navigate cobblestones—but spend a little extra on a solidly built one that can take the bumps, such as Peg Pérego (pegperego.com) or Maclaren (maclarenbaby.com), and make sure it has a basket underneath for storing overflow items. Carriers are great for keeping your hands free and easier than a stroller on subways and buses.

Prepare to tote more than a tot. A combo purse/diaper bag with shoulder straps is ideal. You can always stow it in your stroller's basket, but be on guard: Purse snatchers target parents (especially while busy, as when changing diapers).

For years, we packed along a travel crib and it worked great—providing a safe and familiar zone for our toddler even in iffy hotel rooms. One travel model—the PeaPod—is a lightweight pop-up tent that fits in a small carry bag (kidco.com). BabyBjörn's travel crib is super light-weight and collapses down to the size of a suitcase (babybjorn.com). Portable playpens tend to be too heavy and clunky for travel. At a minimum, bring your child's

sleep sack or blanket, which can be a comforting reminder of home once you are on the road.

Drivers should be aware that child-safety-seat rules are different in Europe. Check out the requirements before you bring a car seat from home. You may want to consider buying a safety seat in Europe or arranging one through the car-rental company (usually the most expensive option). If you bring your own seat, remember to pack a car-seat clip in case you need to secure the car seat to the shoulder-strap seat belt. In addition to being required safety equipment while driving, a car seat can be a stress-saver when traveling by plane, train, or bus. Although it may seem like a bulky carry-on, a car seat is more comfortable for your child to sit in than a seat designed for an adult, and is a familiar place for a nap. Kids are used to car seats and know how to behave in them.

If your child drinks formula, do some research on the manufacturer's website—your usual formula may be available in Europe, but under a different name. Before you fly away, be sure you've packed acetaminophen (easy-dissolving tabs are best), diaper rash cream, a thermometer, and any special medications your baby may need (keeping in mind the air travel rules for liquids).

Older Kids: Technology can make the difference between a dream trip and a nightmare. A tablet or portable gaming device can fill long hours traveling between destinations and soak up time when dinner drags on. Load up on kid-friendly apps, ebooks, movies, and TV shows before you leave. Get a Y-jack so two kids can listen over headphones. There's nothing like a favorite show to help calm your kids before bedtime. Consider giving each of your kids their own digital camera so they can take pictures and make movies from their own perspective. (Back home, encourage older kids to use software to organize and edit photos and video clips.)

Toys: Don't pack too many toys; these take up lots of suitcase space (though it's kind to let a child choose a small toy, such as a stuffed animal, to bring from home for comfort). You can easily buy toys and sports equipment in Europe. The cheapest toy selection is often in large department stores. For the athletic child, a soccer ball guarantees hours of amusement with newfound friends on foreign turf. When you're in France or Italy, consider purchasing a set of bocce balls (called *boules* or *pétanque* in France); this popular form of outdoor bowling is played on public squares. (The balls are heavy, though, so only get them if you're staying in one place or traveling by car.)

A trip to the local toy store can be a fun outing. For quiet time in the hotel room, buy a set of Legos, coloring books, stickers, dolls, or other toys, which can be excitingly different from those found in the US.

Flying with Kids

Deciding whether to buy a separate plane ticket for your child under two years of age is a matter of what you can endure in the air: That cute gurgling baby might become the airborne Antichrist as soon as the seat-belt light goes off. If you elect to keep your child on your lap, you'll still pay the tax on the ticket cost for an international flight. The child doesn't get a seat, but many airlines have baby perks for moms and dads who request them in advance—roomier bulkhead seats, bassinets, and baby meals.

After age two, kids are required to have their own seat. Some airlines offer a children's fare, which is typically 85-90 percent of the adult fare. Other airlines simply charge the full fare—a major financial owie. Children's fares may not appear when booking tickets online, so it's worth calling a travel agent to see if they can get you a discount. Generally, from age 12 on, kids pay full fare.

As soon as you buy your plane tickets, immediately grab seat assignments so your family has a better chance of being seated together. Inquire about food service on your flight; most international flights still offer a complimentary meal, but be prepared to bring snacks for your crew.

Pick flights with few connections; if your child is able to sleep on planes, a red-eye can work well. Decide if you want to sit near the aisle or window. A window seat gives your active child only one escape route, plus the added entertainment of the window. However, a toddler who needs frequent diaper changes and sits quietly may be more comfortable by the aisle.

Watching the in-flight movie can help pass a few hours in the air.

At the airport, you'll have to clear security with your brood. It's easier for you (and everyone else in line) if you're ready before entering the security line: Take off jackets, untie shoes (children under 12 can leave their shoes on), pull out liquids. All your carry-ons, including children's bags, toys, and blankets, must go through the X-ray machine—explain beforehand that even "teddy" has to ride the conveyor belt. Children who can walk without assistance will be expected to go through the metal detector separately from their parents; babies can be carried through. You may encounter a full-body scanner; you and your children can opt out of this type of screening, but you may be subjected to a thorough pat-down instead.

Some airlines are phasing out early boarding for families or have resorted to charging for the privilege. If your carrier doesn't offer early boarding, approach the gate agent at a quiet moment and ask if he or she can help. Tire out your tykes before boarding the plane. Some airports have play spaces—if you can't find one, feel free to take over an empty gate area. If you fly at night, consider having your child skip that afternoon's nap. While you're waiting to board, get your kids up and moving as much as possible. Finally, when you're on the plane and it's time for sleep, follow normal bedtime routines. Change your child into pajamas, tuck her in with a blanket, and read a story or two.

Be prepared. Have at least one change of clothes and plenty of diapers and wipes for your baby or toddler (Mom and Dad might want to have an extra shirt, just in case). Make sure your electronics are fully charged before boarding. You'll also want to pack headphones for everything, including tablets and portable gaming devices (others on the plane will thank you). For younger kids, have lots of activities and surprises, such as books, stickers, paper, washable markers, activity books, and Mad Libs.

Jet lag can be kiddie purgatory. If you can tolerate some—OK, maybe a lot of—crankiness on the first day, keep young children awake until a reasonable bedtime. After Junior passes out from exhaustion, hopefully the whole family will sleep through the night and wake up when the locals do. Take it easy at the beginning (maybe even starting with a rural destination), allowing a couple of low-impact days to get over jet lag (for more on dealing with jet lag, see page 383).

Family-Friendly Lodging

Instead of picking up and moving every few days, some families prefer settling down in an apartment or house, using it as their home base, then side-tripping to nearby destinations. Self-catering flats rented by the week, such as *gîtes* in France

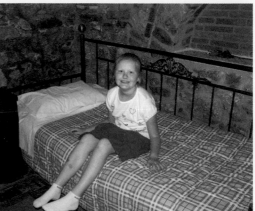

and villas in Italy, give a family a home on the road. To cut costs, try home-sharing services that let you swap houses with a European family. Not only is it cheaper, but you get to spend time together cooking, watching movies, and just hanging out. It's a cultural experience just to see European TV together. But be aware that European standards on televised sex and nudity are much more relaxed than in the US; you might stumble on some uncensored movies, or even unbridled porn, right next to the Nickelodeon channel.

In very tight European hotel rooms, you might have to stow your kids in the closet...or, better yet, ask for an extra bed.

If you're traveling with older kids, consider hostels. Families can hostel very cheaply (especially in high-priced Scandinavia). Family membership cards are inexpensive, and there's no age limit. Hostels typically have members' kitchens where the family can cook and eat for the price of groceries. Some hostels offer family rooms with enough beds for all of you; these are also likely to offer a range of activities designed for kids.

If your kids love camping, rent a camper van or small RV. Kids and campgrounds—with swings, slides, and plenty of friends—mix wonderfully. Suddenly your family and the Spanish kids over at the next tent are best amigos.

Most hotels, especially those catering to business travelers, have large family rooms. London's big, budget chain hotels allow two kids to sleep for free in their rooms. Bonus: They'll sometimes have a swimming pool. Some European chains, such as KinderHotels, appeal to families by providing playrooms, baby equipment, and professional babysitters.

In some countries, you may need to know the necessary phrases to communicate your needs. If you're a family of four and your children are young, request a triple room plus a small extra child's bed. Traveling with teenagers, you may need two rooms: a double (one big bed) and a twin (a room with two single beds). In much of Europe, a "double" bed is actually two twins put together. These can easily be separated.

Be careful about staying in small hotels or B&Bs with a baby. If your child wakes up in the middle of the night, you're going to wake up everybody else. Some B&Bs won't take children, or impose an age limit (such as no kids under 8); ask before booking.

Choosing lodging close to your daytime activities is smart if your little traveler needs to return for a nap or supplies. Having two adjoining rooms can be better for dealing with sleep issues: One jet-lagged person won't keep everyone else up, and napping will be easier. Request quiet rooms away from the street and bar downstairs. If your child is used to sleeping in his or her own space and you're all in one room, ask for one with a partition, large closet, or other area in which you can separate your child when it's bedtime (baby can even sleep in the bathroom).

If you have young children, childproof the room immediately on arrival. A roll of masking tape makes quick work of electrical outlets. Place anything breakable up out of reach. (I find the top of a freestanding dresser works great as a kid-free zone.) Proprietors are generally helpful to considerate and undemanding parents.

With a toddler, budget extra to get a bath in your room—a practical need and a fun diversion. Some European showers have a 6-inch-tall "drain extension" and a high lip to create a kid-friendly bathing puddle.

For more information on the types of accommodations mentioned above, see the Sleeping chapter.

Feeding Kids on the Road

Start the day with a good breakfast (at hotels, kids sometimes eat free). But even with a big breakfast, don't expect them to power through to a late lunch. A short snack break will help in the long run. Make sure to pack along or buy high-quality food as often as possible—a real sandwich, pasta, or yogurt.

Buying bread, cheese, fruit, and drinks in the morning means you can picnic anytime, anywhere. Foreign grocery stores are an adventure for kids, so bring them along and

Find the most scenic perch for your picnic.

let them help shop. In each country, grocery stores have different kinds of kids' treats, some of which may end up being a real hit—sparking both a country-specific passion and great memories. Another fun (and cheap) option is to get takeout food, such as bratwurst, pizza by the slice, crêpes, or sandwiches, from a street stand. You can eat your meals on a square, at a park, or on the top deck of a tour bus.

Since many restaurants don't have high chairs, you might have to do a little juggling at mealtime.

Sample gelato, croissants, or chocolate every day (gelato should be twice a day)—whatever is a "specialty" treat of the country you're in. It's a great way to get off your feet and take a break.

At home, you may try to avoid bribes, but the promise of a treat can make a huge difference to everyone's cooperation when you're out and about—and don't have space for a "time out."

An occasional Big Mac or Whopper between all the bratwurst and kraut helps keep the family happy. You'll get your food relatively quickly, and you'll find kid-friendly food, such as hamburgers, chicken nuggets, and fries. (And, at European fast-food joints, parents can often enjoy their own treat of a beer.)

Eating at European restaurants is a social event, but it can get stressful, since service is much slower than at home. Dinner can easily take two hours, so bring something to occupy the kids while lingering. Skip the white-tablecloth places and hit self-service cafeterias, relaxed cafés, or bars (kids are welcome, though sometimes restricted to the restaurant section or courtyard area). Eat by 7 p.m. to miss the adult crowd. Don't expect high chairs to be available; use your stroller in a pinch.

In restaurants (or anywhere), if your infant is making a disruptive fuss, apologetically say the local word for "teeth" (*dientes* in Spanish, *dents* in French, *denti* in Italian, *Zähne* in German), and annoyed people will become sympathetic.

If you crave a leisurely, peaceful evening out, splurge on a babysitter. Hotels often can get sitters, usually from professional agencies. The service is expensive but worth it. With older kids, we enjoyed an adult break in a nicer, romantic restaurant by giving our teenagers enough money for dinner at a diner and turning them loose for the evening. It was an adventure for them, a welcome break for all involved, and we all shared our stories back at the hotel before bedtime.

Kid-Friendly Sightseeing

Review the day's plan at breakfast with the family. Let your kids make some decisions: choosing lunch spots or deciding which stores to visit. Turn your kid into your personal tour guide and navigator. If you use my guidebooks, deputize your child to lead you on my self-guided walks and museum tours.

Since a trip is a splurge for the parents, the kids should enjoy a larger allowance, too. Provide ample money and ask your kids to buy their own treats, *gelati,* postcards, and trinkets within that daily budget. Expect older kids to carry and use the currency. If you don't want your younger child to carry cash, you can be the "banker" and keep a tally of expenses.

Before buying sightseeing passes for your family, consider how many of the covered attractions will be top choices for your kids. It's not worth setting an exhausting whirlwind pace to race to every attraction just to make the pass pay for itself. Instead, make a short list of the places you and your kids really want to see, and calculate whether a pass makes sense; if not, buy individual admissions. And remember that some museums are free for kids under a certain age.

Make getting somewhere as much fun as the destination. Kids love subway maps, train schedules, and plotting routes. The Paris Métro is especially diverting as many stations have boards that light up the route when you press the button for your destination. Even the automated ticket kiosks are entertaining. Allow time for all of this, rather than just rushing onto a subway train or bus. After a teaching run, let your child lead the family on subway journeys—kids love the challenge. An added perk: Train rides are free for infants and toddlers (and sometimes even for school-age children).

Boat and bus tours can also be a hit. Your kids might not care about the Crown Jewels, but they may go nuts riding the double-decker bus getting there. Boats are also memorable, such as a ride on a Venetian vaporetto or a glide down Amsterdam's canals.

Try a guided walking tour. Some parents are leery of group tours because they're afraid their kids will be the most disruptive

What's more fun than a museum or the Eiffel Tower?

members. But your kids will listen to a guide more than they will listen to you. Being in a group of adults can tone down even the wildest child.

Hands-on tours, from cheesemaking to chocolate factories, keep kids engaged. Go to sports or cultural events, but don't insist on staying for the entire event.

European parks provide a wonderland of fun, including puppet shows, pony rides, merry-go-rounds, small zoos, or playgrounds. One of my favorite places to mix kid business with pleasure is Luxembourg Garden in Paris. They have cafés and people-watching for parents, and a play area full of imaginative slides, swings, jungle gyms, and chess games for kids. You'll also find a merry-go-round, pony rides, toy rental sailboats in the main pond, and *guignols* (French marionette shows).

Hands-on activities, such as this candlemaking demonstration, bring museums to life for kids.

Copenhagen's Tivoli Gardens is like a Hans Christian Andersen fairy tale, with games, marching bands, shows, and rides ranging from vintage cars to a Ferris wheel that resembles a clock to roller coasters. Petzi's World, based on a popular Danish cartoon bear, offers a cuddly array of rides and activities.

Kids need plenty of exercise. Allow time for stops at playgrounds or parks. Many cities have public swimming pools, and bigger cities also have recreation centers or water parks (check out Paris' Aquaboulevard). For family adventures and fun memories, rent bikes, paddle boats, or rowboats. Local tourist offices can help you dig up these treats.

On days when your troupe will need lots of staying power, don't wear them out with too much walking. It's worth taking a taxi to the Louvre to conserve leg power for getting to the *Mona Lisa*. At least every other day, take an extended break. Return to your hotel or apartment after lunch for two hours for napping, reading, or listening to music. What you lose in sightseeing time, you will gain in energy levels.

European amusement parks—such as Denmark's Legoland—are fun for kids of all ages.

Consider visiting an amusement park as an end-of-trip reward—the promise of Legoland in Denmark,

The Steves Kids Vote on Britain's Best and Worst

Imagine being a teenager forced to spend a big part of your summer vacation with robo-tourist Rick Steves (alias Dad). Jackie and Andy did that a while ago. What were the highlights? Here are the results of the post-trip interview:

Best City: Blackpool—England's white-knuckle ride capital! The Big One (one of the world's fastest and highest roller coasters) is still the best. A tip: Avoid the old wooden-framed rides. They're too jerky for parents.

Best Nature Experience: Horseback riding through the Cotswolds with a guide who'll teach you to trot. Wear long pants. One hour is plenty.

Types of Tours: Open-deck bus tours are good for picnic lunches with a moving view. At museums, audioguide tours are nice because you can pick and choose what you want to learn about.

Worst Food: The "black pudding" that so many B&B people want you to try for breakfast...It's a gooey sausage made of curdled blood.

Best New Food: Chocolate-covered digestive biscuits and vinegar on chips (that's British for "French fries").

Most Boring Tour: The Beatles tour in Liverpool: Most kids couldn't care less about where Paul McCartney went to grade school or a place called Strawberry Fields.

Funniest Activity: The Bizarre Bath walking tour is two hours of jokes and not a bit of history. It's irreverent and dirty—but in a way that parents think is OK for kids.

Best Activities: Leisure (LEZH-ur) Centres in almost every town have good swimming pools.

Best Theater: Shakespeare's Globe in London. First tour the theater to learn about how and why it was built like the original from 1600. Then buy cheap "groundling" tickets to see the actual play right up front, with your elbows on the stage. The actors involve the audience...especially the groundlings.

Most Interesting Demonstrations: The precision slate-splitting demonstration at the slate mines in North Wales. The medieval knight at the Tower of London who explained his armor and then demonstrated medieval sword fighting tactics—nearly killing his squire.

Blackpool in England, or Disneyland Paris can keep your kids motoring through the more mundane attractions. Europe's open-air folk museums are a bonanza for families; it's worth a detour if your itinerary takes you near one (see page 294).

Big-Sight Survival with Kids

Europe is rich with amazing museums, churches, and art. But unlike you, kids may not appreciate the magnificence of a Michelangelo statue or the significance of an ancient temple frieze. Still, there are ways to liven up big sights. And whenever possible, go early or book ahead for big sights to avoid long lines (see my crowd-beating tips on page 280).

Audioguides keep kids engaged and entertained at museums and on bus tours.

At Notre-Dame Cathedral, re-enact hunchback Quasimodo's stunt and climb the tower. Kids love being on such a lofty perch, face-to-face with a gargoyle. Using the ArtStart computers in London's National Gallery, kids can enter their interests (cats, naval battles, and so on) and print out a tailor-made tour map for free.

Museum audioguides are great for older children. My kids liked them because they could pick and choose what they wanted to learn about. Bigger sights often have audioguides tailored to the interests of school-age children. For younger children, hit the gift shop first so they can buy postcards and have a scavenger hunt to find the pictured artwork. When boredom sets in, try "I spy" games or have them count how many babies or dogs they can spot in all the paintings in the room. Ask at the information desk for activity packets designed for children; you'll find these especially at museums in Great Britain.

Seek out kid-friendly museums. London's Natural History Museum offers a wonderful world of dinosaurs, volcanoes, meteors, and creepy-crawlies. There are no "do not touch" signs at Florence's two Leonardo da Vinci museums, where kids can use their own energy to power modern re-creations of Leonardo's inventions. If you choose your destination carefully, everyone can enjoy, or at least tolerate, a museum visit.

Precautionary Measures

Even if you have the most well-behaved kids in the world, things happen: Kids wander off, or they get separated from

you in a crowd. Whenever
you're traveling with children
in an unfamiliar place, it's
good to have a go-to procedure in place in case something happens. Be sure to give
each child a business card
from your hotel so they have
local contact information (for
identification your kids can
carry, see page 427).

When using public transportation, make sure everyone
knows the final stop, and have a backup plan for what to do
if you lose each other (for example, plan to meet at your final
stop or reconvene at your hotel).

In a crowded situation, having a unique family noise (a
whistle or call, such as a "woo-woop" sound) enables you to
easily get each other's attention. Consider buying walkie-
talkies in Europe to help you relax when the kids roam
(don't bring walkie-talkies from home, as ours use a different
bandwidth and are illegal in Europe). If your kids don't have
their own phones, you can purchase a cheap pay-as-you-go
mobile phone in Europe (explained on page 254); this can
also be helpful in case of emergencies.

Europe is not the United States of Litigation. Europeans
love children, but their sense of childproofing public spaces
is vastly different from ours. You may find a footbridge across
a raging river has child-sized gaps between the railings.
Windows in fourth-floor hotel rooms may be easy to open
and unscreened. The hot water may scald you in about 30
seconds. Pay attention.

Reflecting and Connecting

Help your kids collect and process their observations. Buy
a journal at your first stop, and it becomes a fun souvenir in
itself. Kids like cool books—pay for a nice one. The journal
is important, and it should feel that way. Encourage kids
to record more than just a trip log: Collect feelings, smells,
tastes, reactions to cultural differences, and so on. Grade-
school kids enjoy pasting in ticket stubs or drawing pictures
of things they've seen (for more on journaling, see page 414).

It can be hard for kids to hang around grown-ups all
day, so help your kids connect with other children. In hot
climates, kids gravitate toward the squares (in cities and
villages alike) when the temperature begins to cool in the

late afternoon, often staying until late in the evening. Take your children to the European nightspots to observe—if not actually make— the scene (such as the rollerbladers at the Trocadéro in Paris or the crowd at Rome's Trevi Fountain).

Just a few phrases spoken by your kids will open many doors. Make a point of teaching them "thank you," "hello," and "good-bye" in the country's language. You'll find nearly everyone speaks English, but small phrases out of the mouths of babes will melt the cool of surly museum guards or harried shop clerks.

Older kids will want to keep in touch with friends at home and European pals they meet on their trip. If they're bringing their smartphones, smart use of Wi-Fi and apps such as Google Talk, FaceTime, or Skype makes staying connected easy and affordable. Otherwise, consider buying an international data plan so they don't run up huge roaming charges (for more on using smartphones in Europe, see page 242).

Journaling trip experiences is fun for kids—and lets them create a personalized souvenir.

During the trip, your kids may complain about being parted from their friends or having to visit yet another museum. But don't lose heart—sometimes the payoff comes years down the road. Your child may surprise you one day by mentioning a painting in Madrid's Prado or recalling a fact about Rome's Colosseum. Besides building memories, your investment in a trip now is a down payment on developing a true citizen of the world.

SAVVY SENIORS

More people than ever are hocking their rockers and buying plane tickets. Many senior adventurers are proclaiming, "Age matters only if you're a cheese." Travel is their fountain of youth. I'm not a senior—yet—so I polled my readers, asking seniors to share their advice (ricksteves.com/travel-forum). Thanks to the many who responded, here's a summary of top tips from seniors who believe it's never too late to have a happy childhood.

When to Go: If you're retired and can travel whenever you want, it's smart to aim for shoulder season (April through mid-June, or September and October). This allows you to avoid the most exhausting things about European travel: crowds and the heat of summer.

Travel Insurance: Seniors pay more for travel insurance—but are also more likely to need it. Find out exactly whether and how your medical insurance works overseas. (Medicare is not valid outside the US except in very limited circumstances; check your supplemental insurance coverage for exclusions.) Pre-existing conditions are a problem, especially if you are over 70, but some plans will waive those exclusions. When considering additional travel insurance, pay close attention to evacuation insurance, which covers the substantial expense of getting you to adequate medical care in case of an emergency—especially if you are too ill to fly commercially. For more on travel insurance options, see page 67.

Packing: Packing light is especially important for seniors—when you pack light, you're younger. To lighten your load, take fewer clothing items and do laundry more often. Fit it all in a roll-aboard suitcase—don't try to haul a big bag. Figure out ways to smoothly carry your luggage, so you're not wrestling with several bulky items. For example, if you bring a second bag, make it a small one that stacks neatly (or even attaches) on top of your wheeled bag.

Carry an extra pair of eyeglasses if you wear them, and bring along a magnifying glass if it'll help you read detailed maps and small-print schedules. A small notebook is handy for jotting down facts and reminders, such as your hotel-room number or Metro stop. Doing so will lessen your anxiety about forgetting these details, keeping your mind clear and uncluttered.

Medications and Health: It's best to take a full supply of any medications with you, and leave them in their original containers. Finding a pharmacy and filling a prescription in Europe isn't necessarily difficult, but it can

LEFT Their fountain of youth is Europe!

RIGHT Seniors can travel as footloose and fancy-free as their teenaged grandkids be time-consuming. Plus, nonprescription medications (such as vitamins or supplements) may not be available abroad in the same form you're used to. Pharmacists overseas are often unfamiliar with American brand names, so you may have to use the generic name instead (for example, atorvastatin instead of Lipitor). Before you leave, ask your doctor for a list of the precise generic names of your medications, and the names of equivalent medications. For more on getting medical help in Europe, see page 391.

If you wear hearing aids, be sure to bring spare batteries—it can be difficult to find a specific size in Europe. If your mobility is limited, see "Travelers with Disabilities," later, for tips and resources.

Flying: If you're not flying direct, check your bag—because if you have to transfer to a connecting flight at a huge, busy airport, your carry-on bag will become a lug-around drag. If you're a slow walker, request a wheelchair or an electric cart when you book your seat so you can easily make any connecting flights. Since cramped legroom can be a concern for seniors, book early to reserve aisle seats (or splurge on roomier "economy plus," or first class). Stay hydrated during long flights, and take short walks hourly to minimize the slight chance of getting a blood clot.

Accommodations: If stairs are a problem, request a ground-floor room. Think about the pros and cons of where you sleep: If you stay near the train station at the edge of town, you'll minimize carrying your bag on arrival; on the other hand, staying in the city center gives you a convenient place to take a break between sights (and you can take a taxi on arrival to reduce lugging your bags). No matter where you stay, ask about your accommodation's accessibility quirks before you book—find out whether it's at the top of a steep hill, has an elevator or stairs to upper floors, and so on.

Getting Around: Subways involve a lot of walking and stairs (and are a pain with luggage). Consider using city buses or taxis instead, and when out and about with your luggage, take a taxi. If you're renting a car, be warned that some countries and some car-rental companies have an upper age limit—to avoid unpleasant surprises, mention your age when you

reserve (for details, see the Driving & Navigating chapter).

Senior Discounts. Just showing your gray hair or passport can snag you a discount at many sights, and even some events such as concerts. (The British call discounts "concessions"; look also for "pensioner's rates.") Always ask about discounts, even if you don't see posted information about one—you may be surprised.

Pilgrims of all ages hike from France to Santiago de Compostela in northwest Spain.

But note that at some sights, US citizens aren't eligible for senior discounts.

Seniors can get deals on point-to-point rail tickets in Austria, Belgium, Great Britain, Finland, France, Germany, Italy, Spain, and Norway (including the Eurostar train between Britain and France/Belgium). Qualifying ages range from 60 to 67 years old. To get rail discounts in most countries—including Austria, Britain, Germany, Italy, and Spain, and a second tier of discounts in France—you must purchase a senior card at a local train station (valid for a year, but can be worthwhile even on a short trip if you take several train rides during your stay). Most rail passes don't offer senior discounts, but passes for Britain and France (as well as the Balkans) do give seniors a break on first class passes.

Sightseeing: Many museums have elevators, and even if these are freight elevators not open to the public, the staff might bend the rules for older travelers. Take advantage of the benches in museums; sit down frequently to enjoy the art and rest your feet. Go late in the day for fewer crowds and cooler temperatures. Many museums offer loaner wheelchairs. Take bus tours (usually two hours long) for a painless overview of the highlights. Boat tours—of the harbor, river, lake, or fjord—are a pleasure. Hire an English-speaking cabbie to take you on a tour of a city or region (if it's hot, spring for an air-conditioned taxi). Or participate in the life of local seniors, such as joining a tea dance at a senior center. If you're traveling with others but need a rest break, set up a rendezvous point. Some find that one day of active sightseeing needs to be followed by a quiet day to recharge the batteries. For easy sightseeing, grab a table at a sidewalk café for a drink and people-watching.

Educational and Volunteer Opportunities: For a more meaningful cross-cultural experience, consider going on an educational tour such as those run by Road Scholar (formerly

Elderhostel), which offers study programs around the world designed for those over 55 (one to four weeks, call or check online for a free catalog, roadscholar.org, tel. 800-454-5768). For ideas on volunteer programs, see page 480.

Long-Term Trips: Becoming a temporary part of the community can be particularly rewarding. Settle down and stay a while, doing side-trips if you choose. You can rent a house or apartment, or go a more affordable route and swap houses for a few weeks with someone in an area you're interested in (for more on apartments and home exchanges, see the Sleeping chapter). If you're considering retiring abroad, two good resources are the *Living Abroad* series (Moon Travel Guides), which offers a country-by-country look at the challenges and rewards of life overseas, and expatexchange. com, where you'll find tips and resources for expatriates.

More Tips: The AARP (American Association of Retired People) provides an extensive library of travel-related articles and advice for seniors at travel.aarp.org, including destination guides, budget travel recommendations, and an interactive trip finder. The AARP also offers info on retiring abroad.

TRAVELERS WITH DISABILITIES

The creaky, cobblestoned Old World has long had a reputation for poor accessibility. It's the very charm of Europe—old, well-preserved, diverse, and different from home—that often adds to the barriers. But Europe has made some impressive advances toward opening its doors to everyone, including travelers with limited mobility.

I'm inspired by the fact that, wherever I go in Europe, I see locals with disabilities. The days of "hiding disability" are over: On the streets, in the museums, in the restaurants, and on the trains, you'll see people using wheelchairs, scooters, walkers, and canes to get around. If people with disabilities can live rich and full lives in Europe, then travelers with disabilities can certainly have an enjoyable and worthwhile vacation there, too.

Anyone with adventure in their soul can take advantage of all Europe has to offer. Levels of personal mobility vary tremendously from person to person. You need to consider your own situation very thoughtfully in choosing which attractions to visit, which hotels to sleep in, which restaurants to dine at…and which things you might want to avoid.

Tips for Travelers with Disabilities

John Sage owns Sage Traveling, which plans and books accessible travel to Europe. John has taken his wheelchair to more than 90 European cities and has run into his share of challenges during his travels—but he also says that the obstacles can almost always be overcome. Here I've included excerpts, in John's own words, from his top tips for traveling in Europe.

Plan ahead, plan ahead, plan ahead. I hear all the time that "Venice is not wheelchair accessible" or "Paris has poor accessibility." While there are certainly some accessibility challenges, the truth is that the more research you do, the more accessible your trip will be. Avoiding bridges in Venice and hills in Paris is entirely possible. Did you know that Herculaneum's ruins are nearly identical to Pompeii's, but are wheelchair-friendly? And that cruise passengers with disabilities don't have to take the "donkey path" up the cliffs when visiting the Greek island of Santorini? Your vacation doesn't need to be a struggle—do your homework and your trip can be filled with fully accessible hotel accommodations, accessible routes between accessible tourist attractions, and wonderful accessible travel experiences.

Book hotels far in advance. It is almost always cheaper to book your accessible hotel accommodation far in advance. Many hotels in European city centers have only one or two accessible rooms. The best ones get booked very early. For travel in the summer, make your reservations in December.

Carefully plan your route. If you know what you're getting into before you arrive in Europe, you'll have a much easier time on your trip. There'll likely be numerous ways to get to the tourist attractions you're so eager to see. Some routes will have wheelchair ramps, smooth pavement, and flat terrain; others may have steep hills, bothersome (and even dangerous) cobblestones, and flights of stairs. Research the accessibility of sidewalks, bus routes, subway stations, and the location of accessible building entrances before your trip. Check for accessibility information in the online visitors guides for your destinations—but be aware that not all guides will offer this type of information.

Stay in the most accessible parts of town. This is one of the hardest parts of planning your trip. You may have found a great accessible hotel, but what will you find when you walk/roll out the front door? Are there hills and stairs in all directions? Will you have to roll over cobblestones? Are there accessible restaurants nearby? It's crucial to research

Breaking Down Barriers

Thanks to Susan Sygall and the staff from Mobility International USA (miusa.org) for this section.

More and more people with disabilities are heading to Europe, and more of us are looking for the Back Door routes. We, like so many of our nondisabled peers, want to get off the tourist track and experience the real France, Italy, or Portugal. Yes, that includes those of us who use wheelchairs. I've been traveling the "Rick Steves way" since about 1973–and here are some of my best tips.

I use a lightweight manual wheelchair with pop-off tires. I take a backpack that fits on the back of my chair and store my daypack underneath my chair in a net bag. Since I usually travel alone, if I can't carry it myself, I don't take it. I keep a bungee cord with me for the times I can't get my chair into a car and need to strap it in the trunk or when I need to secure it on a train. I

Susan Sygall, in Italy's Cinque Terre

always insist on keeping my own wheelchair up to the airline gate, where I then check it at the gate. When I have a connecting flight, I again insist that I use my own chair.

Bathrooms are often a hassle, so I have learned to use creative ways to transfer into narrow spaces. To be blatantly honest, when there are no accessible bathrooms in sight, I have found ways to pee discreetly just about anywhere (outside the Eiffel Tower or on a glacier in a national park). You gotta do what you gotta do, and hopefully one day the access will improve, but in the meantime there is a world out there to be discovered. Bring along an extra pair of pants and a great sense of humor.

I always try to learn some of the language of the country I'm in, because it cuts through the barriers when people stare at you (and they will) and also comes in handy when you need assistance in going up a curb or a flight of steps. Don't accept other people's notions of what is possible–I have climbed Masada in Israel and made it to the top of the Acropolis in Greece.

the hotel's neighborhood. You can use Google Maps' Street View to get the lay of the land, then email the hotel with your questions.

Figure out accessible public transportation options.
When choosing a hotel, don't forget to factor in the price of transportation. If you have to pay for a taxi to get to accessible restaurants, accessible shopping, and the tourist attractions, that hotel "deal" you found won't feel like such a good deal after all. In cities such as London, Paris, and Barcelona, stay near an accessible bus stop. In Berlin, Istanbul, and

If a museum lacks elevators for visitors, be sure to ask about freight elevators. Almost all have them somewhere, and that can be your ticket to seeing a world-class treasure.

I always get information about disability groups in the places I am going. See the resources listed on page 448 for a number of helpful organizations. They have the best access information, and many times they'll become your new traveling partners and friends. They can show you the best spots. Remember that you are part of a global family of people with disabilities.

It can be useful to contact tourism offices and local transit providers before you travel. Some even include information on their websites about accessibility for people with disabilities.

Each person with a disability has unique needs and interests. Many of my friends use power wheelchairs, are blind or deaf, or have other disabilities—they all have their own travel tips. People who have difficulty walking long distances might want to think about taking a lightweight wheelchair or borrowing one when needed—many places in Europe have mobility scooter rentals, and bike shops are excellent for tire repairs if you get a flat. Whether you travel alone, with friends, or with an assistant, you're in for a great adventure.

Don't confuse being flexible and having a positive attitude with settling for less than your rights. I expect equal access and constantly let people know about the possibility of providing access through ramps or other modifications. When I believe my rights have been violated, I do whatever is necessary to remedy the situation, so that the next traveler or disabled person in that country won't have the same frustrations.

Keep in mind that accessibility can mean different things in different countries. In some countries, people rely more on human-support systems than on physical or technological solutions. People may tell you their building is accessible because they're willing to lift you and your wheelchair over the steps at the entryway. Be open to trying new ways of doing things, but also ask questions to make sure you are comfortable with the access provided.

Hopefully more books will include accessibility information, which will allow everyone to see Europe "through the Back Door." Let's work toward making that door accessible so we can all be there together.

Venice, stay near an accessible metro, tram, or boat stop. In Florence, Cambridge, and Edinburgh, stay right in the middle of town so you can walk/roll everywhere.

Rely on the experience of other handicapped travelers. You're certainly not the first person with disabilities to visit Europe. Find out what accessibility challenges other travelers encountered and how they got around them. Check various travel forums (tripadvisor.com, cruisecritic.com, and ricksteves.com, for example) to find previous travelers' experiences—just be sure the information is up-to-date. You

Resources for Travelers with Disabilities

Information

Miusa.org: Mobility International USA's website with work, study, teaching, volunteer, exchange, and research opportunities for people with disabilities; database of disability organizations; and publications including *Survival Strategies for Going Abroad: A Guide for People with Disabilities;* also oversees the National Clearinghouse on Disability and Exchange, which publishes *AWAY (A World Awaits You)*

Sath.org: Society for Accessible Travel and Hospitality's online travel magazine and travel advice

MossResourcenet.org/travel.htm: Clearinghouse of accessible travel resources

EmergingHorizons.com: Travel info for wheelchair users and slow walkers

Flying-with-disability.org: Advice for traveling by air

OverseasInterpreting.com: Help for deaf individuals looking for sign-language interpreting in Britain and the European Union

Ada.gov: US Department of Justice help for those who feel they have been discriminated against under the Americans with Disabilities Act, such as not being allowed on a US tour company's trip to Europe due to a disability (tel. 800-514-0301 or 800-541-0383 TTY)

Dot.gov/airconsumer: US Department of Transportation's Aviation Consumer Protection Division (ACPD); handles complaints regarding the Air Carrier Access Act (disability hotline: tel. 800-778-4838 or 800-455-9880 TTY)

Tours

SageTraveling.com: European trip-planning for people with disabilities, with guides for hire and accessibility reviews of European destinations

DisabilityTravel.com: Accessible Journeys website offering wheelchair-accessible trips to Britain, France, and the Netherlands

FlyingWheelsTravel.com: Escorted cruises and tours to Great Britain, Germany, and Venice and the Mediterranean, plus custom itineraries

Reading

Sites Unseen: Traveling the World Without Sight: Blind author Wendy David's personal experiences (available in Braille and other formats from National Braille Press, nbp.org)

Rick Steves' Easy Access Europe: Guidebook for travelers with mobility challenges, with dated but still helpful information for London, Paris, Bruges, Amsterdam, Haarlem, and the Rhine River (out of print but available free online at ricksteves.com/easyaccess)

can also seek out a travel agent who specializes in accessible travel. See the resources sidebar, above.

Have a backup plan. Even on the most perfectly planned accessible vacation, something can go wrong. If it does, how will you deal with it? If you prepare for all the possible issues, travel with someone who can help you during your trip, and remain flexible, unexpected events won't turn into potential trip-ruining problems. What will you do if a part on your wheelchair breaks? If a train strike occurs in Italy, how will you get from Florence to Rome? With backup plans (such as packing vital spare parts for your wheelchair), you won't have to put your vacation on hold.

If you opt for a tour... A company that specializes in accessibility will lead you on the flattest, smoothest, shortest tour routes.

Before you take a tour or hire a guide, ask these questions:

- Is the tour guide a licensed professional? How much training has the guide received and what tests have they passed?
- What route will the guide use? Does it involve curbs, steps, steep hills, or cobblestones? Where are the accessible bathrooms located? Will the guide physically assist you if needed (i.e., push a manual wheelchair)?
- Is this a private tour, or will you be with other travelers? Are you expected to keep up with able-bodied tour members?
- How many people with disabilities have they guided in the past year? (If it's been a long time, the guide may not be aware of the latest regulations or updates regarding accessibility.)

Enjoy your trip! You've done as much planning as you can. You've relied on the experience of other travelers with disabilities, and you're prepared for what lies ahead. Now it's time to enjoy your trip. Majestic cities, beautiful art and architecture, fascinating history, exquisite food, and wonderful experiences await you.

Bus Tours & Cruises

This book is all about mastering individual, self-directed travel. But while I advocate independent travel, I'm not against organized travel. Far from it—for more than 30 years, I've been organizing tours, taking thousands of travelers to Europe's best destinations. For many people, a bus tour or cruise is the best way to scratch their travel itch. Having someone else navigate for you, arrange where you'll sleep, and make the decisions takes the stress and work out of travel. Whether you join a bus tour or sign up for a cruise, a good organized tour can create plenty of memorable experiences.

Tours can also be the most economical way to see Europe: Large tour companies book thousands of rooms and meals year-round, and with their tremendous economic clout, they can get prices that no individual tourist can match. Similarly, the base price of mainstream cruises beats independent travel by a mile. For people looking to travel comfortably and cheaply, bus tours and cruises can be a good option, especially if you use the tips in this chapter to help you travel smartly—and through the Back Door.

TOURING EUROPE BY BUS

Taking a bus tour can be a good choice if your European vacation time is limited—but you'll want to carefully consider your options before signing up. Offerings range from luxury we-handle-everything bus tours for smaller groups to comfortable midrange tours (like mine, which are also for smaller groups) to low-end, pack-'em-in, big-bus operators for large groups. In nearly all cases, the bus itself will be luxurious and fairly new, with a high, quiet ride, comfy seats, air-conditioning, and a toilet on board.

Choosing a Tour

Would you rather travel with a group of 48 or 28? Change hotels every night or enjoy two-night stays? There are plenty of variables to consider when comparing the fully guided tours offered by travel companies.

And there are hundreds to choose from. The predictable biggies range from high-end expensive (Abercrombie & Kent, Maupintour, and Tauck) to low-end cheap (Cosmos, Globus, Insight, and Trafalgar).

No matter which tour company you go with, it's important to do your research. Start by browsing your options online, asking friends, or talking to a travel agent for advice. In general, a typical big-bus tour has a professional, multilingual European guide and 40 to 50 travelers. The tour company is probably very big, booking rooms by the thousands; it often even owns the hotels it uses. Tour hotels fit American standards—large, not too personal, and offering mass-produced comfort, good plumbing, and double rooms, though often on the outskirts of town. Keep in mind that the goal of most tour companies is to fill every seat on that bus. On the biggest tours, groups are treated as an entity: a mob to be fed, shown around, profited from, and moved out. If money is saved, it can be at the cost of real experience.

When considering tours, remember that some of the best sellers are those that promise more sightseeing than is reasonable in a given amount of time. No tour can give you more than 24 hours in a day or seven days in a week. What a wide-ranging "blitz" tour can do is give you more hours on

Comparing Bus Tours

When you're selecting a bus tour, the cost you're quoted isn't the only factor to consider. Investigate how many people you'll be traveling with as well as what extras you'll be expected to cover. Most tour companies include customer feedback on their websites—look around and see what previous tour members have to say. When comparing prices, remember that airfare is not included. The chart below illustrates what to expect from a range of tour companies.

	High End	Rick Steves	Low End
Price per day	$350-950	$200-350	$150-300
Group Size	20-40	24-28	40-50
Meals	50-75% included	50% included	35-50% included
Sightseeing	All included	All included	Most cost extra
Tips	All except guide's tip included	All included	None included

the bus. Choose carefully among the itineraries available. Do you really want a series of one-night stands? Bus drivers call tours with ridiculous itineraries "pajama tours." You're in the bus from 8 a.m. until after dark, so why even get dressed?

The cheapest bus tours are impossibly cheap. There's literally no profit in their retail price. They can give you bus transportation and hotels for about what the tourist-off-the-street would pay for just the hotels alone. But there's a catch: These tours tend to charge extra for sightseeing, and make money by taking you to attractions and shops from which they receive kickbacks. However, savvy travelers on a tight budget can actually get the last laugh on these tours by thinking of them as a tailored bus pass with hotels tossed in. Skip out of the shopping, don't buy any of the optional tours, equip yourself with a guidebook, and do your own sightseeing every day. Just apply the skills of independent travel to the efficient, economical trip shell that these kinds of organized coach tours provide.

Many who take an organized bus tour could have managed fine on their own.

Having learned long ago what doesn't work when it comes to bus tours, I've made it a priority to give people taking my Rick Steves tours the best possible experience at a midrange price. I keep my groups small (24-28 travelers), stay at least two nights in most locations (at centrally located hotels), and visit the important sights while also seeking out authentic Back Door experiences. I offer a variety of itineraries—Europe-wide, regional, and city tours—and a variety of tour styles—fully guided tours, family-oriented tours, winter tours, and My Way tours, which let you set the sightseeing itinerary (we provide the transportation, hotels, and escort).

The standard European guide does the leading...and you do the following.

Here's my advice for choosing a bus tour and getting the most value for your money:
Go with the smallest possible group. A small group can sightsee, dine, and sleep at places that mainstream groups can only dream of. The bigger the group, the more you're cut off from Europe's charms. When 50 tourists drop into a "cozy" pub, any coziness is trampled.

A good stop for a guide is one with great freeway accessibility and bus parking; where guides and drivers are buttered up with free coffee and cakes (or even free meals); where they speak English and accept credit cards; and where 50 people can go to the bathroom at the same time. *Arrivederci, Roma.*

Avoid one-night stands. Frequent one-night stops can really wear you out. To help you feel settled for a good night's rest, the best tours let you sleep for two nights in the same hotel whenever possible.

Ask where your hotels are located. Hotels set in the historic heart of a city, within walking distance of major sights, make for a far more memorable trip. If the tour brochure says you'll be sleeping in the "Florence area," that could be halfway to Bologna– and you'll spend half your sightseeing time on transportation to and from the city center. Get explicit locations before you decide.

Look for authentic eating experiences. Pick a tour that offers a generous taste of the best local dishes. A common complaint among travelers is that tour meals don't match the country's cuisine. Avoid a tour that offers too many forgettable buffets in big, impersonal hotel restaurants.

Find out about the guide. The quality of your guide can make or break your travel experience. Ask if your tour guide is salaried, or paid through tips and/or commission. Guides from most tour companies make the bulk of their income from tips and merchant kickbacks. A salaried guide can focus on creating memorable travel experiences for you—not on selling you an optional sightseeing or shopping excursion.

Take a close look at what's included—and what's not. Many budget tours expect you to shell out additional cash during your trip to cover "optional" sightseeing, charging as much as $50 or $100 extra for each excursion.

Confirm which sights you'll see. Don't assume that every famous museum or castle will be included in your itinerary. Some companies going to Milan, for example, skip over Leonardo da Vinci's *Last Supper* because it's expensive to visit and its mandatory reservation system is inconvenient.

Some tours deliver exactly what they promise.

Ask if the tour price is locked in once you make your deposit. Some tour outfits reserve the right to increase the price after you've signed up (depending on how

many travelers sign up and/or currency fluctuations). Choose a company that guarantees the price will not change.

Read the fine print. What are the company's policies regarding cancellations, refunds, and trip interruption/cancellation insurance?

Bus Tour Self-Defense

Once you're on board with a bus tour, you'll be part of a group dynamic. But that doesn't mean you can't have any control over your trip. Here are some suggestions to help make sure the good times roll for you while you're on the road:

Be informed. Tour guides call the dreaded tourist with a guidebook an "informed passenger." But a guidebook is your key to travel freedom. Get maps and tourist information from your (or another) hotel desk or a tourist information office. If your tour hotel is located outside the city center, ask the person behind the desk how to catch public transportation downtown. Taxis are always a possibility, and, with three or four people sharing, they're affordable. Team up with others on your tour to explore on your own.

Remember that it's your trip. Don't let bus tour priorities keep you from what you've traveled all the way to Europe to see. In Amsterdam, some tour companies instruct their guides to spend time in the diamond-polishing place instead of the Van Gogh Museum (no kickbacks on Van Gogh). Skip out if you like. Your guide may warn you that you'll get lost and the bus won't wait. Keep your independence (and your hotel address in your money belt).

Discriminate among optional excursions. Some tour companies include certain activities in the price

Questions to Ask Tour Companies

Nail down the price:
- What does the price include? (How many nights and days? How many meals? Admission to sights?)
- If currency values fluctuate, is the tour price adjusted up or down?
- If the tour doesn't fill up, will the price increase?
- Do singles pay a supplement? Can singles save by sharing rooms?
- Are optional excursions offered? Daily? Average cost?
- Will the guide and driver expect to be tipped? Approximately how much?
- Is trip interruption/cancellation insurance included?
- Are there any other costs?

Run a reality check on your dream trip:
- How many travelers will be on the tour?
- Roughly what is the average age and singles-to-couples ratio?
- Are children allowed? What is the minimum age?
- Are hotels located downtown, or are they on the outskirts?
- Does each room have a private bathroom? Air-conditioning?
- How many meals are eaten at the hotel?
- What is your policy if you have to cancel a tour?
- What are your refund policies before and during the tour?
- How can I see tour evaluations from past customers?

(such as half-day city sightseeing tours), then offer one or two optional special excursions or evening activities for an additional cost. While you are capable of doing plenty on your own, optional excursions can be a decent value—espe cially when you factor in the value of your time. But don't feel pressured to join. Your guide promotes excursions because he or she profits from them. Compare prices by asking your hotelier or checking a guidebook for the going rate for a gondola ride, Seine River cruise, or whatever.

You'll find that some options are a better value through your tour than from the hotel concierge, but others aren't worth the time or money. While illuminated night tours of Rome and Paris are marvelous, I'd skip most "nights on the town." On the worst kind of big-bus-tour evening, several bus tours come together for an evening of "local color." Three hundred tourists drinking watered-down sangria and watching flamenco dancing on stage to the rhythm of their digital camera bleeps is big-bus tourism at its worst.

If you shop...shop around. Many people make their European holiday one long shopping spree. This suits your guide and the local tourist industry just fine. Guides are quick to say, "If you haven't bought a Rolex, you haven't really been to Switzerland," or, "You can't say you've experienced Florence if you haven't bargained for and bought a leather coat."

Don't necessarily reject your guide's shopping tips; just keep in mind that the prices you see often include a 10-20 percent kickback. Never swallow the line, "This is a special price available only to your tour, but you must buy now."

Keep your guide happy. Independent-type tourists tend to threaten guides. Maintain your independence without alienating your guide. Don't insist on individual attention when the guide is hounded by countless others. Wait for a quiet moment to ask for advice or offer feedback.

Seek out unjaded locals. The locals most tour groups encounter are hardened businesspeople who put up with tourists because they have to—it's their livelihood. Going through Tuscany in a flock of 50 Americans following the tour guide's umbrella, you'll meet all the wrong Italians. Break away. One summer

A well-chosen tour can be a fine value, giving you a great trip and a table filled with new friends.

night in Regensburg, Germany, I skipped out. While my tour was still piling off the bus, I enjoyed a beer—while overlooking the Danube and under shooting stars—with the great-great-great-grandson of the astronomer Johannes Kepler.

CRUISING IN EUROPE

I once spoke to the CEO of a cruise line, who, in a previous career, sold children's snacks. As bizarre as that connection may seem, he explained to me how adults retain a natural, childlike impulse to explore, coupled with the need for a safe home to return to. While travelers love to get out of their comfort zones, doing so leads many of us to yearn all the more for a refuge or nest. Cruise ships cater to this expertly, by greeting passengers with a welcome table, cold drinks, and friendly smile. On my first cruise, even I remember thinking, as I returned to my ship, "Whew...we're safely back home now."

I'm not pro-cruise or anti-cruise. Taking a cruise can be a fun, affordable, time-efficient, low-hassle, and comforting way to experience Europe—provided you do it smartly. Cruise lines have no incentive to help you have a good time on your own in port—they'd rather you buy an excursion or stay on the ship to spend more money. So it's not only important to choose the right cruise, but also to keep your extra expenses to a minimum and equip yourself with good information to make the absolute most of your time in port. (These strategies are covered in detail by my *Mediterranean Cruise Ports* and *Northern European Cruise Ports* guidebooks, which teach cruisers how to use their precious shore time to their best advantage.) A smart, informed cruiser can have a meaningful and culturally engaging experience while taking advantage of the economy and efficiency of cruising. Here are a few insights and suggestions for deciding whether or not to cruise—and then, if you choose to, how to make the best of your experience.

Is Cruising for You?

Short of sleeping on a park bench, I haven't found a more affordable way to see certain parts of Europe than cruising. On a Mediterranean cruise that includes room, board, transportation, tips, and port fees, a couple can pay as little as $100 per night—that's as much as a budget hotel room in many cities.

Cruising also works well for travelers who prefer to

tiptoe into Europe, rather than dive right in. Cruising can serve as an enticing sampler of bite-sized visits, helping you decide where you'd like to return to and spend more time.

It's also great for retirees (or families traveling with retirees), particularly those with limited mobility. Cruising rescues you from packing up your bags and huffing to the train station every other day. Once on land, accessibility for wheelchairs and walkers can vary dramatically—though some cruise lines offer excursions specifically designed for those who don't walk well. A cruise aficionado who had done the math once told me that, if you know how to find the deals, it's theoretically cheaper to cruise indefinitely than to pay for a retirement home.

Of course, independent, free-spirited travelers may not appreciate the constraints of cruising. For some, seven or eight hours in port is way too short, a tantalizing tease of a place where they'd love to linger for the evening—and the obligation to return to the ship every night is frustrating. If you're self-reliant, energetic, and want to stroll the cobbles of Europe at all hours, cruising probably isn't for you. Even so, some seasoned globetrotters find that cruising is a good way to travel comfortably on a shoestring budget.

There are different types of cruisers. Some travelers cruise because it's an efficient way to experience so many ports of call. They appreciate the convenience of traveling while they sleep, waking up in an interesting new destination each morning, and making the most out of every second they're in port. This is the "first off, last on" crowd that attacks each port like a footrace. You can practically hear their imaginary starter's pistol go off when the gangway opens.

Other cruisers come to enjoy the cruise experience itself. They enjoy basking by the pool, taking advantage of onboard activities, dropping some cash at the casino, running up a huge bar tab, and watching ESPN on their stateroom TV.

If you really want to be on vacation, aim for somewhere in the middle. Be sure to experience the ports that really tickle your wanderlust, but give yourself a "day off" every now and again in the less enticing ports to sleep in or hit the beach.

How Cruises Operate

Understanding how the cruise industry makes money can help you take advantage of your cruise experience...and not the other way around. Cruising is a $30-billion-a-year business. Approximately one out of every five Americans has taken a cruise, and each year about 15 million people take one.

In order to compete for passengers and fill megaships, cruise lines offer fares that can be astonishingly low. In adjusted dollars, the price of cruises hasn't risen for several decades. Your cruise fare covers accommodations, all the meals you can eat in the ship's main dining room and buffet, and transportation from port to port. You can have an enjoyable voyage and not spend a penny more on board (though you'd still have some expenses in port). But the cruise industry is adept at enticing you with extras that add up quickly: alcohol, gambling (at onboard casinos), and cruise-company-run excursions. Other temptations include specialty restaurant surcharges, duty-free shopping, fitness classes, spa treatments, and photos.

It's very easy to get carried away—a round of drinks here, a night of blackjack there. First-timers are often astonished when they get their final onboard bill, which can easily exceed the original cost of the trip. But with a little self-control, you can limit your extra expenditures, making your supposedly cheap cruise *actually* cheap. You always have the right to say, "No, thanks" to these additional expenses.

Choosing a Cruise

Selecting a cruise that matches your travel style and philosophy is critical. Each cruise line has its own distinct personality, quirks, strengths, and weaknesses. Cruise lines fall into four basic price categories: mass-market (Royal Caribbean, Norwegian, Carnival, and Costa), premium (Celebrity, Holland America, and Princess), luxury (Azamara Club, Oceania, and Windstar), and ultra-luxury (Crystal, Regent Seven Seas, and Seabourn).

Here are a few factors to keep in mind:

Price: In addition to the base fare, you'll pay taxes and port fees (which can be hundreds of dollars per person), and an auto-tip of around $10-12/day for each person will be added to your bill. Also remember to budget for all the aforementioned "extras" you might wind up buying from the cruise line.

Destinations: If you have a wish list of ports, use it as a starting point when shopping for a cruise.

Time spent in port: If exploring European destinations is your priority, look carefully at how much time the ship spends in each port; this can vary by hours from cruise line to cruise line.

Ship size: The biggest ships offer a wide variety of restaurants, activities, entertainment, and other amenities (such as resources for kids)—but they can also foster a herd mentality and crowded shore experience for passengers. Smaller ships offer fewer crowds, access to out-of-the-way ports, and less hassle when disembarking, but they also have fewer onboard amenities and generally cost much more.

Onboard amenities: Decide which features matter to you most, including food (both quality and variety of restaurants), entertainment, athletic facilities, children's activities, and so on.

Booking a Cruise

While it's possible to book directly with the cruise line, most cruises are booked through travel agencies. There are two different types of cruise-sales agencies: your neighborhood travel agent, where you can get in-person advice, or a giant cruise agency, which sells most of its inventory online or by phone. Several big cruise agencies have user-friendly comparison shopping websites (such as vacationstogo.com, cruisecompete.com, and crucon.com).

Most cruise lines post their cruise schedules a year or more in advance. The earlier you book, the more likely you'll have your choice of sailing and of cabin type—and potentially an even better price (cruise lines typically offer discounts for booking at least 6 to 12 months before departure). While last-minute deals (usually within 90 days of departure) are fairly common on Caribbean cruises, they're relatively rare for European ones—and last-minute airfares to Europe can be that much more expensive.

Resources for Cruising

Cruisecritic.com: Reviews of cruise lines and ships, tips for visiting ports, cruise-finding tool
Cruisediva.com: Reviews, tips, guide to cruise lines and ships
Cruisemates.com: Travel forums, reviews, cruise planning tips
Avidcruiser.com: Reviews, port profiles, cruise videos, blog

Reading
Rick Steves Mediterranean Cruise Ports
Rick Steves Northern European Cruise Ports
The Unofficial Guide to Cruises (2010)
Fodor's Complete Guide to European Cruises (2013)

Excursion Cheat Sheet

This simplified roundup shows which Mediterranean ports are best by excursion and which are doable independently. For details, see my *Mediterranean Cruise Ports* guidebook, dedicated to helping people cruise "through the Back Door." (Baltic cruisers should look for my *Northern European Cruise Ports*.)

DESTINATION (PORT)	EXCURSION?
Barcelona	No
Shuttle bus from terminal drops you right in town	
Provence (Marseille/Toulon)	Yes
Wide range of worthwhile destinations far from the ugly ports; an excursion can hit several of these with ease	
French Riviera (Nice/Villefranche/Monaco)	No
Entire region is easy to navigate by train or bus	
Florence, Pisa, Lucca (Livorno)	Maybe
These cities are cheap and reasonably easy to reach by public transportation, but excursions offer a no-hassle connection that also includes tours of the major sights in each city	
Rome (Civitavecchia)	Maybe
Easy, direct train trip into town, but an excursion could help you navigate this big city	
Amalfi Coast (Naples/Sorrento)	Yes
Narrow roads of the Amalfi Coast are often snarled by traffic; an excursion gives you peace of mind	
Naples and Pompeii (Naples/Sorrento)	No
Within Naples, everything is easy to reach by foot or bus; the ruins at Pompeii are a quick train ride away	
Venice	No
Getting downtown is easy by public transportation; even walking there is delightful in this unique city	
Split	No
Port is just a few steps from the easy-to-tour Old Town	
Dubrovnik	No
Very compact and easy on your own	
Athens (Piraeus)	Maybe
Getting downtown is relatively easy, but sights benefit from a good guide, and an excursion offers easy connections	
Most Greek Islands	No
Just relax and be on vacation	
Ephesus (Kuşadası)	Yes
Getting from Kuşadası to Ephesus involves considerable hassle, and a local guide is essential to understand this site	
Istanbul	No
The cruise terminals are right in the city	

Like cars or plane tickets, cruises are priced very flexibly. In general, for a mass-market cruise, you'll rarely pay the list price. (Higher-end cruises are less likely to be discounted.) It's common to see sales and other incentives, such as two-for-one pricing, free upgrades, onboard credits, or other extras.

While most cruise lines are willing to arrange your airfare to and from the cruise, you'll typically save money (and gain flexibility) by booking flights on your own. Allow plenty of time—ideally an overnight—before meeting your cruise; if your flight is delayed and you miss your ship, you're on your own to figure out how you'll meet it at the next port.

Cruising Tips

Food and Drink: Most cruise lines offer a wide range of onboard restaurants, including traditional dining rooms (with a semi-formal dress code and assigned seating every night), more casual buffet restaurants, room service whenever you want it, and a variety of specialty restaurants. Avoid this last kind of restaurant if you're on a budget—besides costing you a $10-30 cover charge, certain entrées incur a "supplement" ($10-20). A couple ordering specialty items and a bottle of wine can quickly run up a $100 dinner bill.

In general, water, coffee, tea, milk, iced tea, and juice are included. Other drinks cost extra: alcohol of any kind, name-brand soft drinks, fresh-squeezed fruit juices, and premium espresso drinks (lattes and cappuccinos). To encourage alcohol sales, many cruise lines limit how much alcohol guests can bring on board, or prohibit them from bringing any at all.

Excursions vs. Independent Sightseeing. Whether it's better to sightsee on your own or with an excursion depends on the destination and your own level of comfort with navigating Europe independently. A shore excursion efficiently takes you to a carefully selected assortment of sights, with a vetted local guide to explain everything, and is guaranteed to get you back to the ship in time (if an excursion is late, the ship will wait—but not if you're on your own). If you don't want to hassle with logistics, excursions can be a great option. But they are expensive, ranging from $40-60/person for a three-hour town walking tour to $100-150/person for an all-day bus tour.

Particularly in a place where it's easy to get into the city center on public transportation, you can have a similar experience for far less money. (For a list of Mediterranean cruise ports where excursions make the most sense, see the sidebar on page 460.) If you decide to go it alone, use a good guidebook or visit the local tourist information office in port. Other options are to hire a private guide to meet you at the ship and take you around or to join a scheduled walking tour of the town. As long as you keep a close eye on the time, it's easy to enjoy a very full day in port and be the last tired but happy tourist back onto the ship.

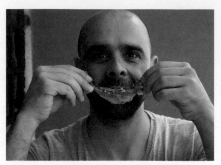

A local guide—such as my Portuguese friend Ricardo, with his "fishy" smile—makes your shore excursion memorable and fun.

Shopping: At every stop, your cruise line will give you an information sheet highlighting local specialties and where to buy them. But be aware that cruise-recommended shops commonly give kickbacks to cruise lines and guides. This doesn't mean that the shop (or what it sells) isn't good quality; it just means you're probably paying top dollar. Many stores—not just the places working with cruise lines—jack up their rates when ships arrive, knowing they're about to get hit with a tidal wave of rushed and desperate shoppers. Before spending big money at the obvious tourist shops, be sure to check out local shopping venues, too.

Perspectives

Beyond all the practical considerations of preparing for your trip, there is one more vital task: calibrating your mind for your European experience. When you travel—whether to Europe or around the world—your best souvenir can be a global perspective. This chapter covers a range of ideas, including broadening your perspective through travel, understanding the current European political structure, recognizing the challenges and social issues facing Europe today, and learning how to travel in a socially and environmentally responsible way. Consider this a bit of food-for-thought pre-trip reading.

BROADENING YOUR PERSPECTIVE THROUGH TRAVEL

In the past few years, I've devoted a lot of time and energy to thinking about travel in a new way: as an invaluable tool for learning how to fit more thoughtfully into our ever-smaller world. I think of this approach as "travel as a political act" (which is also the title of a book I've written; see page 34)

I was raised thinking the world was a pyramid with the US on top and everyone else trying to get there. I believed our role in the world was to help other people get it right... American-style. If they didn't understand that, we'd get them a government that did.

But travel changed my perspective. I met intelligent people—nowhere near as rich, free, or blessed with opportunity as I was—who wouldn't trade passports even if they could. They were thankful to be Nepali, Estonian, Turkish, Nicaraguan, or whatever. I was perplexed. I witnessed stirring struggles in lands that found other truths to be

self-evident and God-given. I learned
of Nathan Hales and Patrick Henrys
from other nations who only wished
they had more than one life to give
for their country. I saw national
pride that wasn't American. It was a
challenging adjustment to my way of
thinking—but it opened my mind to
a whole new world of experiences I'd
otherwise have ignored or derided.

Attitude Adjustment

When American tourists are unhappy, it's usually because
of their stubborn desire to find the United States in Europe.
Meanwhile, the happiest travelers I meet are truly taking a
vacation from America—immersing themselves in different
cultures and fully experiencing different people, outlooks,
and lifestyles.

What a difference perspective makes. When I bragged about how many gold medals our American Olympians were winning, my Dutch friend replied, "Yes, you have many medals, but per capita, we Dutch are doing five times as well."

Even if you believe American ways are better, your trip
will go more smoothly if you don't compare. Things are
different in Europe—that's why you go. And European travel
is a package deal. Accept the good with the "bad." If you
always require the comforts of home, then that's where you'll
be happiest. On the other hand, if you're observant and tune
into all the little differences, you may find great wisdom in
how Europeans do things. Paying for your Italian coffee
at one counter and then picking it up at another may seem
inefficient, until you realize it's more sanitary: The person
handling the food handles no money.

Some Americans' trips suffer because they are treated
like "ugly Americans." Those who are treated like ugly
Americans are treated that way because they *are* ugly
Americans. They aren't bad people, just ethnocentric. These
people act as though they "just got off the boat"—putting
shoes on train seats, chilling grapes in the bidet, talking
loudly in restaurants, snapping flash photos during Mass,
hanging wet clothes out the hotel window, and consuming energy like it's cheap and theirs to waste. But you can't
expect the local people to accept you warmly if you don't
respect their world and their ways of doing things.

Europeans judge you as an individual, not by your nationality. I have never been treated like the ugly American. If
anything, my Americanness has been an asset in Europe. I've
been accepted as an American friend throughout Europe,

The Thoughtless Traveler vs. the Thoughtful Traveler

While the thoughtless traveler slogs through a sour Europe, mired in a swamp of complaints, the thoughtful traveler fully experiences wherever he or she is.

The Thoughtless Traveler	The Thoughtful Traveler
...criticizes "strange" customs and cultural differences. She doesn't respect the devout Spanish Catholic's appreciation of his town's patron saint, or doesn't understand the sense of community expressed by the evening promenade in southern Europe.	...seeks out European styles of living and tries new ways of thinking and doing things. You are genuinely interested in the people and cultures you visit. You accept and try to wrap your head around differences.
...demands to find America in Europe. He throws a fit if the air-conditioning breaks down in a hotel. He insists on orange juice and eggs (sunny-side up) for breakfast, long beds, English menus, ice in drinks, punctuality in Italy, and cold beer in England. He measures Europe with an American yardstick.	...is positive and optimistic. You don't dwell on problems or compare things to "back home," and you focus on the good points of each country. As a guest in another land, you're observant and sensitive. If 60 people are dining with hushed voices in a Belgian restaurant, you know it's not the place to yuk it up.
...uses money as a shield against a genuine experience. She throws money at the locals instead of trying to engage them.	...doesn't flash signs of affluence, especially in poorer countries. You don't joke about the local money or overtip. Your bucks don't talk.
...invades a country while making no effort to communicate with the "natives." He never bothers to learn even the basic survival phrases ("please" and "thank you"), and gets angry when the Europeans he meets "refuse to learn English." Traveling in packs, he looks at and about Europeans in a condescending manner.	...makes an effort to bridge that flimsy language barrier. You find rudimentary communication in any language to be fun. On the train to Budapest, you enter a debate with a Hungarian over the merits of a common European currency—despite only a 20-word shared vocabulary. You don't worry about making mistakes—you communicate!

Russia, the Middle East, and North Africa. I've been hugged by Bulgarian workers on a Balkan mountaintop; discussed the Olympics over dinner in the home of a Greek family; explained to a young, frustrated Irishman that California girls take their pants off one leg at a time, just like the rest of us; and hiked through the Alps with a Swiss schoolteacher, learning German and teaching English.

Go as a guest; act like one, and you'll be treated like one. In travel, as in the rest of life, you often reap what you sow.

UNDERSTANDING THE EUROPEAN UNION

A desire for peace and prosperity is powering some sweeping changes in 21st-century Europe. Over the last several generations, the countries of Europe have gone from being bitter rivals to member states in one of the world's biggest economies: the European Union. Bringing together such a diverse collection of separate nations—with different languages and cultures—peacefully, is unprecedented.

Today, the European Union includes most of Western Europe (except Switzerland), the British Isles, and a large chunk of Eastern Europe and Scandinavia. (The Republic of Macedonia, Montenegro, Serbia, Iceland, and Turkey are seeking to become members.) Essentially, the EU is a free-trade zone with its own currency (the euro, used in most member countries). But it's much more than that: The EU is increasingly a political unit that looks, acts, and quacks like a single unified nation-state. While not quite a "United States of Europe," the EU has an elected Europe-wide parliament that passes laws on economic policy and some social and foreign policy issues.

Everyone has an opinion on how well the EU works. "Eurocrats" and other optimists see it as a bold and idealistic experiment in unity, mutual understanding, and shared priorities. "Euroskeptics" view it as a bloated, overly bureaucratic monster that's threatening to wring the diversity and charm out of the Old World; they especially resent that the EU has lashed economically healthy countries to troubled ones. Here's a snapshot of the EU to help you navigate the many interesting conversations you'll have about it with your new European friends.

The EU: Past and Present

World War II left 40 million dead and a continent in ruins, and convinced Europeans that they had to work together to maintain peace. Poised between competing superpowers (the US and the USSR), they also needed to cooperate economically to survive in an increasingly globalized economy.

Just after the war ended, visionary "Eurocrats" began the task of convincing reluctant European

When I shudder at Switzerland's high taxes, my friend Olle asks, "What's it worth to live in a country with no hunger or homelessness, and where everyone—regardless of the wealth of their parents—has access to good health care and a top-quality education?"

EU Nations

The European Union: Austria, Belgium, Bulgaria, Croatia, Cyprus, Czech Republic, Denmark, Estonia, Finland, France, Germany, Greece, Hungary, Ireland, Italy, Latvia, Lithuania, Luxembourg, Malta, Netherlands, Poland, Portugal, Romania, Slovakia, Slovenia, Spain, Sweden, and the United Kingdom

nations to relinquish elements of their sovereignty and merge into a united body. Starting in 1949, European states gradually came together to form the Common Market (also known as the European Economic Community). In 1992, with the Treaty of Maastricht, the 12 member countries of the Common Market made a leap of faith: They created a "European Union" that would eventually allow capital, goods, services, and labor to move freely across borders. The by-products would be a common currency, softened trade barriers, EU passports, and the elimination of border checks between member countries.

In 2002, most EU members adopted the euro as a single currency, and for all practical purposes, economic unity was a reality. By 2013, EU membership reached 28 nations, encompassing a vast swath of the continent. With passport checkpoints all but obsolete, the EU is now the world's seventh largest "country" (1.7 million square miles), with the third largest population (more than 500 million people). It's also running neck-and-neck with the US for the title of world's biggest economy ($15.6 trillion GDP).

Thank You

Arabic	shukran
Bulgarian	blagodarya
Croatian	hvala
Czech	děkuji
Danish	tak
Dutch	dank u wel
Estonian	tänan
Finnish	kiitos
French	merci
German	danke
Greek	efharisto
Hebrew	todah
Hungarian	köszönöm
Italian	grazie
Polish	dziękuję
Portuguese	obrigado
Russian	spasiba
Slovak	d'akujem
Slovene	hvala
Spanish	gracias
Turkish	teşekkür ederim

As Europe unites, historically subjugated peoples are enjoying more autonomy. The Scottish Parliament originated around 1235, was dissolved by England in 1707, and returned in 1999. Its extravagant and controversial Edinburgh digs (above) opened in 2004.

The EU is governed from Brussels and administered through a complicated network of legislative bodies, commissions, and courts that attempt to complement each country's government without encroaching on sovereignty. The EU cannot levy taxes (that's still done through national governments), and it cannot deploy troops without each nation's approval. Unlike America's federation of 50 states, Europe's member states retain the right to opt out of some EU policies. Britain, for example, belongs to the EU but has not adopted the euro as its currency.

It's a delicate balance trying to develop laws and policies for all Europeans while respecting the rights of nations, regions, and individuals. The European response to the Balkan wars in the early 1990s, the Iraq War of the

US vs. EU by the Numbers

	US	EU
Population	317 million	509 million
Land area	3.7 million square miles	1.7 million square miles
Gross domestic product (GDP)	$16.2 trillion	$15.6 trillion
Life expectancy	78.6 years	79.8 years
Infant mortality rate	5.9 deaths/1,000	4.4 deaths/1,000
Mobile phones	310 million	629 million
Annual military budget	65.5 billion (4.4% of GDP)	25 billion (1.6% of GDP)

Statistics from the CIA's World Factbook, 2014

mid-2000s, and the ongoing debt crisis have demonstrated that Europe isn't always prepared to speak with a single voice. An oft-quoted EU slogan is "promoting unity"—that is, economic and political—"while preserving diversity."

Meanwhile, the EU has been pouring money into an ambitious 21st-century infrastructure of roads, high-speed trains, high-tech industries, and communication networks. The goal is to create a competitive, sustainable, environmentally friendly economy that improves the quality of life for all Europeans. To complete these projects, government and private industry have worked hand in hand in a kind of "democratic socialism" with a global perspective. It's impossible to deny the marked improvements brought about by this investment, as new super-expressways and bullet trains lace the continent ever more efficiently together.

The EU is a bold experiment, and, like any innovation, it's hit a few snags as it's evolved (see next section). But even throughout the debt crisis, the euro remained relatively strong. These economic woes are no more a sign of the total failure of European "socialism" than the economic crisis in the US indicated the final collapse of American capitalism.

The EU has evolved in a stuttering way since World War II—two steps forward, one step backward. While some of the media trumpets the steps backward, the EU is here to stay. Far more important than any of its perceived shortcomings is that France and Germany have woven their economies together to the degree that there will never again be a huge war in Europe. Sure, the French and Germans still mix like wine and sauerkraut. Brits still tell insulting jokes about Italians, and vice versa. But Europeans don't want to go back to the days of division and strife. Most recognize that a strong and unified Europe is necessary to keep the peace and compete in a global economy. Individual nations still duke it out for world domination...but now the battles are on the soccer field.

LEFT The EU headquarters—a vast and shiny complex of skyscrapers in Brussels—welcomes visitors on guided tours to take a peek at Europe at work.

RIGHT New roads (such as this one in Ireland) are bringing the infrastructure in Europe up to speed. These EU-funded projects come with a billboard and EU flag reminding drivers where the funding came from.

EUROPEAN CHALLENGES

Like many places, Europe is grappling with an economic crisis (with resulting strikes and protests) and the ever-present threat of terrorism. Here's a quick rundown on the European reality, and how these issues could affect your trip.

Europe's Economic Crisis

After seeing news reports of violent demonstrations, angry marchers, and frustrated workers rioting, some travelers are wondering if this is still a good time to go to Europe. I'm certainly not an economist. But here's my take on the situation from a travel writer's perspective.

Today Europe is paying the price—in the form of expensive bailouts and painful cutbacks—of what had been taken-for-granted services. Wealthier member countries (mostly in the north) resent being compelled to prop up the euro by rescuing their economically unsound compatriots (the so-called "PIIGS" countries, mostly in the south—Portugal, Italy, Ireland, Greece, and Spain). Meanwhile, troubled countries resent being told what to do by the richer ones, and disgruntled citizens sometimes take to the streets.

When assessing the seriousness of any civil unrest, remember the mantra of commercial news these days: "If it bleeds, it leads." In the era of Walter Cronkite, network news contributed to the fabric of our society by providing solid journalism as a public service without worrying about their bottom line. But today, commercial TV news has to make a profit. In order to sell ads, it has become entertainment masquerading as news. Producers will always grab video footage that makes a demonstration appear as exciting or threatening as possible. Unrest is generally localized—it looks frightening with a zoom lens and much less so with a wide-angle shot.

And also remember that, even when we in the US and Europe consider ourselves in an "economic crisis," the vast majority of people on this planet would love to have our economic problems. By any fair measure, as societies, both the US and Europe are filthy rich. Still, if you're unemployed or if your retirement is suddenly in jeopardy, your times are, indeed, tough.

Europe's economic problems are much like ours here in the US. It seems on both sides of the Atlantic we've conned ourselves into thinking we are wealthier than we really are. Enjoying wild real estate bubbles, we've had houses that were worth half a million suddenly worth a million. Then, when they dropped in value by 50 percent, we felt like we'd lost half a million dollars...or euros. Truth be told, we were never millionaires to start with, and what we "lost" we never honestly gained in the first place.

As societies, we've been consuming more goods than we've been producing for a long time. We import more than we export—and things are finally catching up with us. Here in the US, our priorities are warped. Many of our best young minds are going to our finest schools to become experts in finance: rearranging the furniture to skim off the top... aspiring to careers where you produce little while expertly working the system in hopes of becoming unimaginably rich. Recently, surveying the extravagant châteaux outside Paris—such as Vaux-le-Vicomte—I was struck by how many of them were the homes of financiers. Lately, the US is reminding me of old regime France. It's striking that about 8 percent of the US economy is tied up in the financial industry.

Europeans and Americans have some of the most generous entitlements in the world combined with aging societies. Because of that, our comfortable status quo is not sustainable. Whenever a society gets wealthy and well educated, it has fewer children. That's simply a force of nature. (Western Europe, one of the wealthiest and best-educated parts of the world, has one of the lowest birth rates.)

Europe's generous entitlements were conceived in a postwar society with lots of people working, fewer living to retirement, and those living beyond retirement having a short life span. That was sustainable...no problem. Now, with its very low birth rate, the demographic makeup of Europe has flipped upside down: relatively few people working, lots of people retiring, and those who are retired living a long time. The arithmetic just isn't there to sustain the lavish entitlements.

Politicians in Europe have the unenviable task of explaining to their citizens that they won't get the cushy golden years their parents got. People who worked diligently with the promise of retiring at 62 are now told they'll need to work an extra decade—and even then, they may not have a generous retirement waiting for them. Any politician trying to explain this reality to the electorate is likely to be tossed out, since people naturally seek a politician who tells them what they want to hear rather than the hard truth. And any austerity programs necessary to put a society back on track are also tough enough to get people marching in the streets.

I expect you'll see lots of marches and lots of strikes in Europe in the coming years as they try to recalibrate their economy. Europeans demonstrate: It's in their blood and a healthy part of their democracy. When frustrated and needing to vent grievances, they hit the streets. I've been caught up in huge and boisterous marches all over Europe, and it's not scary; in fact, it's kind of exhilarating. *"La Manifestation!"* as they say in France. All that marching is just too much trouble for many Americans. When dealing with similar frustrations, we find a TV station (on the left or right) that affirms our beliefs and then shake our collective fists vigorously.

When Europe united, the poor countries (such as Ireland, Portugal, and Greece) received lots of development aid from the rich ones (mostly Germany and France). I remember when there were no freeways in any of the poor countries. Now they are laced with German-style (and mostly German-funded) superhighways. These countries traded in their lazy currencies for the euro (which is, in a way, the mighty Deutsche mark in disguise, as the European economy is driven and dominated by Germany).

Today, it's no coincidence that the European countries that have received the most development aid are the ones who are the most debt-ridden and at risk of failing. Even with that aid, their productivity has lagged far behind the stronger economies. And, while their workforce doesn't produce as much per capita as German workers, they have a mighty currency tied to Germany. By earning wages and getting aid in euros, these nations enjoyed a false prosperity that they might not have merited—and the bursting real estate bubble made it worse. Before unity, if a nation didn't produce much and slid into crippling debt, the economy could be adjusted simply by devaluing that nation's currency. Today, there's no way to devalue the currency of a particular country on the euro, so this fix is not an option. It's much easier to get into the Eurozone than to get out.

I'm sometimes asked whether Greece and other struggling economies within the EU are safe and stable places to visit. No one can predict the future for certain. But, as a traveler, I don't worry about it. True, I wouldn't want to be a Greek worker counting on a retirement that may not come. But as a visitor, it's likely that you'll scarcely be aware of these problems. I was just in Greece and enjoyed a warm welcome, great food, and wonderful beaches. Expect a few demonstrations and a few strikes. Expect your loved ones to be worried about you if you are in a country when there's a demonstration. (So be in touch.) But you can also expect rich travel experiences and a society thankful that you decided to spend a slice of your vacation time and money in their country.

Terrorism

Times change. But, it seems, terrorism is always with us—whether in the US (9/11 or the 2013 Boston Marathon bombing) or in Europe (the Madrid train bombings in 2004 or the Oslo shootings in 2011). Every superpower is seen by angry people beyond its borders as an evil empire. All have had insurgents nipping at them. Romans had what they called "barbarians." Habsburgs had "anarchists." And today, Americans and Europeans have terrorists.

Most of the time, travelers can be blissfully oblivious of terrorism. But there's always a chance that terrorists will strike just before, or during, your trip.

If that happens, take a deep breath. Survey the situation. And don't let fear and worry overwhelm the facts. Numbers don't lie. The odds against being killed by terrorists are astronomical. More than 12 million Americans go to Europe every year, and for the last several years, not a single one has been killed by terrorists. I believe that risk is no greater for an American in Milan or Paris than at home in Miami or Pittsburgh. In the mid-2000s, Canada and many European countries issued travel advisories to their citizens for a land they consider more dangerous than their own: the US.

The US State Department issues travel advisories for foreign countries (travel.state.gov). Consider these, but don't follow them blindly. Certain warnings (for example, about civil unrest in a country that's falling apart) could be grounds to scrub my mission. But I travel right through most advisories (which can seem politically motivated). A threat against the embassy in Rome doesn't affect my sightseeing at the Pantheon. For other perspectives, check the British (fco.gov.uk) and Canadian (travel.gc.ca) government travel warnings.

Terrorist threats can have a tangible impact on your travels, usually in the form of increased security lines or disrupted flight plans. If something unusual is happening in

Paris' see-through garbage cans give terrorists one less place to hide a bomb.

the world, be sure to carefully confirm your flight schedule, and allow
plenty of time to get through security.
If I get stuck in a long TSA line, I use
the extra time to meditate on the
thought, "How has America's place in
our world changed...and why?"

Or, if you want to worry about
something, worry about this: Each
year, more than 30,000 Americans
are shot to death in the United States
by handguns (8 times the per-capita gun-caused deaths in
Europe).

Security on
Europe's
premium trains
can be tight.
At this London
train station,
the police keep
a close eye on
who boards
the Eurostar
for Paris.

Having been in Europe during some high-profile terrorist
events, I've been impressed by the local response. Europeans
have a knack for bouncing back and refusing to give in to
the attackers' desire to incite terror. They don't surrender
their emotions and politics to sensational news coverage.
Europeans keep the risk and tragedy of terrorism in perspective. As a matter of principle, it seems, they refuse to be
terrorized by terrorists.

After an attention-grabbing attack, some Americans
choose to put their travel dreams on hold and stay home.
That's OK. I'm still bringing home TV shows that they can
watch from the safety of their living room sofas. But those of
us who are able would rather enjoy the fun and wonders of
Europe firsthand.

Two weeks after 9/11, I was in Padua, the town where
Copernicus studied and Galileo taught. The square was
filled with college students sharing drinks and discussing
America's response to "our new reality." As we talked, I kept
dipping little strips of bread into a puddle of olive oil on my
plate, tiptoe-style. Watching me do this, my new friend said,
"You make the *scarpette*...little shoes."

My Italian wasn't good enough to tell him my thoughts:
Travel is a celebration of life and freedom. Terrorists will
not take that away from me. My mission in life is to inspire
Americans to travel, one by one—"making the little shoes"—
to absorb and savor the wonders of Europe.

Learning from Today's History

The economic crisis and terrorism grab headlines, but
Europe is also wrangling with other forms of friction. For
example, it's next to impossible to keep everyone happy in
a multilingual country. Switzerland has four languages,

but *Deutsch ist über alles.* In Belgium, tension between the Dutch and French-speaking halves led to a caretaker government for 541 days—a world record. And Hungarians living in Slovakia had to rely on European Court intervention to get road signs in their native language. Like many French Canadians, Europe's

linguistic underdogs will tell you their language receives equal treatment only on cereal boxes, and many are working toward change.

Look beyond the pretty pictures in your tourist brochures for background on how your destination's economic and demographic makeup may be causing problems today or tomorrow. A few months in advance of your trip, begin paying attention to political news so you'll know what's happening (information you'll seldom find in guidebooks).

If you've studied up on local politics, you'll get the most out of opportunities to talk with involved locals about complex current situations. At any pub on the Emerald Isle, you'll get an earful of someone's passionate feelings about "the Troubles." In Istanbul, befriend a Turk over a game of backgammon, and ask how he feels about the rise of Islamic fundamentalism in his proudly secular country. Wherever you go, young, well-dressed people are most likely to speak (and want to practice) English. Universities can be the perfect place to solve the world's problems with a liberal, open-minded foreigner over a cafeteria lunch.

Travel broadens our perspective, enabling us to rise above the 24-hour, advertiser-driven infotainment we call "news" and see things as citizens of our world. By plugging directly into the present and getting the European take on things, a traveler gets beyond traditional sightseeing and learns "today's history."

SOCIAL ISSUES IN EUROPE

Tolerance and celebrating diversity are major tenets of the European Union. But for some Europeans, that's easier said than done. This section offers an admittedly oversimplified overview of immigration, race relations, and gay and lesbian rights in Europe.

Immigration and Race Relations

Europe is grappling with an influx of immigrants from the developing world. Racial diversity is nothing new in the melting-pot United States (where one-third of the population is non-white), but about 95 percent of people living in Europe are Caucasian. A few places (such as former colonial powers Great Britain and the Netherlands) have seen a steady influx of transplants from their overseas holdings for many centuries, but most of Europe was largely homogenous well into the 20th century. In the decades since World War II—as Europe has built a new prosperity, and immigrants have arrived seeking a better life—Europe has become much more ethnically diverse.

As immigrants from every corner of the world (mostly Africa, the Middle East, the Caribbean, South Asia, and South America) have come to Europe, many white Europeans have struggled to adapt. Some are frustrated by large numbers of immigrants—and now their descendants— who, the critics claim, stick together in tight communities, cling to the culture of their homeland, and are slow to adopt European culture. The immigrants would likely counter that they've found few opportunities to integrate with their European neighbors. Just as in the US, immigrants are sometimes perceived as challenging lifelong residents for jobs, or as taking advantage of the welfare system. Another thorny issue is the friction between European Christianity and the Islamic faith of many immigrants.

Immigration paranoia came to a head in normally peaceful Norway, where, in July 2011, a deranged white-supremacist Christian bombed government offices in Oslo and then went to a pro-immigrant political party's summer camp and gunned down dozens of people—mostly teenagers. The gunman's fear that Europe is being "taken over by Islamic fundamentalists" revealed a frightening undercurrent of paranoia and hate that represents a small but growing fringe of the European mind-set.

On the other hand, the minority group subject to the most overt racism in Europe isn't made up of new immigrants at all: It's the Roma (or Gypsies). For centuries, white Europeans have regarded this population—which likely shares ancestors with the people of today's India—with suspicion and fear. This feeling is especially pervasive in Eastern Europe, Italy, and Spain, which have large numbers of Roma.

While Europe wrestles with how to accommodate its

Travelers of Color in Europe

People who are not of European descent might be concerned about how they'll be treated abroad. In short, does it matter that you look different from most Europeans? I've collected the following advice from a wide range of people of color who have lived or traveled extensively in Europe.

First off, your Americanness will probably be more notable to the Europeans you meet than the color of your skin. Most Europeans can spot Americans a mile away. And, because American culture is pervasive worldwide, any stereotypes Europeans might have about your race are likely formed by our own popular culture—our actors, musicians, athletes, and characters on TV shows. The Obama presidency has also informed the way Europeans think about black Americans, and Americans in general (mostly positively).

Travelers of color and mixed-race couples tell me that their most common source of discomfort in Europe is being stared at. While this might seem to indicate disapproval, it's more likely a combination of curiosity and impoliteness. Put simply, for some Europeans, you're just not who they're used to seeing. Their response to a person of color likely isn't hostility, but naiveté. (One traveler suggested that this isn't racism, but "rarism"—Europeans reacting not to one's race, but to one's rarity.)

Europeans tend to be opinionated and blunt, and aren't shy about voicing sweeping generalizations about any topic—including race. Many travelers find this jarring and hurtful, while some consider it weirdly refreshing ("at least it's out in the open").

Travelers of color report being frustrated by racial profiling, particularly at border crossings or airport security. (One traveler speculated that this may have to do with targeting immigrants.) It's possible you'll be closely scrutinized before being allowed to continue on your way.

If you're concerned about how you'll be treated in a specific destination, ask fellow travelers of color what their experiences have been there. An excellent resource for African Americans, including destination-specific reports from several travelers, is blacktravels.blogspot.com. Or check out the "Minority Travelers' Forum" at ricksteves.com.

Will you encounter unfriendliness in your travels? Definitely. Everyone does. But be careful not to over-attribute grumpiness to racism. In the words of one traveler of color: "I think we're more likely to interpret bad behavior from non-Americans as being racist because of our history with white Americans. Often their impatience is just because we're American, and we're clueless about other people's cultures and practices."

No matter your race, the best advice for any traveler is to have a positive attitude. If you feel uncomfortable or mistreated, head somewhere else. And remember that most Europeans are as interested in learning about you as you are in learning about them.

new populations, travelers of color may encounter a different social reality than the one they're used to back home. For tips on what to expect, see the sidebar on page 477.

Gay and Lesbian Rights

In keeping with its generally progressive politics, much of Europe tends to be supportive of rights for its gay and lesbian citizens. The European Union specifically includes gay and lesbian citizens in its antidiscrimination laws. The Netherlands—and Amsterdam in particular—has offered equal rights to gays and lesbians for decades. The world's first legal marriage for a gay couple occurred in Amsterdam in 2001.

In general, Northern Europe and larger cities are more progressive when it comes to gay rights. In other places, the record is mixed, with fewer legal rights but pockets of tolerance. Same-sex marriage is legal in many European countries, including the Netherlands, Norway, Sweden, Denmark, Belgium, France, Spain, England, Scotland, and Wales. Austria has a vibrant gay scene in its cities, and in conservative Catholic Ireland, my readers have reported a generally welcoming environment even in country B&Bs. Paris has a gay neighborhood (the Marais), but many rural French communities adhere to an unspoken "don't ask, don't tell" ideology of not flaunting one's sexuality. Italy is a similar story of general acceptance but raised eyebrows in rural areas and in the south. Some of Greece's islands are well-known gay destinations.

Eastern European capitals such as Prague and Budapest have liberal attitudes on par with what you'll find in big Western European cities, and the Czech Republic, Hungary, and Slovenia all have legally recognized same-sex unions. But the farther east and south you venture in the former Soviet Bloc, the less progressive things become. Particularly in rural areas of far Eastern Europe, responses range from reasonably accepting to outright hostility. In places such as Romania and Serbia, laws outlawing homosexuality were lifted in recent decades—but acceptance lags behind. And Russia's intolerance toward gays and lesbians

In progressive Amsterdam, this "Homo-monument"—shaped like a giant pink triangle—honors all gays and lesbians who have been persecuted for their sexual orientation.

nearly overshadowed the 2014 Winter Olympics. (For a country-by-country checklist, search Wikipedia for "LGBT rights in Europe.")

Statistically, gay and lesbian travelers are more likely than heterosexuals to plan vacations overseas—and the travel industry knows it. Gay travelers are now likely to find themselves on the receiving end of European tourism campaigns. Many guidebooks have sections devoted to gay nightlife, especially city guides like the *Time Out* series. Damron publishes guidebooks for gay and lesbian travelers (damron.com). For recommendations online, try websites such as outtraveler.com and purpleroofs.com. The International Gay & Lesbian Travel Association is a useful tool for locating LGBT travel businesses and destinations (iglta.org).

SOCIALLY RESPONSIBLE AND EDUCATIONAL TRAVEL

My travels—whether in Egypt, Afghanistan, El Salvador, Turkey, India, the Holy Land, or the Netherlands—have taught me about my own country as well as the rest of our world. Travel has sharpened both my love of what America stands for and my connection with our world. I've learned to treasure—rather than fear—the world's rich diversity. And I believe that America—with all its power, wisdom, and goodness—can do a better job of making our world a better place. By connecting me with so many people, travel has heightened my concern for people issues: a well-educated electorate, a healthy environment, civil liberties, quality housing, nutrition, health care, and education.

As we learn more about the problems that confront the earth and humankind, more and more people are recognizing the need for the world's industries—including tourism—to function as tools for peace. According to the World Travel and Tourism Council (wttc.org), tourism is a $6.8 trillion-a-year industry (9 percent of world GDP) that directly or indirectly employs more than 260 million people. As travelers become more sophisticated and gain a global perspective, the demand for socially, environmentally, and economically responsible means of travel will grow. Peace is more than the absence of war, and if we are to continue enjoying the good things of life—such as travel—the serious issues that confront humankind must be addressed now. Although the most obvious problems relate specifically to travel in the developing world, European travel also offers some exciting socially responsible opportunities.

"Voluntourism" and Cultural Exchanges

For some travelers, making the world a better place becomes the driving focus of their trip. Various organizations sponsor "volunteer vacations," work camps, and other service projects in needy countries, including Global Volunteers (globalvolunteers.org), Volunteers for Peace (vfp.org), and Service Civil International (sciint.org).

Or consider taking an educational tour; while not explicitly service-oriented, these can do a brilliant job of broadening horizons. I've gone on three trips to Central and South America with the Center for Global Education (at Augsburg College in Minneapolis)—some of the most vivid and perspective-stretching travel experiences I've ever enjoyed (augsburg.edu/global; for trip journals of my CFGE experiences in El Salvador and Nicaragua, see ricksteves. com/centam). For more resources, see the suggestions in the sidebar, or try searching online for "volunteer vacation" or "volunteer travel."

Culturally curious travelers can sign up with one of several hospitality exchange organizations. These groups connect travelers with host families with the noble goal of building world peace through international understanding. Guests sightsee less but engage more in everyday life with their hosts—talking, sharing, and learning. You'll arrive as a stranger at new destinations, but leave as a friend.

Although no money changes hands, these exchanges aren't for people simply out to travel cheap—the logistics involved aren't worth it. Most organizations screen members (with varying degrees of stringency) and set ground rules about length of stay. Opening your own home to visitors is encouraged, but not required. Servas is the oldest and largest of these organizations ($85 to join, plus a $20 deposit for a list of hosts, usservas.org). London-based Globetrotters Club runs a similar network of hosts and travelers ($30 annual membership, globetrotters.co.uk), as do several groups that are free to join, such as the Hospitality Club (hospitality-club.org). Other organizations serve specialized audiences (women, Jewish travelers, touring cyclists, gay travelers). Friendship Force International organizes homestay tours for small groups, also with a goal of fostering international goodwill (thefriendshipforce.org). Many travelers swear by

Resources for Studying, Volunteering, or Working Abroad

Bunac.org: Nonprofit group coordinating work and volunteer experiences for students
CIEE.org: Educational consortium offering for-credit programs in 12 European countries
Helpx.net: Directory of short-term work stints in exchange for food and accommodation
Interexchange.org: Opportunities for both working and volunteering abroad
Transitionsabroad.com: Resource for working or studying abroad
Usservas.org: Service organization for international hosts and travelers
Worldteach.org: Organizes volunteer teaching in developing countries
Wsaeurope.com: Weekend tours for students studying in Europe

these exchanges as the only way to really travel, and they treasure their global list of friends.

Student Travel

I feel strongly about the value of students incorporating a little world travel into their university experience. Ninety-six percent of humanity lives outside our borders—and we risk being left in the dust if our next generation of leaders and innovators doesn't know how to effectively engage the world. Sending our students overseas is not a luxury. It's a necessity. Urge the young people in your lives to get a passport and see the world as a classroom.

Good universities all encourage students to take a semester abroad. Interested students can get the details at their campus foreign-study office.

Here's my personal take—from a parent's perspective—on what's to be gained by spending a semester or two overseas. When my son, Andy, was a college student, he enjoyed a fabulous semester abroad in Rome. The fundamental decision for students like Andy—along with whether they should miss fall football season or the fun of spring on campus—is choosing between Europe and the developing world. A semester in Africa or Latin America gives a real-life experience in the rough-and-tumble reality of poverty and powerfully humanizes the often-quoted statistic that "half of humanity is trying to live on $2 a day." Time spent in China or India (whose economies are growing at a much faster pace than their conventional Western European counterparts) introduces a student to emerging economic powerhouses that will compete with our country throughout that student's work life. And a semester in Europe offers (for many) an opportunity to connect with our roots; follow up on language, art, and history courses already taken; and enjoy that traditional Grand Tour of the Old World.

The real education of a semester abroad takes place outside the classroom. It's hard for students to really focus on lectures and homework with so many cultural experiences so close (and parents so far). Each week the buzz is about who's going where on the weekend and how many classes they're skipping to do it. From his base in Rome, Andy would gather a small gang for each three-day weekend: skiing in the Swiss Alps, hiking in the Cinque Terre, biking the Amalfi Coast, or sharing an apartment in Cefalù, Sicily. It came so naturally to him (I wonder why?) that he even formed a tour company for students abroad (wsaeurope.com).

Learning the language, making new friends from around the world, flirting with foreigners, getting comfortable with a bustling foreign city, and mastering the late-night scene while going through the motions in classes all add up to a life-changing and unforgettable semester. And it's a bonding experience with fellow students who will be friends for life.

Global Warming and Going "Green"

During a heat wave several years ago in Italy, I switched hotels because it was too hot to sleep without air-conditioning. It was the first time I had done that, and it was a kind of personal defeat—since I've always prided myself on not needing air-conditioning.

There's no doubt in Europe (and among Europeans) that things are warming up. Nearly everywhere in the Alps, summer skiing is just a memory, and—even in the winter—ski resorts are in desperate straits for lack of snow. (These days, new ski lifts in Europe routinely come with plumbing for snowmaking equipment.) Eating outdoors in formerly cool-climate Munich or Amsterdam now feels like a traditional way to dine. Dutch boys now wait years for a frozen canal to skate on. Scandinavia is seeing a spike in summertime visitors from Spain and Italy (seeking a break from the heat).

In general, Europeans are ahead of the curve on environmental issues. In particularly "green" Denmark, you pay for the disposal of a car when you first buy it, and entire towns are competing to see which will be the first to become entirely wind-powered. A few years ago, London introduced a $16 "congestion charge" for drivers entering the city center during peak hours. This cuts down on both pollution and traffic, and the money generated helps fund the city's energy-efficient bus system. Other cities have since followed suit. In a similar effort to reduce reliance on cars, many European cities have become aggressively bike-friendly, with well-groomed bike lanes and even free or very cheap loaner bikes for quick rides within town (for details on biking in Europe, see page 304). Next to Amsterdam's Central Station stands a high-rise garage—not for cars, but for bicycles. While these ideas sound laughably idealistic to some oil-addicted American cynics, Europeans are making them a reality, and environmentally conscious travelers can take advantage of them, too.

As they've sweltered through summer after summer, Europeans (and their visitors) have long embraced the "inconvenient truth" that things are heating up.

A day of reckoning is coming, when honest travelers will agree that flying to Europe pumps more carbon into the atmosphere than our earth can handle to sustain the climate we all find comfortable. Europeans are starting to see "carbon taxes" that force consumers to pay for zeroing out the negative impact their purchases have on the environment. I have friends who, despite cheap airfares, ride the train to minimize the environmental cost of their intra-European travel.

Do your part to conserve energy. If your hotel overstocks your room with towels, use just one. Carry your own bar of soap and bottle of shampoo rather than rip open all those little soaps and shampoo packets. Bring a lightweight plastic cup instead of using and tossing a plastic glass at every hotel. Turn the light off when you leave your room. Limit showers to five minutes. Return unused travel information (booklets, brochures) to the tourist information office or pass it on to another traveler rather than toss it into a European landfill.

As a business that promotes travel, my company (Rick Steves' Europe, Inc.) has been exploring the ethics of our work and what we can do to offset our carbon footprint. We're making our office as energy-efficient as possible, and we've made extensive use of 100 percent recycled fabric in the travel bags we manufacture.

There's plenty more that can be done to counterbalance the environmental costs of international travel. Even in small ways, we can make a difference.

Consuming Responsibly

Understand your power to shape the marketplace by what you decide to buy, whether in the grocery store or in your choice of hotels. In my travels (and in my writing), whenever possible, I patronize and support small, family-run businesses (hotels, restaurants, shops, tour guides). I choose people who invest their creativity and resources in giving me simple, friendly, sustainable, and honest travel experiences—people with ideals. Back Door places don't rely on slick advertising and marketing gimmicks, and they don't target the created needs of people whose values are shaped by capitalism gone wild. Consuming responsibly means buying as if your choice is a vote for the kind of world we could have.

Back Doors

Europe is your playground...and it's time for recess.

Traveling Through the Back Door

The travel skills covered in the first half of this book enable you to open doors most travelers don't even know exist. Now I'd like to introduce you to some of my top European destinations, where you'll have a chance to put those skills to work. I'm the matchmaker, and you and the travel bug are about to get intimate. By traveling vicariously with me through this selection of places and sights, you'll get a peek at my favorite parts of Europe. And, just as important, by internalizing this lifetime of magical travel moments, you'll develop a knack for finding your own.

Europe's Top Destinations

This is the first book I ever wrote. In the early days, Back Doors to me were Europe's undiscovered nooks and undeveloped crannies: all-day walks on an alpine ridge, sword-fern fantasies in a ruined castle, and untrampled towns that had, for various reasons, missed the modern parade (like Gimmelwald, Dingle, Salema, and the Cinque Terre). But with ever more sophisticated travelers armed with ever-better guidebooks, places I "discovered" 20 or 25 years ago are now undeveloped and noncommercial only in a relative sense. And certain places that I really raved about now suffer from Back Door congestion.

So now, rather than isolate a few locations and call them "Back Doors," I'm giving you a country-by-country rundown of my favorite destinations throughout Europe and sharing some of my most unforgettable experiences...in the hope that they will inspire you to travel and fill your own journal with your own memories. This approach is less about finding the undiscovered places and more about demonstrating how

Ratings & Map Legend

I use the following symbols to rate destinations in this book:

▲▲▲ Don't miss
▲▲ Try hard to see
▲ Worthwhile if you can make it

I've written these chapters to give you the flavor of each country, not for you to navigate by. My various guidebooks provide all the details necessary to splice your chosen Back Doors into a smooth trip (see page 37).
Bon voyage!

🏰 Castle	········	Ferry/Boat Route
▪ Point of Interest	‑‑‑‑‑	Trails & Paths
▲ Mountain Peak	⊛	Capital City
)(Mtn. Pass	▲	National Park

thoughtful Back Door travel—anywhere you go—can get you beyond tourist traps, broaden your perspective, and enrich your travel experience.

Each corner of Europe has a unique and genuine charm. A destination is worthy simply because it exists, with people who proudly call it home. With a Back Door angle, you can slip your fingers under the staged culture of any destination and actually find a pulse. It's clear to me that the more you understand a region, the more you appreciate and enjoy it.

I've found my niche, and it's teaching people how to be travelers (as opposed to tourists). The lesson: When out wandering, poke around and risk having a door shut in your face—in order to risk being invited in.

Italy

When travel dreams take people to Europe, Italy is often their first stop. There's something seductively charming about this country, its people, and *la dolce vita*. I always feel at home in Italy, whether struggling onto a crowded bus in Rome, navigating the fun chaos of Naples, sipping a cocktail in a Venetian bar, or sitting on the banister of Florence's Ponte Vecchio for a midnight street-music concert.

Italy is the cradle of European civilization. As you explore, you'll stand face-to-face with iconic images from its 2,000-year history: the Colosseum of ancient Rome, the medieval Leaning Tower of Pisa, a cornucopia of Renaissance achievement (Michelangelo's *David* and the Sistine Chapel, for example), and the playful exuberance of the Baroque, perhaps best seen in the Bernini-designed fountains and squares of Rome.

Italy has it all — encompassing German-flavored Alps, romantic hill towns, peaceful lakes lined with 19th-century villas, sun-baked Sicily, the business center of Milan, Mediterranean beaches (like the Cinque Terre), and the art-drenched cities of Venice, Florence, and Rome. The country is reasonably small and laced with freeways and train lines, so you're never more than a day's journey from any of these places. And everywhere you can enjoy Italy's famous cuisine and wine.

I love Italy for its idiosyncrasies—the fun, the unpredictability, and the serendipity. And that comes with frustrations and complications. Precision in Italy seems limited to the pasta (which is exactly and reliably *al dente*). The country bubbles with emotion, traffic jams, strikes, and irate Italians shaking their fists at each other one minute and walking arm in arm the next. Have a talk with yourself before you cross

From fragments of once grandiose Roman statues to bobbing gondolas ready for romance, Italy has sightseeing treats for everyone.

the border. Promise yourself to relax, and remember it's a package deal.

Accept Italy as Italy. Savor your cappuccino, dangle your feet over a canal, and imagine what it was like centuries ago. Ramble through the rabble and rubble, and mentally resurrect those ancient stones. Get chummy with the winds of the past—and connect with the pleasures of the moment. Travel memories here are low-hanging fruit: They're yours to harvest.

FAVORITE SIGHTS AND MEMORABLE EXPERIENCES IN ITALY

Swept Away in Rome

Not long ago in Rome, I spent an entire sunny afternoon in my hotel room, tinkering with changes to the next edition of my guidebook. I had time for just a quick break, but stepping outside was dangerous. There's a strong current of distractions in this city. Just by turning the corner from my hotel, I was swept out into a Roman sea, teeming with colorful and fragrant entertainments. I didn't make it back for hours.

I flowed downhill to the Pantheon, the influential domed temple that served as the model for Michelangelo's dome of St. Peter's and many others. I stopped at the portico—nicknamed "Rome's umbrella," a fun local gathering spot in a rainstorm—from where I saw a symphony of images: designer shades and flowing hair backlit in the magic-hour sun; a flute section of ice-cream lickers sitting on a marble bench in the spritz of a fountain; strolling Romanian accordion players who refused to follow their conductor; and the stains of a golden arch on a wall marking where a McDonald's once sold fast food. The entire scene was corralled by pastel walls, providing the visual equivalent of good acoustics.

As I let go of the Pantheon's columns, the current swept me past siren cafés and out onto Via del Corso, which since ancient times has been the main north-south drag through town. On my swim through the city, this was the deep end. The rough crowd from the suburbs comes here for some cityscape elegance. Today they'd gooped on a little extra grease and were wearing their best leggings, heels, and T-shirts.

Veering away from the busy pedestrian boulevard, I came upon Fausto, a mad artist standing proudly amid his installation of absurdities. While eccentric, he seemed strangely sane in this crazy world. He's the only street artist I've met who personally greets viewers. After surveying his tiny gallery of hand-scrawled and thought-provoking tidbits, I asked for a card. He gave me a handmade piece of wallet-sized art, reminding me that his "secretary" was at the end of the curb: a plastic piggy bank for tips.

Next came the market square Campo de' Fiori, which usually creates its own current in the hours after the fruit and vegetable vendors have packed up. But today the square felt like a punished child. After a Roman teenager drank herself into a coma, police banned the consumption of alcohol in outdoor public spaces. It's like someone turned on the lights at a party before midnight.

I passed a homeless man, tattered but respectfully dressed, leaning against a wall. He was savoring a cigar and a bottle of wine while studying Rome's flow as if it held a secret. Next, I chatted with twins from Kentucky, giddy about their Roman days as they celebrated their 40th birthday together. Their Doublemint smiles and high energy made a great case for embracing the good life.

Moving on to Piazza del Popolo, the vast oval square known for its symmetrical design and art-filled churches, I ducked into the Church of Santa Maria del Popolo just as the ushers closed the doors for Mass. Inside, the white

Fast Facts

Biggest cities: Rome (capital, 2.7 million), Milan (1.3 million), Naples (1 million)

Size: 116,000 square miles (similar to Arizona), population 61 million

Locals call it: Italia

Currency: Euro

Key dates: 5th century A.D., the fall of the Roman Empire; 15th century, the birth of the Renaissance

Biggest festivals: Carnevale (usually February, especially big in Venice), Palio horse races (July 2 and August 16, Siena)

Handy Italian phrases: Buon giorno (good day; bwohn **jor**-noh), Per favore (please; pehr fah-**voh**-ray), Grazie (thank you; **graht**-see-ay), Mi fanno male i piedi! (My feet hurt!; mee **fah**-noh **mah**-lay ee pee **eh**-dee)

noise of Roman streets became the incense-scented hum of a big church with a determined priest—and not enough people. With my hands folded as if here to worship, I slipped down the side aisle to catch a glimpse of a Caravaggio, that late-16th-century thriller of Italian painting.

Stepping back outside, I found myself at the north entrance of the ancient city. Determined to swim back to my hotel and my work, I passed the same well-dressed bum with the cigar and the buzz, still intently caught up in the city. I imagined being in his pickled head for just a moment.

Near him, guys from Somalia launched their plastic fluorescent whirlybirds high into the twilight sky. These street trinkets keep African immigrants from starving. They make me wish I had made a museum from all the goofy things people have sold on the streets of Rome over the years—from flaming *Manneken-Pis* lighters to five-foot-tall inflatable bouncing cigars to twin magnets that jitter like crickets when you play with them just so.

Finally, with a struggling stroke, I made it back to the safety of my hotel, where none of that Roman current is allowed in. The problem: While taking a break from writing, I came home with even more to write about. In Rome, one thing leads to another, and if you're trying to get on top of your notes, it can be perilous to go out.

Tuning in to Tasty Italy

Tuscany is a region fiercely proud of its Chianina beef, from white cows. Recently, while in the town of Montepulciano, I sank my teeth into a carnivore's dream come true. In a stony cellar, under one long, tough vault, I joined a local crowd for dinner. The scene was powered by an open fire in the far back of the vault. Flickering in front of the flames was a huge hunk of red beef, lying on the counter like a corpse on a gurney. Like a blacksmith in hell, Giulio—a lanky man in a T-shirt—hacked at the beef with a cleaver, lopping off a steak every few minutes.

In a kind of mouth-watering tango, he pranced past the boisterous tables of customers, holding a raw slab of beef on butcher's paper as if handling a tray of drinks. Giulio presented the slabs to each table of diners, telling them the weight and price (the minimum was about $40) and getting their OK to cook it. He'd then dance back to the inferno and grill the slab: seven minutes on one side, seven on the other. There was no asking how you wanted it done; *this* was the way it was done.

Eating a steak at Giulio's place—Osteria dell'Acquacheta— is just one of my many memorable Italian dining experiences. And over the years, I've come up with some observations about food and Italy.

If America's specialty is fast food, Italy's is slow food: locally grown ingredients, in season, bought daily, prepared with love, and enjoyed in social circumstances with friends and family. While American food often has to look good, travel well, and be available all year, Italian food does none of that—it just has to taste good.

A perfect example is *vignarola*, a holy trinity of artichoke, peas, and fava beans. It's only available during a brief perfect storm of seasonality in spring, when everything is bursting with flavor. Italian chefs and home cooks religiously prep the vegetables—trimming the artichokes, cleaning the peas, and shelling the fava beans—to create this traditional dish that signals spring at its fullest.

While I've never liked putting up with TV noise when grabbing a simple meal in Italy, I now see that when an eatery has the TV playing, it's often because it's where the

LEFT In Tuscany, enthusiastic carnivores can have the meal of a lifetime at a rustic steakhouse.

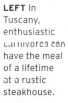

RIGHT For many Italians, "a good marriage" is the relationship between their favorite wine and what's on the plate.

Italy's Top Destinations

Rome ▲▲▲   allow 3-5 days

Italy's capital, studded with ancient architectural remnants, floodlit fountain squares, and Vatican opulence

Top Sights

Colosseum Huge stadium where gladiators squared off
Roman Forum Ancient Rome's main square, with ruins and grand arches
Pantheon Antiquity's best-preserved domed temple
St. Peter's Basilica World's most influential church, with Michelangelo's *Pietà* and dome
Vatican Museum Western civilization's finest art, including the Sistine Chapel
Borghese Gallery Bernini sculptures plus paintings by Caravaggio, Raphael, and Titian

Florence ▲▲▲   2-3 days

Walkable Renaissance wonderland and Tuscan capital with iconic Duomo (and other grand churches), palaces, museums, and Italy's best gelato

Top Sights

Accademia Michelangelo's *David* and powerful (unfinished) *Prisoners*
Uffizi Gallery Greatest collection of Renaissance paintings anywhere
Duomo Imposing Gothic cathedral with bell tower, baptistery, and Renaissance dome
Bargello Sculpture museum of Renaissance greats

Nearby

Pisa Leaning Tower and surrounding Field of Miracles
Lucca Charming city with walled old center
Volterra and San Gimignano Stony, characteristic hill towns

Venice ▲▲▲   1-3 days

Romantic island-city famous for St. Mark's Square and Basilica, the Grand Canal, and singing gondoliers

Milan ▲▲   1 day

Powerhouse city of commerce and fashion, with spiny Duomo, prestigious opera house, and Leonardo's *Last Supper*

Lake District ▲   1-2 days

Low-key resort towns with majestic alpine vistas and aristocratic Old World romance on **Lake Como** and **Lake Maggiore**

Cinque Terre ▲▲▲   1-3 days

Picture-perfect Riviera hamlets strung along a rugged coastline laced with hiking trails

Hill Towns of Central Italy ▲▲   1-3 days

Postcard villages of the Italian heartland: cathedral-capped **Orvieto,** minuscule **Civita,** wine-soaked **Montalcino** and **Montepulciano,** Renaissance-perfect **Pienza,** and classically Tuscan **Cortona**

Assisi ▲▲   1 day

St. Francis' hillside hometown, with a divine basilica decorated by Giotto

Siena ▲▲▲   1 day

Italy's ultimate hill town, with grand square and strikingly striped cathedral

Naples ▲▲   1-2 days

Gritty port city featuring vibrant street life and a top archaeological museum

Nearby
Pompeii Famous ruins of the ancient town buried by Mount Vesuvius' eruption
Sorrento and Capri Seaside resort port and jet-set island getaway
Amalfi Coast String of seafront villages tied together by scenic mountain road

With more time, consider visiting
Dolomites Italy's rugged rooftop, with alpine meadows and a Germanic flair
Padua University town with Giotto's gloriously frescoed Scrovegni Chapel
Verona Town with Roman amphitheater plus Romeo and Juliet sights
Ravenna Coastal town known for its top Byzantine mosaics

local workers drop by to eat—and that indicates a low price and a good value.

To go gourmet and not go broke, I go to a small, classy *enoteca* (wine bar). The bars are owned and operated by food evangelists who thoughtfully design the food menu to complement the wine list. A great wine costs about $10 a glass. Rather than bog down on an expensive entrée, I order top-end on the *antipasti* (starter) and *primi piatti* (first course) list. By doing that, I usually end up with the freshest meats and cheeses and the chef's favorite pasta dish of the day.

I've realized I should stay away from restaurants famous for inventing a pasta dish. Alfredo (of fettuccini fame) and Carbonara (of penne fame) are both Roman restaurants—and they're both much more famous than they are good.

One of my favorite Italian specialties isn't even on the menu: good conversation. In Rome, I talked about dessert with a man at a nearby table. He told me how his grandfather always said, in the local dialect, "The mouth cannot be finished until it smells of cows." In other words, you must finish the meal with cheese.

Another time, I shared a delightful dinner with a local guide, Giuseppe, and his wife, Anna. She greeted each plate with unbridled enthusiasm. Suddenly Giuseppe looked at me and said, "My wife's a good fork." Misunderstanding him, I blushed. My face said, "Come again?" And Giuseppe clarified, saying *"un buona forchetta...*a good fork—that's what we call someone who loves to eat."

To me, Italian cuisine is a symphony—the ingredients are the instruments. The quality is important, and the marriage of ingredients is what provides the tonality. When things are in tune, you taste it.

The Long Italian Meal

For many Italians, dinner is the evening's entertainment. Italians eat in courses, lingering over each one; a three-hour meal is common. A typical meal might start with *antipasti* (such as *bruschetta* or a plate of cold cuts and veggies). Next comes the *primo piatto* (first dish—such as a pasta, risotto, or soup), then the *secondo piatto* (usually meat or seafood), and finally, *dolce* (dessert). For most travelers, the full multi-course meal is simply too much food. A good rule of thumb is for each person to order any two courses, such as an *antipasto* and *primo piatto* (sharing is perfectly acceptable). When you want the bill, you'll have to ask for it (possibly more than once). For Italians, the meal is an end in itself, and only rude waiters rush you. To "eat and run" is seen as a lost opportunity.

Florence: The Cultural Capital of Europe

Geographically small but culturally rich, Florence is home to some of the greatest art and architecture in the world. It was in Florence, in about 1400, that the Renaissance began. After wallowing for centuries in relative darkness, Western civilization was suddenly perky, making up for lost centuries with huge gains in economics, science, and art. And Florence was at the center of it all.

Wealthy merchant and banking families—like the Medici, who ruled Florence for generations—demonstrated their civic pride (and showed off) by commissioning great art. Because of them, in a single day I can look Michelangelo's *David* in the eyes, fall under the seductive sway of Botticelli's *La Primavera*, and climb the modern world's first dome, which caps the cathedral and still dominates the skyline.

In Florence, great art is everywhere—even my hotel. I enjoy staying at Loggiato dei Serviti — a former monastery, crisp with elegance and history. The hotel's entrance is on a quintessentially Florentine square, with a beautifully arcaded building— the first designed by Brunelleschi (the man who engineered the cathedral's famed dome). The building, once an orphanage, now shelters the local down-and-outs on its elegant porch. While these well worn people used to get me down, now I realize that for 500 years, vagabonds and street people who couldn't afford a bedroom like the one I call home in Florence could still enjoy the architecture (or at least the shade). Since the days of the Renaissance greats, they have set up camp for free, under the loggia eave of my fancy front door.

From my room, I can look across the way to the Accademia Gallery and its art school. The courtyard in between is gravelly with broken columns and stones set up for students

Ticket Tricks

Italy's most popular museums and churches can have long lines and lots of crowds. Here are some tips for avoiding lines at the most congested sights.

- Book tickets ahead of time if visiting the Uffizi Gallery or the Accademia Gallery in Florence, to see Leonardo's *Last Supper* in Milan, or to wander the Vatican Museum (including the Sistine Chapel) in Rome.
- Consider getting a museum pass, such as the Firenze Card or the Roma Pass, which puts you in the fast lane at sights like Florence's Uffizi Gallery or Rome's Colosseum. Buy these passes at a tourist-information office or at lesser-visited sights (such as the Church of Santa Maria Novella in Florence or Palatine Hill in Rome) to avoid standing in line. In Venice, a combo-ticket covers the popular Doge's Palace (with long lines) and the less-visited Correr Museum— guess where you should buy the ticket?
- Some sights require a reservation, including the Scrovegni Chapel in Padua and Borghese Gallery in Rome.

to carve. All day long I hear the happy pecking and chirping of chisels gaining confidence as they cut through the stone. If they need inspiration, students only need to dip into the Accademia's exhibition space.

Entering that gallery is like walking into a temple of humanism. At the high altar stands Michelangelo's colossal statue of David, the slingshot-toting giant slayer. This perfect man represents humankind finally stepping out of medieval darkness. Clothed only in confidence, his toes gripping the pedestal, David sizes up his foe, as if to say, "I can take this guy." The statue was an apt symbol for the city, inspiring Florentines to tackle their Goliaths.

Until 1873, *David* lived not in the Accademia, but in the city's great square, Piazza della Signoria. A replica *David* marks the spot where the original once stood. With goony eyes and a pigeon-dropping wig, the fake *David* seems a bit dumbfounded, as tourists picnic at his feet and policewomen clip-clop by on horseback.

One edge of Piazza della Signoria opens into the long arcaded courtyard of the Uffizi Gallery, the museum that once housed the offices of the Medici. A permanent line of tourists waits patiently in the shade to see this best-anywhere collection of Italian paintings. Lounging between the columns, enterprising artists sketch the tourists and display their work. And filling the niches all around are life-size statues of Leonardo, Dante, Lorenzo de' Medici, and a dozen other Renaissance greats—Florentines, every one of them.

My favorite Florentine painter—Botticelli—has a few special paintings inside the Uffizi. His *Primavera* shows the

Botticelli's *Primavera*, a highlight of the Uffizi Gallery

personification of Spring—and the Renaissance in full bloom. Botticelli painted a splendid innocence, where a maiden can walk barefoot through a garden scattering flower petals from a fold in her dress and call it a good day's work—and where the Three Graces can dance naked with no more fanfare than the happy do-si-do of butterflies. To me, the delicate face of Botticelli's Spring is the purest expression of Renaissance beauty in Florence.

In Florence, Brunelleschi's dome towers above much of the finest art in Europe. Yet cross the Arno River, and you're in a rustic zone of traditional artisans.

Today, Florence's artistic legacy lives on across the Arno River, in the Oltrarno neighborhood—home to small shops featuring handmade furniture, enameled jewelry, marbled papers, and finely glazed pottery. One artisan drew me into his shop as if inviting me on a journey. Under a single dangling light bulb, he hammered gold leaf into a dingy halo, breathing life back into a faded statue that had originally been crafted by a neighbor of his—five centuries ago. Hundreds of years after the Renaissance, the spirit of creation remains alive and well in Florence.

The Cinque Terre: Italy's Riviera

"A sleepy, romantic, and inexpensive town on the Riviera without a tourist in sight." That's the mirage travelers chase around busy Nice and Cannes. Pssst! Although hardly free of tourists, the most dream-worthy stretch of the Riviera rests in Italy just across the border, between Genoa and Pisa. It's Italy's Cinque Terre.

Leaving the nearest big city, La Spezia, your train takes you into a mountain. Ten minutes later, you burst into the sunlight. Your train nips in and out of the hills, teasing you with a series of Mediterranean views. Each scene is grander than the last: azure blue tinseled in sunbeams, carbonated waves hitting desolate rocks, and the occasional topless sunbather camped out like a lone limpet.

The Cinque Terre (pronounced CHINK-weh TAY-reh), which means "five lands," is a quintet of villages clinging to this most inaccessible bit of Riviera coastline. Each is a variation on the same theme: a well-whittled pastel jumble of homes filling a gully like crusty sea creatures in a tide pool. Like a gangly clump of oysters, the houses grow on each other. Residents are the barnacles—hungry, but patient. And we travelers are like algae, coming in with the tide.

The rugged villages of the Cinque Terre, founded by Dark Age locals hiding out from marauding pirates, were long cut off from the modern world. Only with the coming of the train was access made easy. Today, the villages draw hordes of hikers, and the castles protect only glorious views. To preserve this land, the government has declared the Cinque Terre a national park. Visitors hiking between the towns now pay a small entrance fee (about $8 for a one-day pass), which stokes a fund designed to protect the flora and fauna and keep the trails clean and well maintained.

The government, recognizing how wonderfully pre-served these towns are, has long prohibited anyone from constructing any modern buildings. For that reason, today there are no big, comfortable hotels in the area—great news for Back Door travelers because it keeps away the most obnoxious slice of the traveling public: those who need big, comfortable hotels. But rugged travelers, content to rent a room in a private home or simple *pensione,* enjoy a land where the villagers go about their business as if the sur-rounding vineyards are the very edges of the earth.

Overseen by a ruined castle, with the closest thing to a natural harbor, Vernazza is my Cinque Terre home base. Only the occasional noisy slurping up of the train by the mountain reminds you there's a modern world out there somewhere.

From Vernazza's harbor, wander through the jumble of a tough community living off the sea...or living off travelers who love the sea. The church bells dictate a relaxed tempo. Yellow webs of fishing nets, tables bedecked with umbrellas, kids with plastic shovels, and a flotilla of gritty little boats tethered to buoys provide splashes of color. And accompany-ing the scene is the soundtrack of a dream...a celebrate-the-moment white noise of children, dogs, and waves.

Vernazza's one street connects the harbor with the train station before melting into the vineyards. Like veins on a

The five pastel ports of Italy's Cinque Terre were established as hideouts from pirates in the Middle Ages. Today, villagers will eagerly rent you a room and drizzle pesto on your pasta.

grape leaf, paths and stairways reach from Main Street into this watercolor huddle of houses. All of life is summer reruns in this hive of lazy human activity. A rainbow of laundry flaps as if to keep the flies off the fat grandmothers who clog ancient doorways.

Residents spend early evenings doing their *vasche* (laps), strolling between the station and the breakwater. Sit on a bench and study this slow motion parade.

Today, at the top end of town, Vernazza's cruel little road hits a post. No cars enter this village of 600 people. Like the breakwater keeps out the waves at the bottom of the town, the post keeps out the modern storm at the top. But Vernazza's ruined castle no longer says "stay away." And its breakwater—a broad, inviting sidewalk edged with seaside boulders—sticks into the sea like a finger beckoning the distant excursion boats.

Barefoot in Venice

When you know where to look, there's so much to see in Venice. Stepping ashore after a boat ride from the airport, I noticed everything seemed particularly vivid in this beautifully decrepit cityscape: the pilings rotten at the water line; a funeral boat with an iron casket-rack lashed to the center of the hull; chandeliers lighting a mansion's ceiling frescoes; white marble inlay lining the edges of the stairs over a bridge. In Venice, always look both ways when you pass over a bridge, as lovely views can hit you from any direction.

But there are times when the magic suddenly stops. I needed to check out the parking situation at the edge of the city, and the traffic appalled me. As I dodged the crazy Italian drivers, the contrast between mainland and island was clear. What a charming world the Venetians enjoy—it's free of traffic noise and, as pedestrians, they completely own their byways.

A boat ride took me to the nearby island of Burano, which is famous for humble fishermen's houses and squinting lacemakers. I noticed how the pastel colors of the homes are getting more and more vibrant. The place is just darling (an adjective I've never used to describe a town before).

But the rising sea has forced Burano to raise its canal-side pavement. I could see a strip of fresh bricks above the water line. Houses that could be made higher have had their ground floors raised, leaving them with shorter ceilings.

Venice has been battling rising water levels since the fifth century. Venice now floods about 100 times a year—usually from October until late winter—a phenomenon called *acqua alta*. During these floods, some high-end hotels lend wading boots to their customers. Wooden benches are placed end-to-end in St. Mark's Square to create elevated sidewalks. But these turn into total gridlock, as the square-sized crowds jostle for space on the narrow wooden walkways.

But on this trip, St. Mark's Square was as dry as ever. At Caffè Florian, the most venerable café on the square, the manager lamented how, in the last decade, the café's elegance has been trampled by poorly dressed tourists (not unlike me, I must admit). Still, I love this place, with its smoke-stained mirrors, white-tuxedoed waiters, and finicky piano and string quartet, which somehow gets called an "orchestra."

While you can enjoy a romantic drink here with live music and all the tourists, I opted for a quiet cup of coffee in the morning, when the square was empty. Surrounded by the patina of faded elegance, I marveled at how the history

Venice is awash with wonders—from the cultural grounding that comes with going barefoot on the flooring "alla veneziana" to the surge of the gondolier's oar as you glide under the Bridge of Sighs.

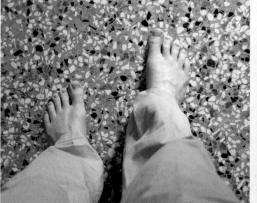

popped with the architecture and without the modern tourism. The Gothic was so lacy, and the Renaissance so capable. It looked like a pure, computer-generated Venetian cityscape—only it was real. In so many ways, when you get up early and stay out late, you enjoy a different, and it seems, more authentic Venice.

Likewise, on the vaporetto water buses, there's a stark contrast between the midday/rush-hour mobs and the easy-going joy of riding at quiet times. Venice is two cities: one garishly touristic and the other so romantic and tranquil that it makes you go *fortissimo* in describing it.

In Venice, I spend my evenings visiting restaurants to consider for my guidebooks, then return to my favorite for dinner. This dining derby is my nightly ritual in Italy. Tonight, when the waiter asked me how I liked my wine, I said, "*Complicato*"—and he served up his house Amarone, a local red. I drank it like a monkey climbs a tree. Just when the branches were getting pretty bendy, he capped the meal with a glass of Sgroppino, a Venetian after-dinner slushy of lemon juice, lemon gelato, Prosecco, and vodka. It's my new favorite taste treat.

Done with dinner, I retreated to my hotel room. The speckled "Venetian pavement"—the city's characteristic floor made of a broken hodgepodge of marble fragments and then polished—greeted my bare feet. While some might mistake it for cheap linoleum, it's far from that—it's treasured here and quite expensive. It flexes with the settling of the buildings and is costly to maintain, but it's so characteristic. My feet connected with that floor in a way my feet have never before connected with flooring—happily grounding me in Venice.

Bella Tuscany

After checking in to my Tuscan *agriturismo*, my host, Signora Gori, takes me on a welcome stroll. Our first stop is a sty dominated by a giant pig. "We call him Pastanetto—'the little pastry.'" While the scene through my camera's viewfinder is pristine and tranquil, the soundtrack is not. As a horrendous chorus of squeals comes from a rustic slaughterhouse on the horizon, she says, "This is our little Beirut." I stow my camera, deciding to simply absorb the attention I'm enjoying from a host who is both old-money elegant and farmhouse-tough. The Gori family estate is Tuscany in the rough.

The Italian landscape is dotted with *agriturismi* like this one—traditional family farms renting out spare rooms to make ends meet. To qualify officially as an *agriturismo*, the

farm must still generate more money from its farm activities—whether growing olives, making wine, or producing prosciutto—and most sell or serve the food they produce to guests. Don't confuse these with farmhouse B&Bs, which aren't actual farms, though they can be fine places to stay. If you want the real thing, make sure the owners call their place an *agriturismo*.

Hiking to the slaughterhouse, we enter a room dominated by a stainless-steel table piled with red sides of pork. Signora Gori says, "Here begins prosciutto." Burly men in aprons squeeze the blood out of hunks of meat the size of dance partners. Then they cake the ham hocks in salt to begin a curing process that takes months. While the salt helps cure the meat, a coating of pepper seals it. In spooky but great-smelling rooms, towering racks of ham hocks age. A man, dressed and acting like a veterinarian, tests each ham by sticking it with a horse-bone needle and giving it a sniff.

Back outside, Signora Gori takes me into the next barn, where fluffy white lambs jump to attention in their hay, kicking up a sweet-smelling golden dust. Backlit by stray sunbeams, it's a dreamy, almost biblical scene. Picking up a baby lamb, she gives it an Eskimo kiss—nose to nose. She explains, "I must really know my sheep." Their milk is turned into Pecorino cheese.

Strolling down another lane, we observe the family's team of vintners just as Signora Gori's brother empties a bucketful of purple grapes into a dump truck. The load tumbles from the truck into a grinder, which munches through the bunches, spitting stems one way and juice with mangled grapes the other. As the juice flows through pipes into a cellar, the brother explains that wine-making is labor-intensive, "but right now the grapes are doing all the work."

And as the new grapes ferment, we taste the finished product. A key word for your Tuscan travels is *corposo*—full-bodied. Lifting the elegant glass to my lips, I sip the wine while enjoying the pride in the eyes of those who made it. Satisfied, I say, "*Corposo*." They say, "*Si, bello*."

That night at dinner, we're joined by the rest of the Gori family. The two sons dress and act like princes home on break from some Italian Oxford. Sitting down to a classic Tuscan table—where things are simple, harmonious, and unhurried—with a glass of good red wine, I nod to my hosts, knowing I've found the art of Tuscany.

After dinner, full and content, we sip port and enjoy a backgammon board that has provided evening fun for 200 years in this very room. Surrounded by musty portraits putting faces on this family's long lineage, I realize that this—a special moment for me—is just another night on the farm here in the Gori home.

Naples: Just Do It

All my life, Naples has been the symbol of chaos, stress, and culture shock for European travel. I remember my first visit as a wide-eyed 18-year-old. I stepped off the train into the same vast Piazza Garibaldi that many years later still strikes everyone who visits it as a big paved hellhole. On that first visit, a man in a white surgeon's gown approached me and said, "Please, we need blood for a dying baby." I made a U-turn, stepped back into the station, and made a beeline for Greece.

The city is calmer now, but Naples remains uniquely thrilling. One of my favorite sightseeing experiences anywhere in Italy is simply wandering Spaccanapoli, the long, straight, narrow street that runs through the historic center and bisects the city. Living in the streets is quintessentially Neapolitan—people here seem perfectly adept at enjoying life with their domestic worlds tumbling right out onto the gritty pavement. Naples may be an urban jungle, but it's a warm and welcoming place. Like Cairo or Bombay, it's appalling and appealing at the same time, the closest thing to "reality

travel" you'll find in Western Europe. But this tangled mess still somehow manages to breathe, laugh, and sing—with a captivating Italian accent.

Lurking deep in old Naples, you know you can't be a local...but you can imagine.

An essential stop on any Naples visit is the Archaeological Museum, which offers the closest possible peek into the artistic jewelry boxes of Pompeii and Herculaneum. The actual archaeological sites, while impressive, are barren—the best frescoes and mosaics ended up here. The Secret Room displays R-rated Roman "bedroom" art. A highlight is the Farnese Collection—a giant hall of huge, bright, and wonderfully restored statues excavated from Rome's Baths of Caracalla. You can almost hear the *Toro Farnese* snorting. This largest intact statue from antiquity (a third-century copy of a Hellenistic original, showing a tangled group of people with a raging bull) was carved out of one piece of marble and later restored by Michelangelo.

Take time to explore Naples. This living medieval city is its own best sight. Couples artfully make love on Vespas, while surrounded by more fights and smiles per cobblestone than anywhere else in Italy.

Paint a picture with these thoughts: Naples has the most intact ancient Roman street plan anywhere. Imagine life here in the days of Caesar, with streetside shop fronts that close up to form private homes after dark. Today is just one more page in a 2,000-year-old story of city activity: all kinds of meetings, beatings, and cheatings; kisses, near misses, and little-boy pisses.

For a peek behind the scenes in the shade of wet laundry, venture down a few narrow streets lined by tall apartment buildings. Black-and-white death announcements add to the clutter on the walls. Widows sell cigarettes from plastic buckets. Buy two carrots as a gift for the woman on the fifth floor if she'll lower her bucket down to pick them up.

In search of cheap eats (near major sights) that I can recommend to my guidebook readers, I walk behind the Archaeological Museum and meet exuberant Pasquale, the owner of a tiny deli. Rather than do the cheapskate "how much?" question, I just let fun-loving and flamboyant Pasquale surprise me.

He turns making a sandwich into a show, and I watch, enthralled. After demonstrating the freshness of his rolls as if squeezing the Charmin, he lays a careful pavement of salami, brings over the fluffy mozzarella ball as if performing a kidney transplant, slices a tomato with rapid-fire machine precision, lovingly pits the olives by hand before hanging them like little green paintings on a tasty wall, and then finishes it all off with a celebratory drizzle of the best olive oil. Five euros and a smile later, I have my cheap lunch and a new guidebook listing.

After saying goodbye to Pasquale, I step outside to look for a bench upon which to enjoy my lunch and watch the spirit of Naples roll by.

Civita: A World Apart

The hill towns of central Italy hold their crumbling heads proudly above the noisy flood of the 21st century and offer a peaceful taste of what eludes so many tourists. Sitting on a timeless rampart high above the traffic and trains, hearing only children in the market as the rustling wind ages the weary red-tile patchwork that surrounds me, I find the essence of Italy.

Of all the hill towns, Civita di Bagnoregio is my favorite. People who've been here say "Civita" (chee-vee-tah) with warmth and love. This precious chip of Italy is a traffic-free community with a grow-it-in-the-valley economy.

Civita teeters atop a pinnacle in a vast canyon ruled by wind and erosion. Over the years its population has dropped, but the town survives to serve a steady stream of tourists. The saddle that once connected Civita to its bigger and busier sister town, Bagnoregio, eroded away. Today a bridge connects the two towns. A man with a Vespa does the same work his father did with a donkey—ferrying the town's goods up and down the umbilical bridge that connects Civita with a small, distant parking lot and the rest of Italy. Rome, just 60 miles to the south, is a world away.

Entering the town through a cut in the rock made by Etruscans 2,500 years ago, and heading under a 12th-century Romanesque arch, you feel history in the huge, smooth cobblestones. This was once the main Etruscan road leading to the Tiber Valley and Rome. Inside the gate, the charms of Civita are subtle. Those searching for arcade tourism wouldn't know where to look. There are no lists of attractions, orientation tours, or museum hours. It's just Italy. Civita is an artist's dream, a town in the nude. Each lane and footpath holds a surprise. The warm stone walls glow, and each stairway is dessert to a sketch pad or camera.

Smile and nod at each passerby. It's a social jigsaw puzzle, and each person fits. The old woman hanging out in the window monitors gossip. A tiny hunchback lady is everyone's daughter. And cats, the fastest-growing segment of the population, scratch their itches on ancient pillars.

Explore the village. The basic grid street plan of the ancient town survives—but its centerpiece, a holy place of worship, rotates with the cultures: first an Etruscan temple, then a Roman temple, and today a church. The pillars that stand like bar stools in the square once decorated the pre-Christian temple. The heartbeat and pride of the village, this is where festivals and processions start, visitors are escorted, and the town's past is honored.

Just around the corner from the church, on the main street, is La Cantina de Arianna Trattoria Bruschetteria, a family-run wine cellar. Pull up a stump and let the family serve you *panini* (sandwiches), wine, and a cake called *ciambella*. The white wine has a taste reminiscent of dirty socks. But it's made right here. After eating, ask to see the cellar with its traditional winemaking gear and provisions

Somehow keeping its head above the flood of the 21st century, the hill town of Civita di Bagnoregio survives and welcomes the adventurous traveler.

for rolling huge kegs up the stairs. Grab the stick and tap on the kegs to measure their fullness.

Explore further through town. At Antico Frantoio Bruschetteria, venture into their back room to see an interesting collection of old olive presses. This local equivalent of a lemonade stand sells bruschetta to visitors. Bread toasted on an open fire, drizzled with the finest oil, rubbed with pungent garlic, and topped with chopped tomatoes—these edible souvenirs stay on your breath for hours and in your memory forever.

At the end of town, the main drag shrivels into a trail that leads past a chapel (once a jail) and down to a tunnel—now barred to entry—that was cut through the hill under the town in Etruscan times. Tall enough for a woman with a jug on her head to pass through, it may have served as a shortcut to the river below. It was widened in the 1930s so farmers could get between their scattered fields more easily.

Civita has only a few restaurants, which cluster near the piazza. At Trattoria Antico Forno ("Antique Oven"), you eat what's cooking. Owner Franco slices and dices happily through the day. Spaghetti, salad, and wine on the Antico Forno patio, cuddled by Civita—I wouldn't trade it for all-you-can-eat at Maxim's.

Spend the evening. After dinner, sit on the church steps and observe the scene. They say that in a big city you can see a lot, but in a small town like this you can feel a lot. The generous bench is built into the long side of the square, reminding me of how, when I first discovered Civita back in the 1970s and 1980s, the town's old folks would gather here every night. Children play on the piazza until midnight. As you walk back to your car—that scourge of the modern world that enabled you to get here—stop under a lamp on the donkey path, listen to the canyon...distant voices...a clicking chorus of crickets.

More Italian Experiences
In Assisi with St. Francis: I have a personal ritual of enjoying a quiet picnic on the rampart of a ruined castle high above Assisi, the town of St. Francis. I look down at the basilica dedicated to the saint, then into the valley, where a church stands strong in the hazy Italian plain. It marks the place where Francis and his friars started the Franciscan order, bringing the word of God to people in terms all could embrace. Hearing the same birdsong that inspired Francis, and tasting the same simple bread, cheese, and wine of

Umbria that sustained him, I calm my 21st-century soul and ponder Francis' message of love, simplicity, and sensitivity to the environment.

A Dove on a Zipline: One spring day, I couldn't resist joining a multitude that had gathered in front of Orvieto's cathedral. For generations, citizens of this small Umbrian town have celebrated the Pentecost—the descent of the Holy Ghost upon the Apostles—in this spot. The anticipation built and built, and then, suddenly, it happened: A dove in a little plastic tube rocketed down a zipline and into a nest of fireworks at the front of the church, setting it all ablaze. After the fireworks exploded, a fireman climbed up to see if the dove was OK. It was. And that was great news, as it brings good luck to the town and fertility to the last couple married in Orvieto.

The Allure of Lake Como: Sleepy Lake Como is a good place to take a break from the obligatory turnstile culture of central Italy. It seems that half the travelers I meet here have tossed their itineraries into the lake and are actually relaxing. The town of Varenna offers the best of all lake worlds. On the quieter side of the lake, with a tiny harbor, narrow lanes, and its own villa, Varenna is the right place to munch a peach and ponder the place where Italy is welded to the Alps. Other than watch the visitors wash ashore with the landing of each ferry, there's wonderfully little to do here. Varenna's volume goes down with the sun. At night, it whispers *luna di miele*—honeymoon. And a good place to enjoy that romance is on its lakefront promenade, the *passerella*. After dark, it's adorned with caryatid lovers pressing silently against each other in the shadows.

Siena Soul: Unlike its rival, Florence, Siena is a city to be seen as a whole rather than as a collection of sights. While memories of Florence consist of dodging Vespas and pick-pockets between museums, Siena has an easy-to-enjoy Gothic soul: Courtyards sport flower-decked wells, churches modestly hoard their art, and alleys dead-end into red-tiled rooftop panoramas. Climb to the dizzy top of the 100-yard-tall bell tower and reign over urban harmony at its best. At twilight, first-time poets savor that magic moment when the sky is a rich blue dome no brighter than the medieval towers that seem to hold it high.

Siena is famous for hosting the frantic Palio horse race, held every year on July 2 and August 16. Dirt is brought in

and packed down over the pavers of Il Campo, the town's main square, to create the track's surface, and mattresses are strapped onto the sharp corners of surrounding buildings. On the big day, the horses are taken into church to be blessed (it's considered a sign of luck if a horse leaves droppings in the church). The snorting horses and their nervous riders each representing a Sienese neighborhood—line up to await the starting signal. Then they race like crazy, while spectators, hungry for victory, wave the scarves of their district. After the winning horse crosses the line (with or without its rider), the prevailing neighborhood goes berserk with joy. If you go, you won't see much—but you'll feel it. It's a real medieval moment.

Whether pondering wisteria villas on Lake Como (left), screaming for your favorite rider in Siena's Palio (center), or struggling on your knees up the steps Jesus climbed on the day he was condemned (right), sightseeing in Italy has an impact on the traveler.

On My Knees in Rome: All of my Protestant life I've watched hardscrabble pilgrims and frail nuns climb Rome's Scala Santa on their knees. These are the "Holy Stairs" of Pontius Pilate's palace that Christ climbed the day he was condemned. This year, a voice inside me said "Do it!" So I picked up the little pilgrim's primer explaining what holy thoughts to ponder on each step, knelt down, and—one by one—began climbing. Knees screaming, weathered faithful struggling up the staircase with me, I climbed the 28 wooden steps. In my pain, the frescoed art surrounding the staircase snapped into action, goading me on. And, while my knees would never agree, the experience was beautiful.

CULTURE AND TRADITIONS: EVERYTHING'S SO...ITALIAN

Style Matters

For Italians, it's very important to exhibit a positive public persona—a concept called *la bella figura*. While some Americans don't think twice about going to the supermarket in sweats, Italians dress well anytime they leave the house— and they'd rather miss their bus than get all sweaty and mussed-up rushing to catch it. An elderly woman will do her hair and carefully put on makeup for her monthly doctor's appointment, and no matter how hot it gets, Italian men wear long pants—never shorts (except at the beach).

Communicating with Italians

Because they're so outgoing and their language is so fun, Italians are a pleasure to communicate with. They are animated and even dramatic. You may think two people are arguing when in reality they're agreeing enthusiastically. Body language is an important part of communicating, especially hand gestures. For instance, the "cheek screw" (pressing a forefinger into their cheek and rotating it) is used to mean good, lovely, or beautiful. A chin flick with the fingers bunched up means "I'm not interested; you bore me." Italians have an endearing habit of speaking Italian to foreigners, even if they know you don't speak their language—and yet, thanks to gestures and thoughtfully simplified words, it somehow works.

Social Time

Italian families and communities are more close-knit than many others in the modern world. Many Italians, especially in rural regions and small towns, still follow the traditional siesta schedule (called *reposo* in Italy). At about 1 p.m., shops

In Italy, the temptations are on parade—in the streets and in the gelato shops. Any town... any evening... *la vita è bella.*

close and people go home for a three-hour break to have lunch, socialize with friends and family, and run errands.

Early evening is the time for the ritual promenade called the *passeggiata*, when shoppers, people watchers, families, and young flirts on the prowl all join the scene to stroll arm in arm and spread their wings like peacocks. In a more genteel small town, the *passeggiata* comes with sweet whispers of *"bella"* (pretty) and *"bello"* (handsome). In Rome, the *passeggiata* is actually a cruder, big-city version called the *struscio* (meaning "to rub"), and people utter the words *"buona"* and *"buono"*—meaning, roughly, "tasty."

Gelato

Gelato is an edible art form. While American ice cream is made with cream and has a high butterfat content, Italian gelato is made with milk. It's also churned more slowly, making it denser. With less air and less fat than American-style ice cream, gelato is more flavorful. To find the best *gelateria*, look for the words *artiginale, nostra produzione,* and *produzione propia*, meaning it's made on the premises. Seasonal flavors and pastel hues (not garish colors) are also good signs. Gelato displayed in covered metal tins (rather than white plastic) is more likely to be homemade. To avoid having your request for a cone turn into a €10 "tourist special," survey the size options and be very clear in your order. My advice is to get plenty of vitamin G. Italy is best explored with long, meandering walks, and nothing refuels the body and spirit like cones of gelato.

Is the Pope Catholic?

Italy, home of the Vatican, is still mostly Catholic. Although Italians will crowd into St. Peter's Square with rock-concert energy to catch a glimpse of "il Papa," they're not particularly devout. And while most people would never think of renouncing their faith, they don't attend church regularly. They baptize their kids at the local church (there's one every few blocks), but they hold modern opinions on social issues, often in conflict with strict Catholic dogma. Italy is now the land of legalized abortion, a low birth rate, nudity on TV, socialist politics, and a society whose common language is decidedly secular. The true dominant religion is life: motor scooters, soccer, fashion, girl-watching, boy-watching, good coffee, good wine, and *il dolce far niente* (the sweetness of doing nothing).

Coffee, Italian-Style

Italians are religious about their coffee. Every coffee drinker has a certain style and a favorite place to buy it. If that place is closed, many would rather skip their coffee altogether. According to Italians, you can tell if coffee is good just by looking at it. When the beans are ground correctly, it comes out of the machine first a creamy brown color, then darker.

Italians tend to drink their coffee with less water than Americans (as one friend put it, "If we are so thirsty, we have a Coke"). In fact, the espresso-based style of coffee that's popular in the US was born in Italy. Most Italian drinks begin with espresso, to which the barista adds varying amounts of hot water and/or steamed or foamed milk. *Un caffè* is just a shot of espresso in a little cup; the closest thing to American-style drip coffee is a *caffè americano*—espresso diluted with hot water. Milky drinks, like *cappuccino* or *caffè latte*, are served to locals before noon...and to tourists any time of day. (Italians believe that milk can be properly digested only in the morning.) If Italians add any milk after lunch, it's just a splash, in a *caffè macchiato*—coffee "marked" or "stained" with milk.

Italy Travel Resources from Rick Steves

Guidebooks

Check out Rick's guidebooks covering all of Italy; Rome; Venice; Florence & Tuscany; Naples & the Amalfi Coast; the Cinque Terre; Milan & the Italian Lakes District; and Central Italy's hill towns; plus his Italian phrase book

Audio Europe

Download Rick's free Audio Europe app, with self-guided audio tours of sights and neighborhoods in Rome (Pantheon, St. Peter's Basilica, Forum, Colosseum, Sistine Chapel, Trastevere, Jewish Ghetto), Florence (Accademia Gallery, Uffizi Gallery, Renaissance Walk), Venice (Frari Church, St. Mark's Basilica, St. Mark's Square, Grand Canal), Assisi (Basilica of St. Francis, Town Walk), and the ancient sites of Ostia Antica and Pompeii

TV Shows

The quintessence of Italy with Rick as your host, viewable on public television and at ricksteves.com. Episodes cover Rome, Venice, Florence, Italian Alps, Cinque Terre, Amalfi Coast, Naples and Pompeii, Italy's hill towns, Milan, Lake Como, and Sicily

Organized Tours

Small group tours, with itineraries planned by Rick: Italy in 17 Days; Village Italy in 14 Days; South Italy in 13 Days; Best of Sicily in 11 Days; Heart of Italy in 9 Days; Venice, Florence & Rome in 10 Days; Rome in 7 Days; My Way: Italy in 13 Days

For more on all of these resources, visit ricksteves.com

France

France is Europe's most diverse, tasty, and, in many ways, most exciting country to explore. With luxuriant forests, forever coastlines, grand canyons, and Europe's highest mountain ranges, France has cover-girl looks. You'll also discover a dizzying array of artistic and architectural wonders—soaring cathedrals, chandeliered châteaux, and museums filled with the cultural icons of the Western world.

Moving from region to region, you feel as if you're crossing into different countries. Paris is in the heart of France. To the west is Normandy, with the historic D-Day beaches and the ethereal island-abbey of Mont St-Michel. To the south is the Loire river valley, filled with luxurious châteaux, and the Dordogne region, with prehistoric caves, medieval castles, and hill-capping villages. Near Spain is Languedoc, crowned by castles, from the fortress town of Carcassonne to remote Cathar ruins. Closer to Italy, sun-baked and windswept Provence nurtures Roman ruins and rustic charm, while the Riviera celebrates sunny beaches and yacht-filled harbors. And to the east, travelers encounter the villages of Germanic Alsace, the vineyards of Burgundy, and Europe's highest snow-capped Alps.

In France, *l'art de vivre*—the art of living—is something every traveler can aspire to learn.

In France, *l'art de vivre*—the art of living—is not just a pleasing expression; it's a building block for a sound life. With five weeks of paid vacation, plus every Catholic holiday ever invented, the French have become experts at living well. It's no accident

that France is home to linger-longer pastimes like café lounging, fine dining, and barge cruising. The French insist on the best-quality croissants, cheese, mustard, and sparkling water; they don't rush lunch; and an evening's entertainment is usually no more than a lovingly prepared meal with friends. France demands that the traveler savor the finer things.

As you travel through this splendid country, slo-o-o-ow down. Spend hours in cafés dawdling over *un café*, make a habit of unplanned stops, and surrender willingly to *l'art de vivre*.

FAVORITE SIGHTS AND MEMORABLE EXPERIENCES IN FRANCE

Circling in on the Arc de Triomphe in Paris

I have a funny ritual I follow whenever I'm in Paris. I ask my taxi driver to take me around the Arc de Triomphe—two times. My cabbie plunges into the grand roundabout where a dozen boulevards converge on this mightiest of triumphal arches. Like referees at gladiator camp, traffic cops are stationed at each entrance to this traffic circus, letting in bursts of eager cars. As marble Lady Liberties scramble up Napoleon's arch, heroically thrusting their swords and shrieking at the traffic, all of Paris seems drawn into this whirlpool. Each time, being immersed in the crazy traffic with my cabbie so in control makes me laugh out loud.

In the mid-19th century, Baron Haussmann set out to make Paris the grandest city in Europe. The 12 arterials that radiate from the Arc de Triomphe were part of his master plan for a series of major boulevards that would intersect at diagonals. At the crisscross points, he had monuments (such as the Arc de Triomphe) erected as centerpieces. As we zip around the circle, it's obvious that Haussmann's plan did not anticipate the automobile.

My cabbie explains to me, "If there is an accident here, each driver is considered equally at fault. This is the only place in Paris where the accidents are not judged. No matter what the circumstances, insurance companies split the costs fifty-fifty. In Paris, a good driver gets only scratches, not dents."

The commotion of cars fights to get to the arch at the center as if to pay homage to the national spirit of France. Cars entering the circle have the right-of-way; those in the circle must yield. Parisian drivers navigate the circle like a comet circling the sun—making a parabola. It's a game of fender-bender chicken. This circle is the great equalizer. Tippy little Citroëns, their rooftops cranked open like sardine lids, bring lumbering buses to a sudden, cussing halt.

While we're momentarily stalled on the inside lane, I pay and hop out. As the cabbie drives away, I'm left feeling small under Europe's ultimate arch. Here the flame of France's unknown soldier—flickering silently in the eye of this urban storm—seems to invite me to savor this grandiose monument to French nationalism.

The Arc de Triomphe affords a great Paris view, but only to those who earn it—there are 284 steps to the top. At the top, I look down along the huge axis that shoots like an arrow all the way from the Louvre, up the Champs-Elysées, through the arch, then straight down the Avenue de la Grande-Armée to a forest of distant skyscrapers around an even bigger modern arch in suburban La Défense. I love the contrast between the skyscrapers in the suburbs and the more uniform heights of buildings closer to the arch. The beauty of Paris—basically a flat basin with a river running through it—is man-made. There's a harmonious relationship between the width of its grand boulevards and the standard height and design of the buildings. This elegant skyline is broken only by venerable historic domes and spires—and the lonely-looking Montparnasse Tower, which stands like the box the Eiffel Tower came in. The appearance of this tower served

Paris is a capital of grand monuments and grand boulevards.

as a wake-up call in the early 1970s to preserve the historic skyline of downtown Paris.

The grandest of boulevards emanating from the arch, the Champs-Elysées, used to be even grander. From the 1920s through the 1960s, it was lined with top-end hotels, cafés, and residences—pure elegance. Parisians actually dressed up to come here. Then, in 1963, the government pumped up the neighborhood's commercial metabolism by bringing in the RER (commuter train). Suburbanites had easy access, McDonald's moved in, and *pfft*—there went the neighborhood. Still, the Champs-Elysées remains the country's ultimate parade ground, where major events all unfold: the Tour de France finale, Bastille Day parades, and New Year's festivities. With its monumental sidewalks, stylish shops, venerable cafés, and glimmering showrooms, this is Paris at its most Parisian.

Joyride in a Loire Valley Restaurant

French cuisine is sightseeing for your taste buds. You're not just paying for the food. A meal can be a three-hour joyride for the senses—as rich as visiting an art gallery and as stimulating as a good massage.

Not long ago, I dined at a fine restaurant in Amboise, in the midst of France's château-rich Loire Valley, with Steve Smith, the co-author of my France guidebook. Aurore, our waitress, was enchanting. She smiled as I ordered escargot for my first course. Getting a full dozen escargot rather than the typical six snails doubles the joy. Eating six, you're aware that the supply is very limited, but with twelve, there's no end to your snail fun. Add a good white wine, and you've got a full orchestral accompaniment.

My crust of bread lapped up the homemade garlic-and-herb sauce. I asked Aurore how it could be so good. With a sassy chuckle she said, "Other restaurateurs come here to figure that out, too." Then she added, "It's done with love." While I've heard that line many times, here it seemed believable.

In France, slow service is good service. After a pleasant pause, my main course arrived: tender beef with beans wrapped in bacon. Slicing through a pack of beans in their quiver of bacon, I let the fat do its dirty deed. A sip of wine, after a bite of beef, seemed like an incoming tide washing the flavor farther ashore.

My crust of bread, a veteran from the escargot course, was called into action for a swipe of sauce. Italians brag

France's Top Destinations

Paris ▲▲▲
allow 3-5 days

World capital of art, fashion, food, literature, and ideas, offering historic monuments, grand boulevards, and corner cafés

Top Sights
Notre-Dame Cathedral Paris' most beloved church
Sainte-Chapelle Gothic cathedral with peerless stained glass
Louvre Europe's oldest and greatest museum, starring *Mona Lisa* and *Venus de Milo*
Orsay Museum Nineteenth-century art, including Europe's best Impressionist collection
Eiffel Tower Paris' soaring exclamation point
Arc de Triomphe Triumphal arch with viewpoint marking start of Champs-Elysées

Nearby
Versailles The ultimate royal palace
Chartres Cathedral Best example of Gothic architecture, statues, and stained glass
Giverny Monet's flowery gardens, which inspired many of his paintings

Normandy ▲▲
2-3 days

Pastoral mix of sweeping coastlines, half-timbered towns, and intriguing cities, including **Rouen** (Joan of Arc sights and soaring Gothic cathedral), artistic seaside **Honfleur,** historic **Bayeux** (famous tapestry), stirring D-Day beaches and museums, and pretty-as-a-mirage island abbey of Mont St-Michel

Brittany ▲
1 day

Windswept and rugged peninsula, with a gorgeous coast, Celtic ties, and two notable towns: medieval **Dinan** and the beach resort of **St-Malo**

Loire Valley ▲▲
1-2 days

Lushly romantic area of picturesque towns (**Amboise** and **Chinon**) and hundreds of castles and palaces

Dordogne ▲▲
2 days

Region of prehistoric cave paintings (including Lascaux), lazy canoe rides past medieval castles, market towns (**Sarlat**), and, for wine lovers, nearby **St-Emilion**

Languedoc-Roussillon ▲
1-2 days

Sunny southern region, highlighted by **Albi's** Toulouse-Lautrec museum, **Carcassonne's** perfectly preserved city walls, and the seaside village of **Collioure**

Provence ▲▲▲
2-3 days

Home to Van Gogh sights in **Arles,** the famed medieval bridge and Palace of the Popes in **Avignon,** Roman history (including a pair of amphitheaters and the Pont du Gard aqueduct), rock-top villages (including **Les Baux**), the **Côtes du Rhone** wine road, and the quintessentially Provençal hill towns of the **Luberon**

French Riviera ▲▲▲
2-3 days

A string of coastal resorts, including cosmopolitan and art-crazy **Nice,** beachy **Villefranche-sur-Mer,** glitzy **Monaco,** easygoing **Antibes** (with a Picasso museum), and hill-capping **Eze-le-Village**

French Alps ▲   2 days

Spectacular mountain scenery featuring the scenic, lakeside city of **Annecy;** Europe's highest peak, Mont Blanc; and the world-famous **Chamonix** ski resort (with lift to Italy)

Burgundy ▲▲   1-2 days

Region of bountiful vineyards, rustic cuisine, and age-old spirituality, with the compact wine capital of **Beaune** (and nearby wine roads), France's best-preserved medieval abbey (**Fontenay**), and a magnificent Romanesque church (**Vézelay**)

With more time, consider visiting

Reims and Verdun Historic cathedral, champagne cellars, and WWI battle sites
Alsace Franco-Germanic region dotted with wine-road villages
Lyon Metropolitan city with Roman ruins and delicious cuisine

about all the ingredients they use. But France is proudly the land of sauces. If the sauce is the medicine, the bread is the syringe. Thanks to the bread, I enjoyed one last encore of the meat and vegetables I'd just savored.

Shifting my chair to stretch out my legs, I prepared for the next course—a selection of fine cheeses. It sounds like a lot of food, but portions are smaller in France, and what we cram onto one large plate they spread out over several courses.

Aurore brought out her cheese platter on a rustic board, the vibrant-yet-mellow colors promising a tantalizing array of tastes. As cheese needs wine, I checked my wine bottle like I would my gas tank before driving home. Noticing the restaurant crowd thinning, I reminded myself that there was no rush. I liked hearing the quiet murmur of other diners, as eating among appreciative patrons is part of the sensory experience.

Finished with the cheeses, I leaned back to stifle a burp, just as Steve announced, "And here comes dessert." Mine was a tender crêpe papoose of cinnamon-flavored baked apple with butterscotch ice cream, garnished with a tender slice of kiwi. That didn't keep me from reaching over for a snip of Steve's lemon tart with raspberry sauce.

Our entire meal cost about $60 each. You could call it $20 for nourishment and $40 for three hours of bliss. Even if you're not a foodie, I can't imagine a richer sightseeing experience, one that brings together an unforgettable ensemble of local ingredients, culture, pride, and people.

In France, luxuriate over a dinner, as if taking your palate out to a spa. And, when it comes to the cheese course, don't hold back.

Well-Fed Geese in the Dordogne

With elbows resting on a rustic windowsill on a farm in France's Dordogne region, I'm watching Denis grab one goose at a time from an endless line of geese. In a kind of peaceful, mesmerizing trance, he fills each one's gullet with corn. Like his father and his father and his father before him, Denis spends five hours a day, every day, all year long, sitting in a barn surrounded by geese.

Denis rhythmically grabs a goose by the neck, pulls him under his leg and stretches him up, and slides the tube down to the belly. He pulls the trigger to squirt the corn in, slowly slides the tube up the neck and out, holds the beak shut for a few seconds, lets that goose go, and grabs the next.

Many of my friends express disgust when I tell them I've witnessed geese being force-fed—the traditional way farmers fatten the livers to make foie gras, a prized delicacy in the Dordogne. Some people want to boycott French foie gras for what they consider inhumane treatment of the geese. That's why I was on the goose farm—to learn more about *la gavage*, the force-feeding process.

Elevage du Bouyssou, a big homey goose farm a short drive from the market town of Sarlat, is run by Denis and Nathalie Mazet. Their geese are filled with corn three times a day for the last months of their lives. They have expandable stomachs and no gag reflex, so the corn stays there, gradually settling as it is digested and making room for the next feeding. Watching Denis work, I wonder what it must be like to spend so much time with an endless cycle of geese. Do geese populate his dreams?

While Denis takes care of the geese, Nathalie meets tourists—mostly French families—who show up each evening at 6 p.m. to see how their beloved foie gras is made. The groups stroll the idyllic farm as Nathalie explains that they

In France, the geese run free on the farm and are force-fed to fatten their livers for foie gras. Being high on the food chain is always nice, but never so nice as when eating in France.

raise a thousand geese a year. She stresses that the key to top-quality foie gras is happy geese raised on quality food in an unstressed environment. They need quality corn and the same feeder.

The Mazets sell everything but the head and feet of their geese. The down feathers only net about 30 cents a goose. The serious money is in the livers. A normal liver weighs a quarter-pound. When done with the force-feeding process, the liver weighs about two pounds. (With a thousand geese, they produce a ton of foie gras annually—Nathalie says, "Barely enough to support one family.")

Like other French supporters of *la gavage*, Nathalie points out that their free-range animals are in no pain and live six months. By contrast, most American chickens live less than two months in little boxes and are plumped with hormones. Who's to say which system is better or worse?

In the Dordogne, farmers in the markets pass out petite goose-liver sandwiches as they evangelize about their foie gras, and every meal seems to start with a foie-gras course. After a few days of this rich eating, I leave with a strong need for a foie gras detox and a plate of vegetables.

Contemplating the Toll of World War II in Normandy

On a small square in a Normandy town, an elderly Frenchman approaches me, singing "The Star-Spangled Banner." In 1944, British, Canadian, and American troops invaded this area, beginning the end of World War II—and the French apparently haven't forgotten. But of course, reminders are still abundant. Seventy-five miles of France's north coast are littered with WWII museums, monuments, cemeteries, and battle remains left in tribute to the courage of the armies that successfully carried out the largest military operation in history: D-Day.

Wandering the beach of Arromanches—ground zero for the D-Day invasion—I take in the remnants of the Allied-built man-made harbor, Port Winston, which gave the Allies a foothold in Normandy, allowing them to begin their victorious push to Berlin and the end of the war. Several rusted floats—once supports for hastily built pontoon roads—are mired on the sand. I can just make out what's left of an anti-aircraft gun on a concrete block in the sea. I'm thankful that, instead of the sound of artillery, all I hear are birds and surf.

Later, I visit Omaha Beach, the eye of the D-Day storm.

In the cemetery, a striking memorial with a soaring statue represents the spirit of American youth. Around the statue, giant reliefs of the Battle of Normandy and the Battle of Europe are etched on the walls. Behind is the semicircular Garden of the Missing, with the names of 1,557 soldiers who were never found.

Nearly 10,000 brilliant white marble tombstones glow in memory of the Americans who gave their lives to free Europe. Wandering among the peaceful, poignant sea of headstones, I read the names, home states, and dates of death inscribed on each, and think of the friends and families affected by each lost life. It's a struggle to reconcile the quiet beauty of the setting with the horrible toll of that battle.

To remember the heroes of Normandy, visit the American Cemetery above Omaha Beach.

Not just in Normandy, but all over France, I'm reminded of the gratitude the French feel for what American troops did for their country. I remember filming one of my public-television shows at a charming little mom-and-pop château. When I'm filming, I'm on a mission—the sun's going down, and we've got work to do. But the aristocratic couple whose family had called that castle home for centuries insisted, "We must stop and have a ceremony because we have an American film crew here working in our castle." They cracked open a fine bottle of wine and brought out—with great ceremony, as if it were a precious relic—the beautiful 48-star American flag they had hoisted over their château on that great day in 1944 when they were freed by American troops. They implored us, "Please go home and tell your friends that we will never forget what America did for us."

Medieval Carcassonne

Before me lies Carcassonne, the perfect medieval city. Like a fish that everyone thought was extinct, Europe's greatest Romanesque fortress-city somehow survives.

Located in southeastern France, medieval Carcassonne is a 13th-century world of towers, turrets, and cobblestones. It's a walled city and Camelot's castle rolled into one, frosted with too many day-tripping tourists. At 10 a.m., the salespeople stand at the doors of their main-street shops, their gauntlet of tacky temptations poised and ready for their daily ration of customers. But an empty Carcassonne rattles in the early morning or late-afternoon breeze. Enjoy the town early or late, or off-season. Spend the night.

I was supposed to be gone yesterday, but it's sundown and here I sit—imprisoned by choice—curled in a cranny on top of the wall. The moat is one foot over and 100 feet down. Happy little weeds and moss upholster my throne. The wind blows away many of the sounds of today, and my imagination "medievals" me.

Twelve hundred years ago, Charlemagne stood below with his troops, besieging this fortress-town for several years. As the legend goes, just as food was running out, a cunning townswoman had a great idea. She fed the town's last bits of grain to the last pig and tossed him over the wall. Splat. Charlemagne's restless forces, amazed that the town still had enough food to throw fat party pigs over the wall, decided they'd never succeed in starving the people out. They ended the siege, and the city was saved. Today, the walls that stopped Charlemagne open wide for visitors.

Carcassonne, in the south of France, is Europe's greatest fortress city.

Paris' Ultimate Market Street

I grew up thinking that cheese was no big deal. It was orange, and the shape of bread was square: slap, fwomp... sandwich. Even though I'm still far from a gourmet eater, my time in Paris, specifically in the Rue Cler street market, has substantially bumped up my appreciation of good cuisine (as well as the French knack for good living). Rue Cler, lined with shops spilling out into the street, feels like village Paris—in the skinny shadow of the Eiffel Tower.

Parisians shop almost daily for three good reasons: Refrigerators are small (tiny kitchens), produce must be fresh, and shopping is an important social event. Strolling down Rue Cler, I soon spot a friend, Marie-Alice. She beckons me to the strawberry display. "You must shop with your nose," she says, burying hers in a basket of lush fruit.

We follow our noses to a long, narrow, canopied cheese table.

Visiting the Eiffel Tower

A stroll along Rue Cler works well with a visit to the nearby Eiffel Tower. There are two ways to get up the tower: smart or stupid. Get a reservation—those who just show up waste lots of time waiting in line. Book an entrance time in advance (tour-eiffel. fr) and scoot right in. Just be sure to reserve well ahead in peak times such as summer; tickets go on sale three months in advance and can sell out within hours.

Marie-Alice bounces her finger over a long line of cheeses: wedges, cylinders, balls, and miniature hockey pucks all powdered white, gray, and burnt marshmallow—it's a festival of mold. *Ooh la la* means you're impressed. If you like a cheese, show greater excitement with more *las. Ooh la la la la.* She holds the stinkiest glob close to her nose, takes a deep, orgasmic breath, and exhales, "Yes, this smells like the feet of angels."

Inside the shop, we browse through some of the several hundred types of French cheese. A cheese shop (known as BOF, for *beurre, oeuf, fromage*) is the place where people go for butter, egg, and cheese products. In the back room are *les meules,* the big, 170-pound wheels of cheese. The "hard" cheeses are cut from these. Don't eat the skin of these big ones—they roll them on the floor. But the skin on most smaller cheeses—like Brie or Camembert—is part of the taste. As Marie-Alice says, "It completes the package."

Across the street we pause at a table of duck, pigeon, quail, and rabbit. Marie-Alice sorts through the dead. With none of the tenderness shown in the cheese shop, she hoists a duck. Rubbing a thumb toughly on its rough and calloused feet, she tells me that well-used feet indicate that the birds run wild on a farm instead of being confined in an industrial kennel.

The ruddy-faced butcher, wearing a tiny plaid beret and dressed in a white apron over a fine shirt, is busy chopping. He's the best-dressed butcher I've ever seen. A battalion of meat hooks hang in orderly lines from the ceiling. The white walls bring out the red in the different cuts of meat.

At the nearby bakery, French women, thick and crusty after a lifetime of baguette munching, debate the merits of the street's rival boulangeries. It's said that when bakers do good bread, they have no time to do good pastry. If the baker specializes in pastry, the bread suffers. But this shop bucks the trend—the women and Marie-Alice agree that this baker does both equally well.

A man with working-class hands steps out the door, cradling a bouquet and a baguette in his arms—and heads off to gather the rest of his daily meal. If you want to learn the fine art of living, Parisian-style, Rue Cler is an excellent classroom.

More French Experiences

Inside the Lascaux Caves: In France's Dordogne region, proud guides compare the prehistoric paintings in the Lascaux caves to Michelangelo's frescoes in the Sistine Chapel. Hyperbole, I thought—until I saw Lascaux II. It's a painstakingly created copy of the actual cave, which the public is no longer allowed to visit. Swept away by its grandeur, I soon forget it's a replica.

The vast cave looks amazingly like my (healthy) colonoscopy scan. Main difference: The cave is covered with paintings made 17,000 years ago, when mammoths and saber-toothed cats roamed the earth. This was a sophisticated project executed by artists from the impressive Magdalenian culture. In the museum, filled with original Magdalenian artifacts, I begin to feel a connection with these people. Looking at the oil lamps, I can imagine the wonder of wandering under flickering flames that lit the Sistine Chapel of the prehistoric world.

Magnificence on a Mudflat: I love to scamper far from shore at low tide, shoes in my hands, across the mud flat in the vast Bay of Mont St-Michel in northwestern France. Splashing across black sand and through little puddles, I head for a dramatic abbey reaching to heaven from a rock surrounded by a vast and muddy solitude, where hermit monks sought seclusion since the sixth century. The

The sights and experiences of France range from caves painted 17,000 years ago, to medieval island abbeys, to cable cars zipping you to thin-air alpine summits.

silhouette of the Gothic Mont St-Michel sends my spirits soaring today, just as it did the spirits of weary pilgrims in centuries past. Though a dreamscape from a distance, Mont St-Michel can be a human traffic jam until late afternoon. It's some consolation to remember that, even in the Middle Ages, the abbey-town was a commercial gauntlet, with stalls selling souvenir medallions, candles, and fast food. I prefer to ramble on the ramparts after dark, when the tourists are gone and the island is magically floodlit. At night, it's easy to ponder the promise of desolation and the simple life of solitude that attracted monks to this striking spot so long ago.

Getting High in Chamonix: Europe's ultimate mountain lift towers high above the tourist-choked French resort town of Chamonix. Ride the Aiguille du Midi *téléphérique* (gondola) to the dizzy 12,600-foot-high tip of a rock needle. Chamonix shrinks as trees fly by, soon replaced by whizzing rocks, ice, and snow, until you reach the top. Up there, even sunshine is cold. The air is thin. People are giddy (those prone to altitude sickness are less giddy). Fun things can happen if you're not too winded to join locals in the halfway-to-heaven tango.

The Alps spread out before you. In the distance is the bent little Matterhorn. You can almost reach out and pat the head of Mont Blanc, the Alps' highest point.

Next, for Europe's most exciting border crossing, get into the tiny red gondola and head south to Italy. Dangle silently for 40 minutes as you glide over glaciers and a forest of peaks to Italy. Hang your head out the window; explore every corner of your view. You're sailing a new sea.

At Helbronner Point, you'll descend into Valle d'Aosta in Italy, the land of cappuccino, gelato, and *la dolce vita*.

Chamonix, the Aiguille du Midi, and the Valle d'Aosta—surely a high point in anyone's European vacation.

CULTURE AND TRADITIONS: EVERYTHING'S SO...FRENCH

Play the Markets

Market days have been a central feature of life in rural France since the Middle Ages. No single event better symbolizes the French preoccupation with fresh products and their strong ties to the soil than the weekly market. Many locals mark their calendars with the arrival of prized seasonal produce, such as truffles in November.

Most markets take place once a week in the town's

main square and, if large enough, spill onto nearby streets. Markets combine fresh produce; samples of wine and locally produced brandies or ciders; and a smattering of nonfood items, like knives, berets, kitchen goods, and cheap clothing. The bigger the market, the greater the overall selection—particularly for nonperishable goods.

Market day is as important socially as it is commercially—it's a weekly chance to resume friendships and get the current gossip. Neighbors catch up on the butcher's barn renovation, see photos of the florist's new grandchild, and relax over *un café*. Dogs sit beneath café tables while friends exchange kisses. Tether yourself to a bench and observe: Three cheek-kisses are for good friends (left-right-left); a fourth kiss is added for friends you haven't seen in a while.

Wine Talk

The French sum up the unique natural conditions where a wine is produced in one word: *terroir* (pronounced "tehr-wah"). It means "somewhere-ness," a particular combination of macro- and microclimate, soil, geology, and the accumulated experience of the winemakers. Two wines can be made from the same grape but be of very different character because of their *terroir*. The best vintners don't force their style on the grape. They play to the wine's

Dealing with the French in French and English

French people value politeness, and take pride in their culture, tradition, and language. You'll get better treatment if you learn and use the simplest of French pleasantries. Begin every encounter with *"Bonjour* (or *S'il vous plaît), madame* (or *monsieur),"* and end it with *"Au revoir* (or *Merci), madame* (or *monsieur)."*

The French are language perfectionists—they take their language (and other languages) seriously. Often they speak more English than they let on. This isn't a tourist-baiting tactic, but timidity on their part about speaking another language less than fluently. If you want them to speak English, say, *"Bonjour, madame (or monsieur). Parlez-vous anglais?"* They may say *"non,"* but if you continue talking and butchering their language, they'll soon say, "Well, actually, I do speak some English."

strength, respecting the natural character of the sun, soil, and vine—the *terroir*.

Grapevines are creepers, with roots going through the topsoil and into the geology deep down. The roots are commonly 150 feet long and deep. While topsoil can be influenced by the vintner, the deep geology cannot, and this gives the wine a distinct character. The French do not allow irrigation, thus forcing the grapes to search deep for water. A good grape, in the French view, must suffer.

Persnickety Perceptions

The good life in France—music, culture, an appreciation of fine wine and food—is seductive but intimidating to Americans. No one wants to make a "mistake" when picking a wine, croissant, or cheese. For a long time, I thought there was something affected and pseudo-sophisticated about all this finicky Frenchness. I once asked a wine merchant in Paris to suggest a good bottle to go with snails, and he wanted to know how I planned to cook them. I had envisioned a good Chardonnay, but *mais non*—not "flinty" enough—only a Chablis would do.

I felt inept for making the wrong pairing and annoyed by the wine seller's hair-splitting choosiness. But then I thought of the way I catalogue the nuances of baseball—it's taken me a lifetime of slowly absorbing the game's rules and situations to simply "know" the game the way the Frenchman "knows" wine. All the stuff that matters to me—how far the runner is leading off first base, who's on deck, how a batter does against left-handed pitchers, when to put in a pinch runner—would be nonsense to a French person. The next time I mortify my French friend by putting a little ketchup on my meat, I'll just remember that with two outs and a full count, he'll have no idea why I know the runner's off with the pitch.

Bowling *Boules*

In small squares in every Provençal village and city, you're likely to find the local gang playing *boules*, the horseshoes of southern France. Every French boy grows up playing *boules* with Papa and *Ton-Ton* (Uncle) Jean. It's a social-yet-serious sport, and endlessly

entertaining to watch—even more so if you understand the rules.

Boules (also known as *pétanque*) is played with heavy metal balls (*boules*, about the size of oranges) and a small wooden target ball (*le cochonnet*—"piglet," about the size of a ping-pong ball). Whoever gets his *boule* closest to the *cochonnet* scores.

I like to pause and watch old-timers while away the afternoon tossing shiny silver balls on gravelly courts—and if I feel like creating a memory, I give it a try myself.

France Travel Resources from Rick Steves

Guidebooks
Check out Rick's guidebooks covering all of France; Paris; Provence & the French Riviera; the Loire Valley; and Normandy; plus his French phrase book

Audio Europe
Download Rick's free Audio Europe app, with self-guided audio tours, including a walk through historic Paris and tours of the Louvre, Musée d'Orsay, and Versailles Palace

TV Shows
The quintessence of France with Rick as your host, viewable on public television and at ricksteves.com. Episodes cover Paris, the Loire Valley, the French Alps, Burgundy, Alsace, Dordogne, Normandy, Provence, and the Riviera

Organized Tours
Small group tours, with itineraries planned by Rick: Paris & the Heart of France in 11 Days; Loire to the South of France in 13 Days; French Riviera in 7 Days; Paris in 7 Days; Eastern France in 14 Days; Basque Country of France & Spain in 9 Days

For more on all of these resources, visit ricksteves.com

Spain

For the tourist, Spain means many things: bullfights, massive cathedrals, world-class art, Muslim palaces, vibrant folk life, whitewashed villages, bright sunshine. You'll find all of this, but the country's charm really lies in its people and their unique lifestyle. From the stirring communal *sardana* dance in Barcelona to the sizzling rat-a-tat-tat of flamenco in Sevilla, this country creates its own beat amid the heat.

Spain is in Europe, but not *of* Europe, thanks largely to the Pyrenees Mountains that physically isolate it from the rest of the Continent. For more than 700 years (711-1492), Spain's dominant culture was Muslim, not Christian. And after a brief Golden Age in the 16th century (financed by New World gold), Spain retreated into three centuries of isolation. Spain's seclusion contributed to the creation of its distinctive customs—bullfights, flamenco dancing, and a national obsession with ham. Even as other countries opened up to one another in the 20th century, the fascist dictator Francisco Franco virtually sealed off Spain from the rest of Europe's democracies. But since Franco's death in 1975, Spaniards have swung almost to the opposite extreme, becoming wide open to new ideas and technologies.

Spain's spread-out geography makes it less a centralized nation than a collection of distinct regions. In the central plain sits the lively urban island of Madrid. Just south is holy Toledo, a medieval showpiece and melting-pot city with Christian, Muslim, and Jewish roots. Farther south is Andalucía, home to sleepy, whitewashed hill towns and three great cities: Granada (topped with the Alhambra palace), Córdoba (with a massive mosque and pretty patios), and Sevilla (where Holy Week is celebrated as if God were watching). Spain's south coast offers a palm-tree jungle of beach resorts along the Costa del Sol, a taste of British fish-and-chips in Gibraltar, and a laid-back launch pad to Morocco (from Tarifa).

To Spain's far north is San Sebastián and the Basque Country, which combine sparkling beaches, cutting-edge architecture, and the *pintxo* (a local—and often gourmet—take on tapas). Nearby is Pamplona, where bulls and tourists run for their lives. Gregarious pilgrims hike through the town on their long journey across northern Spain to the cathedral town of Santiago de Compostela. Along the Mediterranean coast (to the east), Spain has an almost Italian vibe. Trendy Barcelona, where Antoni Gaudí's architecture makes waves, keeps one eye cocked toward trends sailing in from the rest of the Continent.

The Alhambra in Granada, the last Moorish stronghold on the Iberian Peninsula, is a vivid reminder of the splendor of the Muslim society that ruled Spain for centuries.

FAVORITE SIGHTS AND MEMORABLE EXPERIENCES IN SPAIN

Good Morning in Santiago

I'm tucked away in Santiago de Compostela, in the northwest corner of Spain. I have a three-part agenda: to see pilgrims reach their goal in front of the cathedral, to explore the outdoor market, and to buy some barnacles in the seafood section—then have them cooked for me, on the spot, in a café. Whenever I'm here, I make a point to be on the big square at the foot of the towering Cathedral of St. James around 10 in the morning. That's when scores of well-worn pilgrims march in triumphantly from their last overnight on the Camino de Santiago (Way of St. James)—a 30-day, 500-mile hike from the French border.

Humble hikers have trod these miles since the Middle Ages to pay homage to the remains of St. James in his namesake city. (I love the idea that the first guidebook ever written talked up "going local, packing light, and watching out for pickpockets" for pilgrims traveling the Camino de Santiago a thousand years ago.) Arriving in the church square, they step on a scallop shell symbol embedded in the pavement in front of the cathedral. I witness joy and jubilation sweep over those who finish this journey.

Pilgrims often ask me to take their photo and email it

to them. Then they say, "I've got to go meet with St. James," and—as has been the routine for a thousand years—they head into the cathedral.

Two blocks away, the market is thriving, oblivious to the personal triumphs going on over at St. James' tomb. There's something fundamental about wandering through a farmers market early in the morning anywhere in the world: Salt-of-the-earth people pull food out of the ground, cart it to the city, and sell what they've harvested to people who don't have gardens.

Dried-apple grandmothers line up like a babushka cancan. Each sits on a stool so small it disappears under her work dress. At the women's feet are brown woven baskets filled like cornucopias—still-dirty eggs in one; in the next, greens clearly pulled this morning, soil clinging to their roots. One woman hopes to earn a few extra euros selling potent homebrews, her golden bottles stoppered with ramshackle corks.

> ## Fast Facts
>
> **Biggest cities:** Madrid (capital, 3.3 million), Barcelona (1.6 million)
> **Size:** 195,000 square miles (roughly twice the size of Oregon), population 47 million
> **Locals call it:** España
> **Currency:** Euro
> **Key date:** November 20, 1975, Prime Minister Francisco Franco dies, ending nearly four decades of dictator rule
> **Languages:** You'll find four—Castilian (what we call Spanish, spoken country-wide), Catalan (NE Spain), Galego (NW Spain), Euskara (Basque region)
> **Biggest festivals:** Semana Santa (Holy Week, before Easter, best in Sevilla), Running of the Bulls (July, Pamplona)
> **Handy Spanish phrases:** *Hola* (hello; **oh**-lah), *Por favor* (please; por fah-**bor**), *Gracias* (thank you; **grah**-thee-ahs), *Soy rico y soltero* (I'm rich and single; soy **ree**-koh ee sohl-**teh**-roh)

Babushkas sit behind rickety card tables filled with yellow chocolate shaped like giant Hershey's Kisses—or, to locals, breasts. This local cheese is called *tetilla*—that's "tit"—to revenge a prudish priest who, seven centuries ago, told a sculptor at the cathedral to redo a statue that he considered too buxom. Ever since, the townsfolk have shaped their cheese exactly like what the priest didn't want them to see carved in stone. You can't go anywhere in Santiago without seeing creamy, mild *tetilla*.

In vendors' stalls, spicy red chorizo hangs in sausage chains, framing merchants' faces. Chickens, plucked and looking as rubber-like as can be, fill glass cases. A selection of pigs' ears, mixed with hooves going nowhere, fills a shoebox. The ears, translucent in the low rays of the morning sun, resemble neatly flattened conch shells. At the best stalls, short ladies with dusty, blue-plaid roller carts jostle for deals.

The sound of cascading clams and castanet shrimp—red, doomed, and flipping mad—greet me as I enter the seafood

LEFT Venture to the remote northwest corner of Spain for a plate of fresh *percebes* (barnacles)–they go great with beer.

RIGHT Pilgrims hike for weeks to Santiago de Compostela to find meaning in life.

hall. Fisherwomen in rubber aprons and matching gloves sort through folding money. From one vendor I buy my barnacles (*percebes*)—at about $16 a pound, they're one-third the price I'd pay in a bar. I get a little less than a half-pound and hustle my full bag over to the market café called Churro Mania. There, Ramon and Julia boil them up for a few dollars. Feeling quite like a local—sipping my beer so early in the morning—I wait for my barnacles to cook.

Then comes the climax of my morning: Julia brings my barnacles, stacked steaming on a stainless steel plate, as well as bread and another beer. I'm set. Twist, rip, bite. It's the bounty of the sea condensed into every little morsel: edible jubilation in Santiago.

Gaudí's Barcelona Dreaming

Barcelona's most famous architect, Antoni Gaudí, speckled the city with his Art Nouveau fantasies at the beginning of the 20th century. His buildings bloom with flowery shapes, race with galloping gables, and bend with organic curves. A prime example, the apartment building called La Pedrera, has walls of wavy stone and an undulating rooftop, where 30 chimneys play volleyball with the clouds. At Casa Batlló, a green-blue ceramic facade, tibia-esque pillars, and shell-like balconies are inspired by nature, while the humpback roofline suggests a cresting dragon's back.

But Gaudí's best-known and most persistent work is the Sagrada Família church. I've long said that if there's one building I'd like to see in Europe, it's the Sagrada Família... finished. The church, an epic work-in-progress for more than a hundred years, promises to be the most exciting church built in our lifetimes. If there is a miracle anywhere in the world of architecture, it is this church. Climb up stairs between the melting ice-cream-cone spires for a

If there's one building I'd like to see completed, it's Gaudí's wondrous Sagrada Família church in Barcelona. And it's well on its way.

gargoyle's-eye perspective of a living, growing, bigger-than-life building. Local craftsmen often finish up their careers by putting in a couple of years working on the project. The hope: to finish it by 2026—the 100th anniversary of Gaudí's death. By then, it's my bet that Gaudí will be sainted.

Gaudí fans also enjoy the artist's magic in the colorful, freewheeling Parc Güell, a 30-acre hilltop garden once intended to be a high-end housing project. Carpeted with fanciful mosaics, dotted with sculptures (including a famous tiled lizard), and offering grand views of the city and the glittering Mediterranean beyond, this park is a great place to cap a day of Barcelona dreaming.

Strolling Córdoba's Back Streets

The Andalusian town of Córdoba has a glorious Moorish past. The town's centerpiece is its massive Mezquita. Magical in its grandeur, this huge mosque dominates the higgledy-piggledy old town around it. A wonder of the medieval world, the Mezquita is remarkably well-preserved, giving visitors a chance to appreciate the glory days of Muslim rule. But like most big sights, the Mezquita is surrounded by a touristy zone of shops and tour-group-friendly restaurants.

To separate from the crush of tourists, I wander the back streets. Exploring the residential lanes of old Córdoba, I'm quickly all alone with the town. Away from modern-day tourism, it's easy to catch an evocative whiff of the old.

I keep an eye out for colorful patios, framed by decorative ironwork gates. A common feature of houses throughout Andalucía, patios are taken very seriously here. The Romans used them to cool off, and the Moors added lush, ornate

Spain's Top Destinations

Barcelona ▲▲▲   allow 3 days
Catalan capital with atmospheric Gothic old town, elegant new town, and striking art and architecture by resident artists Antoni Gaudí, Pablo Picasso, and Joan Miró

Top Sights
Picasso Museum Works from the artist's early years
Ramblas Colorful pedestrian zone with thriving market
Barri Gòtic Old town maze of streets with towering cathedral
Gaudí's Architecture Sagrada Família Church, La Pedrera, and Park Güell
Catalan Art Museum World-class showcase of this region's art

Nearby
Figueres and Cadaqués Salvador Dalí sights
Montserrat Dramatic mountaintop monastery
Sitges Beach resort

Madrid ▲▲▲   3 days
Spirited Spanish capital, boasting top-notch art treasures, stately squares, a lively tapas scene, and urban Spain at its best

Top Sights
Royal Palace Sumptuous national palace
Prado Museum Masterpieces by Velázquez, Goya, and El Greco
Centro de Arte Reina Sofía Modern art, including Picasso's epic *Guernica*
Thyssen-Bornemisza Museum Especially good Impressionist collection

Nearby
El Escorial Palace and mausoleum of Spanish royalty
Segovia Storybook town with a towering Roman aqueduct

Toledo ▲▲   1 day
Hill-capping former capital, with a colorfully complex history, a magnificent cathedral, and works by hometown boy El Greco

Salamanca ▲   1 day
Spain's quintessential university town, with the country's finest main square

Sevilla ▲▲▲   2 days
Soulful cultural capital of Andalucía, with a spectacular cathedral (the world's largest Gothic church), the Alcázar (labyrinthine Moorish palace), tangled former Jewish Quarter, teeming evening paseo, and fantastic flamenco

Andalucía ▲▲   2-3 days
Classic heartland of southern Spain, home to **Córdoba** (with Spain's top surviving Moorish mosque, the Mezquita) and whitewashed hill towns (including **Arcos de la Frontera** and **Ronda**)

Granada ▲▲▲   1 day
Grand Moorish capital with the magnificent Alhambra palace and Spain's best old Moorish quarter

Basque Country ▲ 3-4 days
Anchored by the culinary capital of **San Sebastián** and the more workaday **Bilbao** (home to the dazzling Guggenheim Museum), with sleepy seaside retreats and colorful villages scattered through the green countryside

Camino de Santiago ▲ 4-5 days
Centuries-old pilgrimage route running across the top of Spain from France to **Santiago de Compostela** in green Galicia, with stops along the way at big cities (**Pamplona, Burgos, León**) and charming villages (**Puente de la Reina, O Cebreiro**)

With more time, consider visiting
Cantabria Rustic northern coast with high-mountain scenery and prehistoric cave art
Tarifa Charming beach-resort town and handy base for day trip to Morocco
Gibraltar A slice of Britain on a giant rock

Córdoba, in the south of Spain, comes with exquisite patios (left) and the biggest mosque Europe ever saw (right).

touches. The patio functioned as a quiet outdoor living room, an oasis from the heat. Inside the see-through gates, roses, geraniums, and jasmine spill down whitewashed walls, while fountains play and caged birds sing.

I continue wandering after dinner. It's almost midnight—everyone's out, savoring a cool evening. I'm drawn to a commotion on a square. Short men with raspy tobacco voices and big bellies—called *curvas de felicidad* (happiness curves)—jostle and bark as a dozen little school girls rattle a makeshift stage with flamenco flair, working on their sultry.

Well after midnight, the city finally seems quiet. I return to my hotel and climb into my bed. Just as I doze off, a noisy and multigenerational parade rumbles down the cobbled lane. Standing in my underwear and wrapped in the drapes, I peer secretively out my window. Below, a band of guitars and castanets funnels down my narrow alley. Grandmothers— guardians of a persistent culture—make sure the children pick up their Andalusian customs. Finally, one woman looks up at me, catches my eye, and seems to nod, as if satisfied that I am witnessing the unwavering richness of their traditional way of life.

Feeling the Heat in Madrid

Changing cultures is always fun. I love to feel disoriented, as I am when I first arrive in a new place. Recently, following a stint in Austria, I switched to Madrid. I felt myself going from crisp rationality to casual disorganization.

When I'm in Madrid, I try to book a room with a balcony overlooking the Times Square of Spain, Puerta del Sol.

This square, like so many in Europe, has gone from a traffic nightmare to a park-like people zone. Within a 10-minute walk I can visit the great Royal Palace; my favorite paintings in the Prado Museum; and Plaza Mayor, the ultimate town square.

To get acclimated, I get up early. Walking around Madrid at 8 a.m., people seem in a kind of fog. It's not clear who is starting their day and who is ending it. As for me, I'm intent on crossing off my rituals for Spain (I have a list for every place I travel): digging into a plate of *pimientos de Padrón* (these lightly fried, little green peppers play Russian roulette with my taste buds...only a few are jalapeño-spicy); savoring a slice of *jamón ibérico*—the most expensive cured ham, made from acorn-fed, black-hooved pigs; people-watching while downing a tall glass of *horchata*, that milky, nutty, refreshing drink; eating really really late; and being really, really hot.

And it is hot in Madrid. Even in the evening, things are so hot, they've moved the times of bullfights two hours later to 9 p.m. People here say, "Be thankful you're not in Sevilla." I catch myself assessing restaurants by the quality of their air-conditioning.

But despite the heat, Madrid is vibrant. Even the living-statue street performers have a twinkle in their eyes. As always, Spain is a festival of life.

Anywhere in southern Europe, enjoy the relative cool of summer evenings by joining the festival of locals out and about. Each summer evening, Madrid's plazas become community gathering places.

Queen of the White-Hill Towns

Arcos de la Frontera smothers its hilltop, tumbling down all sides like the train of a wedding dress. While larger than most other Andalusian hill towns, it's equally atmospheric. The labyrinthine old center is a photographer's feast. Viewpoint-hop through town. Feel the wind funnel through the narrow streets as drivers pull in car mirrors to fit around tight corners.

Residents brag that only they see the backs of the birds as they fly. To see why, climb to the viewpoint at the main square high in the old town. Belly up to the railing—the town's suicide jumping-off point—and look down. Ponder the fancy cliffside hotel's erosion concerns, orderly orange groves, flower-filled greenhouses, and the fine views toward Morocco.

The thoughtful traveler's challenge is to find meaning in the generally overlooked tiny details of historic towns such as Arcos. On one visit, I discovered that a short walk from Arcos' church of Santa María to the church of St. Peter is littered with fun glimpses into the town's past.

The church of Santa María faces the main square. After Arcos was reconquered from the Moors in the 13th century, this church was built—atop a mosque. In the pavement is a 15th-century magic circle: 12 red and 12 white stones—the white ones marked with various constellations. When a child came to the church to be baptized, the parents would stop here first for a good Christian exorcism. The exorcist would stand inside the protective circle and cleanse the baby of any evil spirits.

Small towns like Arcos come with lively markets. On my last visit, I was encouraged by the pickle woman to try a *banderilla*, named for the bangled spear that a matador sticks into a bull. As I gingerly slid an onion off the tiny skewer of pickled olives, onions, and carrots, she told me to eat it all at once. Explosive!

Near the market is a convent. The spiky security grill over the window protects cloistered nuns. Tiny peepholes allow the sisters to look out unseen. I stepped into the lobby to find a one-way mirror and a blind, spinning, lazy Susan-type cupboard. I pushed the buzzer, and a sister spun out some boxes of freshly baked cookies for sale. When I spun back the cookies with a *"No, gracias,"* a Monty Python-esque

Arcos de la Frontera perches on its cliff.

voice countered, "We have cupcakes as well." I bought a bag of these *magdalenas*, both to support their church work and to give to kids on my walk. Feeling like a religious Peeping Tom, I actually saw—through the not-quite one-way mirror—the sister in her flowing robe and habit momentarily appear and disappear.

Walking on, I passed street corners plastered with recycled Roman columns—protection from reckless donkey carts. The walls are scooped out on either side of the windows, a reminder of the days when women stayed inside but wanted the best possible view of any people-action in the streets.

Arcos' second church, St. Peter's, really is the second church. It lost an extended battle with Santa María for papal recognition as the leading church in Arcos. When the pope finally recognized Santa María, pouting parishioners from St. Peter's even changed their prayers. Rather than say, "María, mother of God," they prayed, "St. Peter, mother of God."

The tiny square in front of the church—about the only flat piece of pavement around—serves as the old-town soccer field for neighborhood kids. I joined the game and shared my cupcakes, savoring this idyllic slice of village Spain.

Holy Week in Sevilla

Holy Week (Semana Santa)—the week between Palm Sunday and Easter—is celebrated with intense fervor in Spain. All over the country, Semana Santa processions clog the streets. But nobody does Holy Week better than Sevilla.

Even if all you care about on Easter is chocolate, it's inspiring to witness the intense devotion of Sevillians during Holy Week. The scene is a holy spectacle. Paraders in purple-and-white cone hats shuffle past me, carrying crusader swords and four-foot candles. Like American kids scrambling for candies at a parade, Spanish kids collect dripping wax from religious coneheads, attempting to amass the biggest ball on a stick for their Easter souvenir. In bars, all eyes are fixed on the TVs, watching not soccer or bullfighting... but live coverage of their town's Holy Week procession.

The bell tower of Sevilla's cathedral

When you meet Spaniards, it's common to ask which football team they support. But in Sevilla, you also ask which Virgin Mary they favor. The top two in town are La Virgen de la Macarena and La Esperanza de Triana (same

Mary, different churches). On Thursday during Holy Week, it's a battle royale of the Madonnas, as Sevilla's two favorite virgins are paraded through the streets simultaneously.

The procession squeezes down narrow alleys. Legions of drums crack eardrums in the confined space. Kids sit wide-eyed on parents' shoulders. A gilded, candlelit float rumbles by, edging bystanders against rustic ancient walls. I look up, and high in the sky I see what Good Friday is all about: An extremely Baroque Jesus lurches forward under the weight of that cruel cross, symbolically climbing to his crucifixion. Later, it occurs to me that he floated not on wheels, but on boys. Unseen and unheralded, bent under all that tradition, a team of boys had been trudging for hours through the throngs.

Gilded and glittering floats are parked in churches until they are paraded through the streets on holy days.

The Running of the Bulls in Pamplona

Like a cowboy at a rodeo, I sit atop my spot on the fence. A loudspeaker says, "Do not touch the wounded. That's the responsibility of health personnel." A line of green-fluorescent-vested police sweeps down the street, clearing away drunks and anyone not fit to run. Cameras are everywhere—on robotic arms with remote controls vise-gripped to windowsills, hovering overhead on cranes, and in the hands of nearly every spectator that makes up the wall of bodies pressed against the thick timber fence behind me.

I'm at the Festival of San Fermín in Pamplona. Each July, a million revelers come to this proud town in the Pyrenees foothills for music, fireworks, and merrymaking. But most of all, they come for the Running of the Bulls, when fearless (or foolish) adventurers thrust themselves into the path of six furious bulls each day for a week.

The street fills with runners. Nearly everyone is wearing the standard white pants, white shirt, and red bandana. San Fermín, patron of this festival, was beheaded by the Romans 2,000 years ago, martyred for his faith. The red bandanas evoke his bloody end.

The energy surges as 8 a.m. approaches. The street is so full, if everyone suddenly ran, you'd think they'd simply trip over each other and all stack up, waiting to be minced by

angry bulls. Then it's eight, and the sound of a rocket indicates that the bulls are running. The entire half-mile-long scramble takes about two and a half minutes. The adrenaline surges in the crowded street. The sea of people spontaneously begins jumping up and down like hundreds of red-and-white human pogo sticks—trying to see the rampaging bulls to time their flight.

During Pamplona's famed Running of the Bulls, the mark of a good run is to feel the breath of the bull on the back of your legs.

For serious runners, this is like surfing—you hope to catch a good wave and ride it. A good run lasts only 15 or 20 seconds. You know you're really running with a bull when you feel his breath on your pants.

Like a freak wave pummeling a marina, the bulls rush through. It's a red-and-white cauldron of desperation. Big eyes, scrambling bodies, the ground quaking, someone oozing under the bottom rail. Then, suddenly, the bulls are gone, people pick themselves up, and it's over. Boarded-up shops open up. The timber fences are taken down and stacked. The nine-day cycle of the festival, built around the Running of the Bulls, is both smooth and relentless.

Soaking Up San Sebastián Sunshine

Jostling with enthusiastic eaters at the bar, I munch on my last spider crab open-face sandwich. A tiny plate of toothpicks is all that's left of my meal. I keep them because the bartender will count them to tally the bill.

I'm in the beach resort of San Sebastián, just over the French border in Spain. This is the Basque Country, where bright white chalet-style homes with patriotic red-and-green shutters dot lush, rolling hills. The Pyrenees Mountains soar high above the Atlantic. And surfers and sardines share the waves. Insulated from mainstream Europe for centuries, this plucky region has maintained its spirit while split between Spain and France.

Shimmering above the breathtaking bay of La Concha, elegant and prosperous San Sebastián has a favored location, with golden beaches bookended by twin peaks and a cute little island just offshore. With a romantic setting, a soaring statue of Christ gazing over the city, and a late-night lively Old Town, San Sebastián has a Rio de Janeiro aura.

The Basque resort of San Sebastián is a hit for its crescent-shaped beach and its gourmet tapas.

The highlight of the Old Town is its incredibly busy and colorful tapas bars—though here, these appetizers are called *pintxos*. Local competition drives bars to lay out the most appealing array of petite gourmet snacks. The selection is amazing. Just wander the streets (Calle Fermín Calbetón is best) and belly up to the bar in the liveliest spot.

The bartender insists I drink one more glass of *txakolí*—the local sparkling white wine. It's on the house...and nearly from the ceiling, as he theatrically pours from as high as he can reach to aerate the drink. No one but me marvels as the house wine high-dives expertly into my glass.

More Spanish Experiences

Toledo's Magnificent Cathedral: Just 30 minutes by train from Madrid, Spain's former capital crowds 2,500 years of tangled history onto a high, rocky perch protected on three sides by a natural moat, the Tajo River. Toledo's highlight is its Gothic cathedral, which is shoehorned into the old center, with an exterior that rises brilliantly above the town's medieval clutter. The cathedral's spectacular altar—real gold on wood—is one of the country's best pieces of Gothic art. The sacristy is a mini Prado Museum, with masterpieces by the likes of Francisco de Goya, Titian, Peter Paul Rubens, Diego Velázquez, Caravaggio, and Giovanni Bellini, not to

Toledo's grand cathedral

mention 18 El Grecos. The interior is so lofty, rich, and vast that visitors wander around like Pez dispensers stuck open, whispering "Wow."

Granada at Sunset: Granada's magnificent Alhambra was the last stronghold of the Moorish kingdom in Spain. At the end of the day, I head to my favorite viewpoint in the city—the San Nicolás terrace—and enjoy the breathtaking vista over the palace. It comes with great Gypsy music nearly all day long. Pop a few euros into the musicians' hat, sit down with a nice picnic, and enjoy an open-air concert as good as many you might pay for. And the view can't be beat, as the setting sun makes the Alhambra glow red.

A Taste of Britain in Spain: I can't resist popping into the British colony of Gibraltar whenever I'm in southern Spain. Gibraltar is hardly signposted in Spain, as if Spain wishes the British colony didn't exist. But when you see that famous "Rock of Prudential" standing boldly above the sea, you know it's here to stay. The place is quirkily and happily British: They have big three-pronged English plugs, their own Gibraltar pound currency, and an Anglican church headquarters. The food is a throwback to the days when English food really was as bad as its reputation. Hotels are twice as expensive as those across the border in Spain (and not as comfortable). The imported macaque monkeys might try to steal your bananas. Nevertheless, tourism is booming. Midday, the pedestrian-friendly main street is a human traffic jam. Twice as many planes are landing in the colony every day. When you walk across the airstrip that marks the border between Spain and what's left of the British Empire, it's more important than ever to look left, right—and up.

LEFT The Alhambra

RIGHT Gibraltar's famous rock

CULTURE AND TRADITIONS: EVERYTHING'S SO...SPANISH

Bullfighting

The Spanish bullfight is as much a ritual as it is a sport. Originally a form of military training, with refined knights fighting the noble beast from horseback, bullfighting today consists of a series of six bulls facing off against a matador and his team of fighters. Each ritual killing lasts 20 minutes. Then another bull romps into the arena.

While controversial to many for its brutality, aficionados insist that bullfighting is an art form. The Catalunya region banned the practice in 2012, but it remains popular in places such as Sevilla, Madrid, and Ronda, the birthplace of modern bullfighting. Personally, I find the spectacle rather pathetic and cruel, and prefer to get my bullfight "culture" by popping into a bull bar. My favorite is La Torre del Oro, right on Madrid's Plaza Mayor. Its interior is a temple to bullfighting, festooned with gory decor. For many people, a quick sangria or beer in a bar like this is more than enough nasty for their Spanish vacation.

Flamenco

Although flamenco is performed throughout Spain, this music-and-dance art form has its roots in the Roma (Gypsy) and Moorish cultures of Andalucía. And even if flamenco concerts in Sevilla, Granada, and other Andalusian towns are designed for tourists, they are still real and riveting. For a more local-feeling experience, be at a bar (such as La Carbonería in Sevilla) after midnight, when spirited flamenco singing erupts spontaneously.

At any flamenco performance, sparks fly. The men do most of the flamboyant machine-gun footwork. The women often concentrate on the graceful turns and smooth, shuffling step of the *soléa* version of the dance. I always watch the musicians. Flamenco guitarists, with their lightning-fast finger-roll strums, are among the best in the world. The intricate rhythms are set by castanets or the hand-clapping (called *palmas*) of those who aren't dancing at the moment. In the raspy-voiced wails of the singers, you'll hear echoes of the Muslim call to prayer.

Tapas

Tapas bars are everywhere in Spain. Serving small portions of seafood, salad, meat-filled pastries, and deep-fried tasties, they offer a casual, cheap, and very local way of eating.

Chasing down a particular bar nearly defeats the purpose and spirit of tapas—they are impromptu. Just drop in at any lively place. I look for noisy bars with piles of napkins on the floor (go native and toss your trash, too), lots of locals, and the TV blaring.

You'll generally eat standing up in tapas bars. Standing makes sense

> ## The Spanish Eating Schedule
>
> Spaniards eat late. Lunch is anywhere between 1 and 4 p.m., and dinner doesn't even cross their minds until at least 9. To get by in Spain, you'll either have to adapt to the Spanish schedule and cuisine, or scramble to get food in between. You can have an early light lunch at a tapas bar. Or do as many Spaniards do and have a *bocadillo* (baguette sandwich) at about 11 a.m. to bridge the gap between their coffee-and-roll breakfast and late lunch (hence the popularity of fast-food *bocadillo* chains). Then, either have your main meal at a restaurant around 3 p.m. followed by light tapas for dinner; or reverse it, having a tapas meal in the afternoon, followed by a late restaurant dinner.

if you're on a budget because food and drinks are usually cheapest served at the *barra* (counter). To get started with a basic glass of red wine, you can ask for *un tinto*. But by asking for *un crianza*, you'll get a better aged wine for only a little extra money.

When you're ready to order your food, be assertive or you'll never be served. *Por favor* (please) grabs the guy's attention. Then quickly rattle off what you'd like (pointing to other people's food if necessary). Don't worry about paying until you're ready to leave (your waiter's keeping track of your tab).

Night Owls

Spain comes to life in the cool of the evening, when it's prime time. Whole families pour out of their apartments to stroll through the streets and greet their neighbors—a custom called the *paseo*. Even the biggest city feels like a rural village. The whole town strolls—it's like "cruising" without cars. Streets are polished nightly by the feet of families licking ice cream; buy an ice-cream sandwich and join the parade. Some people duck into bars for a drink or to watch a big soccer match on TV. They might order a bite to eat, grazing on tapas. Around 10 p.m. in the heat of summer, it's finally time for a light dinner. Afterward, even families with young children might continue their *paseo* or attend a concert. Spaniards are notorious night owls. Many clubs and restaurants don't even open until after midnight. Dance clubs routinely stay open until the sun rises, and young people stumble out bleary-eyed and head for work. The antidote for late nights? The next day's siesta.

Spain Travel Resources from Rick Steves

Guidebooks

Check out Rick's guidebooks covering all of Spain; Barcelona; Madrid & Toledo; and Sevilla, Granada & Southern Spain; plus his Spanish phrase book

TV Shows

The quintessence of Spain with Rick as your host, viewable on public television and at ricksteves.com. Episodes cover Madrid, Barcelona and Catalunya, northern Spain and the Camino de Santiago, Andalucía and Sevilla, the Basque Country, Toledo and Salamanca, and the Costa del Sol

Organized Tours

Small group tours, with itineraries planned by Rick: Spain in 14 Days; My Way: Spain in 11 Days; Barcelona & Madrid in 8 Days; Basque Country of Spain & France in 9 Days

For more on all of these resources, visit ricksteves.com

Portugal

Portugal has an appealing mix of hardscrabble cities, sweet port wine, wistful blue tiles, heartfelt ballads, and weather-beaten faces. Tucked into a corner of the Iberian Peninsula, Portugal seems somewhere just beyond Europe—prices are a bit cheaper, and the pace of life is noticeably slower. The traditional economy is still based on fishing, cork, wine, and textiles.

Portugal isn't showy—even its coastal towns lack glitzy attractions. The beach and the sea are enough, as they have been for centuries. They were the source of Portugal's seafaring wealth long ago, and are the draw for tourists today. The country's long coastline has some tucked-away gems that feel authentic—the beach towns of Salema (on the south coast) and Nazaré (on the west).

Portugal is more diverse than its neighbor Spain, as it's inhabited by many people from its former colonies in Brazil, Africa, and Asia. Especially in Lisbon, Portugal's Old World capital, you are as likely to hear lively African music as wistful Portuguese fado. The town of Fátima attracts devout pilgrims, while the university towns of Coimbra and Èvora have a youthful vibe.

With a rich culture, affordable prices, and a salty setting on the edge of Europe, Portugal understandably remains a popular destination. If your idea of travel includes friendly locals,

Portugal's Douro Valley is famed for its vineyards—the birthplace of port wine.

exotic architecture, windswept castles, and fresh seafood with chilled wine on a beach at sunset, you'll love this rewarding corner of Europe.

FAVORITE SIGHTS AND MEMORABLE EXPERIENCES IN PORTUGAL

Lisbon Gold

When I first came to Lisbon in the 1970s, the colorful Alfama neighborhood—then the shiver-me-timbers home of Lisbon's fisherfolk—was one of the places that charmed me into becoming a travel writer. On my last trip here—30-something years later—I noticed that much of the area's grittiness has been cleaned up. Old fishermen's families have been replaced by immigrant laborers. Widows no longer wear black after their husbands die. Once-characteristic fish stalls have moved off the streets and into more "hygienic" covered shops.

But the Alfama, which tumbles down from the castle to the river, remains one of the most photogenic neighborhoods in all of Europe. Wandering deep into this cobbled cornucopia of Old World color, I always get lost. Little streets squeeze into tangled stairways and confused alleys. Bent houses comfort each other in their romantic shabbiness, and the air drips with laundry and the smell of fresh clams and raw fish.

Like its salty sailors' quarter, Lisbon is a ramshackle but charming mix of now and then. Its glory days were the 15th and 16th centuries, when Vasco da Gama and other explorers opened new trade routes, making Lisbon the queen of Europe. Later, the riches of colonial Brazil boosted

Lisbon even higher. Then, in 1755, an earthquake (estimated at 9.0) leveled two-thirds of the city. Within a month, a new city was designed, and downtown Lisbon was quickly rebuilt on a progressive grid plan, with broad boulevards and square squares.

Following the quake, Portugal's rattled royalty chose to live out in suburban Belém, in wooden rather than stone buildings. Three miles from downtown, this district is now a stately pincushion of important Golden Age sights such as the Monastery of Jerónimos, with Vasco da Gama's tomb. The area is guarded by the ornate Belém Tower, which has kept an eye on Lisbon's harbor since 1555. It was the last sight sailors saw as they left, and the first thing they'd see when they returned—loaded down with gold, diamonds, and venereal diseases.

The more modern-feeling Baixa is the rebuilt center of Lisbon. This flat shopping area features grid-patterned streets and utilitarian architecture (buildings are uniform, with the same number of floors and similar facades). The Baixa's pedestrian streets, inviting cafés, bustling shops, and elegant old storefronts give the district a certain magnetism. I find myself doing laps up and down the pedestrian-only main boulevard in a people-watching stupor.

On my must-do list in Lisbon is stopping at a bar to have *pastel de bacalhau*, a fried potato-and-cod croquet. Bacalhau (salted cod) is Portugal's national dish. Imported from Norway, it's never fresh, and kids think it's a triangular fish because of the way it's sold. I think that Portugal must have the only national dish that's imported from far away—strange, and yet befitting of a nation known for seafaring explorers.

Another quintessential Lisbon experience is to take a trolley ride. The city's trolleys—many of which are vintage models from the 1920s—shake and shiver through the old

Fast Facts

Biggest cities: Lisbon (capital, 564,000), Porto (238,000), Coimbra (102,000)

Size: 35,000 square miles (slightly smaller than Indiana), population 10.5 million

Currency: Euro

Key dates: November 1, 1755, a severe earthquake and tsunami nearly destroy Lisbon and coastal communities; April 25, 1974, the Carnation Revolution marks the last gasp of the Salazar dictatorship and the beginning of Portuguese democracy

Biggest festivals: Fátima Pilgrimage (May 13 and October 13), Semana Santa (Easter Holy Week)

Major export: Half the world's cork comes from Portugal

Handy Portuguese phrases: Olá (hello, uh **lah**), Por favor (please; poor fah-**vor**), Obrigado/Obrigada (thank you—said by male/female, oh-bree-**gah**-doo/dah), Fala inglês? (Do you speak English?; **fah**-lah een-**glaysh**)

Portugal's Top Destinations

Lisbon ▲▲▲   allow 2-3 days

Lively, hilly port and capital, with historic trolleys, grand squares, fado clubs, fine art, and distinctive neighborhoods

Top Sights

Bairro Alto and Alfama Areas with glimpses of Golden Age
Belém Waterfront district with Monastery of Jerónimos
Gulbenkian Museum Fine art from Ancient Egypt to Art Nouveau

Nearby

Sintra Fairy-tale castles set in verdant hills

Algarve ▲▲▲   2-3 days

Sunny southern coast, with fishing village **Salema,** end-of-the-road **Cape Sagres,** and beach-party town **Lagos**

Nazaré ▲▲   1-3 days

Traditional fishing village turned surfing capital, and a springboard for nearby sights: **Batalha** (grand monastery), **Fátima** (famous pilgrimage site), **Alcobaça** (huge Gothic church), and **Óbidos** (walled hill town)

Porto and the Douro Valley ▲▲   1-2 days

Gritty hillside port city with charming old town, near the scenic Douro Valley, birthplace of port wine

Évora ▲▲   1 day

Whitewashed little college town with big Roman, Moorish, and Portuguese history encircled by its medieval wall

Coimbra ▲▲   1 day

Portugal's Oxford, home to an Arab-influenced old town and bustling with students from its prestigious university

---

parts of town, somehow safely weaving within inches of parked cars, climbing steep hills, and offering breezy views of the city (rubberneck out the window and you will die). They're perfect for a Rice-A-Roni-style Lisbon joyride. I enjoy hopping off the trolley for the hilltop viewpoint near São Jorge Castle—a good starting point for touring the Alfama district since you'll stroll down rather than hike up.

To complement all your Lisbon sightseeing, be sure to get out and be with the locals. One summer evening I found myself at a fairground watching Portuguese families at play. I ate dinner surrounded by chattering locals ignoring the ever-present TVs, while great platters of fish, meat, fries, salad, and lots of wine paraded frantically in every direction. A seven-year-old boy stood on a chair and sang hauntingly emotional folk songs. With his own dogged clapping, he

dragged applause out of the less-than-interested crowd and then passed his shabby hat. All the while, fried ducks dripped, barbecues spat, dogs squirted the legs of chairs, and somehow local lovers ignored everything but each other's eyes.

Sunny Salema

The Algarve, in southern Portugal, is my favorite stretch of Iberian coastline. I fantasize about being here on a real vacation—nursing a drink in a still-wet bathing suit, hauling in octopus pots, hiking to the beach, and exposing skin that's never seen the sun.

Warm and dry, the Algarve was once known as Europe's last undiscovered tourist frontier. But it's well discovered now, and if you go to the places featured in most tour brochures, you'll find it paved, packed, and pretty stressful.

Still, there are a few great beach towns left along the coast, perfect for soaking up rays in the summer.

My favorite hideaway is the little fishing town of Salema. It's at the end of a small road just off the main drag between the big city of Lagos and the rugged southwest tip of Europe, Cape Sagres. Here the tourists and fishermen sport the same stubble. It's just you, a beach full of garishly painted boats, your wrinkled landlady, and a few other globetrotting experts in lethargy.

When I first came here, in the late 1970s, the road into town wasn't paved. I turned up in the early evening, driving a group of eight tour members in a minivan and with no reservations. I parked at one end of the town, flagged down some locals, and asked for rooms: *"Quartos?"* Eyes perked, heads nodded, and I got nine beds in three homes for 20 bucks each.

While the street looks pretty much the same today, the character of the town is changing. Nowadays, beach towns like Salema are becoming the playgrounds of an international crowd of retirees and vacationers, who stay in newly built gated communities and golf clubs on the inland hilltops. Many of the ladies who once rented out rooms have disappeared, chastened by stricter government regulations (necessary, as southern Europe learns to pay its taxes). There are fewer shoestring-budget backpackers to keep them in business anyway.

On Salema's town square, a flatbed-truck market blitzes in and out weekday mornings. The *1812 Overture* horn of the fish truck wakes you at 8 a.m., followed by a fruit-and-vegetables truck and a five-and-dime truck for clothing and odds and ends. The bakery trailer sells delightful fresh bread and homemade sweet rolls each morning.

Salema is still a fishing village—but just barely. It has a split personality: The whitewashed old town is for locals, and

In Salema, on Portugal's south coast, two worlds merge as fishermen share the beach with travelers.

the other half was built for tourists—both groups pursue a policy of peaceful coexistence on the beach. Tourists laze in the sun, while locals grab the shade.

In Portugal, restaurateurs are allowed to build a temporary, summer-only beachside restaurant if they provide a lifeguard for swimmers and run a green/yellow/red warning-flag system. The Atlântico restaurant, which dominates Salema's beach, takes its responsibility seriously—providing lifeguards and flags through the summer...and fresh seafood by candlelight all year long.

Salema's sleepy beauty always kidnaps my momentum. My typical day begins and ends with the sound of waves. In the morning, I amble over to one of the hidden beaches within walking distance of town. I grab a late lunch overlooking the water, spend the afternoon relaxing on the beach catch the sunset with a drink in my hand, have a nice beachside dinner of grilled sardines, and then fall asleep to the strumming beat of the surf. The next day I do it all over again.

More Portuguese Experiences

Our Lady of Fátima: In 1917, three kids encountered the Virgin Mary near the central Portugal village of Fátima and were asked to return on the 13th of each month for six months. The final apparition was witnessed by thousands of locals. Ever since, Fátima has been on the pilgrimage trail—mobbed on the 13th of each month through the spring and summer.

Wandering around today's modern town, I'm impressed by how it mirrors my image of a medieval pilgrim gathering place: oodles of picnic benches, endless parking, and desolate toilets for the masses. On my last visit, the vast esplanade leading to the site of the mystical appearance was quiet, as only a few solitary pilgrims slowly shuffled on their knees down the long, smooth approach. In the basilica, a forest of candles dripped into a fiery trench that funneled all the melted wax into a bin—to be resurrected as new candles. Just beyond the basilica, 30 stalls lining a horseshoe-shaped mall awaited the 13th. Even without any business, old ladies still manned their booths, surrounded by pilgrim trinkets—including gaudy wax body parts and rosaries that would be blessed after Mass and taken home to remember Our Lady of Fátima.

Nazaré Dreaming: I got hooked on the Atlantic village of Nazaré back when colorful fishing boats littered its beach. Now the boats moor comfortably in a modern harbor outside town, and the beach is packed with sunbathers and surfers. But I still like the place. This fishing town turned resort is both black-shawl traditional and beach-friendly. The back streets are good for a wander and a fine look at Portuguese family-in-the-street life. Older ladies wear skirts made bulky by traditional petticoats, and men stow cigarettes and fish hooks in their stocking caps. Laundry flaps in the wind, kids play soccer, and fish sizzle over tiny curbside hibachis. Squadrons of salted fish are crucified on nets pulled tightly around wooden frames and left to dry under the midday sun. Locals claim they are delightfully tasty—but I'll take their word for it. Off-season Nazaré is almost empty of tourists—inexpensive, colorful, and relaxed, with enough salty fishing-village atmosphere to make you pucker.

The Alentejo Plain: Deep in the heart of Portugal, surrounded by cork trees and the vast, bleak beauty of the Alentejo region, I drive toward the walled city of Évora. It sits on lots of history. Outside of town stand 92 stones—2,000 years older than Stonehenge—erected by long-ago locals to make a celestial calendar. Évora's old center is crowned by

Portugal's top experiences include witnessing pilgrims at Fátima (left), savoring the beach at Nazaré (center), and hanging out with locals in Évora (right).

the granite Corinthian columns of a stately, ruined Roman temple. Tourists wander wide-eyed through the town's macabre 16th-century chapel, decorated with human bones meant to remind worshippers of their mortality.

The people of the Alentejo are uniformly short, look at tourists suspiciously, and are the butt of jokes in this corner of Europe. Libanio, my Évora guide, said it was the mark of a people's character to laugh at themselves. He asked me, "How can you tell a worker is done for the day in Alentejo?" I didn't know. He said, "When he takes his hands out of his pockets." My guide continued more philosophically: "In your land, time is money. Here in Alentejo, time is time. We take things slow and enjoy ourselves." I'm impressed when a region that others are inclined to insult has a strong local pride.

CULTURE AND TRADITIONS: EVERYTHING'S SO...PORTUGUESE

Fado

The songs of fado, the folk music of Portugal, reflect the country's bittersweet relationship with the sea. Fado, which means "fate," originated in the mid-1800s in Lisbon's rustic neighborhoods. These mournfully beautiful and haunting ballads are usually about lost sailors, broken hearts, romance gone wrong, and the yearning for what might have been if fate had not intervened. Fado, like a musical oyster, is sexy and full of the sea.

The singer (fadista) is accompanied by a 12-string guitarra portuguesa (with a round body like a mandolin) or other stringed instruments unique to Portugal. Fado singers typically crescendo into the first word of the verse, like a moan emerging from deep inside. The singers rarely over-act—they plant themselves firmly and sing stoically in the face of fate.

At Portugal's fado bars, you can sip wine while tuning in to these mournful melodies.

One of my favorite fado bars is A Baiuca, in Lisbon's Alfama district. Here mustachioed mandolin pluckers hunch over their instruments, lost in their music, while the kitchen staff peers from a steaming hole in the wall, backlit by their flaming grill. There's not a complete set of teeth in the house. The waiter delivers plates of fish and pitchers of cheap

cask wine to tables. Then, doubling as a Portuguese Ed Sullivan, he stops to introduce the star, who wears blood-red lipstick, big hair, and a black mourning shawl over her black dress—with a revealing neckline that promises that there is life after death.

Convent Sweets and Monks' Treats

Many pastries are called "convent sweets." Portugal, during its days as a trading powerhouse, had access to more sugar than any other European country. Even so, sugar was so expensive that only the upper classes could afford it routinely. Historically, many daughters of aristocrats who were unable to marry into suitably noble families ended up in high-class convents, bringing precious sugar with them. Over time, the convents became famous as keepers of wondrous secret recipes for exquisite pastries, generally made from sugar and egg yolks (which were left over after egg whites were used to starch the nuns' habits). *Barrigas de Freira* (Nuns' Bellies) and *Papo de Anjo* (Angel's Chin) are two such traditional fancies that you'll see in sweets shops.

While nuns baked sweets, the monks took care of quenching thirsts with *ginjinha,* a sweet liquor made from the sour cherry-like ginja berry, sugar, and brandy. Try it with or without berries (*com elas* or *sem elas*) and *gelada* (if you want it poured from a chilled bottle). The oldest *ginjinha* joint in Lisbon is a colorful hole-in-the-wall in the Baixa district, which sells shots for about a buck. In Portugal, when people are impressed by the taste of something, they say, *"Sabe que nem ginjas"* (It tastes like ginja).

Beware of Appetizers

In Portugal's restaurants, there's no such thing as a free munch. If the server puts appetizers on your table before you order, they'll appear on your bill. If you don't want them, push them to the side—you won't be charged if you don't touch the food (which ranges from olives, bread, and pâtés to a veritable mini-buffet of tasty temptations). Simple appetizers usually cost about €1 each, so even if you eat a couple of olives, it won't break the budget.

In Portugal you can discover a new favorite pastry (left), or make a pilgrimage to Porto's harbor—where port wine ages (right).

Barnacles!

Gooseneck barnacles (*percebes*) are a salty delicacy. These little taste treats are expensive because they're so dangerous to harvest—they grow on rocky promontories in narrow inlets where the waves and currents are fierce. (Connoisseurs know that they are fresh only April through September—otherwise they're frozen.) Merchants in coastal towns sell the crustaceans on the street as munchies. They'll happily demonstrate how to eat them and give you a sample, figuring if you try just one briny morsel, you'll buy a kilo. Local bars serve *percebes* with beer, like corn nuts.

Port Party

Much of the world's port wine comes of age in Porto, in northern Portugal. The grapes are grown about 60 miles upstream in the Douro River Valley. A young port is produced, which sits for a winter in silos before being shipped downstream to Porto's Vila Nova de Gaia district. There it ages for years in wooden barrels stored in "lodges" on the cool, north-facing bank of the Douro. For wine connoisseurs, touring a port-wine lodge (*cave do vinho do porto*) and sampling the product is a must-see attraction.

For most people, "port" means a tawny port, which is aged anywhere between 10 and 40 years. But there are multiple varieties of port. Wood ports are aged in wooden vats or barrels, and vintage ports are aged in bottles. *Reserva* on the label means it's the best-quality port (and the most expensive). As for me, I'm not choosy. As I always say, "Any port in a storm..."

Great Britain

From the grandeur and bustle of London, to a rich and royal history that inspired Shakespeare, to some of the quaintest towns you'll ever experience, Great Britain is a delight. Stand in a desolate field and ponder a prehistoric stone circle. Do the Beatles blitz in Liverpool, and walk in the Lake District footsteps of Wordsworth. Discover your favorite pub and have a pint of beer with the neighborhood gang. Tackle some Welsh words, relax in a bath in Bath, and shake paws with a Highland sheepdog. There's something unparalleled yet familiar about traveling in Great Britain.

Three very different countries—England, Wales, and Scotland—make up Great Britain (add in Northern Ireland, and you've got the United Kingdom). England is the center in every way: the seat of government, the economic power-house, the bastion of higher learning, and the cultural heart. Anchored by thriving London, England has everything from castles to cathedrals and sheep-speckled hillsides to dark-wooded pubs.

Humble, charming little Wales is a land of stout castles, salty harbors, slate-roofed villages, stunning mountains, and lusty men's choirs. Traditional and beautiful, Wales sometimes feels trapped in another century. But soon you'll awaken to the distinctive, poetic vitality of this small country.

And then there's rugged, feisty, colorful Scotland—the yin to England's yang. Whether it's the laid-back, less-organized nature of the people, the stony architecture, the unmanicured landscape, or simply the haggis, go-its-own-way Scotland stands apart. Its sights are subtle, but the misty glens, brooding castles, hardy bagpipers, and warm culture are engaging.

I love traveling in Great Britain. It hosts the heritage of the greatest empire the world has ever lived under, yet bears the humiliation of a struggling economy, with remnants of its former empire owning much of its capital city. Its pomp, which seems to serve as a quaint reminder of former grandness, feels almost designed for tourists. Still, a visit here connects you with people, nature, heritage, and culture, all of which combine to make Great Britain such a rewarding destination.

FAVORITE SIGHTS AND MEMORABLE EXPERIENCES IN GREAT BRITAIN

Edinburgh's Royal Mile

There's no better introduction to Edinburgh—the historical, cultural, and political capital of Scotland—than a walk straight down the spine of the old town. Stretching from a hill-topping castle to a queen's palace, this ramble is appropriately called the Royal Mile. Despite being crammed with tourists, it's one of Europe's best sightseeing walks.

I begin my stroll on the bluff where Edinburgh was born and where a castle now stands. Over the centuries, this mighty fortress was home to many of Scotland's kings and queens. Today it's well worth touring to see the old buildings, stunning views, and crown jewels.

As Edinburgh grew, it spilled downhill along the tight, sloping ridge that became the Royal Mile. Back in the vibrant 1600s, this was the city's main street, bustling with breweries, printing presses, and banks. With tens of thousands of citizens squeezed into the narrow confines of the old town,

Edinburgh's Royal Mile entertains from top to bottom, from connoisseur's whisky at Cadenhead's shop to St. Giles Cathedral, where John Knox preached the Reformation.

there was nowhere to go but up. So builders lined the street with multi-story residences (called tenements)—some 10 stories and higher.

Truth be told, these days much of the Royal Mile is a touristic mall—all tartans, sightseers, and shortbread. But it remains packed with history, and intrepid visitors can still find a few surviving rough edges of Auld Reekie, as the old town was once called (for the smell of smoke and sewage that wafted across the city). Exploring back alleys and side lanes, it's easy to imagine Edinburgh in the 17th and 18th centuries, when out-of-towners came here to marvel at its "skyscrapers," and thousands of people scurried through these alleyways, buying and selling goods and popping into taverns.

Scotland is a proud nation, and everywhere I turn, the Royal Mile is littered with symbols of that pride—from a statue of philosopher David Hume, one of the towering figures of the Scottish Enlightenment of the mid-1700s, to its very own Church of Scotland, embodied by St. Giles Cathedral. Filled with monuments, statues, plaques, and stained-glass windows dedicated to great Scots and moments in history, St. Giles serves as a kind of Scottish Westminster Abbey.

St. Giles is also the home church of the great reformer John Knox, whose fiery sermons helped turn once-Catholic Edinburgh into a bastion of Protestantism. Knox's influence was huge. His insistence that every person should be able to read the word of God firsthand helped give Scotland an educational system 300 years ahead of the rest of Europe. Just down the road from St. Giles is the John Knox House, featuring atmospheric rooms, period furniture, and a fun little dress-up corner that lets me play out my Great Reformer fantasy.

But I'm eager to get to one of my favorite stops along the Mile: Cadenhead's Whisky Shop. Founded in 1842,

Fast Facts

Biggest cities: London (capital, 7.8 million), Birmingham (1 million), Glasgow (600,000), Liverpool (450,000)

Size: 95,000 square miles (about the size of Michigan), population 61.5 million

Locals call it: Britain

Currency: British pound

Key date: 1533, King Henry VIII breaks with the Catholic Church and establishes himself as the head of the Church of England, setting the English Reformation in motion

Biggest festivals: Chelsea Flower Show (May, London), Edinburgh International Festival (August, music, dance, and theater)

Language: Predominantly English, but also Scottish Gaelic and Welsh Cymraeg

Handy British phrases: *I'm bloody knackered* (I'm so exhausted), *Don't get your knickers in a twist* (Don't get all upset), *Bob's your uncle* (obviously), *Sod off* (Screw off), *That's a load of bollocks* (That's a bunch of nonsense)

Cadenhead's prides itself on bottling good whisky without watering it down or adding cosmetic coloring. Popping in, I'm shown a shelf of aged wooden casks. The shop owner explains that distillers prefer to drink their whisky rough, from casks like these: "It's like getting your milk straight from the farmer." He draws a wee dram for me, and I taste it. Whoa! Then he pours a little spring water on it. Squinting into the glass, he coaches me along: "Look at the impurities gathering in a happy little pool there on top. The water is like a spring rain on a garden—it brings out the character, the personality." Sipping this whisky with an expert, I see how Scotland's national drink can become, as they're fond of saying, "a very good friend."

Fortified, I walk on to the Royal Mile's next attraction: the modern Scottish parliament building. After three centuries of being ruled from London, the Scots regained a parliament of their own in 1999, and a few years later built this striking, eco-friendly home for it. In the distance is the craggy summit called Arthur's Seat, and this soaring building, mixing wild angles and bold lines, seems to be surging right out of the rock.

My very last stop is the Palace of Holyroodhouse, one of Queen Elizabeth's official residences and a long-time home to Scottish royalty, including James IV and Mary, Queen of Scots. The Scottish monarchs also kept a home at the top end of the Mile, but they preferred the cushier Holyroodhouse to the blustery castle up on the rock.

I've soaked up plenty of Scottish history on my walk from castle to palace. But no Royal Mile walk is complete without popping into a pub—and there's no shortage of them—where a bit of live music and whisky await.

History Comes Alive at Westminster Abbey

Eddie the Verger is posted in his red robe with a warm smile at the exit of London's Westminster Abbey. His responsibility: to sort through those visitors who want to enter the abbey to worship, and those who are masquerading as worshippers in order to sidestep the high entrance fee.

Westminster Abbey is the most famous English church in Christendom, where royalty has been wedded, crowned, and buried since the 11th century. A thousand years of English history—3,000 tombs, the remains of 29 kings and queens, and hundreds of memorials to poets, politicians, scientists, and warriors—lie within its stained-glass splendor, making it a must-see on any London trip. Dropping by, I tell Eddie I'm

Great Britain's Top Destinations

ENGLAND

London ▲▲▲   allow 3-5 days

Thriving metropolis packed with world-class museums, monuments, churches, parks, palaces, theaters, pubs, Beefeaters, double-decker buses, and all things British

Top Sights

Westminster Abbey Britain's most important church
British Museum World's greatest chronicle of Western civilization
National Gallery European paintings from Leonardo, Botticelli, Van Gogh, and more
British Library Top literary treasures of the Western world
Tower of London Castle, palace, and prison housing the crown jewels
St. Paul's Cathedral Christopher Wren's domed masterpiece

Nearby

Greenwich Maritime center with famous observatory
Windsor Queen's primary residence
Cambridge England's best university town

Bath ▲▲▲   2 days

Genteel Georgian city, built around the remains of an ancient Roman bath

Nearby

Glastonbury New Age mysticism, abbey ruins, and a holy hill
Stonehenge and Avebury Prehistoric stone circles
Wells and Salisbury Serene Gothic cathedrals

Cotswolds ▲▲   1-2 days

Quaint villages—cozy market town **Chipping Campden,** popular hamlet **Stow-on-the-Wold,** and handy transit hub **Moreton-in-Marsh**—scattered over a hilly countryside and near one of England's top palaces, Blenheim

Lake District ▲▲   1-2 days

Idyllic lakes-and-hills landscape, with enjoyable hikes and joyrides, time-passed valleys, William Wordsworth and Beatrix Potter sights, and the charming home-base town of **Keswick**

Durham and Hadrian's Wall ▲   1-2 days

Youthful working-class university town with magnificent cathedral, within an easy drive of the Roman ruins of Hadrian's Wall

York ▲▲▲   1-2 days

Walled medieval town with grand Gothic cathedral, excellent museums (Viking, Victorian, railway), and atmospheric old center

WALES

North Wales ▲▲   1-2 days

Scenically rugged land filled with evocative castles, the natural beauty of Snowdonia National Park, and the tourable slate mines at **Blaenau Ffestiniog,** all accessible from the cute castle town of **Conwy**

SCOTLAND

Edinburgh ▲▲▲   2 days

Proud Scottish capital, with an imposing castle on a bluff, attraction-studded
Royal Mile, and Georgian New Town with trendy shops and eateries

Nearby

St. Andrews Famous golf town and Scotland's top university

Highlands ▲   1-2 days

Traditionally Scottish mountainous region, with the handy hub of **Inverness** (near
Loch Ness and Culloden Battlefield) in the north, and the home-base town of
Oban in the south, with boat trips to the historic isles of **Mull** and **Iona**

With more time, consider visiting

Liverpool Gentrified English port city and the Beatles' hometown

Stratford-upon-Avon Shakespeare's home and fine theater

Glasgow Workaday but revitalized city with fun nighttime scene

working on the Rick Steves book, and he says, "I'd like a word with that Rick Steves. He implies in his guidebook that you can pop in to worship in order to get a free visit."

I tell him who I am, and we sort it out. Really charmed by Eddie, I agree that I'll encourage visitors to attend the free worship service for the experience of it, not to dodge the admission fee. (I highly recommend a sung evensong, which takes place six days a week.)

Eddie deposits me in the abbey, and I visit like any other tourist—enjoying the great audio tour narrated by Jeremy Irons. Listening to the actor's soothing voice, I have some private time with great history: the marble effigy of Queen Elizabeth I, modeled after her death mask in 1603—considered the most realistic likeness of her; the coronation chair that centuries of kings and queens sat upon right here on their big day; the literary greats of England gathered as if conducting a posthumous storytelling session around the tomb of Geoffrey Chaucer (Mr. *Canterbury Tales*); the poppies lining the Grave of the Unknown Warrior, an ordinary soldier who lost his life in World War I; the statue of Martin Luther King Jr., added above the west entrance in 1998 as an honorary member of this now heavenly English host; and so much more.

London on the Cheap

London is one of Europe's most expensive cities. Here are some tips for stretching your pennies and pounds:

- Gorge on London's many free museums: the British Museum, British Library, National Gallery, National Portrait Gallery, Tate Britain, Tate Modern, and Victoria and Albert Museum.
- Go to a free evensong service at (the otherwise expensive) Westminster Abbey or St. Paul's.
- Look for free performances such as lunch concerts at St. Martin-in-the-Fields Church, the Changing of the Guard at Buckingham Palace, rants at Speakers' Corner in Hyde Park, and the legislature at work in the Houses of Parliament.
- Join an inexpensive London Walks tour. Or, cheaper yet, take advantage of the free guided London walks in the Rick Steves Audio Europe app.
- Get discounted same-day tickets at theater box offices or from the official TKTS booth at Leicester Square.
- Consider hosteling (yha.org.uk) or staying in dorms (late June to mid-September; the University of Westminster is one option with doubles, westminster.ac.uk/summeraccommodation).

Then Eddie takes me into a place that no tourist goes—the Jerusalem Chamber, where long-ago monks set up shop to translate the Bible from ancient Greek into English, creating the King James Version (finished in 1611). These reformers faced real danger in getting the word of God into the people's language, and knowing the importance of their heroic steps back then, I got shivers and chills (much as I did at Germany's Wartburg Castle, where I saw the room in

With Eddie the Verger (left) at Westminster Abbey (right)

which Martin Luther did essentially the same thing for the German-speaking world).

I thank Eddie on my way out; we part as friends. He's glad that tourists will be less likely to try to sneak into the abbey for free. And for me, it's been worth the visit to look back in time, remembering the writers, reformers, royalty, and soldiers who put the "great" in Great Britain.

The Quaint and Quirky Cotswolds

For three decades, I've said it's a temptation for a travel writer to overuse the word "quaint." I reserve my use of it for describing England's Cotswold villages, in the gentle, hilly region northwest of London. By quaint, I don't mean just thatched cottages and charming teahouses. There's a quirkiness here—a sort of impoverished nobility and provincial naiveté that has something to do with being time-passed. Whatever it is, it charms me to no end.

I like the north Cotswolds best. Two of the region's coziest towns are Chipping Campden, featuring what the great British historian G. M. Trevelyan and I call the finest High Street in England; and Stow-on-the-Wold, with good pubs, antique stores, and cute shops draped seductively around a big town square. Both are close to Moreton-in-Marsh, which has good public transportation connections and lacks the touristic sugar of the other towns. Any of these villages makes a fine home base for your exploration of the thatch-happiest of Cotswold towns and countryside.

Between Stow and Chipping Campden, the tiny hamlets of Snowshill, Stanton, and Stanway get my nomination for the cutest Cotswold destinations. Sweet as marshmallows in hot chocolate, they nestle side by side, each spiced with eccentric characters and odd bits of history.

Snowshill, a little bundle of delight, has a photogenic

triangular square. On one corner stands Snowshill Manor. This dark, mysterious old palace is filled with the lifetime collection of the long-gone Charles Paget Wade. It is one big, musty celebration of craftsmanship, from finely carved spinning wheels to frightening samurai armor to tiny elaborate figurines carved by long-forgotten prisoners from the bones of meat served at dinner. It's clear that Wade dedicated his life and fortune to fulfilling his family motto: "Let Nothing Perish."

The sister villages of Stanton and Stanway are separated by a great oak forest and grazing land, with parallel waves in the fields echoing the furrows plowed by medieval farmers. It's my selfish tradition here to let someone else drive so I can hang out the window, enjoying a windy flurry of stone walls and sheep, all under a canopy of ancient oaks.

In Stanton, flowers trumpet, door knockers shine, and slate shingles clap. It's as if a rooting section is cheering me up the town's main street. The church, however, betrays a pagan past. Stanton is at the intersection of two ley lines (which some new-age types consider a source of special power) connecting prehistoric sights. Many churches such as Stanton's were built on pagan holy ground and are generally dedicated to St. Michael—the Christian antidote to pagan mischief. Michael's well-worn figure, looking down at me from above the door, seems to say, "It's all clear now—good Christians may enter." Sitting in the back pew, fingering grooves worn into the wooden posts by sheepdog leashes (at a time when a man's sheepdog accompanied him everywhere), I'm reminded that it was wool money that built this church.

Stanway, while not much of a village, is notable for its venerable manor house. The Earl of Wemyss (pronounced "Weemz"), whose family tree charts relatives back to 1202,

England's Cotswold villages are made to order for the word "quaint."

occasionally opens his melancholy home to visitors. Musty and threadbare, it feels like a trip back in time. You'll often find his lordship roaming about. The manor dogs have their own cutely painted "family tree," but the earl admits that his last dog, C.J., was "all character and no breeding." Once, while I was marveling at the 1780 Chippendale exercise chair in the great hall, the earl surprised me. Jumping up onto the tall leather-encased spring, and with the help of the high armrests, he began bouncing. A bit out of breath, he explained, "In grandmama's time, half an hour of bouncing on this was considered good for the liver."

The earl's house has a story to tell. And so do the docents—modern-day peasants who, even without family trees, probably have relatives in this village going back just as far as their earl's. If you probe cleverly, talking to these people gives a rare insight into this quirky, authentic slice of England.

A Day in Regal Bath

Shaking off my umbrella, I walked up to my B&B and climbed the stairs to my room, exhausted after a long day exploring Bath. When I blew my nose, I noticed a spray of red dirt on the Kleenex—and I remembered the snuff.

At the Star Inn, the most characteristic pub in town, the manager Paul keeps a tin of complimentary snuff tobacco on a ledge for customers. Earlier that evening I tried some, questioning Paul about it while a drunk guy from Wales tried to squeeze by me holding two big pints of local brew over my head. Paul said that English coal miners have long used it because cigarettes were too dangerous in the mines, and they needed their tobacco fix. He wanted me to take the tin. I put it back on the ledge and said I'd try it again the next time I stopped by.

In Bath, you'll enjoy a lazy picnic surrounded by Georgian elegance.

From the hospitality of its people to its architectural beauty and aristocratic charm, Bath is one of those places that seems made for tourists. Just 90 minutes west of London by train, the city is known for its grand abbey (the last great medieval church erected in England), stately Georgian-era buildings, and restorative thermal baths (said to have cured

Queen Mary of infertility and Queen Anne of gout). Despite its flood of sightseers, I still find Bath to be one of the most enjoyable cities in Britain.

I started my day joining a gang of curious visitors in front of the abbey, where volunteer guides divide up the tourists for a free walk around town. My guide, a retired school-teacher, explained that the volunteer-touring tradition started in 1930, when the mayor—proud of the charms of his historic town—took the first group gathered here on a walk. The mayor's honorary guide corps has been leading free walks daily ever since.

For 2,000 years, Bath's mineral spa has been attracting those in need of a cure.

The musical highlight of my day was a worship service at Bath Abbey. The service was crisp, eloquent, and traditional. I was struck by the strong affirmation of the worshippers' Catholic heritage, the calls for sobriety, and the stress on repentance (including repeated references to how we are such wretched sinners).

The Anglican worship ritual is carefully shuttled from one generation to the next. That continuity seemed to be underlined by the countless tombs and memorials lining walls and floors—worn smooth and shiny by the feet of worshippers over the centuries. With the living and the dead all present together, the congregation seemed to raise their heads in praise as sunlight streamed through windows. This bright church is nicknamed the "Lantern of the West" for its open, airy lightness and huge windows.

The church was packed with townsfolk—proper and still. As I sat among them at offering time, the pastor caught me off-guard with his gentility. He said, "If you're a visitor, please don't be embarrassed to let the plate pass. It's a way for our regular members to support our work."

Later that night, heading home from the Star Inn, I was surrounded by young kids partying. English girls out clubbing wiggled down the street like the fanciest of fish lures—each shaking their tassels and shimmying in a way sure to catch a big one.

The rock star Meatloaf was playing a big concert in the park, and during his performance, much of Bath rocked with him. Although the concert was sold out, I gathered with a hundred freeloaders, craning our necks from across the river for a great view of the stage action.

Bath's an expensive town in an expensive country. The

young couple hired to manage the elegant Georgian guesthouse I was staying in told me they took the gig just to live
in Bath. As they put it, "Workaday English can't really afford
to live here." They have an apartment in the basement, but
they go through the grand front door just to marvel at the
elegant building they live in. I don't blame them. The grandeur of Bath—wonderfully accessible to a tourist—is simply
unmatched.

Highlands Magic

Years ago, I met a dear man on a deserted roadside in the
Scottish Highlands. I was scrambling to make a TV show
about the area, and as if placed there by heaven's Central
Casting, this tender giant of a man was bagpiping to the
birds, the passing clouds, and the occasional motorist. He
had picked a spot that seemed intentionally miles from
nowhere. We stopped, and he graciously demonstrated his
pipes, giving us a tour of that fascinating symbol of Scottish
culture. I've never forgotten that wonderful chance meeting.

The Scottish Highlands are filled with magic and mystery. In the northernmost reaches of Scotland, the Highlands
feature a wild, severely undulating terrain that's punctuated
by lochs (lakes) and fringed by sea lochs (inlets) and islands.
Whenever I want a taste of traditional Scotland, this is where
I come.

About two hours north of Edinburgh, the tiny village of
Kenmore—little more than the fancy domain of its castle, a
church set in a bouquet of tombstones, and a line of humble
houses—offers a fine dose of small-town Scottish flavor. One
day a year, it hosts its Highland Games festival and one year

PIOB MHOR of SCOTLAND
KILTMAKERS &
HIGHLAND OUTFITTERS

I was lucky enough to be there, mixing it up with the locals. The open field was filled with families having a fun day out watching tug-of-wars, little kids' sprints, gunnysack races, bands of marching pipers, and Highland dancing. While the girls impatiently and anxiously awaited their time with the bagpiper on stage, the big boys took turns tossing big things: Stones, hammers, and the caber (a log the size of a small telephone pole) were sent end-over-end to the delight of those gathered.

Loch Tay, near Kenmore, is a fascinating place. All across Scotland, archaeologists know that little round islands on the lochs are evidence of crannogs—circular lakefront houses built by big shots about 2,500 years ago. In the age before roads, people traveled by boat, so building houses on waterways made sense. There are 18 such crannogs on Loch Tay, and one is now the Crannog Centre, a museum dedicated to demonstrating the skills every crannog homeowner needed, such as making fire by rubbing sticks.

There can be very few Scots whose ancestors were not connected to working the land. And sheepdogs have a long rural lineage, too. The dogs herding sheep today are the direct descendants of a long-ago breed domesticated in the British Isles. In the Highlands, the best way to get a taste of this aspect of farm culture is at a good sheepdog show.

Recently, on a remote Highlands farm, I drove up a long rutted drive with one of my tour groups. As we stepped onto the grass, a dozen eager border collies scampered to greet us. Then came the shepherd, whom the dogs clearly loved and followed like a messiah. He proceeded to sit us down in a natural little amphitheater in the turf and explain all about his work. With shouts and whistles, each dog followed individual commands and showed an impressive mastery over the sheep. Then, with good, old-fashioned shears, we each got our chance to shear a sheep—who took it calmly, as if at a beauty salon.

The Highlands' past is written all over its landscape. Perhaps no other place is as evocative as the memorial battlefield of Culloden, near Inverness. In 1746, Jacobite troops (most of them Highlanders) gave it their all to put the Catholic Bonnie Prince Charlie on the English throne... and failed. While only about 50 English soldiers died, the Highlanders lost about 1,500 men. Bonnie Prince Charlie declared, "Every man for himself!" as he galloped away. The Highlanders were routed.

The victorious English pushed an aggressive campaign of cultural assimilation. After Culloden, they banned the wearing of kilts, the playing of bagpipes, and even the Gaelic language—effectively spelling the end of the clan system.

Near Culloden is another fascinating sight—the Clava Cairns. I always knew about England's famous stone circles, but I hadn't realized that Scotland had fancy-pants, over-achieving knuckle draggers, too. At Clava Cairns, set in a peaceful grove of trees, are the remains of three stone burial mounds, each cleverly constructed 4,000 years ago with a passageway that the sun illuminates, as if by magic, with each winter solstice. Wandering through these thought-provoking cairns, knowing they're as old as the pyramids, is a highlight of a Highlands visit.

When in Britain, Take a Hike

After decades of visits to Britain, I finally took some time to slow down and do some real hiking. One thing I learned: Even if you only have two or three hours, taking a hike is about the best time you can invest in places of outstanding natural beauty. Every day has a few hours to spare. What else is so important between 4 o'clock and dinnertime? Because of these walks, I took home vivid memories.

In the Lake District, I struggled up and over Catbells, a 1,480-foot hill above the lake called Derwentwater. The weather had almost kept me in, but I was glad I ventured out. I welcomed the comedic baaing of sheep, and the wind "blowing the cobwebs out" (as my B&B host warned) On previous visits, when I'd stayed down by the lake, I'd look up to see hikers silhouetted like stick figures on this ridge. Now I was one of those sky-high figures myself. With the weather

Hiking in England's Lake District, you can find your own majestic perch overlooking a sunlit valley (left) or stumble upon a surprise view of Derwentwater (right).

storming overhead like a dark army, the wind buffeting in my ears, and 360-degree views commanding my attention—I wanted to turn cartwheels.

Anywhere in Britain, blustery weather is just a part of the scene. Most "bad weather" comes with broken spells of brightness, and it doesn't pay to get greedy for more (like outright sunshine). You wish for and are thankful for brightness. As they say here, there's no bad weather, just inappropriate clothing.

And, oh, the joy of a pub after a good hike. Studying the light on ruddy faces while munching hearty pub grub has always been part of the magic of travel in Britain. When your skin is weather-stung and your legs ache happily with accomplishment, the pub ambience takes on an even more inviting glow.

Dartmoor Calling

A fine way to mix Neolithic wonders and nature is to explore one of England's many turnstile-free moors. You can get lost in these stark and sparsely populated time-passed commons, which have changed over the centuries about as much as the longhaired sheep that seem to gnaw on moss in their sleep. Directions are difficult to keep. It's cold and gloomy, as nature rises like a slow tide against human constructions. A crumpled castle loses itself in lush overgrowth. A church grows shorter as tall weeds eat at the stone crosses and tilted tombstones.

Windswept and desolate, Dartmoor National Park in southwest England is one of the few truly wild places you'll find in this densely populated country. With more Bronze

The stone circles at Dartmoor National Park are as old as the pyramids.

Age stone circles and huts than any other chunk of England, Dartmoor is perfect for those who dream of experiencing their own private Stonehenge sans barbed wire, police officers, parking lots, tourists, and port-a-loos.

On one visit, I trekked from the hamlet of Gidleigh through a foggy world of scrub brush and scraggy-haired goats on a mission to find a 4,000-year-old circle of stone. Venturing in the pristine vastness of Dartmoor, I sank into the powerful, mystical moorland—a world of greenery, eerie wind, white rocks, and birds singing but unseen. Climbing over a hill, surrounded by sleeping towers of ragged, moss-fringed granite, I was swallowed up. Hills followed hills followed hills—green growing gray in the murk.

Then the stones appeared, frozen in a forever game of statue maker. For endless centuries they waited patiently, still and silent, as if for me to come. I sat on a fallen stone, observing blackbirds and wild horses. My imagination ran wild, pondering the people who roamed England so long before written history, feeling the echoes of druids worshipping and then reveling right here.

More British Experiences

My Favorite Welsh Town: In North Wales, miles of green fields are dotted with grazing sheep. My preferred home base for exploring this region is the town of Conwy. Built in the 1280s to give the English king Edward I a toehold in Wales, it also served as a busy port, back when much of Europe was roofed with Welsh slate. Today it boasts the best medieval walls in Britain, a protective castle dramatically situated on a rock overlooking the sea, and a charming harbor that locals treat like a town square. Facing the harbor is the Liverpool Arms pub, a salty and characteristic hangout built by a captain who ran a ferry service to Liverpool in the 19th century. On summer evenings, the action is on the quay It's a small town, and everyone comes out to enjoy the local cuisine—chips, ice cream, and beer—and to savor that great British pastime: tormenting little crabs. If you want to do more than photograph the action, rent gear from the nearby lifeboat house. Mooch some bacon from others for bait, and join in. It's catch-and-release. The scene is mellow, multi-generational, and perfectly Welsh.

Hunting Ghosts in York: Just two hours north of London by express train, York has a rich history—from its Roman origins to its role as a Viking trading center. It's got the largest Gothic church in Britain, and, as locals love to add, "a giant bell." Just as a Boy Scout counts the rings in a tree, you can count the ages of York by the different bricks in the city wall: Roman on the bottom, then Danish, Norman, and the "new" addition"—from the 14th century. With all this history, joining a walking tour makes for a wonderful introduction to the city. Charming old Yorkers volunteer their time to give energetic, entertaining, and free two-hour walking tours every day of the year. Or, for a little more gore, you can pay to join one of the many ghost walks advertised all over town. While generally I find ghost walks to be little more than goofy entertainment, if any city can claim to be legitimately haunted, it would be York. At night, the old town center is crawling with creepy, black-clad characters leading wide-eyed groups of tourists around on various ghost walks. On my last trip, I spent an evening sampling several different walks—and woke up screaming at 2 a.m.

Scotland's Second City: Lately, I've been appreciating what I consider to be the "second cities" of Europe. These places— from Marseille to Porto, Antwerp to Belfast, Hamburg to Bilbao—often have a rough, Industrial Age heritage and a rust-belt vibe that keeps them honest, unvarnished, and nonconformist. Take Glasgow: Even though it is Scotland's largest city, it takes second place to Edinburgh (which wins out for its impressive sights and capital status). Nonetheless, Glasgow has a wonderful energy and plenty of sights, including Art Nouveau architecture from Charles Rennie Mackintosh and fine museums. But the highlight is the city's street scene, which percolates in places like the Golden Zed, a Z-shaped pedestrian shopping zone that zigzags through town. Just strolling up its lanes—listening to buskers, enjoy- ing the people-watching, and remembering to look up at the architecture above the modern storefronts—is a treat. And rather than letting graffiti artists mess up the place with

Britain offers a fine set of experiences: from English garrison towns like Conwy, built seven centuries ago to keep down the Welsh (left), to ghost tours that really grab you in York (center), to fun and spirited public art on the streets of Glasgow (right).

random or angry tagging, the top street artists are given entire walls to paint. These murals are almost sightseeing destinations in themselves.

Walking Hadrian's Wall: For years I've visited Hadrian's Wall, the remains of the 73-mile fortification the Romans built nearly 2,000 years ago. It marked the northern end of their empire, where Britannia stopped and where the barbarian land that would someday be Scotland began. But until recently, I never ventured beyond the National Trust properties, the museums, and the various parking lot viewpoints.

This time, cameraman in tow, I grabbed a sunny late afternoon to actually hike the wall. When you're scrambling along Roman ruins, accompanied by the sound of the wind, surveying vast expanses of Britain from rocky crags that seem to rip across the island—like a snapshot that has frozen some horrific geological violence in mid-action—you need to take a moment and simply absorb your setting. As my cameraman did his work, I did just that. It was a goose-pimple experience, as the Brits would say.

CULTURE AND TRADITIONS: EVERYTHING'S SO...BRITISH

Pubs and Beer

Pubs are a basic part of the British social scene, and whether you're a teetotaler or a beer guzzler, they should be a part of your travel here. For instance, whenever I'm in London, I make it a point to savor a pint at the Anglesea Arms in South Kensington. In my mind, this place is everything a British pub should be: filled with musty paintings and old-timers, beautiful people backlit, dogs wearing Union Jack vests, a long line of tempting tap handles advertising the beers and ales available, and flower boxes spilling color around picnic tables—perfect for a warm summer evening.

Brits take great pride in their beer, and many think that drinking beer cold and carbonated, as Americans do, ruins the taste. At pubs, long-handled pulls are used to literally pull the traditional, rich-flavored "real ales" up from the cellar. These are the connoisseur's favorites: fermented naturally, varying from sweet to bitter, often with a hoppy or nutty flavor. Short-handled pulls at the bar mean colder, fizzier, mass-produced, and less interesting (at least to Brits)—keg beers. Pubs are also a fine (and economical) place to sample traditional dishes, like fish-and-chips, roast beef,

Britain's pubs still provide the best places to hang out with the locals.

bangers and mash (sausages and mashed potatoes), and meat pies—though increasingly, "gastropubs" are raising the culinary bar, with menus that mingle updated English and international fare. For me, eating in a fine pub under ancient timbers is the best and most atmospheric way to dine in Britain.

B&Bs and the British Breakfast

No one does bed-and-breakfasts better than the Brits. You'll find these small, quaint, family-run accommodations everywhere in Great Britain. Besides the company of charming hosts, the best part of staying at a B&B is the huge, home-cooked breakfast, called a "fry-up," a "full English/Scottish/Welsh breakfast," or a "heart attack on a plate." Most B&B owners take pride in their breakfasts. Each morning, you sit down at an elegant and very British table setting in an intimate dining room. You can order whatever parts of the fry-up you desire: Canadian-style bacon, sausage, eggs, broiled tomatoes, mushrooms, greasy pan-fried toast, sometimes potatoes, and coffee or tea. Or, rather than a big plate of cardiac arrest, you can go to the buffet table and help yourself to cereal, juice, yogurt, and fruit.

B&Bs are not without drawbacks. Because they're often housed in older buildings, rooms are commonly smaller and more cramped than hotels. They can have thinner walls and creaky floorboards, so you might hear other guests creeping around at night. And while most rooms have an "en suite" (attached) bathroom, some rooms come with a "private bathroom" instead, which can mean that the bathroom is all yours, but it's across the hall. Yet I happily make the trade-off for the personal touches that B&Bs do offer—whether it's joining my hosts for tea in the afternoon or relaxing by a communal fireplace at the end of the day.

Evensong

One of my top experiences in Britain is to attend evensong at a great church. During this evening worship, a singing or chanting priest leads the service, and a choir—usually made up of both men's and boys' voices—sings the responses. The most impressive places for evensong include Westminster Abbey and St. Paul's Cathedral in London, King's College Chapel in Cambridge, Canterbury Cathedral, Wells Cathedral, York Minster, and Durham Cathedral.

Wherever you attend, arrive early and ask to be seated in the choir. You're in the middle of a spiritual Oz as 40 boys sing psalms—a red-and-white-robed pillow of praise, raised up by the powerful pipe organ. You feel as if you have elephant-size ears, as the beautifully carved choir stalls—functioning as giant sound scoops—magnify the thunderous, trumpeting pipes. If you're lucky, the organist will run a spiritual musical victory lap as the congregation breaks up. Thank God for evensong. Amen.

Afternoon Tea

The best way to experience this most British of traditions is to attend an afternoon tea. This ritual generally takes place around 3 p.m. and is something to be savored over a couple of hours. Menus include several options. "Cream tea" is simply a pot of tea and a homemade scone or two with jam and thick clotted cream. "Afternoon tea" usually comes with a three-tiered platter of dainty sandwiches, scones, and small pastries. Don't confuse afternoon tea with "high tea," which

In Britain, some things never change: The Brits love their afternoon tea (right), and the breakfasts are as traditional and hearty as ever (left).

to Brits generally means a more substantial late-afternoon or early-evening meal, often served with meat or eggs.

Depending on where you go, afternoon tea can get pricey, especially in London (it's nearly $80 per person at the Ritz). You can save money by tucking in at a department store or bookstore café. Still, for maximum opulence and ambience, it can be worth raising a pinky in one of Britain's grand tea rooms, such as the Wolseley or Fortnum & Mason in London, Bettys Café Tea Rooms in York, or my favorite—the Pump Room in Bath, a classy Georgian hall just above the Roman baths.

Great Britain Travel Resources from Rick Steves

Guidebooks

Check out Rick's guidebooks covering London; England; Scotland; and all of Great Britain (including England, Scotland, and Wales)

Audio Europe

Download Rick's free Audio Europe app, with self-guided audio tours, including walks through Westminster and the City of London; tours of the British Museum, British Library, and St. Paul's Cathedral; and a walk down Edinburgh's Royal Mile

TV Shows

The quintessence of Great Britain with Rick as your host, viewable on public television and at ricksteves.com. Episodes cover England (London, Bath, York, Lake District, South England), Wales, and Scotland (Edinburgh, Highlands)

Organized Tours

Small group tours, with itineraries planned by Rick: England in 14 Days; London in 7 Days; Scotland in 10 Days

For more on all of these resources, visit ricksteves.com

Ireland

One of the many reasons I love traveling in Ireland is that it gives me the sensation I'm understanding a foreign language. The Irish have that amazing gift of gab—a passion for conversation. And they're experts at it. Ireland is a sparsely populated island of hardscrabble communities. And along with lush, unforgettable vistas and an endearing heritage, it's the people that make the Emerald Isle such a delight to visit.

This 300-mile-long island, ringed with some of Europe's most scenic coastal cliffs, is only 150 miles across at its widest point—no matter where you go in Ireland, you're never more than 75 miles from the sea. Ireland is dusted with prehistoric stone circles, cliffside fortresses, burial mounds, and standing stones—some older than the pyramids.

Given its small size and geographic isolation, Ireland has had an oversized impact on the world. It was Ireland's Christian monks who tended the flickering flame of literacy through the Dark Ages, and Ireland later turned out some of modern literature's greatest authors (from Jonathan Swift and W. B. Yeats to James Joyce and Oscar Wilde). In the 1800s, great waves of Irish emigrants sought new opportunities abroad, making their mark in the US, Canada, New Zealand, and Australia.

Politics and religion divide Ireland. The Republic of Ireland, to the south, encompasses 80 percent of the island and is an independent nation of 4.6 million predominantly Catholic people. Northern Ireland, with 1.8 million people (roughly half Protestant and half Catholic), remains a part of the United Kingdom—like Scotland or Wales—and pledges allegiance to the Queen.

I'd say no visit to Ireland is complete without a visit to both the North and the Republic. Wherever you venture—from Dublin to Dingle, from bogs to Belfast—you'll find an engaging culture and plenty of locals ready and eager to help you experience and enjoy it firsthand.

FAVORITE SIGHTS AND MEMORABLE EXPERIENCES IN IRELAND

Dublin Spirit

A few years back, I spent a week in Dublin vacationing with my then-teenaged kids. I had a hunch that Dublin would deliver on family fun... and it was grand.

The city is safe, lively, easy, and extremely accessible. Each night we enjoyed spirited and affordable entertainment. Both kids connected with their Irish heritage. We were all pretty wide-eyed at the thriving late-night scene in Temple Bar, Dublin's beer-drinking hotspot. While run-down through most of the 20th century, this now-trendy center feels like the social heart of booming Dublin and is great for people-watching. The girls are wrapped up like party favors, and the guys look like they're on their way home from a rough-and-tumble hurling match.

Nowadays, except for baked beans at breakfast, forget "eating Irish" in Dublin. Going local here is going ethnic. A multinational food court we visited took diversity to extremes: Chinese were cooking Mexican, Poles were running the Old Time American diner, a Spaniard was serving sushi,

Fast Facts

Biggest cities: Dublin (capital of Republic, 1.3 million), Belfast (capital of Northern Ireland, 300,000), Cork (190,000)

Size (entire island): 32,595 square miles (about the size of Indiana), population 6.4 million

Locals call it: Éire

Currency: Euro (Republic of Ireland), British pound (Northern Ireland)

Key date: December 6, 1921, Ireland wins independence from Britain before plunging into a year-long civil war that ends up dividing the country

Biggest festival: St. Patrick's Day (March 17)—although it's a bigger deal for Irish Americans than for people who still live in Ireland

Leprechauns per square mile: 1.7

Handy Irish phrases: *Dia duit* (hello; **jee**-ah gwitch), *Conas atá tú?* (How are you?; Cun-us ah-**taw** too), *Go raibh maith agat* (thank you; guh rov mah **ug**-ut), *Pionta Guinness, le do thoil* (A pint of Guinness, please; pyun-**tah** Guinness leh duh hull), *Slainte!* (Cheers!; **slawn-**chuh)

In Ireland, make a point to connect with the Irish—whether on the streets, at the stadiums, or in the nightlife zones.

and Irish were running the Thai concession. Save your craving for pub grub for the small towns.

We went to Croke Park, the longtime stadium for Gaelic sports, joining 50,000 screaming Irish football fans. (Irish football is a kicking, tackling, running game.) Tickets were $40. I got to talking with a man seated next to us, telling him we went to the Abbey Theater the night before to see a play by Oscar Wilde. He asked me the cost, and I said $40 per person. He said to his wife, "Imagine paying $40 just to see a play." She said that, to a theatergoer, spending $40 to see a football game would be just as strange.

We'd spent another $40 outside the stadium so that my kids and I would each have a scarf or hat with the correct team colors (gold and green—we were rooting for Donegal). I thought back to a game I'd attended here 20 years earlier, when the "colors" were cheaply dyed crepe-paper hats that sold for a buck. In the rain, my colors ran from my paper hat down onto my face, gold and green...I was for Donegal even back then. During both games I recall being careful—for my own safety—to sit with Donegal fans and cheer at the right times. I'll never forget the creative cursing. My vocabulary grew like never before.

Pouring out of the stadium with what seemed like half of Dublin, it occurred to me that we were the only tourists in sight.

Belfast: The Troubles and the *Titanic*

Wandering through energetic downtown Belfast, it's hard to believe that the bright and bustling pedestrian center was once a subdued security zone. That precaution was necessitated by the Troubles (1968 to 1998), the long and violent struggle to settle Northern Ireland's national identity. The

Ireland's Top Destinations

REPUBLIC OF IRELAND

Dublin ▲▲▲   allow 2 days

Bustling Irish capital, with fine museums, fascinating walking tours (history, pubs, literature, music), a passionate rebel history along with the trappings of now long-gone British rule, and a rambunctious pub district

Top Sights

National Museum—Archaeology Interesting collection of ancient Irish treasures
Kilmainham Gaol Historic political prison-turned-museum
Trinity College Home of illuminated Book of Kells manuscript from the Dark Ages

Nearby

Brú na Bóinne Boyne Valley's ancient pre-Celtic burial mounds
Battle of the Boyne Site Location of the pivotal battle that established Protestant rule
Trim Castle Biggest Norman castle in Ireland
Glendalough Evocative Dark Ages monastic ruins set in the Wicklow Mountains

Kilkenny ▲▲   1 day

Inland medieval town, just an hour from the hilltop church ruins known as the Rock of Cashel

Waterford ▲   1 day

Historic port town with famous Waterford Crystal Visitor Centre

County Cork ▲▲   1-2 days

Two quaint harbor towns: gourmet capital **Kinsale** and emigration hub **Cobh**—the Titanic's last stop

Ring of Kerry ▲▲   1-2 days

Mountainous, lake-splattered region with famous loop drive, prehistoric ring forts, and sweet home-base town of **Kenmare**

Dingle Town and Peninsula ▲▲▲   2 days

Fishing village, traditional Irish-music pub paradise, and launch pad for gorgeous peninsula loop drive with plenty of mysterious stone forts and a possible trip to the desolate yet evocative Blasket Islands

County Clare ▲▲   1 day

Rugged western fringe, with the stunning Cliffs of Moher, stone landscape of the Burren, and trad music crossroads of **Doolin**

Galway ▲   1 day

University city with thriving pedestrian street scene and great pubs

Aran Islands ▲▲▲   1 day

Three windswept islands (**Inishmore** is best) laced with rock walls, crowned by Iron Age ring forts, and inhabited by hardy fisherfolk

Connemara and County Mayo ▲▲   1 day

Green, hilly outback of cottages, lakes, and peaks

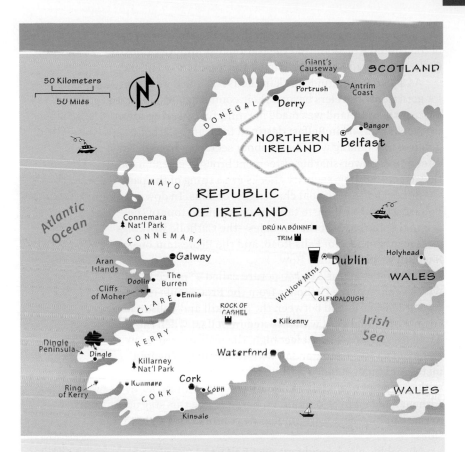

NORTHERN IRELAND

Belfast ▲▲
1-2 days

Industrial Revolution metropolis with stirring political murals and Titanic
museum, near the charming Victorian seaside town of **Bangor**

Antrim Coast ▲▲
1 day

Scenic area embracing the beach resort of **Portrush,** geologic wonderland of the
Giant's Causeway, and cliff-edge ruins of Dunluce Castle

Derry ▲
1 day

Walled city that ignited Ireland's "Troubles"—with an insightful city history
museum and access to the rugged beauty of County Donegal

Unionist majority (mostly Protestant) wanted to remain part of the United Kingdom, and the Nationalist minority (mostly Catholic) wanted to become part of the Republic of Ireland.

As a young tour guide back in the 1970s, I had a passion for getting my travelers beyond their comfort zones. In those days, a trip to Ireland was made meaningful by seeing towering stacks of wood in Belfast destined to be anti-Catholic bonfires and talking with locals about sectarian hatred. Now, after a 1998 power-sharing agreement brought an end to on-the-streets fighting, security checks are a thing of the past.

But evidence of the old challenges remains. In downtown Belfast, I hired a cabbie to take me on a guided tour of the original home bases of the Troubles—the Catholic working-class neighborhood of Falls Road, and the Protestant ones of Shankill Road and Sandy Row.

Our first stop was a sad structure called a "peace wall," which separated the Catholics from the Protestants in the former no-man's-land between the Shankill and Falls roads. It's one of a number of walls erected in Belfast when the Troubles started. Now 40 feet high, the wall started as 20 feet of concrete, was extended with 10 feet of corrugated metal, and finally topped with 10 feet of wire mesh—all with the intent of stopping projectiles from sailing over it. Although meant to be temporary, barriers like this stay up because of lingering fears among the communities on both sides.

My cabbie also brought me past Belfast's Felons' Club—where membership is limited to those who've spent at least a year and a day in a British prison for political crimes. At the Milltown Cemetery, I hopped out of my guide's old black cab to see a memorial to Bobby Sands and nine other hunger strikers, who starved themselves to death for the cause of Irish independence.

Sightseeing in Northern Ireland ranges from political murals remembering a titanic political struggle to exhibits describing the birthplace of a *Titanic* disaster.

To get an up-close dose of the Unionist perspective, I walked along Sandy Row—a working-class-Protestant street. Along the way I passed murals filled with Unionist symbolism, such as a depiction of William of Orange's victory over the Catholic King James II in the Battle of the Boyne.

With more peaceful times, the character of these murals is slowly changing. Paramilitary themes are gradually being covered over with images of pride in each neighborhood's culture. A recurring motif is the *Titanic* ocean liner, built by a predominantly Protestant workforce in Belfast's shipyard. (A typical souvenir T-shirt reads, "Titanic—it was OK when it left here.")

In fact, Belfast has turned its ties to the ill-fated ship into a $155-million touristic landmark. Titanic Belfast, a high-tech, six-story museum, rises adjacent to the dry dock where the *Titanic* took shape. It's part of the quiet optimism that's taken hold in Belfast. Perhaps one day visitors will associate the city more with its proud shipbuilding industry than with political and religious conflict.

Money Matters

The Republic of Ireland uses the euro currency. Northern Ireland, part of the United Kingdom, uses the pound sterling, the same currency in circulation in England, Scotland, and Wales. The pound notes issued by banks in Northern Ireland look slightly different from the British pound sterling, but they are worth the same and are technically interchangeable. Nonetheless, if you're also traveling to Great Britain, note that "Ulster" pounds are considered "undesirable" in England. Banks in either region can exchange them for English pounds at no charge. Don't worry about the coins, which are accepted throughout Great Britain and Northern Ireland.

The Dingle Peninsula

Be forewarned: Ireland is seductive. I fell in love with the friendliest land this side of Sicily. It all happened in a Gaeltacht—an area of traditional culture where the government protects the old Irish ways and Irish is spoken. But Irish culture is more than just the ancient language. You'll find it tilling the rocky fields, singing in the pubs, and lingering in the pride of the small-town preschool that brags "all Irish." Signposts are in Irish only, with many in the old Irish lettering. If your map is in English...good luck.

Green, rugged, and untouched, the Dingle Peninsula is my favorite Gaeltacht. For more than 30 years, my Irish dreams have been set here, on this sparse but lush peninsula where residents are fond of saying, "The next parish is Boston."

Of the peninsula's 10,000 residents, 1,500 live in Dingle town (An Daingean). Its few streets, lined with ramshackle

On Ireland's Dingle Peninsula, humble farms feel haunted with memories of the Great Potato Famine (right) and villages seem built to weather great storms (left).

but gaily painted shops and pubs, run up from a rain-stung harbor. During the day, teenagers—already working on ruddy beer-glow cheeks—roll kegs up the streets and into the pubs in preparation for another tin-whistle night.

Fishing once dominated Dingle, and the town's only visitors were students of old Irish ways. Then, in 1970, the movie *Ryan's Daughter* introduced the world to Dingle, followed in 1992 by *Far and Away*. The trickle of fans grew to a flood, as word spread of Dingle's musical, historical, gastronomical, and scenic charms—not to mention Fungie the friendly dolphin, who hangs out in the harbor.

Dingle town sits on the Dingle Peninsula, which makes a perfect 30-mile loop for a bike ride (or drive). While only tiny villages lie west of Dingle town, the peninsula is home to half a million sheep. Cycling around the peninsula feels like a trip through an open-air museum. The landscape is littered with monuments left behind by Bronze Age settlers, Dark Age monks, English landlords, and Hollywood directors.

Talk with the chatty Irish you'll encounter along the roadside. I once met an elfish, black-clad old man in the little town of Ventry (Ceann Tra'). When I asked if he was born here, he breathed deeply and said, "No, 'twas about six miles down the road." I asked if he'd lived there all his life. He said, "Not yet." When I told him where I was from, a faraway smile filled his eyes as he looked out to sea and sighed, "Aye, the shores of Americay."

The wet sod of Dingle is soaked with medieval history. In the darkest depths of the Dark Ages, peace-loving, book-wormish monks fled the chaos of the Continent and its barbarian raids. They sailed to this drizzly fringe of the known world and lived their monastic lives in lonely stone igloos or "beehive huts," which you'll see dotting the landscape.

Parts of the peninsula are bleak and godforsaken. Study the highest fields, untouched since the planting of 1845, when the potatoes never matured and rotted in the ground. You can still see the vertical ridges of the potato beds—a reminder of that year's Great Potato Famine, which eventually, through starvation or emigration, cut Ireland's population by one-quarter.

Rounding Slea Head, the point in Europe closest to America, the rugged coastline offers smashing views of deadly black-rock cliffs and the distant Blasket Islands (Na Blascaodai). The crashing surf races in like white horses, while long-haired sheep—bored with the weather, distant boats, and the lush countryside—couldn't care less.

The tip of the peninsula is marked by a chalky statue of a crucifix. It faces the sea, but about half the time, it seems it's actually facing an impenetrable cloud and being whipped by sheets of rain. It rains with gusto here. I imagine that Dingle cows have thicker eyelids, evolved over the centuries to survive sideways rain. The Gallarus Oratory, a 1,300-year-old church made only of stone, is famously watertight—unless the rain is hosing in sideways. I've been splattered inside. I've driven over Conor Pass with the visibility at zero, ragamuffin sheep nonchalantly appearing like ghosts in the milky cloud. I've huddled, awaiting a chance to step out, in farmhouses abandoned in the Great Famine. Yes, the weather is a force on the peninsula. But when the sun does come out, everything rejoices.

More Irish Experiences

Slog on the Bog: One of the simple pleasures of Ireland's landscape is bouncing on a springy peat bog. Walk a few yards onto the spongy green carpet. (On wet days, you might squish into a couple of inches of water.) Find a dry spot, and jump up and down to get a feel for it. Have your companion jump; you'll feel the vibrations 30 feet away.

These bogs once covered almost 20 percent of Ireland. As the climate got warmer at the end of the last Ice Age, plants began growing along the sides of the many shallow lakes and ponds. When the plants died in these waterlogged areas, there wasn't enough oxygen for them to fully decompose. Over the centuries, the moss built up, layer after dead layer, helping to slowly fill in the lakes and eventually becoming peat. Peat was Ireland's standard heating fuel for centuries—sliced out of bogs, stacked to dry, and then burned like presto logs in fireplaces and stoves. In the old days, four or five good men could cut enough peat in a day to keep a family warm through the cold Irish winter. Today, a few locals—nostalgic

for the smell of a good turf fire—still come to desolate bogs to cut their own fuel.

Bleak and Beautiful Inishmore: Strewn like limestone chips hammered off the jagged west coast, the three Aran Islands confront the wild Atlantic with stubborn grit. The largest, Inishmore, is nine miles of rock with one sleepy town, a few fishing hamlets, and a weather-beaten charm. The landscape is harsh, with steep, rugged cliffs and wind-swept rocky fields stitched together by stone walls. So barren is this landscape that fishermen had to collect seaweed, sand, and manure to create tiny patches of soil for growing vegetables. This blustery island's stark beauty alone is worth a visit, but the blockbuster sight is Dún Aenghus, an Iron Age stone fortress that hangs spectacularly and precariously on the edge of a sheer cliff 200 feet above the ocean. You'll feel like the westernmost person in Europe, lying down on the rock—your head hanging over the cliff-edge—high above the crashing Atlantic.

LEFT On the far west coast of Ireland, mighty cliffs plunge into the sea while locals gaze out and say, "Ah, the next parish over...is Boston."

RIGHT On the northern coast, the hexagonal basalt pillars of the Giant's Causeway offer a stony playground for visitors.

Giant's Causeway: With camera handy, explore this stretch of Northern Ireland's coastline, famous for its bizarre basalt columns. The shore is covered with largely hexagonal pillars, sticking up at various heights. It's as if the earth were offering God his choice of 37,000 six-sided cigarettes.

Geologists claim the Giant's Causeway was formed by volcanic eruptions more than 60 million years ago. As the surface of the lava flow quickly cooled, it contracted and crystallized into columns (resembling the caked mud at the bottom of a dried-up lakebed, but with deeper cracks). As the rock later settled and eroded, the columns broke off into the many stair like steps that now honeycomb the Antrim Coast.

Of course, in actuality, the Giant's Causeway was made by a giant Ulster warrior named Finn MacCool, who knew of a rival giant living on the Scottish island of Staffa. Finn built a stone bridge over to Staffa to spy on his rival and found out that the Scottish giant was much bigger. Finn retreated back to Ireland and had his wife dress him as a sleeping infant, just in time for the rival giant to come across the causeway to spy on Finn. The rival, shocked at the infant's size, fled back to Scotland in terror of whomever had sired this giant baby. Breathing a sigh of relief, Finn knocked down the bridge. Today, proof of this encounter exists in the geologic formation that still extends undersea and surfaces at Staffa. For cute variations on the Finn story, as well as details on the ridiculous theories of modern geologists, drop by the Giant's Causeway Visitors Centre.

CULTURE AND TRADITIONS: EVERYTHING'S SO...IRISH

Gaelic and the Gift of Gab

Want to really get to know the Irish? Ask for directions to your next destination. It's almost always a rich experience and a fast way to connect with locals. Nearby friends often chime in with additional tidbits that may or may not be useful, and soon it's a communal chitchat session.

That legendary Irish "gift of gab" has its roots in the ancient Celtic culture. With no written language (until the arrival of Christianity), the ancient Celts passed their history, laws, and folklore verbally from generation to generation. Even today, most transactions come with an ample side-helping of friendly banter (called *craic* in Irish). As a local once joked, "How can I know what I think until I hear what I say?"

Traditional Irish Music

The Irish seem born with a love of music. At social gatherings, everyone's ready to sing his or her "party piece." Performances are judged less by skill than by uninhibited sincerity or showmanship. Nearly every Irish household has some kind of musical instrument on a shelf or in a closet.

Live traditional music is a weekly (if not nightly) draw at any town pub worth its salt. There's generally a fiddle, flute or tin whistle, guitar, bodhrán (goat-skin drum), and maybe

an accordion. Occasionally the fast-paced music stops, the band puts down their instruments, and one person sings a heartfelt lament—a sad story of lost love or emigration to a faraway land. This is the one time when the entire pub will stop to listen. Spend a lament studying the faces in the crowd.

In Ireland I enjoy the feeling of understanding a foreign language. And the people you meet love to talk. Whether on a harborside stroll or in a pub between sets of traditional music, try striking up a conversation.

A session can be magic, or it can be lifeless. If the chemistry is right, it's one of the great Irish experiences. The tunes churn intensely while the group casually enjoys exploring each other's musical styles. The drummer dodges the fiddler's playful bow. Sipping their pints, they skillfully maintain a faint but steady buzz. The floor on the musicians' platform is stomped paint-free, and barmaids scurry artfully through the commotion, gathering towers of empty, cream-crusted glasses. With knees up and heads down, the music goes round and round. Make yourself right at home, "playing the boot" (tapping your foot) under the table in time with the music.

Eating and Drinking in an Irish Pub

Pub is short for "public house"—an extended living room where, if you don't mind the stickiness, you can feel the pulse of Ireland. Today the most traditional, atmospheric pubs are in Ireland's countryside and smaller towns.

In much of Ireland, when you say "beer, please" at a pub, you'll get a pint of "the tall blonde in the black dress"— Guinness, Ireland's king of beers. If you want a small beer, ask for a "glass" (a half-pint). Never rush your bartender when he's pouring a Guinness. It takes time—almost sacred time. If you don't normally like Guinness, try it in Ireland; it doesn't travel well and is better in its homeland.

Pub grub is Ireland's best eating value, but don't expect high cuisine. This is comfort food: Irish stew (mutton with mashed potatoes, onions, carrots, and herbs), soups and

chowders, coddle (stewed layers of bacon, pork sausages, potatoes, and onions), fish-and-chips, boxty (potato pancakes filled with fish, meat, or veggies), and champ (potato mashed with milk and onion). In coastal areas, mackerel, mussels, and Atlantic salmon join the menu. Irish soda bread nicely rounds out a meal.

Ireland Travel Resources from Rick Steves

Guidebooks

Check out Rick's guidebooks covering all of Ireland (including the Republic of Ireland and Northern Ireland); Dublin; and Northern Ireland

TV Shows

The quintessence of Ireland with Rick as your host, viewable on public television or at ricksteves.com. Episodes cover the best of Northern Ireland (including Belfast) and the Republic of Ireland, including Dublin, Waterford, the Ring of Kerry, Dingle, Galway, and the Aran Islands

Organized Tours

Small group tours, with itineraries planned by Rick: Ireland in 14 Days; Heart of Ireland in 8 Days

For more on all of these resources, visit ricksteves.com

Scandinavia

Scandinavia is Western Europe's most prosperous, pristine, and progressive corner. For the tourist, it is the land of Viking ships, brooding castles, fishy harbors, deep green fjords, medieval stave churches, and quaint farmhouses—juxtaposed with the sleek modernism of the region's cities. A visit here connects you with immigrant roots, contemporary European values, and the great outdoors like nowhere else.

Denmark is by far the smallest of the Scandinavian countries (although it once ruled Norway and part of Sweden). Danes are proud of their mighty history, and yet they're easygoing with a delightfully wry humor. Denmark's capital, Copenhagen, is freewheeling and modern, while the country's cozy islands seem set in a century gone by.

Norway is stacked with superlatives—it's the most mountainous, most scenic, and, thanks to its offshore oil fields, most wealthy of the Scandinavian countries. Perhaps above all, Norway is a land of epic natural beauty, its steep mountains and deep fjords carved out and shaped by an ancient ice age. The country's capital, Oslo, is wonderfully walkable, its museums reflect its seafaring heritage, and its parks are unforgettable.

Sweden, far bigger than Denmark and far flatter than Norway, is graced with vast forests, countless lakes, and picturesque islands. Its sleek capital, Stockholm, is as appealing as its archipelago, perfect for cruising. This family-friendly land is home to Ikea, Volvo, WikiLeaks, ABBA, and summer vacations at red-painted, white-trimmed cottages.

Residents of the Scandinavian countries are, for the most part, confident, happy, and healthy. They speak their minds frankly, even about subjects others might find taboo, like sex. They're well-educated and well-traveled. Though reserved

and super-polite at first, they're quick to laugh and don't take
life—or themselves—too seriously.

FAVORITE SIGHTS AND MEMORABLE EXPERIENCES IN SCANDINAVIA

Cozying Up to Ærø

The Danish word for "cozy," *hyggelig,* perfectly describes
the little island of Ærø. Few visitors to Scandinavia even
notice this sleepy, 6-by-22-mile isle on Denmark's southern
edge. But Ærø has a salty charm. It's a peaceful and homey
place, where baskets of strawberries sit for sale on the honor
system in front of farmhouses. Its tombstones are carved
with sea-inspired sentiments such as: "Here lies Christian
Hansen at anchor with his wife. He'll not weigh until he
stands before God."

Ærø's main town, Ærøskøbing, is a village-in-a-bottle
kind of place. I wander down cobbled lanes right out of the
1680s, when the town was the wealthy home port to more
than 100 windjammers (today the harbor caters to German
and Danish holiday yachts). Stubby little porthole-type
houses, with their birth dates displayed in proud decorative
rebar, lean on each other like drunken sailors. It's OK to
peek through the windows into living rooms. (If people want
privacy, they shut their drapes.) I notice, mounted to several
old houses, angled "snooping mirrors" that afford someone
seated inside a wide view of the entire street. Antique locals
are following my every move—a thought that fills me with
comfort rather than paranoia.

On the Danish
isle of Ærø,
the town of
Ærøskøbing
is a ship-in-a-
bottle place.

The post office dates to 1749, and cast-iron gaslights still shine in the night. On summer evenings, you can hang out with the farmers in one of the town's two pubs, or even better, join the night watchman, who takes anyone who is interested on a historic stroll through town. That's the only action going on after dark. On midnight low tides it can be so quiet, you can almost hear the crabs playing cards.

A strong social ethic permeates Danish society, and I really feel that on Ærø. Here, you're welcome to pick berries and nuts, but historically the limit has been "no more than would fit in your hat." For years I recommended Mrs. Hansen's bike-rental depot next to the gas station at the edge of town. One day, a big hotel in town (with far more economic clout) decided to rent bikes, too. I saw Danish communalism in the reaction of a local friend: "They don't need to do that—that's Mrs. Hansen's livelihood." In Denmark, looking out for Mrs. Hansen's little bike-rental business is a matter of neighborly decency.

And Ærø's subtle, breezy charms are best enjoyed on a bike. Pedaling into the idyllic countryside, I find myself saying "cute" more than I should as I roll past sweet little hamlets and traditional U-shaped farms (designed to block the wind and protect cows, hay, and people). After struggling uphill to the island's 2,700-inch-high summit—a "peak"

Fast Facts

Biggest cities: Copenhagen (capital of Denmark, 1 million), Stockholm (capital of Sweden, 885,000), Oslo (capital of Norway, 575,000)

Size: Denmark—16,600 square miles (twice the size of Massachusetts), population 5.5 million; Norway—148,900 square miles (slightly larger than Montana), population 5 million; Sweden—174,000 square miles (a little bigger than California), population 9.6 million

Locals call it: Danmark (Denmark), Norge (Norway), Sverige (Sweden)

Currency: Danish crown (*krone*, officially DKK), Norwegian crown (*krone*, NOK), Swedish crown (*krona*, SEK)

Key date: 793 A.D., the Viking Age begins

Biggest festival: Midsummer Eve (summer solstice celebrations—with feasting, music, and dancing around the maypole in Sweden, and with bonfires, picnics, and processions in Norway and Denmark)

Handy Danish phrases: *Goddag* (hello; goh-**day**), *Tak* (thank you; tack), *Ingen ko på isen* (no worries, no problem; literally, "No cow on the ice"; ing koh paw **ees**-ehn)

Handy Norwegian phrases: *God dag* (hello; goo dahg), *Takk* (thank you; tahk), *Det regner trollkjerringer!* (It's raining cats and dogs!; literally, "It's raining troll hags!"; deh **ray**-nehr **trohl**-shehr-ring-ehr)

Handy Swedish phrases: *Goddag* (hello; goh-**dah**), *Tack* (thank you; tack), *Fartkontroll* (speed trap; fahrt kohn-**trohl**)

aptly named Synnes Hoej ("Seems High")—I wind past a fine 12th-century church, a cliffside viewpoint, a 6,000-year-old burial place, and a little brewery.

Then, as I coast back into Ærøskøbing as the sun is setting, I roll right on through to Urehoved beach—where a row of tiny huts lines the strand, and Danes gather to barbecue shrimp and sing songs. The huts are little more than a picnic table with walls and a roof—each carefully painted and carved—stained with generations of family fun, sunsets, and memories of pickled herring on rye bread. It's a perfect Danish scene where a favorite word, *hyggelig*, takes cozy to enjoyable extremes.

Cool, Calm Copenhagen

Copenhagen has always impressed me. Its improbable aspects just work so tidily together. Where else would Hans Christian Andersen, a mermaid statue, Europe's first great amusement park, and lovingly decorated open-face sandwiches be the icons of a major capital?

For the tourist, Copenhagen is compact, with its key sights radiating out from the Rådhuspladsen (City Hall Square), the bustling heart of the city. This used to be the fortified west end of town. In 1843, the king cleverly quelled a revolutionary-type thirst for democracy by giving his people a place to gather in Tivoli Gardens—just beyond the walls.

Tivoli, the granddaddy of amusement parks, is still going strong, but the walls and moats of medieval Copenhagen are long gone. They've been replaced by a ring of lush parks and tranquil lakes that are appreciated by the nearly naked sunbathers who savor the short Danish summer—oblivious to the history all around them.

From Rådhuspladsen, a series of lively pedestrianized streets and inviting squares called the Strøget bunny-hops through the Old Town. Established in 1962, the Strøget was Europe's first major pedestrian boulevard, and it's become the model for people zones throughout the world.

A leisurely stroll through the Strøget leads to Nyhavn

Copenhagen's Nyhavn (New Harbor) is no longer a rollicking quarter of prostitutes and sailor bars. But it does come with good-looking Danes showing off their tattoos.

Scandinavia's Top Destinations

DENMARK

Copenhagen ▲▲▲ allow 2-3 days

Canal-laced, fun-loving Danish capital city with fine museums, well-presented palaces, hordes of bikes, and a flourishing culinary scene

Top Sights
Tivoli Gardens Classic Danish amusement park
National Museum History of Danish civilization
Rosenborg Castle and Treasury Renaissance castle of "warrior king" Christian IV
Christiania Colorful counterculture squatters' colony

Nearby
Roskilde Noteworthy Viking ship museum, plus cathedral packed with royal tombs

Central Denmark ▲▲ 2 days

Peaceful, bike-perfect isle of **Ærø,** with Denmark's best-preserved 18th-century village, and the busy town of **Odense,** with Hans Christian Andersen museum

Jutland ▲ 1 day

Family-friendly region with Legoland park and Denmark's second-largest city, **Aarhus,** with traffic-free core, modern art museum, and open-air folk museum

NORWAY

Oslo ▲▲ 2 days

Norway's businesslike capital city, with stately fjordside setting, innovative architecture, grand palaces and museums, and enjoyable parks

Top Sights
City Hall Palace of good government, slathered with symbolic murals
National Gallery Norway's cultural and natural essence, captured on canvas
Frogner Park Sprawling park with sculptures by Norwegian Gustav Vigeland
Bygdøy Neighborhood of excellent museums about seafaring, Vikings, and folk culture

Sognefjord ▲▲▲ 1-2 days

Norway in a Nutshell, a trip through fjord country—by train, bus, and boat—passing waterfalls, forests, and spectacular vistas, with functional towns **Flåm** and **Aurland** along the way

Gudbrandsdal and Jotunheimen Mountains ▲ 1 day

Lush green valley with touristy **Lillehammer** and access to a rugged mountain range with fine hikes and drives

Bergen ▲▲ 1 day

Salty port city and medieval capital of Norway, with bustling fish market, colorful Hanseatic quarter (Bryggen), and a funicular to great views over town

South Norway ▲ 1 day

Harborside **Stavanger** (with its Norwegian Emigration Center, Petroleum Museum, and Pulpit Rock), time-passed and remote Setesdal Valley, and resort town of **Kristiansand**

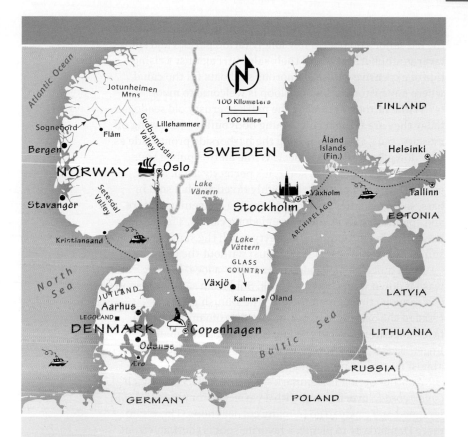

SWEDEN

Stockholm ▲▲▲   2-3 days

Sweden's stunning capital, scattered over 14 islands and bubbling with energy and history

Top Sights
Skansen Europe's first and best open-air folk museum
Vasa Museum Interesting collection centered on ill-fated 17th-century warship
Nordic Museum Fascinating peek at 500 years of traditional Swedish lifestyles
Gamla Stan Picturesque, cobbled Old Town island
Royal Palace Grand collections and pomp-filled changing of the guard

Nearby
Stockholm Archipelago Scenic island chain stretching into the Baltic Sea

Southeast Sweden ▲   1-2 days

Densely forested region punctuated by worthwhile emigration and glass museums in **Växjö;** a 12th-century castle in **Kalmar;** the holiday island of **Öland;** and "Glass Country," famous for its glassworks

harbor, which lounges comfortably around its canal. Here in the old sailor's quarter, a few lonely tattoo parlors and smoky taverns stubbornly defend their salty turf against a rising tide of expensive cafés. Glamorous sailboats fill the canal, where any historic all-wood sloop is welcome to moor.

While tattoos were once the mark of crusty old seadogs, today they are Danish chic. Young bodybuilders, showing off muscles, tans, and tattoos, clog the harborside promenade as they down bottles of local beer. While all this public beer-drinking is off-putting to some, it's perfectly legal. Many young Danes can't afford the highly taxed alcohol sold in bars, so instead they buy their beers at a convenience store and "picnic drink" in squares and along canals. The outdoor beer drinking in Denmark is pretty much the same as consuming a brew in a British pub...just without the building.

For a quick meal, locals grab a *pølse*—a local hot dog—and wash it down with chocolate milk. Sold from sausage wagons (*pølsevogne*) throughout the city, the Danish *pølse* has resisted the onslaught of our global, Styrofoam-packaged, fast-food culture. What the locals call the "dead man's finger" is fast, cheap, tasty, and, like its American cousin, almost worthless nutritionally.

Another option is Denmark's tasty open-face sandwich (*smørrebrød*), overflowing with a variety of toppings and sold wrapped and ready to go in many corner shops. There's no more Danish way to picnic; a favorite spot is the waterfront park where the *Little Mermaid*—of Hans Christian Andersen fame—sits demurely on her rock. The tradition calls for three sandwich courses: herring first, then meat, then cheese, washed down with a local beer. *Skål!*

For the Danes, small really is beautiful.

Delightful, Surprising Oslo

When I was a 14-year-old kid, I traveled through Europe with my parents. One of my best memories from this trip is of sleeping on a ship from Copenhagen to Oslo, and waking up to the pristine Oslofjord. Sitting on the deck and for the first time enjoying the Norwegian scenery—the land of my grandparents—was a thrill. Years later, sailing down the same fjord to Oslo—this time on a giant cruise ship—was a wonderful travel déjà vu.

I love Norway—probably because I'm Norwegian. Three of my grandparents grew up in Norway. (Two homesteaded in Edmonton. One was a relatively famous and often-drunk ski jumper in Leavenworth, Washington.) Yesterday I told my TV producer, "Everyone here looks like my brother." He was shocked (having traveled with me for 12 years) and said, "I didn't know you had a brother." I don't. But if I did, he'd look like the guys around me. It's more than how they look. It's how they are. A fun part of travel is to feel a kinship with people from the land of your forefathers.

Oslo is the smallest of the Nordic capitals, but this brisk little city is a scenic *smörgåsbord* of history, sights, art, and Nordic fun. On May 17, Norway's national holiday, Oslo bursts with flags, bands, parades, and pride. Blond toddlers are dressed up in colorful ribbons, traditional pewter buckles, and wool. But Oslo—surrounded by forests, near mountains, and on a fjord—has plenty to offer the visitor year-round.

Norway is traditionally a seafaring nation, so it's no surprise that Oslo's most popular sights, like the Viking Ship Museum, tell an exciting story of Viking spirit. Rape, pillage, and plunder were the rage a thousand years ago. Back then much of a frightened Western Europe closed every prayer with, "And deliver us from the Vikings, amen." When I gazed up at the prow of one of the museum's sleek, time-stained vessels, I could almost hear the shrieks and smell the armpits of those redheads on the rampage.

Today, Oslo is full of Norwegians rich on oil money. It's an expensive place—so expensive that people share their drinks and munch sandwiches on park benches. I find myself chewing slower and ordering smaller quantities here. The city also has its share of down-and-outers: prostitutes and needle junkies. While wasted people seem to rot on Oslo's curbs, the lack of violent crime here is impressive by any standard.

Overall, I am always struck by how peaceful Oslo feels.

The rooftop of Oslo's shiny new marble opera house slopes into the harbor and is a popular venue for outdoor concerts.

A congestion fee keeps most cars out of the town center, while tunnels take nearly all the rest under the city. The waterfront, once traffic-choked and slummy, has undergone a huge change. With vehicles sent underground, upscale condos and restaurants are taking over.

When the sun's out, Oslo's parks are packed. A common ailment here is *solstikk*, or sunstroke—literally, "sun sting." Wandering through a sunny Frogner Park, where sculptor Gustav Vigeland's 192 bronze and granite nudes strut their stuff, I can't miss the real-life nudity. All of Scandinavia has a casual approach to nakedness (I'm not talking just mixed saunas—many Americans are amazed at what's on prime-time TV here). Women unabashedly sunbathe topless, and parents let their kids run naked in city parks and fountains. It's really no big deal.

Oslo's Frogner Park is a showcase for the work of Gustav Vigeland. Its centerpiece is a towering monolith of life.

For years, I've told the story about my Eureka moment when I was that 14-year-old kid in Frogner Park. I knew my parents loved me very much, and I looked around and saw a vast park speckled with other families—parents loving their children just as much. Right then it occurred to me how our world is filled with equally lovable children of God. I've traveled with this wonderful truth ever since.

As much as I love Norway, goat cheese, and my blond cousins, sometimes I need to inject some color into my days here. Oslo, too, seems to relish the fact that there's more to life than white food and fair hair. The city's rough-and-tumble immigrant zone—a stretch of street called Grønland—is where Turks, Indians, Pakistanis, and the rest of Oslo's growing immigrant community congregates. Colorful greengrocers' carts spill onto sidewalks and ethnic restaurants literally add spice to the otherwise pretty tame cuisine. The area's a hit with locals and tourists, and I love dining streetside here. It's relatively cheap—and seeing a rainbow of people and a few rough edges makes the city feel less Wonder-Bready.

And that's the beauty of Oslo. Just when you think you have it figured out, it gives you a taste of something different.

Norway's Fjordland Beauty

If you go to Norway and don't get out to the fjords, you should have your passport revoked. The country's greatest claim to scenic fame is its deep and lush fjords. Sognefjord, Norway's longest (120 miles) and deepest (more than a mile), is the ultimate natural thrill Norway has to offer.

For the best one-day look at Sognefjord, I like to do "Norway in a Nutshell." This package of well-organized train, ferry, and bus connections lays this beautiful natural feast before you on a scenic platter. Ambitious travelers can see the whole shebang in one very full day, but slowing down and spending the night is more relaxing.

Every morning, northern Europe's most spectacular train ride leaves from Oslo toward fjord country. Cameras smoke as this train roars over Norway's mountainous spine. The barren, windswept heaths, glaciers, deep forests, countless lakes, and a few rugged ski resorts create a harsh beauty. The railroad is an amazing engineering feat. Completed in 1909, it's 300 miles long and peaks at 4,266 feet—which, at this Alaskan latitude, is far above the tree line. You'll go under 18 miles of snow sheds, over 300 bridges, and through 200 tunnels along the way.

When the train reaches the mountain plateau station of Myrdal, a 12-mile spur line drops you 2,800 breathtaking feet to the village of Flåm on the Sognefjord. This is a party train. The engineer even stops the engine for photographs at a particularly picturesque waterfall.

From Flåm, ardent "Nutshellers" zip immediately from the train to catch the most scenic of fjord cruises. The boat takes you up one narrow arm of the Sognefjord—the

On the Sognefjord, Norway shows off its scenic beauty.

Aurlandsfjord—and down the next—the even narrower Nærøyfjord. For 90 minutes, camera-clicking tourists scurry on the drool-stained deck like nervous roosters, scratching fitfully for a photo to catch the magic. Waterfalls turn the black-rock cliffs into a bridal fair. You can nearly reach out and touch the sheer, towering walls. The ride is one of those fine times when a warm camaraderie spontaneously combusts among strangers, all of whom traveled from the farthest reaches of the globe to share this experience.

At the end of Nærøyfjord, the boat docks at the nothing-to-stop-for town of Gudvangen, where waiting buses shuttle passengers back to the main train line and the overnight train to Oslo. You'll sleep through all the scenery you saw on the way out.

While the "Nutshell" trip is fast-paced bliss, if you want to dig deeper into the Sognefjord—just like the glaciers did during the last ice age—spend the night. There's something poetic about summer evenings on a fjord. The mellow, steady, no-shadow light hardly changes from 8 until 11 p.m.

When settled in a village in a Victorian-era fjordside hotel, I spend lots of time sitting on the porch, mesmerized by Norwegian mountains. Rather than jagged, they're bald and splotchy, with snow fields on top and characteristic cliffs plunging into inky fjords.

After dinner, I stroll through the village enjoying the blond cherubs running barefoot through the stalled twilight. Cobbled lanes lead past shiplap houses to rock cliffs—their gullies and cracks green with trees.

I sit on a lonely pier and look up. Half the sky is taken up by the black rock face of the mountain. The steady call of gulls and the lazy gulping of small boats taking on little waves provide a relaxing soundtrack. As I feel my pulse slow, I am thankful to be in Norway.

Stockholm's Island Getaways

One-third water, one-third parks, one-third city, Stockholm is built on an archipelago of 14 islands woven together by 50 bridges. And the islands don't stop at the city limits—they keep going for 80 miles into the Baltic Sea.

The local name for this archipelago is "Skärgården"—literally "garden of skerries." The skerries—meaning rocks—are leftover granite, carved out and deposited by glaciers. The area closer to Stockholm has bigger islands and more trees. Farther out, the glaciers lingered longer, slowly grinding the granite into sand and creating smaller islands.

For years I've simply flown over this famed archipelago, or glided by it on a big cruise ship heading for Helsinki. Finally, I filmed one of my TV shows in Stockholm, diving into the scenic daisy chain stretching out from its downtown. Locals love to brag that there are 34,000 islands (but they must be counting every mossy little rock). A hundred are served by ferries. Even if an island isn't an official stop, ferries will dock on request...or to plop down the day's mail.

With so many islands to choose from, every Swede seems to have his or her favorite. Don't struggle too hard with the "Which island?" decision. Get a quick look on a half- or full-day package excursion from Stockholm's harbor. Or, do it on your own by ferry and overnight on an island.

Vaxholm, the nearest island, is practically a suburb, as it's connected by bridge to Stockholm. Skip past it to the more appealing (and traffic-free) Grinda. It's a rustic isle—half-retreat and half-resort—made to order for strolling through the woods, paddling a kayak, savoring an oh-so-Swedish meal in the rustic-chic lodge, or just chilling out in the floating sauna that bobs in the harbor.

Svartsö ("Black Island"), a short hop beyond Grinda, is the "Back Door" option of these isles. Unlike Grinda, Svartsö is home to a real community of just 80 year-round residents. Leafy and green Svartsö is less trampled than other islands (just one B&B and a top-notch steak house run by Stockholm foodies), but it is reasonably well-served by ferries. There's little to do—walk, bike, eat steak.

Out on the distant fringe of the archipelago—the last stop before Finland—sits the proud village of Sandhamn, on the island of Sandön. Literally "Sand Harbor," the town has a long history as a posh center for boating life—it's Sweden's answer to Nantucket. The headquarters of the Royal Swedish

The archipelago that stretches from Stockholm to the Baltic Sea is an idyllic and watery wonderland for nature-loving Swedes.

Yacht Club is here, making Sandhamn an extremely popular stop for boaters—from wealthy yachties to sailboat racers. A long sandy beach, perfect for families, stretches out on one side of the island.

But honestly, I wouldn't mind if I never get off the ferry. For me, the real highlight of an archipelago trip is the ride itself. Perched on the breezy rooftop sundeck with the Swedes, I position my lounge chair to catch just the right view and sun. It's a pleasure to key in to the steady rhythm of the ferries lacing this beautiful world together. Seeing the contentment of people savoring nature and quality time together, I'm convinced that the journey truly is the destination.

More Scandinavian Experiences

Copenhagen's Alternative Village: In the middle of Copenhagen, you'll find an unlikely hippie commune called Christiania. Surrounded by all that Danish perfection and orderliness, it's a funky enclave of squatters and rebels who operate their own little idealistic society. While hard drugs are emphatically forbidden (that's one of Christiania's rules), marijuana is sold as openly as the current political climate will tolerate—and sellers routinely press whatever boundaries are in place. Somehow, despite the best efforts of developers and the city government, Christiania has survived for more than 35 years. On my last visit, as I entered Christiania, I saw a huge mural that pretty much sums up the spirit of the place: "Only dead fish follow the current."

Remarkably, Christiania has become the third-most-visited sight among tourists in Copenhagen. Move over, *Little Mermaid*. Some visitors see dogs, dirt, and dazed people. Others see a haven of peace, freedom, and no taboos. But watching parents raise their children with Christiania values of peace and freedom, I've come to believe more strongly than ever in this do-your-own-thing haven.

Hobnobbing in Norway: Not long ago, I was at a cousin's dinner party with a dozen people in Oslo. Because I was there, everyone simply spoke English. I felt like it was an inconvenience, but it fazed no one. Topics were fascinating. One man, an author who had just completed a book on FDR, talked with me about the intricacies of American post-WWII politics like no one I've ever met. Someone else suggested that the international phone prefix system must have originated in America, as the US is no. 1—and Norway is a lowly 47. Another guest observed that Midwest Americans

speak louder than other Americans, and wondered if it was for the same reason that West Coast Norwegians talk louder than people from Oslo: They are always trying to be heard above the constant wind. Two new parents gently debated the various ways to split their paid maternal and paternal leave. People seemed very content—these Norwegians were just loving their salmon, shrimp, and goat cheese.

LEFT In Copenhagen's Christiania, a banner proclaims, "Only dead fish follow the current."

Revealing National Galleries: In the space of a week, I visited national galleries in Oslo, Stockholm, and Copenhagen. Each museum was a little palace of culture, showing off the nature of the land and the psyche of its people. In Scandinavia, paintings don't celebrate kings and popes. Instead, artists focus on the tumultuous symphonics of nature, exaggerating its power and awesomeness. When country folk do appear, they're the piccolo section—tiny but in sharp focus, barely surviving, but with grace. Many Scandinavian paintings are people's art—featuring bridal voyages (with traditional jewelry and formal wear), low church devotion (featuring renegade Lutherans who would not follow state dictates, until they ran out of patience and moved to Wisconsin), and solid families at work and play. The slice-of-life scenes seem to just as often be slice-of-death scenes: In one canvas, a stoic family fills their rowboat, carrying the coffin of a dead daughter, her sister clutching the funeral flowers through the bitter ride. And there's evidence of struggles with a puritanical 19th-century Protestant society and the psychological problems that resulted—leading artist Edvard Munch to let out a silent, bloodcurdling *Scream*.

CENTER Edvard Munch's *Scream* at Oslo's National Gallery

RIGHT The traditional *smörgåsbord* is a grand buffet and your chance to feast on many Scandinavian specialties in one sitting.

All Aboard the *Smörgåsbord*: Nobody visits Scandinavia for the cuisine, but there's one culinary tradition I never miss: the Swedish *smörgåsbord* (known in Denmark and Norway as the *store koldt bord*). With so much wholesome Nordic food spread out in front of me, I must pace myself.

Thinking of the *smörgåsbord* as a five- or six-course meal, I take small portions, making several trips to the buffet. I start with the herring dishes, boiled potatoes, and *knäckebröd* (Swedish crisp bread); then, I sample the other fish dishes (warm and cold) and more potatoes; next, it's on to salads, egg dishes, and various cold cuts; and after that, the meat dishes—it's meatball time! I pour on some gravy and plop on a spoonful of lingonberry sauce, and have more potatoes—while other roast meats (hey, is that reindeer?) and poultry tempt me. With a few empty pockets still to fill in my stomach, I sample the Nordic cheeses, delicious seasonal fruits, and bread, and then raid the racks of traditional desserts, cakes, and custards. Stuffed, I cap the meal with coffee to keep from passing out.

CULTURE AND TRADITIONS: EVERYTHING'S SO...SCANDINAVIAN

Mamma Mia!

Sweden spent years trying to find a place for a museum to honor its national treasure: the disco group ABBA. Now ABBA: The Museum is finally open, in Stockholm. For a time, ABBA was a bigger business than Volvo. And even though the group disbanded in 1982, its songs are still on plenty of playlists. They've sold more than 380 million records, and the musical *Mamma Mia*! (based on their many hits) has been enjoyed on screen and in theaters by millions of people. The museum, like everything about ABBA, is slickly promoted and aggressively commercial, with pricey tickets (about $30). But if you like ABBA, it's lots of fun. The museum has plenty of actual ABBA artifacts, re-creations of the rooms where the group did its composing and recording, lots of high-energy video screens, and plenty of interactive stations. The

LEFT At Stockholm's popular ABBA museum, any tourist can hang out with the band.

RIGHT Medieval stave churches are a reminder that Christian Vikings employed their ship-building skills for the Church.

best part is the "digital key" included with admission: You get to record a music video, karaoke-style, as a fifth member of the group, then pick up the production from the museum website (abbathemuseum.com).

Stave Churches

Stave churches are the finest architecture to come out of medieval Norway. These medieval houses of worship—tall, skinny, wooden pagodas with dragon's-head gargoyles—are distinctly Norwegian and palpably historic, transporting you right back to the Viking days. Wood was plentiful and cheap, and locals had an expertise with woodworking (from all that boat-building). In 1300, there were as many as 1,000 stave churches in Norway. Today, 28 remain. See two or three, and they start to look the same—but exploring at least one of them is a must. The fairest stave church in Norway? Two near the Sognefjord are tops: Hopperstad (overlooking a fjord) and Borgund (in a valley with an adjacent excellent museum). These time-machine churches take you back to early Christian days, when there were no pews and worshippers stood through the service. The churches are extremely vertical: The beams inside and the roofline outside lead your eyes up, up, up to the heavens.

Cheap-ish Eats

There are ways to take a bite out of Scandinavia's high cost of dining. First, take full advantage of your hotel's bountiful breakfast buffet. When out sightseeing, grab lunch from a street vendor or a food market, or at a restaurant offering a daily special. In Copenhagen, get a *pølse* (hot dog) from the sausage wagon. In Oslo, hit a *gatekjøkken* (street kitchen) for a quick bite, such as a *pølse med lompe* (hot dog rolled up in a potato flatbread) or *pølse med brød* (hot dog in a bun). In Stockholm, dine at a restaurant advertising *dagens rett*, a cheap lunch special. Affordable cafeterias for local workers—like the one at Oslo City Hall—are often open to the public. In Norway, you'll save 12 percent by getting takeaway food from a restaurant rather than eating inside; even McDonald's has a two-tiered price list.

Anywhere in Scandinavia you can save money by going to a grocery store and shopping for a picnic. In Norway I've even cooked up my own dinner using an *engangsgrill* ("one-time grill"), a disposable foil barbecue that costs just a few bucks at a supermarket. On balmy evenings, Oslo is perfumed with the smoky fragrance of one-time grills as the parks fill up with Norwegians eating out on the cheap.

Coffee Breaks

When sightseeing your way through Stockholm, be sure to join in the local tradition of the *fika*—Sweden's ritual coffee break. People in Sweden must drink more coffee per capita than in just about any other country. The *fika* is to Swedes what the *siesta* is to Spaniards. While typically a morning or afternoon break in the workday, it can happen any time, any day.

Fika fare includes coffee along with a snack or pastry—usually a cinnamon bun. You can get your *fika* fix at just about any café or *konditori* (bakery) in Stockholm. The coffee (drip-style, usually with a refill) and a cinnamon bun cost about what you'd pay at a Starbucks back home.

Dane Mellow

Danes (not to mention Swedes and Norwegians) like to joke about the flat Danish landscape, saying that you can stand on a case of beer and see from one end of the country to the other. Denmark's highest point, in Jutland, is only 560 feet above sea level. But I find Denmark to be simply cute, cute, cute. The place feels like a pitch 'n' putt course sparsely inhabited by blond Vulcans. Poll after poll lists Danes as the most content and happy people on the planet.

Legoland, a wildly popular amusement park built from millions of Lego bricks, crawls with adorable little ice-cream-licking, blond children. Even fueled by piles of sugar, the place is so mellow. Kids hold their mothers' hands and learn about the Lego buildings, or smile contentedly as they whip around on the carousel.

Throughout the countryside, newly paved roads are lined by perfectly smooth bike lanes—one for each direction. Even in the country, there are more bikes than cars. No one's uptight. When there's a little traffic jam, everyone takes it in stride. Damn those Danes.

Scandinavia Travel Resources from Rick Steves

Guidebooks

Check out Rick's guidebooks covering Scandinavia (including Denmark, Norway, and Sweden); Stockholm; Copenhagen & Denmark; and Norway

TV Shows

The quintessence of Scandinavia with Rick as your host, viewable on public television and at ricksteves.com. Episodes cover Denmark (Copenhagen, Ærø Island, Jutland), Norway (fjords, Bergen, Oslo), and Sweden (Stockholm)

Organized Tours

Small group tours, with itineraries planned by Rick: Scandinavia in 14 Days

For more on all of these resources, visit ricksteves.com

The Netherlands

Windmills, wooden shoes, cheese, tulips, and lots of bicycles: These images conjure up the traditional view of the Netherlands, a.k.a. Holland. (While North and South Holland are just two of the country's 12 provinces, they're so dominant that people use the names Holland and the Netherlands interchangeably.) But dig deeper and you will discover that the country also has high-tech culture, far-out architecture, and no-nonsense people with a global perspective.

For many Americans, this is a great place to start your first European vacation. The Dutch generally speak English, pride themselves on their frankness, and like to split the bill. As connoisseurs of world culture, they appreciate Rembrandt paintings, Indonesian cuisine, and the latest French films, but with a non-snooty, blue-jeans attitude.

The capital, Amsterdam, is a laboratory of progressive living, bottled inside Europe's most 17th-century city. Like Venice, this city is a patchwork quilt of canal-bordered islands, anchored upon millions of wooden pilings. But unlike its dwelling-in-the-past cousin, Amsterdam sees itself as a city of the future, built on good living, cozy cafés, great art, street-corner jazz, and a spirit of live-and-let-live.

Because the Netherlands is compact and flat, it's easy to do day trips from Amsterdam (or nearby Haarlem, which also makes a good home base). The slick, efficient train system gets you anywhere in just hours. Choose from an array of activities and sights:

the market in cozy Haarlem, the open-air folk museum in Arnhem, cheese in Edam, porcelain in Delft, or a trip through polder country out to the sea.

Approach the Netherlands as an ethnologist observing a fascinating and unique culture. A stroll through any neighborhood is rewarded with things that are commonplace here but rarely found elsewhere. Carillons chime quaintly in neighborhoods selling sex, as young professionals smoke pot with impunity next to old ladies in bonnets selling flowers.

FAVORITE SIGHTS AND MEMORABLE EXPERIENCES IN THE NETHERLANDS

Amsterdam Street Scenes

Unlike any city in Europe, Amsterdam opens like a fan out of its central train station. It just seems right for a trading center to open up from that lifeline to the world.

Stepping from the train station, I look down Damrak, the main drag, which flushes visitors past cheers of commercial neon into the old center. It's always been this way. After all, long before there was a station, this was a mighty port with a waterway cutting through the center of town, following the route of today's Damrak.

Outside the station, trams glide and room hustlers hawk their offerings. Street people wearing stocking hats over matted hair, black boots, and heavy coats in the sun choose the most public places in town to snooze. Children pedal to school as if in a small town, and pairs of policemen add no stress to the laid-back scene. Tourists pop out of the station, eager to explore.

First-time sightseers leaving the station carry a predictable checklist of sights. The Anne Frank House is on the right, the Red Light District is on the left, and Damrak leads right through the middle toward two great museums—the Rijksmuseum (filled with works by Rembrandt and Vermeer) and the Van Gogh Museum—standing like cultural bulldogs on the opposite side of town.

Fast Facts

Biggest cities: Amsterdam (capital, 820,000), Rotterdam (615,000), The Hague (500,000)

Size: 16,000 square miles (about twice the size of New Jersey), population 16.8 million

Locals call it: Nederland

Currency: Euro

Key date: July 26, 1581, the Dutch declare their independence from Habsburg Spain

Biggest festival: King's Day (April 27)

Bikes per Dutch citizen: 1.3

Handy Dutch phrases: *Hallo* (hello; hol-**loh**), *Alstublieft* (please; **ahl**-stoo-bleeft), *Dank u wel* (thank you; dahnk yoo vehl), *Nou breekt mijn klomp!* (Well, I'll be damned!; literally, "That breaks my wooden shoe"; now brayk men kloomp)

But to me, Amsterdam's unpredictable street scenes—crude one moment, then charming the next—are at least as rewarding as the city's fine museums. Walking down Damrak, I find it a crass perversion of traditional Dutch culture. Wooden shoes hang forlornly on a wall between a bank and a Hooters. Nearby, a sex museum known as the temple of Venus promises a look at "sex through the ages," including the Sado Club, the Torture Tower, and the oldest sex shop in Amsterdam. Visitors are stopped first by the poster of Marilyn Monroe fighting a randy gale, then lured in by a sultry mannequin wearing a provocative dress and a huge smile as she rides a bicycle with a single, hardworking piston.

But slices of Holland survive. Just past a gimmicky torture museum, the sound of an old-time barrel organ revives traditional Amsterdam and cheers me up. It's a two-man affair. While grandpa works the crowd, the boss is in the back spinning the wheel and feeding tunes punched into a scroll, as if feeding bullets into a musical machine gun.

The street organ is a mini-carnival, painted in candy-colored pastels and peopled with busy figurines. Whittled ballerinas twitch to ring bells while Cracker Jack boys crash silver dollar-sized cymbals. Playing his coin-tin maracas and wearing a carved-on smile, the old man looks like an ornamental statue that has just leapt to life. While shoppers trudge by, two tourists break into a merry waltz. Another hugs a day bag between her knees and winks into her camera's viewfinder.

Nearby, the Vlaamse Frites kiosk is painted with take-offs on great art. This art has a purpose: to make you hungry for Flemish-style French fries. On one side of the kiosk, God gives Adam the cone of fries (a variation on this decorates the Sistine Chapel). On the opposite side is Van Gogh's

The Netherlands' Top Destinations

Amsterdam ▲▲▲   allow 2-3 days
Canal-laced city filled with cozy cafés, great art, Golden Age history, and progressive people

Top Sights
Rijksmuseum Premier collection of Dutch Masters art
Van Gogh Museum 200 paintings by the angst-ridden artist
Canal Boat Tours Best cruise through city's fabled waterways
Anne Frank House Young Anne's hideaway during the Nazi occupation
Dutch Resistance Museum Powerful and insightful look at years under Nazi occupation

Haarlem ▲▲   1 day
Classic Dutch town (and handy home base) highlighted by a landmark market square, towering church, Corrie ten Boom House, and the Frans Hals Museum

Delft ▲▲   1 day
Charming, canal-lined hometown of Vermeer and the Delftware pottery factory

Edam ▲▲   1 day
Adorable cheesemaking village with peaceful canals

Arnhem ▲   1 day
Unremarkable city but for Holland's top open-air folk museum and a first-rate modern-art museum

The Hague ▲   1 day
Big-city seat of Dutch government offering the excellent Mauritshuis Gallery and Golden Age art

With more time, consider visiting
Schokland Museum Former island village in the middle of reclaimed farmland
Alkmaar Friday-morning cheese market, near Zaanse Schans Open-Air Museum
Utrecht Bustling student city with charming central zone and top rail museum

---

famous "French Fried Potato Eaters." The peasants, for whom Vincent always had an affinity, are shown solemnly sitting down to a bountiful platter of bright yellow fries. All they need is mayonnaise, the Dutch choice over ketchup.

Warming my hands around my cone of salty fries, I wander down a back street to a charming canal lined with tipsy houses. As their foundations of pilings rot or settle, they lean on each other, looking as if someone has stolen their crutches. Suddenly, away from the tourists and street-scene bustle, I'm in 17th-century Amsterdam, seeing the Dutch Golden Age reflected in the quiet canal.

Seeing Red in Amsterdam

With just a slight swing off Dam Square, I start walking down Warmoesstraat, one of Amsterdam's oldest streets. Lining the street are sex shops, a condom shop with a vast inventory, men-only leather bars, and a smartshop selling "100 percent natural products that play with the human senses." There's no doubt I've entered into Amsterdam's famous Red Light District.

The Red Light District is located in the old sailors' quarter. In fact, the city seems to have taken everything sailors did, put it in a jar, and let it germinate for 200 years. Today that jar is open, and browsers are welcome.

The Dutch have a similarly practical approach to prostitution as they do to the recreational use of marijuana. Rather

Red lights reflect on the canals in Amsterdam, where, as in much of Europe, prostitution is legal.

than criminalize it, they control it with a policy they call "pragmatic harm reduction." Generally, prostitutes (or "sex workers") pay rent for their space and run an independent business with no need for pimps. They are unionized and get their business license only if they are periodically checked by a doctor and are not spreading diseases. If a prostitute has a dangerous client and needs help, she pushes a button to summon not a pimp, but the police.

By the time I reach the area around De Oude Kerk, the oldest church in Amsterdam, I've hit the neighborhood's most dense concentration of prostitution. The church is the holy needle around which the unholy Red Light District spins. Rooms with big windows under red neon lights line the narrow alleys. In window after window, I see women in panties and bras winking at horny men, rapping on the window to attract attention, or looking disdainfully at sightseers. As the steeple chimes, women from Jamaica holler, "Come on, dahling."

Rubbing shoulders with a hungry gaggle of Dutch boy regulars, I rubberneck my way to the most popular window on the street. There, framed in smoky red velvet, stands a sultry blonde. Her ability to flex and shake her backside brings the slow, gawking pedestrian flow to a stuttering stop. And it makes me just one of the faceless, rutting masses. Next up: an exotic woman wearing a black lace power-suit and enough lipstick to keep a third grader in crayons. Just making eye contact leaves me weak—and ready to rejoin the cute and quaint Holland back in the sunshine.

The Dutch remind me that a society has to make a choice: Tolerate alternative lifestyles or build more prisons. And they always follow that up by reminding me that

Americans—so inclined to legislate morality—lock up seven times as many people per capita as Western Europeans do. Either Americans are inherently more criminal people, or we need to reconsider some of our laws.

By the end of my walk, I've seen a lot—from prostitutes to the ghosts of pioneer lesbians to politically active druggies with green thumbs. This is Amsterdam's hardcore, nonstop, live-couples, first-floor-straight, second-floor-gay *paseo*. The kid in me delights in the spectacle. The tour guide in me jumps at this opportunity to give readers such a unique memory as this red light ramble. But the father in me cringes at the sight of a 10-year-old schoolgirl, book bag on her back, studying a window full of vibrators, whips, and sex toys.

In truth, the Red Light District seems to have something to offend everyone. Whether it's in-your-face images of graphic sex, exploited immigrant women, whips and chains, passed-out drug addicts, the pungent smells of pot smoke and urine, or just the shameless commercialism of it all, it's not everyone's cup of tea. Amsterdam is a bold experiment in 21st-century freedom. It may box your Puritan ears. And though I encourage people to expand their horizons, it's perfectly OK to say, "No, thank you."

Now, it's time to go back to my hotel and take a shower.

Haarlem with Herring Breath

A Dutch Masters kind of town, Haarlem is an easy place to start a European trip. While mighty Amsterdam is just a 20-minute train ride away, cute Haarlem provides a comfy base and a more genteel experience.

The centerpiece of Haarlem is its delightful Grote Markt (main square), where 10 streets converge. A noisy traffic circle in the 1960s, the now-car-free area has become the town's social and psychological hub—Haarlem's civic living room.

Today I'm standing on the square under the towering church spire, tempted to eat a pickled herring. The sign atop the mobile van reads: "Jos Haring—Gezond en Lekkerrr" (healthy and deeeeeelicious).

I order by pointing and ask, *"Gezond?"*

Jos hands me what looks more like bait than lunch, and says, *"En lekkerrr."*

I stand there—not sure what to do with my bait—apparently looking lost. Jos, a huge man who towers over his white fishy counter, mimes swallowing a sword and says, "I give

you the herring Rotterdam style. You eat it like this. If I chop it up and give you these"—he points to the toothpicks—"this is Amsterdam style."

As I take a bite he asks, "You like it?"

Even with three "r"s on the delicious, "It's salty" is the only polite response I can muster.

"Yes. This is not raw. It is pickled in salt. Great in the hot weather. You sweat. You need salt. You eat my herring."

It's Saturday—market day, when Haarlem's main square bustles like a Brueghel painting. The scene cheers me with a festival of flowers, bright bolts of cloth, evangelical cheese pushers, and warm, gooey syrup waffles. Gazing at the church, I'm appreciating essentially the same scene that Dutch artists captured centuries ago in oil paintings that now hang in museums. The carillon clangs with an out-of-tune sweetness only a medieval church tower can possess.

Savoring the merry dissonance, and taking tiny Amsterdam-style bites of my Rotterdam herring, I wander deeper into the market, happy that Jos is piling chopped onion on herring, contributing to the amazing ambience of this scene. Dodging flower-laden one-speed bikes, I feel like part of the family here. I'm immersed in Holland—with herring breath.

Haarlem's main square is a community gathering point. And there, like in nearly every Dutch town, you'll find a stand selling pickled herring. Locals declare they are gezond en lekker (healthy and delicious).

The Dutch Made Holland

Today my long-time Dutch friends, Hans and Marjet, are driving me to polder country—the vast fields reclaimed from the sea where cows graze, tiny canals function as fences, and only church spires and windmills interrupt the horizon.

Hans is behind the wheel. He injects personality-plus in all he does, whether running a B&B or leading tours for Americans. And bouncy Marjet, with a head of wispy strawberry-blonde hair, red tennis shoes, and a knack for assembling a Salvation Army-chic outfit for under $20, is the sentimental half of this team.

On each of my visits, they show me a new slice of Holland, renewing my belief that the more you know about Europe, the more you'll uncover what's worth exploring.

It's early summer, and the landscape is streaked with yellow and orange tulip fields. Hans points out a quaint windmill along a dreamy canal.

"Every time I take a tour group through Holland's countryside," I say, "someone in the back of the bus marvels, 'Everything's so Dutch.'"

The windmills were used to pump the polders dry. An area that was once a merciless sea is now dotted with tranquil towns. Many of the residents here are older than the land they live on, which was reclaimed in the 1960s. All this technological tinkering with nature has prompted a popular local saying: "God made the Earth, but the Dutch made Holland."

We motor past sprawling flower mogul mansions, then through desolate dunes. The tiny road dwindles to a trailhead. Hans parks the car, and we hike to a peaceful stretch of North Sea beach. Pointing a stick of driftwood at a huge seagoing tanker, Hans says, "That ship's going to the big port at Rotterdam. We're clever at trade. We have to be. We're a small country."

Holland welcomes the world's business, but Holland is not designed for big-shots. Hans explains, "Being ordinary is being prudent. If you grow above the grains, you'll get your

head cut off. Even our former queen prefers to do her own shopping."

While Hans and I talk, Marjet collects shells with the wide-eyed wonder of a 10-year-old. "Cheap souvenirs," Hans teases. One cliché the Dutch don't dispute is their frugality. Hans quizzes me: "Who invented copper wire? Two Dutch boys fighting over a penny."

Marjet scuffs through the sand, her pockets full of seashells, her scarf flapping in the wind like a jump rope. Under big, romping white clouds, we're surrounded by Holland.

More Dutch Experiences

Wartime Hideaways: Through the ages, the Dutch have given refuge to the persecuted. But they couldn't protect their citizens from the Nazis—more than 100,000 Dutch Jews died in the Holocaust. In Amsterdam, Anne Frank's House gives the cold, mind-boggling statistics of Nazi cruelty some much-needed intimacy. Even bah-humbug types who are dragged in because it's raining and their partners read the diary find themselves caught up in Anne's story. And the small town of Haarlem has Corrie ten Boom's "Hiding Place," which gives the other half of the Anne Frank story—the point of view of those who risked their lives to hide Dutch Jews during the Nazi occupation. During the war, Corrie and her family hid Jews and Resistance fighters in their apartment above a clock shop. One night, with six people hiding behind a wall in Corrie's bedroom, the Nazis raided the house. Though they didn't find the hiding place, they did come across a suspiciously large number of ration coupons and sent the ten Boom family to a concentration camp. Only Corrie survived and later wrote her inspirational book, *The Hiding Place*.

Cannabis and Coffeeshops: Having been decriminalized decades ago, marijuana causes about as much excitement in the Netherlands as a bottle of beer. People can grow their own—cannabis seed sets are even sold in garden centers. Or they simply drop by a coffeeshop—a café that sells marijuana. For tourists, the open use of marijuana can feel either somewhat disturbing or exhilaratingly liberating.

Coffeeshops sell marijuana and hashish both in pre-rolled joints and in little baggies. They loan out bongs and inhalers, and dispense rolling papers like toothpicks. Pot, while sold openly in coffeeshops, is tightly regulated here. It's not sold to minors, and you can only buy a little at a time.

Because they're not allowed to advertise marijuana, you may have to ask to see the cannabis menu. In some coffeeshops, you actually have to push and hold down a button to see an illuminated menu—the contents of which look like the inventory of a drug bust. Coffeeshop baristas warn Americans (who aren't used to the strength of the local stuff) to try a lighter leaf. If you do overdo it, the key is to eat or drink something sweet to avoid getting sick. Cola is a good fast fix, and coffeeshops keep sugar tablets handy.

LEFT In Haarlem, you can tour the Corrie ten Boom house and actually see the "Hiding Place."

CENTER Cannabis starter kits are sold next to the tulip bulbs in the Netherlands, but you're smart not to import them.

RIGHT Each spring the Super Bowl of tulips is held at Keukenhof, an hour south of Amsterdam.

Charming Delft: Delft is a typically Dutch, "I could live here" town. An hour southwest of Amsterdam, it boasts an intelligent exhibit on hometown boy Johannes Vermeer, two grand churches squirreling away royal tombs, and the factory that produces Delft Blue earthenware. But despite some fine sights, Delft is best enjoyed by simply wandering around, watching people, munching local syrup waffles, and daydreaming on canal bridges. Looking out, you'll see reflections in canals that would inspire Monet to set up his easel. On a summer day, the entire town twinkles and ripples like water lilies.

Netherlands in Bloom: The Dutch love plants. And the granddaddy of the European flower festivals is Keukenhof, the greatest bulb-flower garden on earth. Open only for two months in spring, Keukenhof blossoms with seven million tulips, hyacinths, and daffodils that conspire to thrill even the most horticulturally challenged visitor. Located near the city of Leiden, this place is packed with tour groups daily—go in the late afternoon for the fewest crowds and the best light on all those happy flowers. If you can't get out to Keukenhof, try Amsterdam's De Hortus Botanical Garden, with 6,000 varieties of plants spread throughout several greenhouses and a tropical palm house. One of the oldest botanical gardens in the world, it dates from 1638, when medicinal herbs were grown here. Even today, no mobile phones are allowed because "our collection of plants is a precious community—treat it with respect."

CULTURE AND TRADITIONS: EVERYTHING'S SO...DUTCH

Dutch Cheese

Cheese is a staple of the Dutch culture and economy. Cows have always proven to be more reliable than crops in this marshy landscape. And because cheese offered similar nutritional value to milk, but lasted much longer without refrigeration, it was taken on long sea voyages. Holland was the first country to export cheese, and today this small country remains the world's biggest cheese exporter.

The Netherlands' most famous cheeses are Edam (covered with red wax) and Gouda. Gouda can be young or old—*jong* is mellow while *oude* is salty, crumbly, and strong, sometimes seasoned with cumin or cloves. To sample Dutch cheese in Amsterdam, try the Reypenaer Tasting Rooms, which offers a delightful shop and an hour-long cheese tasting in the basement (smart to reserve ahead). Or, for the real deal, head to the town of Alkmaar, Holland's cheese capital, with its bustling Friday-morning cheese market in spring and summer. Early in the morning, cheesemakers line up their giant orange wheels in neat rows on the square. Prospective buyers (mostly wholesalers) examine and sample the cheeses and make their selections. Then the cheese is sold off with much fanfare, as an emcee narrates the action (in Dutch and English). To close the deal, costumed cheese carriers run the giant wheels on something resembling a wooden stretcher back and forth to the Weigh House, just as they have for centuries.

Dutch clichés abound in the Netherlands, where cheese shops are on each corner and classic windmills still churn in the breeze.

Netherlands Clichés

What do windmills, canals, wooden shoes, and tulips have in common? Where did all of these Dutch icons come from? It's all about the land. After diking off large tracts of land below sea level (*Netherlands* means "low lands"), the Dutch used windmills to harness wind energy to pump the excess water into canals. This drained the land, creating pockets of dry ground upon which to build. Wooden shoes (*klompen*) allowed farmers to walk across soggy fields, and since they could float, the shoes were easy to find if they came off in high water. Then in the mid-1500s, the Holy Roman Emperor's ambassador to Constantinople sent some tulip bulbs westward. The people here found that these hardy flowers grew well in the sandy soil near dunes, and tulips have become synonymous with Dutch culture ever since.

Going Dutch on a Bike

If you rent a bike in the Netherlands, you'll need to learn the rules of the road. Use arm signals, follow the bike-only traffic signals, stay in the obvious and omnipresent bike lanes, and yield to traffic on the right. Fear oncoming trams and tram tracks. Carefully cross tracks at a perpendicular angle to avoid catching your tire in the rut. Obey all traffic signals, and walk your bike through pedestrian zones. Use the bell to warn other bikers and pedestrians, and be sure to lock your bike. If you are a pedestrian, look carefully both ways before crossing the brick-colored pavement on the side of the road—this is for bikes. As the Dutch believe in fashion over safety, no one here wears a helmet.

Ethnic Eats

The tastiest "Dutch" food isn't actually Dutch—it's Indonesian. As a former Dutch colony, Indonesia has had a mighty influence on the Dutch cuisine scene. Find any *Indisch* restaurant and experience a rijsttafel (literally, "rice table"). A rijsttafel features an assortment of dishes that shows off the varied cuisines of the different Indonesian islands. You'll get as many as 30 spicy dishes ranging from small sides to entrée-sized plates and a big bowl of rice or noodles. These feasts can be split and easily fill two people.

Surinamese cuisine is also popular in the Netherlands. This mix of Caribbean and Indonesian influences features dishes like *roti* (spiced chicken wrapped in a tortilla) and rice (white or fried) served with meats in sauces (curry and spices). Why Surinamese food in Amsterdam? In 1667, Holland traded New York City ("New Amsterdam") to Britain in exchange for the small South American country of Suriname. When Suriname gained independence in 1975,

100,000 Surinamese immigrated to Amsterdam, sparking a rash of Surinamese fast-food outlets.

Biking

The Netherlands' flat land makes it a biker's dream. And in Amsterdam, bikes are by far the smartest way to travel. Everyone—bank managers, students, pizza delivery boys, and police—use bikes to get around town, and much of my own Amsterdam experience is framed by my black bike handlebars: the shiny wet cobbles, powering up a bridge to coast down it and halfway to the next bridge, getting pinged by passing bikes and pinging my bell to pass others.

The Dutch average four bikes per family. Many people own two: a long-distance racing bike and an in-city bike, often deliberately kept in poor maintenance so it's less enticing to the many bike thieves. The Dutch appreciate the efficiency of a self-propelled machine that travels five times faster than walking, without pollution, noise, parking problems, or high fuel costs. A speedy bicyclist can traverse Amsterdam's historic center in 10 minutes. Meanwhile, pedestrians enjoy the quiet of a people-friendly town where bikes outnumber cars.

Netherlands Travel Resources from Rick Steves

Guidebooks
Check out Rick's guidebooks covering Amsterdam & the Netherlands

Audio Europe
Download Rick's free Audio Europe app, with self-guided audio tours, including walks through the old center of Amsterdam, the Red Light District, and the Jordaan neighborhood

TV Shows
The quintessence of the Netherlands with Rick as your host, viewable on public television and at ricksteves.com. Episodes cover Amsterdam and Dutch side trips

Organized Tours
Small group tours, with itineraries planned by Rick: Heart of Belgium & Holland in 11 Days

For more on all these resources, visit ricksteves.com

Belgium

Belgium falls through the cracks. Nestled between Germany, France, and the Netherlands, it's famous for waffles, sprouts, and a statue of a little boy peeing. But visitors find Belgium to be one of Europe's best-kept secrets. After all, Belgium produces some of Europe's best beer, creamiest chocolates, and tastiest French fries. From funky urban neighborhoods to tranquil convent courtyards, from old-fashioned lace to high-powered European politics, from cows mooing in a pastoral countryside to gentrified medieval cityscapes bristling with spires...little Belgium entertains

It's here in Belgium that Europe comes together: where Romance languages meet Germanic languages; Catholics meet Protestants; and nations meet in Brussels—the capital of the European Union. Its crossroads location has made Belgium strong: Belgians are savvy businesspeople, excellent linguists, and savvy chefs who've learned how to blend delicious culinary influences from various cultures.

When I asked a local, "What is a Belgian?" he answered, "We are a melting pot. We're a mix culturally: one-third English for our sense of humor, one-third French for our love of culture and good living, and one-third German for our work ethic."

Bruges, a wonderfully preserved medieval gem, and Brussels, one of Europe's great cities, are the best two first bites of Belgium. Historic, well-preserved Ghent and big, bustling Antwerp are also worth a visit. To

round out your Belgian experience, spend a few hours in the Flemish countryside around the town of Ypres—both for the pastoral scenery and to visit World War I's Flanders Fields.

While not "undiscovered" (especially popular Bruges), Belgium is certainly underrated. Those who squeeze in a day or two for Belgium wish they had more time. Like sampling a flavorful praline in a chocolate shop, that first enticing taste just leaves you wanting more. Go ahead, it's OK—buy a whole box of Belgium.

FAVORITE SIGHTS AND MEMORABLE EXPERIENCES IN BELGIUM

Bewitched by Bells in Bruges

With Renoir canals, pointy gilded architecture, vivid time-tunnel art, and stay-awhile cafés, Bruges is a joy. Where else can you bike along a canal, quench your thirst with gloriously good beer, savor heavenly chocolate, and see a Michelangelo statue, all within 300 yards of a bell tower that rings out "Don't worry, be happy" jingles?

Whenever I'm in Bruges, I visit the tall bell tower that has shaded the city's Market Square since 1300. With its medieval crenellations, pointed Gothic arches, round Roman arches, flamboyant spires, and even a few small flying buttresses, the tower is a sight in itself. Carillon concerts are played on its bells a few evenings each week. You can hear the tunes ringing out from anywhere in the town center, but to catch the performance while sitting in the tower courtyard is a ritual for me.

One evening I arrived early for the concert, so I had time to climb the tower's 366 steps. Just before the top is the carillon room. On each quarter hour, its 47 bells—tuned to 47 different notes—ring mechanically. It's *bellissimo* at the top of the hour. During concerts, the bells are played by a *carillonneur* on a manual keyboard.

Fast Facts

Biggest cities: Brussels (capital, 1.1 million), Antwerp (508,000), Ghent (249,000)

Size: 12,000 square miles (slightly smaller than Maryland), population 10.4 million

Locals call it: België (Dutch), Belgique (French)

Currency: Euro

Key date: 1830, Belgium declares independence from the Netherlands

Languages: Dutch (to the north; Flemish is the local Dutch dialect), French (to the south)

Biggest festivals: Carnival (Mardi Gras celebrations), Ommegang Pageant (July, Brussels, medieval festival)

Handy Dutch phrases: *Hallo* (hello; hol-loh), *Alstublieft* (please; ahl-stoo-bleeft), *Dank u wel* (thank you; dahnk yoo vehl)

Handy French phrases: *Bonjour* (good day; bohn-zhoor), *S'il vous plait* (please; see voo play), *Merci* (thank you; mehr-see)

After my carillon close-up, I took a seat in the courtyard and gazed up at the lofty brick tower. The *carillonneur* popped his head out a window, and like a kid who checks in with a parent before going down a playground slide, he gave his audience a wave. Then he disappeared and began hammering—literally hammering. A carillon keyboard looks like the foot pedals of a big organ, but it is played by the little-finger sides of bare, clenched fists.

After the concert, the gathered audience clapped, and the *carillonneur* appeared again—his tiny head jutting out the little window to happily catch our applause. The crowd dissipated, but I waited at the tower base to personally thank him.

The bell tower in Bruges

A few minutes later, he was at street level, in his overcoat, looking like any passerby. I shook his hand and found myself gripping a freakishly wide little finger. A lifetime of pounding the carillon had left him with a callus that had more than doubled the width of his pinky.

In a town with a knack for excellence, I'd met just one more artist perfecting his craft.

Bruges Brews

In Bruges, pubs are not just pub... the ... ... appreciate a ... that's not owned by a single brewery, freeing them up to sample a good selection of their country's hundreds of microbrews. Pubs in the old center—places you'd think would be overrun by tourists—are the proud domain of locals, who find the fact that monasteries have historically brewed the finest Belgian beers perfectly in line with their personal theology.

On a recent visit, I plunked myself down on a stool at a local pub with a Dutch Masters ambience. Wanting to check the material I had in my guidebook on Belgian beers, I planned to pick the bartender's brain, but I was surrounded by beer experts—all happy to clue me in on the 300 available choices. They advised me to forego my standard procedure of ordering what's on tap. Because the selection of specialty beers is so vast, no single brew can be consumed quickly

Belgium's Top Destinations

Bruges ▲▲▲ — allow 1-2 days

Perfectly pickled Gothic city with charming cobbles, cozy squares, dreamy canals, divine chocolate, and unbeatable beer

Top Sights
Market Square 14th-century landmark square and bell tower
Groeninge Museum Top-notch 15th-century paintings
Memling Museum Glowing Flemish Primitives masterpieces housed in medieval hospital

Nearby
Damme Charming market town a bike-ride away through the countryside
Flanders Fields Infamous WWI battlefields

Brussels ▲▲ — 1-2 days

Urbane capital of Belgium, the European Union, and NATO, with one of Europe's grandest squares, colorful urban zones, and a beloved statue of a little boy peeing

Top Sights
Grand Place Cobbled main square lined with medieval guild halls and chocolate shops
Royal Museums of Fine Arts of Belgium Old Masters and modern Belgian art

Antwerp ▲▲ — 1 day

Gentrified port city with excellent museums, Belgium's best fashion, and an engaging mix of urban grittiness and youthful trendiness

Ghent ▲ — 1 day

Pleasant, lively university city with historic quarter and breathtaking Van Eyck altarpiece in its massive cathedral

---

enough to keep kegs from going old and stale. Those in the know prefer their beer from the bottle.

Different beers, depending on their taste temperament, are served cold, cool, or at room temperature. A critical part of the beer culture here is that the glass must fit the beer (to best bring out the beer's character). The better pubs have long shelves lined with dozens of slightly different glasses, each marked with a beer's insignia. If the pub runs out of the right glass, the bartender will check to see if you'd like to change your order. Many Belgian connoisseurs will switch beers rather than use the wrong glass.

Soon I had a chemistry lab

of four different beers in front of me. My selection included
Brugse Zot, or "the fool"—the last beer brewed right in
Bruges and considered one of Belgium's best. Kriek beer
is made bitter with cherry. I was told that apple-flavored
Lambic is what you order if you "don't like beer." My favorite
was a complex and creamy Chimay brewed by Trappist
monks. Licking my lips, I thought that Chimay would almost
make celibacy livable.

Brussels' Grand Place

There's no better place to take in Brussels' ambience than
its spectacular main square, the Grand Place. This colorful
cobbled courtyard, encircled by fanciful facades, is the heart
of heart-shaped Brussels. The site where farmers and merchants once sold their wares in open-air stalls today hosts
shops and cafés selling chocolates, waffles, beer, mussels,
fries, and lace. It's the perfect backdrop for concerts, flower

markets, and sound-and-light-shows—and there's always good people-watching.

The Town Hall's 300-foot-tall tower dominates the square, topped by a golden statue of St. Michael slaying a devil. Fancy smaller buildings—former guild halls—give the Grand Place its majestic medieval character.

Just three short blocks away is Brussels' most famous attraction and the most obvious example of Bruxelloise irreverence: the *Manneken-Pis*, a 17th-century statue depicting a little boy urinating. Visiting VIPs have a tradition of bringing an outfit for the statue; he can be costumed as anything from a Beefeater to Elvis as his steady stream carries on.

There are several different stories behind this little squirt: He was a naughty boy who peed inside a witch's house so she froze him. Or the little tyke loved his beer, which came in handy when a fire threatened the wooden city—he bravely put it out. Want the truth? The city commissioned the statue to show the freedom and *joie de vivre* of living in Brussels, where happy people eat, drink...and drink...and then pee.

Brussels has perhaps the grandest square in Europe (La Grand Place) and perhaps the silliest tourist attraction in the world (the *Manneken-Pis,* just a block away). And with each visit, you'll see the little guy peeing through a different outfit.

More Belgian Experiences

Antwerp's Ode to Industrialism: I can't think of a more visit-worthy train station than the Industrial Age-meets-Art Nouveau marvel in Antwerp, giddy with steel and glass. Built at the turn of the 20th century, the station is a work of art and a loud-and-clear comment on a confident new age. Its main facade is like a triumphal arch on a temple of time, crowned by a grand clock. Imagine the station's debut: Just a generation earlier, people thought you might die if you traveled at more than 30 miles per hour. Timetables didn't need to be exact. Now, journeys that previously took days could be done in hours—and things ran according to the clock.

Life and Death in Flanders Fields: In far western Belgium, in the desolate WWI battlefield known as Flanders Fields, poppies were the first flowers to bloom once the dust (and mustard gas) cleared. Hundreds of thousands of soldiers took their last breaths here. Today, the poppy, representing sacrifice and renewal, is the symbol of Flanders Fields.

When touring in this area, I have to remind myself that everything I see—every building, every tree—dates from after the war's end in 1918. The devastation was monumental. You can't drive through this part of Flanders without passing countless artillery craters, monuments and memorials, stones marking this advance or that conquest, and war cemeteries standing stoically between the cow-speckled pastures. Local farmers routinely pull rustic relics of World War I from the earth when they till their fields. Every local has his own garage collection of "Great War" debris fished out of the troubled earth.

The European Union Headquarters in Brussels: This sprawling complex of glass skyscrapers is a cacophony of black-suited politicians speaking 23 different Euro-languages. It's exciting just to be here—a fly on the wall of a place that charts the future of Europe. The Parlamentarium, a high-tech fun and informative exhibit, is designed to let you meet the EU and understand how it works. And you can get inside the European Parliament itself by joining a free tour. The grand finale is the vast hemicycle, where the parliament members sit. It's the largest multilingual operation on the planet. Yet somehow things get done "with respect for all political thinking...consolidating democracy in the spirit of peace and solidarity."

Tiny Belgium has a broad range of attractions, from a mighty Industrial-Age train station in Antwerp (left), to the vast and evocative WWI cemeteries of Flanders Fields (center), to the glassy headquarters of the European Union in Brussels (right).

CULTURE AND TRADITIONS: EVERYTHING'S SO...BELGIAN

World Capital of Chocolate

With a smile, the shop owner handed me a pharaoh's head and two hedgehogs and said that her husband was busy downstairs finishing off another batch of chocolates. Happily sucking on a hedgehog, I walked out of the small chocolate shop with a 100-gram assortment of Bruges' best pralines.

Belgium—home to Godiva, Neuhaus, and Leonidas—is the world's number-one exporter of chocolate, and produces some of Europe's creamiest confections. The two basic types are pralines (what we generally think of as "chocolates"—a hard chocolate shell with various fillings) and truffles (a softer, crumblier shell, often spherical, and also filled). Which is better? It takes a lot of sampling to judge. Locals swear by their personal chocolatier and buy with a concern for freshness—yesterday's chocolate just won't do. This can be disastrous for chocoholics during heat waves: If the weather's too hot, the chocolate makers close down.

Belgian Waffles

Waffles are a famous Belgian treat. There are two kinds: Liège-style (warm, dense, and very sweet—with a sugary crust), and Brussels-style (light and fluffy, dusted with powdered sugar). Although Americans think of Belgian waffles for breakfast, Belgians generally have them as a late-afternoon snack—though the delicious Liège-style waffles are sold 'round the clock to tourists as an extremely tempting treat. You'll see little windows, shops, and trucks selling these *wafels*, either plain (for Belgians and purists) or topped with fruit, jam, chocolate sauce, ice cream, or whipped cream (for tourists).

A Belgian waffle just tastes better in Belgium. And if you're one to gild the lily, there is a world of toppings from which to choose.

Just Say No...to Ketchup

Belgium has some of the tastiest "French" fries in Europe. Get a paper cone of warm fries at a *frituur* (fry shop) or a *frietkot* (fry wagon). One time a local chef took me into his kitchen to witness the double frying that makes the fries taste so good. (The first pass is to cook the potatoes; the second is to brown them.) My friend picked up a single fat fry, gave it a waggle, and then dipped it into its second hot-oil bath. Something about his nervous giggle reminded me of the kid who showed me my first dirty magazine. Belgians dip their fries in mayonnaise or other flavored sauces, not ketchup. But don't worry; most places provide ketchup for Americans.

No Tap Water at Restaurants

I'd rather drink free tap water than pricey bottled water in a European restaurant. But forget about it in Belgium—it can't be had. Belgian restaurateurs are emphatic about that. Tap water may come with a smile in the Netherlands, France, and Germany, but that's not the case in Belgium, where you'll either pay for water, enjoy the beer, or go thirsty.

Belgium Travel Resources from Rick Steves

Guidebooks

Check out Rick's guidebooks covering Bruges, Brussels, Antwerp & Ghent

TV Shows

The quintessence of Belgium with Rick as your host, viewable on public television and ricksteves.com. Episodes cover Bruges and Brussels

Organized Tours

Small group tours, with itineraries planned by Rick: Heart of Belgium and Holland in 11 Days

For more on all of these resources, visit ricksteves.com

Germany

Germany is a young nation (united in 1871) with a long history. It's as modern as it is traditional. You can experience all the cultural clichés you want, from enjoying strudel at the bakery, to shopping for a cuckoo clock, to chugging a stein of beer while men in lederhosen play oompah music. The countryside is dotted with half-timbered villages like Rothenburg, looking as medieval as ever. But despite its respect for traditions, Germany truly is a 21st-century country. Laced together by bullet trains, its cities gleam with futuristic architecture, world-class museums, rejuvenated waterfronts, and people-friendly parks.

The country is blessed with spectacular scenery, and the nature-loving Germans know how to enjoy it: taking lifts to jagged peaks, hiking through the Black Forest, and cruising on rivers such as the moseying Mosel and the raging, castle-lined Rhine. The country boasts hundreds of castles, some ruined and mysterious, and others right out of a Disney fairy tale.

In contrast to its beautiful image, the country has a troubled 20th-century past. In the capital of Berlin and throughout Germany, you'll see respectful acknowledgment of this tumultuous era, with thought-provoking documentation centers, somber monuments, and haunting concentration camps.

Traditionally—and in some ways even today—German culture divides at a sort of North-South Mason-Dixon Line. Northern Germany was barbarian, is predominantly Protestant (thanks to Martin Luther), and tackles life aggressively, while southern Germany (Bavaria) was Roman, is largely Catholic, and enjoys a more relaxed tempo (think of

soaking in spas). Americans' nostalgic image of Germany is beer-and-pretzel Bavaria, probably because that was "our" sector after the war.

Germany is a country of paradoxes. From modern skyscrapers to medieval castles, speedy autobahns to meandering back roads, Nouveau German cuisine to old-fashioned *Wurst*, Germany truly offers something for everyone.

Germany ranges from half-timbered medieval cuteness (Rothenburg) to towering skyscraper zones (Berlin).

FAVORITE SIGHTS AND MEMORABLE EXPERIENCES IN GERMANY

Cruising the Rhine River

Jostling through crowds of Germans and tourists in the Rhine River village of Bacharach, I climb to the sun deck of the ferry and grab a chair. With the last passenger barely aboard, the gangplank is dragged in and the river pulls us away.

I'm captivated by the Rhine. There's a rhythm to the mighty river that merges with its environment: black slate cut from plains above, terraced vineyards zigzagging up hills, husks of crumbling castles, and stoic spires of stone churches slicing vertically through townscapes. While the Rhine is over 800 miles long, the 36 miles from Mainz to Koblenz are by far the most interesting. This is the Romantic Rhine, a powerful stretch of the river

On the romantic Rhine River gorge, cafés at castles offer grand views of busy river traffic.

slashing a deep and scenic gorge. And the best way to see it is to cruise it.

Passengers' parkas flap in the cool wind as the rugged hillscape gradually reveals castles both ruined and restored. All along the Rhine, it seems each castle and every rock comes with a story. Many of the castles were "robber-baron" fortresses built by petty princes and two-bit rulers back when there were several hundred independent little states in what is today's Germany. The castle owners raised heavy chains across the river when boats came—and lowered them only when the merchants had paid their duty. We sail close by one of the many scenic fortresses—Pfalz Castle—which was built on an island in the middle of the river.

As the cliffs get steeper, the rocks darker, and the river faster, the scenery becomes more dramatic. With the boat's sun deck filled mostly with beer-sipping, ice-cream-licking Germans, our collective pulse quickens as we approach the mythological climax of this cruise. Over the ship's blow horns comes the story of the Loreley—a rocky bluff where a maiden seduced sailors into shipwrecks—followed by a lusty rendition of the Loreley song. Parents point to the bluff, featured in the fairytale memory of every German schoolkid.

According to legend, a thousand years of skippers have dreaded the Loreley. Because of the reefs just upstream, many ships never made it beyond the bluff. Sailors (after days on the river) blamed their misfortune on the legendary siren, with her long blonde hair almost covering her body, who'd lured boatloads of drooling sailors to her river bed.

Our boat survives the Loreley and docks in St. Goar, a classic Rhine tourist town. Its massive ruined castle overlooks a half-timbered shopping street and leafy riverside park, busy with sightseeing boats and contented strollers. Sitting like a dead pit bull above St. Goar, Rheinfels Castle—the single best Rhineland

Fast Facts

Biggest cities: Berlin (capital, 3.4 million), Hamburg (1.8 million), Munich (1.5 million)

Size: 138,000 square miles (about half the size of Texas), population 81 million

Locals call it: Deutschland

Currency: Euro

Key date: October 3, 1990, two Germanys become one after the fall of the Berlin Wall (November 1989)

Biggest festivals: Oktoberfest (early autumn, Munich), Christmas markets (late November through Christmas Eve, Nürnberg and elsewhere)

Handy German phrases: *Guten Tag* (hello; **goo**-tehn tahg), *Bitte* (please; **bit**-teh), *Danke* (thank you; **dahn**-keh), *Noch ein Bier!* (Another beer!; nohkh īn beer)

Of all the Rhine castle ruins to tour, Rheinfels is the mightiest.

ruin to explore—rumbles with ghosts from its hard-fought past.

The Rhine Valley is storybook Germany, a world of legends and medieval castles. Through it all, the quiet, deep-gray power of the river flows as steadily as time itself, a dance floor where ferries, barges, and sightseeing boats do their lumbering do-si-do past fabled and treacherous rocks.

Celebrating Democracy at Berlin's Reichstag

In Berlin, a must-see for any traveler is the Reichstag, the country's parliament building. Topped with a glass cupola that visitors can climb, this building is more than just the meeting place for parliament—it's also a symbol of German democracy.

From 1933 to 1999, this historic building—upon whose rooftop some of the last fighting of World War II occurred—sat a bombed-out and blackened hulk, overlooking the no-man's-land between East and West Berlin. After unification, Germany's government returned from Bonn to Berlin. And, recognizing this building's cultural roots, they renovated it—incorporating modern architectural design and capping it with a glorious glass dome.

This old-meets-new building comes with powerful architectural symbolism. The glass dome is designed for German citizens to climb its long spiral ramp to the very top and literally look down (through a glass ceiling) over the shoulders of their legislators to see what's on their desks. The Germans, who feel they've been manipulated by too many self-serving politicians over the last century, are determined to keep a closer eye on their leaders from now on.

The glassy dome of Berlin's Reichstag welcomes German citizens as well as tourists.

I was in Berlin in 1999 during the week that the renovated Reichstag reopened to the public. That day, I climbed to the top of the dome and found myself surrounded by teary-eyed Germans. Anytime you're surrounded by teary-eyed Germans, something exceptional is going on. It occurred to me that most of these people were old enough to remember the difficult times (either during or after World War II), when their city lay in rubble. For them, the opening

Germany's Top Destinations

Berlin ▲▲▲   allow 3-5 days

Vibrant and reunified capital, featuring state-of-the-art museums, cutting-edge architecture, and trendy neighborhoods, along with evocative monuments of the Wall that once divided the city and country

Top Sights

Reichstag Historic parliament building with a modern glass dome
Brandenburg Gate Gateway at the former border of East and West
Memorial to the Murdered Jews of Europe Compelling monument
Topography of Terror Chilling Gestapo/SS exhibit
German History Museum Tells the country's tumultuous story
Pergamon and Neues Museum Classical and Egyptian antiquities
Gemäldegalerie Top collection of Old Master European paintings

Nearby

Potsdam Frederick the Great's palace playground
Sachsenhausen Concentration camp museum and memorial

Munich ▲▲▲   2 days

Lively, livable city with a traffic-free center, good museums, Baroque palaces, stately churches, rollicking beer halls, and sprawling parks

Top Sights

Marienplatz Main square with glockenspiel show
Hofbräuhaus Famous beer hall
Residenz Opulent palace and treasury of Bavarian royalty
Art Museums Alte Pinakothek, Neue Pinakothek, and Pinakothek der Moderne

Nearby

Dachau First Nazi concentration camp, now a museum
Andechs Monastery Monk-brewed beer in bucolic setting

Bavaria ▲▲▲   2-3 days

Alps-straddling region boasting the fairy-tale castles of Neuschwanstein, Hohenschwangau, and Linderhof (with Ehrenberg across the Austrian border); inviting villages such as the handy home base **Füssen** and adorable **Oberammergau;** and the towering Zugspitze and its high-altitude lifts

Rothenburg and the Romantic Road ▲▲   1-2 days

Well-preserved medieval city with half-timbered buildings, cobbled lanes, and walkable walls; a popular stop on the Romantic Road scenic route through lovely countryside and time-passed towns

Rhine Valley ▲▲   2 days

Mighty river steeped in legend, where storybook villages (including charming home-base towns **Bacharach** and **St. Goar**) cluster under imposing castles, such as Rheinfels and Marksburg

Mosel Valley ▲▲   1-2 days

Peaceful meandering river lined with tiny wine-loving cobbled towns, such as handy **Cochem** and quaint **Beilstein,** plus my favorite European castle, Burg Eltz

█aden-Baden and the Black Forest ▲   1-2 days
High-class resort/spa town of **Baden-Baden,** with pampered bath experiences and a grand casino; lively university city of **Freiburg** and cozy village of **Staufen;** and forested countryside rife with healthy hikes, folk museums, and cuckoo clocks

Nürnberg ▲▲   1 day
Old town core and great museums, along with thoughtful reminders of Nazi past and a huge Christmas market

With more time, consider visiting
Dresden Baroque palaces, WWII history, and delightful riverside scene
Erfurt and Wittenberg Martin Luther's stomping grounds
Frankfurt Skyscrapers and modern-day urban Germany
Cologne Riverside city highlighted by spectacular Gothic cathedral
Hamburg Rejuvenated port city with infamous nightlife
Leipzig Bach and Cold War sights in the former East Germany
Trier Roman monuments, including the Porta Nigra gate

of this grand building was the symbolic closing of a terrible chapter in the history of a great nation. No more division. No more communism. No more fascism. They had a united government and were entering a new century with a new capitol filled with hope and optimism.

Castle Day in Bavaria and Tirol

Three of my favorite castles—two famous, one unknown— can be seen in one busy day. If you tackle "Castle Day," you'll visit Germany's Disney-like Neuschwanstein Castle, the more stately Hohenschwangau Castle at its foot, and the much older Ehrenberg Ruins, across the Austrian border in Reutte.

Reutte makes a fine home base. From here, catch the early bus across the border to touristy Füssen, the German town nearest Neuschwanstein. From Füssen, you can walk, pedal a rented bike, or ride a bus a couple of miles to Neuschwanstein.

Neuschwanstein is the greatest of King Ludwig II's fairy-tale castles. It's one of Europe's most popular attractions, so reserve ahead online (otherwise, arrive by 8 a.m. to buy a ticket). If you choose a combo-ticket, you'll first visit Ludwig's boyhood home, Hohenschwangau Castle, and then the neighboring Neuschwanstein on the hill. If you arrive late, you'll spend a couple of hours in the ticket line and may find all tours booked.

Ludwig's extravagance and Romanticism earned this Bavarian king the title "Mad" King Ludwig...and an early death. After Bavarians complained about the money Ludwig spent on castles, the 40-year-old king was found dead in a lake under suspicious circumstances.

Hohenschwangau Castle, where Ludwig grew up, offers a good look at his life. Like its more famous neighbor, it takes about an hour to tour. Afterward, head up the hill to Ludwig's castle in the air.

Neuschwanstein Castle, which is about as old as the Eiffel Tower, is a textbook example of 19th-century Romanticism. After the Middle Ages ended, people disparagingly named that era "Gothic," or barbarian. Then, all of a sudden, in the 1800s it was hip to be square, and Neo-Gothic became the rage. Throughout Europe, old castles were restored and new ones built—wallpapered with chivalry. King Ludwig II put his medieval fantasy on the hilltop not for defensive reasons, but simply because he liked the view.

The lavish interior, covered with damsels in distress,

dragons, and knights in gleaming armor, is enchanting. (A little knowledge of Wagner's operas goes a long way in bringing these stories to life.) Ludwig had great taste for a mad king. Read up on this political misfit—a poetic hippie king in the realpolitik age of Bismarck. After the tour, climb farther up the hill to Mary's Bridge for the best view of this crazy yet picturesque castle.

Fanciful castles decorate the foothills of the Alps along the German-Austrian border. King Ludwig's Neuschwanstein is less than a century older than the castle it inspired at Disneyland.

This is a busy day. By lunchtime, catch the bus to Reutte and get ready for a completely different castle experience. With picnic and directions in hand, walk 30 minutes (or take a taxi) out of town to the Ehrenberg Castle Ensemble, the brooding ruins of four castles. If Neuschwanstein was the medieval castle dream, Ehrenburg is the medieval castle reality. The 13th-century rock pile provides a super opportunity to let your imagination off its leash.

The impressive castle ensemble (once consisting of four buildings) was built to defend against the Bavarians and to bottle up the strategic Via Claudia trade route, which cut through the Alps as it connected Italy and Germany. For centuries, the castle was the seat of government, which ruled an area called the "Judgment of Ehrenberg" (roughly the same as today's district of Reutte). When the emperor came by, he stayed here. In 1604, the ruler moved downtown into more comfortable quarters, and the castle was no longer a palace. After several battles, the castle eventually fell into disrepair, leaving only this evocative shell and a whiff of history.

You can see Ehrenberg's castles reconstructed on Reutte's restaurant walls. Ask at your hotel where you can find a folk evening full of slap-dancing and yodel foolery. A hot, hearty dinner and an evening of Tirolean entertainment is a fitting way to raise the drawbridge on your memorable "Castle Day."

Getting Naked in Baden-Baden

Since the Roman emperor bathed in the mineral waters of Baden-Baden, this Black Forest town has welcomed those in need of a good soak. In the 19th century, it was Germany's ultimate spa resort, and even today the name Baden-Baden is synonymous with relaxation in a land where the government still pays its overworked citizens to take a little spa time.

It's long been a frustration for me that Americans won't go to a European spa because they're too self-conscious to get naked with a bunch of strangers. For me, enjoying the baths at Friedrichsbad in Baden-Baden is one of Europe's most elegant experiences. If you come here, don't miss out.

My experience kicked off with a weight check—92 kilos. The attendant led me under the industrial-strength shower—a torrential kickoff, pounding my head and shoulders and obliterating the rest of the world. He then gave me slippers and a towel, ushering me into a dry-heat room with fine wooden lounges—slats too hot to sit on without the towel.

Finally, it was time for my massage. I climbed gingerly onto the marble slab and lay belly-up. The masseur held up two mitts and asked, "Hard or soft?" In the spirit of wild abandon, I said "hard," not even certain what that would mean to my skin. I got the coarse, Brillo-Pad scrub-down, but it was still extremely relaxing. Finished with a Teutonic spank, I was sent off into the pools.

Nude, without my glasses, and not speaking the language, I was gawky. On a sliding scale between Mr. Magoo and Woody Allen, I was everywhere, careening between steam rooms and cold plunges.

In the end, it all led to the mixed section. This is where Americans get uptight. The parallel spa facilities intersect, bringing men and women together to share the finest three pools. Here, all are welcome to glide under exquisite domes in perfect silence, like aristocratic swans. Germans are nonchalant, tuned into their bodies and focused on solitary relaxation. Tourists are tentative, trying to be cool, but more aware of their nudity. Really, there's nothing sexy about it. Just vivid life in full flower.

The climax is the cold plunge. I'm not good with cold water—yet I absolutely loved this. You must not wimp out on the cold plunge.

Finally, the attendant escorted me into the quiet room

and asked when I'd like to be awoken. I told him closing time.
He swaddled me in hot sheets and a brown blanket and laid
me down warm, flat on my back, among 20 hospital-type
beds. Only one other bed was occupied; he seemed dead. I
stared up at the ceiling and some time later was jolted awake
by my own snore.

Leaving, I weighed myself again: 91 kilos. I had shed
2.2 pounds of sweat. Stepping into the cool evening air, I
was thankful my hotel was a level two-block stroll away.
In my room, I fell in slow motion onto my down comforter,
the big pillow puffing around my head like the Flying Nun.
Wonderfully naked under my clothes, I could only think,
"Ahhhh. Baden Baden."

Standing at the Top of the World

One of my favorite places to be in Europe is atop the
Zugspitze—the highest point in Germany. Standing on this
9,700-foot peak, you can't help but marvel at the thought that
you are above everyone else in the entire country—number
one out of 82 million. From here, facing south, I feel like a
maestro conducting a symphony of snow-capped peaks, as
the mighty Alps stretch seemingly forever to the right and
left.

The Zugspitze also marks the border between Germany
and Austria. There are two separate terraces—Bavarian
and Tirolean—connected by a narrow walk that once
served as the border station. Before Europe united, you had
to show your passport just to walk across the mountaintop.
Crossing was a big deal—you'd get your passport stamped
at a little blue house and shift your currency from shillings
to marks.

Lifts from both countries meet at the top. As if waging
an epic battle of alpine engineering, just a few years after
the Austrians built a cable car to their Zugspitze station, the
Germans drilled through the
mountain (in 1931) so that a cogwheel train could deposit nature
lovers on a glacier just below
their side of the summit.

Today, whether you ascend
from the Austrian or German
side, this is one of the few opportunities to straddle the border
between two great nations while
enjoying an incredible view.

The Zugspitze marks the border of Germany and Austria. Although Germany's highest peak, it's just a wannabe among Austria's mightier Alps.

Once you're done admiring the mountains, you can head to the restaurant that claims—irrefutably—to be the "highest *Biergarten* in Deutschland."

Medieval Rothenburg

Thirty years ago, I fell in love with Rothenburg in the rough. At that time, the town still fed a few farm animals within its medieval walls. Today its barns are hotels, its livestock are tourists, and Rothenburg has turned into a medieval theme park.

But Rothenburg is still the best-preserved medieval town in Germany—and possibly all of Europe. Many also consider it a horrible tourist trap. The place is stampeded midday with visiting tour groups, eager to buy faux traditional Christmas ornaments. The town even created its own traditional pastry—the *Schneeball* (a powdered-doughnut-like "snowball"). Yet when I pass through its medieval gates, I feel like a kid who just got a three-day pass for all the rides at Disneyland. I simply love Rothenburg.

In Rothenburg, medieval life comes alive in its cobbled alleys. The ramparts are intact, still walkable, and come complete with arrow slits for notching an imaginary crossbow. The fish tanks next to the water fountains continue to evoke the days when marauding armies would besiege the town, and the townspeople would survive on the grain in its lofts and the trout in its tanks. The monastery garden still has its medicinal herbs. And the Medieval Crime and Punishment Museum shows graphically how people were disciplined back when life was nasty, brutish, and short. Some travelers react with horror; others wish for a gift shop.

But beyond the medieval ambience, it's the local residents who bring the town to life. Hans-Georg, the night

In Rothenburg, Germany's best-preserved medieval walled town, you can skip the "snowballs" (*Schneeballen*, a "tradition" kept alive for tourists), but don't miss spending a delightful hour touring with the night watchman.

watchman, stokes his lamp and walks wide-eyed tourists through the back lanes telling stories of hot oil and great plagues. Spry Klaus, who runs a B&B above his grocery store, takes travelers jogging with him each evening at 7:30. Another B&B owner, Norry, plays in a Dixieland band, loves to jam, and has invented a fascinating hybrid saxophone/trombone called the Norryphone.

At the English Conversation Club, held every Wednesday night at a town pub, locals enjoy a weekly excuse to get together, drink, and practice their fanciest English on each other and on visiting tourists. Once Anneliese, who runs the Friese shop (my favorite souvenir store in town), invited me to join her. So I meandered into the pub through candlelit clouds of smoke and squeezed a three-legged stool up to a table already crowded with family and friends.

Anneliese poured me a glass of wine, then pulled a *Schneeball* from a bag. Raising a cloud of powdered sugar as she poked at the name on the now empty bag, she said, "Friedel is the bakery I explained you about. They make the best *Schneeball*. I like it better than your American doughnut. Every day i eat one. But only at this bakery."

For years, Anneliese has playfully tried to get me to write good things about *Schneeballen*. I put *Schneeballen* (which originated in a hungrier age as a way to get more mileage out of leftover dough) in that category of penitential foods—like lutefisk—whose only purpose is to help younger people remember the suffering of their parents. Nowadays these historic pastries are pitched to the tourists in caramel, chocolate, and other flavors unknown in feudal times.

Shoving a big doughy ball my way, Anneliese said, "You like to eat this?"

I broke off a little chunk, saying, "Only a teeny-weeny *bisschen*."

After I left the pub for the night, I passed Hans-Georg, the night watchman dressed in medieval garb, finishing up his spiel in the town square with his group: "Now I must call the 'all's well.' You, my friends, should hurry home. Bed is the best place for good people at this hour."

Heading toward my hotel, I heard him calling, "All's well!"

More German Experiences

My Favorite Castle: Nestled in an enchanted forest just above the Mosel River, Burg Eltz is my favorite castle in all of Europe. The castle avoided wars and was never destroyed, remaining in the Eltz family for more than eight centuries. The current owner, an elderly countess who enjoys flowers, always has grand arrangements adorning the public rooms. The castle is furnished throughout basically as it was 500 years ago. That's unusual in castles. For your best approach, start from the Moselkern train station on foot. After hiking for more than an hour through an ancient forest where you'd expect Friar Tuck or Martin Luther to be hiding out, the castle of your fantasies suddenly appears.

Paying Homage in Berlin: Germany's capital city is speckled with touching memorials that honor victims of past sins. The Memorial to the Murdered Jews of Europe, consisting of 2,711 gravestone-like pillars, was the first formal, government-sponsored Holocaust memorial. Using the word "murdered" in the title was intentional, a sign that Germany, as a nation, was officially admitting to a crime. The Monument to the Murdered Sinti and Roma of Europe remembers the roughly 500,000 Sinti and Roma (Gypsy) victims of the Holocaust. The Memorial to Politicians Who Opposed Hitler is a simple row of slate slabs dedicated to the 96 members of the Reichstag who were persecuted and murdered because they didn't agree with Chancellor Hitler. One place where you'll find little signage is the site of the bunker where Hitler committed suicide in 1945. It's just a nondescript parking lot.

Simple, Unspoiled Erfurt: Long ago I gave up looking for an untouristy, half-timbered medieval German town. But recently, I stumbled upon it in the sleepy town of Erfurt. The capital of the German region of Thuringia, Erfurt has history swinging from its eaves. It's most notable as the place where Martin Luther studied and became a monk, essentially planting the seeds from which grew the Protestant Reformation. It's also the rare city in the center of Germany that emerged relatively unscathed from World War II, after

LEFT Burg Eltz, on the Mosel River, is my favorite castle to tour in Germany.

CENTER The Memorial to Politicians Who Opposed Hitler in Berlin is a reminder of the hell Germany lived through in the 1930s and 1940s.

RIGHT For Luther fans, Erfurt is a must-see.

which it became stuck in the strange cocoon of East German communism for half a century. For me, as a Lutheran, coming to Erfurt is a bit like a Catholic going to Rome. Without the pivotal accomplishments of the Reformation, the Bible would still be read in Latin and interpreted for us by priests. The 500th anniversary of Martin Luther kicking off the Reformation in 1517 is quickly approaching, and towns like Erfurt will enjoy lots of attention. But until then, visitors can enjoy this delightful slice of simple, unspoiled Germany in peace.

CULTURE AND TRADITIONS: EVERYTHING'S SO...GERMAN

Beer and *Biergartens*

One of the most satisfying sounds you'll hear in Germany is a big *whop!* as they tap a classic old wooden keg of beer. Hearing this, every German knows they're in for a good, fresh mug.

Germans are serious about their beer. It's regulated by the Reinheitsgebot (Purity Decree) of 1516—the oldest food and beverage law in the world—which dictates that only four ingredients may be used: malt, yeast, hops, and water. There are four main types of Germanic beers: pale lager (*helles Bier*), dark beer (*dunkles Bier*), white/wheat beer (*Weissbier* or *Weizenbier*), and pilsner.

The best place to sample Germanic beer culture is at a *Biergarten*, where long skinny tables stretch beneath shady chestnut trees. This is where Germans meet up with friends and family, relax, and maybe grab a bite to eat. Picnickers can bring their own food or buy it from a self-service stand, then sit at any table without a tablecloth. Covered tables are reserved for people who are being served.

My favorite *Biergarten* (and German beer) is an hour's drive outside Munich at the Andechs Monastery. The stately church stands as it has for centuries, topping a hill at the foot of the Alps. Its Baroque interior—and its beer hall—both stirs the soul and stokes the appetite. The hearty meals come in medieval proportions. Whenever I come here, I get a knuckle of pork, spiral-cut radishes, sauerkraut, a huge pretzel, and a liter of beer (called *eine Mass*, though I'd call it "ein pitcher"). What's more Bavarian than that? Once I asked my German friend if they sell half-liters of beer, to which he replied, "This is a *Biergarten*, not a kindergarten!"

Sausage, Sausage Everywhere

Unless you're a vegetarian, it's hard to leave Germany without sampling sausage *(Wurst)*. Options go far beyond the hometown hot dog. There are literally hundreds of regional variations, including *Nürnberger* (short, spicy, the size of your little finger, and served three in a bun); *Currywurst* (grilled, sliced up, and drenched with a curry-infused tomato sauce); and *Weisswurst* ("white" veal sausage that's boiled, peeled, and eaten with sweet mustard and a fresh soft pretzel).

Most fast-food restaurants *(Schnell Imbiss)* offer sausage on the menu, but I like to go local at a sausage stand *(Würstchenbude)*. In Berlin, I look for human hot dog stands. These hot-dog hawkers don an ingenious harness that hangs off the body, allowing them to cook and serve *Wurst* on the fly.

Munich's Oktoberfest

The 1810 marriage reception of King Ludwig I (the grandfather of "Mad" King Ludwig II) was such a success that it turned into an annual bash. These days, Munich's Oktoberfest lasts just over two weeks—from late September into early October. Every night, eight huge beer tents fill with thousands of people eager to show off their stein-hoisting skills. A million gallons of beer later, they roast the last ox. If you plan to come, reserve a room early (Oktoberfest.de).

Christmas Markets

German towns big and small have been lighting up with Christmas markets *(Christkindlesmarkt)* each December for centuries. One of the biggest is Nürnberg's market, with 200 wooden stalls selling handicrafts from local artisans. A traditional center for toy-making in Germany, Nürnberg offers up market ambience that's classier than your average crafts fair, with no canned music, fake greenery, or plastic kitsch. As far back as 1610, a proclamation warned that "indecent joke articles would be confiscated."

Christmas markets are more than a shopping spree; they're places to enjoy a genuinely homey atmosphere. You'll wrap your mittens around a mug of hot-spiced wine while carolers sing in the background. Because a throwaway cup would ruin the experience, you'll pay a deposit for a nicely decorated ceramic mug. You can either return the mug or keep it as a collectible, as each year there's a different model.

Fast, Dependable Trains

At 12:14, I settle into my seat on the luxurious German bullet train, and at 12:16, we glide out of the station. In no time, I'm rocketing toward my next destination. German trains are as slick as can be—clean, modern, comfortable, and on time. ICE trains are the country's fastest, zipping from city to city at up to 200 miles per hour. IC and EC trains are slower, but only relatively—up to 125 miles per hour. Inexpensive regional trains are substantially slower, but can help stretch a budget.

Fast trains allow you to maximize sightseeing. For instance, on an ICE train, you can get from Munich to Nürnberg in just one hour or from Frankfurt to Cologne in under 90 minutes. German trains are so quiet and efficient that I almost miss the old clackity-clackity rhythm of the rails. It's been replaced by a nearly silent swoosh, as futuristic trains cut like bullets through the green and tidy countryside.

Germany Travel Resources from Rick Steves

Guidebooks
Check out Rick's guidebooks covering all of Germany; Berlin; and Munich, Bavaria & Salzburg; plus his German phrase book

Audio Europe
Download Rick's free Audio Europe app, with self-guided audio tours, including walks through Berlin and Munich and a best of the Rhine tour

TV Shows
The quintessence of Germany with Rick as your host, viewable on public television and at ricksteves.com. Episodes cover Berlin, Munich and the Alps, Cologne and the Black Forest, and Rothenburg and the Rhine River

Organized Tours
Small group tours, with itineraries planned by Rick: Germany, Austria & Switzerland in 14 Days; Berlin, Prague & Vienna in 12 Days

For more on all of these resources, visit ricksteves.com

Switzerland

Mountainous, efficient Switzerland is one of Europe's most appealing destinations. Wedged neatly between Germany, Austria, France, and Italy, Switzerland borrows what's best from its neighbors—and adds a healthy dose of chocolate, cowbells, and cable cars. Fiercely independent and decidedly high-tech, the Swiss stubbornly hold on to their quaint traditions, too.

Despite the country's small size, Switzerland's regions maintain their distinct cultural differences, partly because the wild geography has kept people apart historically. Switzerland has four official languages: German, French, Italian, and Romansh. And yet, regardless of which language is spoken, the entire country is unmistakably Swiss. Everywhere you go, you'll notice a dedication to order and organization, right down to the precision stacking of a woodpile.

Switzerland has more than its share of cosmopolitan cities (Zürich, Luzern, Bern, Lausanne, Lugano), but let's

face it—travelers don't flock to Switzerland for its cities. The Alps are the premier destination. Alpine villages (such as Gimmelwald) give you a taste of rural Switzerland, and are the perfect base for riding lifts to dramatic alpine panoramas and taking unforgettably scenic hikes.

FAVORITE SIGHTS AND MEMORABLE EXPERIENCES IN SWITZERLAND

The Swiss Alps in Your Lap

When I say I'm planning to go to Gimmelwald, Swiss people assume I mean Grindelwald, the famous resort in the next valley. When assured that Gimmelwald is my target, they lean forward, widen their eyes, and—with their sing-songy Swiss-German accent—ask, "Und how do you know about Gimmelwald?"

This traffic-free village, hanging nonchalantly on the edge of a cliff high above the Lauterbrunnen Valley, has more cow troughs than mailboxes. Here, white-bearded old men smoke hand-carved pipes, and blond-braided children play "barn" instead of "house." Big stones sit like heavy checkers on old rooftops, awaiting nature's next move. While these stones protect the shingles from violent winter winds, in summer it's so quiet you can hear the cows ripping tufts of grass. There's nothing but air between Gimmelwald and the rock face of the nearby Jungfrau Mountain. Small avalanches across the valley look and sound like distant waterfalls. Kick a soccer ball wrong and it ends up a mile below, on the valley floor.

Gimmelwald was never developed like neighboring towns because its residents made sure it got rated an "avalanche zone," and developers couldn't get building permits. Consequently, while neighboring villages are

High in the Swiss Alps, in the humble village of Gimmelwald, farmer Peter cuts hay to feed his cows, gathers it on a tarp, and rides his bovine salad down the steep slopes, as if on a barge, to his barn.

Switzerland's Top Destinations

Berner Oberland ▲▲▲   allow 2-3 days
High-mountain region popular for its characteristic villages and scenic hikes, lifts, and train rides, in the shadow of the Eiger, Mönch, and Jungfrau peaks

Top Sights
    Gimmelwald Time-warp village overlooking Lauterbrunnen Valley
    Schilthornbahn Cable car soaring to 9,748-foot Schilthorn peak
    Jungfraubahn Train to 11,333-foot Jungfraujoch saddle, with snow activities
    Männlichen to Kleine Scheidegg Hike Easy, mostly downhill hike with Eiger views

Bern ▲▲▲   1 day
Cozy Swiss capital, lassoed by a meandering river and embedded with shopping arcades, fine museums, and a Gothic cathedral

Appenzell ▲▲   1 day
Traditional Swiss region known for pastoral scenery, appealing folk museums, and remarkably fragrant cheese, and the cliffs of Ebenalp, with its inviting mountain hut

Lake Geneva and French Switzerland ▲▲   1-2 days
Switzerland's best castle, lakeside Château de Chillon; the cute cheesemaking village of **Gruyères;** and the steeply situated, urbane, *très* French-speaking city of **Lausanne**

Luzern ▲   1 day
Thriving city on a mountain-ringed lake, with historic wooden bridges and well-presented museums; Golden Pass scenic rail journey to Montreux starts here

Zürich ▲   1 day
Another tidy city on a pretty lake, bustling with Swiss commerce, upscale shops, and an atmospheric old town

dominated by condos owned by big-city folks who come by only for vacations, Gimmelwald is still inhabited by locals—about 120 in all—and its traditions survive.

Gimmelwald is a poor town whose traditional economy depends on government subsidies for survival. Each year, its citizens systematically harvest the steep hillside outside their windows. Entire families cut and gather every inch of hay. After harvesting what the scythe can reach, they pull hay from nooks and crannies by hand. Half a day is spent harvesting what a machine could cut in two minutes on a flat field. But this is how the farmers of Gimmelwald have made their living forever—lovingly cutting the hay, to feed the cows, to make the cheese, to feed us people.

From Gimmelwald, a modern gondola goes up the nearly

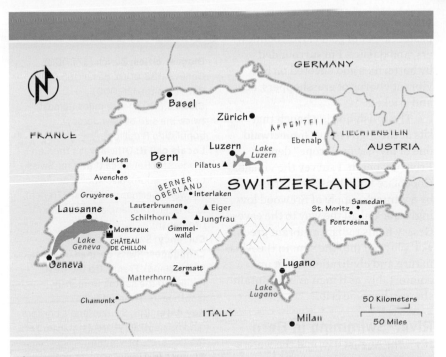

10,000-foot-high peak of the Schilthorn. For the most memorable breakfast around, I ride the early-morning gondola up to the summit and its solar-powered revolving restaurant. There, I sip my coffee slowly to enjoy an entire panoramic rotation of the Eiger, Mönch, and Jungfrau mountains.

Outside, I watch hang-gliders methodically set up and jump into airborne ecstasy. It's possible to hike straight down from the summit, but the first gondola station below the peak, Birg, is the best starting point for high-country hikes. Two minutes from the Birg station and I'm completely alone, surrounded by a harsh and unforgiving alpine world. A black ballet of rocks is accompanied by cowbells and a distant river. Wisps of clouds are exclamation points. After a steep descent, I step out of the forest at the top end of the village I call home. Walking over a pastel carpet of gold clover, bellflowers, and daisies, I'm surrounded by butterflies and cheered on by a vibrant chorus of grasshoppers, bees, and crickets.

The finish line is a bench that sits at the high end of Gimmelwald—one of my "savor Europe" depots. From my perch, I survey the village. Chocolate log cabins are buttressed by a winter's supply of firewood lovingly stacked all the way to the eaves. Grassy fields radiate a vibrant green, as if plugged into the sun. In the Alps, nature and civilization mix it up comfortably, as if man and mountain shared the same crib.

River-Swimming in Bern

It's a hot August day, and the waterfront park along the Aare River, in Switzerland's capital city of Bern, is packed with wet and happy people. They're hiking upstream in swimsuits just to float back into town. I join them—marveling at how this exercise brings out the silly in a people who are generally anything but.

Every hundred yards, concrete steps lead into the swift-flowing river, which looks glacial blue but is surprisingly warm. Leaping in, I'm immediately caught up in the racing current and propelled toward the grand city center, along with other carefree swimmers and a flotilla of rubber rafts.

Nearing downtown, I stroke over to snare a metal stair railing—I'm nervous that I'll miss the last one and rush toward the city's scary weir and, it seems, oblivion. Hanging onto the railing with me is a tanned and wiry grandmother and several giddy children, clearly enjoying an afternoon going up and down the river.

I crawl out, dry off, and put on the clothes that I'd stashed here earlier. Setting out for a stroll, I come across

---

Fast Facts

Biggest cities: Zürich (377,000), Geneva (188,000), Basel (165,000), Bern (capital, 126,000)

Size: 16,000 square miles (almost twice the size of New Jersey), population 8 million

Locals call it: Officially it's the Confoederatio Helvetica (Latin for Swiss Confederation); also known as die Schweiz (German), la Suisse (French), la Svizzera (Italian), and la Svizra (Romansh)

Currency: Swiss franc

Languages: Swiss German (most of Switzerland), French (to the west), Italian (to the south), Romansh (southeastern mountains)

Key date: 1815, Switzerland's borders (and its neutrality) are established at the Congress of Vienna

Biggest festival: Fasnacht pre-Lenten carnival (February/March, countrywide but biggest in Basel, Bern, and Luzern)

Mountain peaks exceeding 10,000 feet: 437

Handy Swiss-German phrases: *Grüezi* (hello; **grit**-see), *Merci* (thank you; **mehr**-see), *Uf Widerluege* (goodbye; oof **vee**-dehr-loo-eh-geh), *Meh schoggi, bitte* (More chocolate, please; meh **shoh**-chih **bit**-teh)

more kids beating the heat, splashing in the squirt fountains spurting from the granite plaza in front of the parliament building. There are 26 fountains—one for each canton, or Swiss "state." Kids happily dance with each watery eruption, oblivious to the fact that half of Switzerland's gold stock is buried under the square, in the Swiss version of Fort Knox.

That evening for dinner, I walk downstream, where a trendy restaurant has been built over the river. I'm seated over see-through floorboards that expose the water where my tasty local trout might have been caught. The noisy roar of the rushing river masks the conversations of patrons sipping beer on open-air sofas.

Bern's old town, packed into a tight bend in the river, is a joy to explore on foot. After dinner, I amble through the lanes lined with miles of shopping arcades. This is my kind of shopping town: Prices are so high, there's no danger of buying. The local slang for the corridor under these arcades is *"Rohr"* (German for pipe). To stroll through the town is to go *"rohren"* (piping).

As the city grew over the centuries, its successive walls and moats were torn down, providing vast, people-friendly swaths of land. Today these elongated "squares" are popular for markets and outdoor cafés—the top places to be seen in the evening. I come upon an open-air performance by a jazz band whose lead instrument is a long alphorn, an improbable meeting of tradition and modernity.

Though I've said it's almost criminal to spend a sunny Swiss day anywhere but high in the Alps, the cities of Switzerland can be a delight and I'd make an exception for urban but easygoing Bern.

> Most people come to Switzerland for the mountains, but its cities are worth visiting, too. Located within a tight bend in the Aare River, the capital, Bern, with its fine arcades, is the most charming

Scared Silly on the *Via Ferrata*

I'm careful not to list activities in my guidebooks that might encourage a traveler to take a risk on something that's

The most I can handle in alpine thrills is a *via ferrata*. Hitched to the cable with carabiners, I worked my way along the cliff high above the Lauterbrunnen Valley floor.

dangerous. So when friends in the Lauterbrunnen Valley started talking about a great new outdoor experience called a *via ferrata*—a mountain route with fixed cables—I had to check it out myself.

I enlisted my B&B host, Olle, to join me. We put on helmets and mountaineering harnesses, clipped our carabiners into the first stretch of the 1.5-mile-long cable, and set off with a local guide. My hike on the "iron way" from Mürren to Gimmelwald proved to be the highlight of my entire trip.

The route took us along the very side of the cliff, like tiny window washers on a geologic skyscraper. About half of the route is easily walked, and I was lulled into wondering, what's the big deal? But for several hundred yards, the path literally hangs out over...nothing. The "trail" ahead of me was a series of steel rebar spikes jutting out from the side of the mountain. The cable, carabiner, and harness were there in case I passed out. For me, physically, this was the max. I was almost numb with fear.

At some points, ladders drilled vertically into the cliff made it easier (in my case, possible) to scramble up or down. There were three thrilling canyon crossings—by zipline, on a single high wire (with steadying wires for each hand), and the "iron way," finished with a terrifying hanging bridge.

After one particularly harrowing crossing—gingerly taking one rebar step after another—I said to the guide, "OK, now it gets easier?" And he said, "No. Now comes *die Hammer Ecke* (Hammer Corner)!" For about 500 feet, we crept across a perfectly vertical cliff face—feet gingerly gripping rebar loops, cold and raw hands on the cable, tiny cows and a rushing river 2,000 feet below me, a rock face rocketing directly above me—as my follow-the-cable path bent out of sight.

Three hours after we had clipped in, we finally reached the end. Olle and I beamed, exhilarated that we had survived our little personal test. We hugged our guide like a full-body high-five, knowing this was the thrill of a lifetime. For the next several nights, though, I awoke in the wee hours, clutching my mattress.

More Swiss Experiences

Switzerland's Best Castle: I like to imagine myself as a member of the aristocracy that inhabited Château de Chillon in the Middle Ages. The castle is set wistfully at the edge of Lake Geneva on the outskirts of Montreux. Remarkably well preserved, it has never been damaged or destroyed—it's always been inhabited and maintained. Because it's built on a rocky island, Château de Chillon has a uniquely higgledy-piggledy shape that combines a stout fortress and dank prison (on the land side) with a visually splendid residence (on the lake side). Over the centuries, the romantic castle has inspired a multitude of writers—Lord Byron, Victor Hugo, Charles Dickens, Goethe, Ernest Hemingway. (You can still see where Byron scratched his name into a column.) All the sumptuous detail indoors can't compare with what's outside, though. At the end of my visit, I curl up on a windowsill to enjoy lake views fit for a king.

Riding High: Switzerland's best attraction might just be hiding between the cities and the villages. In this land of rugged mountains and picture-perfect farms—perhaps more than anywhere else in Europe—the journey is the destination. Several trains, many with special panoramic cars, run

LEFT Château de Chillon

RIGHT Scenic train riding in Switzerland

picturesque routes through the country's prettiest places. The Glacier Express, which traverses southern Switzerland, gets my vote for the most scenic of these rides. Designed to maximize sightseeing thrills, the route is a masterpiece of railway engineering, with the train running through 91 tunnels and crossing 291 bridges. A toothed rack between the tracks helps the hardworking train drag itself up steep gradients, and these same teeth help slow the train on downhill sections. Using powerful snowplow engines to keep the track open through the snowy winter, the Glacier Express runs year-round.

CULTURE AND TRADITIONS: EVERYTHING'S SO...SWISS

Cheese Cuisine

The Swiss eat about 150,000 tons of cheese per year. After a few days of cheese plates for breakfast, cheese sandwiches for lunch, and cheese specialties for dinner, even the biggest cheese lovers might find they need a dairy detox.

There are two kinds of Swiss restaurants—with and without cooked cheese. The Swiss eat out at a "cooked cheese" restaurant because they don't want to perfume their houses with the smell. Some cheese dishes are meant for sharing, like *raclette* and fondue. For *raclette*, cheese is slowly melted on a special grill; as the cheese softens, diners scrape a chunk off and eat it with potatoes, pickled onions, and gherkins. Fondue is Switzerland's best-known cheese dish, made with Emmentaler or Gruyère melted with white wine, garlic, nutmeg, and cherry schnapps. Eating it is a communal affair, with everyone dipping cubes of bread into the melted cheese with a long fork. A Swiss friend told me:

From a steamy fondue treat (left) to cheering the cows along on the day they head up to the high meadows (right), Switzerland's traditions are alive, well, and accessible for travelers.

"When we Swiss plan a cozy party we add *'FIGUGEGL'* to the invitation. It's pronounced like a word: fee-GOO-geck-ul. This stands for *'Fondu isch guet und git e gueti Luune'* (Fondue is good and gives a good mood). When you read this, you know a good time is planned."

More Cowbells

Swiss dairy farming in the mountains isn't lucrative, but a lifestyle chosen to keep tradition alive. Rather than lose their children to the cities, Swiss farmers have the opposite problem: Kids argue about who gets to take over the family herd.

In summer, farmers strap elaborate ceremonial bells on their cows and take them up to huts at high elevations, where they stay for about 100 days. When the cows arrive at their summer home, the bells are hung under the eaves.

Hired hands get up at dawn to milk the cows, take them to pasture, and then milk the cows again in the evening. It's too difficult to transport the milk down to the village, so it is made into treasured "Alp cheese" right on the mountain. The character of each wheel of cheese is shaped by the herbs and flowers consumed by the cows, and locals can tell which valley the cows grazed in by the taste.

Meanwhile, the farmer follows the seasons up into the mountains, making hay while the sun shines and storing it above the huts. In late summer, the cows start down from the high pastures, moving from hut to hut, eating the hay prepared for them. The day the cows return to their home village is an impromptu festival, with the farmers parading their animals through town to their winter barn.

Money, Money, Money

A graffito in Zürich jokes: "Zürich = *zu reich, zu ruhig*" (too rich, too quiet). In a country with a reputation for being one of Europe's most expensive, Zürich is the major hub of international banking and finance. A huge part of the Swiss

Dining on a Budget

Grocery stores and cafeterias are a godsend for thrifty travelers in pricey Switzerland. Larger grocery stores often have a great selection of prepared foods and picnic fixings—perfect for al fresco dining. In most big cities, major department stores have a self-service eatery with lush salad bars, tasty entrées, and fresh-squeezed juices. Swiss hostels usually offer a fine four-course dinner that's often open to non-guests—just call first to reserve a spot.

Quench your thirst at Switzerland's free drinking fountains—with fresh, mountain-chilled water—in squares and other central points around cities and towns. Fill your bottle from the spout of any well-maintained public fountain unless you see a *kein Trinkwasser* ("not drinking water") sign.

economy is based on providing a safe and secret place for wealthy people from around the world to stash their money. (When bank fees are figured in, tax cheats and white-collar crooks actually get negative interest to keep their money anonymously in Switzerland.) Switzerland sticks to its own Swiss franc, partly because adopting the euro currency would require complying with European Union regulations, putting an end to the country's lucrative secrecy.

Switzerland Travel Resources from Rick Steves

Guidebooks

Check out Rick's guidebook covering all of Switzerland; plus his 3-in-1 French, Italian & German phrase book

TV Shows

The quintessence of Switzerland with Rick as your host, viewable on public television and at ricksteves.com. Episodes cover the Alps, Luzern, Lausanne, Bern, and Zürich

Organized Tours

Small group tours, with itineraries planned by Rick: Germany, Austria & Switzerland in 14 Days, My Way: Alpine Europe in 12 Days

For more on all of these resources, visit ricksteves.com

Austria

Austria offers gorgeous alpine scenery, great museums, cobbled quaintness, and decadent pastry. The former head of the Habsburg Empire (one of Europe's grandest), Austria is content to bask in good living and its opulent past. The Habsburgs built a vast kingdom of more than 60 million people by making love, not war—having lots of children and strategically marrying them into the other royal houses of Europe.

Today, this small, landlocked country clings to its storied past more than any other nation in Europe. The waltz is still the rage. Music has long been a key part of Austria's heritage. The giants of classical music—Haydn, Mozart, Beethoven— were born here or moved here to write and perform their masterpieces. Music lovers flock to Salzburg every summer to attend its popular festival. Vienna has the much-loved

The gardens of Schönbrunn Palace, just outside Vienna, are made for endless wandering.

Opera House and Boys' Choir. But traditional folk music is also part of the Austrian soul. The world's best-loved Christmas carol, "Silent Night," was written by two Austrians with just a guitar for accompaniment. And don't be surprised if you hear yodeling for someone's birthday.

The country is much more than its famous cities of Vienna and Salzburg. Awash with mountains and waterfalls, Austria is sprinkled with small towns (like Hallstatt), ruined castles (Ehrenberg), and tucked-away farms (everywhere).

Austrians are relaxed, gregarious people who love hiking in the outdoors as much as enjoying a good cup of coffee in a café. With one of Europe's longest life spans and shortest work weeks, they specialize in *Gemütlichkeit*—meaning a warm, cozy, focus-on-the-moment feeling.

It must be nice to be past your prime—no longer troubled by being powerful, able to kick back and celebrate life, whether engulfed in mountain beauty or bathed in lavish high culture.

Fast Facts

Biggest cities: Vienna (capital, 1.7 million), Graz (265,000), Linz (191,000), Salzburg (148,000)

Size: 32,400 square miles (about the size of South Carolina), population 8.2 million

Locals call it: Österreich ("Eastern Empire")

Currency: Euro

Key date: June 28, 1914, Archduke Franz Ferdinand of Austria is assassinated, setting off World War I

Language: German, with many words (especially for food) exclusive to Austria

Biggest festival: Salzburg Festival (late July and August, classical music)

Handy German phrases: *Grüss Gott* (Austrian version of hello, "May God greet you"; grews goht), *Bitte* (please; **bit**-teh), *Danke* (thank you; **dahn**-keh)

FAVORITE SIGHTS AND MEMORABLE EXPERIENCES IN AUSTRIA

Lovely, Lovable Hallstatt

When I think of my favorite towns in Europe, I'll take the offbeat places, where creaky locals walk gingerly on creaky floorboards, and where each balcony sports a one-of-a-kind flowerbox. The tiny town of Hallstatt, positioned picture-perfectly on the shore of Lake Hallstatt, is just such a place.

Hallstatt, a two-hour train ride east of Salzburg, is the pride and joy of the Salzkammergut Lake District. It's a gentle land—idyllic and majestic—where lakes and mountains are shuffled sloppily together...the perfect place to commune with nature, Austrian-style. Even just arriving at Hallstatt is fun—from the train station, people take a shuttle boat across a lake to get to town. It's rare that a place's charm

LEFT Hallstatt is the cutest town in Austria.

RIGHT The area around Salzburg is dotted with old salt mines, like the one above Hallstatt Dressed up like a miner, you'll slide down from one level to the next on wooden chutes

will get me out of bed early, but there's something about the glassy waters of Lake Hallstatt viewed from the high end of town: The church spire is mirrored in the tranquil water, and then the shuttle boat slices through the reflection—like a knife putting a swirl in the icing on a big cake.

Bullied onto its lakeside ledge by a selfish mountain, Hallstatt seems tinier than it is. Its pint-size square is surrounded by ivy-covered guesthouses and cobbled lanes. It's a toy town, tourable on foot in about 10 minutes. But the ledge couldn't hold Hallstatt forever, and many of its buildings climb the mountainside. Still, land is limited—so limited that there's not enough room for the dead. Remains evicted from the cemetery are stacked neatly in an eerie chapel of decorated bones. Each skull has been carefully named, dated, and decorated. The men's skulls are painted with ivy, and the women's with roses.

Nearly three thousand years ago, this area was the major salt producer of Europe, when salt—a natural preservative for food—was in great demand. The economic and cultural boom put Hallstatt on the map back in Flintstone times. A humble museum next to the tourist office shows off Hallstatt's salty past. For a better look, I took a guided tour of what's said to be the world's oldest salt mine, located a thrilling funicular ride above downtown Hallstatt. Dressed up in an old miner's outfit, I walked through a tunnel dug in 1719 and into the mountain where the salt was mined, explored several caverns, and screamed down a long wooden chute while praying for no splinters.

These days, it can be a challenge to find vivid cultural traditions that survive in well-discovered places like Hallstatt. But on a recent visit, as the sun rose late over the towering Alps, my friend, who runs a restaurant in town, took me for a spin in his classic boat. It's a *Fuhr*, a

Austria's Top Destinations

Vienna ▲▲▲   allow 2-4 days
Genteel and worldly capital city, brimming with a rich Habsburg heritage (spectacular palaces and top-notch art museums), grand classical music, a refined café tradition, and convivial wine gardens

Top Sights
St. Stephen's Cathedral Enormous, historic Gothic cathedral
Hofburg Former winter palace of Habsburg emperors, with a treasury of crown jewels
Schönbrunn Palace Spectacular summer residence, with manicured gardens
Kunsthistorisches Museum Exhibit of Habsburgs' collection of European masters
Vienna Opera Internationally renowned opera house

Salzburg ▲▲   2 days
Musical mecca huddled under a dramatic castle, with an old town full of winding lanes, Baroque churches, Mozart landmarks, and *Sound of Music* kitsch

Salzkammergut ▲▲   1-2 days
Scenic land of lakes and forested mountains, starring the dramatically situated, picturesque village of **Hallstatt**

Danube Valley ▲   1-2 days
Romantic, bikeable valley dotted with ruined castles, offset by the glorious Melk Abbey and poignant Mauthausen concentration camp memorial

Tirol ▲   1-2 days
Austria's mountain-sports region, encompassing view-rich **Innsbruck,** quaint **Hall,** and castle home-base **Reutte**

centuries-old boat design, which was made wide and flat for shipping heavy bushels of locally mined salt across shallow waters. Lunging rhythmically on the single oar, he said, "An hour on the lake is for me like a day of vacation." I asked about the oarlock, which looked like a skinny dog-chew doughnut, and he told me, "It's made from the gut of a bull—not of a cow, but a bull."

Returning to the weathered timber boathouse, we passed a teenage boy with a wooden club systematically grabbing trout from the fishermen's pen and killing them one by one with a stern whack to the noggin. Another man carried them to the tiny fishery to be gutted by a guy who, 40 years ago, did the stern whacking. A cat waited outside the door, confident his breakfast would be a good one. And restaurateurs and homemakers alike—their dining rooms decorated with trophies of big ones that didn't get away—lined up to buy fresh trout to feed the hungry tourists, or a good fish to cook for a special friend.

Traditions are embattled everywhere by the modern world, yet they manage to survive. Despite tourism—and sometimes thanks to tourism—traditional Europe hangs in there. So when I want to cloak myself in *Gemütlichkeit*, flowers, and cobblestones, I visit Hallstatt—where, when friends invite you to visit, they say, "Please come by. I'll cook you a good fish."

Toasting Vienna's Love of Life

If any European capital knows how to enjoy life, it's Vienna. Compared to most modern urban centers, the pace of life here is leisurely. Chatting with friends at a wine garden is not a special event but a regular, frequent occurrence.

For many Viennese, the living room is down the street at the neighborhood coffeehouse, which offers fresh pastries,

From rich chocolate cakes to cozy wine gardens, it's hard not to get caught up in the good life when visiting Austria.

light lunches, a wide selection of newspapers, and a "take all the time you want" ambience (in spite of famously grumpy waiters). One of my ritual stops is at Café Hawelka. Draped in its circa-1900 decor, this smoke-and-coffee-stained café seems frozen in time, with paintings by struggling artists (who couldn't pay for coffee), velvet couches, and a phone that rings for regulars. I could be sitting in a chair that had once been occupied by Trotsky, Hitler, Stalin, Freud, or any number of historical figures who rattled around Vienna 100 years ago. Savoring a *Buchtel* (a marmalade-filled doughnut), I ponder how Vienna was a place of intellectual tumult at the end of World War I, as Europe's family-run empires crumbled.

> ### Fast Food, Austrian-Style
>
> In Austria, you're never far from a *Würstelstand* (sausage stand). Most bakeries sell small, cheap sandwiches; look for *Leberkäsesemmel* (roll filled with Austrian meatloaf) as well as *Schnitzelsemmel* (schnitzel sandwich). *Stehcafés* (food counters) usually offer open-face finger sandwiches (*belegte Brote*) with a wide array of toppings. For a quick bite, have a deli make you a *Wurstsemmel*—a basic sausage sandwich.

Another one of my Vienna rituals is to pop into Demel, the ultimate Viennese chocolate shop and bakery. It's filled with Art Nouveau boxes of choco-dreams come true: *Kandierte Veilchen* (candied violet petals), *Katzenzungen* (chocolate shaped like "cats' tongues"), and an impressive cancan of cakes—including the Sacher torte, a local specialty. Apart from its apricot filling, the Sacher-torte recipe seems pretty simple...chocolate on chocolate. Fancy shops like Demel boast "K.u.K." on their signs, meaning good enough for the "König und Kaiser"—king and emperor (same guy). Easily the saddest thing I witnessed one summer was when, promptly at closing time, all the unsold cakes and pies on Demel's luxurious shelves were unceremoniously dumped into big plastic garbage bags.

For another royally good experience, I head to Vienna's wine gardens—the *Heurigen*. Clustered in foothills at the city's doorstep, mostly in the legendary Vienna Woods, wine-garden restaurants feature cold-cut buffets paired with fine Austrian wines in an old-village atmosphere with strolling musicians. If I'm in town during fall, I try the *Sturm*, the semi-fermented new wine made from the season's first grape harvest. Of the many wine-garden suburbs, I like untouristy Nussdorf.

No matter where I turn in this pleasant city, it's clear that culture is king, and locals are experts at celebrating the art of good living. Here's to Vienna: *Prost!* Cheers!

Alpine Escapes

Even those who know a Rocky Mountain high find something special about the Alps. It's exhilarating to hike on the hilly, wooded trails, passing happy yodelers, sturdy grannies, and dirndled moms with apple-cheeked kids.

In western Austria, the same mountains that put Innsbruck on the vacation map surround nearby Hall. For a lazy look at life in the high Alps around these towns, drive up to 5,000-foot Hinterhornalm and walk to a remote working farm.

Begin your ascent in Gnadenwald, a chalet-filled village sandwiched between Hall and its Alps. Pay at the toll hut, then wind your way upward, marveling at the crazy amount of energy put into this road, to the rustic Hinterhornalm Berg restaurant. This place serves hearty food with a cliff-hanger of a view. Hinterhornalm is a hang-gliding springboard. On sunny days, it's a butterfly nest of thrill seekers ready to fly.

From there, it's a level 20-minute walk to Walderalm, a cluster of three dairy farms with 70 cows that share their meadow with the clouds. The cows ramble along ridgetop lanes surrounded by cut-glass peaks. The ladies of the farms serve soup, sandwiches, and drinks (very fresh milk in the afternoon) on rough plank tables. Below you spreads the Inn River Valley and, in the distance, tourist-filled Innsbruck.

Another alpine escape is Fallerschein, west of Innsbruck. Barely accessible by car, this isolated log-cabin village is smothered with mountain goodness, set in a flower-speckled world of serene slopes, sleepy cows, and musical breezes. Here thunderstorms roll down its valley as if it were God's bowling alley. But the blissfully simple pint-size church on the high ground seems to promise that this huddle of houses will remain standing. The people sitting on benches are Austrian vacationers or clandestine lovers who've rented cabins. Fallerschein is notorious as a hideaway for those having affairs.

More Austrian Experiences

Savoring Salzburg: Salzburg, a musical mecca, is forever smiling to the tunes of Mozart and the *Sound of Music*. The city puts on a huge annual festival as well as constant concerts. With eight million sightseers prowling its cobbled lanes each year, the city can feel pretty touristy. You don't go to Salzburg to avoid the sightseers. You go to experience a town that, in spite of the crowds, is thoroughly entertaining.

After rambling through the old town and past the glorious cathedral, I like to take the funicular up to the towering Hohensalzburg Fortress. One of Europe's mightiest castles, it dominates Salzburg's skyline and offers commanding views of city and countryside.

Another way to take in town and country is on a *Sound of Music* bus tour, sampling Salzburg sights, movie locations, and lovely stretches of the surrounding Salzkammergut Lake District. I took this tour skeptically and actually liked it, even though rolling through the Austrian countryside with 30 Americans singing "Doe, a deer..." is pretty cheesy. But, no matter. With its musical legacies, magnificent scenery, and rich history, Salzburg is a symphony—and you don't have to climb every mountain to enjoy it.

Evocative Castles: Outside the sleepy town of Reutte, not far from the German border, are the ruins of four buildings that once made up the largest fort in Tirol—Ehrenberg. There's the fortified Klause toll booth on the valley floor, which levied duties along the Via Claudia in Roman times; Ehrenberg, the oldest castle on the first hill (from 1296); Fort Claudia, a smaller castle across the valley; and Schlosskopf, the mighty and more modern castle high above. (To combine a visit to Ehrenberg with "Mad" Kind Ludwig's castles just across the border, see "Castle Day in Bavaria and Tirol," page 642.)

When I first visited Ehrenberg, one castle crowned its mountain like an ornery barnacle; the others were lost in a

LEFT Salzburg has a main street lined with traditional business signs.

CENTER One of Europe's biggest castles keeps watch over Salzburg.

RIGHT The stark and evocative Ehrenberg ruins above Reutte

thick forest. Inspired, I hiked up into the misty mountain of meaningless chunks of castle wall pinned down by trees, moss, and sword ferns. But now the hungry forest has been cut away to reveal the castle ensemble, and children and adults with medieval fantasies can leap from rampart to rampart...sword ferns swinging.

CULTURE AND TRADITIONS: EVERYTHING'S SO...AUSTRIAN

Musical Notes

Vienna has a long history as Europe's music capital, and music lovers make a pilgrimage of sorts to see the houses of the composers who lived and worked here. The homes of Schubert, Brahms, Haydn, Beethoven, and Mozart all host museums—but they are mostly small and forgettable. For the best music history experience, I like the Haus der Musik, a museum that honors the great Viennese composers with fine artifacts and fun interactive exhibits. You can try your hand at virtually conducting the Vienna Philharmonic—if you mess up, the "musicians" will refuse to play.

Classical music performances are everywhere in town, booking up to 10,000 seats a night. The Vienna State Opera alone belts out 300 glittering shows a year. Fans of toe-tapping waltzes head to the Kursalon, an elegant hall in the main city park, where Johann Strauss directed concerts 100 years ago. The Vienna Boys' Choir performs in the Hofburg's Imperial Music Chapel. Mozart lovers choose the intimate Theater an der Wien, designed in 1801 especially for Wolfie's operas. This gilded high culture can be surprisingly afford-able—a standing-room ticket for the opera is about the same price as a cinema ticket. Major events can be sold out for

In Vienna's Haus der Musik, you can virtually conduct the city's famed orchestra.

weeks—though there are plenty of live music options available without advance booking.

During the summer, a thriving people scene erupts each evening in the park in front of Vienna's City Hall, where opera and classical music performances are shown for free. Thousands of folding chairs face a 60-foot-wide screen. Scores of food stands and picnic tables are set up. There are no plastic cups, thank you, just real plates and glasses—Vienna wants the quality of the dining experience to be as good as the music. And the people-watching? It's *con brio*.

Mountains

Much of Austria's character is found in its mountains. Austrians excel in mountain climbing and winter sports such as downhill skiing, which was born in Tirol. When watching ski races, you'll often see fans celebrating with red-and-white flags at the finish line: Austria has won more Olympic medals in alpine skiing than any other country. Innsbruck alone—twice the host of the Winter Olympics—is surrounded by 150 mountain lifts, 1,250 miles of trails, and 250 hikers' and skiers' huts. Ski lifts are busy both winter and summer, taking nature lovers to dizzying heights, where the views are big, and the hiking possibilities are endless.

Enjoy some *Germknödel* goodness at high altitude.

Taking a break at a cozy, hospitable hut is a traditional part of Austrian mountain fun. High-altitude huts serve fortifying treats such as *Germknödel* (a sweet dumpling topped with poppy seeds and laced with plum jam), *Kaiserschmarrn* (a cut-up and sugared pancake), and *Glühwein* (red wine mulled with cinnamon and oranges).

Coffee

The story of coffee in Austria is steeped in legend. In the late 17th century, the Ottoman Turks were laying siege to Vienna. A spy working for the Austrians infiltrated the Ottoman ranks and got to know the Turkish lifestyle...including their passion for a drug called coffee. After the Austrians persevered, the ecstatic Habsburg emperor offered the spy anything he wanted. The spy asked for the Ottomans' spilled coffee beans, which he gathered up to start the first coffee shop in town. (It's a nice story. But actually, there was already an Armenian in town running a coffeehouse.)

Take your pick of one of Vienna's many elegant and venerable coffeehouses.

In the 18th century, coffee boomed as an aristocratic drink. In the 19th-century Industrial Age, people were expected to work 12-hour shifts, and coffee became a hit with the working class, too. By the 20th century, the Vienna coffee scene became so refined that old-timers remember when waiters brought a sheet with various shades of brown (like paint samples) so customers could make clear exactly how milky they wanted their coffee.

Austria Travel Resources from Rick Steves

Guidebooks

Check out Rick's guidebook covering Vienna, Salzburg & the Tirol; plus his German phrase book

Audio Europe

Download Rick's free Audio Europe app, with self-guided audio tours, including a Vienna city walk and tours of Vienna's St. Stephen's Cathedral and Ringstrasse

TV Shows

The quintessence of Austria with Rick as your host, viewable on public television and ricksteves.com. Episodes cover Vienna and the Danube, the Austrian Alps, and Salzburg

Organized Tours

Small group tours, with itineraries planned by Rick: Germany, Austria & Switzerland in 14 Days; My Way: Alpine Europe in 12 Days; and Berlin, Prague & Vienna in 12 Days

For more on all of these resources, visit ricksteves.com

Czech Republic

Despite being wedged between Germany and Austria, and battered by 20th-century wars and communist domination, the Czechs have managed to forge one of the most comfortable and easy-to-explore countries of Eastern Europe. Today, the Czech Republic is enjoying an unprecedented prosperity.

The country is composed of two main regions—Bohemia to the west and Moravia to the east, with a tiny slice of Silesia in the upper-right corner. As the longtime home of the Czechs, Bohemia is circled by a naturally fortifying ring of mountains and cut down the middle by the Vltava River. It's best known for its capital city of Prague and its rollicking beer halls. By contrast, the wine-growing region of Moravia is more Slavic and colorful, and more focused on farming.

Prague's Old Town Square

Ninety percent of the tourists who visit the Czech Republic see only Prague...and for good reason. Prague is one of Europe's best-preserved cities. It's an architectural time warp, filled with sumptuous Art Nouveau facades, high art, grand buildings, and back lanes out of the 18th century. You'll feel like royalty strolling down the "King's Walk" from the cathedral into the Old Town. And the city offers a wide-ranging menu of classical concerts and arguably the best beer in Europe.

Outside the capital, you'll enjoy great prices, few tourists, traditional towns, and surprising experiences—whether canoeing through Bohemia, touring the bone chapel in Kutná Hora, or soaking in hot peat soup in Třeboň.

As you travel, talk with Czech people—they bring recent history to life in a way that books can't. And wherever you go, you'll feel the Czech spirit: in the vibrant energy of Prague, the charm of quaint villages like Český Krumlov, and the gentle beauty of the countryside, dotted by wild poppies.

Fast Facts

Biggest cities: Prague (capital, 1.2 million), Brno (380,000), Ostrava (336,000)

Size: 31,000 square miles (similar to South Carolina), population 10.6 million

Locals call it: Česká Republika; Prague is "Praha"

Currency: Czech crown (koruna, Kč, officially CZK)

Key date: January 1, 1993, Czechoslovakia peaceably splits into the Czech Republic and Slovakia

Biggest festival: Prague Spring (May-June, international music)

Handy Czech phrases: Dobrý den (hello; **doh**-bree dehn), Prosim (please; **proh**-zeem), Děkuji (thank you; **dyack**-khuyi), Na zdraví! (Cheers!; nah zdrah-**vee**)

FAVORITE SIGHTS AND MEMORABLE EXPERIENCES IN THE CZECH REPUBLIC

A Historical Walk Through Prague

Prague is a traveler's dream city: exotic but easy, affordable, and with plenty of great sightseeing. My favorite way to soak up the magic is by connecting Prague's major sights with a stroll through its relatively compact core. You'll get an up-close look at charming cobbled streets and fun-loving facades while feeling the sweep of Prague's history, starting at the ninth-century castle from which Czech leaders have ruled for more than 1,000 years and ending at the square where Czechs gained their freedom from communism just a few decades ago.

Perched on a hill overlooking the city, Prague Castle is hailed as being the biggest anywhere, with a 1,500-foot-long series of courtyards, churches, and palaces. If exhausting

Prague's beloved Charles Bridge, straddling the Vltava River, offers one of the most delightful strolls in Europe.

is a measure of big, I'll buy that claim. Whenever I visit the castle, I feel as if I'm in a pinball machine—rolling downhill, bouncing from sight to sight before funneling out the lower gate. The highlight is St. Vitus Cathedral, where locals go to remember Saint Wenceslas, patron saint of the Czechs. This "good king" of Christmas-carol fame was not a king at all, but a wise, benevolent duke of Bohemia. After being assassinated in 935, Wenceslas became a symbol of Czech nationalism. His tomb sits in an extremely fancy chapel.

From the castle, I follow the "King's Walk" into town. This was the ancient route of coronation processions. After being crowned in St. Vitus Cathedral, the new king would walk through the historic town, cross the Charles Bridge, and finish at the Old Town Square. If he hurried, he'd be done in 20 minutes.

The much-loved Charles Bridge gets my vote for Europe's most pleasant quarter-mile stroll. Built in the 1350s, it now features a chorus line of time-blackened Baroque statues towering above a fun string of street vendors and musicians. I love to be on the bridge when the sun is low for the best light, people-watching, and photo opportunities.

After crossing the bridge, I follow the shop-lined street to the Old Town

Avoiding Rip-Offs in Prague

Con artists and pickpockets are definitely an issue in Prague. The city's taxis are notorious for hyperactive meters. At restaurants, tourists are routinely served cheaper meals than what they ordered, given a menu with a "personalized" price list, charged extra for things they didn't get, or shortchanged. Pickpockets—from little children to adults dressed as professionals—target Western tourists. Heed these tips:

- When paying with cash, always count your change.
- In taxis, ask for an estimate up front and insist on using the meter.
- Never let your credit card out of your sight.
- In restaurants, closely examine your bill. Tax is always included in the price, so it shouldn't be tacked on later.

Square. One of the city's top sights, the colorful square is bordered by pastel buildings in diverse architectural styles: Gothic, Renaissance, Baroque, Rococo, and Art Nouveau. This has been a market square since the 11th century, though today, many of the old-time market stalls have been replaced by cafés, touristy horse buggies, and souvenir hawkers. The square's centerpiece is a memorial to Jan Hus, a local preacher who complained about church corruption. Tried for heresy and burned in 1415, Hus has long symbolized the fight for Czech freedom.

Memorial to Jan Palach

Going beyond the "King's Walk," I head to Wenceslas Square, the heart of urban, modern Prague. Whenever I'm here, I'm reminded of the struggles of the Czech people. As my friend Honza explains it, this is where the most dramatic moments in modern Czech history have played out. The Czechoslovak state was proclaimed here in 1918. In 1969, Jan Palach set himself on fire here to protest the puppet Soviet government. And 20 years after his death, massive demonstrations on the square led to the overthrow of the communist government.

"Night after night we assembled here, pulled out our key chains, and jingled them at the president's window, saying, 'It's time to go home now,'" explains Honza. "Then one night the authorities announced he was gone—we had won our freedom." Just being on Wenceslas Square, envisioning the events of November 1989, is compelling. But being here with one of the demonstrators drilled into me the jubilation of a small country winning its freedom from a big one.

Making It Personal with a Local Guide

Prague is one city where, more than just about anywhere else, I recommend hiring a local guide. For about $30 an hour, you get a guide and companion who is expert at giving meaning to your wandering. And if, like me, you are forever fascinated by slice-of-life stories from people who had to live through the Cold War in the Warsaw Pact, it's even more engaging.

On one tour, my guide reminisced about 1989 and how, with the arrival of freedom and the fall of the Iron Curtain,

Russian-language teachers suddenly had to teach English. There were no textbooks, and Russian teachers took cram courses in English so they could teach their students sentences like "Deez eez my bruder" ("This is my brother"). The fun thing for school kids those first few years was that they knew more English from watching Rambo movies than their teachers did from taking the cram courses.

Another guide talked of how, in her youth, she could only dream of drinking a nice cold Coca-Cola. She said, "We couldn't drink Coke, but we could collect the cans tourists threw away. I had five cans. My friend had ten."

Throughout Eastern Europe, guides artfully weave personal memories like these into their time with you.

Boning Up on Kutná Hora

The refreshingly authentic town of Kutná Hora sits upon what once was Europe's largest silver mine. In its heyday, much of the Continent's coinage was minted right here. If you're not claustrophobic, you can don a miner's helmet and climb down to explore the medieval mining shafts. Centuries of mining in the narrow wet shafts have made the ground beneath town resemble a giant honeycomb.

But I'm more fascinated by the Sedlec Church, just outside town. On the outside, the little church looks normal. But inside, the bones of 40,000 people decorate the walls and ceilings. Plagues and wars in the 14th and 15th centuries provided all the raw material necessary for these creepily creative designs. The display was created 400 years ago by monks. Their mission: to remind you (mid-vacation) that before long, you'll be in the same state—so give some thought to how you might be spending eternity. Later bone stackers at Kutná Hora were more interested in design than theology, as evidenced by an illuminating chandelier that includes every bone in the human body.

Czech Republic's Top Destinations

Prague ▲▲▲   allow 2-3 days
One of Europe's most romantic cities, with a remarkably well-preserved Old Town, a thriving New Town packed with Art Nouveau, and fascinating 20th-century history

Top Sights
Old Town Square Beautiful main square with Astronomical Clock
Prague Castle Sprawling hilltop complex of museums, churches, and parks
Charles Bridge Atmospheric, statue-lined bridge enlivened by street music
Jewish Quarter Powerful collection of Jewish sights
Alfons Mucha's *Slav Epic* Massive canvases depicting major events in Slavic history

Nearby
Kutná Hora Workaday Czech town with offbeat bone church
Terezín Concentration camp memorial
Konopiště, Karlštejn, and Křivoklát Trio of impressive castles

Český Krumlov ▲▲   1 day
Charming Bohemian hill town huddled under a colorful castle and hugging a river bend

Southern Bohemian Towns ▲   1-2 days
Třeboň, surrounded by artificial lakes and home to a famous peat spa; **Telč,** with a spectacular main square, and **Třebíč,** with echoes of Jewish history

Olomouc ▲   1 day
Moravian cultural capital, vibrant university city, and home of stinky cheese

With more time, consider visiting
Wallachia Time-passed, mountainous region
Mikulov Wine region, highlighted by the cellars of Pavlov

Spas and Fishy Cuisine in Třeboň

Třeboň, an inviting medieval town in South Bohemia, sits near a biosphere of artificial lakes that date back to the 14th century. Rather than unprofitable wet fields, the nobles wanted ponds that swarmed with fish. Over the years, what was marshland was transformed into a clever combination of lakes, oak-lined dikes, wild meadows, Baroque villages, peat bogs, and pine woods.

These days, people come from near and far to soak in peat, the dark, smelly sludge that's thought to cure aching joints and spines. So I decided to check it out. Immersed in a *One Flew Over the Cuckoo's Nest* ambience, I was ushered to a changing cubicle. The attendant mimed I should take everything off. I climbed into a stainless-steel tub, she pulled a plug, and I quickly disappeared under a rising sea of dark-brown sawdust broth. When finished, I showered off the sludge, then laid face down in what felt like a nurse's office while my attendant gave me a vigorous massage. I walked out with my shirt stuck to my skin by a mucky massage cream...and without a clue what soaking in that peat soup was supposed to accomplish.

Třeboň is also the fish-raising capital of the country. So if you visit Třeboň, you have to eat fish. Like the Italians do with pasta, the Czechs of Třeboň cook fish with both passion and variety. One time, I went to a local eatery and ordered all the fishy appetizers on the menu. The result was a tapas-style meal of "soused" (pickled) herring, fried loach, "stuffed carp sailor-fashion," cod liver, pike caviar, and something my Czech friends translated as "fried carp sperm." I said, "You can't fry sperm." And everyone at my table insisted that, while female fish have a whole trough full of eggs (caviar), the males have a trough full of the male counterpart—and it's cookable. Fried carp sperm tasted like fried oyster, and it had the same texture, too.

While the Czech town of Třeboň sees few American travelers, it's famous locally for its trout.

As we ate, I noticed that the writing on my beer glass said, "Bohemia Regent anno 1379." It occurred to me that I was drinking and eating the same thing that people here have been consuming for over 600 years: local brew and fish from the reservoir just outside the town gate.

More Czech Experiences

Canoeing in Český Krumlov: With its simple beauty and wonderfully medieval feel, Český Krumlov is the quaint, small-town Europe that many people dream of experiencing. An especially pleasant way to connect with this fairytale town is from the waters of the Vltava River. It's easy to rent a canoe or rubber raft from the outfitters in town. Floating down the lazy river, you'll pass through Bohemian forests and other villages, drifting past cafés and pubs happy to welcome you for a break. You'll eventually end up at a 13th-century abbey. From here, hop on the outfitter's shuttle back to town or borrow a bike from them and pedal back along the path.

The Stinky Cheese of Olomouc: Try the sour, foul-smelling, yet beloved specialty of the Haná region, Olomouc cheese sticks (*olomoucké tvarůžky*). The milk goes through a process of natural maturation under chunks of meat. Czechs figure there are two types of people in the world: *tvarůžky* lovers and sane people. The *tvarůžky* are so much a part of the Haná and Czech identity that when the European Union tried to forbid the product, the Czech government negotiated for an official permission to continue to rot their milk. Zip a few of these stinkers in a baggie, and you can count on getting a train compartment to yourself.

In the Czech Republic, you can canoe into the wonderfully medieval town of Český Krumlov (left), dare to eat the infamous "stinky cheese" of Olomouc (center), and exercise your freedom of thought at Prague's Lennon Wall (right).

Prague's Lennon Wall: After John Lennon's death in 1980, Prague's Lennon Wall spontaneously appeared. This was

back in Cold War times, when Lennon's visionary ideas inspired many locals. They'd paint "All You Need Is Love," "Imagine," and other graffiti borrowed from Lennon on the wall. Night after night, the police would paint over the graffiti. And day after day, it would reappear. Until independence came in 1989, travelers, freedom lovers, and hippies gathered here. Silly as it might seem, this wall is remembered as a place that gave hope to locals craving freedom. Though the tension and danger associated with this wall are long gone, it remains a colorful, nostalgic, and poignant place to visit.

CULTURE AND TRADITIONS: EVERYTHING'S SO...CZECH

Classical Music

From Antonín Dvořák to Gustav Mahler, the Czech Republic has a rich heritage in classical music. You'll find it everywhere in Prague, which has museums dedicated to the lives and work of Dvořák, Bedřich Smetana (the father of Czech classical music), and Mozart, who hailed from Austria but spent a lot of time here.

Each day, classical concerts designed for tourists fill delightful Old World halls and churches, including the Art Nouveau Municipal House (where the Prague Symphony Orchestra plays), the classical Neo-Renaissance Rudolfinum (home of the Czech Philharmonic), and the National Theater (great for opera and ballet). Or you can simply drop by Castle Square and see Josef and his Prague Castle Orchestra playing for free on the street. A highlight is hearing them play Smetana's masterwork, *Die Moldau* (the unofficial anthem of the Czech Republic). If I were the mayor of Prague, I'd book this trio for the rest of their musical days to bring joy to the city's many tourists at the gateway to its most visited sight and the orchestra's namesake, Prague Castle.

Czech Beer

Czechs are among the world's most enthusiastic beer drinkers—adults drink an average of 80 gallons a year. Whether you're in a restaurant or traditional beer hall, beer (*pívo*) hits your table like a glass of water does in the States. A new serving will automatically appear when the old glass is almost empty. (You must tell the waiter not to bring more.) On my early trips, I used to have a big beer at lunch and spend the rest of the day wobbly...sightseeing on what I called "Czech

The Czech Republic is a land where classical music bursts out in the streets and the cuisine sticks to your ribs.

knees." Now I resist a momentum-killing beer at lunch and finish each day with a fresh draft beer.

The Czechs invented Pilsner-style lager in Plzeň, and the result, Pilsner Urquell, is on tap in many pubs. Other good beers include Krušovice, Gambrinus, Staropramen, and Kozel. Each establishment serves only one brand of beer on tap (to find out which, look for its sign outside). Unlike many other Europeans, Czechs don't mix beers, and they don't bar-hop. They say, "In one night, you must stay loyal to one woman and to one beer."

Stick-to-Your-Ribs Cuisine

The Czechs have one of Europe's most filling cuisines. Heavy on meat, potatoes, and cabbage, it's hearty and tasty—designed to keep peasants or sightseers fueled through a day of hard work. Expect thick soups, rustic bread, and meaty main dishes such as beef goulash or wild boar. Czech dumplings (*knedlíky*) are a staple. These aren't round, puffy dough balls—they resemble slices of steamed white bread and are meant to be drowned in gravy. There are also sweet dumplings loaded with fresh strawberries, blueberries, apricots, or plums, and garnished with custard and melted butter.

Czech Republic Travel Resources from Rick Steves

Guidebooks
Check out Rick's guidebooks covering Prague & the Czech Republic and Eastern Europe

Audio Europe
Download Rick's free Audio Europe app, with self-guided audio tours, including a walk through Prague

TV Shows
The quintessence of the Czech Republic with Rick as your host, viewable on public television and ricksteves.com. Episodes cover Prague, Olomouc, Třeboň, and Český Krumlov

Organized Tours
Small group tours, with itineraries planned by Rick: Prague & Budapest in 8 Days; Berlin, Prague & Vienna in 12 Days; and Eastern Europe in 16 Days

For more on all of these resources, visit ricksteves.com

Poland

Poland may not appear at the top of many travelers' wish lists, and that's just one reason you may want to visit. With gorgeous towns, evocative sights, an epic history, and low prices, Poland is a diamond in the rough. While parts of the country are still cleaning up the industrial mess left by the Soviets, visitors today are speechless when they set foot on the country's vibrant main squares, in-love-with-life pedestrian drags, and sophisticated shopping boulevards.

Poland is as big as Italy and nearly as populous as Spain. It's also quite flat, with rolling fields. This lack of natural barriers—and Poland's proximity to powerful neighbors (Germany, Russia, Austria, Sweden)—have left the country with a troubled history that's often meant being part of someone else's empire.

This dynamic past has inspired a powerful patriotism among Poles. They are a kind-hearted people: noble, soft spoken, and quite shy. Occasionally they strike first-time visitors as brusque. But extroverts quickly learn that all it takes is a smile and a friendly hello (*Dzień dobry!*) to break through the tough exterior that helped these people survive Poland's difficult times.

The 10 million Americans who trace their roots to Poland find something enticingly familiar here, from the comfort food their Busia cooked them to the kindness of distant cousins they encounter. Many return home with a renewed appreciation for their mother country.

Poland's best attractions are its

big cities: the cultural capital and university burg of Kraków; the picture-perfect old merchant town of Gdańsk; and the cosmopolitan business hub of Warsaw. Leaving these population centers, you're immersed in a gently beautiful countryside, where humble farmers work the same plots and live the same uncomplicated, agrarian lifestyle of their great-grandparents.

The resilience of Poland's culture and the warmth of its people inspire me. Thankfully, these are good times in Poland, a nation with a rich past and an exciting future.

FAVORITE SIGHTS AND MEMORABLE EXPERIENCES IN POLAND

Charismatic Kraków

Kraków is easily Poland's best destination: a beautiful, old-fashioned city buzzing with history, enjoyable sights, tourists, and college students. Even though the country's capital moved from here to Warsaw 400 years ago, Kraków remains Poland's cultural and intellectual center. Of all the Eastern European cities claiming to be "the next Prague," Kraków is for real.

The Old Town, within Kraków's medieval walls, converges on one of the most charismatic squares in Europe: the Main Market Square. I choose a café, sink deep into my chair, and absorb the gorgeously intact buildings around me.

Vast as it is, the square has a folksy intimacy. It bustles with street musicians, cotton-candy vendors, gawking tourists, local teens practicing break-dancing moves for tips, and the lusty coos of pigeons. A folk band—swaggering in their colorful peasant costumes—gives me a private little concert. Feeling flush, I tip them royally. (Perhaps too royally. Be warned: A big tip gets you "The Star-Spangled Banner.")

I suddenly hear a bugle call. Glancing around, I eventually pan up to see its source: a trumpet poking out the window of the tallest tower of

Fast Facts

Biggest cities: Warsaw (capital,1.7 million), Kraków (757,000), Łódź (747,000)

Size: 122,000 square miles (similar to New Mexico), population 38 million

Locals call it: Polska

Currency: Polish złoty

Key date: August 14, 1980, Lech Wałęsa leads the first successful workers' strike in Soviet territory

Biggest festivals: Jewish Cultural Festival (late June-early July, Kraków), St. Dominic's Fair (late July-mid-August, Gdańsk, market stalls, musical performances, and general revelry)

Handy Polish phrases: *Dzień dobry* (hello; jehn **doh**-brih), *Proszę* (please; **proh**-sheh), *Dziękuję* (thank you; jehn-**koo**-yeh), *Na zdrowie!* (Cheers!; nah **zdroh**-vyeh)

the hulking, red-brick St. Mary's Church. Just as I spot the sun glinting off of the trumpet's bell, the song stops abruptly, causing the crowd below to chuckle and applaud appreciatively. This tune—performed every hour on the hour—comes with a legend: During the 1241 Tatar invasion, a watchman saw the enemy approaching and sounded the alarm. Before he could finish, an arrow pierced his throat—which is why even today, the music stops *subito,* partway through.

Ready to move on from my perch, I toss a few zlotys on the table to cover my tab—and head underground into the Rynek Underground Museum. The Main Market Square sits on top of 500 years of history. When it was renovated recently, workers found so many coins, tools, and artifacts of archaeological value that the city opened this excellent museum. Here, at 12 feet below street level, I get an intimate look at medieval Kraków life.

Back on the streets of Kraków, I find that this city, more than any other in Europe, is made for aimless strolling. As I linger my way through town, I'm lucky enough to stumble into Staropolskie Trunki ("Old Polish Drinks"), a friendly little place with a long bar and countless local vodkas and liquors—each one open and ready to be sampled. For about $3, I get a complete vodka education with a cheery local barista who talks me through five different tastes.

Happy after my private vodka tour, I keep walking to clear my head. Eventually I wind up in Kazimierz, the city's historic Jewish Quarter. Once upon a time, the majority of Europe's Jewish people lived in Poland. And Kraków was their most important and influential center. Few Jews still live in the neighborhood, but the spirit of their traditions survives in a handful of synagogues and cemeteries.

Kazimierz is one of the many places where the big events of World War II intersected with ordinary, everyday lives.

Kraków, with its vast yet people-friendly main square and its numerous cafés and pubs, manages to be both trendy and convivial at the same time.

The businessman Oskar Schindler ran his factory here, saving the lives of more than a thousand of his Jewish workers. Now, one of Europe's best museums about the Nazi occupation fills the building where Schindler and his employees worked. While the museum tells the story of Schindler and his workers, it also broadens its perspective to take in the full experience of all of Kraków during the painful era of Nazi rule.

While tourists come to see Kazimierz's historic sights during the day, this isn't a "preserved" neighborhood. It's lively and fun. Throngs of young clubbers clog the streets after dark. The Kazimierz market square retains the gritty flavor of the town before tourism and gentrification. And countless bohemian-chic restaurants make Kazimierz a destination for dinner. On a balmy summer night, it's the perfect spot to end a day in Poland's "second" city.

Historic, Heroic Gdańsk

A port city on the Baltic Coast of Poland, Gdańsk is truly amazing—and amazingly historic. You may associate it with dreary images of striking shipyard workers from the nightly news in the 1980s—but this is one of northern Europe's most historic and picturesque places.

Gdańsk's appealing old town boasts block after block of red-brick churches and narrow, colorful, ornately decorated burghers' mansions. The riverfront embankment, with its trademark medieval crane, oozes salty maritime charm. When the Polish kings came to visit this well-to-do city, they'd gawk along the same route trod by tourists today—which is still called the "Royal Way." Entering through the old town's ornamental gateway, I overheard a fellow traveler gasping, "It's like stepping into a Fabergé egg!"

North of the town center, the charms of the old core fade

Milk Bars

All over Poland, you'll find "milk bars" *(bar mleczne)*—cafeterias that combine good, affordable meals with a fun cultural experience. These are leftovers from communist times, when the government subsidized low-cost eateries for its workers. Despite the misleading name, milk bars serve not just milk, but all sorts of traditional Polish dishes.

The idea of a cheap and hearty meal survived communism, and decades later, you'll still find a wide variety of these budget cafeterias. Some are slick and modern, with excellent food and slightly higher prices. Others are holdovers from the old days (with a certain Soviet je ne sais quoi), where you can snare a fast and forgettable meal for about $5. Just head to the counter and point to what you want.

as you approach the Gdańsk shipyard. For me, the hike to the shipyard isn't about sightseeing; it's a pilgrimage. This is where the Polish Solidarity union was born, kicking off the beginning of the end of Soviet domination in Eastern Europe. It's remarkable to think that it all came down to the gumption of just a motley collection of workers, led by electrician-turned-labor-organizer Lech Wałęsa.

Gdańsk, a rugged port town on Poland's Baltic coast (left), remembers its shipyard workers who heroically helped bring down the Soviet Union (right).

My guide, Agnus, told the story vividly as we stood at the gate under a "Solidarity" banner– draped where a big "LENIN" sign once hung. For 18 days in 1980, protestors huddled behind the shipyard's main gate, refusing to leave until they had won unprecedented concessions from the communists—including the right to strike. A crude yellow board lists the workers' original demands. Their action sparked a wave of strikes and sit-ins that spread along the industrialized north coast of Poland.

When Solidarity negotiated its way to victory in 1980, one of their conditions was that the Soviets let Poland erect a monument to workers killed a decade earlier while demonstrating for the same workers' rights. The government agreed, marking the first time a communist regime ever allowed a monument to be built to honor victims of communist oppression. Lech Wałęsa likened it to a harpoon in the heart of the communists.

The towering monument, with three crucified anchors on top, was designed, engineered, and built by shipyard workers. Just four months after the historic agreement was signed, the monument was finished. Today on Gdańsk's Solidarity Square, the monument, with a trio of 140-foot-tall crosses, honors those martyred comrades and is a highlight of any visit to this city.

I'm inspired when regular people stand bravely in the face of tyranny anywhere in the world. And the Polish

Poland's Top Destinations

Kraków ▲▲▲   allow 2-3 days

Poland's cultural, intellectual, and historical capital, with an easy-to-enjoy Old Town, thought-provoking Jewish quarter, important castle, many churches, and one of Europe's finest town squares

Top Sights

Main Market Square Stunning core of Kraków and a people magnet any time of day
Wawel Castle and Cathedral Poland's historical and spiritual heart
Churches Including St. Mary's (Gothic altarpiece) and St. Francis Basilica (Art Nouveau)
Kazimierz Jewish quarter with synagogues, cemeteries, and Oskar Schindler's factory

Nearby

Auschwitz-Birkenau Notorious Nazi concentration camp, now a compelling memorial
Wieliczka Salt Mine Sprawling underground caverns with sculptures hewn from salt
Nowa Huta Planned workers' suburb, offering an evocative taste of communist times

Warsaw ▲▲   1-3 days

Poland's modern capital, with an appealing urban tempo, stately and sophisticated boulevards, a reconstructed Old Town, and cutting-edge museums (covering WWII history, Fryderyk Chopin, Jewish culture, Polish art, and more)

Gdańsk ▲▲   2 days

Historic trading city, featuring a showpiece old town lined with marvelous facades, a salty maritime charm, and the shipyard where Lech Wałęsa's Solidarity trade union challenged the communists

workers standing up to a repressive and seemingly invincible Soviet empire is a perfect example of courage in action.

Poland's Hometown Hero

A speedy nine years after his death, Karol Józef Wojtyła was made a saint. And today, when you travel in Poland, you'll find John Paul II wherever you go.

The man who would become St. John Paul II lived, studied, and served as a priest and archbishop in Kraków. Many people, including the last Soviet head of state, Mikhail Gorbachev, credit John Paul II for the collapse of Eastern European communism. His Polish compatriots—even the relatively few nonbelievers—saw him both as the greatest hero of their people, and as a member of the family, like a kindly grandfather.

Imagine you're Polish in the 1970s. Your country was devastated by World War II, and has struggled under an oppressive regime ever since. Food shortages are epidemic. Lines stretch around the block even to buy a measly scrap

Pomerania ▲   **1-2 days**

Baltic-hugging region that's home to Malbork Castle (Europe's biggest Gothic fortress) and the red-brick, gingerbread-scented city of **Toruń**

of bread. Life is bleak, oppressive, and seems hopeless. Then someone who speaks your language—someone you've admired your entire life, and one of the few people to successfully stand up to the regime—becomes one of the world's most influential leaders. A Pole like you is the spiritual guide of a billion Catholics. He makes you believe that the impossible can happen. He says to you again and again: "Have no fear." And you begin to believe it. It's not hard to see why many consider John Paul II to be the greatest Pole in history.

Since his sainthood, the entire country has been ramping up celebrations. At the edge of Kraków, the new John Paul II Center is an impressive place to visit. Consecrated in 2013, the church is big and dazzling,

Saint John Paul II is remembered as a favorite son by Poles.

with art in the lower sanctuary highlighting the pope's illustrious ministry. A museum displays his personal effects and gifts given to him from admirers around the world.

About an hour outside Kraków, in the town of Wadowice, the John Paul II Family Home and Museum fills four floors of the tenement building where his family lived through his adolescence. Visitors can see the actual rooms where he grew up and a collection of his belongings.

But for me, one of the best John Paul II experiences is seeing all of the smaller churches throughout Poland, each of which seems to have a chapel dedicated to their saint. Seeing a man of our own time up on the wall, glorified with the apostles and other saints, is powerful. You can almost feel the charismatic presence of this historic figure, who will be honored for ages to come.

More Polish Experiences

Warsaw Reborn: Warsaw is Poland's capital and biggest city. It's huge, famous, and important, but not particularly romantic. (If you're looking for Old World quaintness, head for Kraków.) The fun of Warsaw is to walk through the city's parks, enjoy a little Chopin in the composer's hometown, marvel at its fast-growing skyline, and just connect with big-city people who are as warm and charming as small-town folk.

Warsaw is also an inspiration to visit. To think it was literally bombed flat and rebuilt since 1945 is amazing. When I'm there, I can't help but fixate on the cost of war. I know how lovingly I collect and organize my physical world in my house. But virtually every house in Warsaw was destroyed in 1945...so many cultural and personal treasures simply gone forever.

Warsaw has been rebuilt from the rubble of World War II.

And, now, just two generations later, Germans and Russians stroll through the city on vacation—joking, enjoying ice cream cones, and snapping photos. Of course, we need to forgive and move on. I'm just amazed at how good Poland is at it. Perhaps some other countries—victims of similar horrors—can learn from the Poles.

Look, but Don't Lick: Just outside Kraków is the remarkable Wieliczka Salt Mine, which has been producing salt since at least the 13th century. A tour of the complex, which

spreads over nine levels and 100 miles of tunnels, shows how generations of Wieliczka miners spent their days underground, rarely seeing the sun. Some of these miners carved statues from the salt: legendary figures from the days of King Kazimierz, the famous astronomer Copernicus, and even the region's favorite son, Pope John Paul II. Your jaw will drop as you enter the enormous underground chapel, carved in the early 20th century. Everything, from the altar to the grand chandelier, was chiseled from the rock salt. The remarkable relief carving of the Last Supper looks good enough to lick.

Lessons of Auschwitz-Birkenau: A trip to once-upon-a-time Europe can be a fairy tale. It can also help tell the story of Europe's 20th-century fascist nightmare. While few travelers go to Europe to dwell on the horrors of Nazism, most people value visiting the memorials of fascism's reign of terror and honoring the wish of its survivors—"Forgive, but never forget."

No such sight in all of Europe is as powerful as Auschwitz-Birkenau. This Nazi concentration camp—strategically located in the heart of Jewish Europe, in occupied Poland—was the site of the systematic murder of more than a million innocent people.

Today, visitors make the pilgrimage west of Kraków to tour the grounds, with its vast field of chimneys stretching to the horizon. A visit begins by crossing under the notorious gate with the cruelly mocking message *Arbeit Macht Frei* ("Work sets you free"). The broken-down crematoria and the train tracks that delivered their victims are silent remnants of unspeakable horrors.

Why is this somber place worth a bit of our vacations? Because we can learn from it. Auschwitz-Birkenau is committed to making the point that intolerance lives on—genocide is as recent as conflicts in Rwanda, Sudan, and Syria. Even today, Machiavellian politicians can hijack great nations, artfully manipulating fear, patriotism, and mass media to accomplish their destructive agendas.

CULTURE AND TRADITIONS: EVERYTHING'S SO...POLISH

Churchgoing Catholics

Poland is arguably Europe's most devoutly Catholic country. Nearly all Polish children are baptized as Roman Catholics, and almost everyone who gets married has a church wedding. In small Polish towns, there's a strong contemporary tradition of building huge, architecturally daring churches as a sign of civic pride and deep respect for the Catholic faith. The architecture of these modern houses of worship sometimes feels more slapdash and done-on-the-cheap than the great churches of an earlier age (which were often built over centuries). But the spirit that fills them is powerful.

When you travel around Europe, you rarely see new churches. And the old churches you see often feel more dead than alive...kept going more for tourists than for worshippers. But in Poland, churches are alive with the faithful.

Polish Food

Polish food is hearty and tasty, with lots of "cold-weather" ingredients: potatoes, dill, berries, beets, and rye. Polish soups are a highlight, especially *barszcz* (borscht, the savory beet soup) and *żurek* (a hearty sourdough soup with

LEFT During communist times, Poles built bold new churches as a statement.

RIGHT A plate of Polish food fills the stomach and warms the body.

a hard-boiled egg and pieces of *kiełbasa* sausage). Another familiar Polish dish is pierogi, ravioli-like dumplings with various fillings: minced meat, sauerkraut, mushroom, cheese, or even blueberry.

And, of course, there's *wódka* (vodka). The most famous brand, Żubrówka, comes with a blade of grass from the bison reserves in eastern Poland. The bison "flavor" the grass...then the grass flavors the vodka. It's strong—but if you down your vodka quickly, it only hurts once. Poles often mix Żubrówka with apple juice, creating a cocktail called *szarlotka* ("apple cake"). *Na zdrowie!*

Poland Travel Resources from Rick Steves

Guidebooks

Check out Rick's guidebooks covering Kraków, Warsaw & Gdansk, and Eastern Europe

TV Shows

The quintessence of Poland with Rick as your host, viewable on public television and at ricksteves.com. Episodes cover Kraków, Auschwitz, and Warsaw

Organized Tours

Small group tours, with itineraries planned by Rick: Eastern Europe in 16 Days

For more on all of these resources, visit ricksteves.com

Hungary

A proud oddball planted firmly in the center of Europe, Hungary mixes a refined elegance (from its days as Vienna's powerful sidecar of the Austro-Hungarian Empire), post-communist rejuvenation, cultural artifacts of a unique Asian heritage, spicy food, exotic thermal baths, endearingly eccentric locals, and Europe's single most underrated capital city. The more you know Hungary, the more you grow to love it.

Throughout history, various cultures from the mysterious East have stampeded to Europe, terrorized the Continent, and eventually retreated home. But only one group stuck around. The original Hungarians—called the Magyars—arrived here in A.D. 896, after a long migration from the steppes of Central Asia. After a few generations of running roughshod over Europe, they decided to convert to Christianity, adopt European ways, and integrate with their neighbors. And even though modern-day Hungarians are fully European, there's still something about the place that's distinctly Magyar.

Budapest—the sprawling Hungarian capital on the banks of the Danube—is a city of nuance and paradox. But those who grapple with it are rewarded with great sights, excellent restaurants, and vivid memories.

While one in five Hungarians lives in Budapest, the countryside plays an important role in Hungary's economy—this has always been a heavily agricultural

The grand spas of Hungary recall the glory days of the Austro-Hungarian Empire.

region. The country's large towns and small cities—including my favorites, Eger and Pécs—offer the visitor a refreshing contrast to the congested metropolis at the country's heart.

FAVORITE SIGHTS AND MEMORABLE EXPERIENCES IN HUNGARY

Budapest Remembers the Cold War

Traveling in Europe in the 1980s, I got in touch with my Czech friend, Lída, and told her I was coming to Prague for a visit. "If you don't mind," she said, "maybe we can meet in Budapest instead? I have been dying to try a Big Mac!"

If communism was a religion during the Cold War, Budapest was sin city. Offering tourists from communist countries a taste of the decadent West, Budapest had a famously progressive economic system dubbed "goulash communism." Meeting up with Lída in Budapest, we strolled down the shopping street called Váci utca. An excited mob gathered in front of a shop that was selling Adidas shoes. Lída explained that this was the only place in all of Eastern Europe where wannabe capitalists could drool over window displays featuring fancy sportswear that cost two months' wages. Up ahead, Ronald McDonald stood on the street corner like a heretic prophet cheering on the downtrodden proletariat. I'll never forget waiting an hour—in a line that stretched around the block—for American "fast" food. But as I finally bit into that long-awaited Big Mac, a deeply satisfied smile spread across her face. That evening, we went to hear Bruce Springsteen at the local stadium. With 50,000 rock fans, you could feel freedom ready to combust all around.

Today, that time feels like ancient history, and Hungarians under age 30 have no living memory of communism. But Budapest still has one of Eastern Europe's best sights for those fascinated by the Red old days: Memento Park.

When regimes come crashing to

Fast Facts

Biggest cities: Budapest (capital, nearly 2 million), Debrecen (205,000), Miskolc (170,000)
Size: 36,000 square miles (similar to Maine), population 10 million
Locals call it: Magyarország
Currency: Hungarian forints (Ft or HUF)
Key date: A.D. 896, seven original Magyar tribes arrive in the Carpathian Basin after a long migration from Central Asia, creating what would become Hungary
Biggest festivals: Formula 1 races (July, Budapest), Sziget Festival (August, Budapest, one of Europe's biggest rock and pop music events)
Handy Hungarian phrases: Jó napot kívánok (hello; yoh **nah**-pot kee-vah-nohk), Kérem (please; **kay**-rehm), Köszönöm (thank you; **kur**-sur-nurm), Egészségedre (cheers; **eh**-gehs-shay-geh-dreh)

the ground, so do their monuments. And, while most Eastern Europeans quickly disposed of any statues of Stalin, Lenin, and their local counterparts, some clever entrepreneur collected Budapest's into an open-air museum. The result is Memento Park, located in the countryside several miles outside the city center, boasting an entertaining jumble of once fearsome, now almost comical statues, gesturing frantically in an otherwise empty field, as if preaching their ideology to each other for eternity.

In Budapest's Memento Park, the sculpted figures that once glorified the communist goals of the state are now gathered together in a nostalgic game of statue maker.

A visit to Memento Park is a lesson in Socialist Realism, the art of communist Europe. They took censorship to new extremes: Under the communists, art was acceptable *only* if it furthered the goals of the state. Aside from a few important figureheads, individuals didn't matter. Everyone was a cog in the machine, a strong and stoic automaton, an unquestioning servant of the nation.

The gift shop hawks a fun parade of communist kitsch. On my last visit, I picked up a CD featuring 20 patriotic songs—*The Greatest Hits of Communism*—and a Stalin vodka flask. Observing the capitalist bustle of today's Budapest, it occurs to me that Stalin, whose estate gets no royalties for all the postcards and tacky souvenirs featuring his mug, must be spinning in his communist grave.

Heat Wave in a Budapest Ruin Pub

Budapest's trendiest clubs are called "ruin pubs." Inhabiting ramshackle old buildings in the city center, they feel like a gang of squatters made a trip to the dump yesterday and grabbed whatever was usable, moved in today, and are open for business tonight.

This fast-combusting nightlife scene fills the city's long-derelict, now-gentrifying Jewish Quarter. On hot nights, the pubs spill out into shoddy courtyards, creating the feeling

Hungary's Top Destinations

Budapest ▲▲▲   allow 2-3 days

Grand, Danube-spanning cityscape peppered with opulent buildings, fine restaurants and cafés, rejuvenated streets and squares, and avant-garde "ruin pub" nightlife

Top Sights
Thermal Baths Fun Széchenyi, genteel Gellért, and classic Rudas
Hungarian Parliament Riverside behemoth with over-the-top interior
Hungarian State Opera House Neo-Renaissance splendor and affordable opera
House of Terror Remembrance of Nazi and Soviet crimes
Buda Castle Historic hilltop ensemble of palaces, churches, and museums

Nearby
Memento Park Open-air museum of communist statues
Szentendre Colorful, Balkan-feeling riverside artist colony
Esztergom Unassuming town with Hungary's biggest and most important church
Gödöllő Palace Summer palace of Habsburg monarchs

Eger ▲▲   1 day

Strollable town with inviting main square, gorgeous Baroque buildings, invigorating thermal baths, and fine wines

Pécs ▲▲   1 day

City featuring a unique mosque-turned-church, good museums, and colorfully tiled facades

With more time, consider visiting

Sopron Charmingly well-preserved Old Town
Hollókő Intriguing open air folk museum, still inhabited by villagers

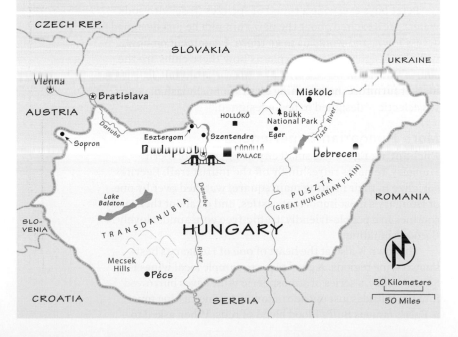

of a cozy living room missing its roof...under the stars. Enjoying a drink here, I'm reminded of creatures that inhabit discarded shells in a tide pool. The formula really works. With the come-as-you-are atmosphere, these clubs attract people who make a point not to be fashion slaves. And, for adventurous travelers of any age, it's easy to meet people.

Budapest's ruin pubs provide a great chance for travelers to connect with locals (and the local hard liquor).

I end up sitting with Peter (who designs ruin pubs), Laura (who works at a hotel), and Sandra (whose father's company introduced pornography to Hungary after freedom in the 1990s). I say how much I like the shabby lounge atmosphere of a ruin pub, and Laura declares that this one, Szimpla Kert (which means "Simple Garden"), is the mecca of ruin pubs.

Ruin pubs come with a bit of communist kitsch. Many of the regulars who love these lounges were toddlers during the last years of communism. Never having experienced its downside, they have fond memories of those "good old days," when the pace of life was slower and families were tighter-knit. Ruin pubs sell nostalgic commie soft drinks along with cocktails.

Peter buys everyone a round of spritzes (rosé with soda water). He's excited about the new ruin pub he just designed across town, and wants us to go there. I comment on how well the design works. He explains how these clubs are the soul of underground culture here. It's the anti-club: flea market furniture, no matching chairs, a mishmash of colors. It's eclectic—"designed to be undesigned."

More Hungarian Experiences

Enchanting Eger: The small city of Eger, in northern Hungary, remains refreshingly off the tourist trail. Egerites socialize in their inviting main square, watched over by one of Hungary's most important castles, and go about their daily routines in a people-friendly, traffic-free core amidst lovely Baroque buildings.

The town is also at the heart of one of Hungary's best-known wine regions. A good place to sample local wines is Sirens' Valley, a series of atmospheric wine caves burrowed into the hillsides just outside of town. A wine-tasting must is Eger's famous Bull's Blood blend of reds. When asked to

Eger, with striking architecture (left), and Pécs, with decorative tilework (right), are the two most interesting towns in Hungary outside of Budapest.

explain the name, one vintner told me: "In 1552, when the Ottomans laid siege to Eger, they were astonished by the ferocity of the town defenders. Local wine sellers knew that the Muslim invaders wouldn't drink alcohol, so they told them it was bull's blood." Of course, since locals only started making this wine in the 1850s, the story is bunk. But as the vintner says, "If it convinces visitors to buy a bottle, where's the harm?"

Colorful Pécs: It takes a lot to get me excited about decorative tiles. But the small Hungarian city of Pécs at the southern tip of the country—somehow manages. This is the hometown of the Zsolnay family, who innovated the "pyrogranite" method for creating architectural tiles that are as delicate-looking and vibrantly colorful as a fine vase, but frostproof and as hard as stone. During Hungary's late-19th-century heyday, buildings all over the country were slathered with vibrant ornamentation. Today, Pécs retains the highest concentration of this distinctively Hungarian form of art, the old tile factory has been turned into a crisp and colorful cultural center, and local museums and shops explain the story of the Zsolnay clan and their finest creations. My favorite tiles are glazed with eosin, another Zsolnay invention that shimmers with a unique range of subtly shifting colors—like the gossamer wing of a butterfly.

The Tricky Hungarian Tongue

The Hungarian language is of Asian origin—unrelated to any other tongue in Europe (except distant cousins Finnish and Estonian). The language befuddles their neighbors and tourists alike. For example, the letter s by itself sounds like "sh," while the combination sz is "s." That's why the capital is called "boo-daw-pesht," while "Liszt" sounds like "list." Like other Eastern cultures, Hungarians list a person's family name first, and the given name last. So the composer Franz Liszt is called "Liszt Ferenc" in his homeland.

Hungarians tend to be traditional and formal in the way they speak—a waiter greets diners with *Tessék parancsolni* (Please command, sir) while a polite young man greeting an older woman might say, *Kezét csókolom* (I kiss your hand). On the other hand, Hungarians use two different words as a *ciao*-like informal "hi" and "bye": the local word *szia* (which sounds like "see ya") and the English word "hello." So you may hear a Hungarian begin a conversation with "See ya!" and end it with "Hello!"

CULTURE AND TRADITIONS: EVERYTHING'S SO...HUNGARIAN

Thermal Baths

Locals brag that if you poke a hole in the ground anywhere in Hungary, you'll find a hot-water spring. Budapest alone has 123 natural springs and some two dozen thermal baths (which are actually part of the health-care system—doctors might prescribe a soak and a massage instead of medicine). While it may sound intimidating, enjoying Hungary's thermal baths is a quintessential experience—and very accessible, even to tourists. It's a mix of sightseeing, a cultural experience, and ultimately, relaxation. Easing into steaming water, submerging yourself nostril-deep, you'll feel the accumulated impact of your busy day ebb away.

At most baths, men and women are usually together, and you can keep your swimsuit on the entire time. But there are also a few gender-segregated, clothing-optional areas. A typical bath complex has multiple pools: Big pools with warm water are for serious swimming, while the smaller, hotter thermal baths are for relaxing and soaking. You'll also usually find a dry sauna, a wet steam room, a cold plunge pool, and sunbathing areas. Many baths have fun flourishes: bubbles, whirlpools, massage jets, wave pools, and so on. Baths feature some of Europe's most memorable people-watching. Hungarians of all shapes and sizes stuff themselves into tiny swimsuits and strut their stuff. Housewives float blissfully in warm water while potbellied, Speedo-clad elder statesmen stand in chest-high water around chessboards, pondering their next moves.

One of my favorite bath experiences is at Budapest's Széchenyi Baths—a big, yellow, copper-domed complex in the middle of City Park. Stepping into the lobby, I survey the long price list. I then try to explain what I want to the cashier: a bath ticket with a private changing cabin (for just a few dollars more). Once inside, I'm immediately lost in a labyrinth of hallways, until a white-smocked attendant directs me to my cabin. After I rent a towel and slip into my swimsuit, I'm finally ready for some hot-water fun. Also in Budapest are the genteel, touristy Gellért Baths, located in a fancy hotel, and Rudas Baths, huddled

under a mysterious-feeling, 35-foot-
tall, 500-year-old dome first built
by the Ottoman Turks. Great bath
experiences outside of Budapest
include Hévíz, a huge thermal lake,
and the delightful Egerszalók Salt
Hill Thermal Spa, just outside Eger,
which boasts a cutting-edge and
luxurious bath complex huddled
under a natural terraced formation
called the salt hill.

Budapest's Cafés

In the late 19th century, a vibrant
café culture boomed in Budapest,
just as it did in Vienna and Paris.
The *kávéház* (coffeehouse) was a
local institution, allowing urbanites
to escape their tiny flats (or get a jolt
of caffeine to power them through
a 12-hour workday). Locals didn't want to pay to heat their
homes during the day. So instead, for the price of a cup of
coffee, they could come to a café to enjoy warmth, companionship, and loaner newspapers.

Realizing that these neighborhood living rooms were
breeding grounds for dissidents, the communists closed the
cafés or converted them into *eszpresszós* (with uncomfortable stools instead of easy chairs) or *bisztrós* (stand-up fast-
food joints with no chairs at all). Today, nostalgia is bringing
back the *kávéház* culture. A favorite activity is whiling away
the afternoon at a genteel coffeehouse, sipping a drink or
nibbling a delicate layer cake. Budapest has many impressive
cafés, but the undisputed champ is the palatial New York
Café—which makes other fancy coffeehouses feel like a strip-
mall Starbucks.

Hungarian Cuisine

Hungarian cuisine features meat, tomatoes, and peppers
(*paprika*) of every shape, size, color, and flavor. Peppers can
be stewed, stuffed, sautéed, baked, grilled, or pickled. For
seasoning, red shakers of dried paprika join the salt on tables.
There are two main types of paprika spice: sweet (*édes*), used
for cooking, and hot (*csípős* or *erős*), used to adjust your own
plate to your preferred amount of heat.

On menus, chicken or veal *paprikás* comes smothered in

a spicy, creamy red stew, and is served with dumpling-like boiled egg noodles. Hungarian *gulyás leves* (shepherd's soup) is a clear, spicy broth with chunks of meat, potatoes, and other vegetables—not the thick "goulash" stew you may be expecting. Cold fruit soup *(hideg gyümölcs leves)* is a sweet, cream-based treat—generally eaten before a meal, even though it tastes more like a dessert.

Wine and Spirits

Hungary boasts 22 designated wine-growing regions, scattered across the country. In addition to the standard international grapes (such as Riesling and Chardonnay), Hungary corks up some interesting alternatives. Tokaji—which French King Louis XV called "the wine of kings, and the king of wines"—is a sweet, late-harvest, honey-colored dessert wine made from noble-rot grapes, which burst and wither on the vine before being harvested.

Hungary is also proud of its fruit-flavored firewater *(pálinka)* and—most of all—Unicum, a bitter liquor made of 40 different herbs and aged in oak casks. Featured in a series of whimsical, vintage, Guinness-like ads, Unicum is a point of national pride and has a history as complicated as its flavor. To sample this local answer to Jägermeister, look for the round bottle with the red-and white cross.

Hungary Travel Resources from Rick Steves

Guidebooks
Check out Rick's guidebooks covering Budapest and Eastern Europe

TV Shows
The quintessence of Hungary with Rick as your host, viewable on public television and at ricksteves.com. Episodes cover Budapest

Organized Tours
Small group tours, with itineraries planned by Rick: Eastern Europe in 16 Days; Prague & Budapest in 8 Days

For more on all these resources, visit ricksteves.com

Slovenia

Tiny Slovenia is one of Europe's most unexpectedly rewarding destinations. At the intersection of the Slavic, German, and Italian worlds, Slovenia blends the best of each culture. And though it's just a quick trip away from the tourist throngs in Venice, Munich, Salzburg, and Vienna, Slovenia has stayed off the tourist track—making it a more authentic Back Door destination.

Though only half as big as Switzerland, Slovenia will surprise you with all it has to offer. You can hike on alpine trails in the Julian Alps, go spelunking in some of the world's best caves in the Karst, get your urban fix in the vibrant capital of Ljubljana, and ride a romantic *pletna* boat across beautiful Lake Bled. And be sure to make time to relax with a glass of local wine and a seafood dinner while watching the sun dip into the Adriatic.

Today, it seems strange to think that Slovenia was ever part of Yugoslavia. In fact, Slovenia feels more like Austria both in its landscape and in the personality of its people. Slovenes are more industrious, organized, and punctual than their fellow former Yugoslavs...yet still friendly, relaxed, and Mediterranean. They won't win any big wars (they're too well-adjusted to even try), but they're exactly the type of people you'd love to chat with over a cup of coffee. And the Slovenian language is as mellow as the people. The worst they can say in their native tongue is, "May you be kicked by a horse." Rather than say "Damn it!" they'll exclaim, "Three hundred hairy bears!"

Slovenia is an endearing, undiscovered gem. Just make sure when planning a trip to Slovenia that you allow enough time to explore this delightful land.

FAVORITE SIGHTS AND MEMORABLE EXPERIENCES IN SLOVENIA

Bells and Bridegrooms in Lake Bled

With its sweeping mountain panoramas and Romantic Age aura, Lake Bled is Slovenia's top alpine resort. Since the Habsburg days, this is where Slovenes have taken their guests—from kings to cousins—to show off the country's natural wonders.

The focal point of any Lake Bled visit is to ride a *pletna* boat to the fairy-tale island in the middle of the lake. Boarding my *pletna*, I strike up a conversation with the oarsman, Robert. With close-cropped blonde hair and piercing blue eyes, he's younger than I'd expect for such a traditional profession. He explains that he built his boat by hand, following a design passed down from father to son for centuries. There's no keel, so Robert must work hard to steer the flat-bottomed boat with each stroke. Leaning back, I appreciate his rhythmic rowing, which sends us gliding smoothly across the lake's mirrored surface—neatly bisecting a perfect reflection of the cliff-capping castle overhead.

From the boat dock where Robert drops me off, I look up a long, stony staircase. Lake Bled is a popular wedding location, and after the ceremony, it's traditional for grooms to carry—or *try* to carry—their brides up all 99 of these steps to prove themselves "fit for marriage." On summer Saturdays, you'll see a steady procession of brides and grooms here. Trudging up the stairs carrying only my camera—and getting winded near the top—I'm glad not to be hauling a spouse.

Summiting the island, I'm face-to-face with the pretty Baroque Church of the Assumption. Inside, a long rope hangs down in front of the altar. Visitors take turns grabbing hold, pulling hard, and being lifted momentarily off their feet to the sound of a clanging bell in the adjacent campanile. Supposedly, ringing the bell three times with one pull will make your fondest wish come

Fast Facts

Biggest cities: Ljubljana (capital, 270,000), Maribor (158,000)
Size: 7,800 square miles (size of New Jersey), population 2 million
Locals call it: Slovenija
Currency: Euro
Key date: June 25, 1991, Slovenia declares independence from Yugoslavia
Language: Slovene
Biggest festivals: Ljubljana Festival (summer-long music fest), Kurentovanje (spring Mardi Gras celebration, town of Ptuj)
Handy Slovene phrases: *Dobar dan* (hello; **doh**-behr dahn), *Prosim* (please; **proh**-seem), *Hvala* (thank you; **hvah**-lah), *šnopc* (schnapps; "schnapps")

The Slovenian mountain resort of Lake Bled has an enchanting church on its island and hardworking boatmen who are standing by to get you there.

true. While I'm usually skeptical of these touristy traditions, I can't resist giving the rope a tug.

After Robert gives me a lift back to shore, I begin strolling the promenade around Lake Bled. Handsome villas line the lake, including what was once the vacation getaway of the Yugoslav president for life Tito, who huddled here with foreign dignitaries like Indira Gandhi and Nikita Khrushchev. After Tito died in 1980, his villa was converted into a classy hotel with a James Bond ambience. In one suite, you can actually sleep in the dictator's bed. And guests can use Tito's personal desk for something I bet he never imagined—sending an email.

Completing my circle around the lake, I settle in at a waterfront café and dig into a Lake Bled specialty: a delicate layer cake of vanilla custard, whipped cream, and crispy wafers. Slovenes are proud of their local pastries—and the beauty of their land. Tasting my delicious cream cake, surrounded by the majesty and serenity of Lake Bled, it's easy to see why.

Laid-Back Ljubljana

As a tour guide, I enjoy introducing my American travelers to Slovenia's capital, Ljubljana. Although Slovenia is known as the most industrious of the Balkan countries, this vest-pocket capital's mellow ambience and lively riverfront café scene are a revelation. The leafy riverside promenade crawls with stylishly dressed students sipping *kava* and polishing their near-perfect English. Surveying this scene, invariably one of my tour members wonders aloud, "Doesn't anybody here have a job?"

Ljubljana's residents work hard. But, with the country's main university campus right downtown, the city also knows

Slovenia's Top Destinations

Ljubljana ▲▲   allow 1-2 days

Vibrant capital oozing with cobbled ambience, trendy
boutiques and eateries, unique architecture by Jože Plečnik,
and inviting riverside promenade

Lake Bled ▲▲▲   1-2 days

Alpine lake resort with a church-topped island, cliff-hanging castle, famous desserts, and proximity to mountain thrills

Julian Alps ▲▲   1 day

Cut-glass peaks, tranquil Soča River Valley, adventure-sports capital Bovec, and
fine WWI museum in Kobarid, all connected by a twisty mountain road

Karst Region ▲   1 day

Arid plateau with world-class caves (Škocjan and Postojna), Lipizzaner stallion
stud farm at Lipica, scenically situated Predjama Castle, great wines, and "slow
food"

With more time, consider visiting

Logarska Dolina Remote mountain valley with traditional lifestyles
Piran Atmospheric seaside resort town
Ptuj Charming-if-sleepy historic town topped by a castle

how to play hard. Socializing and people-watching seem to be the national pastime.

While Ljubljana has slick and endearing new museums opening each year, ultimately this town is all about ambience. The cobbled core of Ljubljana is an idyllic place that sometimes feels too good to be true. The spunky mayor is on an eternal crusade to pedestrianize the entire city, block by block. Fashion boutiques and al fresco cafés jockey for control of the Old Town, and people are out enjoying a Sunday stroll any day of the week. Easygoing Ljubljana is the kind of place where graffiti and crumbling buildings seem elegantly atmospheric instead of shoddy.

Ljubljana, the trickiest capital in Europe to pronounce, is shaped by the artistic genius of Jože Plečnik, the greatest Slovenian architect of the 20th century.

The Ljubljanica River, lined with cafés, restaurants, and a buzzing market hall, bisects the city. The outdoor farmers market is a hive of activity, where big-city Slovenes buy directly from the producers. Some farmers still use wooden carts to hand-truck veggies in from their garden patches in the suburbs.

After being damaged by an earthquake in 1895, Ljubljana was rebuilt in the Art Nouveau and Art Deco styles that were so popular in Vienna, the empire's capital at the time. A generation later, the homegrown architect Jože Plečnik bathed the city in his distinctive classical-meets-modern style: sleek and eye-pleasing, artfully ornamented with columns and geometrical flourishes.

Like Gaudí shaped Barcelona and Bernini shaped Rome, Plečnik made Ljubljana what it is today. Because he walked to work each day and had to live with what he designed, Plečnik was particularly thoughtful about incorporating aesthetics, nature, and human needs into his work. The result is like feng shui on an urban scale. Enjoy his picturesque market colonnade, Triple Bridge, and Cobbler's Bridge.

For a more personal look at the architect, I enjoy visiting his home, decorated exactly as it was the day Plečnik died in 1957. On my first visit, this nondescript house underwhelmed me. But as the docent, Ana, proudly walked me from room to room—revealing the quirky but beautiful furniture and artful bric-a-brac he designed, as well as souvenirs from around the world that inspired him—I found myself seduced by his genius.

Standing in Plečnik's bedroom, Ana seemed to be fighting back tears as she explained how important this great man was to her tiny nation. Inspecting a table strewn with his drawings, equipment, and personal items (including his glasses and the hat that he was famous for wearing), I began to feel as though Plečnik himself had invited me over for dinner.

That's a feeling I get again and again throughout Slovenia. This cozy land and its welcoming people just have a way of making visitors fall in love with it.

High in the Slovenian Alps

The northwestern corner of Slovenia is crowned by the Julian Alps, which are laced with hiking paths, blanketed with deep forests, and speckled with ski resorts and vacation chalets. Beyond every ridge is a peaceful alpine village nestled around a quaint Baroque steeple.

> ### Don't Skip the Sticker
>
> Slovenia's sleek network of expressways is one of Europe's best—but these aren't "free"-ways. Drivers using expressways must display a toll sticker, called a *vinjeta*. If renting a car in Slovenia, it probably comes with a toll sticker (ask just to be sure). If you're driving in from elsewhere, you can buy one at a gas station near the border. Be warned: This rule is taken very seriously. Police check frequently, and drivers without stickers are given a large fine on the spot.

The single best day in the Julian Alps is spent driving up and over the breathtaking Vršič Pass and back down via the Soča River Valley. The pass consists of 50 hairpin turns—24 on the way up, 26 on the way back down—each one numbered and labeled with the altitude in meters. Curling on twisty roads between the peaks, I am treated to stunning high-mountain scenery and charming hamlets. But as beautiful as this area is, it has a dark side.

Originally a military road, the pass was built during World War I by 10,000 Russian prisoners of war. At switchback #8, I park my car by a rushing mini-waterfall and hike up through the woods to a humble little Orthodox chapel, rustically crafted from wood. In 1916, an avalanche thundered down the mountains, killing hundreds of workers. The chapel, built where the final victim was found, offers today's visitors a chance to pay their respects to those who made this scenic drive possible.

Just after switchback #24, I reach the summit at just over 5,000 feet, where a mountain hut offers amazing alpine

Slovenia's beautiful Julian Alps were the scene of fierce and bloody fighting during World War I, as the mausoleum at Kobarid attests.

views. Twisting back down the other side of the mountains—and getting dizzy from all of the serpentine roads—I get my first view of the Soča River Valley. The Soča—with water somehow both crystal clear and spectacularly turquoise—is a mecca for kayakers and other whitewater adventurers, who call it "Adrenaline Valley."

Nearing the end of the switchbacks, I enter the Soča River Valley. Though peaceful now, this area saw some of the fiercest fighting of World War I. Known as the Soča Front—or the Isonzo Front in Italian—the million casualties here gave it the nickname "Valley of the Cemeteries." The fighting between the Italian and Austro-Hungarian armies was waged not in the valleys, but at the tops of the mountains.

Finally, I reach the humble village of Kobarid, with the valley's best collection of World War I sights. The town was immortalized by Ernest Hemingway, who drove a Red Cross ambulance nearby (and later wrote about Kobarid in *A Farewell to Arms*).

I stop at Kobarid's excellent museum, which tells the story of the Soča Front and humanizes the suffering of this horrific but almost forgotten corner of World War I. The tasteful exhibits, with a pacifist tone, focus not on the guns and heroes, but on the stories of the common people who fought and died here. I gaze into the eyes of a generation of young men—imported from the farthest reaches of the Habsburg Empire to fight a hopeless battle on a frigid mountaintop. Graphic images of war injuries are juxtaposed with a display of medals earned—suggesting the question, was it worth it?

After visiting the museum, I head up to the hilltop mausoleum just above town. The octagonal pyramid holds the remains of 7,014 Italian soldiers—victims of just one battle. Standing on the broad terrace at the top of the gigantic monument, I'm surrounded by a 360-degree panorama of cut-glass peaks. Visually tracing the twinkling Soča River back the way I've come, I think: Only Slovenia combines epic scenery and poignant history, all in one dizzying corkscrew drive.

More Slovenian Experiences

Spectacular Spelunking: About an hour south of Ljubljana, Slovenia's Karst region is honeycombed with a vast network of caves and underground rivers. Spelunkers agree that this region has some of the most remarkable caves on the planet, including my favorite, the Škocjan Caves. Visitors begin by seeing a multitude of formations in a series of large caverns. Guides tell the story as, drip by drip, stalactites grow from spaghetti-thin strands to mighty sequoia-like stone pillars. The experience builds and builds as you go into ever-more-impressive grottoes, and you think you've seen the best. But then you reach the truly colossal final cavern, where the sound of a mighty river crashes through the mist. It's a world where a thousand evil Wizard of Oz monkeys could comfortably fly in formation. Crossing a breathtaking footbridge 150 feet above the torrent gives you faith in Slovenian engineering. Finally, the cave widens, sunlight pours in, and you emerge—like lost creatures seeking daylight—into a lush canyon.

World-Class Horses: Lipizzaner stallions—known for their noble gait and Baroque shape—were made famous by Vienna's Spanish Riding School. The Lipica Stud Farm, near the Škocjan Caves, was founded in 1580 to provide Lipizzaners for the Habsburg court in Vienna. While the stuffy Viennese cousins of Slovenia's Lipizzaners still perform under chandeliers, the horses at Lipica provide a more intimate look. Here visitors can get nose to nose with the stallions, learn how they're raised and trained, and—on most

LEFT The Škocjan Caves

RIGHT The Lipica Stud Farm

days—watch them train or perform. The Lipizzaners' clever routine—stutter-stepping sideways to the classical beat and hopping in the air on their hind legs—thrills horse lovers and casual viewers alike.

CULTURE AND TRADITIONS: EVERYTHING'S SO...SLOVENIAN

Hayracks and Beehives

Coming from such a small country, locals are proud of the few things that are distinctly Slovenian. Two such icons of Slovenian culture are roofed hayracks and beehive panels.

Because of the frequent rainfall in Slovenia, hayracks are covered by a roof that allows the hay to dry. You'll see these distinctive roofed hayracks scattered across the hillsides, especially in the northwest. Souvenir shops sell postcards and miniature wooden models of this unlikely national symbol.

Slovenia also has a strong beekeeping tradition. Slovenian beekeepers believe that painting the fronts of the hives makes it easier for bees to find their way home, so for centuries, they have illustrated their hives with vivid, whimsical scenes of folk life, bible stories, historical events, and so on. A lovable beekeeping museum in the village of Radovljica (near Lake Bled) explains the history of beekeeping. But if you can't make it there, replica beehive panels—a favorite form of folk art—are sold everywhere as souvenirs.

Slovenian Food

Traditional Slovenian food has a distinctly Germanic vibe—including the "four G's," sausages, schnitzels, strudels, and sauerkraut. One local dish to look for is *štruklji*, a dumpling-like savory layer cake, which can be stuffed with

Slovenia's charms are subtle—like its trademark laid-back and its passion for the berry-flavored cola, Cockta.

cheese, meat, or vegetables. But cosmopolitan Slovenia—at an intersection of cultures—isn't too hung up on traditional grub. Locals favor a wide range of cuisines: Mediterranean, French, Asian, Mexican, and so on. Ljubljana has some of the best—and most varied—restaurants in the former Yugoslavia.

Drinking in Slovenia

Slovenia is proud of its good wines, its many varieties of flavored brandies, and the local lager with a warm-and-fuzzy name that suits the culture: Smile. But its most unusual beverage is Cockta, a cola with an unusual flavor (which supposedly is made from berry, lemon, orange, and 11 herbs). Originally called Cockta-Cockta, the drink was introduced during the communist period as an alternative to the difficult-to-get Coca-Cola. These days, even though Coke is widely available, nostalgic Slovenes still have a taste for the Cockta they grew up on. Be adventurous, buy a bottle to drink, and ponder the power of an acquired taste.

Slovenia Travel Resources from Rick Steves

Guidebooks

Check out Rick's guidebooks covering Croatia & Slovenia and Eastern Europe

TV Shows

The quintessence of Slovenia with Rick as your host, viewable on public television and at ricksteves.com. Episodes cover Ljubljana, Lake Bled, Soča Pass, Škocjan Caves, Predjama Castle, and Lipica Stud Farm

Organized Tours

Small group tours, with itineraries planned by Rick: Eastern Europe in 16 Days; Adriatic in 14 Days

For more on all these resources, visit ricksteves.com

Croatia

Sunny beaches, succulent seafood, and a taste of *la dolce vita*...in Eastern Europe?

Croatia, with thousands of miles of coastline, is Eastern Europe's Riviera. Holiday makers love its pebbly beaches, predictably balmy summer weather, and dramatic mountains. Croatia is also historic. With ruined Roman palaces, Byzantine mosaics, Venetian bell towers, medieval walls, Habsburg villas, and even communist concrete, past rulers have left their mark.

One tragic exception to Croatia's mellow history came in the early 1990s, when the country declared independence from Yugoslavia, sparking an ugly war. Today the bloodshed is in the past. While a trip to Croatia offers thoughtful travelers the opportunity to understand a complicated chapter of recent history, most visitors focus instead on the appealing towns and natural wonders the country has long been known for.

Dubrovnik is still the "Pearl of the Adriatic," with its old town encircled by a medieval wall. The town of Split is—astonishingly—built in, on, and around a Roman palace. The stunning Plitvice Lakes National Park, sparkling with waterfalls, attracts hikers and photographers. And for a coastal getaway, it's easy to fall in love with the village of Rovinj, on the Istrian Peninsula.

Over the last several years, Croatia has reclaimed its status as a tourist hotspot. In the summer, its long coastline is crawling with a Babel of

Dubrovnik, with its mighty walls and inviting beach

LEFT Rovinj, on the tip of the Istrian Peninsula, is my favorite stop between Venice and Dubrovnik.

RIGHT Croatians are clever at turning their rocky shores into romantic cocktail bars.

international guests. And yet, despite the tourists, this place remains distinctly and stubbornly Croatian.

FAVORITE SIGHTS AND MEMORABLE EXPERIENCES IN CROATIA

Romantic Rovinj

Idyllic Istria, a wedge-shaped peninsula at Croatia's northwest corner, is an engaging mix of Croatia and Italy. While most of the Croatian coast was Italian-dominated for centuries, Istria remained part of Italy for even longer. Today, bilingual street signs remind visitors that both languages are still official.

My favorite little town on the Istrian coast is Rovinj. Surrounded by the Adriatic on three sides, this town is like a little hunk of Venice draped over a hill. A visit here produces a collage of vivid travel memories: Boats laden with kitschy shells for sale bob giddily in the harbor, while the bell tower's rickety staircase tests climbers' faith in the durability of wood. From the top, on a clear day, you can see Venice. And capping the tower, a patron-saint weathervane valiantly faces each menacing cloud front that blows in from the sea. She swivels with the breeze to provide locals with a primitive, but eerily accurate, weather report.

Walking through the market puts me in a good mood. I feel like Marilyn Monroe singing to a bunch

Fast Facts

Biggest cities: Zagreb (capital, 780,000), Split (178,000), Rijeka (129,000)

Size: 22,000 square miles (similar to West Virginia), population 4.5 million

Locals call it: Hrvatska

Currency: Croatian kunas (kn)

Key date: October 8, 1991, Croatia declares its independence from Yugoslavia

Biggest festivals: Dubrovnik Summer Festival (July-August, music), Moreška sword dance (twice a week in summer, on the island of Korčula)

Handy Croatian phrases: *Dobar dan* (hello; **doh**-bar dahn), *Molim* (please; **moh**-leem), *Hvala* (thank you; **hvah**-lah), *plaža* (beach; **plah**-zhah)

of sex-starved GIs. Babushkas push grappa and homemade
fruit brandies on me. Istria is one of Europe's top truffle
regions, and small, pricey bottles of pungently flavored oils
invite me to bring that taste home with me. The merchants'
sample walnuts are curiously flavorful. I'll buy a bag on my
way out of town.

Strolling the cobbled back lanes, I wander into a time-
warp bar that takes "untouristy" to almost scary extremes.
The town fishermen and alcoholics (generally, it seems, one
and the same) are smoking, bantering loudly, and getting too
drunk on cheap homemade beer to notice the nude pinups
plastering the walls. Suddenly, all eyes are on me...and I
feel like a rabbit at the nocturnal house at the zoo. But they
quickly go back to their chattering, laughing, and drinking.
My friend explains that they're speaking the local Istrian
vernacular—a Croatian-Italian hybrid tongue.

That evening, walking along "restaurant row"—the
seafront promenade where interchangeable fish joints
desperately vie for diners' attention—I stumble on Valentino
Cocktail Bar, where travelers nurse cocktails on the rocks...
literally. Patricia, the elegantly coiffed and exactingly made-
up owner, hands out pillows and invites you to plunk down in
your own seaside niche. Fish, attracted by the bar's under-
water lights, swim by from all over the bay. The sun sets on
a gorgeous Istrian evening, classy candelabras twinkle in
the twilight, and couples cozy up to each other and the view.
Sipping my white Croatian wine, I keep thinking, simply,
"romantic."

Wandering Dubrovnik's City Walls

Jockeying my way between cruise-excursion groups, I climb
the steep steps to the top of the still-stout medieval walls
that surround Dubrovnik. As I begin a slow, circular, hour-
and-a-half walk around the fortified perimeter of one of

My B&B host
holds a mortar
shell—a souvenir
of the 1991
shelling of
Dubrovnik.
Houses that
were hit are
the ones with
newer, brighter
red tiles.

Croatia's Top Destinations

Dubrovnik ▲▲▲   allow 1-3 days
The "Pearl of the Adriatic," highlighted by walkable medieval walls; great beaches; and Mount Srđ, a Napoleonic fortress with spectacular views

Nearby
Mljet National Park Undeveloped island retreat
Cavtat Art-packed resort village
Pelješac Peninsula Dramatic coastal scenery and Croatia's best vineyards
Ston Small town with giant fortifications

Dalmatian Islands ▲▲   1-2 days
Low-key **Korčula**, with walled Old Town and fjord-like backdrop, and ritzy **Hvar**, with seductive beaches

Split ▲▲   1 day
Bustling city with extensive Roman palace ruins and busy seaside promenade

Istria ▲▲   2-3 days
Italian-feeling region with Croatia's prettiest town **(Rovinj)**, Roman ruins **(Pula)**, and picturesque wine-and-truffles hill towns **(Motovun)**

Plitvice Lakes National Park ▲▲▲   1 day
Forested canyon filled with crystal-clear lakes, stunning waterfalls, and easy trails

Zagreb ▲▲   1-2 days
Capital city boasting quirky museums, lush parks, and a colorful urban bustle

Europe's best-preserved medieval towns, I snap photos like crazy of the ever-changing views. On one side is a sea of red rooftops; on the other side, the actual sea.

Near the Pile Gate, I pause to enjoy a full frontal view of the Stradun, the 300-yard-long promenade that runs through the heart of Dubrovnik's Old Town. In the Middle Ages, merchants lined this drag; before that, it was a canal. Today this is the main artery of the city: an Old World shopping mall by day and sprawling cocktail party after dark.

Farther along, I look down and see a peaceful stone terrace perched above the sea, clinging to the outside of the city walls. Generously shaded by white umbrellas, this is my favorite Dubrovnik escape, a rustic outdoor tavern called Buža. The name means "hole in the wall"—and that's exactly what you'll have to climb through to get there. Filled with mellow tourists and bartenders pouring wine from tiny screw-top bottles into plastic cups, Buža comes with castaway views and Frank Sinatra ambience.

Looking inland from my ramparts perch, my eyes fall on a random arrangement of bright- and dark-toned red roof tiles. In this complex and often troubled corner of Europe, even a tranquil stroll around the walls comes with a poignant history lesson. After Croatia declared independence in 1991, the Yugoslav National Army laid siege to this town and lobbed mortars over the hill. Today, the new, brighter-colored tiles mark houses that were hit and have been rebuilt. At a glance, it's clear that more than two-thirds of the Old Town's buildings suffered bomb damage.

Surveying the rooftops, my thoughts turn to Pero, my B&B host, who spent years after the war turning the bombed-out remains of his Old Town home into a fine guesthouse. Upon my arrival last night, Pero uncorked a bottle of *orahovica* (the local grappa-like firewater). Hoping to write that evening with a clear head, I tried to refuse the drink. But this is a Slavic land. Remembering times when I was force-fed vodka in Russia by new friends, I knew it was hopeless. Pero made this hooch himself, with green walnuts. As he slugged down a shot, he handed me a glass, wheezing, "Walnut grappa—it recovers your energy."

Pero reached under the counter and held up the mangled tail of a mortar shell, describing how the gorgeous stone and knotty-wood building he grew up in suffered a direct hit in the siege. He put the mortar in my hands. Just as I don't enjoy holding a gun, I didn't enjoy touching the twisted remains of that mortar. Pero explained that he gets a monthly retirement check for being wounded in the war, but he got bored and didn't want to live on the tiny government stipend—so he went to work rebuilding his guesthouse.

I took Pero's photograph. He held up the mortar and smiled. I didn't want him to hold up the mortar and smile, but that's what he did. He seemed determined to smile—as if it signified a personal victory over the destruction the mortar had wrought.

It's impressive how people can weather tragedy, rebuild, and move on. In spite of the terrors of war just a couple of decades ago, life here is once again very good, and, from my perch here atop the city walls, filled with promise.

> ### Croatian Beaches
>
> Croatia is known for its glimmering beaches. However, most are pebbly or rocky rather than sandy—and spiny sea urchins are not uncommon. In addition to your swimsuit, pack a pair of water shoes for wading, as well as a beach towel. Good sunscreen, a hat, bug spray, and sturdy shoes (for hiking to some of the more secluded beaches) can also be handy.
>
> Many of Croatia's beaches are nude. If you want to work on an all-around tan, seek out a beach marked *FKK* (from the German *Freikörper Kultur*, or "free body culture"). But don't get too excited—these beaches seem to be most beloved by people you'd rather see with their clothes on.

Magical Motovun

Croatia is more than the sea, and diverse Istria offers some of the country's most compelling reasons to head inland. In the Istrian interior, between humble concrete towns crying out for a paint job, you'll find vintners painstakingly reviving a delicate winemaking tradition, farmers pressing that last drop of oil out of their olives, trained dogs sniffing out truffles in primeval forests, and a smattering of fortified medieval hill towns offering sweeping views over the surrounding terrain. The best of these hill towns is Motovun, featuring a colorful old church and a rampart walk with the best spine-tingling vistas in the Istrian interior.

On my first visit to this region, I drove halfway across Croatia and arrived late at night. Through a driving rainstorm, I wound and wound up through the dark to

Croatia's Istrian Peninsula is famed for its hill towns (like Motovun, left) and its a cappella singing groups.

Motovun's summit. The road got narrower and narrower. When I ran out of road, I parked, got out, and walked to my hotel, with no sense of what the town even looked like. The next morning, I awoke before my alarm rang and pushed open my lumbering shutters. The heavy rainstorm had cleaned the air, and an early-morning light invigorated the colors of the glistening red-tile roofs, the rustic stone rampart, and a lush landscape of rolling hills and simple farms.

The next year, I returned to Motovun with my film crew. During a break, while strolling the town's cobbles and marveling at how dead it was, I heard a men's a cappella group practicing. I snooped around to find out where they were. Around the corner, I went up a short flight of stairs and stared at a closed door separating me from their heavenly singing. I gently pushed the door open just a crack to see the group. It was a traditional *klapa* group consisting of a dozen men sitting in a half-circle with their backs to me. Standing before them was the group's director, a woman with springy hair who looked like a mad, young, female Beethoven. She saw me, ran to the door, and invited me in. I pulled out a chair and savored the chorus.

A short time later, I ran to get my film crew. We unanimously agreed it was a magic moment, and we filmed it. The group ended up kicking off our Croatia episode with a wonderful bit of serendipity. Not only did it make for good television, but it was also a reminder to me of an important travel lesson: When out wandering, be bold. Remember, it's worth running the risk of having a door shut in your face—in order to risk being welcomed in.

More Croatian Experiences

Quirky Zagreb: In addition to its cosmopolitan bustle, generous parks, and in-love-with-life café-and-restaurant scene, Croatia's capital is home to some of Europe's most

delightfully offbeat museums. The Museum of Naive Art showcases a uniquely Croatian art form: paintings by untrained peasant artists. (In the early 20th century, art-world highbrows embraced this sort of unschooled art as evidence that artistic ability is inborn rather than taught.) The movement's founder, Ivan Generalić, typically painted wintry scenes on glass (in winter, he wasn't busy working the fields, and glass was the cheapest material available).

Just across the street is the equally endearing Museum of Broken Relationships, featuring true stories of failed couples from around the world, told in their own words. Displayed alongside their story is an actual item that embodies the relationship (from angry gnomes to sex toys to discarded wedding albums), in addition to the predictable "he cheated on me so I broke his favorite fill-in-the-blank" items. The collection has struck such a chord, they've taken it on the road, garnering fans in cities worldwide.

Croatia's charms range from the Museum of Naive Art in Zagreb (left), to Plitvice, a dramatic natural wonderland (center), to the town of Split, whose nucleus was the fourth-century palace of Roman emperor Diocletian (right).

Hiking in a Waterfall Wonderland: Plitvice Lakes National Park, two hours south of Zagreb, is one of Europe's most spectacular natural wonders. Imagine Niagara Falls diced and sprinkled over a heavily forested Grand Canyon. There's nothing like this lush valley of 16 terraced lakes, laced together by waterfalls, boat rides, and miles of pleasant plank walks. Countless cascades and water that's both strangely clear and full of vibrant colors make this park a misty natural wonderland. Before I came here, I thought I really knew Europe. Then I discovered Plitvice and realized you can never exhaust Europe's surprises.

Layers of History in Split: Croatia's "second city," Split, has an atmospheric Old Town core that's built amid the foundations of a fourth-century Roman palace. When the Emperor Diocletian retired, he built a vast residence for his golden years here in his native Dalmatia. After Rome fell and the palace was abandoned, a medieval town sprouted from its shell. The hallways of the palace became streets, the rooms morphed into squares, and to this day, residents are actually living inside the walls of Diocletian's palace. Squeezed between the Old Town and the harborfront is a nicely landscaped pedestrian promenade called the Riva, where the sea of Croatian humanity laps at the walls of the palace. Strolling locals finish their days in good style here—just enjoying life's simple pleasures in a city that so seamlessly weaves its past and present into one.

CULTURE AND TRADITIONS: EVERYTHING'S SO...CROATIAN

Staying with Locals

Private accommodations throughout Croatia (and especially along the coast) offer travelers a characteristic alternative to big, overpriced resort hotels. There are *sobe*—individual rooms for rent—or *apartmani*, which are a bit larger and have a kitchen. The simplest *sobe* allow you to experience Croatia on the cheap, at nearly youth-hostel prices, while giving you a great opportunity to connect with a local family. The fanciest *sobe* are still affordable and can be downright swanky, with hotelesque amenities (private bathroom, air-conditioning, satellite TV, and so on) and as much or as little contact with your host family as you like.

Succulent Seafood

While Italian-style pastas and pizzas are common throughout Croatia, it's more memorable to splurge on a seafood dish, especially when vacationing on the coast. Croatians say that a fish should swim three times: first in the sea, then

in olive oil (as you cook it), and finally in wine (when you eat it). But be careful when ordering: Most fish dishes are priced by the kilogram or by the 100-gram unit, rather than by the portion (a one-kilogram portion feeds two hungry people or three light eaters).

Be open and adventurous. Seafood items that may sound unappetizing can be a delicious surprise. For instance, a good, fresh anchovy, when done right, has a pleasant flavor and a melt-in-your-mouth texture. The menu item called "small fried fish" is generally a plate of deep-fried minnows. Another specialty is octopus salad, a flavorful mix of octopus, tomatoes, onions, capers, and spices.

Harmonious Croatian Voices

Traditionally found in Dalmatia, *klapa* music features the hauntingly beautiful sound of men's voices harmonizing a cappella, like a barbershop quartet with a soothing Adriatic flavor. Typically the leader begins the song, and the rest of the group follows behind him with a slight delay. Mariachi-style *klapa* groups perform in touristy areas, including what was once the entry vestibule of the Emperor Diocletian's palace in Split. Just listening to a few glorious tunes in this grand space with grand acoustics provides an unforgettable soundtrack for your trip.

Croatia Travel Resources from Rick Steves

Guidebooks
Check out Rick's guidebooks covering Croatia & Slovenia; Dubrovnik; and Eastern Europe

TV Shows
The quintessence of Croatia with Rick as your host, viewable on public television and at ricksteves.com. Episodes cover Split, Plitvice Lakes National Park, Zagreb, Rovinj, Dubrovnik, and the Dalmatian Coast

Organized Tours
Small group tours, with itineraries planned by Rick: Eastern Europe in 16 Days; Adriatic in 14 Days

For more on all of these resources, visit ricksteves.com

Greece

With its classical past and hang-loose present, Greece offers something for every traveler. As the cradle of Western civilization, Greece boasts some of the world's greatest ancient monuments. But it also has plenty more to offer, including succulent seafood, inviting islands, whitewashed houses with bright-blue shutters, and a mellow, Zorba-the-Greek ambience.

Most tourists come here for a quick visit to Athens to bask in the greatness of the Acropolis and then head to an island to bask in the sun. But for a true Back Door experience, consider some of my favorite destinations on the mainland, such as the home of the ancient oracle at Delphi, the birthplace of the Olympics in Olympia, the Gibraltar-style fortress at Monemvasia, the stark Mani Peninsula, or the elegant-but-cozy port town of Nafplio, near two of Greece's greatest ancient sites—Mycenae and Epidavros.

Greece is easy on travelers. The people are welcoming

and accommodating. Greeks pride themselves on a concept called *filotimo*—literally "love of honor," but roughly translated as openness, friendliness, and hospitality. Social faux pas by unwary foreigners are easily overlooked by Greeks.

The country is going through some tough economic times, but the pace of life remains relaxed. People work in the mornings, then take a midafternoon siesta, when they gather with their families to eat the main meal of the day. On warm summer nights, they stay up very late, even kids. Families spill into the streets to greet their neighbors on the evening stroll. For entertainment, they go out to eat, ordering large amounts and sharing it family-style.

It's a joy to surrender to the Greek way of living. All the things you're looking for—deep-blue water, mouth-watering food, striking scenery, and the thrill of connecting with ancient history—are here waiting for you. With its long history and simple lifestyle, Greece has a timeless appeal.

> **Fast Facts**
>
> **Biggest cities:** Athens (capital, 800,000), Thessaloniki (375,000), Piraeus (172,000)
> **Size:** 51,485 square miles (roughly the size of Alabama), population 10.8 million
> **Locals call it:** Hellas
> **Currency:** Euro
> **Key date:** 776 B.C., the first Olympic Games are held
> **Biggest festivals:** Athens & Epidavros Festival (June and July in Athens and Epidavros on the Peloponnese), Carnival Season, a.k.a. Apokreo (weeks prior to Orthodox Lent)
> **Annual per-capita cheese consumption:** 55 pounds (mostly feta, highest in the world)
> **Handy Greek phrases:** *Gia sas* (hello; yah sahs), *Parakalo* (please; pah-rah-kah-**loh**), *Efharisto* (thank you; ehf-hah-ree-**stoh**)

FAVORITE SIGHTS AND MEMORABLE EXPERIENCES IN GREECE

Cockcrow on Hydra

Hydra—less than two hours south of Athens by hydrofoil—offers the ideal Greek island experience, without a long journey across the Aegean.

Hydra has one real town, no real roads, no cars, and not even any bikes. Zippy water taxis whisk you from the quaint little harbor to isolated beaches and tavernas. Donkeys are the main way to transport things here. These surefooted beasts of burden, laden with everything from sandbags and bathtubs to bottled water, climb stepped lanes. Behind each mule-train toils a human pooper-scooper; I imagine picking up after your beast is required. On Hydra, a traffic jam is three donkeys and a fisherman.

While the island is generally quiet, dawn here taught me

On Greece's idyllic isle of Hydra, the only traffic is donkeys.

the exact meaning of "cockcrow." On Hydra, the end of night is marked with much more than a distant cock-a-doodle-doo: It's a dissonant chorus of cat fights, burro honks, and what sounds like roll call at an asylum for crazed roosters. After the animal population gets that out of its system, it's like one of the old gods hits "snooze" and the island slumbers a little longer.

Tourists wash ashore with the many private and public boats that come and go, but few venture beyond the harborfront. Today, after my barnyard awakening, I decided to head uphill, and my small detour became a delightful little odyssey. While I had no intention of anything more than a lazy stroll, one inviting lane after another drew me up, up, up to the top of the town. Here, shabby homes enjoyed grand views, tired burros ambled along untethered, and island life trudged on, oblivious to tourism.

Over the crest, I followed a paved riverbed down to the remote harbor hamlet of Kaminia, where 20 tough little fishing boats jostled within a tiny breakwater. Children jumped fearlessly from rock to rock to the end of the jetty, ignoring an old man rhythmically casting his line.

As I trudged into town, a rickety woven-straw chair and a tipsy little table at Kodylenia's Taverna were positioned just right, overlooking the harbor. The heavy, reddening sun commanded, "sit." I did, sipping ouzo and observing a sea busy with taxi boats, hydrofoils connecting this oasis with Athens, freighters—like castles of rust—lumbering slowly along the horizon, and a silhouetted cruise ship anchored like it hadn't moved in weeks. Ouzo, my anise-flavored drink of choice on this trip, and my plastic baggie of pistachios purchased back in town were the perfect complements to the setting sun. Blue and white fishing boats jived with the chop. I'd swear the cats—small, numerous as the human residents of this island, and oh so feminine—were watching the setting sun with me. An old man flipped his worry beads, backlit by

Greece's Top Destinations

Athens ▲▲▲ allow 2-3 days

Greece's sprawling, congested capital, featuring first-class ancient ruins, atmospheric old Plaka quarter, and thriving ramshackle nightlife

Top Sights

Acropolis Hilltop capped by architectural jewel, the Parthenon
Acropolis Museum Glassy modern temple for ancient art
Ancient Agora Marketplace and meeting point of ancient Athens
National Archaeological Museum World's best collection of ancient Greek sculpture

Nafplio ▲▲▲ 1-2 days

Tidy midsized town with a cozy port, elegant Old Town, hilltop fortress, and easy day trips to two amazing ancient sites

Nearby

Mycenae Ancient fortress city with iconic Lion Gate and beehive tomb
Epidavros Best-preserved theater of the ancient world, with astonishing acoustics

Hydra ▲▲ 1-2 days

Idyllic car-free island with picturesque harbor, casual beaches, and enticing coastal hikes

Santorini ▲▲ 1-2 days

Black-sand beaches and postcard-perfect towns clinging to the rim of a caldera (flooded volcano crater)

Mykonos ▲▲ 1-2 days

Quintessential Greek isle with whitewashed village and pulsating nightlife

---

the golden glitter on the harbor. Three men walked by, each reminding me of Spiro Agnew.

As darkness settled, my waiter—who returned here to his family's homeland after spending 20 years in New Jersey, where he "never took a nap"—brought a candle for my table. My second glass of ouzo came with a smudge of someone's big fat Greek lipstick. Wiping it off before sipping seemed to connect me with the scene even more. The soft Greek lounge music tumbling out of the kitchen mixed everything like an audio swizzle stick. I glanced over my shoulder to the coastal lane home. Thankfully, it was lamplit.

Walking home, under a ridge lined with derelict windmills, I tried to envision Hydra before electricity, when spring water flowed and the community was powered by both wind and burros. At the edge of town I passed a bar filled with noisy cruise-ship tourists, and was thankful I'd

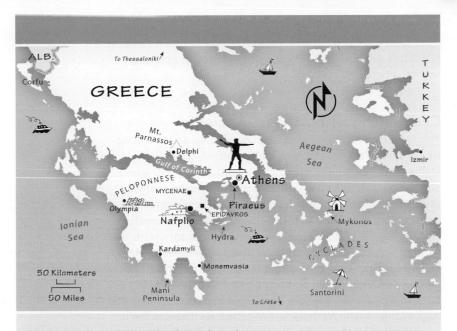

Kardamyli and the Mani Peninsula ▲   1-2 days

Unspoiled beach town of **Kardamyli** and jumping-off point for the Mani Peninsula's dramatic hill towns and jagged coastlines

With more time, consider visiting

Olympia Stunning temple and stadium ruins at birthplace of the ancient games
Monemvasia Gibraltar-like rock peninsula with million-dollar views
Delphi Where ancients came to consult the oracle

taken the uphill lane when I left my hotel that morning. Locals, proud of the extravagant yachts moored for the night, like to tell of movie stars who make regular visits. But the island is so quiet that, by midnight, all the high rollers seem to be back on board watching movies. Sitting on a ferry cleat the size of a stool, I scanned the harbor—big flat-screen TVs flickered from every other yacht.

Back in Hydra town, I observed the pleasant evening routine of strolling and socializing. Dice clattered on dozens of backgammon boards, entrepreneurial cats seemed busy, children chased soccer balls, and a tethered goat chewed on something inedible in its low-profile corner. From the other end of town came the happy music of a christening party. Dancing women filled the building, while their children mimicked them in the street. Farther down, two elderly, black-clad women sat like tired dogs on the curb.

Succumbing to the lure of a pastry shop, I sat down for some honey-soaked baklava. I told the baker I was American. "Oh," he said, shaking his head with sadness and pity, "you work too hard."

I answered, "Right. But not today."

Communing with Athens' Ancients

For decades, I recommended that travelers to Athens—long infamous for its sprawl, noise, and pollution—see the big sights, then get out. But visiting it recently, I saw a dramatic change. New driving laws, along with a marvelous subway system, have made the city less congested. While it used to turn my hanky black in a day, the air now seems much cleaner. And the city is much more people-friendly, with welcoming pedestrian boulevards and squares filled with benches, shade-giving trees, and inviting cafés rather than parked cars. But the big draw still remains its ancient sites. Nowhere else in the world will you feel like you've journeyed back in time to the birthplace of Western civilization itself.

Crowned by the mighty Parthenon, the Acropolis rises ethereally above the sprawl of modern Athens. I consider the Parthenon the finest temple from the ancient world: Simple, balanced, and orderly, it sums up the Greek Golden Age. Unlike most ancient sites, the Acropolis we see today was started and finished within two generations—a snapshot of the Golden Age set in stone. I visit late in the day, as the sun goes down, when the white Parthenon stone gleams a creamy golden brown, and what had been a tourist war zone is suddenly peaceful.

While the Acropolis was the city's ceremonial showpiece, the ancient Agora, at its foot, was the real heart of classical Athens. For some 800 years, this marketplace was the hub of

Still stately after all these centuries, the Parthenon tops Athens' majestic Acropolis. And at the base of the hill is the new, state-of-the-art Acropolis Museum.

all commercial, political, and social life, as well as home to many of the city's religious rites.

Little remains of the Agora, other than one very well-preserved temple and a rebuilt portico. But wandering this field of humble ruins with an Athenian guide reminds me of the value of connecting with great local guides. Fay ("like Faye Dunaway," she explained) was a wealth of insights mixed with attitude: "We Greeks smoke, hate breakfast, and just can't get along with each other. But give us a common enemy and we become tight as a fist."

She also explained that Greeks designed on a human scale—appropriate for their democracy. When the Romans came, they added gigantism. As Romans didn't have democracy, their leaders had a taste for grandeur—putting an "un-Greek" veneer of power on the Agora with pompous staircases, fancy pavement, and oversized temples and statues. You can tell Roman statues from Greek ones because Roman ones are larger than life, not freestanding (always propped on something), with "too much robe" and interchangeable heads. Masters of both imperial ego and efficiency, they reused stone bodies, economically replacing just the head with each new emperor. That's why lots of Roman statues are headless, with scooped-out necks.

From the Agora, it's on to Athens' best new attraction, the Acropolis Museum. Housed in a striking, glassy building that gives a postmodern jolt to the otherwise staid, concrete cityscape, the museum houses various artifacts from the Acropolis. It's

Travel Through "the Crisis"

Don't expect your visit to museums and ancient sites to go like clockwork. Virtually all of the big sights are run by the troubled Greek government, so the opening and closing times can be erratic. It's smart to arrive well in advance of listed closing times and to hit your must-see attractions in the morning, especially if traveling outside of summer. While museum websites may claim they list the latest hours, you'll get more reliable, up-to-date information by asking your hotelier or calling the places directly. Watch out for the switch between high-season and low-season schedules, which can come without much warning.

While Greece's economic crisis is real for its workers (and I wouldn't want to be a local counting on my retirement), it's no big deal for travelers. If you're a tourist looking for a place in Athens' countless trendy eateries and watering holes, you'll be impressed not by an economic slowdown but what feels like boom time. Don't let news of turbulent demonstrations scare you away from Athens. Sure, there are some angry marches that come with the imposition of austerity programs. They're designed to make it on the evening news. And there will be a few closures and strikes. But this is the reality: Traveling in Greece is safe, your vacation dollar is needed, you'll enjoy a particularly warm welcome, and you'll likely return home with a better sense of how sensational commercial media coverage in the USA can wrongly shape our perceptions.

well worth a visit, though for me, the main attraction will always be the Parthenon itself.

At the end of the day, a ritual for me is to wander the old town under the floodlit Parthenon, munching a souvlaki rolled in greasy pita bread and pretending that Athens is the same small, charming village at the foot of the Acropolis that it was a century ago.

Greece Goes Wild

The Mani Peninsula—the southern tip of mainland Greece—feels like the end of the road. It's stark and sparse. If Greece had an O.K. Corral, this is where it would be. And the town of Kardamyli would be the saloon where everyone goes for a drink.

Today the Mani is a peaceful region of rustic villages and untrampled beaches. Only goats thrive here. While mountains edged with abandoned terraces hint that farming was once more extensive, olives have been the sole major Mani export for the last two centuries. Many Mani towns feature sumptuous, old, fresco-slathered churches—pockets of brightness in this otherwise parched land.

Sealed off from the rest of the country by a ridge of mountains, the peninsula has—over the centuries—harbored refugees, fleeing whatever crises were gripping the rest of Greece. People would hide out in the mountains, far from the coast and marauding pirate ships. And when they weren't fighting foreign invaders, they would fight each other.

Clambering up ridges are empty, ghostly villages fortified with towers. The most characteristic is Vathia. Built on a rocky spur, Vathia was an extreme example of what can happen when neighbors don't get along. In this vendetta-ville, 80-some houses were split north/south into two rival camps, which existed in a state of near-permanent hostility.

After spending a day driving around the Mani, exploring its rugged landscape and contentious history, I enjoy

Greece's rugged Mani Peninsula is dotted with ghost towns, souvenirs of a tough environment and a hard-fought past.

unwinding in Kardamyli, a humble beach town with a "Bali in a dust storm" charm. This handy base for exploring the Mani Peninsula works like a stun gun on my momentum. On my last trip, I felt as if I could have stayed for days, just eating well and hanging out. It's the kind of place where travelers plan their day around the sunset.

Having dinner at my favorite beach taverna under a leafy canopy brings back memories of my first meal here 20-some years ago: I had settled my chair into the sand under a bare and dangling lamp, and felt a faint but refreshing spritzing. Looking around for the source of the mist, I saw a tough Greek teenager in a swimsuit the size of a rat's hammock tenderizing a poor octopus to death by whipping it like a wet rag, over and over, on a big flat rock. The octopus would be featured that night on someone's dinner plate—but not mine.

These days, light bulbs still swing in the breeze—but, no longer naked, they're dressed in gourd lampshades. I sit under an eave enjoying the view. I love gazing into the misty Mediterranean, knowing the next land is Africa. The inky waves churn as the red sun sets.

More Greek Experiences

The Allure of Nafplio: My vote for the most charming town in Greece is Nafplio, on the Peloponnesian Peninsula. Nestled under cliffs at the apex of a vast bay, Nafplio has a unique pride. Its role as the first capital of independent Greece once made it a prestigious port town. And although its glory days have faded, the town retains a certain genteel panache, with palm-tree waterfronts, and narrow and atmospheric back arrouus that are lined with stately Venetian houses and invit- ing shops. Owing to its prestigious past, Nafplio's harbor is guarded by three castles (all wonderfully floodlit at night): one on a small island, another just above the Old Town, and a third capping a tall cliff above the city. With its harborfront setting and pleasant present-day vibe, Nafplio doesn't even need tourists—and doesn't disappoint them.

Nafplio also serves as a handy home base for touring the historic ruins of Mycenae and Epidavros. Mycenae, as ancient to Golden Age Greeks as Socrates and Plato are to us, has an archaeological mystique to it. And Epidavros entices visitors to actually try out the famed acoustics of the best-preserved theater in the ancient world.

Olympic Original: For more than a thousand years, the Olympic Games were held in their birthplace—Olympia,

a sacred village in the Peloponnese. Besides the stadium, Olympia's Temple of Zeus was one of the great tourist destinations of the ancient world, boasting a then-world-famous 40-foot statue of Zeus by the great sculptor Phidias. Today, Olympia is one of the best opportunities for a hands-on antiquity experience. Despite the crowds that pour through here, Olympia is a magical place, with ruins nestled among lush, shady groves of pine trees. Its once-majestic temple columns—toppled like a tower of checkers by an earthquake—are as evocative (with the help of the excellent museum) as anything from ancient times. And you just have to play "On your mark, get set...go!" on that original starting block from the first Olympic Games. As you line up, crank up your imagination, light a torch, and refill the stadium with 40,000 fans. Olympia can still knock you on your discus.

Magnificent Monemvasia: This gigantic rock juts up improbably from the blue-green deep, just a few hundred yards offshore from the Peloponnese peninsula. Often referred to as the "Gibraltar of Greece," it is a fascinating showcase of Byzantine, Turkish, and Venetian history dating back to the 13th century. Its remarkably romantic walled Lower Town hides on the sheltered side of the burly rock, tethered to the mainland by only a skinny spit of land (Monemvasia means "single entry"). A steep, zigzag path leads up to the even bigger Upper Town, whose fortress, in its day, was considered the mightiest in Byzantine Greece. Today its scant ruins sprawl evocatively across the broad summit. Climbing Monemvasia takes only about half an hour, but on top, spend as long as you want, getting lost in the Middle Ages.

CULTURE AND TRADITIONS: EVERYTHING'S SO...GREEK

Greek Cuisine

The food in Greece is simple...and simply delicious. The Greeks have an easy formula, and they stick with it. The four Greek food groups are olives (and olive oil), salty feta cheese, ripe tomatoes, and crispy phyllo dough. Virtually every dish you'll have here is built on a foundation of these tasty building blocks.

My favorite way to eat in Greece is to order a main dish and a medley of *mezedes* (appetizers) to share with my companions. The selection, while predictable and routine after 10 dinners, never gets old for me: *tzatziki* dip, garlic dip, fava bean dip, or a mix of all three on a single serving platter; fried eggplant or zucchini; Greek salad; and big grilled peppers—red or green—stuffed with feta cheese. Usually there's also something from the sea, such as grilled calamari, sardines, or a plate of fried small fish (three inch), very small fish (two inch), or very, very small fish (one inch). With three-inch fish, leave the head and tail on the plate (and try not to wonder about the once inky, now dry black guts). With the smaller fish, you'll leave nothing but a line of greasy fingerprints on the fringe of your paper tablecloth.

Religion

The Greek Orthodox Church remains a strong part of everyday life here. Ninety-five percent of all Greeks consider themselves Orthodox, even if they rarely go to church. Their faith was a rallying point during centuries of foreign occupation, and today the Greek constitution recognizes Orthodox Christianity as the prevailing religion of Greece. Greek lives are marked by the age-old rituals of baptism, marriage, and funeral.

Orthodox elements appear everywhere. Icon shrines dot

the highways. Orthodox priests—with their Old Testament beards, black robes, necklaces, cake-shaped hats, and families in tow—mingle with parishioners on street corners. During the course of the day, Greeks routinely pop into churches to light a candle, asking for favors. Greek lotharios in track suits reverently bend at the waist to kiss an icon, which is already slathered with lipstick from a steady stream of devout visitors. Even local teens who seem far from religious make the sign of the cross when passing a church.

Orthodox Easter, which is often later than the Catholic/Protestant Easter, is celebrated with gusto and tradition. For instance, on Good Friday in Kardamyli, a processional passes through town and the priest blesses each house. At midnight on Holy Saturday, townspeople turn off their lights and come to the main square. The priest emerges from the church with a candle and spreads light through the candle-carrying crowd, who then take the light home with them. Gradually the entire town is illuminated...and the fireworks begin.

Drinking in Greece

Greece is a rough land with simple wines. A local vintner told me there's no such thing as a $50 bottle of fine Greek wine. I asked him, "What if I want to spend $30?" He said, "You can buy three $10 bottles." With dinner, I like to order the infamous resin-flavored *retsina* wine. It makes you want to sling a patch over one eye and say, "Arghh." The first glass is like drinking wood. The third glass is dangerous: It starts to taste good. If you drink any more, you'll smell like it the entire next day.

With its new affluence and a new generation of winemakers (many of them trained abroad), Greece is getting better at wine. More than 300 native varietals are now grown in Greece's wine regions. But like many locals, I often skip the wine and go for a cold beer, or the cloudy, anise-flavored ouzo, supposedly invented by monks on Mount Athos.

Greek Dance

In Greece, dancing is a part of everyday life. If you go to a special occasion such as a wedding or baptism, you can see all ages dancing together. With arms outstretched or thrown across one another's shoulders, Greeks form a circle to perform their traditional dances. (In the old days, mixed couples were linked by handkerchiefs instead.) Often they dance to folk songs accompanied by a *bouzouki*, a long-necked mandolin. These days the music is usually amplified, fleshed out with a synthesizer, and tinged with pop influences.

Some of the dances you might see are the graceful *kalamatianos* circle dance, the *syrtaki* (famously immortalized by Anthony Quinn in *Zorba the Greek*), and the dramatic solo *zimbetikos*. A few dancers might get carried away, "applaud" by throwing plates or flowers, and then dance on the tables into the

wee hours. Wherever you are in Greece, ask locals where you might enjoy some live music and dancing with dinner or after. It can be a smashing time.

Greece Travel Resources from Rick Steves

Guidebooks
Choose from Rick's regional and city guides on Greece and Athens

Audio
Download Rick's free Audio Europe app, with self-guided audio tours, including a walk through Athens and tours of the Acropolis, Ancient Agora, and National Archaeological Museum

TV Shows
The quintessence of Greece with Rick as your host, viewable on public television and at ricksteves.com. Episodes cover Athens, the Peloponnese Peninsula, and the islands of Hydra, Santorini, Samos, and Lipsi

Organized Tours
Small group tours, with itineraries planned by Rick: Athens and the Heart of Greece in 14 Days

For more on all these resources, visit ricksteves.com

Books, Films & TV for Travelers

Here's a country-by-country list of recommended reading and viewing for thoughtful travelers. For more recommendations, see ricksteves.com/travelreading.

AUSTRIA

Nonfiction
Beethoven: The Music and the Life (Lewis Lockwood, 2005). The musician's life in Vienna and his contributions to Viennese culture.
The Story of the Trapp Family Singers (Maria von Trapp, 2001). True story behind the famous singing family.
World of Yesterday (Stefan Zweig, 1964). Autobiography of a famous writer who lived through Vienna's golden days, World War I, and the Hitler years.

Fiction
Embers (Sándor Márai, 2001). Cobblestoned, gaslit Vienna just before the empire's glory began to fade.
Henry James' Midnight Song (Carol de Chellis Hill, 1995). Literary mystery with a cast of famous historical characters in fin-de-siècle Vienna.
Radetzky March (Joseph Roth, 1932). Classic novel follows four generations of an aristocratic family during the decline and fall of the Habsburgs.

BELGIUM

Nonfiction
The Guns of August (Barbara Tuchman, 2004). Pulitzer Prize-winning book about the outbreak of World War I and events along the Western Front, including Belgium.

A Tall Man in a Low Land: Some Time Among the Belgians
(Harry Pearson, 1999). A wry look at contemporary
Belgium through the eyes of an outsider.

Fiction

The House of Niccoló series (Dorothy Dunnett, 1999). A three-
volume series tracing an audacious apprentice who rises
to lead a mercantile empire in 15th-century Flanders.

Resistance (Anita Shreve, 1997). A wounded American
WWII bomber pilot is sheltered in a Nazi-run village in
Belgium.

The Square of Revenge (Pieter Aspe, 2013). The medieval
architecture of Bruges conceals a bizarre mystery for
Inspector Van In to solve.

Film and TV

In Bruges (2008). A dark and violent comedy filmed just
where you'd think.

CROATIA

The Balkan Express and *Café Europa: Life After Communism*
(Slavenka Drakulić, 1993/1999). Insightful essays about
surviving Communism.

Black Lamb and Grey Falcon (Rebecca West, 1941). Definitive
travelogue of the Yugoslav lands (written during a journey between the two World Wars).

They Would Never Hurt a Fly (Slavenka Drakulić, 2004).
Profiles of Yugoslav war criminals.

A Traveller's History of Croatia (Benjamin Curtis, 2015).
Readable history of Croatia.

Yugoslavia: Death of a Nation (Laura Silber and Allan Little,
1996). Thorough explanation of how and why Yugoslavia
broke apart.

Film and TV

Underground (1995). Award-winning satire follows two
friends—and the history of Yugoslavia—through World
War II, the Cold War, and the Yugoslav wars.

CZECH REPUBLIC

The Cowards (Josef Škvorecký, 1970). A Czech teen comes of
age in post-WWII Bohemia.

Rick Steves' Europe on Public Television

Our television series, *Rick Steves' Europe,* airs in high definition on nearly 300 public television stations across the United States. The three shows on Travel Skills help illustrate this book. We've also produced several specials, including *Rick Steves' The Holy Land, Rick Steves' Andalucía, Rick Steves' European Christmas* (celebrating family holiday traditions in seven different European cultures), *Rick Steves' Iran* (made in the hope of humanizing that proud if perplexing nation), and *Rick Steves' Symphonic Journey* (a

Producer Simon Griffith, cameraman Karel Bauer, writer/host Rick Steves, and David–working together to bring the best of Europe home to you on public television.

visual and musical tour of European composers and countries, ranging from Edvard Grieg in Norway to Giuseppe Verdi in Italy).

All 100 TV shows are available on demand at ricksteves.com/tv, which also has all the scripts, plus a behind-the-scenes look at filming *Rick Steves' Europe.*

Dita Saxová (Arnošt Lustig, 1962). Young concentration camp survivor struggles to restart her life.

The Garden Party and Other Plays (Vaclav Havel, 1994). Political commentary infused with dry humor by Czechoslovakia's first post-communist president.

Good Soldier Švejk (Jaroslav Hašek, 1923). Hilarious Czech classic, following the fortunes of a soldier in World War I's Austro-Hungarian army.

How I Came to Know Fish (Ota Pavel, 1974). Memoir juxtaposing the simple act of fishing with the complexities and terror of World War II.

I Served the King of England and *Too Loud a Solitude* (Bohumil Hrabal, 1971/1976). Enchanting fictions that deftly express the Czech spirit and sense of humor.

The Twelve Little Cakes (Dominika Dery, 2004). Delightful memoir of a childhood spent near Prague at the end of the communist era.

These are just some of the places covered on my TV show, *Rick Steves' Europe*.

DENMARK

Conquered, Not Defeated (Peter Tveskov, 2003). The author's childhood memories of Denmark under WWII German occupation.

Music and Silence (Rose Tremain, 1999). Seventeenth-century Denmark through the eyes of a lute player at court.

We the Drowned (Carsten Jensen, 2010). The love, wars, and adventures of the seafaring men of the port town of Marstel.

Winter's Tale (Isak Dinesen, 1942). Short stories, most set in the author's native Denmark, by a gifted storyteller.

Film and TV

Babette's Feast (1987). The original foodie movie, set in rural 19th-century Denmark.

FRANCE

Nonfiction

Almost French: Love and a New Life in Paris (Sarah Turnbull, 2003). An amusing look at adopting a famously frosty city.

I'll Always Have Paris (Art Buchwald, 1996). American humorist recounts life as a Paris correspondent during the 1940s and 1950s.

Is Paris Burning? (Larry Collins and Dominique Lapierre, 1991). A German general disobeys Hitler's order to destroy Paris.

Long Ago in France: The Years in Dijon (M. F. K. Fisher, 1929). Remembrances from the celebrated American food writer of her life in France.

The Longest Day (Cornelius Ryan, 1959). An account of the hours before and after the D-Day Normandy invasion.

A Moveable Feast (Ernest Hemingway, 1964). Paris in the 1920s is recalled by Hemingway.

My Life in France (Julia Child, 2006). The inimitably zesty chef's recounting of her early days in Paris.

Paris to the Moon (Adam Gopnik, 2000). A collection of essays and journal entries exploring the idiosyncrasies of life in France.

The Road from the Past: Traveling Through History in France (Ina Caro, 1994). A chronological journey through France's historical sights.

Sixty Million Frenchmen Can't Be Wrong (Jean-Benoit Nadeau and Julie Barlow, 2003). Insight into what makes the French tick.

Wine & War: The French, the Nazis, and the Battle for France's Greatest Treasure (Don and Petie Kladstrup, 2001). The compelling story of how French vintners preserved their valuable wine amidst the chaos of WWII.

A Year in Provence and *Toujours Provence* (Peter Mayle, 1989/1991). Mayle's humorous anecdotes about restoring and living in a 200-year-old farmhouse in a remote area of the Lubéron.

Fiction

Chocolat (Joanne Harris, 1999). A woman and her daughter stir up tradition in a small French town by opening a chocolate shop two days before Lent (also a film).

City of Darkness, City of Light (Marge Piercy, 1996). Three French women play pivotal roles behind the scenes during the French Revolution.

Les Misérables (Victor Hugo, 1862). A Frenchman tries to escape his criminal past, becoming wrapped up in Revolutionary intrigues.

A Place of Greater Safety (Hilary Mantel, 2006). Three young men come to Paris in 1789—Maximilien Robespierre, Camille Desmoulins, and George-Jacques Danton—and the rest is history.

Suite Française (Irène Némirovsky, 2004). Account of the chaos of the evacuation of Paris during World War II.

A Tale of Two Cities (Charles Dickens, 1859). Gripping tale of the French Revolution.

Film and TV

Amélie (2001). Charming young waitress searches for love in Paris.

Grand Illusion (1937). French WWI prisoners of war hatch a plan to escape a German POW camp.

Jean de Florette (1986) and *Manon of the Spring* (1986). Marvelous tale of greed and intolerance follows a hunchback as he fights for the property he inherited

Jules and Jim (1962). A classic from François Truffaut, a film maker of the French New Wave school.

Marie Antoinette (2006). Kirsten Dunst stars as the infamous French queen (with a Californian accent) at Versailles.

Midnight in Paris (2011). Woody Allen's sharp comedy shifts between today's Paris and the 1920s mecca of Picasso, Hemingway, and Fitzgerald.

Saving Private Ryan (1998). Steven Spielberg's intense and brilliant story of the D-Day landings and their aftermath.

GERMANY

Nonfiction

Berlin Diary: The Journal of a Foreign Correspondent (William Shirer, 1941). Stationed in Berlin from 1934 until 1940, CBS radio broadcaster Shirer delivers a vivid, harrowing account of the rise of Nazi Germany.

In the Garden of Beasts (Erik Larson, 2011). A chronicle of 1930s Berlin, seen through the eyes of America's ambassador to Nazi Germany and his daughter.

Martin Luther: A Life (Martin E. Marty, 2004). A short, vivid biography of the irascible German reformer who transformed Western Christianity.

Night (Elie Wiesel, 1960). Candid and horrific account of survival in a Nazi concentration camp.

Peeling the Onion (Günter Grass, 2007). Memoir of the Nobel Prize-winning author's childhood in Danzig and experiences as a drafted member of the Waffen SS.

Stasiland: Stories from Behind the Berlin Wall (Anna Funder, 2002). A powerful account about the secrets of the Stasi, the East German Ministry for State Security, and how it affected the citizens of East Germany.

Fiction

Address Unknown (Kathrine Kressmann Taylor, 1939). Published before World War II and banned in Nazi Germany, a series of letters between a Jewish art dealer living in San Francisco and his former business partner, which warns of the terrors yet to come.

All Quiet on the Western Front (Erich Maria Remarque, 1929). Young German classmates enlist in the German Army of World War I, only to find that war is not about glory and pride.

Berlin Noir (Philip Kerr, 1993). An ex-policeman turned detective struggles with secrets and crime in 1930s and '40s Berlin.

The Book Thief (Markus Zusak, 2007). Award-winning novel about a German girl who steals books and shares them with victims of World War II.

Brother Grimm (Craig Russell, 2007). Detective novel evocatively set in modern-day Hamburg.

The Good German (Joseph Kanon, 2001). A foreign correspondent in postwar Berlin covers the Potsdam Conference while searching for a love he left behind.

The Silent Angel (Heinrich Böll, 1994). Soldier Hans Schnitzler returns from World War II unknowingly secreting a will that will change his life.

Simple Stories (Ingo Schulze, 2001). Written 10 years after the reunification of Germany, this novel traces the human impact of the reunion.

Stones from the River (Ursula Hegi, 1994). Story of a dwarf in Nazi Germany who seeks compassion and humanity in her small town affected by the war.

The Tin Drum (Günter Grass, 1959). A young boy stands defiant against the Nazis, armed with only a drum and a piercing scream.

Film and TV

The Baader Meinhof Complex (2008). The still-fragile
German democracy is rocked in 1967 by acts of terrorism
committed by radicalized Germans.

Cabaret (1972). With Hitler on the rise and anti-Semitism
growing, the only refuge in Berlin is in the Cabaret.

The Lives of Others (2006). A member of East Germany's
secret police becomes too close to the lives he surveils.

The Marriage of Maria Braun (1979). Gritty meditation on
post-WWII Germany, seen through the romantic woes of
a young woman.

Mephisto (1981). Allegorical tale about one man's artistic
approach to the Nazis' rise to power.

Run Lola Run (1998). Art-house phenomenon set in Berlin,
combining action, love, and mobsters with a time-twist-
ing plot.

Sophie Scholl: The Final Days (2005). Beautiful, devastating
account of a student who defied Hitler.

Wings of Desire (1987). Set in Berlin, Wim Wenders' best film
depicts an angel who falls in love and falls to earth.

GREAT BRITAIN

Nonfiction

Cider with Rosie (Laurie Lee, 1959). Boyhood memoir set just
after World War I in the Cotswolds.

Crowded with Genius (James Buchan, 2003). Exploration of
Edinburgh during the Scottish Enlightenment

The Emperor's New Kilt (Jan-Andrew Henderson, 2000).
Deconstructs the myths surrounding the tartan-clad
Scotts.

Fever Pitch (Nick Hornby, 1992). Memoir illuminating the
British obsession with soccer.

The Guynd (Belinda Rathbone, 2005). An American woman
married to a Scottish man details how their marriage
endures through cultural gaps and household mishaps.

How the Scots Invented the Modern World (Arthur Herman,
2001). An exploration of Scotland's cultural and social
revolution in the 18th and 19th centuries.

Longitude (Dava Sobel, 1995). The story of the clockmaker
who solved the problem of keeping time aboard a ship—a
timely read for visitors to Greenwich.

My Love Affair with England (Susan Allen Toth, 1994). A
traveler's memoir exploring the country's charm and
eccentricities.

Notes From a Small Island (Bill Bryson, 1997). An irreverent but delightful account of the island country that was the author's home for two decades.

Fiction

Atonement (Ian McEwan, 2001). Disquieting family saga in upper-middle-class England in which the consequences of a childhood lie play out badly.

Brideshead Revisited (Evelyn Waugh, 1945). Celebrated novel about the intense entanglement of a young man with an aristocratic family.

The Pillars of the Earth (Ken Follett, 1990). Cathedral epic about the birth of Gothic architecture, set in a fictional town in 12th-century England.

Rebecca (Daphne du Maurier, 1938). Mysterious tale about upper-class English lives and the secrets they keep, set on the Cornish Coast.

The Warden (Anthony Trollope, 1855). Moral dilemmas in the 19th-century Anglican church.

Wolf Hall and *Bring Up the Bodies* (Hilary Mantel, 2010/2012). The court of Henry VIII seen through the eyes of Thomas Cromwell.

Film and TV

Braveheart (1995). Mel Gibson helps the Scots overthrow English rule in the 13th century.

Downton Abbey (2010-). A crisis of inheritance in an aristocratic family with no male heirs is at the heart of this Edwardian-era drama.

The Elephant Man (1980). Stark portrayal of the cruelty of Victorian London.

Hope and Glory (1987). Semi-autobiographical story of a boy growing up during WWII's London blitz.

The King's Speech (2010). Colin Firth as the stuttering King George VI.

My Beautiful Laundrette (1985). Compelling story of two gay men in urban London.

Persuasion (1995). The classic Jane Austen tale of status, partially filmed in Bath.

Pride and Prejudice (1995). One of the many versions of Jane Austen's classic.

The Queen (2006). The life of Elizabeth II in the days after Princess Diana's death.

Rob Roy (1995). The Scottish rebel struggles against feudal landlords in 18th-century Scotland.

Sammy and Rosie Get Laid (1987). A portrayal of the racial tensions found in multiethnic London.

Shakespeare in Love (1999). Clever, romantic taste of Tudor-era London set in the original Globe Theatre.

Sweeney Todd (2007) and *Sherlock Holmes* (2009). Two highly stylized films capturing the gritty Victorian milieu.

GREECE

Nonfiction

Eleni (Nicholas Gage, 1996). Riveting account of a *New York Times* investigative reporter's quest to uncover the truth behind his mother's assassination during the Greek civil war.

The Greek Way and *Mythology* (Edith Hamilton, 1993). The classic interpretations of classic myths and cultures.

The Greeks (H. D. F. Kitto, 1950). Standard text on ancient Greece by a leading scholar.

Sailing the Wine Dark Sea: Why the Greeks Matter (Thomas Cahill, 2003). Understanding the relevance of Greek ancient culture to today.

The Spartans and *Alexander the Great* (Paul Cartledge, 2002/2004). Illuminating narratives of iconic Greek figures and their heroic tales.

The Summer of My Greek Taverna (Tom Stone, 2002). American expat's take on running a bar on the island of Patmos.

Fiction

Corelli's Mandolin (Louis de Bernières, 1994). Ill-fated lovers on a war-torn Greek island.

Fire from Heaven and *The Persian Boy* (Mary Renault, 1969/1972). Historical novels about Alexander the Great.

Gates of Fire (Steven Pressfield, 1998). Re-creates the Battle of Thermopylae, where 300 vastly outnumbered Spartans held back the Persian army.

Little Infamies (Panos Karnezis, 2002). Fine collection of short stories written in a magical realism style.

Pascali's Island (Barry Unsworth, 1980). A tale of treachery and duplicity, in which a Greek spy operating in the declining years of Ottoman rule regrets his activities.

The Walled Orchard (Tom Holt, 1990). Amusing and well-researched pseudo-autobiography of the comic playwright Eupolis.

When the Tree Sings (Stratis Haviaras, 1981). Events during

World War II and the subsequent Greek civil war, as witnessed by a young boy.

Film and TV

Clash of the Titans (1981). The myth of the Greek hero Perseus, who takes on the dark forces of the underworld.

Never on Sunday (1960). An American tries to educate a beautiful prostitute in postwar Greece.

Troy (2004). Brad Pitt portrays the petulant warrior Achilles from Homer's *The Iliad*.

Z (1969). Thriller about the assassination of a crusading politician—and the rise of the Greek junta—in the 1960s.

Zorba the Greek (1964). Shows how Greek culture can free even the most uptight Englishman (based on the novel by Nikos Kazantzakis).

HUNGARY

Fatelessness (*Sorstalanság*, Imre Kertész, 1975). Semi-autobiographical novel by a Hungarian-Jewish Auschwitz survivor.

Memoir of Hungary, 1944-1948 (Sándor Márai, 2000). A telling account of Hungary's transition from the horrors of World War II to Soviet occupation and the beginning of a communist regime.

Prague (Arthur Phillips, 2002). Five American expats negotiate young-adult life in post-communist Budapest.

The Radetzky March (Joseph Roth, 1932). The fortunes of the aristocratic von Trotta family rise and fall with the fate of the Austro-Hungarian Empire.

Film and TV

The District! (2004). Animated farce about star-crossed lovers in a Budapest ghetto.

Sunshine (1999). A somewhat melodramatic account of three generations of an aristocratic Jewish family in Budapest.

IRELAND

Nonfiction

Angela's Ashes (Frank McCourt, 1996). Evocative memoir of an Irish family's struggles in the Great Depression.

Are You Somebody? The Accidental Memoir of a Dublin Woman (Nuala O'Faolain, 1996). A woman steps out of the traditional shoes she was always told to fill.

How the Irish Saved Civilization (Thomas Cahill, 1995). How the "island of saints and scholars" changed the course of world history.

Ireland: A Concise History (Máire and Conor Cruise O'Brien, 1972). A riveting account of Irish history from pre-Christian Ireland to the Belfast civil rights movement.

O Come Ye Back to Ireland (Niall Williams and Christine Breen, 1987). Two New Yorkers adjust to life in a tiny Irish village.

To School Through the Fields (Alice Taylor, 1988). Well-written memoir of growing up in a rural Irish town.

Fiction

The Barrytown Trilogy and *A Star Called Henry* (Roddy Doyle, 1992). Gritty novels capturing the day-to-day life of working-class Dubliners.

The Bódhran Makers (John B. Keane, 1986). The struggles of hard-living farmers in 1950s Ireland.

Dublin Saga (Edward Rutherfurd, 2004). Historical saga tracing the lives of rich and poor families through key events in Irish history.

Dubliners (James Joyce, 1914). Irish life in the 1900s, told through the experiences of 15 ordinary Dubliners.

Finbar's Hotel and *Ladies' Night at Finbar's Hotel* (Dermot Bolger, 1997/1999). Written collaboratively, with each chapter penned by a different modern Irish author.

Long Lankin (John Banville, 1970). Short-story collection by the Man Booker Prize-winning Irish author.

Film and TV

The Commitments (1991) and *The Secret of Roan Inish* (1994). Two comedic films adapted from books by Roddy Doyle and set in Dublin and charming Donegal County, respectively.

The Field (1990). An Irish farmer fights to keep his land.

In the Name of the Father (1993). A biopic of accused bomber Gerry Conlon, starring Daniel Day-Lewis.

Michael Collins (1996). Liam Neeson as the Irish Free State revolutionary.

Odd Man Out (1947). Film noir about the early IRA, with a great scene filmed in Belfast's Crown Bar.

Philomena (2013). Poignant but clear-eyed story of a young Irish girl forced to give up her child for adoption in the 1950s.

Ryan's Daughter (1970). David Lean's epic WWI love story,
filmed near Dingle.

The Wind That Shakes the Barley (2006). The struggle for
independence from Britain told through the story of two
brothers.

ITALY

Nonfiction

Brunelleschi's Dome (Ross King, 2000). Description of the
innovative building of Florence's magnificent Duomo.

Christ Stopped at Eboli: The Story of a Year (Carlo Levi, 1944).
A doctor and philosopher, the author is banished in 1935
to southern Italy because of his opposition to Fascist
Italy's Ethiopian war.

City: A Story of Roman Planning and Construction and *Rome
Antics* (David Macaulay, 1974/1997). Illustrated books
about the Eternal City.

The City of Falling Angels (John Berendt, 2000). Real-life
mystery of Venice's La Fenice Opera House fire.

*Excellent Cadavers: The Mafia and the Death of the First
Italian Republic* (Alexander Stille, 1995). This story
about the Sicilian Mafia in the 1990s is part-history/
part-thriller.

The House of Medici (Christopher Hibbert, 1974). The story of
Florence's first family.

Italian Days (Barbara Grizzuti Harrison, 1998). Appealing
travel essays on destinations ranging from Milan to
Naples.

Italian Neighbors (Tim Parks, 1992). An Englishman's humorous and sometimes difficult attempt to live as a local in a
small Italian town.

Michelangelo and the Pope's Ceiling (Ross King, 2003). The
story behind the creation of the Sistine Chapel.

The Seasons of Rome (Paul Hofmann, 1997). Journal chroni-
cling the eccentricities of Rome often overlooked by
tourists.

Under the Tuscan Sun (Frances Mayes, 1996). Living *la dolce
vita* in the Tuscan countryside.

Venice Observed (Mary McCarthy, 1963). Penetrating memoir
detailing the Venetian ethos.

Fiction

Death in Venice (Thomas Mann, 1912). Classic tale of an
author's liberation from writer's block in the Floating

City, published on the eve of World War I.

The First Man in Rome (Colleen McCullough, 1990). Historical novel set in 110 B.C. that pits a low-born Roman soldier against a corrupt aristocrat.

Galileo's Daughter (Dava Sobel, 1999). Historical memoir that centers on Galileo's correspondence with his oldest daughter and confidante.

I, Claudius (Robert Graves, 1934). The history of ancient Rome told by Claudius, who lives through the reigns of Augustus, Tiberius, and Caligula before becoming emperor himself.

Invisible Cities (Italo Calvino, 1972). The imagined conversations of Marco Polo and Chinese ruler Kublai Khan.

The Leopard (Giuseppe Tomasi di Lampedusa, 1958). Sicilian life during the Risorgimento.

Pompeii (Robert Harris, 2003). The engineer responsible for Pompeii's aqueducts has a bad feeling about Mount Vesuvius.

A Room with a View (E. M. Forster, 1908). A young Englishwoman visiting Florence seeks liberation.

A Soldier of the Great War (Mark Helprin, 1991). A young Roman lawyer falls in love with an art student, but World War I rips them apart.

A Thread of Grace (Mary Doria Russell, 2005). How more than 43,000 Jews were saved by Italian citizens.

Film and TV

Ben-Hur (1959) and *Spartacus* (1960). Two campy big-budget Hollywood flicks bring ancient Rome to life.

Bicycle Thieves (1949). A poor man looks for his stolen bicycle in busy Rome in this inspirational classic of Italian Neorealism.

Bread and Tulips (2000). A harassed Italian housewife discovers beauty, love, and her true self in Venice.

Cinema Paradiso (1988). Drama about the friendship between a film projectionist and a little boy in post-WWII Sicily.

La Dolce Vita (1960). Director Federico Fellini tells a series of stories that capture the Roman character.

Enchanted April (1991). Filmed in Portofino, an all-star British cast falls in love, discusses relationships, eats well, and takes naps in the sun.

Gladiator (2000). An enslaved Roman general (Russell Crowe) fights his way back to freedom in this Oscar winner.

Life Is Beautiful (1997). Comedy-drama set in a Tuscan town, in which an imaginative Jewish-Italian man protects his son from the truth about Nazi death camps.

Il Postino (1995). Poet Pablo Neruda befriends his Italian postman, using a newfound love for Italian poetry to woo a local beauty.

Rome, Open City (1945). Roberto Rossellini's war drama, set in the Eternal City during the WWII Nazi occupation.

Roman Holiday (1953). Audrey Hepburn and Gregory Peck sightsee the city on his scooter.

THE NETHERLANDS

Nonfiction

Amsterdam (Geert Mak, 1998). Academic but an engaging and thorough look at centuries of the city's history.

A Bridge Too Far (Cornelius Ryan, 1974). A story of the battle of Arnhem.

Daily Life in Rembrandt's Holland (Paul Zumthor, 1994). Focuses on the everyday concerns of Dutch society in the 17th century, covering art, history, culture, sports, holidays, and more.

Dear Theo: The Autobiography of Vincent van Gogh (edited by Irving Stone, 1995). A look into the psyche of Vincent van Gogh through letters to his brother.

The Diary of a Young Girl (Anne Frank, 1952). Remarkable diary of a young Jewish girl hiding out from the Nazis in Amsterdam.

The Embarrassment of Riches: An Interpretation of Dutch Culture in the Golden Age (Simon Schama, 1997). A comprehensive overview of Dutch culture and the attitudes of Dutch citizens from their early beginnings and most famous struggles.

The Hiding Place (Corrie ten Boom, 1971). The story of a Christian family caught hiding Jews in Haarlem.

My 'Dam Life: Three Years in Holland (Sean Condon, 2003). Humorous account of adventures in a low country.

Spice: The History of a Temptation (Jack Turner, 2005). Holland was at the center of the spice trade back when a pinch of cinnamon was worth its weight in gold.

Tulipmania (Mike Dash, 2001). The Golden Age tulip craze of the 1600s.

The Undutchables: An Observation of the Netherlands, Its Culture and Its Inhabitants (Colin White and Laurie Boucke, 2001). Irreverent guide to modern Dutch culture.

Fiction

The Black Tulip (Alexandre Dumas, 1850). A classic swash-
buckling tale of fortunes won and lost.

Girl with a Pearl Earring (Tracy Chevalier, 2005). Historical
portrait of artist Johannes Vermeer and his maidservant
in 17th-century Delft (also a fine film).

*Max Havelaar: Or the Coffee Auctions of the Dutch Trading
Company* (Multatuli, 1860). Satirical novel denouncing
the injustices of the Dutch colonial system in Indonesia.

Film and TV

Antonia's Line (1995). A portrait of five generations of Dutch
women.

The Diary of Anne Frank (1959). A fine version of Anne's story.

Soldier of Orange (1977). Epic tale about the Nazi occupation
and Dutch Resistance during WWII (and a good book).

NORWAY

Growth of the Soil (Knut Hamsun, 1917/2007). Epic tale of
man and nature in back-country Norway, winner of the
Nobel Prize in Literature.

The Ice Palace (Tarjei Vesaas, 2009). A legendary tale of two
young girls, a tragic disappearance, and its shattering
aftermath.

Kon-Tiki (Thor Heyerdahl, 1950). Norwegian biologist
Heyerdahl records his historic 1947 journey from Peru to
Polynesia on a balsa-wood raft.

Kristin Lavransdatter (1995). A condensed version of the epic
novel about the life of a Norwegian woman in the 14th
century.

Out Stealing Horses (Per Patterson, 2003). A widower in
remote Norway meets a neighbor who stirs up memories
of a pivotal day in 1948.

POLAND

The Eagle Unbowed (Halik Kochanski, 2012). A comprehensive overview of Poland during World War II.

The Lullaby of Polish Girls (Dagmara Dominczyk, 2013).
Three young Polish girls befriend each other, reuniting as
adults due to a mysterious murder.

The Painted Bird (Jerzy Kosiński, 1965). Dark tale of a boy
abandoned by his parents during World War II.

Poland (James Michener, 1984). Historical fiction that serves as a fabulous guide to the country's hectic past.

Skeletons at the Feast (Chris Bohjalian, 2008). WWII refugees from all walks of life take the dangerous trek from Warsaw to the Rhine.

Film and TV

The Decalogue (1989). Television drama that explores the meanings of the Ten Commandments with a fictional narrative set mostly in modern Warsaw.

The Pianist (2002). Oscar-winning movie about the plight of a Jewish musician hiding in Warsaw during the Holocaust.

Schindler's List (1993). Oscar winner about a German factory owner's inspirational efforts to save his Polish-Jewish employees from deportation to concentration camps.

PORTUGAL

Baltasar and Blimunda (José Saramago, 1998). Early 18th-century Lisbon at the height of the Inquisition.

The Book of Disquiet (Fernando Pessoa, 1982). A collection of poetry and thoughts left behind in the trunk of a famed Portuguese writer.

The First Global Village (Martin Page, 2002). How such a small country has had such a big influence.

Film and TV

Amália (2008). The story of Portugal's beloved fado singer Amália Rodrigues.

Capitães de Abril (2000). The 1974 coup that overthrew the right-wing Portuguese dictatorship, told from the perspective of two young army captains.

Letters from Fontainhas (2010). Series of three short films following three troubled lives in Lisbon.

SPAIN

Nonfiction

Barcelona (Robert Hughes, 1993). Engaging history of the city and its people.

The Basque History of the World (Mark Kurlansky, 2001). An essential history for understanding the Basque region (divided between Spain and France).

The Dangerous Summer (Ernest Hemingway, 1960). Vivid look at brutal, dramatic season of bullfights.

Discovering Spain: An Uncommon Guide (Penelope Casas, 1992). Blends references to history, culture, and food with travel information.

Driving Over Lemons (Chris Steward, 2001). Real-life account of a family relocating to Spain and adjusting to new cultures and traditions.

Homage to Catalonia (George Orwell, 1938). Gripping account of Orwell's Spanish Civil War experiences, fighting Franco's Fascists.

The Ornament of the World (María Rosa Menocal, 2002). Vivid depiction of how Muslims, Jews, and Christians created a culture of tolerance in medieval Spain.

The Road to Santiago (Kathryn Harrison, 2003). Beautifully written portrait of the pilgrimage trail.

South from Granada (Gerald Brenan, 1957). British expat's 1920s experiences of village life in the mountains south of Granada.

Fiction

The Carpenter's Pencil (Manuel Rivas, 2001). Unsentimental tale of an imprisoned revolutionary haunted by his troubled past.

For Whom the Bell Tolls (Ernest Hemingway, 1940). Tale of idealism and harsh reality, with the Spanish Civil War as a backdrop.

The Last Jew (Noah Gordon, 2000). One man's story of survival in Inquisition-era Spain.

The Shadow of the Wind (Carlos Ruiz Zafón, 2005). Best-selling thriller set in 1950s Barcelona; sequels include *The Angel's Game* and *The Prisoner of Heaven*.

Tales of the Alhambra (Washington Irving, 1832). Whimsical fact, mythical tales, and descriptions of Granada and the Alhambra.

Film and TV

L'Auberge Espagnole (2002). The loves and lives of European students sharing an apartment in Barcelona.

Vicky Cristina Barcelona (2008). A macho Spanish artist romances two American women when his stormy ex-wife suddenly re-enters his life.

Women on the Verge of a Nervous Breakdown (1988), *All About My Mother* (1999), and *Volver* (2006). Director Pedro Almodóvar's piquant films about relationships in the post-Franco era.

SWEDEN

The Girl with the Dragon Tattoo series (Stieg Larsson, 2008). Three-part thriller featuring a punky computer hacker and a disgraced journalist (also a film).

Hanna's Daughters (Marianna Fredriksson, 1998). Epic novel that follows the lives of three remarkable Swedish women, from the 1870s through World War II.

Pelle the Conqueror (Martin Andersen Nexø, 1988). This classic follows the fortunes of a Swede and his son as they immigrate to Denmark in the 19th century.

The Red Room (August Strindberg, 1879). Biting satire on Stockholm society from Sweden's literary giant.

Film and TV

My Life as a Dog (1985). Bittersweet tale of a young boy in 1950s Sweden.

The Seventh Seal (1957), *Smiles of a Summer Night* (1955), and *Fanny & Alexander* (1983). Iconic films from Oscar-winning Swedish director Ingmar Bergman.

SWITZERLAND

Hotel du Lac (Anita Brookner, 1995). A writer of romance novels attempts to recover from her own misguided love affair by fleeing to Switzerland.

The Magic Mountain (Thomas Mann, 1924). An exclusive sanatorium high in the Alps is a microcosm for European society in the days before World War I.

La Place de la Concorde Suisse (John McPhee, 1984). Journalistic look at the role of the army in Switzerland's efficient, orderly society.

Target Switzerland: Swiss Armed Neutrality in World War II (Stephen Halbrook, 2003). How the Swiss dealt with neutrality during WWII.

Film and TV

The Eiger Sanction (1975). Spy thriller partially shot in Kleine Scheidegg.

Jonah Who Will Be 25 in the Year 2000 (1975). A Big-Chill look at former student activists living in Geneva.

North Face (2008). The disastrous 1936 attempt by an Austrian/German team to scale the Eiger's "wall of death."

Index

Start your trip at

your travel dreams into affordable reality

Radio Interviews

Enjoy ready access to Rick's vast library of radio interviews

covering travel tips and cultural insights that relate specifically to your Europe travel plans.

Travel Forums

Learn, ask, share! Our online community of savvy travelers is

a great resource for first-time travelers to Europe, as well as seasoned pros. You'll find forums on each country, plus travel tips and restaurant/hotel reviews. You can even ask one of our well-traveled staff to chime in with an opinion.

Travel News

Subscribe to our free Travel News e-newsletter, and get monthly updates from Rick on what's happening in Europe.

Audio Europe™

Rick's Free Travel App

Get your FREE Rick Steves Audio Europe™ app to enjoy...

- Dozens of self-guided tours of Europe's top museums, sights and historic walks

- Hundreds of tracks filled with cultural insights and sightseeing tips from Rick's radio interviews

- All organized into handy geographic playlists

- For iPhone, iPad, iPod Touch, Android

With Rick whispering in your ear, Europe gets even better.

Find out more at ricksteves.com

Pack Light and Right

Gear up for your next adventure at ricksteves.com

Light Luggage

Pack light and right with Rick Steves' affordable, custom-designed rolling carry-on bags, backpacks, day packs and shoulder bags.

Accessories

From packing cubes to moneybelts and beyond, Rick has personally selected the travel goodies that will help your trip go smoother.

Rick Steves has

Experience maximum Europe

Save time and energy

This guidebook is your independent-travel toolkit. But for all it delivers, it's still up to you to devote the time and energy it takes to manage the preparation and logistics that are essential for a happy trip. If that's a hassle, there's a solution.

Rick Steves Tours

A Rick Steves tour takes you to Europe's most interesting places with great guides and

great tours, too!

with minimum stress

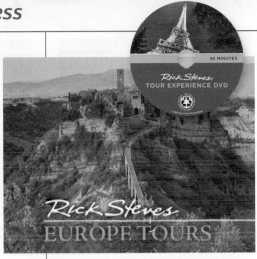

small groups of 28 or less. We follow Rick's favorite itineraries, ride in comfy buses, stay in family-run hotels, and bring you intimately close to the Europe you've traveled so far to see. Most importantly, we take away the logistical headaches so you can focus on the fun.

Join the fun

This year we'll take 18,000 free-spirited travelers— nearly half of them repeat customers— along with us on 40 different itineraries, from Ireland to Italy to Istanbul. Is a Rick Steves tour the right fit for your travel dreams? Find out at ricksteves.com, where you can also get Rick's latest tour catalog and free Tour Experience DVD.

Europe is best experienced with happy travel partners. We hope you can join us.

See our itineraries at ricksteves.com

![Rick Steves]

EUROPE GUIDES

Best of Europe
Eastern Europe
Europe Through the Back Door
Mediterranean Cruise Ports
Northern European Cruise Ports

COUNTRY GUIDES

Croatia & Slovenia
England
France
Germany
Great Britain
Ireland
Italy
Portugal
Scandinavia
Spain
Switzerland

CITY & REGIONAL GUIDES

Amsterdam & the Netherlands
Belgium: Bruges, Brussels, Antwerp & Ghent
Barcelona
Budapest
Florence & Tuscany
Greece: Athens & the Peloponnese
Istanbul
London
Paris
Prague & the Czech Republic
Provence & the French Riviera
Rome
Venice
Vienna, Salzburg & Tirol

SNAPSHOT GUIDES

Basque Country: Spain & France
Berlin
Copenhagen & the Best of Denmark
Dublin
Dubrovnik
Hill Towns of Central Italy
Italy's Cinque Terre
Krakow, Warsaw & Gdansk
Lisbon
Loire Valley
Madrid & Toledo
Milan & the Italian Lakes District
Naples & the Amalfi Coast
Northern Ireland
Norway
Scotland
Sevilla, Granada & Southern Spain
St. Petersburg, Helsinki & Tallinn
Stockholm

POCKET GUIDES

Amsterdam
Athens
Barcelona
Florence
London
Munich & Salzburg
Paris
Rome
Venice
Vienna

Rick Steves guidebooks are published by Avalon Travel, a member of the Perseus Books Group.

HOW WAS YOUR TRIP?

If you enjoyed a successful trip with the help of this book and would like to share your discoveries, please fill out the survey at ricksteves.com/feedback. Thanks in advance for your feedback—it helps a lot. We're all in the same traveler's school of hard knocks...and it's OK to compare notes. Your feedback helps us improve this book for future travelers!

For our latest travel tips, tap into our information-packed website: ricksteves.com. For any updates to this book, check ricksteves.com/update.

Rick Steves' Europe is more than Rick Steves. All 100 of us are pooling our travel experience and working hard to help you enjoy the trip of a lifetime!

ACKNOWLEDGMENTS

Danke to Cameron Hewitt for his travel savvy, editing, and commitment to excellence. *Dank u wel* to Risa Laib for her vision and helping build our guidebook series over the years, and *obrigado* to Jennifer Davis for managing my guidebook series so capably. And *grazie* to the following for sharing their knowledge in their fields of travel expertise: Dave Hoerlein (artful maps, public-transit tips); Wide World Books & Maps (guidebooks, wideworldtravelstore.com); Tim Tattan (radio); Brooke Burdick (audio tours); Joan Robinson and Margaret Cassady (women's packing tips); Kent Corrick (travel insurance); Todd and Carla Hoover (cruisers extraordinaire); Elizabeth Holmes (travel agents, overseas flights); Laura Terrenzio and Gretchen Strauch at RSE (train travel); Alfred Celentano at Europe by Car and our colleagues at Auto Europe/Kemwel (car rental and leasing); Chris Rae (driving and navigating); Steve Breedlove at Bank of America Merrill Lynch (money); Cory Mead (technology); Ruth Arista (wine transport); Alan Spira, M.D., and Craig Karpilow, M.D. (health for travelers); Lisa Friend (family travel and health advice); Amy Lysen (couchsurfing); David Shore (camping); France Freeman (home exchange); Kevin Williams (alternative accommodations); Tara Swenson (health advice); Arlan Blodgett, Stewart Hopkins, Chris Luczyk, and Sabine Schrader (photography); Deanna Russell (tours); John Sage and Susan Sygall (travelers with disabilities); Jennifer Hauseman (gay travelers); Audrey Edwards and Leiane Cooke (travelers of color); Rich Sorensen (website); Andy Steves (foreign study abroad); and Aaron Harting (green travel).

Merci for support from my entire well-traveled staff at Rick Steves' Europe, including Gene Openshaw, Steve Smith, Rich Sorensen, and in particular, Anne Kirchner for keeping things in order while I'm both in and out. *Spasiba* also to Pat Larson, Sandie Nisbet, and John Givens at Small World Productions for introducing so many travelers to this book through our original public television series, *Travels in Europe with Rick Steves*. *Muchas gracias* to Simon Griffith for directing and producing our current *Rick Steves' Europe* television series with such passion and artistry.

Finally, *tusen takk* to my parents for dragging me to Europe when I didn't want to go.

CONTRIBUTOR

Cameron Hewitt

Cameron Hewitt has researched and written for the last 10 editions of Europe Through the Back Door. He has researched various guidebooks and led tours for Rick Steves' travel company since 2000. While he's visited almost every European country, his favorite area is Central and Eastern Europe, where he co-authors Rick Steves' guidebooks on Eastern Europe, Croatia & Slovenia, and Budapest. When he's not traveling, Cameron lives in Seattle with his wife, Shawna.

PHOTO CREDITS

Cover: Lake Bled, Slovenia © Jan Wlodarczyk/Alamy

Title Page: Berner Oberland, Switzerland © Dominic Bonuccelli

Frontispiece: Pisa, Italy © Dominic Bonuccelli

Chapter Banners: Dominic Bonuccelli © pp. 77, 243, 274, 301, 342, 382, 405, 420, 454, 493, 537, 555, 588, 641, 657, 668, 710; Cameron Hewitt, pp. 701, 720; Dave C. Hoerlein, p. 180; Sandra Hundacker, p. 95; Rhonda Pelikan, p. 63; Rick Steves, pp. 14, 25, 111, 150, 196, 263, 312, 327, 358, 467, 489, 520, 567, 601, 618, 632, 679, 690, 730.

Additional Photography: p. 327, right, © Jacob Ammentorp Lund/istock.com, John Adkins, Marcella Benson, Dominic Bonuccelli, Julie Coen, Anna Conley, Robyn Cronin, Jennifer Madison Davis, Lizanne Fowler, Sonja Groset, Ron Haas, Jennifer Hauseman, Cameron Hewitt, David C. Hoerlein, Anne Jenkins, Jane Klausen, Suzanne Kotz, Lauren Mills, Pat O'Connor, Rhonda Pelikan, Michael Potter, Randy Ratzlaff, Carol Ries, Sabine Schrader, Allen Shoemaker, Benjamin Shoemaker, Rich Sorensen, Jackie Steves, Rick Steves, Gretchen Strauch, Bruce VanDeventer, Laura VanDeventer, Ragen Van Sewell, Deanna Woodruff, Rachel Worthman, Robert Wright (photos are used by permission and are the property of the original copyright owners).

Avalon Travel
a member of the Perseus Books Group
1700 Fourth Street
Berkeley, CA 94710

For a complete list of Rick Steves guidebooks, see page 35.

Printed in China by RRD Shenzhen.
First printing August 2015.

For the latest on Rick's lectures, guidebooks, tours, public television series, and public radio show, contact Rick Steves' Europe, 130 Fourth Avenue North, Edmonds, WA 98020, tel. 425/771-8303, fax 425/771-0833, ricksteves.com, rick@ricksteves.com.

ISBN 978-1-63121-175-1
ISSN 1096-794X

Rick Steves' Europe
Special Publications Manager: Risa Laib
Managing Editor: Jennifer Madison Davis
2016 Edition Leads: Sandra Hundacker, Suzanne Kotz, Cathy Lu
Editors and Researchers: Glenn Eriksen, Tom Griffin, Carrie Shepherd, Gretchen Strauch
Editorial & Production Assistant: Jessica Shaw
Editorial Intern: Kate Clark
Maps & Graphics: David C. Hoerlein, Lauren Mills, Mary Rostad

Avalon Travel
Senior Editor and Series Manager: Madhu Prasher
Editor: Jamie Andrade
Associate Editor: Maggie Ryan
Copy Editor: Patrick Collins
Proofreader: Kelly Lydick
Indexer: Stephen Callahan
Design and Typesetting: McGuire Barber Design
Maps & Graphics: Kat Bennett, Mike Morgenfeld, Brice Ticen
Cover Design: Kimberly Glyder Design

ABOUT THE AUTHOR

Rick Steves

Since 1973, Rick Steves has spent 100 days every year exploring Europe. Along with writing and researching a bestselling series of guidebooks, Rick produces a public television series (*Rick Steves' Europe*), a public radio show (*Travel with Rick Steves*), a blog (on Facebook), and an app and podcast (*Rick Steves Audio Europe*); writes a nationally syndicated newspaper column; organizes guided tours that take over 20,000 travelers to Europe annually; and offers an information-packed website (www.ricksteves.com). With the help of his hardworking staff of 100 at Rick Steves' Europe—in Edmonds, Washington, just north of Seattle— Rick's mission is to make European travel fun, affordable, and culturally enlightening for Americans.

Connect with Rick: ☐ facebook.com/RickSteves
                   🐦 twitter: @RickSteves